THE MEDICI

Citizens and Masters

VILLA I TATTI SERIES, 32

THE MEDICI
Citizens and Masters

ROBERT BLACK *and*
JOHN E. LAW, *Editors*

VILLA I TATTI

THE HARVARD UNIVERSITY CENTER FOR ITALIAN RENAISSANCE STUDIES

LIBRARY OF CONGRESS CATALOGING-IN-PUBLICATION DATA

The Medici : citizens and masters / Robert Black and John E. Law,
editors. — First edition.

pages cm — (Villa I Tatti ; 32)

Most of these papers were presented at a conference, held at Villa I
Tatti, Florence, 12–14 October 2011.

Includes bibliographical references and index.

ISBN 978-0-674-08844-3 (alkaline paper)

1. Renaissance—Italy—Florence—Congresses.

2. Florence (Italy)—Civilization—Congresses.

3. Arts—Italy—Florence—Congresses.

4. Medici, House of—Congresses.

5. Power (Social sciences)—Italy—Florence—History—To 1500—Congresses.

6. Statesmen—Italy—Florence—Biography.

7. Florence (Italy)—Politics and government—1421–1737—Congresses.

8. Florence (Italy)—History—1421–1737—Congresses.

I. Black, Robert.

II. Law, John E. (John Easton)

DG533.M43 2015

945'.51107—dc23

2015004982

Book and cover design: Melissa Tandysh

Book production: Dumbarton Oaks Publications

COVER ILLUSTRATION: Benozzo Gozzoli, detail of the wall with portraits of the Medici,
as well as Sigismondo Malatesta and Galeazzo Maria Sforza, *Procession of the Magi*, fresco.
Palazzo Medici Riccardi, Florence. (Photo: Scala/Art Resource, New York.)

TITLE PAGE ILLUSTRATION: Bertoldo di Giovanni, attrib., pre-restoration detail
of the right side of the portico frieze, Poggio a Caiano, early 1490s, glazed terracotta.
(Photo: Warburg Institute, London.)

Contents

Part III: Religion and the Church

Part IV: The Medici and Their Image

Abbreviations

Dizionario biografico degli italiani (Rome, 1960–)	DBI
Florence Archivio di Stato	ASF
Arte della lana	AL
Capitani di Parte Guelfa	CPG
Carte Strozziane	CS
Consulte e pratiche	CP
Dogana di Firenze	DF
Signori, Legazioni e commissarie	LC
Mediceo avanti il principato	MAP
Signori, Missive, Iᵃ Cancelleria	Missive
Notarile antecosimiano	NA
Otto di guardia e balìa	Otto
Provvisioni, Registri	PR
Signori, Dieci, Otto, Legazioni e Commissarie, Missive, Responsive	Sig.X.VIII
Florence Biblioteca Medicea Laurenziana	BML
Florence Biblioteca Nazionale Centrale	BNCF
Magliabechi	Magl.
Florence Biblioteca Riccardiana	BRF

Indice generale degli incunaboli delle biblioteche d'Italia, edited by T. Guarnaschelli and D. Valenziani, Rome, 1943–81, 6 vols.	IGI
Mantua Archivio di Stato	ASMn
Archivio Gonzaga	AG
Milan Archivio di Stato	ASMi
Potenze estere, Firenze	Pot. est.
Registri delle missive	Missive
Milan Biblioteca Ambrosiana	BA
Modena	ASMo
Carteggio tra principi Estensi, casa e stato	CS
Vatican City Archivio Segreto Vaticano	ASV
Registra vaticana	RV
Vatican City Biblioteca Apostolica Vaticana	BAV
Paris Bibliothèque Nationale de France	PBNF
Rome Biblioteca Nazionale Centrale	BNCR
sine data (undated)	s.d.

NB: All dates have been modernized unless otherwise indicated.

Preface

JOHN E. LAW

THE CONFERENCE AT WHICH most of these papers were read—held 12–14 October 2011—was inspired by the late Professor Francis William Kent. Following an earlier exercise in comparative history held at Brasenose College, University of Oxford, in September 2007, which explored the legacy of Philip Jones's comparison of communal and "despotic" regimes, Bill suggested that a similar approach could be usefully applied to the quattrocento Medici in the context of a northern Italy largely dominated by signorial regimes. Among the interesting themes to emerge from the conference—helping to justify the enterprise—was the fact that regimes, both signorial and Medicean, could vary in terms of influence, authority, and perception, both at home and abroad, depending on political, military, financial, and dynastic circumstances.

As organizers, Robert Black and I are grateful for the interest offered at the outset by Joseph Connors and Louis Waldman at Villa I Tatti, the Harvard University Center for Italian Renaissance Studies; and for the decisive support from I Tatti's new director in 2010, Lino Pertile, and the incoming assistant director for academic programs and publications, Jonathan Nelson. We were also greatly aided by Peter Howard and his colleagues at the Prato Centre established by Monash University. In both institutions, the importance of the subject was acknowledged, as was their close association with Bill Kent: he was the "founding father" of the Prato Centre and a frequent—and productive—visitor to I Tatti, when, on the death of Nicolai Rubinstein, he took over the editorship of the Lorenzo de' Medici letters.

We are also extremely grateful for the participation in the Planning Committee of Peter Howard, Lino Pertile, and Jonathan Nelson, and for the guidance given to us by those who anonymously read the papers and by the other members of the Academic Committee: Alison Brown, Peter Howard, Amanda Lillie, Christine Meek, Bernadette Paton, and Brian Richardson. We are grateful to William McCuaig for his translation of the papers originally written in Italian; his translations have been subsequently revised extensively by Robert Black. We are grateful to Magda Nakassis and Sara Taylor for their professional copyediting services; further extensive editorial work was undertaken by Robert Black, with the invaluable assistance at crucial moments of Jane Black and Lorenz Böninger. The hospitality and support offered in Prato and at I Tatti were much appreciated, as was the concert *La chiesa e la corte: Renaissance Polyphony for Florence, Ferrara, Mantua, and Milan* held at I Tatti by Singer Pur and organized by Kathryn Bosi. Without the generous financial backing of I Tatti, this concert could not have taken place (nor indeed the entire conference).

Of course, not even a conference and a collection as wide-ranging as this can cover everything. How were these regimes resourced? The Sforza were not bankers like their allies the Medici, though they borrowed from banks. John Paoletti drew our attention to the fact that, while many rulers, and some individuals, had celebratory and commemorative medals cast in bronze, the quattrocento Medici were remarkable in having copies cast in gold, posthumously in the case of the elder Cosimo, but in the lifetime of his grandson Lorenzo. This could perhaps be seen as an exercise in signorial "magnificence"; magnificence was an attribute—and "magnificent" a title—adopted by signorial regimes as major as the Visconti of Milan and as minor as the Varano of Camerino.[1] Lorenzo could routinely address the governors of republican Siena and Lucca in these terms, as is clear from his published letters.[2] Philippe de Commynes, who knew Italy well, addressed the *signoria* of Florence in January 1493 as "magnifici amplissimi viri." A foreign view of how to address Italian regimes could be revealing. Commynes, for example, addressed Lorenzo as "singnor" on 23 September 1478 and Piero as "seigneur" on 8 May 1493.[3]

Such observations suggest that the comparative approach adopted by this conference and in this volume could be taken further, but, in themselves, the papers presented at Prato and I Tatti represent a considerable and welcome advance in the study of quattrocento Italy. As editors, Bob and I would like to thank all those who attended and contributed, while gratefully acknowledging the inspiration provided by Bill Kent. Sadly, he could not be with us at an event he would have appreciated.

1   Green 1990; Law 2010, 170–173.
2   See Medici, 1977–, 7:302–303 (to Siena, 23 August 1483), 7:369 (to Lucca, 11 March 1484). On 10 March 1484, Lorenzo addressed the *gonfaloniere* and priors of Arezzo—a city subject to Florence—as "magnifici" (ibid., 7:366–368).
3   Commynes 2001, 39–42 (September 1478), 175–177 (January 1493), 180–182 (May 1493).

Introduction

ROBERT BLACK

THE POSITION OF THE MEDICI in fifteenth-century Florence and in comparison to signorial regimes has been an issue of vigorous historical debate for decades if not centuries. In Italian historiography of the early twentieth century, the tendency was to see the early Medici as signori in all but name. For Vicenzo Ricchioni, writing in 1913, "there was no doubt that Lorenzo de' Medici was, in practice, *signore*"[1] of Florence. Similarly, Giovanni Soranzo wrote in 1953 of Lorenzo de' Medici's "first leap toward a *signoria*."[2]

Since the eighteenth century, and even before, the Medici had an allure for British writers. William Roscoe (1753–1831), who laid the foundations for extended study of the Medici in Britain, was the first in a notable series of British Medici historians, including Edward Armstrong (1846–1928), Janet Ross (1842–1927), and Cecilia Ady (1881–1958). However, some of these writers were as much dilettantes as serious historians, and it was only with the arrival of Nicolai Rubinstein (1911–2002) in Britain that Medici studies were put on a solidly professional footing, with a firm foundation in archival research.

Rubinstein had a lifelong fascination with constitutional history. His teaching at Westfield College, University of London, included at one time English texts such as John Fortescue's *De laudibus legum Angliae*. It is a matter of speculation what inspired his attraction to limited and constitutional monarchy: perhaps it was

1 Ricchioni 1913, 4: "Che in pratica egli fosse Signore non v'è dubbio."
2 Soranzo 1953, 70: "primo balzo verso la signoria."

his patriotic love for the adopted country that provided him with a haven in 1939. There is no doubt that Rubinstein always approached the position of the Medici in Florence from a constitutional and limited-monarchical perspective. Cecilia Ady (see below, 4) and her Italian counterparts such as Ricchioni or Soranzo (see above, 1) had bracketed the Medici with the despots of north and central Italy; in contrast, Rubinstein emerged as a radical revisionist, viewing the Medici as civic leaders, heading an ever narrowing oligarchic ruling group.

For Rubinstein, the power of Cosimo "il vecchio" de' Medici (1389–1464) was restricted. "The eulogists who praised Cosimo as [the Roman emperor] Augustus," he wrote in 1967, "greatly exaggerated his real authority."[3] In his classic work, *The Government of Florence under the Medici*,[4] he wrote in a similar vein regarding Cosimo's grandson, Lorenzo the Magnificent (1449–1492): "Lorenzo is...denounced [by his contemporary Alamanno Rinuccini (1426–1499)] as [a] 'perniziossimo e crudelissimo tiranno.' Such denunciations, like the eulogies of Lorenzo, give an exaggerated picture of his power."[5] "In fact, [Lorenzo] respected the structure of the republican constitution," he wrote in 1980, "and during his life his official and legal position in Florence was no different from what any other member of the ruling class would have held."[6]

A prominent theme in Rubinstein's analysis of early Medici power was the failure of foreign observers to understand—indeed their tendency to misrepresent—Florentine practices and customs. "The Milanese ambassadors tended to stress, and sometimes to overstress, Lorenzo's authority in Florence ... and their reports, though broadly accurate, are consequently liable to give an over-simplified picture of the complex structure of Lorenzo's ascendancy."[7] Furthermore, "the Milanese ambassador wrote, after Lorenzo's death, that whoever wanted an office would apply to him, and...this was clearly exaggerated..."[8] Indeed, "Lorenzo was eulogized as head of the State.... It was not surprising that [foreign rulers] should consider him the virtual ruler of Florence, and that this in turn should react on his position at home, despite his protests that, like his grandfather, he was no more than a private citizen."[9]

Rubinstein also put forward this view with regard to Pope Pius II (1405–1464): "already during [Cosimo's] lifetime, Pius II wrote of him that, after Medicean controls were restored and reinforced in 1458, he was considered 'not so much a citizen

3   Rubinstein 1967, 35.
4   Rubinstein 1966. A second edition was published in 1997.
5   Rubinstein 1997, 252.
6   Rubinstein 1980, 30: "In effetti [Lorenzo] rispettò la struttura della costituzione repubblicana e durante la sua vita la sua posizione ufficiale e giuridica in Firenze non fu diversa da quella che qualche altro membro della classe dirigente avrebbe potuto tenere."
7   Rubinstein 1997, 255–256.
8   Ibid., 257.
9   Rubinstein 1967, 38.

as a lord,' to whom 'nothing was denied' . . . non-Florentines like Pius II were likely to be impressed by Cosimo's wealth and his dominant role in the foreign policy of his city."[10] But Rubinstein extended the same argument to Florentine citizens too: "even a Florentine patrician like Giovanni Rucellai [1403–1481] could comment in 1461, when recording in his *Zibaldone* the engagement of his son to a granddaughter of Cosimo's, that Cosimo and his two sons 'had our city and its government at their disposal as if they were *signori a bachetta*'[11]—that is, according to republican terminology, signori, or despots. Giovanni Rucellai had personal reasons for emphasizing the power of the grandfather of his daughter-in-law; but he was also, at the time of writing, largely ignorant of the inner workings of the Medici regime, having, since its establishment, been excluded from it."[12]

Rubinstein vigorously distinguished the Medici from contemporary Italian despots: "Cosimo's authority in Florence was of an entirely different kind from that of a despot";[13] "[Cosimo's] position was far removed from that of an Italian despot, a *signore a bacchetta*";[14] "[Lorenzo] met the Milanese ambassador's arguments in favour of a determined policy to increase his power in Florence by insisting that, while he was seeking the *stabilimento del stato suo*, he did not wish to *dare alteratione a la terra*, but that he wanted to achieve it by indirect methods. This remained the guiding principle of the constitutional reforms under Lorenzo, as it had been under Cosimo; if the duke of Milan [Galeazzo Maria Sforza, 1444–1476] thought, in January 1471, that Lorenzo, having 'begun to understand what medicine he needed,' might make a bid for despotic government, he was clearly mistaken."[15]

Rubinstein particularly emphasized the contrast between Lorenzo and the Gonzaga rulers of Mantua when analyzing the differences between *De optimo cive* and *De principe* by the humanist Bartolomeo Platina (1421–1481): "we can follow Platina adapting a treatise dedicated to an Italian despot to fit the very different position the Medici occupied in Florence," stressing "the different political systems within which the Gonzaga and the Medici operated. However much Platina would try to equate the virtues of the *optimus princeps* with those of the *optimus civis*, he could not help explaining at some point the difference of their constitutional position and political status . . . Unlike Mantua, Florence was a republic, and it was accordingly the Florentine citizens, not, like the Marquess of Mantua, Lorenzo, who elected the magistrates."[16]

For Rubinstein, the key word to describe early Medicean Florence was oligarchy: "Cosimo's ascendancy after 1434 did not materially change the oligarchical

10 Rubinstein 1992, 11–12.
11 Rucellai 2013, 20. For a technical definition of this phrase, see Brown, this volume, 115.
12 Rubinstein 1992, 11–12.
13 Rubinstein 1997, 145.
14 Rubinstein 1992, 12.
15 Rubinstein 1997, 261.
16 Rubinstein 1985, 385–388.

pattern of Florentine politics; it did not eliminate the republican ideas underlying it . . . as before, the Florentine upper class occupied a prominent position in the government of the city."[17] Furthermore, when "in 1458 Medicean controls were restored and decisively reinforced, contemporaries could then describe this fact as a victory not only of Cosimo and of Luca Pitti [1398–1472], but, in more general terms, as that of a group of eminent families under their leadership, and actually as a victory of a party rather than of one or two men."[18] Florence had "a political system which remained, under the personal leadership of Lorenzo, basically oligarchical."[19] Indeed, like "his father [Piero de' Medici, 1416–1469] and grandfather, [Lorenzo] did not occupy an official post that could not have been held by other patricians, and he exercised his *de facto* ascendancy with the help of a group of loyal followers . . . the patriciate continued to be heavily represented in the highest councils and offices. And if Lorenzo collaborated, in every-day affairs, with a small number of friends, he had also to rely on the loyalty of a larger group of less influential supporters."[20] "During much of the fifteenth century, Florence had been . . . deeply rooted in its medieval traditions. Politically this continuity was expressed by the survival of a basically oligarchic structure of government . . ."[21]

Rubinstein's interpretation of the Medici's position, however, did not go unchallenged in twentieth-century British historiography. Unlike Rubinstein, Philip Jones (1921–2006) was not a Florentine specialist, although he did write several important articles on Florence and Florentine Tuscany. Even as an undergraduate at Oxford in the 1940s, his inclinations were far removed from Rubinstein's. To quote Trevor Dean, "within months [after March 1943] he had returned to Oxford and was writing essays on Italian history. . . . In response to the question, 'Had Cosimo or Lorenzo de' Medici the more secure hold upon the government of Florence?,' Jones's very monarchical answer drew the tutorial response that Lorenzo 'must conform to the republican tradition.'"[22] Although criticized by his unnamed tutor, Jones's monarchical perspective on the Medici in fact reflected the traditional British interpretation of Lorenzo's position in Florence: as Cecilia Ady wrote in 1955, Lorenzo's "will became law both in politics and society. . . . A law was . . . passed declaring an attempt to assassinate Lorenzo to be high treason. Such was the extent to which he was recognized as the uncrowned prince of Florence."[23]

---

17 Rubinstein 1967, 36.
18 Rubinstein 1980, 34: "Quando nel 1458 i controlli medicei furono ristabiliti e decisamente rafforzati, i contemporanei poterono quindi descrivere il fatto come una vittoria non soltanto di Cosimo de' Medici e di Luca Pitti, ma, in termini più generali, come quella di un gruppo di famiglie eminenti sotto la loro guida, e veramente come la vittoria di un partito piuttosto che di uno o due uomini."
19 Rubinstein 1972, 25.
20 Rubinstein 1967, 38.
21 Ibid., 42.
22 Dean 2009, 209.
23 Ady 1955, 78, 81.

Jones's mature interpretation was reinforced by his initial research on Italian despotism. As a result, in his famous essay on "Communes and Despots," he wrote about the Medici in terms unthinkable for Rubinstein, aggregating them to the ruck of Italian despots: "Not only did most despots derive from the upper class, as feudatories like the Visconti, or plutocrats like the Medici…"[24]

For Jones, the Medici were typical examples of despotism: "'Be especially careful,' wrote Leo X to the young Lorenzo de' Medici [1492–1519], 'not to give offence to the notables.' The impolicy of doing other was proved by more than the Medici. Whenever, in the fourteenth and fifteenth centuries, *signorie* were overthrown, the occasion, more often than not, was offence to the notables, in their property, their persons, or their honour. Despotism, in its fall as in its rise, was regulated by the same class interests."[25] This approach reached a high level of sophistication in Jones's famous study, "Economia e società nell'Italia medievale. La leggenda della borghesia" (Economy and Society in Medieval Italy: The Myth of the Bourgeoisie):

> According to some, contemporaries as well as later writers, the new like the old generation of *signorie* were characterized by a variety of social affinities, in certain cases aristocratic (for example the Baglioni or the Petrucci), in others popular (the Adorni and Fregosi, Bentivoglio and, in particular, the Medici). Among the new "tyrants," moreover, some were more popular or mercantile in origin than in the past; at the moment of their accession to power, however, all, except the Medici, were landed nobles or *anoblis*, the majority, like the first *signori*, asserting ancient rights or descent from feudal lineages, and the rest claiming family ties or lifestyle; the different traditions notwithstanding, if we examine their class affiliations, we shall find them to be in almost all cases more fundamentally patrician than popular: the *popolo* seem rather to be associated with reaction to a *signoria* or an aristocratic regime, as at Bologna in 1376 and 1402, or at Florence in 1494 and 1527. In pre-Medicean and Medicean Florence, the nobles and the optimates (with a certain support from the lower orders) were the class that inclined or aspired to a *signoria*. The Medici, it has now been demonstrated, were not notably popular by party affiliation or ruling style (they were only less aristocratic than the Albizzi); but they rehabilitated, and contracted marriages among magnates, further closed the ruling class, and governed by alliance (albeit somewhat uncertain) with clans and families [of importance]; and these were the clans in the end who remained outside the wider regimes (however undemocratic they were) of 1494 and 1527; and burdened

24 Jones 2010, 9.
25 Ibid., 23.

by the nightmare of 1378 [the Ciompi revolt], they promoted or accepted the principate.[26]

Philip Jones's skepticism about Rubinstein's republican interpretation of the Medici regime was echoed by his friend and Rubinstein's friend and colleague Daniel Waley, who described Lorenzo as in "practice the city's signore."[27] This view, first published in 1964, has been modified along lines even more reminiscent of Jones's oligarchic interpretation of the Italian city states[28] in the third edition of *Later Medieval Europe*, prepared by Waley's friend and Jones's pupil Peter Denley, in 2001: "Florence . . . survived as a republic in name only, first undergoing sustained evolution towards explicit oligarchy, and then moving to a hybrid system of a largely cosmetic constitution with an unofficial signore who could more than hold his own on Florence's behalf in the Italian political arena."[29]

The debate carried on across the Atlantic too. Gene Brucker, writing in 1969, adopted Rubinstein's interpretation:

> The regime established after Cosimo's return from exile in 1434, and continued by his son Piero and his grandson Lorenzo, was based upon the close cooperation of the Medici and a small group of patrician families, for their mutual advantage and security. The social composition of this ruling group did not change perceptibly during the sixty years of Medici rule. Cosimo and Lorenzo did introduce certain techniques to secure their control— the selection of priors by hand instead of by lot, the creation of councils with special authority—but these devices had their precedents in earlier regimes. The application of these institutional controls was very gradual

---

26 Jones 1978, 344–346: "Secondo taluni, contemporanei e più tardi, la nuova come la vecchia generazione di signorie era caratterizzata da varie affinità sociali, in certi casi aristocratiche (per esempio Baglioni, Petrucci), in altri 'popolari' (Adorni e Fregosi, Bentivoglio e, in particolare, Medici). Fra i nuovi 'tiranni', inoltre, ce n'erano di origine popolare o mercantile più che nel passato; al momento della loro ascesa al potere, però, tutti, tranne i Medici, erano nobili terrieri o *anoblis*; la maggioranza, come i signori di prima, per antico diritto, discendenza da 'lignaggi' feudali, e il resto per accampate pretese, relazioni familiari, o stile di vita; nonostante le tradizioni contrastanti, se esaminiamo le loro relazioni di classe, le scorgiamo in quasi tutti i casi più fondamentalmente patrizie che popolari: il popolo sembra piuttosto associarsi con la reazione alla signoria o al regime autocrato, come a Bologna nel 1376 e nel 1402, a Firenze nel 1494 e nel 1527. Nella Firenze premedicea e medicea, i 'grandi' e gli 'ottimati' (con un certo appoggio dei 'minuti') erano la classe che più inclinava o aspirava alla signoria. I Medici, è stato ormai dimostrato, non erano segnatamente popolari per affiliazione di partito o sistema di governo (erano solo meno aristocratici forse degli Albizzi); ma si riabilitarono e contrassero matrimoni fra i magnati, chiudendo ulteriormente il ceto dirigente, e governando con l'alleanza (sia pure un po' incerta) delle 'case' e 'famiglie'; e furono le 'case' alla fine che, rimaste estranee ai 'governi larghi' (per quanto poco democratici fossero) del 1494 e del 1527—e sotto l'incubo dei ricordi del 1378—promossero o accettarono il principato."
27 Waley 2001, 194.
28 Jones 2010.
29 Waley 2001, 196.

and sporadic, and legislative opposition sometimes forced the Medici to abandon temporarily their plans for electoral and constitutional reform. Even though Medici authority in the regime increased progressively, it never became absolute, and the republic was not transformed into an autocratic despotism.[30]

In contrast, closer to Jones than to Rubinstein (or Brucker) is Lauro Martines. In 1979, he wrote of a "veiled signory";[31] in 2004, that the Medici "went about the business by appearing to respect the constitutional norms, and all the while subverted a constitution that allowed for the representative input of different groups and voices";[32] in 2006, that "Florence was still a republic in name, if only partly so in fact. In the 1480s, Lorenzo de' Medici was the supreme political boss, much more than first among equals."[33] Least Rubinsteinian among leading American historians is John Najemy:

> After 1466, no ambiguities remained about the regime. The myth of the Medici as "first among equals" was now recognized as the fiction it had always been...Piero [the Gouty] had re-established his family's power and asserted a de facto right of succession.... Lorenzo [the Magnificent]'s marriage...to a woman from a Roman branch of noble Orsini confirmed that the Medici no longer wished to be seen as mere Florentine citizens and bankers...[there was an] immense difference...between the regime of "first citizen" Cosimo and that of the boy "prince" Lorenzo.[34]

Furthermore, Najemy has argued,

> Lorenzo's power in the 1480s was unprecedented in Florence and perhaps unmatched even by some of Italy's princes. No one held or even became eligible for important offices without his approval. No action or communication was undertaken by the foreign policy magistracy without his instructions. Lorenzo controlled fiscal policy through his "minister" of the Monte.... Elite families did not contract marriage alliances of which he did not approve. Intervening in the administration of justice, he compelled magistracies to carry out punishments on his orders.... These were the powers of a prince above the law.[35]

30 Brucker 1969, 257.
31 Martines 1979, 158, 278.
32 Martines 2004, 51.
33 Martines 2006, 16.
34 Najemy 2006b, 306.
35 Ibid., 363.

The chapters published in the present volume continue to show scholars divided into two camps, which can be roughly called "republican" or "signorial." Among the "republicans," Gian Maria Varanini suggests how in all regimes of north and central Italy, "the city-state remained the inescapable point of reference, the true touchstone against which all else was measured."[36] Lorenz Böninger sees the Medici and particularly Lorenzo the Magnificent as reluctant to assert prerogatives with regard to the control of immigration and reprisals. For Alison Brown, Piero di Lorenzo de' Medici was regarded abroad as just as or even more powerful than the pope was in Rome, although at home "Piero was unable to control his own family and friends, let alone the city."[37] Dale Kent is perhaps the most unreservedly republican voice: Cosimo de' Medici's position, for her, was different to that of a signore, based as it was on his patriarchal position as paterfamilias of Florence itself, rather than on a constitutional position or on the abuse of the constitution. For Amanda Lillie, castellation was an ambivalent gesture: what the Medici were doing in their villas differed little from the patronage of other families such as the Pazzi. David Peterson emphasizes continuity under the Medici in the history of the Florentine church, which retained "many of the institutional structures ... devised by the Albizzi ... to curb the church's judicial prerogatives and ... to monitor the movement of ecclesiastical wealth," while recognizing greater efforts by the Medici to "to justify their family's dominant position."[38] Blake Wilson suggests that, though strong models for the patronage of music as a princely sign of magnificence and courtly refinement had emerged elsewhere in late fifteenth-century Italy, the Medici appear not to have emulated them; "the ephemerality of musical performance and the persistent orality of native Florentine musical practices were not conducive to the creation of substantial monuments ... to combine signorial splendor with civic pride."[39] For Alison Wright, the "physical and social contexts in which imprese were employed by the Medici within their city were necessarily different to those of princely dynasties"; "their precise lack of a formal court and of legal title remain important distinctions."[40] Carolyn James reveals differences between political culture in Florence and Ferrara vis-à-vis dominant women in politics. In Ferrara, women could and did assume active political roles, but in Florence they were impeded by the city's republican traditions, having to exercise their influence behind the scenes. Paola Ventrone uncovers a contrast in the Medici's self-presentation: at home they maintained their image as *primi inter pares* (first among equals), while abroad they endeavored to portray themselves as princes. For Stephen Milner, the name was and is the thing: "for republican and signorial partisans in the fifteenth and sixteenth century," rhetoric "was a question of political life

36 See Varanini, this volume, 37.
37 See Brown, this volume, 121.
38 See Peterson, this volume, 172–173.
39 See Wilson, this volume, 278, 280.
40 See Wright, this volume, 303, 310.

and its stability," just as controversy between Rubinstein and Jones was not about words but about genuine "intellectual leaning."[41] Marco Gentile unearths a deep divergence in the political culture not only of local societies but also of officialdom between Sforza Milan and Medici Florence.

In contrast, "signorial" voices are clearly audible. Giorgio Chittolini shows how difficult it was to find a new language and a new conceptual framework for political power in the fifteenth century. Although the idea and, arguably the reality, of the "civitas" remained vital in Florence, Genoa, Milan, and Venice, nevertheless, when new vocabulary did gradually emerge, it reflected homogeneity rather than difference among various types of regimes. For Francesco Bausi, the image of the Medici in humanist literature changed from republican to princely in the transition from Cosimo "il vecchio" to Lorenzo the Magnificent. Jane Black, moreover, writes that the Medici and the Sforza both had their myths: in reality, the Medici had more signorial power than their endemically weak counterparts in Lombardy. Melissa Bullard suggests that Lorenzo de' Medici "enjoyed a more effective and weighty political presence in the Italian theater of power as the non–head of state of a mercantile republic than he would have had as an aspiring or actual signore of Florence."[42] For David Chambers, persistent Medici efforts to obtain a cardinal's hat for their family reflect their signorial or princely pretensions. Franco Franceschi suggests that the Medici's policy of privileging their clients and certain subject towns distanced their economic policies from the centralizing program of the earlier fifteenth-century Albizzi regime. The Medici approach was more comparable to the policies of the dukes of Milan, who had to recognize that the regional economy of their Lombard dominions was polycentric and ultimately not susceptible to centralizing direction. Riccardo Fubini observes how little was left of the Florentine traditional communal constitution, dissolved by a series of extraordinary measures which culminated in the creation of the Council of Seventy. Its core membership set aside the time-honored tradition of popular geographical representation, suggesting that Lorenzo the Magnificent aimed to cap this process by making himself constitutional head of state, as gonfalonier of justice for life (according to Francesco Guicciardini). Paolo Orvieto depicts literature, culture, and religion as reflecting the rise of the Medici *signoria*, with Lorenzo becoming not only Florence's philosopher king but replacing the pope as the head of Florence's church. John Najemy suggests, through the voice of Machiavelli, how closely the regimes of the Sforza in Milan and the Medici in Florence converged. Andrea Zorzi points to the absence of legitimation as a problem not only for the Medici but for all the *signorie*; alternation between signorial and republican regimes—evident in Florence beginning at the end of the thirteenth century—was a characteristic phenomenon throughout central and north Italy: in the end, as Philip Jones argued half a century ago, the regime

41   See Milner, this volume, 294.
42   See Bullard, this volume, 53.

in Florence under the Medici was hardly distinguishable, in fact, from signorial despotisms throughout Italy.

So the controversy is just as much alive today as it was in the second half of the last century, when Nicolai Rubinstein and Philip Jones were engaged in this debate—unspoken, since neither Rubinstein nor Jones alluded by name to each other's contrasting views of the Medici—but nevertheless keenly articulated and felt.

PART I

Power and Legitimacy

ONE

Dominant Cities

*Florence, Genoa, Venice, Milan, and Their Territories
in the Fifteenth Century*

GIORGIO CHITTOLINI

ONE PURPOSE OF THIS CHAPTER is to try to assess how the term *civitas* was used in the fifteenth century, and what shifts in meaning or what replacements by other terms it may have undergone. In particular, the focus will be on Florence, Genoa, and Venice—three *civitates* (cities) that evolved into "new principates." This new species of principate was the ruling city (*città dominante*), a city-state exercising lordship directly over a territorial state replete with other *civitates*—what might be called a "multi-city-state state." Another aim is to see what terminology such ruling cities themselves adopted to provide their sovereignty with a legitimacy that the conceptual language of the city-state was evidently ill-suited to confer. The same problem does not arise for a city such as Milan, which was not a ruler (*dominante*), but a capital, the city of residence for a ruler (*dominus*) to whom it was subject and who held a personal title to lordship over Milan itself and over all the other cities in his possession.

The Concept of *Civitas*

From the dawn of the communes, in chancery and legal usage, the term *civitas* designated a town that was an episcopal see of ancient standing and that, in north-central Italy, had evolved politically into a fully self-governing commune. To such communes alone—ancient *civitates* possessing, as episcopal seats, patron saints— was the term "city" reserved, and, in the juridical language of the late Roman empire, now fully revived, the concept of *civitas* implied that the urban center in question controlled a territory tending to coincide with the confines of the ancient ecclesiastical diocese: a territory that came to be known as the *comitatus*—the *contado*.[1] Hence every village, territory, and cluster of habitation within those confines was embraced by the larger *civitas*. A few localities and strongholds (*castra*) might have tried to proclaim themselves free and exempt from such inclusion, but it was difficult (except in the Papal States) to make such claims effective. The law was against them. As the renowned jurist Bartolo of Sassoferrato (1313–1357) wrote, any *castrum* "located within the *contado* of any city cannot properly be called a free people [*populus*], and residents of such habitations are to be considered part of the citizenry."[2] What had already struck Otto of Freising in the twelfth century was now truer than ever: northern Italy was a land *tota inter civitates divisa*, a space fully articulated into an array of city-states, each "not recognizing a superior" (*superiorem non recognoscens*, as it was later put), each with a well-defined and demarcated territory, an ensemble of *civitates* of equal status, their *libertates* guaranteed by the empire. At the start of the fifteenth century, "in the legal language of the day Florence, like Milan and other Italian city-states, was a *provincia*, or *civitas* within the *respublica* of the Holy Roman Empire."[3]

So as Leonardo Bruni, echoing Bartolo, was at pains to emphasize,[4] the concept of the *civitas* as an autonomous and, in fact, sovereign political community governing itself and its surrounding territory provided the basis for a city's legitimate rights over its *contado*. Not only was it the basis for each city-state's autonomy, it was the cornerstone of the entire state system's legitimacy: north-central Italy as a distinct component of the Holy Roman Empire. It was a complex state system: each actor was a city-state and the system extended seamlessly over the whole region, its coverage virtually uninterrupted by seats of power of a different nature. In the age of the communes, the foundation for the north Italian state system's legitimacy was the Peace of Constance of 1183, or rather, its interpretative superstructure as created by lawyers.[5] Such a state system sets Italy apart from the rest of Europe; its like can scarcely be found elsewhere in the empire, or in France or England. Not even Flanders, with its wealth of

---

1   The word *districtus* (district) can sometimes be used interchangeably with *comitatus*, but not always with the same meaning: see note 14 below.
2   Bartolo on D. 49, 15, 7 (De captivis et de postliminio, l. Non dubito) Rubr., paragraph 1: "Nota quod ista castra, quae sunt in comitatu alicuius civitatis possunt dici proprie non liber populus; et homines de illis castris dicuntur cives illius civitatis." *Civitas* enjoyed a distinct status within the universal and steeply graduated juridical hierarchy comprising all *communitates*: the *iura propria* and *iurisdictio* of a *civitas* had a specific and higher status than the law and jurisdiction to which any generic *communitas-universitas* could lay claim. See Tanzini 2012, 84–85.
3   Witt 1983, 385.
4   As Nicolai Rubinstein notes with reference to Leonardo Bruni's *Laudatio florentinae urbis*, where Florence is declared sufficient "ad totius orbis dominium imperiumque adipiscendum" (to acquire dominion and imperium over the entire world). See Fubini 1990, 31. Fubini highlights similar perspectives in Bruni's *Historiae florentini populi*: ibid., 51–57.
5   Magni 1937, 65–72. More recently, Dilcher and Quaglioni 2007.

illustrious and autonomous cities, is comparable to the Italian state system in the communal period.[6]

Old *Civitates,* New *Dominanti*

But over the course of the fourteenth century, the political and territorial system in north-central Italy underwent profound structural modifications, and the terminology of the *civitas* now proved entirely inadequate. Out of shifting frontiers, alignments, and balances of power, and decades of war, there emerged a handful of "great powers": Milan, Florence, and Venice. A state system composed of free communes was evolving into a system—starting to take shape by the early fifteenth century—dominated by larger territorial states, ones corresponding in embryo to the regions of Italy.[7] On a smaller scale, the same scenario had already been played out when, for example, Siena had expanded its territory by absorbing ancient but decaying *civitates* nearby such as Roselle and Sovana. It had been played out in Milan too and more episodically in Perugia.[8]

But when, starting in the late fourteenth century, important cities such as Florence and Genoa, and (albeit with its own distinctive tradition of legitimacy) Venice, found themselves in charge of broad sections of Italy, the linguistic adequacy of *civitas* and *commune*, whatever their aura of heritage and tradition, came seriously into question as a medium for conceiving this new kind of territorial power. Few were prepared to contend that the rights of war and conquest alone were enough to justify such territorial aggrandizement. In theory, it was the Roman law (*ius commune*) of war that applied when sovereign entities such as *civitates superiorem non recognoscentes* resorted to arms, with captivity and enslavement resulting for the losers. But according to Bartolo and other authoritative jurists, Roman law had disallowed such practices: *civitates* conquered by other *civitates* retained their sovereignty. Therefore, Roman law was not structured in such a way as to contemplate territorial expansion through war, nor the total subjugation of the losers to the victors.[9]

As for cities reduced to subjugation, forced to acknowledge the higher authority of a stronger ruler (*dominus*) in the impersonal form of a stronger city (*civitas*)—what value or content could they assign to the term *civitas*, to which they remained so tenaciously faithful? There was a whole nexus of terminology, from *civitas* to *civilitas*, from *comitatus* to *districtus*, that no longer corresponded to an altered reality wherein a few ruling cities (*città dominanti*) were exerting political sway and

---

6   A few comparative remarks in Chittolini 2010.

7   Fubini 2003, 91–97.

8   On Siena's actions, seemingly aimed at erasing the very identity and urban physiognomy of resisting localities, see, for example, Redon 1994.

9   Montorzi 1997, 68 n. 13. Nor, as the author notes, was the *augmentum regni* (extension of rule) an applicable model: Florence was not a *regnum*, nor had the *res publica florentina* ever been a *provincia*, to which it would have been formally possible to annex, as to a *regnum*, another *civitas* and its territory by mere territorial *adiunctio*.

rights of jurisdiction over other, lesser cities (*città*),[10] and where the citizens of the dominant town enjoyed privileges and prerogatives superior to those of the subject towns' citizens—indeed at their very expense.[11] The concrete reality to which the term *civitas* now corresponded was a situation of opposition, with one *civitas* suppressing the long-standing rights of another.[12] From their sister cities, the rulers (*dominanti*) demanded juridical, judicial, and fiscal subjection that was emphasized in rituals and ceremonies. Subject towns were compelled to take part in processions and the consignment of canopies and wax to honor the patron saint of the ruling city (*dominante*).[13] Campaigns of conquest against other *civitates* were depicted in large colored paintings, or in miniatures illuminating codices that belonged to the victorious commune. In Perugia, the dominated territories near Chiusi and Lake Trasimene are represented visually in the stone "encyclopedia" erected in the city's most prominent location, the figural decorations on the Fontana Maggiore.

In what follows, some examples will be examined of how this conflict of power was reflected dialectically in the political language that developed over the course of the fifteenth century.

Florence

As it went about organizing and consolidating its territories during the fourteenth and early fifteenth centuries, Florence by and large remained tied to the doctrine of a communal city-state (*stato cittadino*, "citizen state"). Terms such as *commune*, *populus*, and *civis* retained their distinctively Guelf flavor. But this was a city-state bent on expanding its own *contado*. And indeed the term *comitatus* was still being used in the early decades of the fifteenth century to mean the expanded state that resulted, though the newly added territories had never been part of the ancient Florentine *contado*—an ambivalence that casts an aura of legitimacy over the new

---

10   That is, the *iurisdictio* exercised by the *dominante* was different in kind (Montorzi 2009, x), and its statutes of greater force, prevailing across the whole *territorium* (Savelli 2003, 100, 120 n. 382, 122).

11   Compared to citizens and inhabitants of other urban centers and territories in Tuscany, the citizens of the *dominante* were privileged in property transactions (permission for acquisition, and fiscal and jurisdictional protection), which meant they rapidly acquired land throughout the dominion. They were also privileged with respect to grain provision and manufacturing and commercial activity. Such privileges were normally not forthcoming for inhabitants of cities that were merely capitals or princely seats (the Milanese, for example, with respect to the residents of other cities in the dominion). The princely presence might even depress their status, overriding the power of city magistracies.

12   The paradox of this consequence, which derives from Bartolo's very concept of *civitas superiorem non recognoscens*, is emphasized by Ryan 2000.

13   A practice dating back to the time of the city-state communes, when it signified the subjection of *contado* communities to the city: Chittolini 1996b. On the influence of the nascent Florentine regional state on the city's festival of San Giovanni, see Ventrone 2007a. For Perugia, see Pecugi Fop 2008, 48–60. The rights of communes over subject localities were explicitly expressed by communal chanceries in "solemn communal codices, solemnized and at the same time used and updated, read and expounded, and never absent from the mental horizons of the civic governing class" (Cammarosano 1994, 458).

possessions. In chancery documents and in the city's statutes, conquered territories are referred to as *comitatus civitatis Florentiae*, "*contado* lands of the city of Florence," even if they had originally belonged to the *contado* of another city, such as Pistoia or Pisa. Sometimes documents even add the specification *olim comitatus Pistorii, olim comitatus Pisarum*, "formerly *contado* lands of Pistoia or Pisa," before adding emphatically *et nunc comitatus civitatis Florentiae*, "but now *contado* lands of the city of Florence." A clear distinction between the inner *contado*, on one hand, and the outer *distretto* of conquered lands, on the other, had not yet arisen.[14]

And yet Florence was increasingly taking on the profile of a city-state obliged to venture beyond its original and legitimate confines, albeit more tentatively than some princely dynasties were then doing: in a laborious fashion, almost strip by strip, through the acquisition of one castle or village or small plot of territory after another. Florence needed a stronger doctrinal justification for its new principate than the pacts of submission that the conquered towns were forced to sign. Only with difficulty could territories won by conquest be portrayed as enlargements by accession (*per accessionem*), as though they had come about by a natural process (as *per vim alluvionis*, when a change in the course of a riverbed "shifts" a plot of land from one bank to the other).[15] The need for a fully legitimate mantle was increasingly felt in the fourteenth century, as the dominion expanded and challenges were mounted by the Visconti, by Florentines in exile, or by countless "competitors." One way to acquire full legitimacy for the conquests was to seek an imperial privilege, especially a vicariate, following the lead of numerous communes and dynasties. Another was to look to interstate accords with other Italian powers.

Recourse to the Holy Roman Empire's validating authority was unattractive to Florence and other Tuscan cities. According to the nineteenth-century historian of Florence, Gino Capponi, it would have "amounted to acknowledging foreign domination" (*quasi che fosse tirarsi addosso una straniera dominazione*).[16] Other cities—Pisa, Lucca, Siena, and Perugia—presumably displayed similar reluctance, though they had to accept that an actual imperial descent into Italy probably

---

14 On the distinction between *contado* and *distretto*, which long remained without a precise formulation, see Zorzi 1994, 345; Guidi 1981, 1:24. The distinction "was ultimately based on the fact that the *contado* lands were subject to the *estimo rurale*": Montorzi 2009, ix, based on Kirshner 1971, 241. See also Fasano Guarini 1973, 13–17. A *contado/distretto* distinction is also found in the Sienese territories and other areas of Italy, sometimes under different names but always conveying the same notion that the fiscal status of those dwelling in the *distretto* was more favorable: the *contado* was completely subject to Sienese power, while the *districtus* preserved greater autonomy because Sienese intrusions, especially fiscal in nature, had (formally at any rate) to be contractually stipulated. Elsewhere the terms *contado* and *distretto* assume inverted meanings—*districtio* being the effective power the commune was able to exert over areas closest to the city, with the *contado* ranging more widely. From the sixteenth to eighteenth centuries, nevertheless, the trend was for the two fiscal and administrative regimes to converge.

15 Montorzi 1997, 68; Fubini 1990, 51–53, 57, and passim; on policy regarding statutes and legal norms, see Tanzini 2007a, 2007b.

16 Capponi 1875, 1:241 (book 3, chapter 6).

involved seeking a corresponding imperial privilege.[17] When Florence resolved to come to terms with the Luxembourg emperor Charles IV of Bohemia in 1356, there was internal resistance and the pact (which awarded Florentine magistrates the status of imperial vicars) was acknowledged only grudgingly in the city.[18] This was an empire with little Roman and a great deal of German to it, an *imperium Alamannorum*, as Matteo Villani and others put it, not the *imperium Romanum* that the Florentines saw as the font of their liberty.[19] And in the months leading up to the pact, the commune had pointedly refused to allow the German entourage onto its territory. Nevertheless, the behavior of competitor states meant that the option of seeking imperial legitimation could never be ruled out—nor was it down to the very end of the fifteenth century, though Florence took care to keep its constitutional lexicon free of contamination with any terminology implying dependency, or an external delegation of power.

The other way to give the process of state consolidation an aura of legitimacy was to obtain indirect recognition from other Italian states. In numerous diplomatic *démarches*, when the moment came to stipulate peace treaties, leagues, and alliances, nuanced forms of words were chosen that acknowledged de facto Florentine dominion over other territories and cities while circumventing any formal claims. Thus, the Florentine syndics stated that they were agreeing to the truce of Sarzana in 1343 in the name of the commune "for the lands and places which it holds," and in the name of three *civitates* (Pistoia, Arezzo, Volterra); in the name of six fortified places (*castra*), with their territories (Prato, San Gimignamo, S. Miniato, Colle Valdelsa, Vernio, Barga); in the name of the *castrum-comitatus* "de Puteo" and, generically, for the *castra* of *Vallis Nebulae et Vallis Adrianae* (Valdinievole, Valdarno).[20]

Adherence was stipulated to various peace treaties of the 1470s and 1480s, "not just for the commune, *contado*, and district of Florence," but also for the *civitates* and *terrae* over which the commune had jurisdiction, in other words preeminence, force, custody, overlordship (*giurisdizione, ovvero preminenza, fortezza, custodia, maggiorìa*). The other signatories (Bologna, Perugia, Siena, etc.) also took care to

---

17 Ercole 1929, 285. On the case of the imperial vicariate presumably (indeed probably) obtained in 1355 by Perugia (which belonged to the *terrae ecclesiae*, had extended its dominion outside its *contado*, particularly in Tuscany, and was threatened at that juncture by Cardinal Albornoz), see Segoloni 1962; Pecugi Fop 2008, 61–89. The statement of Bartolo, "the city of Perugia is subject neither to the church nor the empire" (commenting on C. 10, 32, 61 [De decurionibus et filiis eorum, l. Neque Dorotheum] Rubr. "Civitas Perusina non subsit ecclesiae nec imperio"), might be datable to the period following the revocation of the imperial vicariate and prior to the restoration of papal dominion. In this period, the apostolic vicariate had a similar function of legitimizing the annexation of territories and towns: De Vergottini 1953–54.

18 Capponi 1875, 238–243, app. 5, 576–578, for the texts of Matteo Villani. Capponi, writing in the nineteenth century from a chauvanistic Guelf perspective, draws attention to the silence and the deliberate disregard of this event by contemporary Florentine chroniclers and historians.

19 And of which they would soon boast themselves to be the heirs: Fubini 1990, 30–31, 51–53, 57; Hankins 2000b, 146–147.

20 Chittolini 2009a.

distinguish between what their own *contadi* and *distretti* (districts) legitimately comprised, and what they held or occupied de facto. In the same period, Florence entered into treaties of alliance or protection with numerous minor lords and castellans who possessed lands on its borders; these were subsequently incorporated into the agreements reached with major powers, and had the effect of demarcating a zone of influence around the republic.[21]

Certainly the fullest and most explicit manifestation of Florence's growing need to distinguish its proper and preeminent nature as a *civitas* with respect to other *civitates* is to be found in the famous proem *Urbem nostram*, written for the statutes of 1409 and incorporated with some trimming into the text as "published" in 1415. This was a time when Florence "exercised more power in Italy than at any other time in her history.... The Florentines were riding high, and dreams of empire were in the air."[22] In *Urbem nostram*, the wavering formulations and ambiguities of the past are swept aside by a new and blunter turn of phrase: the adjective *potens* in the expression *potens civitas* raises the city of Florence to a position of superiority over what in the proem itself are acknowledged to be *civitates* too, but are nevertheless openly declared to be subject to the commune of Florence.[23] Sections of the statute were rescinded in 1417, but others enjoyed extensive application for many years over a wide geographical ambit. It is well known that, through court decisions, legal opinions, and legal commentaries, the statute served for centuries as the basis upon which judges, lawyers, and commentators constructed the "conceptual apparatus justifying the basis of imposed political subjection upon which the Tuscan territorial state was then being built."[24] It is remarkable that the notion of *florentina libertas*, as Hans Baron called it, could be seriously defended at the same time: if such a thing existed, it ought to have entailed respect for the *libertas* of the other Tuscan cities, and moreover a will to ensure that city-states

21 Fubini 2003, 94–97; Chittolini 2009a, 207–209; Somaini 2011.

22 Hankins 2000b, 145, 146–147, 155; de La Roncière 2004. On the elaboration of the text of the statute, with its attendant manipulations, see Tanzini 2004. The redaction of the statutes, completed under the supervision of Maso degli Albizzi, is known to be the work of Paolo di Castro. On the strongly assertive character of the *consilia* drawn up by the same jurist a few years later on behalf of Venice with respect to the rights of the *dominante* over the Terraferma dominion, see Mazzacane 1981, 589–595; Greenwood 2011, 89–93; and note 32 below. On the institutional transformations in Florence that concentrated government authority in the hands of what was coming to be called the *signoria* during the second half of the fourteenth century, see the lucid overview of Fubini 1995, with further bibliography.

23 Fubini 1994, 28–32; Tanzini 2004 emphasizes that the "selection of the norms" that went into the statute was keenly pondered so as to make it "all-embracing" (62, 66, 68), and stresses as a "fundamental fact" its "absolute originality with respect to previous compilations of statutes" (255). On contemporary juridical and humanist thought about the problem of war, see Greenwood 2011, 66–118, 119–154.

24 Montorzi 1997, 69. As noted previously by Martines (1968, 412–415), from mid-century jurists claimed for the territorial dominion the attributes of full sovereignty, thanks to an analogous extension of the meaning of *civitas* combined with Bartolo's principle of the "civitas per se sufficiens et sibi princeps" (city sufficient unto itself and a prince unto itself).

throughout Italy should coexist in peace. But it has been noted how, in Leonardo Bruni's *Laudatio* and other works from that period, the panegyric of Florentine liberty always goes hand in hand with pride in Florence's territorial expansion within Tuscany and along the Apennines.[25] And about the same time, or at any rate within a few decades, a new and heavily laden term—*imperium*—came into use, as Alison Brown has pointed out,[26] to denote the whole territory under the republic's control, overriding the distinction between *contado* and *distretto*. At the end of the fourteenth century, *dominium/dominio* was still the word the Florentines used to refer to their territory (though Bruni does use the repetitive pairing *dominium imperiumque*). In the proem of 1409, the distinction is made between the city itself, *urbs*, and the wider juridical entity, *civitas*, and the claim is advanced for the first time that the city and its *territorium* are subject to Florentine law, that together they depend upon "our jurisdiction, our power, our dominion" (*nostrae iurisdictioni potestati dominioque*). Within a few decades, the term *imperium* starts to turn up in chancery documents as well, though it is used with caution, and sometimes prudently replaced by *jurisdictio*.[27] By the end of the fifteenth century, *impero* seems to have become standard usage, certainly for Girolamo Savonarola, and a little later for Niccolò Machiavelli and Francesco Guicciardini. But by Guicciardini's time, the emerging key concept was principate, not empire.[28] In the mid-sixteenth century, the ducal power of the Medici, with all its attributes of full sovereignty and power, was still defined by the "substitution" (*subrogatio*) of "the duke of Florence and Siena for the aforementioned cities, which are among the most important in Italy" (*Dux Florentiae et Senarum in locum praedictarum civitatum, quae sunt de maioribus Italiae*). This indeed was the title borne by the Medici until the eighteenth century.[29]

Venice and Genoa

The acquisition of a large, landed dominion was less urgent for the maritime powers than for the inland cities. What did interest them, however, was establishing a buffer zone of landing sites, ports, fortifications, and even small-scale dominions around the capital city and along the principal entry and exit routes (the Ligurian coast for Genoa, the "Adriatic gulf" for Venice, the outposts on the Tyrrhenian islands in Sardinia and Sicily for Pisa). Large-scale territorial penetration into the hinterland was not a goal in itself. Venice began planning for an enlarged dominion

---

25 Hankins 2000a, particularly Najemy (2000) on the political implications of the concept of *florentina libertas*, and Brown (2000a) on the changes in meaning the concept underwent during the Medici period.

26 Brown 2000b.

27 Ibid., 34–35.

28 Ibid., 34–37; Hörnqvist 2000.

29 Montorzi 1997, 67, 93 n. 6, with reference to Sebastiano Medici, *De legibus, statutis et consuetudinibus* (Cologne, 1574).

on the Terraferma only during the violent clash with Gian Galeazzo Visconti, and in the power vacuum created in northern Italy by his death. But the project was always subordinate to its Mediterranen mercantile interests—what can be termed the principle of maritime empire that continued to prevail in the city, "by virtue of which the sea was considered self-evidently as Venetian property of indubitable legitimacy. Paradoxically, it was a possession in some sense firmer and less alienable than any conquest on [the mainland] of Italy."[30] Genoa, girded by the Ligurian Apennines, never seriously undertook a policy of conquest beyond the ridges. Pisa, weakened by its conflict with Genoa, was no longer a major player in Italian power politics by the end of the fourteenth century, and indeed fell prey to Florence within a few years.

Therefore, it was less pressing for Venice than for Florence to legitimize its dominion over territories conquered with extraordinary rapidity at the same time as Florence was seeking to extend its power—a dominion which the former expanded further in subsequent years. Venice famously laid claim to a special status which jurists came to acknowledge: it was a city "founded upon the sea" (*fundata in mari*), animated by a kind of dominion unknown to other communes. "By the law of nations, cities built upon the sea belong to their builders," as the preeminent jurist Baldo degli Ubaldi (1327–1400) puts it.[31] They had not arisen on territory over which neither pope nor emperor had ever held power: the sea was regarded as nobody's property (*res nullius*). Venice declared and portrayed itself as existing neither within the *terrae imperii* (lands of the empire) nor the *terrae ecclesiae* (lands of the church), but as a third sort of power standing apart from the empire and the papacy.[32]

There was no doubt, however, that the lands occupied on the mainland in the early fifteenth century were subject to the empire: the imperial vicariate for these territories had already been granted in the fourteenth century to Scaligeri and Carraresi rulers. Emperor Sigismund protested at their abusive occupation by "our Venetian rebels" (*rebelles nostri Veneti*), and the "rebels" for their part strove in the usual way to acquire legitimation from a superior authority, the pope in the case of the Patriarchate of Aquileia, and the emperor in Vienna for the rest. Bargaining did in fact lead to a new, fuller vicariate,[33] although Venice never succeeded in gaining,

---

30 Tenenti 1991, 46.

31 Comment on D. 1, 8 [De divisione rerum, Rerum omnium], paragraph 8: *de iure gentium civitates in mari edificatae sunt ipsorum qui aedificant.*

32 Law 1988, 136. On how this theme was conveyed, see Zenatti 1905, 127–162; Robey and Law 1975, 57–59. On various occasions from the fourteenth to sixteenth centuries, the republic commissioned fresco and panel paintings to emphasize that it was extraneous to the twin monopolies of *terrae ecclesiae* and *terrae imperii*, that its role was virtually that of a "third power" with respect to the papacy and the empire: Ortalli 2004, 514.

33 In 1421, after the annexation of Friuli, a delegation was sent to Pope Martin V, perhaps to seek this investiture, but it failed (the assertions of some chroniclers notwithstanding). The *patria* was acknowledged to belong to Venice only in 1445: Law 1988.

and perhaps never really exerted itself to obtain, a proper imperial duchy, with all its attendant validity and prestige.[34]

Even in Venice, there was a shift during the early fifteenth century in the language defining the republic's institutional identity. *Civitas* had never borne much weight in Venetian political discourse, where sovereignty was expressed in terms of *comune Veneciarum*. Now, just as in Florence, *signoria* ("lordship") came to denote Venetian sovereignty, just as *dominio* did for the subject territories.[35] The doge's title remained "Dux Venetiarum et cetera," with no specific mention of the Terraferma dominion, and the absence of any articulated and elaborated theory of "sovereignty" was the norm in Venice.[36] Nevertheless, clear awareness of the new reality of the territorial state is detectable, for example, in a famous *consilium* that Paolo di Castro (the codifier of the Florentine statutes of 1409) drafted sometime between the late 1420s and the late 1430s.[37] There may have been a trend to "recuperate" the validity of local customs, feudal privileges, and contractual treaties in favor of the Terraferma towns, but "the local magistracies were marginalized, energetically subordinated to the authority of the *princeps* [as Venice was termed], and above all every relationship was set in terms of an 'ordinary' [Venetian] regime whose outlines were beginning to emerge. The result was a determination to override the dualism that allowed corporations and social orders to defend [against the pretensions of the center] prerogatives going back to the feudal traditions of the Middle Ages; such a defense was now diverted into a rigid and conservative conception of the social hierarchy, in full accord with the policies of the Serenissima [Venice]."[38] In any case, the legitimacy of the Terraferma dominion remained an undisputed cornerstone of Venetian policy, as evident in the ill-tempered response, reported by Philippe de Commynes, of the Venetian *signoria* to expressions of doubt about the legitimacy of Venice's Italian possessions advanced by the French at the time of Charles VIII: "from the time this city was founded, [the Venetians] have always done their duty to remain at peace with their neighbors. And when they have been unable to do otherwise, they have defended themselves, and for this reason they have justly acquired that which they possess, both with their own blood and money. And just as they have acquired it, so they intend to defend it against all who may attack them": just as the king of France would defend his own French possessions, and the Kingdom of Naples as well, "which your forefathers won with

34 Law 1979, 15–17.

35 Cozzi 1982, 100–101. The abolition in 1421 of the institution of the *arengo* should perhaps be interpreted as a sign of growing awareness that Venice was becoming a territorial state, rather than as an aristocratic maneuver. See further Romanin 1973, 98.

36 Mazzacane 1981, 580–581 and passim.

37 Paolo di Castro, *Consilia*, Book 1, 318, "Viso et examinato puncto."

38 Mazzacane 1981, 590. See Viggiano 1996, 533 and passim as well. On the tempered stance of the dominion's jurists, see various suggestive remarks in Rossi 2009, especially in the articles by Gian Maria Varanini, Giovanni Rossi, and Umberto Santarelli.

similar efforts" ("che vostri predecessori hano acquistato con simili fatiche ... ").[39] The same viewpoint is set out in a letter dispatched to the Venetian ambassador in Milan, on the same date: it is perfectly natural for a free city to be an "empowered city," indeed a major territorial state; self-defense and self-assertion (i.e., expansion) amount to the same thing.[40] A few fundamental imperatives remained in force: throughout the dominion there was full Venetian sovereignty, full validity for Venetian law, and overriding authority of Venetian magistracies with respect to judicial and administrative practices.[41]

Over the ports and landings of the Ligurian coast, Genoa had exerted a precocious control, one that gradually assumed the shape of a territorial dominion. With equal precocity, two different districts were distinguished. The narrower coincided approximately with the boundaries of the bishopric of Genoa (from 1113, the archbishopric), and was directly subject to the city's consuls. This district was defined with the expression "da Gesta a Roboreto." The second covered almost the whole Riviera, and was defined with the expressions "da Monaco a Portovenere" (or "al Corvo") and "da Voltaggio, Montealto e Savignone [or *a jugo*, i.e., from the ridgeline], sino al mare [down to the sea]." In the first district, only the statutes of Genoa applied; in the second, the statutes of cities and communities of varying sizes were in force. The legitimacy of this dominion was said by the Genoese annalist Stella to derive from a concession by Emperor Frederick I. In truth, it was imposed by force of arms, its stages marked by the *submissiones* (submissions), attended by *pacta* (pacts) and *capitula* (capitulations), of one locality after another to the *dominante* (ruler).

This precocious (and relatively unopposed) imposition of dominion over adjacent territories did not lead to sudden constitutional shifts of the kind noted in Florence and Venice, nor, in chancery and political language, did it lead to a search for foundations, concepts, and formulas capable of expressing the republic's dominion over its *contado* or Liguria as a whole. At the turn of the fifteenth century, nevertheless, it is possible to catch a glimpse of a heightened consciousness of dominating a territory, of an effort to upgrade the framework of statute, and of a more rigidly hierarchical definition of the sources of law, including occasional authoritarian

39 "dicendo che, poi che questa città è stata facta, continuamente hano facto el debito suo per restare in pace con li vicini soi. Et quanto non hanno possuto fare altramente, se sono defesi, et per questo hano acquistato quelo che hano per iusticia, et col sangue et facultate sue, et in questo proprio modo col quale l'hano acquistato lo voleno defendere contra tucti che li vorano offendere." Commynes 2001, 246–257, 251: a letter of Commynes to King Charles VIII, dated 24 May 1495; the original French is no longer extant, but the Italian translation quoted here survives in the ASMi, Pot. est., cartella 555.

40 Preserved in Venice, Archivio di Stato, Senatus Secreta, 35, fol. 107v–108r, and published by Segre 1904.

41 Viggiano 1996. The question of Venice's assertion of sovereignty leads to the problem of the pacts of surrender entered into with subject communities: Ventura 1964, 40–45; 1982; Cozzi 1982, 257–263. The efforts of Verona and Padua to interpret the *bullae aureae* or *pacta* they obtained upon surrendering in 1405 and 1406 as warranties against innovations the Venetian government might introduce were met with little success: Law 1979, 14–15.

initiatives. For example, the requirement imposed, like in Florence, on subject communities to revise their statutes and to submit their draft texts to the *dominante* (ruler) for approval.[42] Nor did Genoa fail to seek imperial privileges, which were acquired in the fourteenth century and renewed in the fifteenth. But the Genoese republic was so detached politically from the empire that these could not constitute a significant foundation for its ambitions. Paradoxically, it was only in the late sixteenth century, with its Ligurian dominions at stake, that Genoa's status as an "imperial city" became a useful card to play against France.[43]

Milan

Problems analogous to those arising in the city republics did not emerge in the fourteenth and fifteenth centuries for Milan, a city not in itself "dominant" but subject, since the late thirteenth century, to the dominion of a ruling family, the Visconti, and hence at most a capital, simply the seat of a ruler (*dominus*) who possessed a personal *signoria* over Milan, just as over various other cities.[44] But when Filippo Maria Visconti died without legitimate heirs in August 1447, Milan found itself without a lord and beset by ducal claimants. At this juncture, the political will coalesced to restore republican institutions, the city returning to its illustrious communal past—with little hope, perhaps, that the experiment would endure, but ad hoc, so as to have a government in place to negotiate with the pretenders. So came into being the "magnifica Repubblica Ambrosiana."

The new republic now had to decide the extent of the territorial dominion to which it could lay claim. There existed a precise notion of the scope of the *comitatus Mediolani*: its boundaries more or less coincided with the archbishopric, enclosing a large territory (about six thousand square kilometers) subdivided into distinct areas (il Seprio, la Martesana, etc.). Over that far-flung *contado*, which, after the imperial enfeoffment of Gian Galeazzo Visconti began to be called "the duchy," the city sought to maintain and defend its own rights as a *civitas*, rights pertaining to *commune Mediolani* (commune of Milan) rather than to its ducal *dominus*, rights which, for their part, the Visconti dukes had done their best to erode and attenuate. So when the Visconti dynasty expired in 1447 and the Ambrosian Republic came into being, what territories could rightfully be claimed as its dominion? Its *contado* (or "duchy") alone? Or the array of cities—Como, Pavia, Lodi, Parma, Novara, Cremona—formerly subject to the Visconti dukes?

---

42 See Savelli 2003, 70–87, 141–146, with extensive bibliography (see 144 on how the statutes of the *dominante* functioned as "connective tissue" for the territory). On the search for foundations, concepts, and formulas adequate to express the dominion of the Genoese republic not only over its *contado* but over all of Liguria, see also Piergiovanni 1984.

43 Schnettger 2006.

44 Even Milan's rank as capital was contested, primarily by Pavia, which laid claim to a dignity loftier than that of Milan because it had been the capital and residence of the Lombard kings, and later the seat of the *palatium regium* (royal palace): Majocchi 2008, 223–225.

The Milanese had an exceptional interlocutor with whom to discuss the matter: the imperial envoy Aeneas Silvius Piccolomini (spokesman at the time for a policy of imperial "restoration"). His employer Emperor Frederick III regarded the Visconti domains as having "devolved" back to the empire, just like the Venetian territories according to Emperor Sigismund. Milan was offered the high rank of *Reichstadt* (imperial city). But agreement had to be reached with the Milanese on the form of government the city would assume once it was imperial. Piccolomini visited twice, in 1447 and 1449, and on both occasions the major stumbling block was the Ambrosian Republic's stubborn claim to the broader territorial dominions. The republic maintained that the rights enfeoffed to Gian Galeazzo to hold the other Lombard cities in subjection had not died out with the Visconti: they had reverted to Milan rather than devolved to Vienna, and at most the empire retained a right of confirmation. The Ambrosian Republic adopted this stance from the very start, projecting an image of itself not just as a free commune but as a *città dominante*, a city endowed with a dominion of its own. Tellingly, the word *communitas* was used repeatedly to refer to the territory as a whole rather than just to the Ambrosian community of Milanese citizens: this was a community comprising the city *cum eius territorio sive dominio* (with its territory or dominion), in other words, the entire Visconti state.

Thus, the Ambrosian Republic was playing a double game. On one hand, it insisted that, after the duke's death, the commune had found itself *suis legibus relictum* (left to its own laws) and that its right to direct self-government had been recognized by the empire since the twelfth century: "this, they affirmed, was stipulated in the Peace of Constance at the time of Emperor Conrad."[45] A long interlude of despotic lordship there may have been, but now it was over, and the city had regained its authentic communal institutions. The Ambrosian Republic was a new *regimen* (regime), elective and "more divine" than any simple transmission of the ducal title to a new signore.[46] But on the matter of territorial claims, it simultaneously clung

---

45 Piccolomini 2009, 1:50: "sic enim in pace Constantiae diffinitum fuisse tempore Conradi Caesaris affirmabant." Commentators have wondered why the name of Conrad rather than that of Frederick I sprang to Piccolomini's mind in connection with the Peace of Constance. A few lines further on, in his excursus on the history of Milan (1:50–59), he alludes again to the Peace of Constance "imperante Conrado facta," specifying that the *magna libertas* granted to the Lombard cities by the empire did not extend to Milan, "quod per vicarios Caesares regebant" (1:51–52). This may be a reminiscence on Piccolomini's part of the so-called *Constitutio de feudis* issued by the Salian emperor Conrad II, another cornerstone of the city's history. For a full account of Piccolomini's Milanese mission of 1447, see Piccolomini 1912, 263–278.

46 "Regimen quod est per electionem est magis divinum quam illud quod est per successionem" (rule acquired by election is more divine than rule obtained by succession), as Bartolo put it, a quotation that effectively conveys the climate of opinion prevailing in Milan at that time: Spinelli 1988, 48. See ibid., 31, 48–51, for an analysis, based on a wide range of documents produced by the republic, of the semantic significance of the terms *communitas*, *universitas*, and others linked to them (*populus*, *res publica*, *libertas*). He shows clearly how they were used to emphasize that the Ambrosian Republic had the full status of a state, and that all those holding Milanese citizenship were members of one united body of citizenry.

to the heritage of the Visconti duchy. The captains of Milan's citizenry declared that they themselves possessed the *plenitudo potestatis* that had previously been awarded to the Visconti (or that the Visconti had awarded themselves). Their decisions were arrived *at ex certa scientia et motu proprio ac de nostre plenitudine potestatis* (from the certain knowledge and spontaneously from our plenitude of power). They did not, unlike other communes, publish *riformagioni* or *provvigioni*, laws approved in the city councils: they promulgated edicts and decrees (*decernimus, statuimus, absolvimus, declaramus*) in formulas that imitated the style of the ducal chancery. They acted, in short, as a collectivity wielding ducal power.[47]

This was the sticking point—these pretensions half communal and half princely—that prevented an agreement with the imperial envoy. For his part, Piccolomini, in the account he gives of his missions, presents himself as less hostile to Milanese pretensions than the rest of the imperial delegation, more sensitive to the aspirations of a *civitas*. In any case, political and military events did not favor the republic: "its" cities and territories were occupied by others, or set themselves up as *magnifiche comunità* (magnificent communities) in their own right. By Piccolomini's second mission, Francesco Sforza's forces were closing in on Milan. Even then an agreement proved unattainable, though *in extremis* the Milanese condescended to offer the remaining free cities in Lombardy a federal option with recognition of Milan's preeminence rather than subjection to a *dominante*. But it was too late: the Sforza era was about to dawn.[48]

Civitas, then, a concept pregnant with meaning in the thirteenth and fourteenth centuries, subsequently lost ground. The focus became the principate and the prerogatives the *princeps* might now exercise over a territorial state. And yet the concept of the *civitas* lived on: the cities in question never surrendered their claim to quasi-sovereign control over their historic *contadi*, and jurists never failed to acknowledge the special status that was naturally inherent in ancient city-states, "authentic *civitates*," in contrast to urban centers that had come into being since the communal age.[49] Adduced now in defense of subject cities' rights vis-à-vis princes and *dominanti*, the rights of a virtual "small state" within a larger state,[50] the concept of *civitas* remained laden with meaning throughout early modern Italian history—for better and for worse; indeed, it animated opposition to the reforms instigated in the eighteenth century by Italy's enlightened despots.

47 Black 2009, 80–81.
48 See Chittolini, forthcoming, for full citation of documents and bibliography.
49 Thus, among others, Giovan Battista De Luca, referring specifically to north-central Italy: Chittolini 2009b. For Lombardy and the sharp distinction over the whole early modern period between the episcopal *civitas* and other *oppida* (towns) and *terre grosse* (fortified towns), see Magni 1937, 189–193.
50 Mannori 1999.

TWO

Medicean Florence and Beyond

Legitimacy of Power and Urban Traditions

GIAN MARIA VARANINI

IN RECENT HISTORIOGRAPHY, THE SYSTEMATIC comparative study of Renaissance (or, to be precise, late medieval) Italian states began at Villa I Tatti almost forty years ago, with the celebrated volumes *Florence and Venice: Comparisons and Relations.*[1] In these, comparisons and contrasts were drawn between the two republics. This approach continued in the early 1980s with the seminars on Florence and Milan organized by Sergio Bertelli, Craig Hugh Smyth, and Nicolai Rubinstein. Their proceedings were published at the end of the decade,[2] with the terms of comparison extended to the Medici and Sforza "courts." Scholarly colloquia with similar comparative formats continued to be held in Italy, including one in Milan on the Lombard and Burgundian duchies.[3] Two further memorable occasions were the Italian-American meeting at Chicago on the *Origins of the State,*[4] and the 1996 gathering at San Miniato on the Florentine territorial state.[5]

In the brief remarks that follow, the focus will be political and ideological: How was the control exercised by the Florentine, Milanese, and Venetian states throughout their respective dominions juridically organized and legitimized? To what extent did communal traditions live on and exert an impact, both in the capital cities and in the subject towns?

1 Bertelli, Rubinstein, and Smyth 1979–80.
2 Bertelli, Rubinstein, and Smyth 1989.
3 Cauchies and Chittolini 1990.
4 Chittolini, Molho, and Schiera 1994.
5 Connell and Zorzi 2000.

In her comparison of the Florentine and Milanese states, Jane Black states a point of fundamental importance.[6] No matter what image the two regimes strove to project (toned-down understatement in Tuscany, unrestrained display of power in Lombardy), in both cities the basis of legitimate power was still formally the popular will as manifested in the *parlamento*, the assembly of all the citizens in the central town square acting virtually as a constituent assembly, an institution descended from the popular assembly of the communal age.

In Florence, the *parlamenti* of 1434, 1458, and 1466 were key moments in the history of the Medici regime: in each case, the *parlamento* ratified Medici authority. These assemblies could be held only in the presence of heavy security, but they could not be dispensed with because the institutional machinery, and more than that, the communal tradition, insisted that sovereignty had a popular basis. The force of that tradition was stressed almost fifty years ago by Nicolai Rubinstein,[7] who argued that the republican tradition embodied in the *parlamenti* still counted heavily in Medicean Florence. In a number of papers, Riccardo Fubini has distanced himself from Rubinstein's republican formalism, and, widening the chronological purview, has emphasized that this impressive series of formal ratifications, of approvals delivered under duress by the people summoned to the piazza by the *signoria*—an institution unique to Florence[8]—commenced in 1378 and was continued in 1382 and 1393. The Medici resumed the use of *parlamenti* after a forty-year gap, and there matters stood until 1480, when Lorenzo's reform and the creation of the council of seventy (*consiglio dei settanta*) put an end to the tradition of ad hoc legislative assemblies. This was the turning point for the tradition of popular sovereignty: the creation of an incipient life senate to replace the *consulte*,[9] which had theoretically been not legislative but consultative, and to override the ancient principle of territorial representation based on the *popolo*, as represented in the *gonfaloni* (the city's sixteen local districts).

In Milan, the jurists consulted by the Sforza were split over how best to legitimize Sforza power across the range of territorial entities that made up their dominion. But overall they tended to look upon the princely claim to *plenitudo potestatis* with a caution and reserve that contrasted strikingly with the recognition, assent, and favor shown by their trecento predecessors.[10] Gian Galeazzo Visconti's request to the emperor Wenceslas in 1396 for the Lombard duchies to be vested in him had been a juridical act of "willful defiance of the communal and urban source of his own authority." The terms of the Peace of Constance (1183) were evaded with the help of *consilia* composed by Baldo degli Ubaldi, among others. And during

---

6   See Jane Black, this volume, 86–87.
7   See in particular Rubinstein 1997, 99 ff. (chap. 5, "The *Parlamento* of 1458 and the Consolidation of the Régime").
8   See Fubini, this volume, 62.
9   See ibid., 65.
10   See Black 2009, chap. 6 ("Lawyers and the Repudiation of Ducal Absolutism").

Filippo Maria Visconti's time (the historical backdrop to the theoretical writings of Martino Garati of Lodi), the "restructuring of the urban *contado*" and the "territorialization project of Gian Galeazzo and Filippo Maria which aimed to unify the former 'city states' into a single regional state" appeared to gain ground. But with the advent of Francesco Sforza, "the various cities once again started demanding the restoration of their individual rights over their *contadi*," and the project stalled. Similarly, the Ambrosian Republic (1447–49) showed no less zeal than the preceding princely regime for imposing centralized administration upon the dominion.[11]

In other words, in contrast to Tuscany, where Florence had incorporated rural districts once belonging to Prato, Pisa, and Pistoia[12] into a single *contado*, all the Lombard cities retained the power to defend local liberties by renegotiating the terms of their various capitulations and pacts with the Sforza regime, both during the changeover from Visconti to Sforza and at the moments of succession in 1466 and 1483. Even the Visconti's ducal decrees—no matter how peremptorily worded, and even though it had been explicitly declared in 1441 that they were to override local statutes—often had to be issued repeatedly as they clashed with the legal codes of the subject towns, and local councils fiercely obstructed their enforcement. These cities may have been subject to a lord, but formally they were still *civitates superiorem non recognoscentes*,[13] and the sovereign's decrees took effect there only once the subject towns had permitted them to be publicly proclaimed.[14]

So in the political and institutional context of the Florentine and Milanese quattrocento, the problem of the ineluctably "citizen/civic" and "communal" wellspring of public authority, and its unsuitability for hereditary transmission, was often explicit, sometimes latent, but never absent from theoretical debate. It is important to stress this fact: the ideal of the city-state retained great vitality in Italian life.

In north-central Italy, where a number of formerly sovereign communes had fallen under the rule of dynasties (*signorie*) relatively early,[15] there was a tradition of political discourse and debate about the problem that already had a 150-year history at the turn of the quattrocento. It has its modern counterpart in a trenchant strand of historiography which in any discussion of the Italian Renaissance state ought not to be overlooked. In 1910, Francesco Ercole, a historian of law and political theory, published his research on dynastic regimes in the Veneto during the late due- and early trecento.[16] He perceived the interface between the communes and the dynastic families as a functioning "diarchy," a perspective recently revived by

11 For the above, see Cengarle 2006, 66, 95, and 107, respectively, for the quoted passages.
12 Zorzi 1994. Giorgio Chittolini makes this point as well in his contribution to this volume, see above, 16–17.
13 See, on this principle, Costa 1999, 213.
14 Cengarle 2006, 97.
15 See the synthesis in Zorzi 2010.
16 The title of the 1910 volume was *Comuni e signorie nel Veneto. Scaligeri Caminesi Carraresi* (see Ercole 1929).

John Law.[17] In 1924, Pietro Torelli highlighted the case of Mantua under the rule of the Bonacolsi, showing how the imperial vicariate, on one hand, and the captaincy of the *popolo*, on the other, were the "constituent elements" of the Bonacolsi *signoria*.[18] In the 1940s, before research on dynastic regimes went out of fashion (an intellectual and historiographical reaction of the 1950s to fascism),[19] Giovanni De Vergottini and Gino Sandri probed the specific problem of the relation between the dynastic regimes and the imperial or papal vicariate beginning early in the trecento.[20] To be appointed vicar for one of the universal authorities was a way for a signore to obtain the legitimization from above that would allow him to break free of the "communal" shackles binding him from below—reminders of the origins of his own authority in the city-state and obstacles to his ambitions to hand that authority on to his heirs. Reflecting on this aspiration in the middle decades of the trecento, Bartolo of Sassoferrato defended the view that the rulers of particular domains (*reges particulares*) could indeed transmit power "per successiones" in *De tyranno*.[21] But ingrained traditions continued to have their effects, and in many towns under signorial rule during the second half of the trecento, the election of a new ruler had to be ratified by the citizens assembled in an *arengo*. Dynastic regimes even advertised this fact for its public relations value.[22] In sum, even in towns where a *signoria* was deeply rooted—towns that Florentine propagandists in the trecento and early quattrocento customarily branded as tyrannies—there persisted a profound and ineradicable sense that the citizens themselves, the members of the commune, were the ultimate font of local power. The same feeling is detectable in Florence in the *parlamenti* that the Medici always regarded with apprehension and managed with such vigilance and finesse.

A few examples will suffice to show how deeply and viscerally the memory of their history as communes survived in towns under signorial rule. In mid-fourteenth-century Bologna, even after the Pepoli had made themselves signori of the city, the council of four thousand retained the right to elect the civic magistrates *ad brevia*—that is, by a random sortition in which, in principle, the names of all full citizens could be entered.[23] The procedure could be bypassed with a direct plea to the signore, but the principle of popular sovereignty remained firmly in

17 Law 2010.
18 Torelli 1924.
19 On this stasis, a reaction to the favor shown by historians with links to the Mussolini regime toward "authoritarian" styles of government (with Ercole himself in the vanguard—his 1910 book was reprinted in 1929 under the title *Dal comune al principato*), and the subsequent reprise of studies on the *signorie* under the stimulus in particular of a famous article by Ernesto Sestan (1961), see Zorzi 2012b.
20 De Vergottini 1977 (first published 1941); Sandri 1969 (first published 1939).
21 Quaglioni 1983, 166–167.
22 Here the example of the Carrara *signoria* at Padua can suffice: Kohl 1998.
23 The word *breve* means a ballot or slip of paper bearing the name of a candidate and inserted with the other *brevia* into an urn. On these procedures, see Waley 2010.

place, and election to office clearly survived under Visconti lordship in the middle decades of the trecento. Nor were the Bolognese oblivious to the fact that not all people lived as subjects to a dynastic family as they did. In 1376, they stated what they would ideally have preferred: "it would be good to rule and govern the city of Bologna in the manner of other cities where the *popolo* is sovereign, above all like the Venetians and Florentines."[24] As one historian remarks, the institutional and constitutional history of Bologna between 1376 and 1506 is "the history of the ongoing conflictual relation between, on one hand, the practice and culture of government by the *popolo* in a free state, and on the other the practice and culture of untrammeled papal dominion."[25]

The "small councils" (*consigli ristretti*) that emerged in many dynastically ruled cities of north-central Italy during the trecento kept the memory of the "communal" origins of local power alive in practical terms of everyday administration.[26] Composed of eight, twelve, or twenty-four members (*deputati ad utilia civitatis*), these councils were primarily executive bodies with limited competence. And yet the representative function they fulfilled was not insignificant, meeting, as they did, the desire for political participation that was still potent among the elites of fourteenth-century Italian towns. These were ruling classes who harbored no anachronistic aspirations to "democracy," but who did seek a degree of participation in government.

Mantua under the Gonzaga is an interesting and well-known case where the specter of the popular will, the ill-defined but deeply rooted awareness of the need for general consultation so that *quod omnes similiter tangit ab omnibus comprobetur,*[27] can be seen, for example, in the so-called referendum that Gianfrancesco I Gonzaga, signore of Mantua, conducted and recorded in 1430.[28] It is worth noting that at this time he still held power as *capitano del popolo*—power legitimized from below by the citizen body. Only in 1433 did the title and office of marquis confer princely power upon him.[29] The point of interest here is not the upshot of the referendum (which was certainly predetermined), but rather the procedure that was followed, and the very fact that it was followed at all, at a time so close to the creation of the marquisate. A century and a half after the seizure of power

---

24 "Bonum esset regere et gubernare civitatem Bononie secumdum quod faciunt alie civitates que habent statum popularem, et maxime ut faciunt Veneti vel Florentini": De Benedictis 2007, 899. For the references to earlier Bolognese history, see Trombetti Budriesi 2007.

25 See De Benedictis 2007, 903.

26 The Scaligeri of Verona are a pertinent example of a strongly consolidated and robust *signoria*: see Varanini 1979; 1992, 185–196 ("I consigli civici veronesi tra la dominazione viscontea e quella veneziana"). On the general topic of urban executive councils with a quasi-representative function, see now Tanzini 2013a, which focuses, however, on the duecento.

27 "What affects all similarly should be approved by all": the classic formulation from the Codex Justinianus, 5.59.5.2.

28 Grignani 1990.

29 Mozzarelli 1990, 17.

in Mantua by Pinamonte Bonacolsi in 1272, despite the many subsequent generations of Bonacolsi and Gonzaga rule, the memory of the communal origins of signorial power was not yet extinct. The Gonzaga, who took power in 1329, might have repressed communal opposition more successfully than the Bonacolsi, but in Mantua an equilibrium between commune and signore never vanished altogether, and the referendum of 1430 signified that in those 150 years no new political culture had arisen to match the new territorial structures and princely power. The Gonzaga still felt that they lacked legitimacy, which is why Gianfrancesco sought sporadically (and soon afterward successfully) the title of marquis and recognition from the empire.[30]

The principle of the hereditary transfer of power was never, or almost never, formally recognized in the political life of the Italian dynastic principalities of the trecento.[31] There continued to be discussion about the *civitas* (the city) and the consent the *civitas* granted to the princely regime. So the idea of Italy as the land of both "communes and despots," associated with the name of Philip Jones,[32] retains all its force, no matter whether the holder of the *signoria*, the signore in the abstract sense, was a signore in person (a "despot"), or a sovereign commune of citizens (a "republic," such as Florence and Venice). In certain respects, it would continue to do so down to the end of the *ancien régime*. Giorgio Chittolini's work, focused on Lombardy but with results applicable to other Italian regional states, has shown not only how a persistent and abiding civic identity was a crucial and indispensable element of the late medieval and early modern history of north-central Italy, but also that in practice there were wide opportunities for the exercise of administrative and judicial power on the part of the citizen communes.[33] Additionally, recent research on the Venetian Terraferma has confirmed that the urban mentality persisted there perhaps even more decisively than among the Lombard cities, at least in Brescia, Verona, Vicenza, and even Padua.[34] It persisted in the teeth of a policy emanating from Venice to centralize government throughout its dominion in the later quattrocento, a tendency not unconnected with the enhanced role of the council of ten.[35] The same is true of the Lombard cities.

A related aspect is what might be called the disquiet in political thought provoked among the governing classes of the towns in the regional states by their faint awareness that their conceptual schemes and linguistic formulations were inadequate to the task of defining and organizing the new territorial entities that had

---

30 Lazzarini 1996, 34.
31 On these problems, see now Canzian 2013.
32 Jones 1965 (republished 2010).
33 See Chittolini's collection of articles (Chittolini 1996a); and in general for his publications, see Covini 2011.
34 See especially Law 2000b (sixteen articles from 1971 to 1993); Varanini 1992, especially the *Introduzione*, lix–lxvi, on the strong sense of local citizen identity felt by the governing classes in each town.
35 The first to highlight this connection with the council of ten (*consiglio dei dieci*) was Knapton 1981.

arisen. The territorial states were supra-civic dominions that did not match the categories framed by current terminology.[36]

The Florentine governing class, starting in the 1350s (and with the utmost reluctance), also resorted to the imperial vicariate, an office that the priors were granted by Emperor Charles IV,[37] but at that time the territorial dominion of Florence in Tuscany was still in its infancy. Over the following decades, as they acquired Arezzo, Pistoia, and Pisa,[38] the Florentines chose a different method of imparting structure and organization to their new *imperium*. The urban centers were separated from the country districts attached to them and these districts were "reduced to *contado* status," thus creating a single, large territory that was in principle uniformly subject to Florence. Andrea Zorzi calls the Florentine territorial state a *contado* state (*stato contado*), characterized by "a policy of dominion, rather than integration," and by the emergence of Florence as the hub.[39] In relation to Pistoia, Charles de La Roncière asks, "what was the status of Pistoia with respect to the dominant city: *libertas, devotio,* or *dominatio*? All three words were used, but the reality was *dominatio*."[40] Hence, as Chittolini opportunely notes,[41] in the proem to the statute of 1409, the Florentines introduced a gradation among *urbs, civitas,* and *civitas potens,* and used the triad "iurisdictio, potestas et dominium" to indicate the ensemble of the subject territories, placing strong emphasis on the unitary dimension of the new territorial entity that had come into existence. Naturally the subject cities did not lose all their individuality, but local autonomy was reduced in the case of Pisa, and at the very least kept under firm surveillance in that of Pistoia.[42]

A strikingly similar pattern emerges with the Ambrosian Republic, that brief political experiment that brought the glory days of the Milanese commune briefly back to life in 1447–49.[43] Their heritage of institutions and values inevitably caused its leaders to view the Lombard territorial state, at the head of which they now found themselves, in exclusively "civic" and "communal" terms. The revived communal government of Milan now tried surreptitiously to extend to the entire Visconti dominion built up by Gian Galeazzo and Filippo Maria the traditional, twofold classification of *città* and *contado*. For the Milanese elite, this was the obvious alternative to the array of juridical expedients used by the Visconti to assert dominion over the Lombard duchies. In a paradox more apparent than real, the Ambrosian Republic acted according to principles identical to those characteristic of the most

36 See Gamberini, Genet, and Zorzi 2011.
37 Luzzati 1986, 97–98; Zorzi 2000, 31.
38 Luzzati 1986, 127 (1380), 122 (1402), 170–172 (1406), respectively.
39 Zorzi 2000, 31; the second passage quoted is from Elena Fasano Guarini (1994, 173).
40 De La Roncière 2004, 18 n. 6.
41 See Chittolini, this volume, 19. On these problems see also Tanzini 2004.
42 See Connell 2000a; Tognetti 2010a, both with full bibliographies.
43 See Spinelli 1986–1987.

extreme princely absolutism, and tried to impose its own direct rule throughout Lombardy. It has been astutely observed that "the Capitani assumed the role of the collective duke," and the republic emitted not *provvisioni* or *riformagioni* (resolutions, in other words, adopted in civic councils) but decrees, in the manner of the Visconti dukes.[44] The documents for the period define as Ambrosian *territorium sive dominium* even the cities that the Visconti had juridically governed as civic signori rather than as dukes (Milan and Pavia being the obvious exceptions). Another sign of the municipal mind-set that animated the elites of Lombardy is the fact that at Pavia, too, a short-lived "repubblica di san Siro," named for the city's patron saint, was proclaimed.[45]

So the Ambrosian Republic and the Florentine commune present two instances of the same phenomenon: the civic *signoria*, the princely *dominium*, of a capital city with strong communal roots over conquered cities whose communal roots were just as strong. Shifts in political vocabulary are telling: the near-contemporary innovation in Venetian sources is no accident. Beginning in 1423, the expression *commune Veneciarum* was replaced in official documents by the couplet *signoria-dominium* —a reflection of the dominion on the Terraferma instituted in the same year.[46] The way archival documents are organized is an indicative sign of genuine institutional change, and the new direction in Venetian policy toward the Terraferma did not fail to leave its mark in this respect. In 1440, the series of registers of the Venetian senate were divided into two distinct streams whose designations, *Senato-Terra* and *Senato-Mar*, indicate the two primary categories of senate business.[47] And yet there was stubborn resistance in the Veneto and Lombardy. The lexical shift in the Venetian documents had less significance for the Venetian Terraferma than the parallel shift in the Florentine documents had for the conquered towns in the fifteenth-century Florentine state. Apart from the use of the term *dominium*, Venetian sovereignty had been imposed in the years leading up to 1423 through the mechanism of submissions (*dedizioni*). It is well known that these putatively spontaneous acts making the cities subject to the *dominante* were sometimes no more than camouflage for military conquest (as at Padua, which fell in 1405 after a long siege), but sometimes they did in fact express willingness to submit. In every case, these *dedizioni* (stipulated for Vicenza and Verona, for the communities of Friuli, and in 1427 and 1428 for Bergamo and Brescia) ostensibly presented the relation between Venice and the subject city as a bilateral pact. This circumstance would lead to endless rounds of negotiation over the coming decades and even centuries.[48]

44 Black 2009, 80.
45 Roveda 1992b, 83, also cited by Black 2009, 80 n. 64.
46 Law 2000a, 153–155; 2000c, 20–21; Finlay 1980, 43. See also Viggiano 1993.
47 Varanini 2012, 393.
48 There exists a vast literature on this crucial aspect of the history of the Venetian Terraferma state: see the perspicacious survey in Ortalli 2002.

The adoption of the term *dominium* corresponded to no profound change in the political outlook of the Venetian patriciate, nor did it elsewhere. Such a change certainly lay ahead, and it did in the long run bring about a different attitude toward the Terraferma state, but that change came about over the long term, and was not complete before the second half of the cinquecento. In 1437, the emperor Sigismund granted the Venetian Republic a celebrated diploma, creating Francesco Foscari as imperial vicar over Treviso, Feltre, Belluno, Ceneda, Padua, Brescia, Bergamo, Casalmaggiore, Soncino, Piadena, and S. Giovanni in Croce (the greater part of the Terraferma, in other words, but not Verona and Vicenza, to which the last Scaligeri still laid claim). It was a significant enactment, but it changed nothing in substance. Some time ago, Aldo Mazzacane observed that Venice "never rethought its own sovereignty in theory."[49] The political culture of the Venetian patriciate remained tied to localism, as shown by treatises such as the *De bene instituta republica* of Domenico Morosini, dating from the end of the quattrocento.[50] Venetian historiography likewise remained municipal and rhetorically incapable of facing up to the problem of the construction of the Venetian state. The quattrocento historiography of the Terraferma cities mirrors this municipal focus, leaving the *dominante* out of of the picture.[51] Significantly, it was a Friulian noble, Jacopo da Porcìa, who set out the problem of the Terraferma *dominium*'s structure as a state with the greatest clarity. In his *De reipublicae Venetae administratione domi et foris liber*, he dwelt on the relation between the Venetian patriciate and the local governing classes of the Terraferma (with special emphasis on the Friulian nobility to which he belonged), treating such technical matters as the military organization of the state.[52]

When it comes to comparing the Florentine and Venetian states, one can do no better than cite the remarks of Francesco Guicciardini in one of his *ricordi*:

> I have said many times, and it is very true, that it was harder for the Florentines to achieve their small dominion than for the Venetians to achieve their large territorial gains. For the Florentines are in a region that knew many liberties, and these are very hard to extinguish. These provinces are very hard to conquer and, once conquered, are no less hard to keep. Besides, the Florentines have the Church nearby, which is strong and immortal. Though it sometimes seems to stagger, in the end it reaffirms its rights more strongly than ever. The Venetians have conquered lands accustomed to servitude,

---

49 Mazzacane 1981, 599, for the reference to the diploma granted by Sigismund, and 601 for what follows.
50 For this text see Morosini 1969, and the assessment of Cozzi 1970. For further discussion see Casini 2001, 2002.
51 See Gaeta 1980.
52 On da Porcìa see Mazzacane 1981, 605; Stefanutti 2006.

stubborn neither in defense nor in rebellion. And as neighbors they have had secular princes, whose lives and memories are not everlasting.[53]

The strong localism of the cities of Tuscany, that "region that knew many liberties," had, at the turn of the quattrocento, been violently suppressed by Florence from the moment of conquest, and the revolt of Pisa in 1494–1509 is there as a reminder of the brutal methods employed to give birth to the Florentine dominion.[54] Guicciardini doubtless had Pisa in mind when he wrote the above *ricordo*. The cities brought under Venetian rule and integrated into their Terraferma *dominium* may indeed have been "accustomed to servitude," having already fallen under the rule of dynastic regimes during the trecento. Nevertheless, the greater margins of autonomy and local self-government that Venice in fact granted the Terraferma cities, through the legal mechanism of the *dedizioni* (especially those most remote from the capital, such as Brescia, Bergamo, Verona, and Vicenza), created no bond of affection or allegiance, no real consent to the rule of the *dominante*. In 1509, when the Venetian army was defeated at Agnadello (Vailà), the Terraferma state disintegrated precipitately and the self-serving loyalty of the Terraferma elites was patently evident, as they looked to their own interests, in choosing Emperor Maximilian I as their new ruler.[55]

The turmoil of the Italian Wars also gave rise to a few isolated reminiscences of ancient communal, *popolano* government as opposed to elite rule. An interesting example here is the Brescian humanist Carlo Valgulio in his treatise *De concordia brixianorum*, published in 1516 (when, following the collapse of the Venetian Terraferma state in 1509 and the French interlude, Brescia reverted to Venetian subjugation). Valgulio took the fictitious name of a Brescian *popolano*, Benedetto Massimo, but the political aspirations he expressed were really those of the *popolari* of every Lombard city. "Benedetto Massimo" stringently criticizes the oligarchic dispensation at Brescia, where the city council "is restricted to a handful of the rich, almost all interrelated by marriage alliances, family connections, and friendship. They alone enjoy public honor and profit." But the aspiration for more broadly based government, in which the majority of citizens would not feel themselves "exiles in their own home," and in which the city would not be "utterly laid waste through

---

53 "Ho detto molte volte, e è verissimo, che più è stato difficile a' Fiorentini a fare quello poco dominio che hanno, che a' Viniziani el loro grande: perché e' Fiorentini sono in una provincia che era piena di libertà, le quali è difficillimo a estinguere—però si vincono con grandissima fatica e, vinte, si conservano con non minore. Hanno di poi la Chiesa vicina, che è potente e non muore mai, in modo che se qualche volta travaglia, risurge alla fine el suo diritto più fresco che prima. E Viniziani hanno avuto a pigliare terre use a servire, le quali non hanno ostinazione né nel difendersi né nel ribellarsi, e per vicini hanno avuto principi secolari, la vita e la memoria de' quali non è perpetua." Guicciardini 2013, *ricordo* n. 29; English translation from Guicciardini 1965, 48–49. See in general, on the assessments by the Florentines of Renaissance Venice (the city alone, not the Terraferma towns), the classic article by Gilbert 1968.

54 Luzzati 1973.

55 Varanini 2011.

incessant jealousies, hatreds, and hostilities," was destined to remain unfulfilled: Venice chose to maintain the status quo, forging its alliance with the powerful local patriciate.[56]

Once more, then, there is a "muncipally oriented" mind-set and a total incapacity to think in terms of the "modern state."[57] In the political culture and structure of the Italian regional states of the quattrocento, the city-state remained the inescapable point of reference, the true touchstone against which all else was measured.

56 Ventura 1993, 185.
57 Ibid., 180–183 was the first to remark on the importance of this text and the whole episode.

THREE

Communal Traditions and Personal Power in Renaissance Florence

The Medici as Signori

ANDREA ZORZI

THE COLLOQUIUM OUT OF WHICH this volume has risen is important for at least two reasons. The time was ripe for an assessment of the rich period of scholarship opening in 1966 with Nicolai Rubinstein's study of the government of Florence under the Medici.[1] The image of the Medici as Renaissance princes of the fifteenth century has since been transformed. The works of Dale Kent on Cosimo "il vecchio" and those of Melissa Meriam Bullard and Francis William (Bill) Kent on Lorenzo the Magnificent[2] have projected an image of the Medici as political operators, indeed as "bosses." The last term, laden with negative connotations, is chosen deliberately. Anthony Molho, for example, contrasted Cosimo's public image as *pater patriae* (father of his homeland) and his private role as a "godfather" (*padrino*), while Bill Kent used expressions such as "boss" (*padrone*) and "Big Man" in his portrait of Lorenzo.[3] In recent decades, the perspective introduced by Rubinstein has prevailed: the Medici were *primi cittadini*, "leading citizens," operating within institutional structures—those of the communal city-state—that properly pertained to republics, not principates.

Another reason to reassess this established perspective is to profit from Philip Jones's alternative and contrasting interpretation of governmental forms in the Italian city-states. From Jones's viewpoint, the Medici regime fits neatly into the

---

1 Rubinstein 1966; a second edition was published in 1997.
2 See Dale Kent 2000; Bullard 1994; F. W. Kent 2004b.
3 See Molho 1979; F. W. Kent 2004b, especially 7, 45, 71.

category of despotism. First, in his 1965 essay on "Communes and Despots: The City-State in Late-Medieval Italy,"[4] and ultimately in his 1997 political history of the Italian city-states,[5] Jones showed himself indifferent to the romantic spell cast over the Italian "despots" by writers such as John Addington Symonds[6] and unmoved by the older and sometimes cherished notion that the Italian cities had been the locus of a dramatic confrontation between republican (or "democratic") and despotic (or "tyrannical") systems of government. Jones emphasized instead that oligarchy, no matter what its form, was the key feature of Italian cities. This included the personal *signoria*, which he interpreted as a political response to the communal regime's failure, the "outcome of a political drive, oligarchic or factional, toward restriction,"[7] combating and conquering opposing "popular" political forces that sought legitimacy in the will of the *popolo* (people).[8]

This colloquium is well timed too on account of the revival of scholarly interest in the *signorie*. In recent publications, Gian Maria Varanini has issued an invitation to break free of prejudice in favor of the communal regime as a model of participatory democracy (especially in the case of Florence), and to reject the stereotype of tyrannical *signoria* versus republican commune.[9] As for Giorgio Chittolini, the passage from commune to *signoria* appears "less sharp and brutal, a less dramatic process," inasmuch as "communal regimes no longer look so communal and 'democratic,' and autocratic alternatives commanded numerous supporters."[10] In 2010, the Italian Ministero dell'Istruzione, dell'Università e della Ricerca supported a research project coordinated by Jean-Claude Maire Vigueur—*Le signorie cittadine in Italia (metà XIII secolo–inizi XV secolo)*—which investigated signorial government as a political form from its medieval origins down to the Renaissance,[11] and compiled a systematic online *repertorio delle esperienze di potere personale e signorile nelle città italiane* (repertory of cases of personal and signorial power in the Italian cities).[12]

It is worthwhile, against this background, to try and assess to what extent Florence remained a communal republic under the Medici, or to what degree it fits the profile of a *signoria*. Here it would be profitable to go back to the 1960s as well,

---

4   Jones 1965; republished 2010.

5   Jones 1997.

6   On his influence, see Law 2005; Kohl 2010.

7   "Prodotto di tendenze politiche restrittive, oligarchiche o di fazione": Jones 1980, 516.

8   The tendency to view the *signoria* as a "reaction" to the rise of *popolo* regimes appears still to prevail in Anglophone historiography; for a recent example, see Dean 2004.

9   Varanini 2004, 137.

10   "Meno brusco e traumatico, suscettibile di una interpretazione meno drammatica," because "i regimi comunali ci appaiono meno comunali, meno 'democratici,' e i regimi autocratici ci appaiono non sprovvisti di consenso": Chittolini 2007, 146.

11   See now Zorzi 2013a; Maire Vigueur 2013.

12   See *Repertorio delle esperienze di potere personale e signorile nelle città italiane*, accessed 23 September 2014, http://www.italiacomunale.org/resci.

even earlier than Rubinstein's 1966 book and Jones's 1965 essay, to Ernesto Sestan's 1961 article on the origins of civic *signorie*. The topic had occupied center stage during the Fascist period, exploited for examples of acclamation by plebiscite so as to provide precedents for the assumption of dictatorial powers; it will come as no surprise to learn that the theme has been the victim of embarrassed silence ever since.[13] Sestan put to one side the prevailing Italian historical-juridical approach, concentrating instead on the signori's social profile. He proposed a two-phase model, with the signori who gained power in the thirteenth and fourteenth centuries emerging from the rural nobility, in contrast to those of the later fourteenth and fifteenth centuries, who rose from the merchant aristocracy. Families such as the Estensi, Carraresi, Scotti, Maggi, Faggiolani, Bonacolsi, and Antelminelli typify the early phase, all with backgrounds "in feudal society, or in societies half-feudal, half-communal." Only when the signorial age had reached its "second or third, or even subsequent, generation" are signori encountered emerging from the mercantile bourgeoisie, for example the Pepoli, the Gambacorta, the Guinigi, the Petrucci—and, of course, the Medici.[14]

Sestan viewed "the early Medici *signoria* in Florence" as a "textbook example" of a species he called *crypto-signoria*, in which the de facto signore was a "leader of an oligarchic faction held together by densely interwoven interests, licit and illicit." The *crypto-signorie* were

> *signorie* in fact, where the signore might not even allow himself to be identified as such and might permit all or most traditional communal institutions (such as deliberative councils) to continue, while he deftly pulled the strings from behind the scenes, ensuring that they were guided with a firm hand by trusted individuals, beholden to his orders.[15]

Though such observations would appear to suggest a convergence between Sestan and Rubinstein, the latter curiously failed to acknowledge the interpretative precedent provided by Sestan's article (which goes unmentioned in both 1966 and 1997 editions of his work). Jones, of course, knew the article well, citing it in his own 1965 paper in support of his oligarchic, and in 1980, feudal interpretation of the *signorie*'s origins.[16] Rubinstein cannot have been ignorant of Sestan's article; perhaps the omission was due to a deep incompatibility between their perspectives: for Sestan

---

13 Sestan 1961. I have proposed a rereading of Sestan's essay in Zorzi 2012b.

14 Sestan 1961, 56–57: "alla società feudale o ad una promiscua società feudale-comunale"; "seconda o terza generazione ed oltre."

15 Sestan 1961, 49: "cripto-signorie tenute di fatto dal capo di una oligarchia faziosa, saldata insieme da una fitta rete di interessi leciti ed illeciti"; "signorie sostanziali, nelle quali il signore, talora nemmeno assumendo questo titolo, lascia sussistere tutti o buona parte degli istituti comunali tradizionali, tirando abilmente i fili dietro di essi e facendo sì che gli istituti comunali sopravviventi siano tenuti fermamente da persone di sua fiducia e a lui subordinate."

16 Jones 1965, 71 n. 2, and 2010, 3–4 n. 3; Jones 1980, 503.

the fifteenth-century Medici were de facto signori—a view Rubinstein found thoroughly uncongenial. Sestan grounded his interpretation on a comparative survey of previous and contemporary signorial regimes; Rubinstein, on assiduous documentary research in the Florentine archives. In her paper at this colloquium, Dale Kent points to differences in research methods between Rubinstein and Jones (see below, 236–237).

Fundamental questions such as the nature of the Medici regime are more than just problems; they are genuine quandaries that have engaged generations of historians. I view the question as essentially methodological. Over the years, the quantity of published documentary research has swelled, enriching historians' knowledge, but the problem remains as challenging as it was for Rubinstein, Jones, and Sestan a half a century ago. It is still fundamentally a matter of interpretation, and should be addressed as such, starting with a fresh reading of the sources. The most useful way to go about assessing the nature of the Italian city regimes is arguably to break free of the historiographic models and a priori assumptions that have long conditioned such assessments,[17] and that have resulted in numerous qualifications or added shades of meaning: cripto-*signoria*, proto-*signoria*, para-*signoria*, pseudo-*signoria*, pre-*signoria*, substantial *signorie*, veiled *signorie*, *signorie* de facto, shadow *signorie*, informal *signorie*, virtual *signorie*, and so on. All such otiose expressions are based on hypotheses of what a *signoria* is. Such hypotheses are arguably little other than historiographical constructs, no more helpful than their variants, elaborations, or qualifications in comprehending practices of government that prevailed in the Italian cities over the centuries.

When, in contrast, a broad criterion of what constitutes signorial government is adopted—one not tied to formal definitions but open to the wide variety of forms that personal preeminence and personal government might have taken—then, at a stroke, the political panorama presented by the north Italian city-states looks far richer and more variegated than from a narrowly "philo-communal" perspective. The fact is that, from the second half of the thirteenth century, a range of different, often hybrid, regimes came and went. None could shake off the burden of civic traditions and ideology, and while many were fragile and short-lived, some were stable and durable. The point is not to blur the differences among governmental forms that were perceived by contemporaries to constitute a range of diverse constitutional structures,[18] but to see how they all emerge from the same political matrix, the Italian city-state in its many local variants, while giving rise to new and diverse configurations of power, institutional arrangements, and political languages.[19]

---

17 Already argued in Zorzi 2010, ix–xii, 8–10; Zorzi 2012b, 1261–1264.

18 It is telling that when the signore's government shows signs of mutation from a shared expression of the civic will into undisguised authoritarianism no longer aimed at the common good, terms such as "tyrant" and "tyranny" start to appear in the contemporaneous political lexicon, becoming the focus of political and juridical debate: Zorzi 2010, 108 ff., 145–155; 2013b.

19 For a first synthesis, see Zorzi 2010.

Many of the chapters in this volume, then, constitute a useful starting point for considering the quandary posed by the Medici regime.[20] Dale Kent analyzes the registers of the consultative assemblies known as the *pratiche*, where Cosimo de' Medici exerted strong direct influence until the 1440s, continuing thereafter to make his influence felt indirectly through reliable supporters, as well as via his son Giovanni. She highlights how far short Cosimo fell, despite the enormous authority he wielded, of exerting absolute control over the mechanisms of consensus within the regime.[21] His growing authority had to be constantly renegotiated, not just in the councils and the *balìe* (extraordinary assemblies), but vis-à-vis the core members of the Medici *reggimento* (regime). This authority was nurtured by the patriarchal ideal (itself promoted by humanism) of the paterfamilias who extends his protection to friends and neighbors like a baptismal godfather, including non-Florentines (to Francesco Sforza he stood almost *in loco patris* [as a second father]), and ultimately to the *patria* (homeland or native city) itself, as has been immortalized in his posthumous epitaph (*pater patriae*). Kent rightly points out that this style of leadership is not to be confused with condescending paternalism; on the contrary, it arose out of the formidable patronage network that Cosimo had been weaving since the days of the Albizzi regime.[22] Cosimo rose to power and continued to operate as a faction leader: of the other leading members of the regime, only Luca Pitti could count on a powerful patronage network; significantly, he alone would mount the most serious challenge the Medici leadership had hitherto had to confront.[23]

Authority and the power to dispense patronage could ensure political preeminence, but they could prove ineffectual in daily life, with respect to non-Medici clients, and especially at the death of the *pater*, when power had to be transferred to the heir in the absence of the ritualistic procedures available to dynastic *signorie*. Cosimo's authority was grounded, so Kent stresses, in part on the threat that those who refused to join his alignment might be excluded from office or suffer fiscal discrimination; for this reason, the reintroduction of the *catasto* (wealth tax) was proposed in 1458.[24] But inevitably his control over the regime's members could never be absolute, a fact that constituted a structural weakness in Medici power. At Cosimo's death, his son Piero found himself on uncertain footing with the regime's other leaders, who were dispensing advice to him in "fatherly" fashion, but who would eventually have to come to terms with the filial status inherent

---

20 There is always the risk of an interminable hunt for endless individual cases. But the risk has to be run, because only through comparing numerous specific cases (and I mean comparing empirically, not through model-building) can an understanding of the numerous profiles assumed by signorial and personal powers in the Italian cities be arrived at.

21 See Kent, this volume, 221–237.

22 See Dale Kent 1978; Molho 1988.

23 Rubinstein 1997, 155 ff.

24 A further example of Cosimo's fiscal policy is studied in Tognetti 2009.

in the patriarchal ideal, upon which the Medici family's own particular authority was grounded. In these circumstances, Francesco Sforza's external support proved decisive, with exile ensuing inevitably for Dietisalvi Neroni and Agnolo Acciaiuoli.

Lorenz Böninger also suggests a quasi-patriarchal approach in his analysis of the role of intermediary, played by Lorenzo, in aid of national minorities who had become embroiled in conflicts.[25] His interventions took place against a background in which commercial reprisal was commonplace, and the custom of entrusting the resolution of economic disputes to one or more private arbiters was equally widespread—yet another opportunity for the kind of mediation which the Medici, and Lorenzo in particular, employed with dexterity to reinforce their preeminence. This has been exemplified recently in research by Thomas Kuehn, William Connell, Patrizia Salvadori, Lorenzo Fabbri, and Robert Black.[26] Patronage practices of this kind were, in the case of national minorities, necessarily episodic. Böninger highlights Lorenzo's ability to vary his approach, performing the role of eminent citizen generously granting protection to private individuals, on the one hand, and playing the part of political leader, on the other, capable of achieving diplomatic resolutions to the most vexatious conflicts.

Giorgio Chittolini had already remarked, so Dale Kent notes, on the continuous interaction between public and private spheres in the political practices of Renaissance states.[27] In the case of the Medici, such interplay constituted a key feature of their statecraft. Kent and other colloquium participants repeatedly highlight Cosimo's and his successors' insistence on their status as "private" citizens. Kent rightly notes how in Florence (and Venice) the interests, especially economic, of the elite were closely identified with the public good, with what contemporaries were already calling *lo stato*, whereas the elites who gravitated toward signori such as the dukes of Urbino or Milan owed their fortunes to the personal bonds they were able to forge with such rulers. The republic's welfare, for both the Medici and their principal backers, was identified with maintaining their own social and political preeminence.

And yet such oscillation between private space and public stage—the ability to switch roles as contexts and circumstances dictated—might turn out to be problematic, especially in moments of crisis. Relations with the church, for example, were always fraught: David Peterson has highlighted the ongoing difficulty that the Medici had in influencing the selection of Florentine bishops, while David Chambers has shown the futility of Cosimo's repeated efforts to obtain a cardinalate for his family, and how hard fought was Lorenzo's successful struggle to win a red hat for his son Giovanni.[28] In the bull of 1 June 1478 with which he excommunicated

25 See Böninger, this volume, 155–168.
26 See Kuehn 1991; Connell 1994a, 1994b, 1996; Salvadori 2000a, 2000b, 2003; Fabbri 2000; Robert Black 2000.
27 Chittolini 1995.
28 See Peterson, this volume, 181–184; Chambers, this volume, 205–217.

Lorenzo, Sixtus IV struck hard at Lorenzo's public profile, accusing him of persecuting some pilgrims on their way to Rome "in a pharaonic manner." Böninger shows that in fact these pilgrims were a pair of Germans being made to pay for the capture of two Florentine galleys four years earlier by pirates in league with the Hanse. The boundaries between public and private might grow blurred to the point of constituting a vulnerability, as Alison Brown shows in her chapter on the crisis that overwhelmed Piero di Lorenzo in 1494.[29] Lorenzo the Magnificent's son inherited his father's "princely" prestige in diplomatic relations beyond Florence, but was incapable of asserting similar authority within the regime. As Charles VIII's menace loomed, he behaved in his dealings with the French king as though he were signore of Florence at a time when formally he had no special status in the city. Everyone knows the upshot.

Franco Franceschi for his part introduces a field of research less frequented among students of the early Medici—economic policy—and from a comparative perspective attempts to hone in on policy elements specific to the Medici.[30] The exercise is opportune, both for the originality of the results and for the contribution made to the wider problem of gauging the signorial profile of the Medici regime. Franceschi notes several elements of discontinuity in policies with respect to their predecessors, for whom, in parallel with the acquisition of the territorial dominion, there had been an indubitable tendency to centralize decision-making, a "regional" approach to problems, and an undisguised orientation toward public regulation of trade. The Medici were prepared to reorganize structures when necessary and to tighten controls, as with the law on *passeggieri* (customs officers) of 1461, which allotted the costs of infrastructure maintenance among local communities in a consistent manner, and relocated toll stations in order to better capture commercial traffic passing along Tuscan roads, or with the revision of customs at Livorno and Pisa in 1475, lightening exit duties and rationalizing entrance tolls. And yet their policy appears to have been guided by the overriding need to achieve consensus and to quell tension in communities that in many cases had been under Florentine rule for no more than a few decades. It is striking that the Medici gave a higher priority to commerce than to the needs of industrial production, which had enjoyed priority in the communal period. Striking too is what Franceschi calls their "policy of privilege-granting"—that is, grants of fiscal exemptions and prerogatives (generally the concession of the right to hold a fair or market) to individual communities within the dominion. Here, the Medici themselves sometimes expended considerable effort: Piero di Cosimo, for example, played the role of intermediary in 1461 when the Aretines were seeking the right to hold an annual duty-free fair, as did Lorenzo in 1473 when the Cortonesi sought a similar concession—a privilege

29 See Brown, this volume, 113–125.
30 See Franceschi, this volume, 129–154, and also Franceschi 1993a, 1994.

they had long been denied. Such discontinuities give Medici economic policy in the dominion a distinctive character of pragmatism and opportunism.

Kent, in particular, focuses her analysis on the practices through which Cosimo exerted his authority, and refers throughout to Rubinstein's analysis of institutional mechanisms. Rubinstein took a stand against those who viewed the Medici regime as a species of principate, emphasizing that the government of Florence "under the Medici" kept its republican institutions, essentially the deliberative councils, and retained (however much tampered with) the communal modes of election to office as well. Relevant here is an observation made by Giovanni Tabacco about the way many *signorie* actually operated: in numerous cities "there were signorial regimes of what can be called a perfectly communal type," in which "the *signoria* functioned within, not above and beyond, the political world of the city," operating "as one of its recurrent institutional elements."[31]

So the situation of the Medici in fifteenth-century Florence as illuminated by Rubinstein scarcely differs from the practices of other signori beginning in the second half of the thirteenth century. In nearly all these cities, communal institutions such as deliberative councils were retained (and manipulated), communal modes of election to office were preserved (and interfered with), and city statutes retained validity. Communal institutions might have been rendered hollow by emergency measures and *balie*, but they were not overturned. They underwent transformation, as personal and dynastic domination gradually acquired the capacity to represent its self-interest as coterminous with the welfare of the city, so winning effectual consensus not so much demagogically as from social and economic elites, including merchants, bankers, and manufacturing entrepreneurs. In short, Cosimo and his descendants did what many other signori had done for two hundred years: they acted as pilots in a complex (and conflict-ridden) political environment, in line with tradition and precedent.[32]

Riccardo Fubini likewise revisits the relation of the Medici to communal tradition.[33] He observes that the epoch of the Medici's rise was marked by ever more frequent recourse to "extraordinary" measures that temporarily violated existing statutes: *parlamenti, balie*, electoral purses filled with increasingly fewer carefully selected name tickets. The fact is that recourse to emergency measures had been widespread in city government ever since the mid-thirteenth century, with "popular" regimes in the vanguard, as recent research has shown.[34] Emergency measures did not, in other words, constitute a discontinuity: on the contrary, they were tools of political power, available and in good working order. In Florence, the Albizzi had been the first to resort systematically to such mechanisms (though Lorenzo

---

31 Tabacco 1974, 242–243.
32 Tradition and precedent that historians, not without some oversimplification, tend to call "communal." This too is a historiographical construct.
33 See Fubini, this volume, 62 ff.
34 See, for example, Milani 2009; Menzinger 2009.

Tanzini points out that similar practices are attested from the middle of the thirteenth century),[35] and Cosimo did no more than adopt and refine practices that had belonged to the city's political traditions for generations.

Discontinuity came with Lorenzo, who was preoccupied with laying a new basis of legitimacy for his own personal power. There are two crucial moments in the process he launched: the institution of the council of seventy in 1480, a *balìa* coopted from above (its members nominated for five-year terms), meant to assist Lorenzo in taking important decisions and conceived as a more stable and formal version of the *collegio della consulta* ("consultative committee": hence endowed with deliberative powers, making it an embryonic life senate, as Fubini notes); and the *scrutinio generale* (general scrutiny) of 1484, an electoral reform that broke once and for all with the criterion of territorial representation as the basis for access to office. It is well known that in the *Storie fiorentine* (*Florentine Histories*), Francesco Guicciardini characterized Lorenzo in 1491 as engaged, "according to report, in reforming the regime and making himself gonfalonier for life."[36]

A deficit of legitimacy was not a problem for the Medici alone; it had been felt since the end of the thirteenth century by every *signoria* in the course of its rise. The standard response was to have *arbitrium* (authority to rule) conferred on the signore by the communal councils, or sometimes by popular acclamation—the procedure followed by Cosimo in 1434 and 1458, and by Piero in 1466.[37] One expedient adopted during the fourteenth century was to obtain from the pope or emperor the concession of a vicariate; this was done so often that Bartolo of Sassoferrato decried such ostensible delegation as a devaluation of the two universal sovereigns' *iurisdictio* (jurisdiction), with the result that petty local despots were succeeding in legitimizing their tyrannies. Nevertheless, even the priors of Florence showed little reluctance in seeking the vicariate from Emperor Charles IV.[38] In 1395, Gian Galeazzo Visconti succeeded in acquiring the title of "prince and duke" of Milan, which allowed him to employ feudal law to impose new forms of dependence on territories in the dominion.[39] All those holding power in the Italian cities had long been aware that they were afflicted by a deficit of legitimacy. Such a deficiency, as suffered not least by Cosimo, Lorenzo, and indeed Piero de' Medici, was not only inevitable but time-honored.

Another aspect of the problem is why Florence arrived later than other political entities at an explicit manifestation of signorial power. Part of the answer was given by Sestan: the Medici were a "third-generation" *signoria* of bourgeois origin,

35 Tanzini 2010a; see also Isenmann 2011.
36 "L'anno sequente 1491 sendo Lorenzo tutto vòlto per la quiete publica alle arti della pace, e tra le altre cose, come dicono alcuni, in riformare lo stato e crearsi gonfaloniere a vita, volse lo animo a rassettare Pisa [...]": Guicciardini 1931, 71.
37 Rubinstein 1997, 1, 80, 117 ff., 187, 190.
38 Quaglioni 1983, 61 ff.; Fubini 2009, 26–29.
39 Black 2009, 69 ff.; 2010.

in contrast to signori who had come to power in the cities of the Po valley beginning in the thirteenth century, individuals of indubitable noble status, often with feudal roots.[40] Regional differences, especially the economic and political precocity of Lombardy and the greater influence there of signorial powers of rural origin as compared to Tuscany, are important factors, but it is also the case that Pisa, Arezzo, and Lucca experienced historically significant signorial episodes as early as the end of the thirteenth and early fourteenth centuries.

It is time to expose the historiographical myth of Florence as the cradle of republican, popular, and mercantile "buon governo," the myth of Florence as the model of communal democracy,[41] which has until recently obscured the fact that the city had been the locus of recurrent alternations of regime ever since the 1260s, when it embraced the *signoria* of its powerful new ally, Charles I of Anjou. Between the 1290s and the first decade of the fourteenth century, the city was buffeted by powerful authoritarian tempests, as Dino Compagni notes in his *Cronica*, with reference to Manetto Scali, the Cerchi, and Rosso della Tosa, one of the leaders of the faction of the Neri, "whose every action and achievement was aimed at gaining a *signoria* in the manner of the signori of Lombardy."[42] In 1313, the house of Anjou once again obtained a *signoria* over Florence, in the person of King Robert of Naples; Florence yielded to Angevin *signorie* for twenty-six of the seventy-seven years between 1267 and 1343 (i.e., one-third of the time).[43] Like demons demanding continuous exorcism, historians of Florence have clung to the prevalent interpretation of such *signorie* as interludes (the temporary result of military emergencies and the vicissitudes of peninsular politics) that left no trace on the republican evolution of the Florentine political system. In reality, Florence looks like an exemplary case of the complex social and political processes at work in all other cities experiencing oscillations between communal and signorial regimes. The dramatic case of the duke of Athens in 1342–43 was manipulated in hindsight into an extraordinary and exceptional despotic episode, demonized in historical memory.[44] The obsession with tyranny that pervades Matteo Villani's chronicle starkly mirrors the political sentiment that dominated Florence in the third quarter of the fourteenth century. But not long afterward, the Albizzi, in the persons of Maso and subsequently Rinaldo,[45] presented Florence with yet another episode of authoritarianism, signorial in profile and yet exploiting all the instruments of humanist propaganda in defense of republican liberty against the menace of Visconti tyranny.

40 Sestan 1961, 56–57.
41 A myth that will not die, see Maire Vigueur 1997.
42 "il quale tutto ciò che facea e procurava nella città, era per avere la signoria a guisa de' signori di Lombardia": Compagni 2000, 87 (bk. 3, chap. 2). A first analysis can now be found in Zorzi 2012a.
43 See De Vincentiis 2001.
44 See De Vincentiis 2003, 2010.
45 See Tanzini 2013b.

It is little wonder then that, from the earliest days of Cosimo's regime, as Francesco Bausi notes, the Medici too strived to appear as defenders of liberty.[46] Discussing such works as Platina's *De principe*, dedicated to Federico Gonzaga in 1471 and then rededicated to Lorenzo in 1474, with a change of title to *De optimo cive*, or Aurelio Lippo Brandolini's *De comparatione reipublicae et regni*, designed to celebrate the government of the king of Hungary, Matthias Corvinus, and then dedicated to Lorenzo in 1490, Bausi emphasizes their "bivalent" (albeit not in the least ambiguous) character. In fact, they appear to be the mature fruit of the Italian cities' long history, in which oscillation from communal regime to one form or another of personal *signoria* and back again had been the distinctive mark of political culture since at least the mid-thirteenth century.

To put it another way, the Medici regime in the fifteenth century was arguably the sole form of *signoria* that Florentine political culture was able to permit. The Medici were indeed signori.[47] But for almost sixty years, over the course of the fifteenth century, they were signori to the extent and through the modes that the context in which they exercised their leadership permitted. Finally in the following century they returned to establish their *signoria* in Florence for good.

46   See Bausi, this volume, 239–251.
47   John Najemy points out how, in the wake of Piero de' Medici's flight in November 1494, the Florentine political elite was faced with "reinventing" republican government: Najemy 2006b, 375 ff.

FOUR

Diplomacy, Language, and the "Arts of Power"

MELISSA MERIAM BULLARD

THE 2011 CONFERENCE AT VILLA I TATTI took as its point of departure an invitation to reflect on an unarticulated dialogue between two eminent historians, Nicolai Rubinstein and Philip Jones, concerning the nature of the early Medici regimes in Florence. At issue for them was how to characterize Florentine government—grossly stated, whether, as in Jones's interpretation, the Medici trod the beaten path toward despotic rule as leaders in an otherwise unremarkable urban oligarchy, or, as in Rubinstein's more hybrid view, the Medici regimes were worthy of note for how they functioned in and around governmental structures that retained elements of Florence's communal and republican traditions. Their different approaches to political and institutional history—in Jones's case informed by sweeping economic analysis of rural Italy, and in Rubinstein's by penetrating archival research—spoke to their generation of historians who were maturing after World War II. In the decades since Rubinstein and Jones began publishing, the scholarly agenda regarding the early Medici has changed, particularly in light of fresh perspectives offered by social history, feminist critique, and the new cultural history with its linguistic turn. Focus has shifted away from attempts to pin down the institutional character of early Florentine regimes under the Medici. Rather, historians seem more intrigued today by the manner of Medici political conduct, what I will call the Medicean "arts of power." Thus, this chapter leaves aside the question of whether or not the early Medici were signori of Florence, but rather seeks to examine Lorenzo the Magnificent's role in Florence through a different kind of lens—namely, a rhetorical lens that interrogates his style of governance from the perspective of the impressions and images he and his circle wished to convey of his position in Florence and in Italy. The Medici "arts of power" reached a high level of development during the last years of his life. By "arts of power," I refer to conscious political posturing for particular ends that relies upon subtle, quite deliberate manipulations of language, whether in oral, written, visual, or gestural communications.

Language is capable of playing many tricks in any circumstance. It is by nature equivocal, in that any act of speech includes numerous layers, at minimum from intent and expression to reception and interpretation. Those aspects multiply and complicate as more actors become involved in an exchange. When language is used deliberately to simulate and dissimulate diplomacy, in an environment in which trust is at best negotiable, it becomes even trickier. Communications become densely packed with possible meanings, fraught with uncertainty as the players extrapolate, interpolate, read between the lines, and second-guess each other's intentions. I would argue that the Medici showed themselves to be nimble, superior gamesmen in the theater of fifteenth-century Italian politics and diplomacy. The question remains, however, as the arts of power became more skilled and purposeful in their and their agents' hands, whether diplomatic discourse became a more or less effective means of negotiation and persuasion.

The work of editing Lorenzo's letters from the mid- to late 1480s brought me a heightened sensitivity to how language can be a very artful tool of diplomacy. This was the period when Lorenzo was ratcheting up his dynastic ambitions with the papacy and jockeying for position among the other powers of Italy in the aftermath of the Barons' War (1485–86).[1] Lorenzo's surviving correspondence captured many exchanges between him, his agents, and the Florentine ambassadors, and included their reflections upon leading political players, their representatives, and Italian peninsular politics in general. The surviving correspondence reveals how the edifice of Medici political power was artfully constructed, maintained, and manipulated at a remarkable level of consciousness. As argued elsewhere using the concept of shared agency, the evolution of heightened Florentine political consciousness and the ability to articulate that consciousness developed in Medici circles at the end of the fifteenth century and subsequently found wider currency in the political and historical writings of the early sixteenth century among analysts such as Francesco Guicciardini and Niccolò Machiavelli.[2] This heightened consciousness produced a new language of diplomacy. But it was not the product of a single mind or voice, namely Lorenzo's, but rather the fruit of dialogic exchange that built upon frequent epistolary and spoken interactions among a limited group of intimates within Medici circles composed of secretaries, agents, and ambassadors. In what

1   Medici 1977–, vols. 10 and 11, passim.
2   Bullard 1994, 109–130.

follows, I hope to illustrate the artfulness of their endeavors to buttress Medici power and, most of all, Medici prestige.

Viewed through an "arts of power" lens, the Florentine republic was alive and well in late fifteenth-century Florence. This republicanism was not evidenced by the persistence of representative elements and dissent in Florentine city councils of the sort that Rubinstein investigated,[3] but rather republicanism in a more rhetorical sense, as a foil, or posture, or mode of representation aimed primarily at an external diplomatic audience. Guicciardini's posthumous claim that had Lorenzo lived longer, he would have made himself signore of the city is open to skepticism.[4] Rather, I would argue, retaining the Florentine republic as a rhetorical facade had too many advantages even, or especially, for someone with the driving dynastic ambitions of Lorenzo the Magnificent.

This "rhetorical republic" was not just a shadowy holdover from the bygone days of medieval corporatism, or even a chimeric fantasy to which people paid solemn lip service. It was a deliberate political tool. In the diplomatic world of the late fifteenth century, the "rhetorical republic" was a Medicean strategy, a creative hybrid response to the all-too-real circumstance of Florence's weakness in Italy relative to the more militarily powerful regimes of Milan and Naples, with whom the city maintained an uneasy alliance, and to the papacy with its territorial base in central Italy and pan-European sway. The ambassador Giovanni Lanfredini aptly described Lorenzo's relatively disadvantaged position in Italy: "He is neither duke of Milan, nor king of Naples, and he does not spend personal funds for the state."[5] This was a true enough description of Lorenzo and Florence's actual situation, but also, in context, a deliberate rhetorical statement to underscore that Lorenzo could not (or did not want to) take certain actions—in this case commit Florentine military resources on an ally's behalf.

Given Florence's position as an important, but, according to some, second-tier state both militarily and politically, Lorenzo de' Medici found it advantageous to maintain a republican facade. He had more maneuverability behind a rhetorical curtain that obfuscated and blurred the extent of his power in the city. Sometimes he played the role of *primus inter pares* in the style of the Roman emperor Augustus; at other times, he could be a directing, de facto head of state; at yet others, he could be someone who deferred to the wishes of his fellow citizens, though usually on less important issues. Ironically, he enjoyed a more effective and weighty political presence in the Italian theater of power as the non–head of state of a mercantile republic than he would have as an aspiring or actual signore of Florence. As late as 1491, Lorenzo indicated as much in a message directed to the pope, in which he

---

3   Rubinstein 1997, passim.
4   Guicciardini's actual term was "gonfaloniere a vita" (standard bearer for life): Guicciardini 1931, 71 (ch. 8).
5   "non è duca di Milano, né re di Napoli, et non spende el suo": 12 July 1487, ASF, MAP 40, 91.

asserted that he considered himself far more useful to the papacy operating as he did from a foundation of good will among the Florentines, rather than if his position were dependent on or accessory to any other type of political *fondamento* ("foundation").[6] As signore he would have had to jockey more directly, and from a disadvantaged position, with the muscular regent for the young duke of Milan, with the king of Naples, or even the pope. As it was, when it suited, he could present himself as just one among many private citizens. At other times, he clearly called the shots for Florence. In the late fifteenth century, this Florentine "rhetorical republic" was a multivalent foil—a thin covering layer, and simultaneously an active instrument of diplomatic swordsmanship.

Ambassadors used the metaphor of testing and weighing a counterfeit coin to characterize the equivocal rhetorical world they inhabited and helped fashion. In diplomacy, where the coin of exchange depended heavily upon spoken, written, and gestural language and its subtle interpretation, words were easily and frequently counterfeit. Like a fake coin, diplomatic parlance was impure from the very moment of fabrication. Florentine ambassadors well understood the growing equivocality of language as they pulled and stretched it to convey subtle distinctions and used it, or suspected others of using it, to deceive. Like a suspicious coin, they felt the need constantly to test the purity and sincerity of the language they received from others. Back then, one tested a debased coin by weighing or biting it. They did the same with language. One ambassador described literally how he was *caratando*, or weighing and measuring, words. He advised Lorenzo, "If [the pope] *pays* in good words, *repay* [italics mine] him in the same kind of money, this to see how things go and subsequently how he acts toward us."[7]

In the art of power, Lorenzo's "rhetorical republic" was similarly counterfeit. It worked like the gauzy theater curtain that separates the audience from the actors on stage. A change of lighting determines what the audience can see. Illuminated from the front, the scrim becomes opaque. Lit from behind, it becomes translucent. Only then can the viewers see hazily through it to the action behind. Actual scrims had not yet been invented in theaters, but the idea of the scrim was present in the language of fifteenth-century Florentine diplomacy.[8] A vital aspect of and interpretive key to Lorenzo's mastery of politics and diplomacy lay in his ability to manipulate the scrim and allow only a filtered view of Florentine policies and of himself.

---

6   "è molto più utile et comodo questo fondamento naturale che uno accessorio et dependente da fondamento mancho acto": Lorenzo de' Medici to Piero Alamanni, 17 September 1491, ASF, Medici-Tornaquinci 3, 157. Originally cited in Rubinstein 1966, 228 (see now Rubinstein 1997, 263).

7   "Io sono ito assai caratando le parole et modi di San Marco per vedere se in questa pratica va con arte. . . . Et se in questo mezzo il papa dà buone parole, pagarlo della medesima moneta, per vedere più inanzi dove le cose s'adirizeranno et che dimostrationi facessi il papa verso di noi": Pier Filippo Pandolfini to Lorenzo, 17 January 1487, ASF, MAP 51, 369.

8   According to the *Oxford English Dictionary*, the loosely woven gauzy fabric used in scrims probably did not appear until the late eighteenth century. The *Online Etymological Dictionary* finds earliest reference to it in 1792, of unknown origin as the gauze used in upholstery lining: Harper 2011.

One observes subtle changes in the meaning of words contemporaries used in diplomatic discourse to express their heightened awareness of ambivalence and anxiety about conflicting messages.[9] A word such as *arte* (art) came to be used in two senses: in its traditional meaning of careful guild craftsmanship, but increasingly in diplomatic parlance, referring to the craftiness and artifice of intentional deception.[10] Managing the scrim for the "rhetorical republic" was an essential aspect of Lorenzo's *arte* in the shadowy, often deceptive, high-stakes game of Italian interstate relations.

Lorenzo's "rhetorical republic" also worked like a stage set or an architectural facade or facing that makes its own visual statement and simultaneously points to what lies behind. Sometimes facades invitingly beckon toward the interior, such as the portico of the Pantheon in Rome. Other times, like stage scenery, the facade deceives and belies what, if anything, stands behind. Sometimes it shapes expectations only to jolt them off-center, like the Florentine cathedral today with its elaborate nineteenth-century facade covering the cleaner lines of a late Gothic/Renaissance interior, or the Rucellai palace, whose classicizing Renaissance facing creates a visual disguise covering three adjacent buildings behind it. The praxis and language of Florentine diplomacy were no different in that they too presented a constructed facing, intrinsically double-natured, showing an outside and pointing within. But in diplomacy, with its higher callings of effective communication to find common ground and work through differences, the more the facade differed from what lay behind, the more it became quite literally two-faced, masking its lack of sincerity. Using the approach of German sociologist and philosopher Jürgen Habermas, Peter Burke aptly described Italian politics as a theater culture with a low level of sincerity.[11] His characterization, however, did not do justice to the artistry of Florentine diplomacy and the calculation behind its use. The Florentine skill lay in developing the ability to improvise and glide more effectively than others along a spectrum of overt and covert meanings and representations—in other words, from behind the facade, to work the scrim, changing the lighting from in front and behind.

In the late fifteenth century, doubleness in all these senses—as foil, facade, fakery, and the newly expanded meaning of *arte* as artifice—found expression not only in the language and metaphors used in diplomatic letters, but also in the very praxis of diplomacy, where Florentine ambassadors were literally double agents. Under Lorenzo, Florentine diplomats functioned both as official representatives of the Florentine state and unofficially, and more importantly, as private agents for Lorenzo himself. They routinely maintained two sets of correspondence, one official with the *otto di pratica*, the Florentine foreign office, and the other more

---

9   On the language of diplomacy in this period, see Bullard 1994, 81–108.
10 Ibid., 97–99.
11 Burke 1987, 13; and more generally for the idea of diplomacy as a "theater of power," see Cohen 1987.

extensive and informative with Lorenzo or his personal secretaries.[12] These dual correspondences were not always kept separate, in that Lorenzo frequently read reports going to the *otto*, and he sometimes shared with them portions of letters sent directly to him. To keep up the guise of republican government, he occasionally made a show of consulting the *otto* after the fact—for example, after he and the ambassador to Rome had already secretly arranged the marriage of his daughter to Pope Innocent VIII's son.[13] With this marriage, together with the betrothal of his son Piero to the daughter of Roberto Orsini, Lorenzo (in the space of little more than a year) departed twice from a long Florentine preference for marriages arranged among Florentine families, not to foreigners.[14] The marriage made obvious diplomatic and strategic sense. His consultation of the *otto di pratica* after the fact was a gesture that had importance particularly in the context of impression management.

At other times, Lorenzo had to remind his ambassadors to keep the *otto* better informed. "There is no set rule about this," he wrote to one, "for discretion will dictate," but it is prudent "to satisfy their [the *otto*'s] appetite" for information, especially on less critical matters.[15] On those occasions, the ambassador should send fuller reports to the *otto* and fewer to him, so that it would not be noticed, in this case in Rome, just how many separate dispatches the ambassador was sending to Lorenzo.[16] Similarly, on another occasion when Lorenzo did not care to assist the duke of Ferrara, he extricated himself, feigning deference to the *otto*, claiming that it was their prerogative to handle secret matters of state.[17]

Manipulating the appearances of republican government gave Lorenzo more maneuverability at home and in foreign relations. It was disconcerting, perhaps confusing, for heads of state such as Duke Ercole d'Este, who knew Lorenzo had the reins of government in hand, and who preferred to deal directly with him, only to be unexpectedly rebuffed when Lorenzo wished to hide behind the facade of the Florentine republic.[18] Stepping behind the *otto* was often a strategy to delay action in order to gain time to assess a situation further. Sometimes Lorenzo would delay action physically, by removing himself to one of his villas, ostensibly to take a cure for his gout. When he did not want to see Cardinal Giuliano Della Rovere,

---

12 See Rubinstein 1977, 92.

13 ASF, Signori, Missive 49, fol. 175.

14 Negotiations for the marriage of Maddalena de' Medici to Franceschetto Cibo had begun in late 1486: Medici 1977–, 10:481–492. In 1488, Piero de' Medici married Alfonsina from the powerful Orsini clan. These were not the first extra-Florentine marriages for the Medici: in 1469, Lorenzo's father had arranged his union with Clarice di Jacopo Orsini.

15 Lorenzo to Giovanni Lanfredini, 22 December 1487, Medici 1977–, 11:533.

16 Lorenzo to Alamanni, 26 April 1487, BAV, MS Patetta 1739, fol. 31v.

17 Antonio da Montecatini to Ercole d'Este, 24 May 1480, ASMo, Archivio Segreto Estense, Ambasciatori, Firenze 2.

18 Ibid. For other examples of his verbal craftiness with the Estense ambassador, see Medici 1977–, 10:381–388, 11:293, 502.

due to pass through Florence, he left town precipitously, leaving management of the visit to Florentine officials.[19] When relations with Milan began to deteriorate, he frequently frustrated the Milanese ambassador with his unavailability, a ploy that Ludovico Sforza would subsequently repay with his refusal to grant an audience to the Florentine ambassador in Milan.[20] Absenting himself also permitted Lorenzo to conduct political business in private, such as when he briefed a special papal envoy at one of his villas on matters he did not want leaked in Florence.[21]

Difficulties surfaced when Lorenzo's interests ran at odds with those of the Florentine state, such as during negotiations to impose taxes upon the local clergy. When it came to deciding in what proportion the collections should be divided between the papacy and the city of Florence, Lorenzo pushed for ever larger amounts to go to Rome, not Florence, because his agents could privately scoop off the pope's share in repayment of papal debts to the Medici bank.[22] In another example of a tension-producing situation pitting Lorenzo against the city, in order to mollify Ludovico Sforza in the late 1480s, Lorenzo agreed secretly to restore the *castello* of Villa to Milanese control, against Florentine wishes to retain jurisdiction. In 1486, much to Ludovico's anger, Villa had voluntarily placed itself under Florentine protection.[23]

The ambassadors who had to handle these situations lived in a pressure-cooker atmosphere, having constantly to maintain credibility in their double roles as government representatives and as Lorenzo's private agents. To their external audiences, they had to effect Lorenzo's will and make it appear that his will and Florence's coincided. At the same time, they had to convey appropriate impressions or misrepresentations of foreign affairs in their correspondence back to the *otto*, often to pressure them on Lorenzo's behalf.[24] In addition, ambassadors had to keep a stream of observations and reports of conversations flowing back to Florence and directly to Lorenzo.

The Florentine ambassadors found themselves caught uncomfortably in the middle. Like veritable jugglers keeping so many rhetorical balls in the air or like troupers playing so many different, simulaneous roles, handling delicate situations so skillfully put Florentine ambassadors under tremendous strain. Often they had to spend years abroad away from their families and business interests.[25] No wonder

19 Medici 1977–, 11:138.
20 Ibid., 11:575.
21 Lorenzo met privately with Giacomo Gherardi at his villa in Spedaletto in September 1487: ibid., 11:159–161.
22 23 December 1490, ASF, MAP 52, 92.
23 Medici 1977–, 11:124–125. See also ibid., 10:40, 394.
24 For example, Lorenzo instructed Piero Alamanni, his ambassador in Milan, what to write to the *otto*: ibid., 10:91.
25 For example, Giovanni Lanfredini, Lorenzo's bank manager in Venice and then in Florence, served as Florentine ambassador to Naples from 1484 to 1486 before becoming ambassador to Rome in 1487 until his death in 1490. Ibid., 10:245–246.

they sought release from their appointments, citing illness or the need to attend to family business. Even though the ambassadors were carefully handpicked by Lorenzo and usually served in a revolving capacity between membership on the *otto di pratica* and ambassadorial service abroad, a few, such as Francesco Gaddi, were not up to the task, evidently too inept to represent the Florentine state and Lorenzo's private interests simultaneously.[26] Piero Alamanni, though a close personal friend of Lorenzo's and a seasoned ambassador, was judged by a Medici bank agent in Rome to lack the necessary grit and finesse to fulfill his dual role as ambassador of Florence and Lorenzo's personal representative, while at the same time acting aggressively enough in order to squeeze benefices and privileges out of the pope on Lorenzo's behalf.[27] One of the most successful of Lorenzo's men to play all the requisite roles as Florentine ambassador to the Holy See was Giovanni Lanfredini. Like Alamanni, he was an experienced ambassador, but unlike the latter, he was also an accomplished merchant banker. Perhaps his previous employment in the Medici bank gave him the necessary pluck: he was posthumously credited as the principal architect of young Giovanni de' Medici's appointment as boy cardinal. Lanfredini, however, died on the job, relatively young in his fifties, taken ill perhaps because of the incredible pressures to which he was subject.

This overview does not permit an exhaustive examination of how Lorenzo and his collaborators managed others' perceptions of the Florentine republic. Ample evidence exists in more than a dozen volumes of his published letters, each with extensive historical commentary. These letters, mainly diplomatic in nature, constituted a useful proving ground for the rhetorical arts of power in late fifteenth-century Florence and their outgrowth, namely the highly nuanced and more complex conceptualization and, hence, language of diplomacy and politics—the language that the next generation of thinkers such as Machiavelli and Guicciardini used in their treatises and histories. The diplomatic language of the Florentines, I would maintain, had no equal, even among the humanists at the Neapolitan court, traditionally the most rhetorically savvy in Italy.[28]

In conclusion, the double, even duplicitous game that Lorenzo and his circle of ambassadors and secretaries played to maintain the "rhetorical republic" as a political and diplomatic foil indicates a subtle shift in Florentine policy precisely during the period when Lorenzo's dynastic ambitions were accelerating; he had set his sights first on a marriage alliance with the pope, to be followed by the elevation

26 Ibid., 10:202. Gaddi was interim ambassador to Rome in April 1487. A month later, the more skillful Giovanni Lanfredini replaced him.

27 25 February 1491, ASF, MAP 42, 25.

28 This reputation derives from the period of King Alfonso (1442–58), whose brilliant court received much humanist praise and who was aided in his disagreements with the papacy by the able pen of Lorenzo Valla. Under Alfonso's son Ferrante I, humanist chancellors and ambassadors, among them Antonio D'Alessandro and Giovanni Pontano, continued the tradition. Their writings in the late fifteenth century do not contain the same subtlety and sensitivity to shades of meaning and possible duplicity prevalent in Lorenzo de' Medici's correspondence with his ambassadors.

of his young son as prince of the church. As the gap widened between his diplomatic pretensions and his civic pretences in an aristocratically dominated republic, I would argue that his effective power actually increased. More collaborators joined with him in recognizing the inevitable, namely that their best future lay with Lorenzo. His son and heir Piero was not so skilled at the republican game, and one wonders, had he been a more adept player, despite the peninsular disruptions brought by the French invasion of Italy in 1494, whether he might have remained in the Medici palace conducting both public and private family business as usual. As it turned out, it was left to Machiavelli to put into his own words the importance for the prince of both being and seeming to be.[29]

A later Renaissance appreciation of such matters comes from Shakespeare, that master of double roles and duplicity. In *The Merchant of Venice*, he wrote, "What a goodly outside falsehood hath!"[30] More recently, post-structuralist Turkish author and Nobel Prize winner Orhan Pamuk recognized the subtle but real power of intentional duplicity. In *My Name Is Red*, set in sixteenth-century Istanbul, he speaks intriguingly of a counterfeit Venetian gold ducat, used in trade with unsuspecting Ottomans, who believed the coin to be authentic because it bore all the proper inscriptions of an undebased coin. Pamuk gives the coin a voice, made to declare, "As my actual value drops, however, my metaphorical value increases, proof that poetry is consolation to life's miseries."[31] Lorenzo's "rhetorical republic" was similarly counterfeit, but I hope to have shown that, since it was used consciously as a political tool, it was more than just an empty facade. It did not fool many people into believing that Florence operated as a true citizen republic nor that Lorenzo was just another of its citizens, but, like Pamuk's eloquent counterfeit coin, it could sometimes pass as genuine. It looked and seemed to function like the real thing. Even if one suspected its fraudulance, it beguiled and confused. Lorenzo's arts of power may not have achieved Pamuk's level of poetry, nor provided much consolation in his adult life, but they certainly gave ample evidence of his ability to use the Florentine republic rhetorically as a political stratagem, with what Baldassare Castiglione would later call *sprezzatura*, that studied ease that simulates by dissimulating its own artifice.

29 *The Prince*, ch. 18.
30 *The Merchant of Venice*, 1.3.
31 Pamuk 2002, 127.

FIVE

Lorenzo the Magnificent's Regime
Aims, Image, and Constitutional Framework

RICCARDO FUBINI

THE MEDICI REGIME IN FLORENCE has been a topic of lively debate ever since the publication of Nicolai Rubinstein's *The Government of Florence under the Medici* in 1966.[1] Rubinstein's main purpose was to counter the prevalent image of the Medici as creators of a virtual principate, making a radical break with Florence's republican traditions. It was an image with a long rhetorical pedigree (both encomiastic and vituperative)—one still having enjoyed wide currency in twentieth-century historiography—for reasons not so much political as cultural and artistic.[2] Following a meticulous and methodical excavation of the archives, Rubinstein came to the view that, even under Medici government, the traditional constitutional structures of Florence held firm. The electoral purses continued to be filled with the names of citizens as the result of periodic scrutinies, and officials were still selected through extraction by lot from the purses, even though the scrutinies and the sortitions might both have been tampered with in particular cases. Approval by the councils of the commune and the people (the so-called *consigli opportuni*) was still mandatory for legislative proposals issuing from the *signoria* (the priors and the gonfalonier of justice), flanked by the two colleges (the sixteen gonfaloniers of the companies and the twelve good men). Finally, on the matter of social representation, Rubinstein noted the high degree of continuity in the city's governing class,

---

1   Rubinstein 1966. I cite the second edition (1997).
2   Fubini 2009, 187–194.

as demonstrated by membership lists of successive assemblies with plenary powers known as *balìe*, published in his appendices.

Nicolai Rubinstein's work is an indispensable point of reference, a book always consulted with profit, even though his interpretation, valid as far as it goes, remains too narrowly focused to satisfy scholars after nearly half a century. In the first place, Rubinstein relies on the concept of "constitution," understood as a complex of procedures and magistracies. But what did the communal constitution amount to in the wake of the profound alterations of the late fourteenth century and especially in light of the striking succession of *parlamenti* that have no counterpart in other Italian towns? One should not be fooled by the term *parlamento*: it no longer meant the free deliberation of the assembled citizenry, but the compulsory ratification, by a crowd summoned to attend, of measures proposed by the *signoria*—and on significant occasions, of genuine reform programs that the ordinary councils would never, following normal legal procedures, have approved.[3] It is enough to list the dates: 1378, 1382, 1393, 1433, 1434, 1458, and 1466. These were the key moments at which the Albizzi and Medici regimes were established and consolidated. The list might be regarded as ending in 1494 when, after Piero de' Medici had fled, a *parlamento* manipulated by the oligarchy attempted to install an oligarchic regime controlled by the twenty *accoppiatori* (electoral supervisors);[4] or in 1512, when (despite the ban on *parlamenti* approved in 1495 by the great council [the supreme legislative council created at the end of 1494]) it was a *parlamento* that restored to Florence the regime established by Lorenzo the Magnificent, with all its legacies, partisans, and structures.[5]

The epoch in which the Medici rose to power was marked, therefore, by what were known as extraordinary measures—exceptions to the law, justified by necessity and urgency, which, taken together, created an ever wider sphere of discretion for the *signoria*, and exceeded even the *signoria*'s authority by creating committees (*balìe*) that assumed and extended the *signoria*'s own powers.[6] The result was an informal configuration of power, in whose name and at whose direction the *signoria* itself operated (generating endemic conflict with the traditional councils). The real seat of power was the *reggimento*, or regime. Formally, this term denoted all the citizens selected in the scrutinies to be eligible for the three major offices (*tre maggiori*), but in reality it connoted the far narrower clique of decision-makers who, by managing the electoral scrutinies, exerted control over city politics.[7]

---

3   On the *parlamento* in communal tradition from the twelfth century onward, understood as a collective manifestation "of that will and consensus . . . representing . . . a fundamental grant of legitimacy," see Gualtieri 2009, 80–81. The *parlamento* of 1 September 1378, the first of the series mentioned in the text, was summoned in order to restore legitimacy in the wake of the expulsion of two Ciompi from the *signoria*: see Trexler 1978b.

4   See the provision of 2 December 1494 in Cadoni and Di Sciullo 1994–2000, 1:1–30.

5   For the ban on holding *parlamenti*, passed with backing from Girolamo Savonarola on 28 July 1495 (thus delegitimizing the twenty *accoppiatori*), see Villari 1887, 309.

6   See Rubinstein 1997, 77 ff.

7   On *reggimento* (here translated throughout as regime), see Kent 1975; Fubini 1994, 41–61.

The personal factor was of importance in the Albizzi and Medici regimes, precisely because of the need to control the *signoria* and the electoral mechanism directly in order to maintain power and to impart continuity to the administration. So Rubinstein's notion of a Florentine "constitution" is questionable in a period when the city's own statutes and traditions had already been set aside, and when a state of permanent and irreversible crisis prevailed, without achieving a new form of recognized legality. The *reggimento*, a fundamental political fact, had no juridical warrant to exist. If one turns back to the fourteenth century, to the time of Giovanni Villani's *Cronica* and of the frescoes depicting "good government" in Siena, *reggimento* is the abstract term denoting the offices of government in their entirety. In the following century, the notion becomes concrete, coming to signify the group of families whose members were selected (in proportions that varied) for inclusion in the purses for the *tre maggiori* (the *signoria* and the two colleges) during secret scrutiny proceedings. The *reggimento* was, in fact, the political class of Florence, stakeholders in the enterprise as it were, with shares of varying size affording varying degrees of access to power. Hence the control exerted over the *reggimento* as a whole, which meant control over city politics, constituted the unwritten instrument of real power. It should be noted as well that this essential notion, to which the word *stato* (in Latin, *status*) was also applied and which is familiar to anyone acquainted with the relevant archival documentation,[8] scarcely forces its way to the surface in the chronicles and treatises constituting the forum in which public affairs were openly discussed. It was Leon Battista Alberti, in book three of *Della famiglia* (a work not intended for public dissemination), who coined the pejorative term *statuali* for participants in the regime: "Every other way of life has always appealed to me more than that of *statuali*, the participants in the regime."[9] A more traditional term was used immediately before by the character in the dialogue Giannozzo Alberti to refer to the allure of political power: "fummi"—the fumes, in the sense of the infatuations with political office.[10] The word and the concept (*i fumi degli uffici*) are employed to convey a sense of disapproval by the chronicler Marchionne di Coppo Stefani, writing at the end of the fourteenth century.[11] But the best formulation of this notion can be found in a public letter written on 30 November 1384 by Coluccio Salutati to the citizens of Perugia, which, under the pretense of admonishing the

---

8   See Fubini 1994, 48, 54. The Medici *balìa* of 1452 laid down the rule that henceforth council members would also have to be chosen from among those *imborsati* for membership of the regime (i.e., those whose name tags had been selected for insertion into the electoral purses).

9   "Ogni altra vita a me sempre piacque più troppo che quella delli, così diremo, statuali." Alberti 1969, 218. These words are put into the mouth of Giannozzo Alberti, who continues, "Vita molestissima, piena di sospetti, di fatiche, pienissima di servitù. Che vedi tu da questi i quali si travagliono agli stati essere differenza a pubblici servi?" (Ibid.) (A burdensome life, filled with suspicion and distress, and especially filled with servitude. What difference do you see between those who struggle for political power and public slaves?)

10   Ibid.

11   See Green 1972, 93; Cabrini 2001, 25–33.

recipients, actually describes the poisonous atmosphere prevailing at a *scrutinio generale* (general scrutiny):

> On top of that, whoever is not admitted and included among the potential holders of one of the three major offices starts to imagine that he is not trusted and is being cast aside, and in the end all those who find themselves excluded become foes of the regime, whether they were overlooked, or whether there was some pressing reason, or whether it just happened inadvertently.[12]

A more tangible and, for that matter, better known indication that, at the turn of the fifteenth century, the political atmosphere in Florence was thick with suspicion, comes from a minor figure in the regime, Giovanni di Pagolo Morelli; his advice to his own son was to keep clear of politics.[13] But it is the historian Giovanni Cavalcanti who most scathingly excoriates the system of government by regime, in words that reverberate down to the time of Niccolò Machiavelli. He worked on his *Nuova opera* during two separate periods spanning the transition from the Albizzi to the Medici regime, and spoke for all members of the citizenry "outside the regime, those insulted and wronged."[14]

It was a higher priority for Lorenzo the Magnificent than for his predecessors to put Medici rule on a sound legal footing, maintaining control while justifying its power. So during his first tumultuous year in government—unlike his father Piero and although under pressure from his ally and protector, Duke Galeazzo Maria Sforza of Milan—he refused to resort to force and to stage a *parlamento*. He clung to this policy, even when resorting to *balìe* to force through momentous reforms, as in 1471 and 1480, or during the electoral scrutinies of 1471 and 1484.[15] In other words, Lorenzo's preferred methods were within normal political bounds, and this paradoxically was the underlying cause of the Pazzi conspiracy.[16]

The Pazzi, a family of magnate origins, had been brought into the regime through a pact with the Medici, sealed by the marriage of Lorenzo's older sister

---

12 "Accedit ad hoc quod quicunque non fuerit admissus et inter maximorum magistratuum presules numeratus, tanquam suspectus se cogitat aliisque superatus, ut tot efficiantur regiminis inimici, quot per oblivionem aut necessitate, etiam inconsulte, reperiantur exclusi." De Rosa 1980, 122; Fubini 2009, "Propaganda e idee politiche da Coluccio Salutati a Leonardo Bruni," 152.

13 See "Morelli, Giovanni di Pagolo (1371–1444), *Ricordi*," in Branca 1986, 203–204. A Morelli family descendant took the same view, although he rose to far greater power: see Pandimiglio 1999.

14 "i quali sono, senza il reggimento, sostenitori di ingiurie e di torti." Cavalcanti 1944, 15; on the author, see Fubini 2007, 180–185.

15 In this regard, see the significant words directed by Lorenzo in December 1470 to the Milanese ambassador Sacramoro da Rimini, in response to the solicitations and offers of military assistance he was receiving from the duke of Milan: he did not intend, he said, to deal with his internal adversaries by staging a *parlamento* as in 1466 (see below, 73).

16 See Fubini 1994, "La congiura dei Pazzi: Radici politico-sociali e ragioni di un fallimento," 87–106. See also Daniels 2013a.

Bianca Maria to Renato de' Pazzi. But the head of the family, Jacopo, took advantage of the regime's weakness during the transition from Piero's to Lorenzo's predominance, as well as of the general turbulence, both within the city and without, of the period from 1469 to 1471. Emboldened by his popularity among the citizenry, Jacopo worked the levers of power in a manner exceeding what had been informally understood with the Medici, advancing his own man, Bardo di Bartolo Corsi, to the position of gonfalonier of justice for May to June 1471. Without warning, Corsi put forward a plan for administrative reorganization that presupposed a policy of pacification, and thus a virtual renunciation of the key alliance with the Sforza dukes of Milan that had guaranteed the regime's security ever since the dominance of Cosimo "il vecchio." Lorenzo's response was typical: instead of taking steps to punish Jacopo Pazzi, all he did was to ensure, under the formal cover of secrecy afforded by the scrutiny of November 1471, that the Pazzi were excluded from the customary distribution of extra electoral tickets (or *polizze*). To receive such extra tickets was a badge of membership in the regime, and the converse was a tacit sign of exclusion from the inner circle. But to the Pazzi, this constituted a violation of the 1458 pact admitting them to the regime, and thus a justification for revenge. They showed their hand as early as 1473–74, as relations deteriorated, on the one hand, between Florence and the Holy See, and, on the other, between the two allies—themselves rivals—Milan and Naples. This is the background behind why, immediately after the Pazzi war in March 1480, Lorenzo's main concern was to secure a constitutional reform, with the primary aim of guaranteeing the principal families a broader and more solidly grounded share of power as members of the new "institution of the seventy" (*ordine dei settanta*). This institution or council was created through the co-optation of forty members to the *balìa* of thirty, with membership renewable quinquennially, so making tenure virtually permanent. Formally it was meant to function as a consultative council (a *pratica*), but in fact it sapped the *signoria's* powers, becoming Florence's supreme executive organ—a position enhanced by Lorenzo's personal power and membership.[17]

At this point, it is opportune to recall that, in fifteenth-century Italy, such methods of narrowing and tightening access to power and of overriding long-established civic magistracies through appointed, nonelective institutions constituted the rule rather than the exception. The less-than-obvious workings of clan and lineage can elude scholars, though these had an impact even on the legally conformist Venetian oligarchy,[18] not to mention the two allies upon whom Lorenzo's regime especially relied (except during the Pazzi war): the duchy of Milan and the kingdom of Naples. In the former, the claim to *plenitudo potestatis* inaugurated by the signori and later first dukes, the Visconti, and transmitted to their successors, the Sforza,

17 See Rubinstein 1997, 228–244; Fubini 1996, "Diplomazia e governo in Firenze all'avvento dei reggimenti oligarchici," 93–98.
18 In general, see Martin and Romano 2000.

was strongly contested, on grounds no less political than doctrinal. In her valuable book, Jane Black illustrates the resistance this claim met from the members of the law faculty at the University of Pavia—the public voice, as it were, of the Milanese nobility.[19] Franca Leverotti for her part had already portrayed in detail the strains caused by the abrupt centralization of power on the part of Duke Galeazzo Maria Sforza.[20] As for the kingdom of Naples during the transfer of power from the Angevin to the Aragonese dynasty, especially in the reign of King Ferrante (1458–94), it is enough to mention the Barons' Wars of 1458–65 and 1485–86 to indicate the endemic friction between the court and the feudal nobility, a topic now coming into clearer focus thanks to the publication of the dispatches from Naples of the Milanese and Florentine ambassadors.[21]

As far as Lorenzo's regime is concerned, the creation of the seventy was conceived as an improvement on the previous device of constituting exceptional *balìe*. Still, the problem of legitimacy could not be dodged. Lacking roots in tradition and co-opted from above, the seventy could have acquired legitimacy only as a senate under a prince. The converse also holds true: the only possible outcome of the formalized creation of a senate would have been mutual formal recognition between it and a permanent head of the city. This is the core of Lorenzo's constitutional strategy: the progressive enervation of the statutory organs of government was meant to be capped, as Francesco Guicciardini hints in the *Storie fiorentine*, by the creation of a legitimate headship in the form of a lifelong gonfalonierate of justice. Although Lorenzo never held the title, the suggestion remains credible, comforted as it is by other circumstances, including the fact that he had not reached the requisite age of 45 when he died. The most telling argument in its favor is that, beginning with the Medici's expulsion in 1494, the idea of a perpetual gonfaloniership was in the air, coming to fruition in 1502 when Piero Soderini was elevated to the rank. The constitutional crisis in Florence was to furnish the indispensable backdrop for the new political thought of Machiavelli and Guicciardini.[22] But one aspect of these developments may not have fully engaged the attention of scholars. The essential feature of the commune's governing institutions was that they rose from below, out of territorial representation. The priors, as well as the guilds, specifically represented the quarters and the *gonfaloni* (subsections of the quarters, or districts); only in the case of the head magistracy, the gonfalonierate of justice, did the quarters take turns. The more authoritative of the two colleges, the *sedici gonfalonieri di compagnia* (the sixteen gonfaloniers of the sixteen militia companies), gave a consultative and deliberative voice to each of the sixteen *gonfaloni* making up each quarter of the city. Even for extraordinary magistracies such as the *dieci di balìa* (ten of war),

19 Black 2009. See also Fubini 1994, "La crisi del ducato di Milano nel 1477 e la riforma del Consiglio Segreto ducale di Bona Sforza," 107–135; Arcangeli 2002.

20 Leverotti 1994.

21 See especially, with extensive bibliography, Lanfredini 2002.

22 See Fubini 2009, 194–203.

the criterion of territorial representation was retained, with appropriate modifications. It was this fundamental norm that was violated by the seventy, because its core, the *balìa* of thirty, had no territorial basis (though the forty adjunct members did).[23] As Guicciardini put it much later, it was no longer important for those chosen to represent a quarter, but only to be worthy to hold the office: the ancient constitution of the commune had in effect been superseded.[24]

Because the seventy lacked legitimacy, a full permanent record of their deliberations was not kept; in fact, in spite of a special chancery rule on the subject in 1483, whatever survives is scant and fragmentary.[25] A record of such executive meetings was meant to furnish the raw materials for an official history, responsibility for which was assigned to a chancery secretary. The model here was Giovanni Simonetta's *De rebus gestis Francisci Sfortize commentarii*, which Cristoforo Landino, the most eminent of the chancery secretaries, had been assigned to translate into the vernacular.[26] More important, this projected official history provided the cue to Niccolò Machiavelli when working as second chancellor under the life gonfalonier, Pier Soderini. And it remained a chancery project when on commission from Giulio de' Medici, Machiavelli resumed work, albeit in an altered format, but remaining within the traditions of the Florentine chancery (ultimately producing his *Istorie fiorentine*).[27]

If the seventy was the first bulwark of Lorenzo's regime, the general scrutiny of 1484 was the second. By creating the seventy, he had marked the limits within which optimate power would be exercised. With the scrutiny of 1484 (the first since 1471), he tried to set definitive boundaries to what might be called the wider regime, in the sense of all politically eligible citizens—those with a hereditary right to be considered for office, or for membership in a deliberative or consultative body. The social effects were felt well into the age of the grand duchy. One aspect of the 1484 scrutiny may not have been sufficiently stressed. In an unusual proem to the register of the *accoppiatori* (selection officials) who carried out the scrutiny, the names are given of the *accoppiatori* elected by the *balìa* of September 1466 to fill the electoral purses for the *signoria* (the pardoned rebel Luca Pitti heading the list), but the scrutiny of 1471 is passed over in silence. This omission is a mark of rupture with respect to the circumstances of thirteen years before, out of which had originated, in the manner seen above, the Pazzi's projected vendetta against the Medici.[28] A final point is that, under Lorenzo, the established statutory rule that periodic scrutinies

23 Rubinstein 1997, 359–360. In the lists for 1489 there is no longer any indication of quarters of origin: ibid., 361–362.
24 Fubini 2009, 235–236; Guicciardini 1994a, 175.
25 Rubinstein 1997, 373–375.
26 Ianziti 1988, 230–231.
27 For an official historiography in Florence on the project, dating from the time of the chancery reforms of 31 December 1483, see Fubini 2007, "Machiavelli, i Medici e la storia di Firenze," 193–207, in particular 197–198.
28 Viti and Zaccaria 1989, 239; and, in general, Rubinstein 1997.

should be held every five years was suspended, and with that a new basis of political representation was as good as defined once and for all. And it was a basis for a state, not just a regime, though for the moment it still lacked the final component—a legitimate and recognized head. The passage from regime to state with a permanent, juridically defined constitutional structure would be the main focus of the political thought of Francesco Guicciardini, particularly in the *Dialogue on the Government of Florence* (*Dialogo del reggimento di Firenze*). Drawing upon the fund of political experience acquired in the creation of the Great Council and then of the life gonfalonier, he sought a republican equivalent to the design for a principate sketched by Lorenzo and effected subsequently by his heirs.[29]

With regard to the image of personal power, which Lorenzo himself transmitted, more or less deliberately, to posterity, one point needs to be made at the outset. It would have been inappropriate for Lorenzo to project a triumphal image of himself, in the way that his ducal and grand-ducal successors did, for example in the Vasari frescoes. So it was easy for an art historian such as André Chastel, in his book *Art et humanisme à Florence au temps de Laurent de Médicis*, to reject the "Medici legend," or for an architectural historian such as Manfredo Tafuri to go on about Lorenzo's refusal "to represent himself triumphally in Florence."[30] In formal terms, Lorenzo was a private person, as he himself never failed to recognize. Triumphal representation was a privilege reserved for the public person of an anointed prince—the formal status of the dukes and grand dukes of Tuscany. The celebration, from the sixteenth to eighteenth centuries, of Lorenzo as Maecenas was an anachronism of the Medici principate, which traced its own recent magnificence to the distant ancestor who bore the title of "il Magnifico."

But while it was literally anachronistic, it was not, so to speak, an absolute anachronism. As recent research by Francis William Kent and Caroline Elam, among others, has revealed, it is possible to detect the formal outlines of an inchoate principate already taking shape in Lorenzo's mind.[31] When he came to power in December 1469, Lorenzo enjoyed a position at the heart of the regime different to his father Piero's. He had to beware of the same narrow oligarchy, headed by his uncle through marriage, Tommaso Soderini, that had ensured that the regime passed to him, virtually like a private inheritance. As Lorenzo noted in his *Ricordi* (a strictly private document),

> (i)l secondo dì dopo la sua (di Piero) morte... vennono a noi [Lorenzo e Giuliano] i principali della città et dello stato a confortarmi che pigliassi la cura della città et dello stato, come havevano fatto l'avolo et padre mio; le

29 Fubini 2009, 227–248.
30 Chastel 1959; Tafuri 1992, 93–94.
31 Elam 1994; Kent 2001. But see too the important observations in Rubinstein 1995.

quali cose, per essere contro alla mia età e di gran carico e pericolo, mal volentieri accettai e solo per conservatione delli amici e substantie nostre, perché a Firenze si può mal vivere ricco sanza lo stato.[32]

On the second day after the death of Piero, the principal men of the city and of the regime visited us [Lorenzo and Giuliano] to press me to assume the care of the city and the regime, like my grandfather and father. As I was not of age and the burdens and dangers were great, I accepted reluctantly, and only to keep our friends and our assets safe, because in Florence the rich are at risk if they did not belong to the *stato*.

Here in the usual format of a family diary (*libro di ricordi*), by definition a private composition, every word has an obvious justificatory intent. Power (or rather, "the care of the city") had been offered to Lorenzo, when not yet of age, by the regime's leading citizens. He had accepted it ("reluctantly") in order to safeguard his family's patrimony and social standing ("because in Florence the rich are at risk if they are not members of the regime"). The last remark would not have sounded out of place if it had come from the pen of Giovanni di Pagolo Morelli. The reality that Lorenzo's words conceal is entirely different, indeed diametrically opposed. It is possible to reconstruct the true significance of these events with the help of the dispatches sent to Milan almost daily by the Milanese resident ambassador in Florence, Sacramoro da Rimini. They reveal the secretive efforts made by "the principal men" of the regime, the very individuals who, led by Tommaso Soderini, had ensured his succession, to set bounds to Lorenzo's power as *primus inter pares*. From their perspective, it was essential to reduce external intervention from the Sforza, whose support had buttressed the Medici regime ever since Cosimo and Francesco Sforza had first formed their alliance. Lorenzo for his part knew he could not shrink from his inherited position of civic leadership. As he confided to Sacramoro, he held "the firm conviction that, when someone in his position suffers a loss of status, total ruin soon follows."[33] From the beginning, his strategy was not to let his personal, private interests be confounded with those of the regime, in the institutional sense of the term.

In this regard, it is worth mentioning the particular question of knightly honors. These were normally conferred by sovereign potentates and required the obligatory confirmation of the city councils. But they could also be conferred directly by

32 I cite the sixteenth-century transcription in Morelli Timpanaro, Manno Tolu, and Viti 1992, 31. The full title of the fragment is "Narratione breve del corso di mia vita o d'alcune altre cose d'importanza degne di memoria per lume e informatione di chi succederà, massime de' figli nostri, cominciata questo dì 15 marzo 1473" (Brief narrative of the course of my life and other things of importance worth recording for the enlightenment and information of my successors, especially my children, begun today 15 March 1473).

33 "per constante che dopo la bassezza de uno suo paro el ce vene apresso la total ruina." Sacramoro to Galeazzo Maria Sforza, Florence, 26 November 1470, Medici 1977–, 1:235.

the *signoria* on deserving citizens, who were then known as *milites populi*. Piero de' Pazzi, for example, had been made a knight by the French king Louis XI, but shortly after his death the same title was conferred by the *signoria* on his younger brother Jacopo. Though it was a relic of the medieval past, a knightly title had acquired fresh political relevance in the 1460s. A particularly solemn occasion was the conferral of a knighthood on Luca Pitti on 15 December 1463—with the death of Cosimo de' Medici imminent—*ob multiplicia eius erga rem publicam benemerita* (for his many meritorious services to the republic). This event was a prelude to the civic revolt, headed by Luca Pitti himself, against Piero's succession.[34] At about the same time, coinciding with Bartolomeo Scala's appointment as first chancellor in 1465, a procedural innovation in the meetings of the *pratiche* (consultative assemblies summoned by the *signoria* on matters of pressing importance) gave knights rather than jurists the privilege of speaking first, and so of setting the debate's direction.[35] Knightly investiture, both within the city and without, had once again become important, and when Sacramoro da Rimini, the Milanese ambassador in Florence, alludes to the snares laid for Lorenzo by the regime's oligarchy, he refers to them as *questi cavallari* (these knights). At a moment of great tension, and in need of a loyal ally, Lorenzo obtained a knighthood for Bongianni Gianfigliazzi on 26 December 1470. The new knight, who belonged to a family branch that had stayed loyal to the Medici, thus attained the same level of distinction as his ancestor messer Rinaldo Gianfigliazzi, one of the most distiguished figures of the Albizzi regime.[36] Although Lorenzo was not a knight himself as custom prescribed, he claimed the right, as *sindaco* in the name of the *signoria*, to dub the new knight with the traditional insignia in person. Since Cosimo's day, the Medici had taken care not to give the appearance, through the dignity of knighthood, of figuring as *primi inter pares*, that is as first among equals. A *sindaco* by definition acted in the name of a commissioning party; now, in defiance of every rule and precedent, Lorenzo performed this symbolic act on no basis other than his own authority. As Sacramoro wrote on 29 December 1470, "they maintain that his own authority will replace legal validity" (*tengono che'l vallerà per l'auctorità*). And indeed Gianfigliazzi, unfailingly, at least until 1478, appears on the list of Lorenzo's most trustworthy adherents, starting with the embassy swearing obedience to Pope Sixtus IV in August 1471, of which Lorenzo himself was a member.[37]

---

34 Salvemini 1896, 133–135 (*Appendice A, 83*). It may be relevant that the construction of the ambitious Palazzo Pitti began in the 1450s, which is why Luca's faction was called "del Poggio" (of the hill on which the palace was built).

35 Fubini 2009, 178.

36 Salvemini 1896, 136, 151 ff.; and also Kent 1978, 147–148; Rubinstein 1997, 123 n., 142 n. Bongianni di Bongianni Gianfigliazzi appears among the *arroti* (adjunct members) of the *balìe* from 1466 onward, for the quarter of Santa Maria Novella. In 1469, he figures for the first time among the even more select *accoppiatori*, and in 1471, he is included among the forty privileged members of the *balìa*: Rubinstein 1997, 276, 339, 344.

37 Medici 1977–, 1:337. See also Klein and Arrighi 2013.

The official posthumous award to Cosimo of the honorific title *pater patriae*, approved by the councils on 15–16 March 1465, was a distinction enhancing at the very least the house of Medici's stature as citizens of unique moral worth. When, for example, on 12 December 1479, as Lorenzo was preparing to sail to Naples, the ten of war entrusted him with full powers to make peace with the Neapolitan king, they justified this extraordinary delegation not just on the grounds of his eminent intellectual and practical abilities (*confidentes de summa prudentia ac multarum rerum experientia*), but also by his descent from that eminently deserving citizen, Cosimo: *dominum Laurentium Petri olim sapientissimi viri Cosme de Medicis decreto pubblico "Patris Patrie."*[38] Lorenzo himself was exhorted more than once, in a literary context at any rate, to assume that very title. One needs to leave aside Marsilio Ficino's essentially self-serving point that his own devotion to the Medici was justified by their deserving deeds, loftier than any princely title, which made them *in libera civitate patres patriae* (fathers of their country in a free city). In this letter from 1476, Lorenzo was thus implicitly contrasted to the idealized Cosimo "il vecchio," in order to nurture aims incompatible with the status of citizen. The diarist Marco Parenti took a similar view: according to him, from the time of his wedding to Clarice Orsini, Lorenzo "wished to ally himself in matrimony only with lords, for his frame of mind already looked beyond the city" (*si volse riserbare a imparentarsi con signori, che già aveva l'animo sopracittadino*).[39] But Lorenzo was also urged to assume the honorific title borne by his grandfather in a different, more poetic way. A literary figure from the cardinal of Mantua's circle, Paolo Emilio Boccabella, addressed Lorenzo in these elegiac couplets immediately after the Pazzi conspiracy, predicting for him the same honor previously accorded to Cosimo and Cicero:

Ad Laurentium Medices.
Vive diu, Medice, firmissima cura tonantis / Et patriae numen praesidiumque tuae / [. . .] / Restat ut "assertae" dignum "Pater Urbis" honorem / Excipias, Cosmus quem tulit et Cicero.[40]

Live long, Medici, under the firm care of the Thunderer, both inspirer and guardian of your homeland.... It remains for you to take up the worthy honor "Father and protector of the City," which both Cosimo and Cicero bore.

38 Medici 1977–, 4:367. The title of *pater patriae* is highlighted in the contemporary *priorista delle riformagioni* with capital letters, repeated here with initial capitals.

39 Marsilio Ficino to Giovanni Cavalcanti, undated (but 1476), Fubini 1996, 275; Parenti 2001, 141. The *Ricordi*, while dealing essentially with the anti-Medici disturbances after the death of Cosimo, date from the years 1478 to 1479, and are linked to anti-Medici propaganda during the Pazzi war.

40 My student and friend Tobias Daniels, whom I thank, supplied me with these unpublished verses: see now Daniels 2013a and 2013b. On Boccabella, see Chambers 1988, 243.

Aurelio Lippo Brandolini, the Florentine exile in Naples, had addressed similarly flattering words to Lorenzo not long before, invoking him as father of his country (*Ergo pater patriae communi est voce vocandus*, and also "sole protector and defender of the poor, orphans and exiles").[41] The same Brandolini, who was later appointed to the University of Pisa in 1490, dedicated his treatise *De comparatione reipublicae et regni* to Lorenzo, celebrating him, if not as a prince, with a flattering "princely image" capable of resolving discords: *aliquam etiam illius regii principatus imaginem*.[42] But, as Rubinstein notes, titles such as these were never among his official attributes. After the death of Lorenzo in 1492, the provision that declared Piero his heir "did not go beyond calling him *vir primarius nostrae civitatis*" (foremost man of our city).[43]

It is a question not so much of honorific titles as of underlying political strategies. In Lorenzo's eyes, in order to keep the regime united, it was necessary to exert control from a position outside the regime itself, with no further disruptive *parlamenti* and *balìe*—in other words, with no further recourse to those extraordinary measures used by Cosimo to achieve power that had subsequently rendered his son Piero's authority so precarious. It had been possible to use such extraordinary measures repeatedly over several decades only because of the pact made by Cosimo at the start of his regime with Francesco Sforza. As military captain, and even more as duke of Milan, Sforza intimidated internal opposition in Florence with the threat of armed intervention. His heir Galeazzo Maria similarly reassured Lorenzo, faced with powerful internal resistance toward the end of 1470:

> Dicimo cossì, che debbiate stare de buona voglia et franco animo et con prudentia et animosità conservare el loco, conditione et reputatione vostra con l'aiuto delli amici vostri là, certificandove che nui dal canto nostro tanto mancaremo per la conservatione del bene, honore et stato vostro quanto per lo nostro proprio, immo per mantenerlo et accrescerlo ... metteremo lo stato, le gente et tucte le nostre facultate, et in questo non facia dubio alchuno

> you should keep up your positive mood and firm resolve, and with prudence and courage preserve your position, situation, and reputation with the help of your friends there; be assured that we for our part should no more fail to preserve your welfare, honor, and rule than our own; indeed, to maintain and enhance it, we should employ our regime, our troops, and all our assets, and of this you should have no doubt.

41 Rubinstein 1997, 252.
42 Lenzuni 1992, 99–103.
43 Ibid.; Rubinstein 1997, 264; and further Lenzuni 1992, 99–103 (2.85, 2.86, entries by Ida Giovanna Rao).

Galeazzo Maria recommended emphatically to Sacramoro that in Florence a forced plebiscite should be conducted by way of a *parlamento*,

> dove se vedi de mandare fora quatro o sey o quelli paresse de li più cativi et inimici de Lorenzo, acciò che'l se possi meglio conservare senza havere obiecto alcuno[44]

> which would see to exiling four, or six, or however many it seems best, of the worst characters and enemies of Lorenzo, so that he can preserve himself better, without opposition.

Typically, in his reply Lorenzo reserved the option, should circumstances require, "of holding a *balìa* in a manner neither scandalous nor dangerous, and without soldiers" (*de fare una balìa cum modo né schandaloso né periculoso et senza soldati*).[45] Such was exactly the sort of *balìa* summoned by simple decree of the *signoria* on 5 July 1471, under the name, used again in 1480, of *consiglio maggiore* (great council). Nor was this merely a euphemism: it betrays a political intention to transform the regime into an institution, under the guidance, if not precisely institutionalized, then at any rate entrenched, of Lorenzo, who thus enlarged his sphere of personal authority. The 1471 reforms paved the way for those of 1480, and were meant to free Lorenzo from dependence, internal or external, on the restive Florentine oligarchy, as well as from Sforza interference. It was thanks to the powers conferred upon him by the *balìa* of 1471 that he began to practice (no matter with what success in the short term) the policy of mediation in the endemic conflicts between his Milanese and Neapolitan allies—an approach that came to be known as his "balance of power policy." The political and institutional aspects of the 1471 reforms have already been mentioned, but there is one element, typical of Lorenzo, that deserves emphasis. In his campaign to put the regime on a more regular footing, without further possible disruption, he was reverting to the policies not so much of his father Piero, who had been generally unpopular when he died, as of Piero's adversaries. The tendency to stabilize the regime by way of carefully managed access to the privilege of political office (which was already being referred to by the technical term *beneficio*) was at the heart of the constitutional proposals of Niccolò Soderini in 1465. Guidance of the regime by a prestigious citizen, publicly recognized and authorized, characterized the ambitions of Luca Pitti, the true architect of the reforming *parlamento* of 1458. Jacopo de' Pazzi enjoyed wide popularity in the city as well: his position was enhanced by the close marriage connection formed with the Medici in 1459, but suffered from his open dissent from Medici

---

44 Galeazzo Maria Sforza to Lorenzo de' Medici, Milan, 16 August 1470, Medici 1977–, 1:207; Galeazzo Maria Sforza to Sacramoro, 2 November 1470, ibid., 1:209.

45 Sacramoro to Galeazzo Maria Sforza, Florence, 16 December 1470, ibid., 1:209.

policy in 1469–71, and in the electoral scrutiny of November 1471—as stated above (65)—his house saw its quota of electoral *polizze* reduced with respect to the other families in the regime's inner circle. The greatest threat arose when Jacopo de' Pazzi, with the complicity of Pierfrancesco de' Medici, the family's dissenting member, had one of his followers, Bardo di Bartolo Corsi, installed as gonfalonier of justice for the bimester May to June 1471. Corsi delivered a speech in the *pratica* proposing to distance the city from the duke of Milan's reckless policies, and to effect a rapprochement with the king of Naples.[46] This was the origin of the rupture between Lorenzo and the Pazzi clan, leading to the celebrated conspiracy. Corsi for his part was silently sidelined (*quasi amunito e privato delli uffici* [as though banned and deprived of office] according to Alamanno Rinuccini's *Ricordi*)[47]—but not immediately. Bardo Corsi's speech dealt with the need for peace, the precondition for a broad economic and administrative reorganization of the city. This had been the policy advanced by Jacopo de' Pazzi ever since Piero's death, and the opportunity to put it into effect came with his client's gonfalonierate (*anima et corpo de d. Jacomo de Pazi* [Jacopo de' Pazzi's in soul and body] is how Sacramoro da Rimini characterized the gonfalonier, Bardo Corsi).[48]

But Lorenzo shrewdly made this program his own: he had a second *balìa* convoked alongside the main *balìa* of 5 July (which was meant to decide the framework of power and the guidelines of foreign policy), with distinct and specific responsibilities for economic and administrative reorganization. Its membership was, in typical fashion, composed of individuals in whom Lorenzo had full confidence, but the link to the program put forward in Corsi's speech is evident in the fact that Corsi was chosen on this occasion as a *monte* (publicly funded debt) official, and so was able to participate in the second *balìa*'s work.[49] That is not all: the *consiglio maggiore* undertook "a complete restructuring of the city's guilds," placing them under centralized political control.[50] This was a responsibility that Lorenzo, as will be seen, personally assumed. And yet for the moment Jacopo de' Pazzi was not removed from his influential position in the wool guild: he was a member, for example, of the committee elected on 24 September 1472 to divert the income from Volterra's alum mines to this guild, a committee transformed not long afterward

46 Fubini 1994, 240, 242–243. In ASF CP 60, fol. 125r, the discourse, which is censored, with the space left blank, is described as "most eloquent" ("ex eloquentissima oratione").

47 Rinuccini, Rinuccini and Rinuccini 1840, cxvii; Medici 1977–, 1:320.

48 Sacramoro to Galeazzo Maria Sforza, 5 May 1471, Fubini 1994, 243.

49 Fubini 1996, "Prestito ebraico e Monte di Pietà a Firenze (1471–1473)," 174–175. The archival records for this committee are found in ASF Balìe 33; its activities were inaugurated on 23 July (hence it was distinct from the so-called *consiglio maggiore* of 5 July, whose records are preserved in ASF Balìe 31). The members were Tommaso Soderini (who had resolved his disagreements with Lorenzo through a personal *intelligenza*, or sworn pact, following Milanese intervention), Antonio Ridolfi, Bernardo Del Nero, Lorenzo Niccolini, Roberto de' Lioni, Bongianni Gianfigliazzi, Leonardo Bartolini, ser Niccolò di Michele Fei, Matteo Palmieri, and Antonio di Taddeo Taddei. With regard to Soderini's agreement with Lorenzo at the end of 1470, see Medici 1977–, 1:209.

50 Franceschi 1996, 1346.

into the *Proveditori diputati per l'arte della lana sopra l'allumiera* ("overseers deputed by the wool guild to supervise the alum mines"), alongside such typical members of Lorenzo's inner circle as Antonio Taddei, Domenico Bartoli, and Roberto de' Lioni, who were joined shortly after by Lorenzo himself.[51] Beneath such feigned continuity, a genuine shift of control was taking place from the Pazzi to the Medici at this nerve center of civic political and social life.

There is a salient moment in the career of Lorenzo in which the twofold aspect of his control over the city—as head of the regime and as external arbiter and regulator of all political and social power—emerges with particular clarity: namely, his eminently personal mission to Naples in search of an accord with the Aragonese king Ferrante at the end of 1479, in the midst of the Pazzi war. Lorenzo was then a member of the *dieci di balìa*, but, officially at least, he conferred neither with them nor with the *signoria* prior to announcing his decision, not at a consultative *pratica* but before "an extremely large number of citizens" convoked by the two offices jointly.[52] The *dieci* were, incidentally, figures who enjoyed Lorenzo's full confidence; the most authoritative member was Tommaso Soderini, bound to Lorenzo by a sworn *intelligenza*, while his companions on the Neapolitan voyage included Tommaso's eldest son Pagolantonio.[53] In other words, the personal pact between Lorenzo and Tommaso Soderini, and then Lorenzo's voyage, will have contributed to the continuing ambitions of the Soderini family beyond the fall of the Medici regime in 1494. To return to Lorenzo, he stubbornly refused diplomatic accreditation in the name of the Florentine *signoria*, despite the sleight of hand exercised by the chancellor Bartolomeo Scala, who went beyond customary legal language in drafting the mandate: the new *dieci* who took office on 13 December delegated powers to Lorenzo "so that, as always, his private interest might be conjoined with the public interest." Lorenzo, therefore, "as ambassador of the Florentine people, would consider what was most advantageous for the republic," concluding a treaty with the king of Naples.[54] In fact, Lorenzo declined to accept these credentials. The *dieci* had no recourse but to take note, and to write the following exceptional letter

51 Kent 2001, 347.

52 Medici 1977–, 4:249.

53 Ibid., 4:376, for Lorenzo's act delegating Ippolita, duchess of Calabria, and Niccolò Michelozzi as his procurators for the conclusion of the peace accord, executed at Gaeta on 6 March 1480; signing with Lorenzo, as a witness and before the Neapolitan dignitaries, was Pagolantonio Soderini ("Io Paulo Antonio de Sodorino de Florentia come testimonio chi me sottoscrivo de manu propria"); on the composition of the *dieci*, see ibid., 4:365.

54 "Mandatum Decemvirum Balie civitatis Florentie in Laurentium de Medicis: [...] ut esset cum sua re privata etiam coniuncta publica, ut semper fuit. Videat ergo Laurentius Medices, populi florentini legatus, quid e republica sit; agat cum gloriosissimo principe Ferdinando rege Neapolitano [...] Quicquid Laurentio Medici visum fuerit cum ser.mo rege [...] de pace, de amicitia deque omni re publica transigeret, magistratus et populus Florentinus probabit, confirmabit et constantissime observabit." (Mandate of the Dieci di Balìa of the city of Florence to Lorenzo de' Medici: ...Whatever Lorenzo de' Medici sees fit to transact with the most serene king ... concerning peace, friendship, and all public matters, the magistrates and people of Florence will approve, confirm, and continuously observe.) Ibid., 4:369–370. It scarcely needs to be said that

of accreditation to the king on 15 December: "Since Lorenzo de' Medici is coming to you *primarily for private reasons,* we have thought it fitting that he should not arrive without public credentials as well."[55] When he had to abandon peace negotiations in order to return quickly to Florence, Lorenzo, as he was about to embark at Gaeta, empowered his trusted secretary Niccolò Michelozzi to act in his name ("I bind myself by this letter from my own hand, as though by a legal instrument").[56] Hence, when the peace treaty was signed at Naples on 13 March 1480, Florence was represented by two classes of signatories: the representatives accredited by the *dieci* (on Lorenzo's strict instructions), Agostino Biliotti and Niccolò Michelozzi, who signed in the name of the republic; and those accredited personally by Lorenzo, in the persons of Michelozzi (again) and the duchess of Calabria, Ippolita Sforza, wife of the heir to the Neapolitan throne, Alfonso of Calabria.[57]

These details are far from mere formalities. Apart from the matters explicitly dealt with in the negotiations (restitution to Florence of the lands conquered by Siena, assurances for the signori of the Romagna), there was Lorenzo's promise to the king—the real reason for his trip. As Lorenzo himself instructed his delegates Michelozzi and Biliotti on 16 March, when he was back in Florence, they were to tell King Ferrante, "I am the same Lorenzo I told him I was at my departure, and am prepared either to execute *what I promised to his majesty* or to die; he will see the proof of this, should the case arise."[58] The proof was seen in 1485–86, when Lorenzo took a leading role, both among his fellow citizens and among Naples's allies, in supporting King Ferrante during the Barons' War against the papacy and the eventuality of a new French-Angevin expedition. The ambassador he sent to Naples, in 1485–86 as selected in 1479–80, was his close confidant, albeit an outsider to the city's

---

the document was illegal: the nomination of an ambassador, and a fortiori the delegation of powers to conclude a treaty, fell within the competence of the Council of 100.

55 "Cum ad te Laurentius Medices *privatis de rebus satis veniret,* visum est ut veniret etiam publica persona": Medici 1977–, 4:269; italics mine.

56 "per questa lettera di mia mano me obligo, come se fusse per instrumento." Lorenzo to Niccolò Michelozzi, Gaeta, 28 February 1480, ibid., 4:326.

57 See Lorenzo to Michelozzi, Gaeta, 5 March 1480, ibid., 4:327 ff.: "La procura mia privata ho fatto in Madonna Duchessa et in te" (my private delegation I have conferred upon the lady Duchess and you); and the delegation of the *dieci* to Niccolò Michelozzi and Agostino Biliotti, 2 March 1480: "con questa sarà il mandato in amendue" (with this the mandate will be for both), ibid., 4:321. Biliotti was a merchant with interests in the Sicilian and Catalonian maritime trade; having gained the Medici's trust, he was director of the Medici bank's Neapolitan branch in 1471–75, in January, he joined Lorenzo at Naples: ibid., 4:321; and also 3:201. The text of the treaty, dated 13 March 1480, can be found ibid., 4:377–389.

58 "ch'io sono quello Lorenzo che li dissi al mio partire, et disposto o a morire o a fare *quanto promissi alla Sua Maestà*: vedrassene experientia, se'l caso sarà." Ibid., 4:338; italics mine. Also Lorenzo to Michelozzi, Pisa, 13 March 1480, ibid., 4:333: "Se harò gratia o reputatione, io le ho tucte a spendere nel modo ragionai costì colla Maestà del Re: e tanto valerà questo capitale, tanto potrà spendere per sempre la Sua Maestà" (If I enjoy favor or reputation, I have them all to spend in the way I discussed with His Majesty the king when I was there; and as long as this goodwill exists, His Majesty can always put it to use).

inner political circles—Giovanni Lanfredini, a director of the Medici bank.[59] But the most direct confirmation of the anti-French commitment made by Lorenzo to Naples came from the French king Louis XI himself. Initially, the king had Philippe de Commynes write a letter of simulated congratulations to Francesco Gaddi, a trusted agent who had acted on Lorenzo's behalf at the Roman court, guaranteeing his "honor and glory."[60] But when Lorenzo dispatched an embassy to France in the person of Gaddi the following year, it was spurned.[61] Worse still, the following year Louis XI arranged for Lorenzo to receive a letter from Commynes, dated 30 November 1481, threatening military intervention in unmistakable terms: "And it seems to me that, although I am insufficiently wise to offer you advice, nevertheless you ought to take pains to keep yourself in the king's good graces, and not to underestimate the situation here: even though the road from our territories to yours is long, the king enjoys great power everywhere—more perhaps than many people in Italy imagine."[62]

With the Neapolitan treaty and the constitutional reforms in Florence, which were put into immediate effect, Lorenzo was freed from the twin contrasting restraints that had made his rise to power so arduous: dependence on factions within the city's oligarchy, and excessive interference by the Sforza dukes of Milan in Florentine affairs. On the one hand, the oligarchy's demands for a share of power were satisfied by access to the newly constituted council of seventy. On the other, with the personal guarantee given to the king of Naples, the old bond, by nature entirely personal and dynastic, between Cosimo de' Medici and Francesco Sforza and then their respective heirs, became a thing of the past. The other side of the coin was that the twofold nature of Lorenzo's power—public and private, civic and dynastic—was enhanced.

Not that Lorenzo grew careless about appearances. On 26 November 1484, he wrote to his son Piero, who had been attached as a "youth" to the Florentine embassy to swear obedience to Pope Innocent VIII: "At times and places where

59 Lanfredini 2002, 2005. For the cooling of the Milanese alliance, and the difficulties encountered by Lorenzo at home in 1484, see Medici 1977–, 8:vii (to quote from the introduction by Humfrey Butters): "Lorenzo had to employ almost as much energy to convince the other members of the Florentine regime that his analysis of the Neapolitan situation was correct [as he did to convince Ludovico il Moro]."

60 Medici 1997–, 4:343. Francesco Gaddi, a merchant and a figure trusted by Lorenzo, was put forward by him as chancellor to the *dieci di balìa*; to overcome the irregularity (because he was neither a notary nor a lawyer), he was enrolled ad hoc in the guild of judges and notaries: see Morelli Timpanaro, Manno Tolu, and Viti 1992, 92, and also Arrighi 1998.

61 Medici 1977–, 5:54–61, 67–71. These are letters to Leonetto de' Rossi, the Medici's banking agent at Lyon and an individual trusted by King Louis XI, who wanted a meeting with him: "io credo che la cagione per che il Re ti domandi sia per havere poca fede nel Gaddo" (I believe the reason the king is asking for you is that he has little faith in Gaddi) (ibid., 5:55).

62 "Et me semble que, encores que je ne soye bien saige pour vous conseiller, que vous devez mectre paine de vous entretenir en l'amour du roy, et que vous ne le devez point peu estimer ne les choses de par de ça et, ancore que le chemin soit long d'icy la, si peut le roy beaucoup par tout, et plus par aventure qu'il ne semble à beaucoup de gens d'Italie." Commynes 2001, 55.

the other ambassadors' sons join you, bear yourself gravely and with good manners toward your equals and make sure not to go before them if they are older than you, for you may be my son, but you are still no more than a citizen of Florence, just as they are."[63]

Lorenzo's language here is that of his *Ricordi* from the long past days of his accession to power, alert to propriety and to the distinction between public and private. And yet the language is belied by the message's substance, which betrays a dynastic perspective: Piero was taking a particularly prominent part in an embassy that recalled his father's when Sixtus IV came to power. Reserve was in any case entirely cast aside in another text, semiofficial in character, and directed to the young Piero too. This was the dedication composed by Cristoforo Landino, a Florentine university professor and also a "secretary" or high-ranking chancery functionary, for the printed edition of his Virgil commentary, which departs from standard practice in recounting Lorenzo's triumphant career. Landino had likewise rehearsed Ferrante of Aragon's deeds when, three years earlier, he dedicated his Italian translation of the elder Pliny to the king. In the Virgil preface, Lorenzo too was portrayed as the statesman upon whom the equilibrium not just of Florence but of all Italy depended: *ut in rebus maximis agendis ac domi forisque administrandis universa Italia primas prudentiae partes illi sine controversia concedat* (such that in the handling and administration of great matters at home and abroad, all Italy unhesitatingly awards him first place for prudence).[64] Addressing Piero di Lorenzo, Landino felt warranted in abandoning cautious formality, endorsing for the first time in a public composition the eminent role of the Medici family, or indeed dynasty: "Your house has for long achieved preeminence in this republic... [through merit not fortune] it has claimed first place in the city, to such an extent that, among the entire citizenry, every other house comes a poor second."[65]

A year later, another chancery employee, albeit of inferior rank, Filippo Redditi, joined Landino in addressing to the heir, Piero di Lorenzo, a panegyric on his father.[66] Redditi too, and even more explicitly than Landino, insisted on

---

63 "Ne' tempi e luoghi dove concorrano gl'altri gl'altri giovani degli'ambasciatori, pòrtati gravemente et costumatamente et con humanità verso gl'altri pari tuoi, guardandoti di non preceder loro, se fussino di più età di te, perché per essere mio figluolo non se' però altro che cittadino di Firenze, come sono ancor loro." Medici 1977–, 8:70.

64 Landino 1974, "In P. Vergilii interpretationem prohemium ad Petrum Meduces Magni Laurentii filium," 1:211–225. The imprint is dated 28 March 1488; for the dedication of the Pliny translation to the king of Naples, ibid., 1:81–93; see in this regard Fubini 1996, 303–332. Lastly, it is a key point that Landino's encomiastic composition came in the wake of events such as the peace between the king of Naples and Innocent VIII, Giovanni Lanfredini's mission to Rome (May 1487, on behalf of Lorenzo in particular), and the marriage pact between Lorenzo and Pope Innocent VIII by which Franceschetto Cibo was engaged to Maddalena de' Medici: see Scarton 2007, 242–276.

65 "Est iam diu, Petre Medices, princeps in republica vestra domus tua [...]; ita primum locum sibi in civitate vendicavit, ut ex ceteris omnibus nulla civibus fuerit nisi longo intervallo sibi secunda." Scarton 2007, 217.

66 Redditi 1989.

the peninsular role of Lorenzo, upon whom reposed "all Italy's common safety as well" (*communem quoque totius Italiae salutem*). But, unlike Landino, he insisted on Lorenzo's meritorious religious actions, such as the protection afforded to Giovanni Pico della Mirandola, who in his profound speculations on divine mysteries had revived the virtues of the holy fathers Jerome, Augustine, Gregory, and Ambrose.[67] In a postscript added after Lorenzo's death, the message became more explicit: Lorenzo had protected the distinguished theologian against malign curial enemies, "to the glory of God the highest and for the resilience of the Catholic faith" (*ad gloriam summi Dei et robur catholicae fidei*).[68] In the proem containing Pico's dedication of his *Heptaplus* to Lorenzo—the work in which he had vindicated the orthodoxy of his own Christian interpretation of the Jewish kabbalah in the teeth of papal condemnation, and which Lorenzo defended[69]—it was Pico himself who celebrated Lorenzo's most glorious achievement, the appointment of his son Giovanni to the cardinalate. "This fruit of my cogitations reaches you at an opportune moment, when your son Giovanni, at an age younger than anyone before him, has been elected by the lofty pontiff Innocent VIII to the highest college in Christendom."[70] Giovanni di Lorenzo de' Medici had been created cardinal in a bull of 9 March 1489, with the stipulation that the appointment should be kept secret for three years to avoid the scandal that his youth might have provoked. This stipulation was disregarded by Lorenzo, who perhaps spread the news without delay, not just throughout Florence but to every Italian chancery;[71] on the other hand, the news is known to have spread independently.[72] Political motivation was more compelling than the papal bull's strictures, while Pico's rhetoric managed to turn the new cardinal's precocity into a source of pride for the dynasty, if not an outright mark of spiritual election.

This relationship of simultaneous collusion with and challenge to the papacy, along with the unwritten Neapolitan pact, were reflected at home in the image that Lorenzo projected, as well as in his architectural program there. To intervene at the highest levels in ecclesiastical affairs, in the unadulterated style of princely absolutism, was a distinctive mark of Lorenzo's power. In February 1474, with the death of Pietro Riario, Lorenzo obtained the appointment of his brother-in-law Rinaldo

---

67   Ibid., 21; and also Fubini 2009, 210–211.

68   Redditi 1989, 25.

69   Medici, 1977–, 16:43–44.

70   "Opportune igitur nostra haec lucubratio ad te venit, quo tempore Ioannes filius ea aetate, qua nemo antea, summo christianorum ordinum collegio a pontifice summo Innocentio VIII destinatus est": Pico della Mirandola 1942, 182–184.

71   Morelli Timpanaro, Manno Tolu, and Viti 1992, 146–148. Writing to Giovanni Lanfredini from Florence on 11 March 1489, Lorenzo justifies himself thus: "né io ho potuto negare o non accettare la congratulatione di tucta questa città insino a' minimi; se pure è inconveniente, era impossibile che non fussi" (nor was I able to deny or fail to accept the congratulations of this whole city, all the way to the humblest individuals; while it may be inconvenient, it was impossible for this not to happen). See ibid., 148. See now Medici 1977–, vol. 15.

72   See Medici 1977–, 15:6–7.

Orsini as Florentine archbishop; at the very moment of his election, Orsini granted Lorenzo full discretion in diocesan administration: *o de vicario o de altri offitiali che ad ciò sian necessari, la Vostra Magnificentia poterà in mio nome provedere secondo gli pare* (Your Magnificence may appoint, in my name, vicars or other officials as required and as you see fit).[73] F. W. Kent, in the essay cited above (68), has dealt exhaustively with Lorenzo's virtual government of the *opera del duomo* (supervisors of the cathedral) via the direct control he exercised over the wool guild. One point deserves notice. In 1485, there appeared the posthumous *editio princeps* of Leon Battista Alberti's *De re aedificatoria*, edited by his cousin Battista Alberti and printed by Lorenzo Alemanno. Lorenzo had supported it, and the official stamp of approval was marked by Angelo Poliziano's prefatory epistle.[74] Alberti's doctrines were implicitly referred to in the deliberations of the wool guild's consuls on 12 February 1490 (working under the auspices of *provveditori* and, through them, of Lorenzo himself): the dilapidated facade of the cathedral (previously known as Santa Reparata) had been built at a time, so the deliberation states, when the proper rules of architecture were unknown ("sine aliqua ratione aut iure architecture").[75] The provision (which, as is known, was canceled following the Medici's fall) is of special interest here, also because it indirectly recalls the episode—a source of lively civic dispute at the time—of the construction by Alberti of the choir (*tribuna*) of the Servite church Santissima Annunziata. That initiative's patron had been the marquis of Mantua, Ludovico Gonzaga, who bore the costs. The episode is important because it testifies to the deep reluctance of Florentine society (and the Servites as well) to introduce a Roman centrally planned model, which was regarded as princely in style. Lorenzo had been reluctant to go against local prejudice in his first years in power, and only after an ultimatum from the marquis did he agree to back the project.[76] The individual in charge of this ultimate phase of the project was Leon Battista Alberti, but its executant—or so at least scholars assume— was the Florentine architect Luca Fancelli, who had long been in the service of the Gonzaga, and was a collaborator of Alberti's.[77] Now it was Fancelli who was chosen, at Lorenzo's instance, as chief architect (*capomastro*) of the cathedral, and who prepared a model for a new facade. Comparison of the two structures shows, better than anything else, the new direction of Lorenzo's policy, indeed his will to impose on the reluctant city an architecture rivaling the princely style on view elsewhere.

His consultant architect here was Giuliano da Sangallo, who had drafted the plans for the building work at Poggio a Caiano as early as 1480. Rather than a villa, for Lorenzo the structure had become a kind of rural palace, a visual symbol of his detachment from day-to-day civic government. (When at Poggio a Caiano he

73 Rinaldo Orsini to Lorenzo, Rome, 26 February 1474, ibid., 142.
74 Alberti 1989.
75 Kent 2001, 362.
76 Lorenzo to Ludovico Gonzaga, 22 May 1471, Medici 1977–, 1:275–278.
77 See the DBI entry by Ghisetti Giavarina 1994; Vasic Vatovec 1996, 73–93.

maintained contact with the city through his secretaries, Niccolò Michelozzi and subsequently Piero Dovizi.) Apropos of this villa's architecture, it has been said that "an idea as original as the use of a pediment for a private dwelling, and of decorating the entablature with a frieze in terracotta is absolutely unheard-of at that time," given that, according to ancient sources (Livy, Plutarch), such a feature was "an attribute of regality or power."[78] This unique character is accentuated by the arcane allegories on the frieze, where, within a complex frame of philosophical-religious allegory, an indirect allusion is made to the theme of concord achieved after discord, of peace and order under the government of one ruler, and finally of promised glory, represented by the ascent of the sun's chariot, which indirectly alludes to Giovanni di Lorenzo's appointment as cardinal.[79] It is significant that an architect so close to Lorenzo was assigned (before the villa was finished) first to the project (never realized) for a regal residence for King Ferrante of Naples (1488), and then for the construction, in succession, of the Florentine palaces of Filippo Strozzi and Giuliano Gondi (1489–90). Both men had supported Lorenzo's mission to Naples in 1479–80: Gondi, a rich banker in exile as an adversary of the regime, had conducted the negotiations as Alfonso of Aragon's and Federico da Montefeltro's agent,[80] while Strozzi's participation was even more essential. He carried out a preliminary informal diplomatic mission on behalf of Lorenzo, whom he had preceded by land a month or so before his departure, with a sumptuous entourage of sixteen mounts, and had been charged by the king with preparing Lorenzo's lodgings.[81] Indicative of the climate of trust existing henceforth in Filippo Strozzi's relations with Lorenzo were the huge loans that Strozzi made to the Florentine treasury, for which the quid pro quo was Lorenzo's favor during the 1484 electoral scrutiny.[82] The proximity in time between the Strozzi and Gondi building projects, and the recognition of status that they entailed, would seem to indicate a mark of recognition on Lorenzo's part for services rendered at the vital moment when a new Neapolitan link was being forged. This is the source of the idea, turned posthumously into a virtual myth, of Lorenzo as arbiter of a new civic construction program, which emerges first in the *Vita di Lorenzo de' Medici* by Niccolò Valori (1495), who celebrates the regal splendor of Filippo Strozzi's palace, along with Lorenzo's wise counsel:

> infra e' quali [*scil.* edifici costruiti per consiglio di Lorenzo] Filippo Strozzi, famosissimo cittadino … ne cominciò uno da' fondamenti, che non solo superava la magnificenza degli altri edifici privati della nostra città …, ma

78 Landi 1986, 127.
79 I am working together with Massimo Giontella on this subject; see Giontella and Fubini, forthcoming. On the topic, the fullest contribution remains Cox-Rearick 1982.
80 Medici 1977–, 4:363–365.
81 Ibid., 4:249–250, 274.
82 Lorenzo to Filippo Strozzi, 28 October 1484, ibid., 8:32–35.

tutti li altri di che s'ha notizia non solo per ornamenti, ma per la mirabile et ordinata struttura.[83]

among the buildings constructed with the benefit of Lorenzo's counsel, Filippo Strozzi, an eminent citizen, began the erection of a fabric from its [very] foundations, not only surpassing in magnificence our city's other private edifices, but all the rest we know of, not just in its decoration, but in its admirable and orderly structure.

All this forms the background to a new residential palace projected for the Medici in the renovated zone of via Laura, which was once again entrusted to Giuliano da Sangallo's expertise. The long-standing Medici residence in via Larga (today via Cavour) should not be overshadowed by Filippo Strozzi's extravagant new edifice. The prospect of Lorenzo's becoming gonfalonier for life in the near future required the ostentatious erection of a suitable, and no longer private, residence. As Caroline Elam observes, "the kernel of the project is indeed very close to the King of Naples' plan."[84]

If one descends from the artistic and architectural plane to the more modest realities of everyday life, there is a group of people who testify better than anyone (or anything) else to Lorenzo's virtual elevation from citizen to prince: chancellors and secretaries—not so much the public functionaries of the chancery, the highest-ranking of whom were raised by the reforms of 1483 to the status of *segretari* (a term in use at princely courts such as Milan, Naples, and the papal curia) and who were qualified to handle complex political affairs (*ad quaecumque etiam magna negotia gerenda*, "for managing all, even major, matters");[85] but instead, although the distinction is not perfectly sharp, those, employed in his personal chancery or in various other offices, who enjoyed a particular bond of trust with Lorenzo. These were what might be termed his firstborn subjects, bound by emotional fidelity to both the nascent principate and the dynastic lineage. In this context, Filippo Redditi, mentioned already as the author of a precocious panegyric on Lorenzo, addresses him as the "great Lorenzo" (*magne Laurenti*) when requesting his favor in the

---

83 Fubini 2009, "Lorenzo de' Medici tra eulogia e storia. La *Laurentii Medices vita* di Niccolò Valori," 205–226, here at 215. Lorenzo's role is given greater emphasis in the Latin version, which with numerous alterations Valori dedicated in 1517 to Leo X: "Multi enim [*scil.* cives] multa regia aedificia de Laurentii consilio estruxere, in quibus Philippi Stroctiae insulares aedes, quae . . . venustate et magnificentia superant sine ulla controversia non solum privatas domus sed regias." (Numerous citizens erected numerous regal buildings upon Lorenzo's advice, among them Filippo Strozzi's palace, an entire block, which in beauty and magnificence surpass, without doubt, not only private houses but royal palaces.) Ibid., 216. The two versions are published together in Valori 1991. The supposed Italian translation by Filippo Valori is a fiction by Niccolò to mask his own preceding text in Italian, written for different purposes in 1495.

84 Elam 1994, 375.

85 Morelli Timpanaro, Manno Tolu, and Viti 1992, 80.

electoral scrutiny of 1484;[86] Simone Grazzini appeals to Lorenzo as his *padrone* and *benefattore*, and in his will of 1489 imposes on his heirs a duty of loyalty to Lorenzo and his lineage, *pro quorum statu vitam etiam exponatis si oportebit*, "for whose regime you must risk even your life if necessary."[87] But most telling is arguably ser Pace di Bambello, recently studied by Alison Brown.[88] He too is careful to profess himself "a servant of the house of Medici." He too makes his career as an underling and client of Niccolò Michelozzi, first secretary to Lorenzo, and in that role conducts on his behalf the essential business of managing the wool guild. Ser Pace even passed up the chance of an independent bureaucratic job, the chancellorship of the *parte guelfa*. At Lorenzo's death, he declared himself lost, blaming the doctors through whose ineptitude "our homeland has lost such a leader" (*ha perduto questa patria uno tanto capo*), asserting that Lorenzo died "in the most Christian manner" (*cristianissimamente*), and reporting the popular devotion shown at the funeral for "this holy house" (*questa sancta casa*).[89] Ser Pace, as he demonstrated elsewhere, was far from a religious enthusiast: his concern was rather to legitimize, indeed sacralize, the house of Medici. The same concern and sentiment are later encountered in Giovanni da Strada detto lo Stradino, servant to Lorenzo's daughter Lucrezia Salviati, who gave to the panegyric written by Niccolò Valori the title *La vita del magnifico, anzi santo Lorenzo* (*The Life of the Magnificent, or Rather Holy, Lorenzo*), copied "at the instance of my mistress Madonna Lucrezia" (*ad instanzia di Madonna Lucrezia mia padrona*).[90]

What then was the direct outcome of Lorenzo de' Medici's regime—the eventual principate, or the reformed republican system of 1494–1512? The question requires caution, and not just because Lorenzo's early death left his project unfinished. The Medici who returned to power in Florence in 1512 could lay claim to the Laurentian heritage, but so could the republican regime of the great council. The governments inspired by Savonarola and later headed by Pier Soderini completed the annihilation of the ancient communal constitution, the consolidation of the regime and its membership, and finally the election of a permanent head. They were following a track mapped out by Lorenzo and pursued in different terms by Savonarola. Even more so in the case of the chancery, the *segretario fiorentino* par excellence, Niccolò Machiavelli, as far as his chancery role is concerned, was direct heir to his Medici predecessors. Of course, there were major differences: Savonarolan and Soderinian Florence turned to a French alliance that Lorenzo had declined. But just as in the Laurentian period, the politics and government of the city were bound up with international politics, and inconceivable outside that framework.

86 Ibid., 73.
87 Ibid., 91.
88 Brown 2008.
89 Ibid., 244, 252.
90 Martelli 1964, here at 237; Fubini 2009, 215.

These are challenging problems, to which only analytical research, free of rigid and preconceived theses, can supply an answer. That is a lesson I have learned in collaborating on the edition of Lorenzo's letters, and that I continue to learn from the work of the colleagues and friends who were or are participants in the project. Chief among them is of course Nicolai Rubinstein, from whom I received my start in research on Lorenzo, and in whose name it is right to conclude this discussion.

SIX

Medici and Sforza—Breeds Apart?

JANE BLACK

"I AM NOT SIGNORE OF FLORENCE but a citizen with some authority," wrote Lorenzo de' Medici at the peak of his power.[1] Francesco Guicciardini described Lorenzo's style of living: "His way of life was that of a citizen—he lived more like a private person than a statesman."[2] The Medici palace was a family home; government business continued in the Palazzo della Signoria; the *signoria* and other officials carried on with their normal duties; and, despite his role as an energetic diplomat on Florence's behalf, Lorenzo insisted that ambassadors' reports should go through the proper channels.[3] Jurists corroborated, making no mention of the Medici as rulers. But people saw through the masquerade. Alamanno Rinuccini, an opponent, famously described how Lorenzo "took all eminence, power and public authority for himself, eventually seizing control of the republic, just like Julius Caesar."[4] Even Guicciardini conceded that Lorenzo's power was that of any fully fledged signore.[5] Still, the republican image was a vital prop: as Melissa Bullard put

1   Lorenzo de' Medici to Pier Filippo Pandolfini, 26 November 1481, Medici 1977–, 6:100.
2   Guicciardini 1933, 227.
3   See Bullard 1994, 54–55.
4   Rinuccini, Rinuccini, and Rinuccini 1840, cxlvii.
5   Following the crisis of the Pazzi conspiracy, Guicciardini said that Lorenzo "lived his whole life ruling and ordering the city entirely as he wanted, just as if he were a proper signore" ("visse insino alla morte governandosi e disponendosi la città tanto interamente a arbitrio suo, quanto se ne fussi stato signore a bacchetta"): Guicciardini 1931, 73. For further contemporary assessments of Lorenzo as signore of Florence, see Rubinstein 1980, 29–30; 1997, 250–252; Brown 1992e, 103–104; 1994.

it, Lorenzo's ability "to pull strings behind the scenes depended on there being a convincing facade behind which to operate."[6]

Less appreciated is the fact that the Sforza too depended on the conscious projection of an image—they attempted to disguise their weakness just as the Medici disguised their power.[7] The duke had to be presented as a great prince: so, where the Medici dressed as ordinary citizens, the duke and his household were kitted out in extravagant luxury;[8] while the Medici pretended to live in a private house, Francesco Sforza built himself a vast fortress in Milan; his son, Galeazzo Maria, in turn redesigned the interior to accommodate the hierarchical ritual of a grand court.[9] As with the Medici, the myth of the Sforza should be seen for what it was. For behind the imposing facade, the regime struggled to enforce its authority.

Medici and Sforza both depended on the principle, or pretense, of popular sovereignty. The Medici claimed that their system had been ordained by the citizens: it was the three crucial meetings of the Florentine *parlamento*—in 1434, 1458, and 1466—that consolidated their control. That assembly was authorized to represent "the full, free, total, and absolute power and authority of the whole people."[10] The Medici well understood that recourse to a *parlamento* was the nuclear option: it required meticulous planning to guarantee that the issues to be addressed on each occasion would elicit a favorable response.[11] To forestall any unintended outcome, all three *parlamenti* were accompanied by an intimidating military presence: six thousand armed *contadini* watched over the meeting of 1434; mercenary troops including three hundred cavalry, as well as armed citizens, guarded that of 1458; and between six and ten thousand men were on hand in 1466.[12] Risky though it was, the *parlamento* proved a perfect mechanism for the creation of a quasi-princely regime: as proclaimed in the warning inscribed in the chamber of the great council after the fall of the Medici, "he who wishes to convene a *parlamento* is aiming to take control of government away from the people."[13]

---

6   Bullard 1998, 349.

7   Francesco Sforza's position, like that of many Renaissance princes, depended on "a personality capable of holding together a scattered, disaggregated, fragile political order." Chittolini 1989c, 698–699.

8   On Galeazzo Maria's court, see Lubkin 1994.

9   Welch 1995, 203–212.

10 This was the description given in the act of 1382, which first established oligarchic government in Florence (Najemy 1982a, 268). The meeting of 1434 allowed Cosimo de' Medici to take over from the Albizzi; that of 1458 facilitated his defeat of internal opposition, creating the council of 100; that of 1466 ensured that the regime, now led by his son Piero, would prevail in the face of a threatened coup.

11 On preparations for the *parlamento* of 1434, see Dale Kent 1978, 336–338. Discussions in the *pratica* in July 1458 show the regime's fear of the unknown consequences of a *parlamento*; the question put to that assembly was almost inaudible, but the result was presumed favorable (Rubinstein 1997, 114–117). Similar anxiety was felt in 1466: that *parlamento* was asked simply to authorize a short term *balìa* (ibid., 187).

12 On armed intervention, see Najemy 2006b, 277, 295, 305; Rubinstein 1997, 117, 187.

13 Najemy 2006b, 390.

In terms of popular sovereignty, the Sforza had much in common with the Medici: Francesco Sforza's role had been conferred by the people too. In Milan, he had been proclaimed hereditary ruler, "true and legitimate prince, duke and signore" by the heads of all households.[14] In Pavia, the title of count had been bestowed on Francesco by the same method: "all the city's power and jurisdiction was transferred with full rights by representatives appointed by the citizens for the purpose."[15] In Piacenza, Francesco's accession was endorsed by the equivalent of a *parlamento*: after agreeing to terms, the *anziani* summoned the council and the entire populace to consider the issues; Francesco was then acclaimed signore by the citizenry.[16] In Parma, it was the general assembly who "elected him signore of the city."[17] The Sforza would have liked to dissociate themselves from their populist credentials, but so long as Frederick III was on the imperial throne, there was no hope of a grant of authority from above.[18] In January 1469, Galeazzo Maria was presented with the only alternative. He had consulted two senior jurists from his council on the question of an official investiture. Raffaele da Busseto was convinced of the need for imperial recognition, but Luca Vernazza gave a different view. Having refused to invest Francesco Sforza, the emperor had forfeited all right to interfere in questions involving the government of the dominion: election and popular acclamation were enough.[19] Other lawyers were surprisingly willing to go along with Vernazza's judgment. As Francesco Corte, professor of civil law at the University of Pavia, wrote, "the emperor can do nothing in the duchy of Milan, except insofar as he is given permission by the duke, any more than he can in the lands of the Turkish sultan or of any other ruler who de jure or de facto does not recognize him."[20] With Frederick III unwilling to budge, the Sforza would have to live with self-declared independence until after the emperor's death in 1493.

So a basis in popular sovereignty was shared by the Medici and Sforza regimes. But whereas the Medici managed to minimize the risks associated with *parlamenti*, the Sforza found their subjects' claims to supremacy a perpetual menace. Giovanni Simonetta, secretary to the council, warned Galeazzo Maria that the emperor's refusal to recognize the regime was a danger: "Such matters should not come to the

---

14 "verum et optimum principem, ducem et dominum": 11 March 1450, Colombo 1905, 88.

15 "omnis civitatis potestas jurisditioque omnis in Franciscum ipsum ejusque posteros pleno jure transfertur": 18 September 1447, Simonetta 1932–59, 188. There are no surviving documents relating to these proceedings, which took place in the cathedral.

16 Castignoli 1962, 153–154.

17 Pezzana 1837–59, 2: Appendix, 50.

18 On a diplomatic trip to Rome in January 1469, the emperor refused even to acknowledge the duke's envoys, ordering them out of the room on the grounds that they did not represent any authorized ruler (Soranzo 1915, 259).

19 Giovanni Simonetta to Galeazzo Maria Sforza, 26 January 1469, ASMi, Sforzesco 887; see Vaglienti 1997, 113 n. 105.

20 Corte 1580, 65 ("Super praemissa narratione"), paragraph 15: "nihil potest imperator in terris ducatus Mediolani nisi quatenus sibi permitteretur a praefato duce, sicut nec posset in terris Soldani vel Turci vel alterius non recognoscentium imperatorem de iure vel de facto."

ears of all and sundry; it is damaging for things like this to be debated in Milan."[21] The government knew that the theory of popular sovereignty was understood even by ordinary people, who assumed it was open to them to take to the streets in pursuit of regime change. At the moment of his life-threatening illness in 1462, as rebellion took hold in Piacenza, Francesco saw too well how the foundations of his regime could be used against him. The rebel leader, "il Pelloia," mimicking the duke himself, appeared mounted and dressed as a condottiere, his followers shouting "long live Pelloia, our prince!" The local chronicler, Antonio Da Ripalta, referred to this figure as "emperor and signore of the contadini."[22] Francesco was cruelly reminded of his debt to popular sovereignty when the rebels had their demands drawn up and notarized in an apparent reenactment of the original *capitoli* of 1448 for the submission of the city; its terms were supported by a giant assembly of a thousand members. In an attempt to salvage the ducal image, Francesco's representatives were adamant that no part of the subsequent negotiations with the rebels should be recorded.[23]

An even more threatening figurehead was the local aristocrat, Onofrio Anguissola, who believed that he could become signore of Piacenza by putting himself at the head of disaffected *contadini*.[24] In Tortona and Alessandria, the rumor that Francesco was dying persuaded the Guelfs to propose making a present of their cities to the king of France; the inhabitants of Castellazzo (in the district of Alessandria) promised that, with a few thousand men behind them, their community too could be his, hinting that the whole area north of the Po, and even Pavia, would be willing to transfer allegiance to the French king.[25] Similarly, when, after Galeazzo Maria's death, his brothers Sforza Maria, duke of Bari, and Ludovico il Moro attempted to take power in Milan, they naturally claimed to be acting at the behest of the populace. The duchess Bona described how shouts of "Bari, Bari! Moro, Moro!" were heard in the streets "as if they had become signori of the city."[26] The following year, Ludovico, accompanied by the mercenary leader Roberto Sanseverino, again attempted to harness popular power in the territory of Piacenza, the *contadini* shouting "Adorno, Gatto e Fregoso!" in support of their Genoese allies.[27] In the end, it was indeed Sforza subjects who dictated events. In 1499, Ludovico il Moro's troops melted away in the path of Louis XII's invasion. Among the first to surrender were the inhabitants of Tortona, Alessandria, and Castellazzo, who had already threatened to hand themselves over to the French

21 "simili cose male sonno in pratica in Milano [. . .] e ancora tale cose no li pare debiano andare per aures quorumcumque": 26 January 1469, ASMi, Sforzesco 887.
22 Da Ripalta 1731, cols. 907, 908.
23 These events are described in Andreozzi 1994, 70–76.
24 Pezzana 1837–59, 3:220.
25 De Mandrot 1916–23, 1:165, 182.
26 Bona Sforza's speech to councillors, 4 March 1477, Rosmini 1815, 2, 22. Bernardino Corio said six thousand people were involved (Corio 1978, 2:1414).
27 Andreozzi 1993, 103 n. 65.

king under Francesco. The contemporary Venetian observer Girolamo Priuli described the dynamic:

> The French king's expedition really went very smoothly, but not because the troops he had were superior. With that number of men he could not possibly have taken the duchy by force. Rather, it was the fact that the whole populace was so unhappy with Ludovico's tyranny that they could hardly wait for the chance to expel him. People looked forward to the arrival of the French with bated breath, and as [the troops] approached each area and city, they went to meet them with open arms.[28]

So the principle of popular sovereignty appears to have been more of a threat to the Sforza than to the Medici. But surely the Sforza had the advantage when it came to the issue of succession. They were, after all, hereditary dukes, even though they owed their title to popular acclamation. But as it turned out, the Medici were able to pass on their position more easily than the Sforza. On Cosimo's death, it is true, the Florentine elite, including Medici supporters, showed themselves loathe to accept that the ruling family had become a dynasty.[29] Dietisalvi Neroni's warning to Piero de' Medici probably came as no surprise: "The citizenry would like more freedom and a more broadly based government, such as there ought to be in a republican city such as ours."[30] Resentment within the ruling class led to one of the biggest crises faced by the regime when four hundred leading citizens agreed to reverse Medici innovations. Piero owed his ultimate victory to luck as well as to military force when, despite the abolition of electoral controls, a sympathetic *signoria* emerged from the draw of August 1466. But such was the power of the Medici machine that, with Piero's success, the hereditary principle was won. On his death, with a show of support from the party, Lorenzo slipped effortlessly into the role of head of the regime. Then again when Lorenzo himself died in 1492, the handpicked statutory councils ensured that the succession would pass smoothly to his eldest son, Piero.

It was not so easy for the Sforza. Popular acclamation had provided an alternative to imperial investiture for Francesco in Milan and Pavia, granting him titles that could be handed down. But that hereditary mechanism was not available when it came to his other cities. The Visconti had had the advantage, in contrast to the

---

28 Priuli 1912–41, 1:173: "Questa impresa del re di Franza contra il stado de Milanno, come di sopra se pol legere, veramente andava molto prospera et non per potentia di gente che 'l havesse, che se havesse abutto altratante gente non haveria potuto conquistar tal ducato per forza, ma perché tutti li populi heranno sì mal contentti de questo tirano del signor Ludovico, che non vedevanno l'hora di poter cazarlo del stato, et aspectavanno questo campo francese cum la bocha aperta, et quando si acostava ale terre et ale citade li andavanno in contra a quelli cum la palma in manno."

29 See Rubinstein 1997, 155–183; Najemy 2006b, 298–302.

30 Dietisalvi Neroni to Francesco Sforza, 5 September 1465, Rubinstein 1997, 160–161: "la cittadinanza vorrebbe più libertà et più universale governo come si conviene nella città popolari come è la nostra."

Sforza, of the second ducal title (created by Wenceslas in 1396), which covered their other dominions. But the second duchy could not be conferred on the Sforza by their subjects because, as separate entities, the cities were powerless to cooperate in the necessary process of acclamation.[31] Lack of the second ducal title meant that, for the Sforza, there was no automatic right of inheritance outside of Milan and Pavia. Francesco well understood his position: immediately after his election in Milan, he called himself duke of Milan, count of Pavia and Angera, but mere signore of Cremona, Parma, Piacenza, Novara, Lodi, and Como.[32] In the interests of his princely image, he called himself "duke of Milan etc."[33] But in reality, outside of Milan and Pavia (with the exception of Cremona and Pontremoli, which had been part of Bianca Maria's dowry), Francesco's only formal connection with his cities were the terms agreed at the time of surrender, together with a citizens' oath of loyalty.[34] And when it came to hereditary rights, it was an unfortunate fact that *capitoli* were agreed with him personally; there was no mention of his heirs. A significant proportion of subjects therefore were under no absolute obligation to accept the Sforza succession.

What made matters worse for Francesco's successors was that the Sforza regime was widely resented: it was reported in 1461 that the only places then demonstrating no open discontent were Milan, Pavia, and Cremona. Bianca Maria's actions on Francesco's death betray genuine fear that her son would not be accepted.[35] With Galeazzo Maria away in France, she wrote to local officials on the very night Francesco died, ordering them to take whatever steps were necessary to secure the regime.[36] She was particularly worried about Milan itself, summoning councillors and leading citizens to forestall trouble.[37] She knew that, despite the deficit of five hundred thousand ducats bequeathed by Francesco, she would have to make immediate tax cuts to win continuing allegiance.[38] Giacomo Ardizzi, *referendario* in Piacenza, scene of the uprising in 1462, revealed the dangers. On the day after Francesco's death, he informed Bianca Maria that he had already announced the lowering of duties, but that his own recommendation would be for a reduction in the *macina*, because that levy (a tax on milling) was a particular burden on the

---

31 Sforza cities covered by the second title included Como, Novara, Alessandria, Tortona, Piacenza, Parma, Cremona, Lodi, Soncino, Bormio, Borgo San Donnino, and Pontremoli. The investiture is published in Lünig 1725–35, 1:cols. 425–432.

32 "Privilegia communitatis Modoetiae," 19 March 1450: *Antiqua ducum Mediolani decreta* 1654, 332.

33 Black 2011, 19.

34 On Francesco's *capitoli* with subject communities, see Chittolini 1978. The contractual nature of the relationship between Sforza and his territories is highlighted in Della Misericordia 2011.

35 Galeazzo Maria was technically a minor. Having acted as regent during Francesco's absences, Bianca Maria had governed almost single-handedly during his last year. On her role in the succession, see Terni de Gregori 1939, 82–84.

36 "Fare tutte quelle cose che sonno necessarie per conservatione de questi citadi": ASMi, Carteggio interno, Milano città, 878.

37 Giulini 1854–57, 6:567.

38 Chittolini 1996a, 145. On the financial crisis, see Leverotti 1994, 31–40.

poor.[39] Military preparations were made and repressive measures ordered in the *contado*.[40] Conflict in Parma throughout April and May between opponents and supporters of the government necessitated a military occupation.[41] Outright rebellion in Alessandria led to an immediate reduction in one of the most hated forms of taxation, the *tassa dei cavalli*.[42] Ferrante, king of Naples, joined Bianca Maria in imploring Como to stay loyal.[43] There was disorder in Pavia[44] and more and more desertions (even among troops that had been paid), showing there was little faith in the new duke.[45]

The price Galeazzo Maria had to pay for the continuing obedience of some of his subjects was the renewal of their *capitoli*. We have no complete list of places that had their terms of submission reissued, but the scale of the process is perhaps indicated by Piacenza's comment that they themselves had not demanded fresh *capitoli* before accepting Galeazzo Maria as signore: "the people are devoted to your lordship giving the governorship of the city freely and without any prior conditions."[46] There are allusions to a confirmation by Galeazzo Maria in 1466 of Vigevano's agreement,[47] and mentions of requests for renewal in Soncino, Sonvico, Caravaggio, Gera d'Adda, and Como.[48] We know that the request from Brianza in the *contado* of Milan, where the Sforza enjoyed hereditary rights, was refused, presumably because Galeazzo Maria did not feel his authority there was in any sense conditional.[49]

Piero de' Medici had faced a difficult accession to power too. But, in contrast to the Medici experience, Galeazzo Maria's troublesome takeover from Francesco did not spell the end of problems over the succession. On Galeazzo Maria's assassination in December 1476, the hereditary titles passed, as expected, to the seven-year-old

---

39 ASMi, Sforzesco 861, 9 March 1466.
40 Andreozzi 1997a, 155.
41 Covini 1998, 174–177.
42 Covini 1992, 23.
43 Rovelli 1789–1802, 3:pt. 1, 324.
44 Roveda 1992b, 99–100.
45 Vaglienti 1994, 128.
46 "Questo populo, di sua signoria affectionato, senza alcuni precedenti capituli, liberamente deti ad sua signoria il dominio di questa città": 21 January 1467, quoted by Bellosta 2001, 45.
47 There is a reference to such in a council debate on a proposed salary increase for the *podestà* (Fossati 1914, 142).
48 In the strategic fortress of Soncino on the Venetian border, Galeazzo Maria had to reissue the *capitoli* with further tax cuts: 7 September 1468, Galantino 1869–70, 1:219–220, 3:274–276. Caravaggio, according to the *commissario* of Gera d'Adda, wanted to agree terms as if control over the area had only just been acquired: "capitulare cum prelibata Excelentia, como se pur hozi la acquistasse lo dominio de questa terra et del paese" (14 May 1466, ASMi, Sforzesco, 805, quoted by Della Misericordia 2004, 187); the author discusses in detail the *capitoli* of subject communities in the subalpine region. For Sonvico, in the lakes, see Chiesi 1999, 405. The people of Como told their envoys to Milan to take with them the city's *capitoli* for ratification (Rovelli 1789–1802, 3:pt. 1, 325).
49 Bianca Maria felt the people of Brianza deserved to have their *capitoli* confirmed on account of their conspicuous loyalty, but Galeazzo Maria agreed to do so only after years of delay, in March 1476 (Beretta 1966, 177–180).

Gian Galeazzo Maria (in the care of his mother and secretary, Bona of Savoy and Cicco Simonetta). But again, beyond the hereditary lands, nothing was certain. Lorenzo de' Medici believed it more than possible that Sforza dominions would fall into the hands of the Venetians.[50] The level of anxiety can be judged from the government's willingness once more to agree to tax cuts in the middle of a financial crisis, and once more subjects were quick to press their advantage. Because the young duke enjoyed the hereditary title of count of Pavia, that city's request for a renewal of their *capitoli* was rejected.[51] But elsewhere there was further haggling over terms. Among the many requests for a renegotiation was one from the citizens of Parma, who submitted a dozen new demands.[52] The *podestà* of Bormio wrote that their continuing allegiance depended on a renewal of tax exemptions and a reduction of the town's debt to the treasury: the envoy sent to swear loyalty to the new duke took the local statutes with him for confirmation, along with "certain additional capitoli."[53] There were new demands from Como[54] and Monza.[55]

Cities under Florentine rule endured, in general, a more subservient position than those under the Sforza.[56] In terms of jurisdiction, towns in the *distretto*, such as Pistoia, Arezzo, and San Gimignano, were considered to have the same status as those in the Florentine *contado*: in other words, they were deemed to have lost their independent status.[57] Subjection was agreed for all time with the result that, once a town had passed into the dead hand of Florentine rule, there was limited opportunity for a renegotiation of terms. Although local tax exemptions and other privileges came up for renewal when they lapsed (generally after either five or ten years),[58] Florentine subjects never benefited from a shared opportunity to press for better conditions, as occurred at Sforza accessions. It is true that the Medici themselves curried favor by approving more liberal terms with subject communities, and that towns that had come under Florentine rule since 1434 enjoyed particularly advantageous agreements. The *capitoli* arranged with Poppi in 1440 under Cosimo's auspices, for example, were strikingly generous, exempting the inhabitants from

---

50 Lorenzo to Gianetto Ballerini, 29 December 1477, Medici 1977–, 2:450 (quoted in Fubini 1978, 66).

51 Robolini 1823–38, 6:pt. 1, 99.

52 1 February 1477 (Pezzana 1837–59, 4:7 n. 2).

53 The *podestà*'s letter is dated 2 March 1477 (Colò 1892, 137); on Bormio's negotiations, see also Della Misericordia 2004, 186. Similarly, as well as a confirmation of their earlier *capitoli*, the people of Mattarella wanted the duty on their iron trade to be abolished (Cavalli 1845, 3:193).

54 Rovelli 1789–1802, 3:pt. 1, 340–341.

55 Frisi 1794, 1:193.

56 Florence's heavy hand, exercised through official channels as well as informal networks, is illustrated in Salvadori 2000b, 211–214; Zorzi 2000, 24–26; Chittolini 1979, 244–255.

57 San Gimignano's terms of submission in 1353 stated that the inhabitants were to be deemed "veri e originari contadini e popolari della città di Firenze" (Guasti 1866–93, 1:303); Pistoia's in 1401 said its people would be considered "veri et originales comitatini civiatis Florentie" (De Angelis 1995, 1165); according to those of Pietramala, agreed in 1404, the people would be considered "come del contado e contadini" (Guasti 1866–93, 2:266).

58 See Epstein 2000b, 102.

tax for twenty-five years (a concession renewed in 1468).[59] The terms agreed with Sarzana in 1467, with which Piero di Cosimo was closely involved, were similarly accommodating.[60] For the most part, on the other hand, the Medici took advantage of the rigorous control that the city itself exercised: the fact that local judicial and military officials were almost always Florentine citizens allowed the regime to monopolize posts for their own supporters and so handle territorial affairs from the center.[61]

In terms of lawmaking, the obvious contrast is between Medici policies implemented from behind the scenes and Sforza decrees issued from on high. Personal input by the Medici into local legislation was not unknown,[62] but usually the process was indirect: government-backed policies were introduced in the form of local statutes and provisions. Significant enactments in communal assemblies took place under the eye of Florentine officials, who by Lorenzo's day were supporters of the regime.[63] Backroom participation by the Medici grew relentlessly. As Lorenzo Tanzini has demonstrated, so many disputes were settled and privileges granted under Lorenzo's personal auspices that the traditional mechanism for the control of local statutes by Florentine officials (the *approvatori degli statuti*) hardly functioned.[64]

In some respects, the process of legislation under the Sforza was not so very different: ducal officials supervised the deliberations of local councils. Admittedly the Medici felt they had cause to envy the duke's explicit right to legislate: it was Lorenzo's belief that when it came to raising new taxes, it was easy for the Sforza "because they do not have to summon colleges and councils."[65] Ducal decrees and orders were binding, taking precedence over other laws. Under Florentine rule, by contrast, local statutes came first.[66] In addition, the duke enjoyed absolute power, or plenitude of power, enabling him to override the rights of individual subjects. But in reality the Medici need not have envied the Sforza's ability to issue decrees, which were not all they appeared to be. Certainly they were no panacea when it came to getting things done. The Sforza frequently complained that edicts were ignored even by their closest associates.[67] Their absolute power was subject to a multitude of restrictions and in any case the concept itself was falling

---

59 The *capitoli* are published in Bicchierai 2005, 283–287; Cosimo is mentioned in clause 32.

60 The terms were concluded in the Medici palace: see Guasti 1866–93, 1:655–659.

61 Zorzi 1997, 203; Salvadori 2000b, 217–219.

62 Lorenz Böninger has shown that it was Lorenzo who drew up new eligibility rules for the general council of the little town of Santa Croce sull'Arno: the reform was subsequently referred to as a way of avoiding disputes, "come per lo magnifico Lorenzo de' Medici fu ordinato" (Böninger 2006b, 322).

63 Tanzini 2007a, 133–135; Salvadori 2000a, 97–100; 2000b, 209–213.

64 Tanzini 2007a, 135–136.

65 Lorenzo to Girolamo Morelli, 14 November 1478, Medici 1977–, 2:285: "lo possono fare facilmente, non havendo a ragunare né collegi né consigli."

66 See Jane Black 2000, 50–51.

67 On the inability of ducal officials to implement government policies, see Chittolini 1989b, 105–108.

out of favor in government circles. For example, when a transfer of property was decreed, grounds for defiance on the part of the injured party were easily found: the new owner might have misrepresented the facts, or used improper means to win favor; it could be alleged that property rights had been wrongly overturned, testamentary provisions ignored, or a previous owner denied the right to defend his case. [68]

Lawyers were not afraid to condemn such decrees: two of Galeazzo Maria's concessions were described by the leading Sforza jurist, Giasone da Maino, as "unlawful and invalid, having been granted on grounds that were patently unjust." [69] The threat of litigation was enough to deter some people from accepting the offer of confiscated property. [70] Ducal decrees of a more general nature often amounted to little more than wishful thinking. Galeazzo Maria ordered in 1472, for example, that all roads, bridges, and embankments in the district of Parma were to be repaired. In an admission of defeat, the decree was reissued nine years later. [71] Such repetition was evidence of the duke's impotence and, moreover, had the effect of undermining acts that had not benefited from such confirmation. A case in point was the decree *De maiori magistratu*, issued by Filippo Maria in 1441 with the aim of limiting the jurisdiction of feudatories in favor of urban courts. The act was ostensibly one of the century's most important pieces of ducal legislation, but its renewal by Galeazzo Maria in 1468 for Pavia left its status in other places ambiguous, while councillors confessed that the measure was hardly enforced. [72]

A feature of the legislative process that the Sforza shared with Florence was that promulgation was decentralized. While ducal decrees took precedence, they depended on local publication for their validity: as the contemporary jurist Alessandro Tartagni put it, a decree has no force over those who are unaware of it. [73] In his edict for reforms in Cremona, Francesco Sforza declared that the terms were to be widely disseminated, "lest anyone have the possibility of excusing himself [from obeying] under the cloak of ignorance." [74] Having been read aloud to the citizens, a new ducal act was transcribed either as an add-on at the end of the communal statute book, or in a separate local collection. Published in this way, decrees

---

68 See Black 2009, 30–35, 150–152, 160–165.

69 Del Maino 1581, 2, 177 ("In praesenti consultatione"), Introduction: "dictae literae ducales reddantur iniustae et nullae, cum sint ex causis notorie iniustis concessae."

70 Covini 2007, 128.

71 Pezzana 1837–59, 4:233.

72 Vaglienti 1997, 120–122.

73 Tartagni 1610, 6, 181 ("In causa et lite"), paragraph 13: "this decree was never published in Tassignani and it ought to have been published there, despite having been published in other places . . . for the decree cannot bind those who are ignorant [of it]" ("dictum decretum nunquam fuit publicatum in castro Tassignani, et quod debuerit ibi publicari, non obstante quod fuerit per alia loca publicatum [. . .] non enim potest dictum decretum ligare ignorantes"). As Paolo di Castro had explained earlier in the century, a punishment cannot be imposed without a crime—and the ignorant do not commit crimes (Di Castro 1580, 1, 199 ["Licet ista sit"], paragraph 3).

74 *Statuta civitatis Cremonae* 1578, 255.

came to be seen as an aspect of community law. Some could simply fall into disuse, and, as Bartolomeo Cipolla, professor at Padua, put it: "when an act is not approved by actual use, those who do not observe it are deemed not to have broken the law."[75] Other decrees, having proved their worth over time, became embedded, indistinguishable from local statutes. Examples of the latter were the acts on judicial procedure dating from the mid-fourteenth century that had quickly made their way into statute books across the dominion. Significantly, Pavia, Vigevano, and Novara made an exception for those particular decrees when, as the price of submission to Francesco, they demanded the abolition in their area of all Visconti legislation.[76] The list of "ducal decrees in force in the city of Parma" in this period is strikingly meager—only a dozen are mentioned.[77] The Visconti themselves had shown that decrees could be canceled wholesale without any dire consequences: Gian Galeazzo had declared Bernabò's acts invalid; Filippo Maria had abolished all those issued since the collapse of Visconti rule in 1402; Francesco likewise annulled acts concerning the taxation of feudatories that had been issued by his predecessor since 1433.[78] Lawyers for the most part concerned themselves with ducal legislation only when an individual concession was involved: in their commentaries and *consilia*, the focus was overwhelmingly on statutes. Clumsily drafted and poorly integrated with local law, decrees were seen as extraneous.[79]

The contrast between image and reality is well demonstrated in the management of faction by the Medici and the Sforza. For the Medici, the main target was Pistoia, where antagonism between Cancellieri and Panciatichi was proving an impediment to Medici influence. Cosimo decided that the old system of dividing offices equally between the two parties should not be allowed to continue. The resultant reforms were implemented in the roundabout way that was the Medici trademark: Alessandro degli Alessandri, a strong Medicean, was commissioned by the Florentine government to find a way of settling dissension in Pistoia; Alessandri advised the Pistoiese authorities to establish a panel of *riformatori*, who in turn recommended to the *podestà* that the practice of sharing posts between the parties should be discontinued; the *podestà* consulted Cosimo and in 1457, the reform was enacted in Pistoia.[80] The factions themselves had not been suppressed: their

---

75 Cipolla 1555, 13 ("Stante quodam decreto"), paragraph 7: "Quando constitutio non est moribus utentium approbata, illi qui non servant legem non dicuntur transgressores legis."

76 Robolini 1823–38, 6:pt. 1, 308; Colombo 1903, 514; Morbio 1841, 157.

77 ASMi, Sforzesco 1635 (s.d.). The measures listed are decrees concerning taxation and currency, the jurisdiction of feudatories, appeals, the acquisition of property in the *contado*, assaults on citizens by *contadini*, the obligation of students to remain within the dominion, the sindication of *notarii bancharum*, rules on the provision of guardians for orphans and widows, and the naming of parties.

78 Leverotti 2003, 185.

79 Covini 2007, 126–130; Chittolini 1991, 25.

80 This complicated process is charted in Milner 2000b, 312–314. The statute abolished the traditional system: instead of two bags per quarter containing the names of those eligible for office, there would be only one, with no differentiation of candidates according to party.

resurgence after the fall of the Medici led to civil war from 1499 to 1502 for control of the city.[81] Nevertheless, Cosimo's scheme may be regarded as a success, leaving the regime strengthened in a key dependency.

The dukes of Milan had to deal with entrenched parties in all parts of their possessions. Filippo Maria Visconti abominated faction: in his reforms of 1417, he referred to "the disorder and corruption arising from the pernicious influence of parties."[82] Like Cosimo, he wanted to end all official recognition of such groups; in the decree of 1440 concerning the appointment of officials, he ordered that every three years, each city was to elect 150 citizens not by party, but by income level, one-third from each sector.[83] Modeling himself on Filippo Maria, Francesco Sforza was eager to demonstrate that he too was above party; in practice, however, he was unable to eradicate faction from political life. In Pavia, despite contrary statutes passed with his approval in 1454, it soon became clear that Bianchi and Neri would remain key elements of the system.[84] In Piacenza in 1451, the citizens suggested a mechanism for elections to the general council and governing executive that would be based on the four quarters of the city rather than on party. Francesco subsequently decreed that he himself would initially choose who should qualify for the *anziato* and appoint all members of the general council; thereafter, it would become a process of co-option. Significantly, there was no mention of parties, but again it soon became obvious that the Anguissola, Landi, Fontana, and Scotti continued to dominate all aspects of political life.[85]

Far from eradicating faction from government, Francesco showed himself to be heavily dependent on partisan support. The trouble was that in general his allies were weaker than his opponents.[86] In some places, under the guise of eliminating parties, he was actually hoping to strengthen his own side. Parma was the most notorious nest of family rivalry: government had been divided among the four leading houses, the Pallavicini, Sanvitale, Da Correggio, and Rossi, for the best part of a hundred years. Francesco aimed to consolidate his own authority by strengthening that of his supporters, the Rossi. He expressed his purpose, as befitted a prince, not in the language of party politics, but in terms of the settlement of internal conflict.[87] In 1456, he banned all reference to party in the selection of members of the general council and governing executive. But the real aim of the abolition of party quotas was so that at least some governing officials could be appointed at will by the duke; and so it turned out: after the reform, the Rossi and their followers were given

---

81 See Connell 2000a, 181–237.
82 Filippo Maria's letter is reproduced in Cognasso 1955, 484. On the entrenched position of parties in Reggio Parma and Piacenza, see Gamberini 2008, 6.
83 *Antiqua ducum Mediolani decreta* 1654, 286–287.
84 Roveda 1992b, 86–87.
85 Andreozzi 1997a, 152–154.
86 Chittolini 1990, 24.
87 Gentile 2009c, 122.

more positions.[88] The consequence, unfortunately for Francesco, was that he now became the focus of local conflict: it was reported in 1461 that "there was no area more likely to organize an uprising than Parma."[89]

In Cremona, there were three dominant groups—Guelfs, Ghibellines, and Maltraversari. In 1457, as Cosimo confronted the party system in Pistoia, Francesco ordered a wide-ranging reform of Cremona's government. Again, his stated aim was to restore internal harmony. Noting the "assaults, quarrels, feuds, and hatred" that beset public life, he decreed that the size of the council should be increased from 100 to 150, and that of the governing executive from 10 to 12.[90] Since these numbers were divisible by three, it appears that the practical effect had been to enable the party system in Cremona to function even more effectively.[91] Francesco's dependence on faction in the city was revealed in private by his agent: "the Guelfs are more numerous than the Ghibellines, but because the Maltraversari are allied with the latter, our side is stronger."[92] In Vigevano, the return to power of anti-Sforzeschi in the early 1460s was accompanied by intolerable violence; as in Cremona, the ostensible purpose of the reforms initiated by Francesco in 1463 was to settle party conflict. But a parallel aim was to bolster the position of the duke's own supporters.[93]

The futility of Francesco's attempt to gloss over the role of parties was revealed under his successor when Galeazzo Maria acknowledged faction as an inescapable aspect of government in the localities. In Parma, on Francesco's death, the Rossi came under attack from the other three houses, requiring the intervention of two hundred armed men; the duke had no alternative but to recognize the former four-party system.[94] The domination of parties in Cremona was once more accepted: in 1472, at the request of the communal executive, Galeazzo Maria ordered, "the 150 citizens [in the general council] will be chosen from each party or color in equal numbers."[95] Factions were sanctioned too in the governments of Lodi, Alessandria, Piacenza, and Novara.[96] Lists were drawn up of candidates suitable for ducal appointments, such as *podestà* and *referendario*, each name identified by party.[97]

The Medici found that the suppression of party influence in Pistoia was hugely beneficial: once the two factions could no longer depend on statutory rights, access

---

88 Somaini 2007, 131–132; Gentile 2009b, 156.

89 Ghinzoni 1892, 874.

90 Decree of 9 November 1457 (*Statuta civitatis Cremonae* 1578, 255–263). Details on the reforms of 1457 can be found in Gualazzini 1978, 126–129.

91 Gamberini 2008, 31; Arcangeli 2003, 372 n. 34.

92 Ghinzoni 1892, 870.

93 Roveda 1992a, 73–76; Belloni 1997, 269–271. The changes involved elections to Vigevano's general council; the reform itself is not extant.

94 Zaccaria Saggi to Ludovico Gonzaga, 15 April 1466, Leverotti and Lazzarini 1999–, 7:63; Somaini 2007, 131–132.

95 Gualazzini 1978, 131.

96 Arcangeli 2003, 373.

97 Leverotti 1997, 59–61.

to civic office depended on Medici favor.[98] The Sforza, on the other hand, dependent on the cooperation of local factions, had to put up with the inevitable consequences. When it came to the distribution of tax burdens, for example, it was
difficult to obtain a realistic assessment when council members were concerned
primarily for the interests of their own people.[99] Crimes would go unpunished
when party supporters were accused.[100] In Pavia, factional jealousy was responsible
for continuous unrest, violence brought under control only during the period of
Galeazzo Maria's residence in the city in the 1470s.[101] Ever present was the danger
that outside powers would take advantage of conflict, allying with one of the great
houses.[102] Party rivalry led to upheavals that shook the regime to its core. The final
act of the drama, which saw the defeat of Pietro Maria Rossi's armies at the hands
of Ludovico il Moro in 1482, had begun on Galeazzo Maria's death, with Pietro
Maria's attempt to reestablish the dominance he had enjoyed under Francesco, an
ambition in which he was violently opposed by the other houses.

In practice, while the Medici and Sforza shared significant elements of authority and policy direction, it was the Medici who had more control. The reasons are
not hard to find. While the Medici dominated Florence through political networks,
there was little trust between the Sforza and the Milanese elite, with many of the
leading families being excluded from government circles.[103] Resentment was made
worse by the scant loyalty shown by the regime to governing officials: Galeazzo
Maria sacked many of his father's functionaries; others did not survive his own
demise.[104] With regard to the dominions, Florence, like the Sforza, had the role of
vero signore, circumventing the remnants of autonomy embedded in local statutes,
offices, and assemblies. But unlike Sforza cities, Florence's subject communities—
impoverished and underpopulated as a result of Florentine rule—had long since
been cowed. Standing on the shoulders of Florence, it was the Medici who reaped
the benefit.

The Sforza would have liked to unify their dominions in a similar way, ele-
vating Milan into a capital or, as Gian Galeazzo Maria called it, "the head of our
principality."[105] But there were too many obstacles: Milan lacked any official status
as a dominant city outside the confines of its own *contado*, and the Sforza themselves

---

98 On Lorenzo's role as patron and mediator in Pistoia, see Milner 1996, 246–252.

99 That was the situation in Piacenza, for example (Andreozzi 1994, 68). On the strength of parties in
    Piacenza and Sforza dependence on them, see Bellosta 2003; on the weakness of the duke's posi-
    tion in the localities, see Chittolini 1989b.

100 There is a graphic example in Chittolini 1989b, 113–114.

101 Roveda 1992b, 100; Covini 2007, 227.

102 Bartolomeo Colleoni planned to make use of support from within Parma itself for his threatened
    siege of the city in 1466 (Covini 1998, 176); Pietro Maria Rossi was encouraged by the Venetians
    in his rebellion against Ludovico il Moro in 1482: see Gentile 2007b, 35.

103 Chittolini 1990, 25–26; Vaglienti 1992, 647; Fubini 1978, 54–55.

104 Leverotti 1994, 12–18; 1997, 25, 42.

105 *Antiqua ducum Mediolani decreta* 1654, 396; the issue is examined in Leverotti 1997, 43–44.

were without the necessary unifying title. Above all, the general liberation that had taken place after Gian Galeazzo's death, and again after that of Filippo Maria, had served to revitalize local autonomy. As a result, the dukes found their hereditary rights questioned, appointments circumscribed, and policies challenged by cities, aristocrats, and *contadini* alike: for all their princely trappings, it seems it was the Sforza rather than the Medici who had trouble imposing their will.

SEVEN

Tuscans and Lombards

The Political Culture of Officialdom

MARCO GENTILE

THIRTY YEARS HAVE NOW PASSED since Nicolai Rubinstein, Sergio Bertelli, and Craig Hugh Smyth organized two memorable scholarly conferences at Villa I Tatti on relations between Milan and Florence. The conference papers were published in 1989 under the title *Florence and Milan: Comparisons and Relations*.[1] The first volume included a paper by Giorgio Chittolini on the officials of the Sforza duchy, entitled "L'onore dell'officiale," in which he looked for signs of the emergence of what he called "a budding self-awareness of a new social order."[2] Chittolini analyzed the contribution of this social order (*ceto*) to the emergence of what can anachronistically be called a bureaucratic apparatus, within a broader historical perspective on the Renaissance state that goes back to Federico Chabod. It was a line of research subsequently pursued by Franca Leverotti and Maria Nadia Covini in particular.[3]

In general, to study the officials who were thinly dispersed throughout territories governed by exiguous political structures, such as those possessed by the Italian states in the fifteenth and sixteenth centuries, is to investigate a series of wearisome and desultory careers punctuated by endless setbacks suffered by the representatives of central authority in their dealings with local social groups. Typical are the

1   Bertelli, Rubinstein, and Smyth 1989.
2   Chittolini 1989b, 103.
3   See Leverotti 1992, 1994; Covini 1998, 2007. On Sforza officialdom, see Leverotti 1997. On officials as a social order (*ceto*) in the Italian Renaissance states, see Castelnuovo 2012.

well-known letters written by Ludovico Ariosto while serving as commissioner (*commissario*) in Garfagnana[4]—not to mention the famous lines from his fourth *Satira* that brilliantly and succinctly portray the precarious position of the state official who found himself, especially in remote, peripheral, and frontier districts, having to confront problems of public order and violence without adequate instruments of coercion.[5]

What was worse for the functionary was that the problem was institutionalized: central government had little will to undertake the active policing sufficient to meet Max Weber's criterion of a "monopoly on the legitimate use of violence"; to do so would have upset the equilibrium, codified as pacts, that underpinned numerous Renaissance states.[6] In the Sforza dominions, where the general problem of public order was compounded by the ruling family's lack of legitimacy, the gap between means and ends is palpable,[7] as revealed in a remarkable source highlighted by Chittolini in his 1989 paper: the *Carteggio interno*, consisting of thousands of letters written by ducal officials that disclose the vivid meeting, interacting, and clashing of political cultures.[8]

A significant change to the system of ducal administration was delivered by the decision of Francesco Sforza and his successors to employ a number of functionaries from outside the Milanese dominions. A quota came from Florence and Tuscany, thanks to the close alliance between Cosimo de' Medici and Francesco.[9] In fact, their appointments can be seen as a form of extraterritorial Medici patronage for Florentine clients. Chittolini noted that "a consciousness of the norms of civic and public life that in many Sforza officials is overridden by the demands of personal fealty to the duke … is more often apparent among officials from Tuscany or other areas with republican traditions, when they point forcefully to the dignity of officeholders and their noble duties."[10]

Did such a cultural (and anthropological) difference between Tuscans under the Medici and Lombards under the Sforza in fact exist? The number of Tuscans holding politically important offices (functioning, that is, as *podestà* and *commissari*) in the Sforza duchy was not large. According to the registers of the Sforza territorial administration published by Caterina Santoro (a fundamental source, although not quite complete), there were about sixteen. There were possibly a few but not many

4   Ariosto 1965, 55–341. On Este officialdom, see Folin 1997; 2001, 208–213.
5   Ariosto, *Satira IV*, lines 142–165. See Folin 2001, 116.
6   See Chittolini 1989b; Gentile 2010; Della Misericordia 2012.
7   The Sforza dynasty's difficulty in achieving legitimacy is a classic theme in the historiography of the Milanese state. Among recent contributions (with abundant bibliography), see Somaini 1998, 710–728; Black 2009. In general, see Del Tredici 2012.
8   See the groundbreaking article by Massimo Della Misericordia in 2004, who stressed the importance of using the concept of "dialogue" non-metaphorically to "represent the relation between the prince and the social and territorial corporations." Della Misericordia 2004, 148.
9   On the close links between Cosimo and Francesco, see Ilardi 1989; Fubini 1994, 79–85.
10 Chittolini 1989b, 130.

more.[11] Most of their posts were prestigious, not *podesterie* in minor towns: at least nine of the Florentines in Santoro's registers were *podestà* of Milan itself.[12]

The outstanding Florentine functionary was Gabriele Ginori, who between 1484 and 1497 was *podestà* of Novara, Parma, and Alessandria. He was subsequently *podestà* of Milan, and during the crisis of 1499 was active at Pavia and Cremona.[13] He was also the author in 1492 of some strong words on the dignity of the function and office he was meant to exercise, and on how it was cheapened and humiliated by the failure of the commune of Parma to pay his salary, even though his position was "more necessary than bread and wine to the son of man."[14] Ginori was not the first Florentine official to have trouble at Parma, a problematic city and territory where social differences north and south of the Apennines between Tuscany and Emilia emerge with striking clarity.[15] The territory of Parma was chock-full of those *gentiluomini* (members of the landed nobility who held castles and enjoyed power of jurisdiction), whom Machiavelli would characterize as "pernicious in every dominion and province" because they were "profoundly hostile to civic mores."[16]

Forty years before the experiences of Gabriele Ginori, whose career was, all in all, untroubled, his fellow Florentine Andrea Della Stufa had a tough time of it in this environment so remote from any form of "civic life."[17] He arrived in Parma as ducal *commissario* at the beginning of January 1452, officially taking the place of his cousin Angelo Della Stufa, well known as a confidant of both Cosimo de' Medici and Francesco Sforza.[18] The salary (120 florins per month) was handsome, but the job was no sinecure:[19] less than ten days after arriving, Andrea was already trying to disentangle himself from the pervasive conflict among several potent lineages of Parma's territorial aristocracy (the Rossi and the Sanvitale, and not long after the

11   The list is Pietro Vespucci, Pietro Capponi, Francesco Altoviti, Bernardino de' Monteluci da Arezzo, Gabriele Ginori, Manno Donati, Luigi Pitti, Altobianco Giandonati, Bartolomeo da Firenze, Andrea Della Stufa, Vanni de' Medici, Baldassarre Carducci, Giovanni Gianfigliazzi, Bartolomeo Gianfigliazzi, Luigi Guicciardini, and Francesco Guasconi. To these can be added two holders of minor *podesterie* in the *contado* of Milan, Cantù, and Desio, administered respectively by Giovanni da Cortona and by Cristoforo Toscano. Giovanni da Cortona was also *podestà* and *castellano* of San Colombano al Lambro (Lodi) in 1450. See Santoro 1947, 15, 138, 139, 140, 141, 142, 144, 163, 206, 211, 281, 289, 294, 316, 318, 403, 408, 409, 411, 439, 457, 459, 460, 461, 482, 515, 530, 633.

12   Vespucci, Capponi, Altoviti, Ginori, Pitti, Medici, Guicciardini, and both the Gianfigliazzi. Santoro 1947, 138–142.

13   Santoro 1947, 142, 294, 318, 411, 461, 530.

14   Chittolini 1989b, 130 n. 66.

15   On Parma in the second half of the fifteenth century, see Gentile 2009b.

16   "perniziosi in ogni republica ed in ogni provincia [. . .] al tutto inimici d'ogni civiltà": Machiavelli 2001a, 266 (1:55.19, 21). See Arcangeli 2003, ix–xxxiv.

17   Machiavelli 2001a, 266 (1:55.21)

18   Francesco Sforza to the *podestà* and the *anziani* of Parma, 8 January 1452, ASMi, Missive 14, fol. 16r; Francesco Sforza to Angelo Della Stufa, 2 January 1452, ibid., fols. 41r–v. On Angelo Della Stufa, see Vivolo 1989; Fubini 1994, 131, 220–221, 283, 290–291.

19   Francesco Sforza to the referendary (*referendario*) and the treasurer of Parma, 31 January 1452, ASMi, Registri delle Missive 14, fol. 42v.

Da Correggio as well) in a situation made even more complicated by the war against Venice.[20] Awareness of the dignity of office could take many forms. According to Angelo Ardizzoni, who wrote to the duke of Milan on 4 February 1452 "per sua consolazione," Della Stufa was "an extremely fine looking and well dressed man" who, when taking office, presented himself with fifteen splendid horses and twenty "well dressed" servants—altogether a "highly respectable entourage."[21] But although he looked the part and had the right family connections, Andrea Della Stufa's tenure was a failure, unable as he was to manage the aftermath of a feud that broke out in June between two families belonging to Parma's governing class, the Zaboli and the Ferrari. The political shock waves spread, fomenting a conflict between factions led by Da Correggio and Sanvitale *gentiluomini*.[22] Andrea, who sportingly admitted in a letter to the duke that he was not up to the task, was removed from office at the beginning of July and replaced by the older and more experienced Oldrado Lampugnani, a Milanese citizen who had previously been governor of Parma under Filippo Maria Visconti.[23]

The experiment of a Florentine *commissario* at Parma was not repeated,[24] although the Sforza government did on occasion choose Florentines for the far less politically sensitive role of *podestà*. But in July 1457, Vanni de' Medici, who had been in Parma since April, also felt impelled to voice a complaint in a letter to Francesco Sforza: "the injury done to me is also done to your illustrious lordship in two ways: first because I am your official, and second because I am Vanni, son of Alamanno de' Medici, a blood relative of Cosimo; and we have been and will be servants and partisans of your illustrious lordship unto death." Vanni relayed to the duke the knotty details of a dispute between Count Guido da Correggio and the local family of the Cantelli, adding, "We shall do justice to those in the right without respect for persons, as your illustrious lordship wishes; and although it is hard to deal with these nobles (*grandi*), who are numerous and powerful in every way, we shall fearlessly carry out all the duties of government, and with less difficulty if your illustrious lordship should see fit to grant us full powers."[25] It is striking how arguments

---

20 Francesco Sforza to Della Stufa, 17 January 1452, ASMi, Missive 14, fol. 29r. See Gentile 2009c, 111–112.

21 "homo de belissimo aspeto e beni vestito [...] [famigli] molto bene vestiti [...] [una] honestisima famìa": Angelo Ardizzoni to Francesco Sforza, 4 February 1452, ASMi, Sforzesco 744. Andrea himself confirmed this account in a letter to Francesco Sforza, reminding the duke of the expense incurred in presenting himself to the city "honoratissimamente."

22 On the affair, see Gentile 2009c, 256–267.

23 Francesco Sforza to the referendary and the treasurer of Parma, 12 June 1452, ASMi, Missive 14, fol. 151r.

24 Although Arnolfo Salutati was initially considered to replace Della Stufa: Francesco Sforza to the referendary and the treasurer of Parma, 12 June 1452, ASMi, Missive 14, fol. 151r.

25 "La ingiuria mia in duo modi hè della Vostra Illustrissima Signoria: prima, io sono officiale di Quella; secondario, io sonno Vanni, di misser Alamanno de' Medici figliuolo e stretto di sangue di Cosimo, et siamo stati et saremo in fino alla morte servidori et partesani della Vostra Illustrissima Signoria" / "Noi senza guatare in viso persona faremo ragione a chi l'arà, seguitando la intentione

referring to the dignity of his role as the prince's representative are interwoven with others emphasizing the bonds of clientage between him and the prince.[26] And yet it is well known that it was no easier to perform effectively as a functionary in outlying towns of the Florentine territorial state without exploiting ties of clientage than it was in the Milanese state.[27] The difference is the more highly developed capacity of the Medici regime (and the Florentine governing class in general) to orient personal bonds of this kind, with all their political importance, toward the center. In the case of Lombardy, any attempt to exert state authority from the center had to reckon with the countervailing powers of local lords, and the bonds of factional solidarity that, different to Tuscany, were a structural feature of the Sforza duchy, where political networks and alliances were encouraged on a provincial and regional scale that often wore the ancient badges of Guelf and Ghibelline.[28] In short, it would appear that on top of the feeling of otherness provoked in officials from Tuscany (or, in general, officials from anywhere outside the duchy of Milan)[29] by contact with Lombards, whose culture and way of life these officials disdainfully referred to as "servile,"[30] there was more: not so much a refusal on the part of these officials to respect informal power relations and the self-organizing logic of local societies, as a feeling of helplessness caused by the fact that their own clientage relationships counted for little or nothing in Lombardy, plus the fact that it was extremely difficult to construct new ties of this kind from scratch. It is noteworthy that Vanni de' Medici's arrival at Parma was unwelcome: a few months before his appointment as *podestà*, the *anziani* (the equivalent of the Florentine priors) had asked the duke to appoint a Milanese citizen, Giorgio del Maino. They were worried at the prospect of having as their *podestà* "someone ill informed about the Lombard way of life, and ours especially."[31] But this concern went unheeded. The particular flavor of political life in Parma is well known: the city was renowned for its unusual level of tension between urban factions.[32] The upshot of a failure to take due account of the "Lombard way of life," especially forms of political and military organization from the communal past that had become almost extinct in

della Vostra Illustrissima Signoria: nonostante che con questi grandi mal si può fare, sendo in numero assai et potenti in qualunche qualità, senza paura faremo ogni cosa del nostro reggere, et con men fatica se ne darà qualche arbitrio la Vostra Illustrissima Signoria." Vanni de' Medici to Francesco Sforza, 5 July 1457, ASMi, Sforzesco.

26 See Black 1996, 223–24; Robert Black 2000, 300.

27 In general, see Zorzi 1989. See Salvadori 2000a, 100–110, on the age of Lorenzo, and De Angelis 2000, 171–179, on the trecento and the early quattrocento. For a few significant cases, see Robert Black 2000 (Arezzo); Fabbri 2000 (Volterra); Milner 2000b (Pistoia).

28 See Arcangeli 2003; Gentile 2007a.

29 For example, typical was Lorenzo Terenzi from Pesaro: see Gentile 2009c, 126–127.

30 "usi a servire": the famous expression is Guicciardini's: Guicciardini 2013, 87. (Series B n. 131 in Domandi's translation: Guicciardini 1965, 127.)

31 "persona non informata del vivere lombardo e *precipue* del nostro": the *anziani* of Parma to Francesco Sforza, 12 September 1456, ASMi, Sforzesco 747.

32 Gentile 2009c.

Florentine Tuscany, can be seen in the case of Pietro Vespucci, who served as *capitano* of the Valle di Lugano and of Alessandria and Tortona.

Like the other Florentines mentioned above, Pietro launched his career in Sforza officialdom at the center as *podestà* of Milan in 1474. He does not seem to have been daunted by the challenges he encountered in the capital city.[33] It was later on, and in the periphery rather than at the center, that he, like so many others, first discovered how tough the life of a ducal official could be. Tainted by the Pazzi conspiracy, and with ties to Roberto Sanseverino, count of Caiazzo (1418–87),[34] he was appointed *capitano* of an outlying territory, the Valle di Lugano, in 1481. The valley had been enfeoffed to the Sanseverino two years earlier by the Sforza. This was an area that harbored real challenges (which may be why Luigi Pulci had turned the job down). The Rusca, the most powerful local clan, was one of the strongest and most deeply rooted noble dynasties in all Lombardy, to say nothing of the robust, rural communities there. The Sanseverino did not find it easy to establish themselves in the Valle di Lugano as feudal overlords, and indeed they were disenfeoffed in January 1482.[35] Above all, the valley was a zone of fierce conflict between Guelf and Ghibelline factions.[36] After he had been there for a year, Pietro Vespucci was confirmed as *capitano* by the effective duke, Ludovico il Moro, even though alarm bells were sounding. On 18 January 1482, the ducal *commissario* in Como, Antonio Crivelli, reported that Pietro was "held in low regard by most of the men of Valle di Lugano" and had not dared set foot out of his house since the day of Sanseverino's disenfeoffment.[37] The same day, the representatives of the Valle di Lugano communities wrote to Milan asking to have Vespucci removed.[38] Instead he was confirmed, and the reaction to the presentation of the letter of confirmation was unequivocal. The *procuratori* and civic notables of Lugano "responded that for no price would they have him continue as *capitano*, growing extremely heated as they said so." In a display of defiance, they warned the ducal *commissario* Giacomo Seregni that Vespucci "showed little sense in wishing to carry on as an official where he was not wanted, and if he were ever so arrogant as to mount the bench and administer justice, they would cause him to regret it."[39] Vespucci wrote to Lodovico il Moro to defend himself and denounce vigorously the principal Ghibellines, in particular Ettore Rusca and Albertino Pocobelli, whose insolence had brought things "to a point where it seems that there

---

33 Santoro 1947, 140. For information about his (apparently unsatisfactory) career as a Florentine official, see Salvadori 2000a, 29–30.

34 Fubini 1994, 285, 321.

35 On the lordship of the Sanseverino, see Motta 1880.

36 Motta 1884.

37 "malveduto dalla magior parte de li homini de la Valle di Lughano": ibid., 154–155.

38 Ibid., 155–156.

39 "resposeno che *nulo pacto* el volevano *amodo in antea* più per capitaneo, et molto se scaldarono de parole" / "l'era poco savio a volere essere offitiale al despecto di chi nol voleva, et s'el voleva essere sì presumptuoso ch'el volesse montare in bancha per ministrare justitia, che lo farìano essere mal maestro." Ibid., 97.

is no more fear or obedience in this valley of yours, and that your dominion lies in ruin." He asked for appropriate punishment to be meted out on them all, because, "if not, it would encourage others to act similarly or worse, discrediting your excellency's regime."[40] It was the Ghibelline faction (*parte ghibellina*) that showed Vespucci the most defiance, but his local support came more from the Sanseverino clan—as is suggested by Antonio Crivelli's remark about staying indoors—than from the Guelfs as such. Indeed, in a letter to the duke dated 22 January 1482, the valley council ironically applauded his success in turning all parties against him: "so efficacious and incisive has his bad conduct been in this valley of yours that he has succeeded where even God could not and united the Guelfs and the Ghibellines . . . divided since the time of Christ."[41] By way of comparison, Giannozzo Manetti had achieved diametrically opposite results at Pistoia in 1446, where "his dealings with the two Pistoiese factions were so even handed that both parties joined in sending an embassy to Florence with the controversial proposal—not approved by the Signoria—that Manetti's term be extended for another six months."[42]

Pietro Vespucci tried once more to make the case that to allow public officials to be dishonored by "coarse vulgar common folk" was to undermine the credibility of the ducal state itself. As he wrote to the duke, "although your excellency dispatched me here with the title of *capitano* and with the duty of administering justice . . . I command no more obedience than any lowly private person. What is worse, they threaten that, if I do seat myself on the bench and administer justice, they will hack me to pieces." Once more, he insisted that, if central government was not prepared to use coercive force and impose rigorous justice, the result would be "great detriment and harm to the effectiveness of the regime."[43] In a subsequent letter to the ducal secretary Bartolomeo Calco, Vespucci specified that his adversaries had reportedly said, "if the ducal regime won't do something about him, we'll hack him to pieces ourselves."[44] Yet again, he implored that coercive measures be taken to set "an example to other malefactors in the ducal dominion . . . not so much out of fear for myself as out of concern for the honor of our Illustrious and most excellent lord."[45] Unhappily for him, this identification of ducal government's honor with

---

40 "ita che al pare che non sia più thema né obedientia in questa vostra valle, et che sia ruinato il vostro stato" / "se altramente se facesse, se darebe materia ad altre persone de fare simile et pezore cossa che redondarebbe in grandissimo detrimento del stato de vostra excellentia." Ibid., 98–100.

41 "De tanta efficatia et ponteroxitade sonno stati li soi mal deportamenti, sonno stati di tanta efficatia che in questa vostra valle, hanno poduto più non poté may dio, ha confirmato insema gibellini et gelfi [. . .] che da Christo in qua mai più non fòno unitti." Ibid., 101.

42 Connell 2000b, 151.

43 "popullo vulgare et grosso" / "Non obstante che Vostra Excellentia me habia deputato qui per suo capitaneo et per fare ragione [. . .] non ho obedientia alchuna più comme fosse una persona privata et abieta, *et quod deterius est* me menazano se asendarò ad bancha per fare ragione me taliarano a pezo" / "grandissimo detrimento et detractione del Stato." Motta 1884, 99–100.

44 "S'el stato ducale non li vole providere tagliamelo a pezi nui." Ibid., 102.

45 "exemplo ad altri nel ducale dominio che fosseno malcostumati [. . .] non tanto per paura di me, ma per honore del nostro Illustrissimo et Excellentissimo Signore." Ibid., 164. Requests for exemplary

that of its representatives did not command unanimous assent at Milan, where the representations of Ettore Rusca, who had appeared at court in person, carried greater weight: an inspector of finances for Vespucci's territory was appointed on the advice of Rusca, and Vespucci himself was sacked.[46]

Appointed *capitano* of justice in Milan for 1483 as compensation, Pietro was dispatched once again to the periphery in 1485 as *commissario* of Alessandria and Tortona. Once again, the periphery proved to be a different world from the metropolis. The tragic end of Pietro Vespucci's career is well known: he was lynched by the Ghibellines of Alessandria in May 1485, an episode that both Letizia Arcangeli and I have recently examined in detail.[47] Let it suffice to say here that Vespucci showed little respect for the power relationships inherent in local politics. As in the Valle di Lugano, he went about his work overlooking the importance of factions, demonstrating outright incomprehension of them as vital political phenomena.[48] Vespucci had barely assumed office when, in a letter of 7 January 1485, he displayed confidence in his ability to "pacify these insolent bands, who have perpetrated so many homicides and offences because there were no vigorous officials there [at Varzi and elsewhere] to punish them; and the same disease is at work here [in Alessandria]."[49] For Vespucci, lack of assertiveness in executing an office was a "disease," and he believed he had the cure. A few months later, he heaped further blame on his colleagues: scandals were occurring at Alessandria

> because past infractions went unpunished, as the criminal registers of the city for the last six years reveal. No trial, or almost none, was brought to a conclusion, and in truth you [sc. the duke] have never seen such a disorderly set of registers. Having learned before taking office of the crimes and scandals that had occurred, I brought with me a strong law enforcement team [*una bona et bella compagnia*] to coerce the insolent and the seditious locals, and for as long as this police squadron [*essa famiglia*] was at my disposal the

---

punishment are standard in the letters of Sforza officials. As Massimo Della Misericordia notes, "The recurring insistence that the punishment should be exemplary shows not just the will to assert power by means of 'the splendor of the suffering inflicted,' but the vitality of the culture of custom [*cultura consuetudinaria*] itself. It was in fact from *exemplum* that custom was generated." Della Misericordia 2012, 256–257.

46 Motta 1884, 103–104. It was not extraordinary for a community to succeed in getting rid of an unwelcome official, or even to prevent him from taking office in the first place. Making difficulties for officials in charge of law enforcement was part of the normal dialogue between the sovereign and territorial corporations in the Milanese state. See Della Misericordia 2012.

47 Factions were not absent from Milan either, but they manifested themselves in far more informal and muted ways than in the towns and territories of the Sforza dominions. Arcangeli 2003, 414–418; Gentile 2010, 60–62.

48 On Milanese factions, see Somaini 2005, but also Arcangeli 2005; Gentile 2007a.

49 "pacificare quelle brigate molto insolente le qualle hanno perpetrato tanti homicidii et mancamenti per non essere stato in quilli logi offitialli vigorosi che li habia puniti, et questo medesimo morbo lavora qui." Pietro Vespucci to Gian Galeazzo Maria Sforza, 7 January 1485, ASMi, Sforzesco 1145.

city was peaceful and quiet, and, in the words of the citizens, felt as if it had been reborn.[50]

But these bold intentions proved illusory as the police squadron was whittled down, and worse still, as tension rose between Alessandria's Guelfs and Ghibellines during the winter of 1485. Vespucci declared that he was prepared to act "irrespective of persons," adding, "I shall show Your Excellency [sc. the duke] whether I make a distinction between Guelfs and Ghibellines."[51] His incomprehension of the phenomenon of faction is demonstrated by the manner of his death: he reinforced his own squadron with men supplied by the Guelfs, and raided the house of the Ghibelline Carrante Villavecchia, whom he captured and hanged— without trial, and without permitting him a final confession—from the balcony of the communal palace. The Ghibellines resolved to impose a death sentence on the ducal commissioner himself as reprisal, and did so solemnly in the course of a regular meeting of their faction—a case almost unique in the history of the Sforza dominions. As the investigator of the case, Giovanni Andrea Cagnola, later put it, the Ghibellines of Alessandria took the view that Carrante Villavecchia had been hanged "more out of extreme partiality, and to do them harm, than out of zeal for justice: both because [Carrante] was seized with the help of some Guelfs and subjected to maltreatment in his own house, and also because, as they saw it, the late commissioner was a supporter of the *parte guelfa*."[52] Vespucci was assailed, captured, and hanged at the location designated for executions in Alessandria— the same balcony of the communal palace from which he had hanged Carrante Villavecchia. Even though his body suffered postmortem indignities, the city managed to avoid being charged with *lèse-majesté*, and indeed the ducal government disavowed the work of its Florentine *commissario*.[53] It is hard to credit the suggestion that Pietro Vespucci suffered some kind of cleverly disguised revenge at the hands of Lorenzo de' Medici for his involvement in the Pazzi conspiracy. It would have been impossible to orchestrate in advance a scenario such as the one

50 "per non essere state punite le culpe comisse per lo passato, come appare per li libri del maleficio de dicta città de anni sey, che non se trova processo alchuno o vero pochi esser stati finiti, che in verità non vedete may cosa più inordinata quanto sono stati quelli libri; de le quale culpe et scandali se comettivano, habiandone io noticia inanze l'intrata mia d'esso officio, condusse megho una bona et bella compagnia per ripremere li insolenti et sediciosi, et per quel tempo è stata essa famiglia megho la dicta città è stata pacifica, quieta et pariva renovata, secondo dicevano li citadini." Vespucci to Gian Galeazzo Maria Sforza, 4 March 1485, ASMi, Sforzesco 1145.

51 "non guardando in faza a homo del mondo" / "farò intendere a Vostra Excellentia se io cognosco che cossa sia ni gelfo ni gebelino." Vespucci to Gian Galeazzo Maria Sforza, 4 March 1485, ASMi, Sforzesco 1145.

52 "più presto processa per passione e per fare iniuria a loro che per zello de justicia, sì per essere mandato a prendere per alcuni de parte gelfa et fatoli quelli oprobrij in casa, sì etiam perché hano questa opinione, ch'el dicto condam comissario fosse fautore de parte gelfa." Andrea Cagnola to Gian Galeazzo Maria Sforza, 19 May 1485, ASMi, Comuni 3.

53 Arcangeli 2003, 414–418; Gentile 2010, 60–62.

played out in Alessandria in May 1485. Vespucci was the victim, certainly, of his own character, but also of the absolutist velleities of Ludovico il Moro, who on this as on other occasions sought to shift local political equilibria to the advantage of the central government, with mixed but ultimately disastrous results, as shown by the events of 1499 and the French invasion of the duchy.[54] With hindsight, sending Pietro Vespucci to Alessandria in the wake of his troubled tenure in the Valle di Lugano was shortsighted. It is unconvincing to suggest that the rigid attitude shown by the Florentine *commissario* in his management of the situation was based on a "lofty" conception of his role. As an outsider, he lacked the mantle of protection afforded to various Lombard colleagues, independently of Milan and the court, by inherited bonds of faction and clientage. It is understandable that, in the situation he faced, coercion appeared the only possible answer to the problems of public order the factions were causing, though the means of coercion at his disposal were inadequate. But even today, without the backing of a strong political will, a controversial magistrate can be discredited; and loss of credit is the prelude to failure.[55] Florentine functionaries working away from home were not much different from their Lombard colleagues when it came to asserting the nobility of public office and identifying the honor of the ducal government with that accorded its officials. The dignity of the officeholder was generally invoked after the first and most effective option had failed—that is, government through mediation, through clientage, through factional networks. These were tools unavailable to Florentine officials (nor to non-Lombard officials in general), and the power they did derive from their direct link to the court and the central administration of the duchy of Milan was often insufficient when it came to actually governing cities and territories not at all like those in Tuscany.

So real differences of social and political structures between Lombardy and Tuscany did play an undeniable role. Significant is the experience of Goro Gheri as pontifical governor at Piacenza in 1515 (and again in 1522–23).[56] Anyone from Pistoia, as he was, would have known all about factions, and for that matter he seems to have been a leader of the Panciatichi.[57] His letters to various members of the Medici family contain detailed and acute analyses of the phenomenon of faction. Even so, his consternation at finding out just what Piacenza was like is striking. Not only was the city unable to control its own *contado* because of the feudal jurisdictions retained by noble families; not only did members of the Guelf and Ghibelline factions live in different neighborhoods and attend different churches; not only were the keys to the gates of the city held by individual nobles:

---

54 On Ludovico il Moro's approach to government, see Arcangeli 2003, 123–148.
55 On these problems, see Gentile 2010.
56 On Goro Gheri's government in Piacenza, see Andreozzi 1997b, 148–154, 158–159; Arcangeli 2003, 352–353, 368, 404–407.
57 On Goro Gheri's role as party leader in Pistoia, see Connell 2000a, 160, 192, 207.

I find there is another serious problem pertaining to both parties. The offices of city government are filled neither by appointment by the sovereign regime nor by the commune. Instead there are four main houses, two Guelf and two Ghibelline, each of which designates a quarter of the candidates for office, and (what is yet more shocking) there are four different urns, one for each of the four families. And when the name tags are drawn to fill the offices, they say actually in front of the sovereign's representatives, "this is the urn for this or that house." Your excellency can well imagine how vexatious this is to the population, and how dishonorable and detrimental to those who represent the sovereign. I was thinking that, when things settle down a bit in Lombardy and there is less need for caution, two measures could be taken: first, the tax leases and offices that currently go exclusively to the Guelf faction should be shared among the members of the Ghibelline faction as well: they are Piacentini too. And moreover this scandalous method they use to designate the holders of municipal office should be suppressed. While the practice could serve the interests of the two factions' four families, nevertheless its suppression would please the people, and enhance the authority of the sovereign's representatives.[58]

Gheri was particularly appalled by the failure to respect protocol (*"actually in front* of the sovereign's representatives" [italics mine]) and stressed the fact that many Piacentini, although full citizens, were excluded from office. His summary judgment was, "I found this city in great disorder, with social life undisciplined and hardly civic."[59] The last phrase ("poco civile") is probably the key expression, and the remedy for the disorder in Gheri's eyes was the promotion of civic identity: "To gratify the people and win them over entirely, so that their only thought is the preservation of magnificent signore's rule, I would have the *anziani*, that is the priors, who at present are accorded no ceremony or reputation, granted some honorific ceremonials, as we do in Tuscany, so that they feel they have achieved something

58 "Io ci trovo anco un altro gran disordine, che è nell'una e l'altra parte. Gli offizii che ordinati sono per il governo della città, non si fanno né dal superiore né dalla Comunità, ma ci sono quattro case principali, due guelfe e due ghibelline, le quali ognuna di quelle per la quarta parte imborsa i cittadini di quelli offizii e (che ancora è più disonesto) sono quattro borse; una per ognuna delle quattro famiglie; e quando si estraggono [corrected from "cstraggono"] li offizii, si dice etiam alla presenzia de' superiori: questa è la borsa della Casa; di modo che se questa cosa è esosa al popolo, e poco onorevole ed utile ai superiori, la Vostra Eccellenzia lo può pensare. Io andavo pensando, come le cose qua di Lombardia saranno un poco più quieto, e che non si abbi ad aver tanti rispetti, che si provvedessi a queste cose: all'una, che questi dazii ed offizii che sono soli dati a queste parti guelfe, si facessino che ne partecipassino anco quelli dell'altra fazione, perchè ancora loro sono Piasentini: ed in su questa si potria provvedere a quest'altra esorbitanzia del modo che servono a fare questi loro offizii; e benché sia questo interesse delle quattro famiglie dell'una ed altra fazione, tamen se ne farìa piacere al popolo, e l'autorità de' superiori resteria maggiore." Goro Gheri to Giuliano de' Medici, 27 June 1516, Gheri 1848, 44–45.

59 "questa città ho trovata in tanto disordine e vivere licenzioso e poco civile." Goro Gheri to Giuliano de' Medici, undated but clearly from June 1516, Gheri 1848, 23.

significant. I do not mean they should be given real authority, only ceremonies and smoke."[60]

That is, what remained of north-central Italy's celebrated political civic culture (*civilitas*; never mind "republicanism") amid the crisis of the Italian Wars: the "smoke" of liberty. When Michel de Montaigne was traversing the grand duchy of Tuscany in May 1581 and came to Pistoia, he made a revealing observation:

> This poor town compensates for its lost liberty with the empty image of its ancient constitution. They have nine priors and a gonfalonier whom they elect every two months. These men are in charge of the administration and are paid by the duke, as they once were by the public. Lodged in the palace, they never step outside unless as a group, being permanently confined there. The gonfalonier walks in front of the *podestà* sent by the duke, but it is the *podestà* who wields all the power. Meanwhile the gonfalonier acknowledges no one, in imitation of some petty imaginary royal. It was pitiful to see them feeding on this sham while the grand duke extracts ten times more revenue from them than before.[61]

---

60 "per gratificare bene il popolo, ed acquistarlo tutto, che non pensassino mai se non alla conservazione dello stato del Signore Magnifico, che farei che li Anziani, cioè lì Priori, quali adesso stanno senza alcuna cerimonia o reputazione, si desse loro qualche cerimonia di onoranze al modo nostro di Toscana; perché paresse loro aver acquistato assai: non dico già dare loro autorità dì valore, ma *solum* cerimonie e fumo." Goro Gheri to Giuliano de'Medici, undated but clearly from July 1516, Gheri 1848, 66. The passage did not escape the notice of Carlo Dionisotti: see Dionisotti 1980, 105.

61 "Cette pauvre ville se paie de la liberté perdue sur cette vaine image de sa forme ancienne. Ils ont neuf premiers et un gonfalonier qu'ils élisent de deux en deux mois. Ceux-ci ont en charge la police, sont nourris du duc, comme ils étaient anciennement du public, logés au palais, et n'en sortent jamais guère que tous ensemble, y étant perpetuellement enfermés. Le gonfalonier marche devant le potesta que le duc y envoie, lequel potesta en effet a toute puissance; et ne salue, ledit gonfalonier, personne, contrefaisant une petite royauté imaginaire. J'avais pitié de les voir se paître de cette singerie, et cependant le grand-duc a accru les subsides des dix parts sur les anciens." Montaigne 1983, 265–266. See Connell 2000b, 44–45.

EIGHT

Piero in Power, 1492–1494

A Balance Sheet for Four Generations of Medici Control

ALISON BROWN

THE TWO AND A HALF years between Lorenzo de' Medici's death in April 1492 and the fall of the regime in November 1494, following the French invasion, encapsulate the strengths and weaknesses of Medici power. Piero de' Medici, then aged twenty, inherited his father's position as de facto head of a republican regime without either the experience or legal status to act authoritatively in a time of crisis. Having refused to grant Charles VIII free passage, he then single-handedly ceded Florence's recently built fortresses at Sarzana and Pietrasanta to the French king and negotiated the handover of Pisa and Livorno to him before returning to Florence to be ejected from the city the following day. In what follows, I shall use Piero's brief period in power to evaluate his family's status in Florence at a particularly revealing time. For although he acted like a prince in his dealings with the king and was accepted as such by the castellans who meekly handed over the fortresses, he was nevertheless immediately ejected from the city on his return for lacking a constitutional mandate for his actions.[1] These events reveal the fault line between the Medici's status abroad and at home. It is illustrated by two contrasting incidents I shall use to throw light on the difficulties they—like other early modern rulers— faced in balancing both princely and civic roles. Yet it was from the crisis of these

---

1   ASF, Otto di Pratica, Missive 25, fols. 25r–v, 33r–v, 41v–42v, 55r–57r (29 October–6 November 1494); ASF, Signori, Deliberazioni in forza di ordinaria autorità, 96, fol. 96r (20 November 1494); Parenti 1994–2005, 1:114–125.

years, I shall argue, that a new, more flexible definition of government developed that more accurately describes the Medici's position at this time.

The Medici were certainly not military rulers, or signori, of Florence, nor were they, as yet, its princes. As Piero's old tutor, Gentile Becchi, put it when writing to Piero on the eve of the revolution in 1494, "it's difficult to play the role of prince in a republic unless you appear to be a wholehearted republican in the eyes of the people."[2] Republicanism remained "the only language in town," for no other terms were available in which to praise them or to deprecate their unofficial status in the city as tyrants.[3] So despite the recent emphasis of historians such as Francis William (Bill) Kent and Melissa Bullard on the Medici's role as patrons or bosses, the republicanism-despotism antonym still dominates Renaissance historiography— whether it takes the form of the recent reassessment of the historical debate initiated by Philip Jones or the linguistic deconstruction of the rhetoric of liberty.[4] We now distinguish these approaches as belonging to different methodologies, but they were in fact all in use in fifteenth-century Florence. Even before Lorenzo de' Medici died, republican ideology was being subverted by critics who saw how it was being used to "dazzle" and mislead people, and already the old normative typologies of good and bad government were being replaced by neutral, "transgressive" definitions of power that described Lorenzo as an arbiter or mediator (*mezzadro*) and as the pivot, or "tongue," of the balance of power.[5] So in what follows, I use the metaphor of balance to convey both the flexibility and the instability of Piero's "pivotal" role as his father's heir, uncertain of his present status in Florence and ignorant of what the future held in store for him and his family. The metaphor can describe our position, too, as we weigh up the events of these years: did they encourage progression toward military lordship, regression to republican nostalgia, or did they instead contribute to new thinking about the state?

On the death of his father on 8 April 1492, Piero acquired no powers that can be called signorial. Aged twenty, he was well below the statutory age for holding office, so that, by transferring to him "all the powers" enjoyed by Lorenzo, the councils were simply allowing him to be a member of the Cento or Council of One Hundred (the ultimate legislative authority), and the supremely powerful Seventy (which also enabled him to be an all-important electoral official, or *accoppiatore*, as well as a member of the equally important foreign affairs and financial executive committees). In addition, as the chronicler Piero Parenti reported, he was given his father's positions as a palace *operaio* (supervisor of building works) and a governor of the

2   Gentile Becchi to Piero de' Medici, October 1494, Picotti 1928, 555: "difficile est gerere personam principis in republica se non si pare republicone in oculis populi."
3   See Milner, this volume, 281–294, and in the following note.
4   See Law and Paton 2010; Milner 2000a; 2005b, 166–169; Kent 1993, especially 281; Bullard 1994, 109–130.
5   Brown 2000a, 179–180, repr. 2011c, 225–245; 2012, especially 55–57.

wool guild with "all the other dignities."[6] A semi-hereditary legacy, then, that nevertheless depended on a majority vote of approval in Florence's three legislative councils, the 100 and the councils of the Commune and the People—and the fact that Piero's entourage betrayed a certain nervousness about the outcome shows that it was by no means to be taken for granted.[7]

As "ignoble merchants,"[8] the Medici conspicuously lacked the military authority symbolized by the *bacchetta*, or baton of command, that condottieri lords such as the Este displayed on statues of themselves on horseback in the main city square: an open display of power for which the Medici waited another century before imitating.[9] Far from being "lord of Florence" and able to get Florence to do what he wanted "with signs," Lorenzo claimed he lacked the credit and authority to do even what was necessary.[10] The slow progression toward military lordship even after the Medici's return to power in 1512 shows how much resistance there still was to the idea. One milestone on the military route, the appointment of Piero de' Medici's son Lorenzo as Florence's captain general in 1516, was widely opposed, not least by Lorenzo's uncle, Pope Leo X.[11] Another, the building of Florence's first fortress, the Fortezza da Basso, met with similar opposition, despite the fait accompli of Alessandro de' Medici's dukedom in 1532: the outcry when this "bridle" was slipped into place provided more visible and concrete evidence than the constitutional changes that—as John Hale put it in 1968—"freedom was in fetters."[12] The same is true of the other powers that constitute sovereignty: control of finance and law. As Lorenzo complained in 1487, he was not "the duke of Milan nor the king Ferrante," and unlike them he could not use his "own money" for public expenses such as paying condottieri or ambassadors, building fortresses, and so on, all of which had to be approved by councils or by the Ten of War with *balìa* (full powers).[13] Similarly, the Medici lacked the absolute or arbitrating legal powers enjoyed by lords in the field of law and, according to the judge of appeals in Florence, Lorenzo would very wisely often say that, although a ruler needed to defend himself, he shouldn't mix politics with individual concerns.[14]

6   Parenti 1994–2005, 1:26; Guidi 1981, 1:103.

7   Ser Pace Bambello to Niccolò Michelozzi, 11–12 April 1492, Brown 2011c, 64–65; on the votes, see Rubinstein 1997, 264 n. 6.

8   Medici 1977–, 2:117, citing the Milanese diplomat Francesco Maletta: "Uno vile mercatante et citadino."

9   Gibbons 2001, 77–95.

10   Medici 1977–, 5:268–269 (3 July 1481): "co' cenni," "non ho tanto credito et auctorità quanto bisognerebbe." See ibid., 6:100 (26 November 1481).

11   Giorgetti 1883, 204–211.

12   Hale 1968, 502; see Machiavelli 2001a, 463–477 (*Discorsi* 2.24).

13   Medici 1977–, 10:402 (7 July 1487): "perché io non sono né duca di Milano né il re Ferrando, né spendo in queste cose del mio."

14   Andrea Recuperati of Faenza to Piero, 5 June 1494, ASF, MAP 73, 90: "prudentissimamente dire," "non essere convenienti fare mixtura del stato cum el dare et havere intra particulari."

Of course, as postmodernists, we know better than to believe Lorenzo's denial of lordship, relying instead on his family's many hints or "innuendos" of rulership to assess their status—such as using porphyry in their tombs and palaces, dressing up as kingly magi, reordering sacral space and processional routes to give themselves prominence, founding universities, building libraries, creating family cardinals, and promoting themselves as cult images that seemingly gave them the position, if not yet the title, of princes as well as saints "with holy bones."[15] Racing was an activity that usefully combined elitism with populism, as Michael Mallett has suggested, since it was both "a symbol of princely status" and—thanks to the early practice of betting on horses—populist.[16] Despite this, other cultural giveaways document the constraints on Medici power with equal subtlety, such as the absence of biographies of the Medici (until the late 1490s) to compare with the fulsome lives of Neapolitan kings and Sforza dukes.[17] Similarly, no portraits were painted of the Medici (as opposed to sculpted busts) unless they served a votive or commemorative function.[18] And their display of arms and other feudal attributes was strictly limited, the only exception being the king of France's concession of his arms to Piero di Cosimo in 1467; the fact that the Medici's arms were removed and defaced after 1494 and then proliferated wildly after 1513 speaks for itself of their contentious role as status symbols.[19] The same is true of dress. By always dressing himself like other citizens, in a cloak and scarlet hood, Lorenzo proclaimed his citizen status as clearly as he did by his behavioral "tell" of always putting citizens older than himself—according to Giovanni Cambi—on his righthand side, and if there were more than one, he always put the oldest in the middle. He similarly refused to allow his children to wear scarlet cloth in case they should be thought to be wearing the prohibited luxury crimson cloth, suggesting that we must interpret his son Piero's later extravagance in dress as an open step toward princely status.[20]

All this demonstrates that, on one side of the balance, the Medici were constrained by the strong tradition of republicanism in Florence. On the other side, however, it is clear that the boundary between public and private was becoming increasingly indistinct. One critic thought Lorenzo was "worse than a *signore a bacchetta*, since he was always accompanied by ten lackeys armed with swords when he went out," a privilege that was also extended (and repeatedly renewed) to Lorenzo's

15 Among a vast bibliography, see, on "innuendos," Hatfield 1992, 238; McKillop 1992a, especially 289–291; on family cardinals, Medici 1977–, 1:400–401, 9:370–371, and Chambers, this volume; on sanctity, see Bullard 1994, 18; Kent 1994b, 209–210 and 2013, 94–100.
16 Medici 1977–, 5:34–37; Mallett 1996, 256–262.
17 Bentley 1987, 222–241; Ianziti 1988; Brown 1992c, 3–40, 259–261; Fubini 2009, 205–226.
18 Wright 1996, 80; Langedijk 1981, 1:13–38.
19 McKillop 1992b, especially 654 n. 36. According to McKillop (personal communication), the Medici family were granted royal privileges they never used or displayed. See ASF Diplomatico, Spoglio 90/1, nn. 145, 155, 442, 679.
20 Cambi 1785, 65; Guicciardini 1994b, 57–58 and n. 167; Brown 2011c, 70, 73–74.

cousins and to his son Piero.[21] In the fields of finance and justice, the boundary was equally indistinct. It seems clear that Lorenzo enjoyed some access to public money, partly as a result of the Medici's role as moneylenders to the state and partly thanks to the special privilege Lorenzo was awarded to prevent him losing office through debt.[22] He frequently intervened in criminal, if not civil, legal processes. In 1485, for instance, he was told by Pierfilippo Pandolfini that the *otto di guardia* (eight of ward or magistracy for internal security) would "willingly hear your opinion and then find a good means of putting it into effect," and in 1489 he personally ordered a man to be hanged who was fleeing justice.[23] Although the summary justice inflicted on Giuliano de' Medici's assassins by the *otto di guardia* (when Lorenzo was a member) was condemned as illegal by lawyers, its continued use for the crime of *lèse-majesté* against Lorenzo "indeed attributes honor and respect to Lorenzo," as startled observers commented.[24]

The Medici undoubtedly enjoyed their greatest prestige in the field of foreign affairs, thanks partly to their diplomatic skills and renown as bankers, partly to the need of other rulers to treat them as part of the club and (almost) one of themselves. Following Cosimo de' Medici's dramatic change of alliance in the later 1440s from Venice to Milan that realigned the balance of political power in Italy for most of the fifteenth century, his grandson Lorenzo acted with equal dexterity as the "tongue of the balance" (*examen della bilancia*), as his tutor Gentile Becchi put it in 1470.[25] Despite the crisis of the Pazzi conspiracy, his prestige as peacemaker and arbiter of power in Italy seemed assured by the time of his death, with one son a cardinal, another married to the princely Orsini, a daughter married to the pope's son, and he himself the pope's principal banker (holding the papal tiara as surety for his bank's massive loan of ninety-five thousand florins to Innocent VIII), as well as his close adviser on foreign policy.[26] Ten years earlier, in 1482, a revealing image linked his reputation abroad with his status at home by describing him as an "idol" of the elite in Florence, for—as Antonio Montecatini, the Este ambassador in Florence, explained to Duke Ercole d'Este—Lorenzo's reputation consisted in the esteem in which Italian and outside powers held him, without which he would lack the reputation he enjoyed at home, "and without this idol [*hiidolo*], those in power would be just like everyone else."[27] As a precocious intellectual, poet, lover, and discerning

---

21 Cambi 1785, 65, and see 10, 63, 67; e.g., ASF, Otto 5, fol. 2v (July 1481); 63, fol. 22v (November 1482); 71, 2bis[r] (July 1486); 95, fol. 1v (July 1493).

22 Brown 1992b, 151–183; 2011c, xix–xx; see Goldthwaite 2009, 495 (on the contrasting fiscal practices of republican and princely states).

23 ASF, MAP 26, 448 (24 September 1485): "Intenderassi volentieri il parere vostro et poi per buona via si metterà a efetto"; Brown 1992d, 99.

24 Cavallar 1997; Brown 2011c, 88–91.

25 Fubini 1994, 185–219, especially 215.

26 Bullard 2008, 391–392; Medici 1977–, 15:185–188; Guicciardini 1931, 72–73; 1975, 1:4–7.

27 Medici 1977–, 7:57 (introd. note): "quando non havesseno quello hiidolo, seriano como gli altri" (17 December 1482).

collector of antiquities, Lorenzo was by the time of his death, as Bill Kent put it, a "proto-prince" himself and well able to hold his own in princely circles.[28]

This was Lorenzo's legacy to his son in 1492: great personal prestige and idolization but no official title or constitutional role in mercantile Florence. On one hand, as the chronicler Piero Parenti put it, Lorenzo's "greatness" made Piero accustomed to issuing commands and being obeyed; on the other, the limitations on his authority made it difficult to curb the rivalries that had led to his brother Giuliano (Piero's uncle) "being cut to pieces" in 1478 and Lorenzo himself "always living in fear, deprived of all peace of mind and body."[29] Lorenzo might well have intended to become Gonfalonier of Justice for life when he reached the age of forty-five, as Riccardo Fubini—following Francesco Guicciardini—suggests; but his death two years short of the requisite age meant that Piero enjoyed no legal primacy in Florence, only the practical experience that according to one of the Pucci family "placed the regime almost entirely on his shoulders."[30] Nor do we know how the ailing Lorenzo would have responded to the challenges that faced his young son: the newly inherited claims of the French king to the kingdom of Naples, the new Borgia pope (no longer Lorenzo's *parente* [relative]), and the new league of San Marco that for the first time since the 1450s excluded both Florence and Naples from an Italian alliance of powers.[31] A letter from the banker Lorenzo Spinelli in the French court to Lorenzo on 30 March 1492 (which he probably never read) reported that France was putting the blame for its putative invasion of Italy on Lorenzo, and that he was also being criticized by the pope for Francesco Cibo's sale of his castles to the Orsini. Since both were seen as the seeds that brought about the French invasion and the Medici's downfall, the letter suggests that Lorenzo should be blamed as much as Piero for the eventual outcome.[32]

In this situation, with the French ambassador already in Florence to discuss Charles's claim to the throne of Naples, Piero apparently kept all his options open in his attempt to hold the balance of power in Italy as his father had done. Far from "throwing himself" at Ferrante and "totally alienating" Milan, as Guicciardini suggested, Piero remained in close contact with the Sforza in Milan and with the pope in Rome.[33] He had already established a friendly relationship with Lodovico il Moro during his visit to Milan for Gian Galeazzo Sforza's marriage in 1489, when Lodovico was so impressed with his behavior and his repartee that he gave Piero precedence over the young Annibale Bentivoglio by placing Piero next to himself;

28 Kent 2007, 41; 2013, 62–63.

29 Parenti 1994–2005, 1:25.

30 Fubini 2009, 179, citing Guicciardini 1931, 71; Piero Pucci to his brother Giannozzo Pucci, Florence, 24 December 1491, Florence Archivio Pucci, *filza* 2, 7, fol. 73: "parmi che lo stato se riposi già quasi tuto in sulle sue spalle."

31 Mallett 1995, 154–155; see Negri 1923, 13–14.

32 ASF, MAP 20, 32; see Lorenzo Spinelli to Piero, 14 April 1492, ASF, MAP 14, 269; Mallett 1995, 156–158.

33 Brown 2011a, especially 308–309; Grimani 1900, 229; see Guicciardini 1931, 87–88.

and although Lodovico apparently thought Piero had too high an opinion of himself after 1492, he and the Sanseverino brothers nevertheless continued Lorenzo's double diplomacy by writing separately to Piero through secretaries such as Bernardo Ricci and Piero Dovizi. [34] Similarly in Rome, Piero reinforced the success of his earlier visits in 1484 and 1487 (in the time of Pope Innocent VIII) by returning in 1492 as a member of the Florentine embassy offering homage to Alexander VI. As the youngest of the six ambassadors, he bore the papal train, for which he was rewarded, eighteen months later, by Alexander's promise to help him attain the great glory and favor enjoyed by his grandfather Cosimo and his father in Florence and Italy, "who were deservedly on a par with every great prince." [35] This sums up his close relationship with Italy's rulers, who treated him as a son to be protected and as a prince—like themselves—of taste and culture, a champion jouster, and huntsman too. [36] And although the same is true of his relationship with Ferrante and Virginio Orsini, Piero's long hesitation about his course of action in 1494 suggests he was not as deeply committed to the Neapolitan alliance as Guicciardini implies— influenced, perhaps, by the advice of one of his intimates, messer Puccio Pucci, that he should behave as "master of the workshop" (*maestro della bottegha*) by not getting too close to the Aragonese nor to Virginio Orsini, who wanted to control him. [37]

Messer Puccio introduces the first of my two contrasting vignettes of Piero's standing with Italy's rulers and with the ruling elite in Florence. The Pucci were "the most valued friends" of Cosimo, Lorenzo, and especially of Piero, who called Giannozzo Pucci his "alter ego." [38] They served Piero in key embassies in Italy: Giannozzo's half brother, messer Puccio, first in Faenza and then in Rome (where he joined another brother, the future cardinal Lorenzo), and Puccio's son Dionigi in Naples. Since messer Puccio was married to Geronima Farnese, sister of Alessandro (later Pope Paul III) and the beautiful Giulia Farnese (Pope Alexander VI's current mistress), he provided the Medici, as well as the Pucci, with an invaluable link to Rome, as Lorenzo Pucci's letters reveal. Through them, we know of a plan hatched there by the Farnese for Piero de' Medici to broker a marriage for the one-year-old daughter of Giulia and the pope; the dowry would be large (since the pope liked to do well by his daughters, as he had done for "madonna Lucrezia"), and it would enable Piero to profit from the pope's affairs as effectively as by any other means, "and many good results would follow"—among them, influence in the church and in the papal states—"and the patron of everything, as I see it, would be his

34 Brown 2011a, 305–306, 309; 2011c, 74–78.

35 Brown 2011c, 72, 83; Antonio da Colle to Piero, 3 May 1494, ASF, MAP 55, 177, fol. 293v: "quali [. . .] meritamente si possono equiparare ad ogni gran principe."

36 Parenti 1994–2005, 1:55; Martelli 1978, 187.

37 Puccio Pucci to Piero, 16 June 1494, Canestrini and Desjardins 1859–86, 1:494: "Confortovi [. . .] dimostrare di volere essere recognosciuto per el Maestro della Bottegha."

38 Piero to Michelozzi, 26 November 1491, BNCF, Ginori Conti 29, 35, fol. 8r: "el quale (se gl'è vero che *amicus est alter ego*) fia costì io"; see Parenti 1994–2005, 1:111.

magnificence [i.e. Piero]."³⁹ Although the initial proposal was to marry the baby Laura to Astorre Manfredi, the young lord of Faenza—as a way of securing his strategically important state from the clutches of Milan following his father's murder in 1488—another name then came into play: that of Piero's brother Giuliano, who had been "born after 1478 as a reborn Giuliano [Lorenzo il Magnifico's murdered brother] and so couldn't be more than fourteen or fifteen years old" and, despite the loss of a finger in a fight a few months earlier, was "beautiful, wise, and loved by the *magnifico* as much as he loved his own life."⁴⁰

Although negotiations continued into the spring, nothing came of them and Laura was eventually married to Niccolò Della Rovere, Julius II's nephew.⁴¹ Nevertheless, they throw revealing light on Piero's status in curial circles as a potential marriage broker and patron, as well as on his mutually supportive relationship with the Pucci. While Piero expected to receive a third of the dowry for brokering the deal, Lorenzo Pucci was assured by Alessandro Farnese that, if the Farnese and the Medici did well out of it, Piero would have to reward the Pucci as well—as indeed happened, when Lorenzo was among the first batch of cardinals created by Piero's brother Giovanni after he became pope in 1513.⁴² Since the negotiations were seen by the cardinal of Alessandria (Giovanni di San Giorgio, "l'Alessandrino") as a way of securing Piero's allegiance to Ferrante and the pope, who feared the Florentines might desert them for France because of their trading interests, they also confirm that, at the end of 1493, Piero was still uncommitted in the face of the threatened French invasion: "if he decides to come to an agreement with the French, he won't conclude it [the marriage agreement]; if he decides for the pope, he will."⁴³ Although the situation was soon to be changed by the death of Ferrante of Naples on 25 January 1494 and the growing certainty of the French invasion, Piero also appeared much less committed to the Orsini than has been suggested, for on 7 January, Lorenzo Pucci reported that if Piero brokered the marriage, it would not be for a relationship with the Orsini family, to whom he was already related through

39 Lorenzo Pucci to Giannozzo Pucci, 24 December 1493, ASF, CS, ser. 1, 340, fol. 98v: "ne seghuirebbe molti buoni efeti [...] e il padrone di tutto sarebe il magnifico, secondo pare a me"; see Mathew 1912, 82, 85–86; Picotti 1960, 198.

40 Pellegrini 1999, especially 112–113; Lorenzo Pucci to Giannozzo Pucci, 24, 26 December 1493, 7, [19] January 1494, ASF, CS 1, 340, fols. 95v, 124r–125r, 133r: "era nato doppo il '78 essendo rifatto Juliano e però non potea passare 14 o 15 anni [...] e che era bello, savio e amato del Magnifico quanto la propria vita"; Parenti 1994–2005, 1:58. Probably Piero is meant here by "Magnifico" but both he and his father Lorenzo are referred to in the letter.

41 Piero to Puccio Pucci, Faenza, 13 March 1494, ASF CS 1, 340, fol. 162r: "per hora né a questi anni io non sono in proposito di resolvermene interamente"; Mathew 1912, 85.

42 Mathew 1912; Lorenzo Pucci to Giannozzo Pucci, 26 December 1493, 11 January 1494, ASF, CS 1, 340, fols. 95v, 135v.

43 Lorenzo Pucci to Giannozzo Pucci, 26 December 1493, ASF, CS 1, 340, fol. 98v: "se delibera intendersi con i Franciosi, non lo concluda; quando diliberasi intendersi col papa, lo faccia e chredo farà per lui la a/3 parte." See Lorenzo Pucci to Giannozzo Pucci, 1 January 1494, ASF, CS 1, 340, fol. 114r: "se il magnifico Piero si voltava con i Ghalli, non vi porgerebbe orechio; se con il papa, che lo concluderebe."

his wife and others, but for one with the Farnese, Alessandro, his brother Angelo, and Giulia."[44]

Within these courtly circles, Piero was grandiosely described as a figure who enjoyed as much power in Florence as the pope did in Rome, for the Florentines (Pucci told the cardinal of Alessandria) "had a God in the sky and a lord on the earth, who was the magnificent Piero, who could dispose of that city of Florence as our lord [Pope] could the miter, and more."[45] Within Florence, however, Piero was unable to control his own family and friends, let alone the city, as my second vignette will demonstrate. As Florentine ambassador in Faenza, messer Puccio had passed on to Piero in May 1493 a report about divisions within the ruling elite in Florence, on one side Bernardo Rucellai and Pagolantonio Soderini, on the other Bernardo Del Nero, Niccolò Ridolfi, and Pierfilippo Pandolfini, with some young men forming a third group, and dissension "even within your own Medici family."[46] The dissension with his own family referred not only to Piero's earlier quarrel with his brother, Cardinal Giovanni, over their respective spheres of influence—benefices being Giovanni's sphere and temporal matters Piero's, as Giovanni told his brother Piero in August 1492[47]—but to his much more serious quarrel with his cousins, Lorenzo and Giovanni di Pierfrancesco. In 1493, the cousins accepted high offices from the king of France and became involved in incipient plans for revolution in Florence.[48]

Messer Puccio's letter to Piero from Rome a year later was much more disturbing. It revealed that Francesco Soderini, bishop of Volterra, was so ambitious for a cardinalate that he was seeking it through these cousins and Cosimo Rucellai, despite all the favor he had received from Lorenzo.[49] When visited by Soderini in Rome in June 1494, messer Puccio told him, Piero was so angered by this that— unless Soderini did penance by leaving the papal court and abandoning his intrigues there at once—Piero threatened to "wage open war and publish you as his enemy and treat you as an enemy everywhere." Describing him to Piero in his

44 Lorenzo Pucci to Giannozzo Pucci, 7 January 1494, ASF, CS 1, 340, fol. 124r; see Lorenzo Pucci to Giannozzo Pucci, 24 December 1493, ASF, CS 1, 340, fol. 98v: "queste cose di Virginio et de Magnifico Piero [...] non sono però molto chiare." Orsino Orsini was the baby Laura's putative father.

45 Lorenzo Pucci to Giannozzo Pucci, 26 December 1493, ASF, CS 1, 340, fol. 95r–v: "noi avavamo [...] uno Idio in cielo e uno signore in terra che era il magnifico Piero, il quale poteva così disporre di quella città di Firenze come potessi nostro signore della mitra e più." See Lorenzo Pucci to Giannozzo Pucci, 7 January 1494, 8 February 1494, ASF, CS 1, 340, fols. 117r, 147r.

46 Puccio Pucci to Piero, 25 May 1493, ASF, MAP 54, 168; Rubinstein 1997, 266 n. 2.

47 Picotti 1928, 627–628 (21 August 1492); see Brown 2011c, 119.

48 Brown 2011c, 119–126. In April 1494, they were imprisoned and later exiled to their country estate before leaving to join the French king on his progress into Italy in mid-October 1494. See also the following note.

49 Zanobi Acciaiuoli's detailed confession in ASF, CS Append. 3, fols. 185r–190v, confirms messer Puccio's letter, in describing the co-involvement of the cousins and Cosimo Rucellai in the plan to make Soderini a cardinal, which replaced an earlier scheme to marry Lorenzo di Pierfrancesco's son to a daughter of Pope Alexander VI and make his brother Giovanni a cardinal, now seen as "cosa difficile, essendo egli secolare" (ASF, CS Append. 3, fols. 185r, 186r).

letter as "a man of spirit and intelligence who knows how to simulate and dissimu-late whatever he wants, and for a cardinalate he'd go to Christ, not just to you," Puccio continued that, despite liking Soderini well enough personally (Soderini was a potential source of patronage for the Pucci in Rome, since his niece was mar-ried to Puccio's brother Roberto), he had nevertheless told him that what was "most deadly" was not his admitted desire for "honors and status" (*dignità et grado*), which Piero and his father had supported, but his attempt to acquire them through the favor of men who opposed not only the regime, but Piero in person and the republic of Florence: "'You shouldn't have sought the cardinal's hat through Lorenzo and Giovanni di Pierfrancesco and through Cosimo Rucellai.' He was silent."[50]

The letter speaks for itself of the internal rivalries that contributed to Piero's downfall. In the mid-fifteenth century, Francesco's uncle Niccolò Soderini had formed part of an opposition group in Florence (with links to the philo-Ghibelline Bracceschi) that "planned to overturn Cosimo de' Medici's regime."[51] Although Niccolò's brother Tommaso had agreed to support the young Lorenzo as the city's unofficial head after Piero di Cosimo's death in 1469, the family remained the Medici's chief rivals, especially after the young Giovanni de' Medici had pro-cured a cardinalate in 1489, fourteen years before Francesco Soderini's eventual success. Thwarted by Piero's opposition, it was not until 1503 that Francesco finally achieved his ambition, a year after his brother Piero Soderini had been appointed Florence's first life gonfalonier.[52] So perhaps it was not surprising that the Soderini regarded Piero as a "tyrant" and wanted to elevate Lorenzo di Pierfrancesco in his place—in order "to have an idol more to their taste," as Gianvettorio Soderini wrote in his diary some years later.[53] As Sergio Bertelli has argued, the Soderini were more ambitious rivals for power and honor than some have been led to believe.[54]

These rivalries made Piero's inheritance in Florence difficult for the reasons that Parenti described.[55] His ambivalent legacy made Piero as inconsistent as his father, on one hand proud and assertive ("proud and bestial, fierce and cruel" is how Guicciardini described him) and on the other negligent and careless, as a twenty-two-year-old more intent on bodybuilding, jousting, playing football in the streets, and bird-catching than on engaging in politics—in November 1493, he even

50 Puccio Pucci to Piero, 13 June 1494, ASF Sig. X. VIII 65, fols. 40v–42r: "la vuole fa con voi *aperto marte* et publicarvi per suo inimico, et come inimico tractarvi in omni loco [41r] [. . .] È huomo di spirito, d'ingegno, che sa simulare et dissimulare ciò che vuole, et per venire al cappello, la farebbe Cristo, non che ad voi [41v] [. . .] questo era portato mortalissimo. 'Non dovevate', dix'io, 'cerchare el cappello per mezo di Lorenzo e Giovanni di Piero Francesco et di Cosimo Rucellay.' Obmutuit [42r]." On Roberto Pucci's marriage to Margherita di Tommaso Soderini, see Rubin 2007, 238–240.

51 Ferente 2005, 632 n. 23, 646–647; 2013, 102–103.

52 Brown 2011c, 27 and n. 74; Pesman Cooper 2002, 101; Eubel 1901, 26 (31 May 1503).

53 Bertelli 1987, 584 (see 1980, 476 n. 54): "insino al tempo del tyranno [1492–94]," "per havere idolo più a loro modo."

54 Bertelli 1980, especially 481–494.

55 See note 29 above.

enclosed a long stretch of public space along the walls for jousting, "an unheard-of thing for a private citizen to do," according to Parenti.[56] Yet he had made a good impression immediately after his father's death, not wanting to influence elections and cutting down on unnecessary expenditure, such as his Barbary horses and his falcons.[57] He was initially careful to consult with "our leading members of the government," "my elders and fathers," as he called them, and in February 1494, when the French invasion seemed inevitable, he had long and detailed discussions with these men to weigh up the pros and cons of possible actions.[58] He was also careful to distinguish his private from his public commitments to Virginio Orsini;[59] and in May 1494, when Alfonso of Naples attempted to bolster Piero's status after his cousins' threatened coup by offering him an estate in his kingdom, Piero was equally careful to stress his private status. Declining the gift, he replied to the king (through Dionigi Pucci) that, if the former wanted to favor him, he should do so in the normal way, through the personnel of his bank in Naples, for, as the king was well aware,

> my ancestors have always lived as citizens (*civilmente*) from their commerce and possessions, nor have they ever sought any but a private status. I don't intend to lapse from their way of life, any more than his royal majesty would want me to lapse from my hereditary devotion to his majesty.[60]

Similarly, he justified his apparent clemency toward his cousins at this time as behavior "befitting our civic lifestyle," which he also followed in adopting his father's republican etiquette when escorting them out of Florence by putting Lorenzo (the elder) in the middle and Giovanni to his right.[61] And although Piero was warned by the pope, as well as by Alfonso, to protect himself and not "go round at night in search of pleasure," since his nocturnal sorties had already been targeted by would-be assailants, their warnings had little effect.[62] On the eve of the revolution, Piero

56 Parenti 1994–2005, 1:55 ("alla gagliardia del corpo voltosi"), 61–62 (see Najemy 2006a, 45); Martelli 1978, 187; Guicciardini 1931, 94–95.

57 Parenti 1994–2005, 1:28–29.

58 For example, Piero to Dionigi Pucci, Naples, 6 May 1493, ASF, MAP 138, 260, fol. 255r; Piero to Dionigi Pucci, Naples, 13 February 1494, ASF, MAP 138, 274, fol. 269r; Piero to Dionigi Pucci, Naples, 16 February 1494, ASF, MAP 138, 253, fol. 248r.

59 Dionigi Pucci to Piero, 1 August 1493, ASF, MAP 49, 310; Dionigi Pucci to Piero, 14 August 1493, ASF, MAP 49, 326, fols. 537v–538r; Dionigi Pucci to Piero, 30 August 1493, ASF, MAP 49, 333, fol. 554v.

60 Dionigi Pucci to Piero, 6 May 1494, Capponi 1842, 346–347; see Pieraccini 1924–25, 1:166.

61 Piero to Dionigi Pucci, Naples, 11 May 1494, ASF, MAP 138, 278, fol. 273bis^r: "secondo el stilo et vivere nostro civile"; Martelli 1978, 192, citing Poliziano's letter of 20 May 1494: "a dextra Ioannes, a sinistra Petrus, recepto in medium Laurentio" (see Cambi 1785 in note 20 above); on conflicting accounts of events, see Brown 2011c, 122–124.

62 See the letters from Antonio da Colle to Piero, Rome, 3 May 1494, ASF, MAP 55, 177, fol. 293v; Puccio Pucci to Piero, Rome, 13, 16 June 1494, ASF, Sig.X.VIII, 65, fols. 35r, 42v; Pierfilippo Pandolfini to Piero, Naples, 20–21 April [1493], ASF, Sig.X.VIII, 65, fol. 10v; Filippo Valori to

apparently left his chamber open day and night, when there were unknown for-eigners and none of his own men about. What he needed to protect himself against attack—according to his old family friend and general of the Servites, Antonio Alabanti—was five hundred trusted soldiers, who would defend him from traitors such as the men who had assaulted his grandfather and father, and assassinated his uncle and rulers such as Galeazzo Maria Sforza, Girolamo Riario, and Galeotto Manfredi. Although Alabanti clearly ranked the Medici among Italy's lords, his unheeded advice shows how far Piero still was from adopting their military lifestyle and—as Guicciardini would point out—their "blood and violence."[63]

Piero's republicanism must be treated as cautiously as the princely rhetoric of his friends, but it was vigorous enough to influence and constrain him and his family in the ways I described initially in this chapter. The tension between the Medici's princely and civic roles created a precarious balance when the day of reck-oning came. Their standing in Italy was counterbalanced on the debit sheet by the restless ambition of their rivals and by a republican populace at home, where their fluctuating success as brokers or *mezzadri* held an uneasy equilibrium of power. For the elite was prepared to revere the Medici as idols only as long as the Medici furthered the elite's ambitions to prosper in business, to marry up, and to attain the cardinalate in a process of mutual interchange. As Lorenzo Pucci put it so well, the marriage scheme would benefit the Pucci as well as the Medici, for if it turned out well for the Medici, "it would also turn out well for us, and the magnificent Piero would have to do us some good."[64] When Piero was unwilling to promote Francesco Soderini's cardinalate, however, he became a fallen idol and the Soderini transferred their allegiance to Piero's cousins, who returned to Florence victors after the 1494 revolution.

I suggested initially that Piero's two years in power are interesting as years of transition between the old, normative definition of rulership according to typolo-gies of good and bad government and the flexible pragmatism of the new neutral, "transgressive" political ethos. Although the restoration of republican government during the Savonarolan years (from late 1494 to 1498) might suggest that Piero's incompetence, or "tyranny" as his critics called it, encouraged a return to old val-ues rather than a progression to lordship or to the princely rule that was eventually imposed by force, we can define their status better by the gap that needed filling after their fall. For Savonarola, this meant replacing a private head of state with "a public head," and although his suggestion of "Christ for your king" was less than

Piero, Naples, 16 October 1494, Canestrini and Desjardins 1859–86, 1:466; Lorenzo Spinelli to Piero, Chambéry, 26 August 1494, Buser 1879, 552–553.

63 Antonio Alabanti to Piero, 22 October 1494, Brown 2011c, 84–85; Guicciardini 1932, 25; 1994b, 24 (see 169–170, *ricordo* 21).

64 Lorenzo Pucci to Giannozzo Pucci, 11 January 1494, ASF, CS 1, 340, fol. 135v: "havendo questa cosa a resultare bene a luy e la casa loro non dubitava resultassi ancora a noi et che la magnificenzia di Piero ce havessi a fare qualche bene."

possible, it conveyed the quality of *maestà* (majesty) that the Medici had enjoyed as idols, protected now by the Roman law of *lèse-majesté*.[65] The Medici's role as arbiters or *mezzadri* was also acknowledged by the creation in 1502 of a life gonfalonier as "head of justice" (*capo di giustizia*), whose "preeminence and authority" would enable him to intervene in all criminal decisions.[66] The dual roles played by the Medici, as idols and as masters of the workshop, subsequently contributed to the *maestà* of Machiavelli's and Guicciardini's model heads of state, for Machiavelli, the Medici during their lifetimes and then an inner elite of sixty-four citizens, for Guicciardini, a "superhead" (*sopracapo*) inspiring fear and reverence through his majesty and oracular status: he was not to be "a lord who rules," but, as a fixture, someone who would devote the thought and care to the city's affairs that bosses give to their own business. Together, these qualities created the aura of sovereignty, or Hobbesian "reputation of power," that offered de facto justification of Medici authority before their status as dukes and grand dukes made it less necessary.[67] Non-normative and flexible enough to cover a wide range of functions and roles, they describe the Medici's position in Florence better than the formal titles on offer at the time.

65 Brown 1992c, 265–268.
66 Cadoni and Di Sciullo 1994–2000, 2:238.
67 Machiavelli 2001b, 634 (*Discursus florentinarum rerum post mortem iunioris Laurentii Medices*): "essersi renduto la maestà e la reputazione al capo dello stato". Guicciardini 1931, 178: "uno sopracapo chi e' temino o riverischino"; 1932, 104, 109; 1994b, 101, 106.

PART II
Economic Policy

NINE

Medici Economic Policy

FRANCO FRANCESCHI

T HE PRACTICE OF WHAT WAS classically known as political economy and is now called economic policy has been a topic that long remained at the margins of twentieth- and twenty-first-century research on fourteenth- and fifteenth-century Florentine history. Greater interest was shown in economic history as such. The picture started to change only with the wave of research in the 1980s on the formation of a "regional" economy in Tuscany; on the relationships between different institutions and authorities in the management of the Florentine industrial sector; and on the key role of the state in the "crisis" of the late Middle Ages.[1]

Few aspects of the exercise of sovereignty tell more about the nature of the central power than the capacity to steer economic policy. But the field of Medici economic policy is vast, and a preliminary survey of the situation before Cosimo and the Medici family came to power is indispensable, so I shall limit the focus to a few key areas: the development of the regional economy, the incentives provided to international trade, the support given to manufacturing, and the stimulus imparted to innovation. In conclusion, I shall try to assess the Medici administration's overall economic policy and to attempt a few comparisons.

1   For an overview of these trends in Florentine historiography, and more generally in the history of the Renaissance Italian states, see Franceschi and Molà 2012.

The Development of the Regional Economy:
Roads, Customs and Excise, Markets

Before the age of rapid territorial expansion, Florentine commercial policy had three main objectives: to ensure the continued flow of foodstuffs into the city itself, to promote trade in a city that based its prosperity on cloth manufacture and mercantile activity, and to increase tax revenue. In concrete terms, this meant making the road system more efficient; establishing the number and function of marketplaces; setting customs duties in such a way as to encourage the flow of provisions and raw materials into Florence and to discourage their export; attempting to standardize the city's weights and measures across the *contado*; and being ready, in times of dearth, to intervene directly in the collection and distribution of agricultural produce. The same objectives guided policy toward other regional communities with whom it sought to make pacts that reciprocally lowered or abolished tariffs. Florence negotiated with Pisa, Lucca, and Siena in particular for access to the ports on the Tyrrhenian Sea, which the latter three cities controlled.[2]

The submission of Arezzo (1384), Pisa (1406), and Cortona (1414) was followed by the acquisition (fundamental for securing Florence's supply of grain and raw materials used in the textile industry) of Livorno and Porto Pisano (1421). A new, enhanced territorial entity had come into being, requiring an up-to-date economic policy to match its dimensions and characteristics.[3] This change was primarily made possible thanks to the increased role played by small decision-making bodies at the heart of city government such as the *balìe* (ad hoc assemblies with full or limited powers), the *signoria* with the colleges, the provisors of gabelles, and the *monte* (publicly funded debt) officials. New offices came into being too, such as the sea consuls created when the republic took full responsibility for the Pisa-Livorno ports. From the start, those elected to this board included not only men of proven business experience, but also figures prominent in politics, members of the Albizzi regime such as Niccolò da Uzzano and Schiatta Ridolfi.[4] It was the sea consuls who guided the ambitious project to equip the republic with its own fleet modeled on the *mude* of Venice, but they also took a leading role in the exploitation of internal resources: in 1422, they were asked to seek measures to boost industrial activity throughout Florentine territory. This twofold aspect of the responsibilities of the sea consuls was highlighted when, on 22 June 1423, the magistracy was split into a branch operating in Florence and another in Pisa,[5] where the ships were actually built. The branch in Florence had the task of setting out administrative guidelines for the galley system (regulations, route planning, the tender process, appointment

2 See Franceschi 1993a, 865–876; Epstein 1996, 880–881; De La Roncière 2005, pts. 2–3; Goldthwaite 2009, 489.
3 Epstein 1996, 882; Tognetti 2010b, 163–165.
4 Mallett 1967, 23.
5 ASF, PR 113, fol. 51r.

of captains and shipowners), and was subsequently allotted jurisdiction over legal disputes connected with shipping and given the prerogative of appointing ambassadors and representatives of Florentine communities abroad. The branch in Pisa oversaw the fleet's construction, exercised a degree of supervision over customs, and coordinated and controlled direct and indirect taxes applicable to Pisa and its former *contado*. Hence they held authority over commerce in general and over the issuing of licenses to export grain in particular.[6]

A main aspect of public intervention regarding infrastructure was care of the road network—always essential to the Florentine transport system. The principal agents here were the tower officials, a magistracy to which the central government had entrusted primary responsibility for public works since the fourteenth century (as well as for public property and some duties and tolls).[7] The activity of this agency, which despite various vicissitudes remained in existence until the middle of the sixteenth century, extended both to the narrower *contado* of Florence and the wider *distretto* (the newly conquered cities and territories). It supervised the construction, repair, and maintenance of roads and bridges.[8] Assisted by the *viai*—functionaries tasked with inspecting the road network and drawing attention to urgent problems—and in constant contact with the territorial judicial rectors, the tower officials showed themselves keenly aware of which itineraries were most strategic for Florentine interests: the "road leading from Florence to Siena, Rome, and other parts of the world";[9] the "master road that goes to Pistoia and then to Lombardy and Genoa,"[10] perhaps the route best equipped, with its numerous bridges and overpasses;[11] but above all the road to Pisa, defined in one law as "the main roadway" of the city,[12] usable by wagons since the early trecento.[13] Those in charge knew full well how traffic would suffer from any blockage and how urgent it was therefore for them to be cleared expeditiously. Thus, in September 1445, the tower officials expressed concern at the state of the bridge over the river Elsa on the road to Pisa: one of the pilasters had collapsed, creating danger especially in wintertime "for our merchants and travelers and their merchandise, to the shame of our commune and

---

6   See Mallett 1959, 160–162; Fasano Guarini 1976, 20–22; Ciccaglioni 2009.

7   Guidi 1981, 2:286–291.

8   See Pansini 1989, 11–12.

9   "[la] strada per la quale si va da Firenze a Siena e a Roma e ad altre parti del mondo": ASF, CPG, numeri rossi 105, fol. 66r (a. 1415). (This register, known as the Libro della Luna, contains legislation relating to the tower officials from 1349 onward.)

10 "[la] strada maestra che va a Pistoia et in Lombardia e a Genova": ASF, CPG, numeri rossi 106, fol. 158v. (This volume is an eighteenth-century copy, in a better state of preservation, than the Libro della Luna cited in the previous note.)

11 De La Roncière 1976, 3:902.

12 "la strada principale": ASF, CPG, numeri rossi 105, fol. 79v (a. 1445).

13 De La Roncière 1976, 3:851.

their [i.e., merchants' and travelers'] great detriment."[14] To deal with this emergency, the tower officials appointed an ad hoc committee on which sat such important figures as Luca di Maso degli Albizzi, Neri di Gino Capponi, and Alamanno di Jacopo Salviati.[15] The officials subsequently decided to entrust the repair work to maestro Domenico di Matteo da Firenze, who in turn would execute "according to plan" the design for a new bridge drawn up by the young Antonio Manetti.[16]

And yet, despite their best efforts, the myriad instances of damage brought to their attention bear witness to a losing battle against the degradation of the road system. A law of 1454 stated that the main roads of the *contado* were "in a state of ruin" (*destructe*) and their condition posed a threat to foreign merchants and Florentine guildsmen.[17] The root of the problem was probably structural, inherent in the limited powers of the magistracy and its functionaries, but neither were the environmental and social contexts favorable. The central government repeatedly showed its dissatisfaction with the performance of the *viai*, who were unable to halt the degradation of the road network, dilatory in drawing attention to communities that had failed to perform their road maintenance duties, and often susceptible to bribery from local administrations and property owners with road frontage: between 1445 and 1464, the office was twice abolished and twice reactivated.[18]

The main problem, however, was obtaining full cooperation from the localities responsible for road maintenance and for taking remedial action. The tower officials were charged with redistributing this burden more equitably, and adapting to the profound changes that were occurring across Florentine territory owing to the demographic upheaval that had commenced a century before[19]—a task rendered more difficult than anticipated by the resistance encountered from residents of the *contado* (*comitatini*) and of the district (*districtuales*). Only in the summer of 1461 did the project take concrete form with the specification of seventy "main roads" (*vie maestre*) and a denser network of "public roads" (*vie pubbliche*) to facilitate local travel. Every stretch of road, with an indication of its "length and boundaries" (*quantità di braccia e confini*), was assigned to one of the "parishes, communes, villages, men, and inhabitants" (*popoli, comuni, ville, huomini e persone*) constituting the Florentine dominion, along with responsibility for its ongoing maintenance.[20]

But local authorities were not simply shirking. In some areas of the dominion, they had to contend with scarce resources and challenging environmental problems. Such—so the tower officials conceded in 1455—was the situation in Pisa,

14 "a nostri mercatanti et viandanti et alle loro mercatantie, in vergogna del nostro comune et danno grandissimo d'essi": ASF, CPG, numeri rossi 105, fol. 79v.
15 ASF, CPG, numeri rossi 105, fols. 79v–80r.
16 ASF, CPG, numeri rossi 105, fol. 80v.
17 ASF, PR 145, fol. 288r.
18 See Pansini 1989, 10–11.
19 ASF, PR 145, fol. 288r–v.
20 Pansini 1989, 10–11; Rombai 1987, 9–10.

where water management difficulties were hindering not only agriculture but viability, "with the result that all roads are in a state of ruin." Meanwhile "numerous communes and parishes" were trying to evade their obligations by alleging "exemptions and privileges."[21] In this case, the institutional response was to entrust the work of repairing roads and dykes and of clearing ditches to a Pisan *viaio*, Lorenzo di Giovanni de' Sardi, under the supervision of the sea consuls. The latter received wider authority in 1457, while in 1463 the canal officials became involved in the effort to rehabilitate land in the Pisan *contado*.[22] All the immunities, special favors, and penalty discounts for communities that failed to meet their obligations were abolished by decree—all of which, however, might not have had much concrete effect. In fact, as shown by the Medici correspondence, residents of the subjects' centers sought and often obtained through the direct intervention of Lorenzo the Magnificent changes to or cancellations of decisions made by the tower officials. In 1478, for example, the inhabitants of Terranuova sent ambassadors to Lorenzo to complain, "because our commune had been harassed by the tower officials for certain transgressions contrary to their orders, committed by mistake." These envoys obtained satisfaction, which the inhabitants acknowledged by naming Lorenzo as "father and protector" (*padre et protectore*) of their community.[23]

Related to roads were *passi*, the stations where duties on the transit of goods were collected. Aiming to extend to the district as a whole the relationship already established with the communities of the *contado*, the Florentine government stripped the subject towns, except for Pistoia, of the prerogative of setting commercial tolls and excises independently. This new authority was occasionally used to reduce or even abolish the tariff barriers between Florence and its bordering communities, mainly to the advantage of the former. But central government had no vision of a genuinely uniform system: various customs regimes continued to exist throughout Florentine dominions, possessed of their own bureaucracies and distinctive

21 ASF, CPG, numeri rossi 105, fol. 102r: "Per parte degli ufficiali della torre e di beni de' ribegli del comune di Firenze si dice chome a lloro notitia è venuto che per le guerre che ssono state per lo passato la città e chontado di Pisa è in grande disordine per chagione che i fiumi e aqueducti del detto chontado non vanno pe' letti loro, perché le fosse sono spianate et guaste et non sono state rimesse et annieghano tucto el paese, et tucte le semente vi si fanno si perdono; e però cavalchano le strade e stannovi su tucta la vernata in modo sono tucte guaste et ongni chosa si perde [...] Et voluto intendere il modo del provedere dice che molti chomuni et popoli si schusano alleghando loro exenzioni e brivilegi e non intendono chonchorrere a tali aconccimi chome sono usati, e gli altri non vogliono fare la parte loro e chosì rimanghono le chose di più necessità indrieto."

22 Mallett 1968, 430. In the latter half of the quattrocento, the government devoted increasing efforts to keeping the Pisan countryside from turning into a swamp by reviving the traditional system for maintaining the banks, ditches, streams, and bridges, and limiting the pasturing of animals (especially water buffalo) on the vast tracts of uncultivated land, in order to benefit agriculture (see Petralia 1996, 962–966).

23 "per cagione di certa molestia data al nostro comune dall'ufficio della torre, per certa trasgressione facta ignorantemente contro a' lloro ordini": Salvadori 2000a, 82–83.

regulations and giving rise to myriad particular liberties and local exemptions.[24] Paradoxically, the never-ending struggle against the evasion of customs duties militated against simplification: in order to escape payment, merchants and carriers sought byways in place of roads with customs stations, forcing the authorities to close these alternative routes (as within the territory of Arezzo in 1451) or else to multiply the number of guards and customs officers (*passeggeri*).[25]

Progress did come with the creation in 1448 of the *dogana dei traffichi*, which was meant to facilitate the collection of commercial duties and impede the movement of contraband. The procedure was straightforward: goods subject to gate tolls were deposited in a customhouse for the customs officers to register their entry, their itemized contents, and their exit, recording the proprietor's name and his agents. These data were checked against those detailed on the waybill (*bullecta*) issued by the first Florentine official encountered in the course of the journey. Once the duties owed to the treasurer (*camarlingo*) of the customhouse in Florence, Pisa, or Arezzo had been paid, the goods could be sold at the local market or continue their journey, always accompanied by the waybill, which was surrended only to the final customs officer whom the merchant or transporter encountered.[26]

A yet more radical scheme was the so-called *legge dei passeggeri* (law regarding customs officers), passed in 1461 to deal with functionaries who failed "to do their duty," and businessmen "who schemed to carry and dispatch their goods and merchandise by little-used passes, roads, and places, so as to elude customs officers and appointed customs stations."[27] Closely linked to the redistribution of the burden for road maintenance, this disposition rationalized the geography of the toll stations, funneling all commercial traffic and livestock into selected routes, especially those that, like spokes of a wheel, connected the towns of Tuscany to Florence. Whatever its genuine capacity for reducing fraud, the law did reinforce the central role of Florence in the dominion-wide system of distribution, and at the same time facilitated commercial taxation. Moreover, by limiting the number of roads carrying heavy traffic, it had the effect of concentrating repair work on the principal arteries.[28] This was not an insignificant outcome, given the wretched state, as has been seen, of much of the dominion's road network.

The location of the toll collectors was gradually adjusted, particularly in 1465 and 1474. In 1490, the question of customs, ports, and gabelles in all the Florentine dominions was again on the agenda of the seventeen reformers—a special committee, including Lorenzo the Magnificent himself, with wide powers over economic

24 See Epstein 1996, 882–883; Fasano Guarini 1976, 16–17.
25 Dini 1984, 23.
26 Dini 1986, 289–290.
27 "che portano et mandano le loro robbe et mercantie per gli passi, vie et luoghi inusitate et per fuggire i passegieri et passi deputate": Benigni, Carbone, and Saviotti 1985, 24.
28 See Epstein 2000b, 94, 116–117; Dini 1986, 290–292.

policy.[29] However, despite their intention to correct the most patent discrepancies in the system, these officials appear to have introduced no significant reforms. There were still numerous internal *passi*, including nine in the lower Valdarno between Florence and Pisa, or three concentrated in a short stretch of the upper Valdarno (Montevarchi, Terranuova, Levane). At the same time, the number of stations in border areas such as the Pisan Maremma, the territories between Pisa and Lucca, the Valdinievole, and the Pistoia mountains were decidedly inadequate. Such lack of uniformity was not the simple result of organizational dysfunction. While the multiplication of customs points was paradoxically due to closer controls, or to the need for greater tax revenue, often the small number, or complete absence, of such barriers in a given area is explained by the existence of more or less extensive exemptions from customs duties enjoyed by local communities, usually until the moment they had come under Florentine rule. Thus the scarcity of *passi* along the roads of the Lucchesia and the western Apennines is a facet of the privileged regime from which Pistoia, San Miniato, and the Valdinievole had benefited ever since the mid-fourteenth century.[30] Nor should one overlook the numerous privileges, some never meant to be permanent, enjoyed by a particular type (or a whole category) of merchandise. Such privileges continued to be a feature of the excise system, and indeed of the whole complex of indirect taxes. Examples would include the abolition in 1453 of duty on the transit of wine and vinegar destined for consumption in Pisa,[31] or the cancellation in 1458, under pressure from local authorities, of the duty on wool, which producers in Sansepolcro brought to Anghiari for spinning, as well as on bolts of woolen cloth acquired at Sansepolcro by the residents of Anghiari.[32]

The picture changes little when turning to Florentine policy with respect to fairs and markets. According to Stephan Epstein's data, between 1350 and 1550 no fewer than thirty-eight seasonal fairs were founded or revived: at fifteen of these, debtors who attended were granted immunity from arrest, and at seventeen, a total exemption from duty on goods traded was conceded. Over the same period, at least thirty-four new weekly markets were established, twelve with immunity for debtors and another twelve with exemption from customs duties. Most of these new markets were established in the Medici period, in particular from the 1430s to the 1480s. Their territorial distribution suggests that a main goal of the Florentine authorities was to create a series of trading sites along the borders, particularly with Siena, Umbria, and the Marche, so as to stimulate the importation of agricultural produce and livestock. Another interesting facet is that, in general, Florence was not averse

29 This committee, comprising the *monte* officials and twelve additional citizens, operated for two brief spells: from 4 August 1481 to 24 July 1482, and from 15 July 1490 (with extensions) until 31 July 1491 (Brown 1992b, 155–159).
30 Epstein 1996, 882–883; 2000b, 94–96.
31 ASF, Dogana di Pisa 4, tomo I, fol. 121r.
32 ASF, DF, Dogana antica e campioni 373, fol. 240r. See also Scharf 2003, 111–112.

to requests from minor centers or those lacking political clout to establish fairs and markets of their own—requests that were opposed by the towns to which they had once been subject. Such an attitude is confirmed by the fact that the attempt in 1446 by some communities of the former Pistoiese *contado* to obtain new markets, in defiance of Pistoia's ban, was supported by Florentine lawyers. [33]

But even here it would be a mistake to attribute too much coherence to Florentine economic policy. The former *contadi* of Pistoia, Pisa, Arezzo, and Volterra had few fairs able to compete with the urban fairs, and rural fairs were concentrated for the most part in communities that, thanks to long-standing privileges, were exempt from urban jurisdiction: such facts testify to cities' capacity to protect their own commercial interests by influencing the decisions of central government. In the end, negotiation, not diktat from the center, prevailed, comforted by the very mechanisms that regulated the creation or cancellation of fairs and markets. Florentine authorities might have had the last word on creating new points of exchange, and on granting (or revoking) corresponding customs and judicial relief, but the bureaucratic process was generally set in motion by the community in question, [34] which tended to mobilize political will at various levels: with Florentine territorial rectors, implored to speak up for local interests (for example, the vicar of Lari was urged in 1472 to seek reinstatement of a recently suppressed fair), [35] and with influential Florentines, including the Medici. First Luca Pitti and then Piero de' Medici, gonfalonier of justice in January and February 1461, undertook a *démarche*, initiated by the Aretines, to gain a permanent, duty-free annual fair, [36] while in 1473, Lorenzo the Magnificent backed a petition from Cortona's priors "for the duty-free status of our fair, which has so often been improperly subverted." [37]

Reviving Exchange

Following the acquisition of Livorno and Porto Pisano and the creation of the sea consuls, the Albizzi regime became convinced that setting the city free of dependence on foreign merchant navies would stimulate an economy described as stagnant at the start of the 1420s. And so, with strong backing from the merchant-entrepreneurs of Florence, the government devoted itself enthusiastically to fitting out a commercial fleet. [38] Rapidly constructed in the shipyards of Pisa, the galleys first plowed the waves in 1422, and within a few years had established four strategically important shipping routes. One led to Aragonese ports in Sicily and Catalonia. Another went to Flanders and England, with stops along the Andalusian and Portuguese coasts; the main purpose here was to furnish the Florentine textile

33 Epstein 2000a, 153–154.
34 See Epstein 2000b, 106.
35 Salvadori 2000a, 88.
36 Black 1993, 24. For further details, see Franceschi 2012, 247.
37 "per la franchigia della nostra fiera, la quale tante volte ci è stata rotta a torto": Salvadori 2000a, 88.
38 See Brucker 1977, 426–432.

industry with wool, silk, and dyestuffs, the secondary aim being to supply the Pisan tanning industry with hides. Florentine wool and silk cloth was exported to the Levant along the third route, with silk, cotton, alum, and coloring agents loaded for the return journey, not to mention, of course, spices. The latter were for the most part unloaded in southern Italian ports, and foodstuffs brought onboard for the last lap of the journey. The fourth main destination was "Barbary"—Tunis and Tripoli, with intermediate stops in Sicily—where the goods loaded included hides and once again foodstuffs.[39] In assuming the huge cost of launching a state-run merchant navy, was the Albizzi regime's goal "to compete with other maritime powers— Genoa, Venice, the kingdom of Aragon, Naples—for Mediterranean trade"?[40] Probably not. Their priority was to enhance the commercial network connected with Florentine industrial production.[41] But there is no doubt that becoming a player, if not a leading competitor, in the arena of long-distance trade transformed Florence. Florentine businessmen entered the spice trade, expanded their footing in the North African ports, and from their bases in the western Mediterranean and the North Sea established more rapid and reliable links back to their home city.[42] By demonstrating a capacity to manage regular transport and communication linkages over long distances, Florence inevitably laid down a marker to the Mediterranean powers of its autonomy and political clout.[43]

Seaborne trade remained a central feature of Medicean public policy, although not without ups and downs. The communal galley fleet thrived between 1436 and 1447, but suffered from the outbreak of the Aragonese wars in the kingdom of Naples, leading to a reduced number of voyages because of the increased risk. The peace of Lodi in 1454 and Cosimo de' Medici's consolidation of power in 1458 heralded a period of further expansion.[44] Along with significant institutional changes that year, a report "on maritime trade" (*sopra li fatti del navichare*) was commissioned, ostensibly because such a review was overdue. At the same time, leading figures in the Medici regime began to participate in the management of galley contracts.[45] Sharing common interests in the maritime trade, they drove the decision to shift responsibility for a relaunch of public shipping from the Pisan branch of the sea consuls to the five governors and conservators of the city, *contado*, and district of Pisa. This new magistracy remained in office for three years and included among its members important figures such as Tommaso Soderini and the

---

39 Tognetti 2010b, 163–164.
40 As stated by Brucker 1977, 430.
41 This view is stressed in Ciccaglioni 2009, 102, according to whom the traditional equation between industrial prosperity and collective well-being continued to be the dominant ideology, overshadowing "the idea that the wealth of the city might be capable of further growth if the republic were to give its full backing to maritime trade."
42 Dini 2001, 118–119.
43 Tognetti 2010b, 167.
44 See Mallett 1967, 144.
45 Ciccaglioni 2009, 115.

merchant-statesmen Bartolomeo Lenzi and Francesco Neroni.[46] Even the Guelf party, over which the regime was asserting ever stricter control, was temporarily drawn into maritime affairs: a law of 1461, initiated by the newly formed council of 100 (the institutional vehicle for enhanced Medicean predominance),[47] required those who had obtained safe-conducts and privileges necessary to sail to foreign countries, either for themselves or as representatives of the commune, to deposit the originals for safekeeping with the captains of the Guelf party.[48]

Over the coming years, which saw the sea consuls restored to their former role, the regime passed a series of measures intended to improve the service on offer and to encourage the merchant class to use public shipping: regulations were revised, hiring rates were made more attractive, subsidies were offered to shipowners, and crews were selected with greater care.[49] In addition, an effort was made to boost trade with Levantine ports and regions, an area where the position of the Genoese and the Venetians had been weakened by the fall of Constantinople to the Ottomans, creating room thereby for the Florentines,[50] who, unlike the two major north Italian maritime powers, did not possess territories with coastlines threatened by the Turkish advance. Perhaps as early as 1456, but certainly starting in 1458, Florentine galleys returned to making regular stops at Constantinople, and in 1459, thanks to accords reached with the emperor of Trebizond, David II, they penetrated the Black Sea region, touching at Caffa (modern Feodosia) and Trebizond (Trabzon) itself.[51]

An initiative closely tied to relaunching the Florentine commercial fleet was the decision to canalize the stretch of the Arno between Florence and Pisa. As matters stood, in order to reach Pisa from Porto Pisano, vessels had to pass through the Pisa canal, while closer to Florence, the Arno was regularly navigable only up to the bridge at Signa, and then only by craft of limited size. The 1458 law authorizing the new canal stated that this was essential in order to encourage young men to embark on trading careers, but the project itself was undertaken with the ambitious goal of allowing "barges and other large boats, and perhaps galleys" to navigate as far as Florence itself.[52] In order to manage the project, which limped along until the late 1470s, a dedicated agency was created and specific sources of financing earmarked, but soon the canal officials were assigned tasks of higher priority, and the only place where any work was actually done was the stretch of the river lying within the urban boundaries of Florence.[53]

46   Clarke 1991, 65–66.
47   Rubinstein 1997, 128–137.
48   See Ciccaglioni 2009, 113–118.
49   Mallett 1967, 144.
50   See Hoshino 2001; Dini 2001, 121–122.
51   Mallett 1967, 58; Müller 1879, 186–189.
52   "le schafe et altre barche grosse et forse galee": ASF, Balìe 29, fols. 23v–24v; the passage cited is on fol. 23v.
53   See Rombai 1996, 866.

The intense activity of the Florentine fleet in the early 1460s was driven partly by the discovery of alum deposits in the Tolfa hills of the Papal States—a prized substance used as a mordant in dyeing textiles, whose commercial exploitation was entrusted to the Medici bank.[54] The communal galleys, on their voyages to Flanders and England, now stopped regularly at Civitavecchia to load alum from Tolfa. So did ships fitted out by private entrepreneurs, among them galleys owned by the Medici, which in 1470 alone transported three hundred tons of alum.[55] Vice versa, when relations between Pope Sixtus IV and Lorenzo the Magnificent began to deteriorate, and the pontiff's involvement in the Pazzi conspiracy of 1478 led to open warfare between Florence and the papacy, the Florentine galleys lost a key article of trade with northern Europe.[56]

This last circumstance probably played some part in the government's decision to terminate the entire system of public shipping, although there were wider and more profound causes. By the late 1470s, Florentine manufacturing, closely linked to the activity of the communal galleys, was relying less upon raw materials imported from abroad than sixty years before: wool and silk were increasingly supplied by land from Italian sources, or if they did come from abroad, were carried by ships of Castilian, Biscayan, Andalusian, or Portuguese origin sailing to the Pisa-Livorno or Adriatic ports, chiefly Ancona. The outlets for textile products had also shifted: the largest part of the precious silk cloth produced in Florentine workshops was now sent overland to Rome or Naples, and especially to France, where the fairs of Lyon had become the main marketplace for retailing Italian velvet, satin, and damask, as well as the most important clearing house for international payments.[57] In contrast, there was not the slightest decline in importance for Florentine producers selling woolen textiles of middling quality in the Ottoman empire, especially in the cities of Bursa, Adrianopolis (modern Edirne), Gallipoli, and Constantinople. This circumstance certainly played a part, along with other political and cultural factors, in the friendly attitude toward Sultan Mehmed II assumed by Lorenzo de' Medici from the start of his ascendancy, a diplomatic *démarche* that paid off handsomely when in 1483 the new sultan, Bayezid II, guaranteed Florence the export of about five thousand bolts of cloth per annum into imperial territory.[58] But the enhanced trade with the Ottoman Empire moved increasingly along routes—sometimes by both land and sea—that reached Constantinople and Adrianopolis from the Adriatic coast (via Ancona, Lecce-Valona, or Ancona-Ragusa), undercutting the maritime routes followed by communal galleys sailing from the Tyrrhenian.[59]

---

54 See Delumeau 1962, 19–25; De Roover 1963, 153–154.
55 Mallett 1967, 136–137.
56 De Roover 1963, 164; Mallett 1967, 137.
57 See Tognetti 2010b, 166–167; Dini 1995b, 198–199.
58 Tanzini 2010b, 273–275, 280; Hoshino 2001, 113–115.
59 See Dini 1995a, 259–261.

The increased availability of foreign ships in Tuscan ports at the end of the 1470s not only made it less urgent for Florence to have a fleet of its own; it is also an indicator of the wider economy: state-directed economic policy, by developing infrastructure at Porto Pisano and Livorno and along the transport network leading to Florence, had stimulated, not throttled, the flow of commercial traffic through the two ports. Here too, however, the main lines of policy had been laid down before the Medici took power—for example, the 1419 law that aimed to provide incentives for trade at Pisa through a complex system of reductions and exemptions, most prominently the complete dispensation from duty of all merchandise arriving by sea and destined for maritime reexport to distant destinations within a year. Such lowered tariffs were also applied to goods (except woolen cloth) exported to Lombardy, exported through Lombardy to any other destination, or imported from Lombardy. Goods brought in that were not intended for onward shipment but for sale at market in Pisa were subject to exit duties only, while those for export overland or for loading onto vessels headed for ports north of Rome or south of Genoa remained subject to regular gabelles both upon entry and exit.[60]

These tariff reductions were trimmed back to some extent in 1430 and 1440,[61] but thereafter they (or enhanced versions) became established economic policy. Beginning in 1441, for example, it was decided that operators using the port of Livorno for transit would enjoy "the same privileges or immunities from excise as at Pisa"—in other words, total exemption, as decided in 1419.[62] Moreover, specific concessions were granted repeatedly to mercantile communities from Germany, Lucca, and above all Catalonia.[63] In 1451, when the import duties were increased on foreign bolts of cloth entering Florentine territory, it was stipulated that the new arrangements applied neither in Pisa nor Livorno.[64] A clause favoring transit of cloth through the two ports was also inserted into measures to defend the domestic market in 1458.[65]

Even more important was the general revision of customs tariffs at Pisa and Livorno in 1475. Exit duties were abolished for imports of Lombard, Lucchese, and Bolognese merchants arriving by sea and re-exported overland within six months; tariffs were reduced on articles exported by other merchants; and above all duties payable upon entry were rationalized. To gabelles as such, in fact, were added a series of additional "tributes" variously earmarked to finance projects such as the Florentine Spedale degli Innocenti, the restoration of Empoli's walls, or the Arno

60 ASF, DF, Dogana antica e campioni 371 (a volume assembling the legislative output of various organs of central government pertaining to customs and excise), fols. 167r–168v. The same document, from a copy in the Archivio di Stato of Pisa, was published in Silva 1909, 312–314, but it figures already in Uzzano 1766, 45–46.
61 Mallett 1968, 414.
62 "quello medesimo brivilegio o immunità della ghabella che avessino a Pisa": ASF, DF, Dogana antica e campioni 371, fols. 184v–186v, at fol. 185r–v.
63 Mallett 1968, 414; Böninger 2006a, 97–103.
64 ASF, DF, Dogana antica e campioni 371, fol. 209r–v.
65 ASF, Balìe 29, fols. 18v–19v.

canal (mentioned above, 138). The result was a fiscal jungle bewildering to foreign traders: "it seems strange to merchants from abroad, because, believing they have a set amount of excise to pay, they discover they have to pay far more on these routes. They cannot precisely calculate the actual costs, and they cannot get full information from our own merchants, because, never mind them, the system is incomprehensible even to its own administrators."[66] And yet the declared goal of the provisions was to augment the movement of goods and merchants so as to extract more revenue from indirect taxation. This source was thought to be underperforming, given the potential of Pisa and its surrounding territory—a zone that, thanks to the nearby seaboard and the internal frontier with the Florentine *contado*, was meant to assume crucial importance for Florence's trading economy.[67]

The nature of the 1475 reform and similar policy initiatives reveal a fundamental limitation of Florentine economic policy with respect to Pisa: the urgent needs of the fisc outranked more farsighted plans to consolidate the economy of the city and its former *contado*. Other factors, not strictly economic, worked to hinder effective planning too. In the first half of the fifteenth century, and until the peace of Lodi (1454) at the very earliest, Florence's preoccupation with maintaining a grip on its conquest, and with crushing all opposition from Pisa's former governing class, led—in Giuseppe Petralia's words—to a policy of "unremitting suspicion," characterized by "an inevitable schizophrenic split between the stated policy of good and equitable government and the growing repression of the subject population and its leading families."[68]

Viewed in this light, even the demographic measures introduced by the Florentine government appear ambiguous: to repopulate a city and an area short of inhabitants, but at the same time to "reclaim" Pisa and much of its territory in the political sense by expelling families most closely associated with the former regime, to be replaced with immigrants from Florence and its *contado*, or from other states.[69] From 1408, all exiles from Florence could move to Pisa, while all residents of the Florentine *contado* with unpaid fines could similarly settle in Pisa or its territory. In 1410, the opportunity to live in Pisa for five years was extended to all criminals, except political rebels. In 1413, foreigners moving with their families to Pisa within a year were guaranteed a ten-year exemption from direct taxation and the cancellation of previously contracted debts and obligations, while in 1419, similar privileges were granted to such foreigners for twenty years.[70]

---

66 "a' mercatanti forestieri pare strano, perché credendo havere a pagare uno tanto di gabella, truovono avere a pagare per queste vie più assai et non possono bene fare loro conti, et da' nostri mercatanti non ne possono havere aviso interamente, perché non che loro ma i proprii ministri che sono sopra ciò vi si smarriscono drento": ASF, PR 166, fols. 108r–109r, at fol. 108r.

67 Petralia 1996, 958.

68 Petralia 1987, 316.

69 Ibid., 317; Tognetti 2010b, 161.

70 See Silva 1909, 314; Mallett 1968, 413; Petralia 1987, 317–318.

The last concessions were renewed in 1441, while between 1435 and 1448—that is, during a period of tension between Florence and the communities of Pisa's former *contado*, where spontaneous uprisings occurred during Niccolò Piccinino's military campaign against Florence—another series of laws, all employing fiscal incentives, continued the pre-Medicean policy of encouraging the transfer of inhabitants from Florence and its *contado* to Pisa and its environs, as well as the simultaneous displacement of Pisan citizens and *contadini* in the other direction. A shift in policy can be detected at the end of the 1450s, when the political-military situation improved and the Medici regime emerged stronger following the crisis of 1458. The enactments of the council of 100 and the five governors of Pisa between 1458 and 1461 assumed a more markedly demographic-economic character, and encouragement to immigration was actually accompanied by measures facilitating the return of Pisan rebels, and all who had previously left the city, through granting pardons and canceling old debts. Nevertheless, the repopulation of Pisa was still a matter of concern thirty years later when, in 1491, the seventeen reformers planned to encourage removal to Pisa and Livorno by guaranteeing to non-Pisan subjects suspension of outstanding monetary fines, and to Florentine emigrants and their families exemption from taxation for sixty years; additionally, a ten-year fiscal moratorium was granted to all new dwellers in the Pisan *contado*.[71]

Although the overall effectiveness of the above provisions remain entirely undemonstrated, the fact remains that a few entreprising Florentines did indeed move to and even prosper in Pisa, thanks in part to the lighter fiscal burden available there. These included Ridolfo di ser Gabriello, a minority partner in the Salviati bank of Pisa between 1446 and 1449, and a correspondent of the Cambini bank; Riccardo di Jacopo Riccardi, forebear of the future purchasers of the Medici palace; Francesco di Lorenzo Cambini, a functionary and merchant; and Piero Vaglienti, an apothecary and chronicler of the Pisan rebellion in 1494.[72] In another sense, this was just part of a wider and more noteworthy phenomenon: the rapid replacement of Pisa's most economically dynamic class by a thrusting group of Florentine companies, which became commercial intermediaries between the port area, the city center, and the rest of Tuscany. Accounting documents, the *accomandita* contracts registered with the *mercanzia* (commercial tribunal) of Florence, as well as the registers of several fifteenth-century Pisan notaries, all testify to the massive presence in Pisa of firms managed by leading Florentine business families (Martelli, Capponi, Salviati, Uguccioni, Quaratesi, Serristori, and Rucellai). These companies were engaged in international trade and banking, but were increasingly active as traders in the Tyrhennian Sea too. Direct control of one of the major ports in the Mediterranean, and the establishment of state-backed shipping, had enabled the Florentine mercantile elite to capitalize on opportunities in areas hitherto

---

71 Petralia 1987, 320; 1996, 959–961, 979; Salvadori 2000a, 86.
72 Meli and Tognetti 2006, 76–77.

little frequented (the Maghreb, Mamluk Egypt, the Ottoman Levant, Andalusia, Portugal), and at the same time to establish themselves in nearer trading systems, commercially exploiting iron from the island of Elba, and also salt and agricultural products from Sardinia.[73]

A Policy for Manufacturing

A policy for manufacturing concerned, in the first place, industries central to the Florentine economy: the production of wool and silk cloth. The governance of these fundamental sectors was largely entrusted to the respective wool and silk guilds, the latter originally known as the Arte di Por Santa Maria.[74] There were at least three policy concerns, however, where these textile guilds inevitably proved inadequate, given that central authority was needed to impose decisions that, while protecting particular interests, had general consequences. The first has already been mentioned: the building and maintenance of the infrastructure, in particular the road network and waterways. The second was the protection of the domestic market, the guiding principle being to prevent the import of any fabric that could, in theory at least, have been produced in Florence. The third was direct support for what might be termed innovative start-ups—promising new product lines or production techniques.

Once again, the accolade of priority must go to the Albizzi regime. The first tangible sign of public protectionism for manufacturing appears in 1393, when, at the initiative of the oligarchic, Albizzi-dominated *balìa* and at the instigation of the wool guild, and during the gonfaloniership of Maso degli Albizzi himself (from a family with long-standing ties to the textile industry),[75] a prohibitive duty was imposed on introducing into Florence or Florentine territory Italian, French, and especially English cloth not intended for the transit trade.[76] In 1418, the wool producers complained again of the difficult economic climate requiring even more drastic relief, but the legislative councils twice turned down the request, which was then withdrawn.[77]

In these years, with the wool sector increasingly threatened and the wool guild on the defensive,[78] the silk guild sought policy relief for further expansion of its industry, already a growth sector: in 1406, to ensure a constant supply of the precious metals necessary for the production of silk and gold cloth, the duty on the import into Florence of gold and silver was abolished.[79] Two years later, to try and prevent raw silk currently within Florentine territory from being re-exported,

73 Tognetti 2010b, 169–173.
74 See Franceschi 1994, 82–98.
75 See Hoshino 1980, 305–327.
76 ASF, Balìe 19, fols. 28v–29v; Franceschi 1993a, 896–898.
77 ASF, Libri fabarum 51, fols. 203r, 206r.
78 See Hoshino 1980, 231–244; Franceschi 1993b, 30–31.
79 ASF, DF, Dogana antica e campioni 371, fol. 129v.

tariffs on the import of different types of silk were made uniform and those on the transshipment of silk raised.[80] In 1423, the government sought to establish sericulture and silk-reeling in Florence, while three years later, to favor local producers, restrictions were placed on trade in silk fabrics from abroad. Finally, in 1429, silk workers forced out of the city by debt were offered fiscal incentives to return.[81]

Until about 1420, tariff protection as a means of assisting Florentine manufacturing was used with moderation, but after the acquisition of Porto Pisano and Livorno and the creation of the sea consuls, protectionism became a core policy to stimulate internal industrial development, as well as a means, of course, to respond to fiscal demands, never absent and especially pressing between 1424 and 1433.[82] Accordingly, in December 1422, the newly constituted office of the sea consuls was charged with revitalizing, through a revised tariff system, industrial activity in the city of Florence and (a novelty in public legislation) in its territories.[83] Just under four years later, the sea consuls presented their proposals: to counter declining wool manufacture and to discourage producers from moving their operations outside Florence, they would raise tariffs on the export of wool and on equipment used to work cloth.[84] At the same time, to protect the silk cloth market by penalizing the trade in textiles arriving from competing cities, they threatened whoever used the communal galleys for the transport of foreign silks with the same fines as applied for failure to respect the 1393 customs tariffs relating to woolen cloth.[85] Lastly, to encourage cotton manufacture and the metal industry, both experiencing robust demand, they subjected corresponding foreign articles to heavy import duties, added to the customary internal gabelles.[86]

Apart from declarations of principle on the need to boost economic activity throughout the dominion, the above provisions were not accompanied by specific measures to support the productive sector in the subject towns, except for relief

---

80 ASF, DF, Dogana antica e campioni 371, fol. 130r (1408): the duty on silks in transit was set at the same level as the exit duty, whereas the principle applied normally, and reemphasized in the general tariff of 1402, was that "tutte le merchatantie vanno per passo, paghino la metà dell'uscita, che viene il terzo dell'entrata" (all merchandise in transit pays half of the exit fee, which amounts to one-third of the entry fee): Uzzano 1766, 34. A copy of the provision in Latin is printed in Dorini 1934, Appendix 1, 785–787.

81 Franceschi 1994, 86, 89–90, 93–95.

82 See Molho 1971, 63; 1991, 821–822.

83 As Scipione Ammirato later put it succinctly, "volendosi ridurre i mestieri et le arti della città et del dominio in florido, et introdurne di quelle che non vi fossero, ne fu data la cura et balìa a Consoli di mare, a' quali fu poi anche ampliàta per dar loro occasione di prèmere maggiormente in questa faccenda" (with the intention of helping the trades and guilds of the city and dominion to flourish, and introducing ones currently lacking, the sea consuls were assigned the task and possibility of so doing, which was later enhanced so that they could act more forcefully): Ammirato 1641–47, 999.

84 ASF, Consoli del mare 3, fols. 21r–22v. A copy in the vernacular can be found in ASF, DF, Dogana antica e campioni 371, fols. 152v–154r.

85 ASF, DF, Dogana antica e campioni 371, fol. 153v.

86 Ibid.

measures to stimulate shipbuilding at Pisa, where the project to fit out the commercial fleet was based.[87] Indeed, policy in the pre-Medici era perpetuated the privileges traditionally granted to manufacturing in Florence vis-à-vis the same sector in the subject communities—a regime based primarily on the peculiar organization of the guild system. Guildsmen from the Florentine *contado* had to be matriculated in the corresponding Florentine guild, of which they constituted a minor section (*matricola minore*), and were subject to its coercive powers.[88] With the extension of Florentine jurisdiction to areas beyond the historical *contado*, however, the application of these principles grew more elastic. "A basically laissez-faire attitude toward most trades and crafts" may have prevailed, but there was "a firm policy of marginalizing the most feared rival industries."[89] But there were exceptions even to this rule: Prato, which had boasted a strong textile industry since the start of the trecento, succeeded in retaining its guild autonomies, and Arezzo, San Gimignano, San Miniato, Montepulciano, and other minor localities under Florentine control were treated the same way. Things were different when it came to Cortona and above all to Pisa. The better-known example of the latter testifies clearly to Florentine determination to proceed with a sort of *reductio ad comitatum* (reduction to the *contado*) of its long-standing rival. Although the forms of dependence varied in their extent according to the guild in question, the guildsmen of Pisa were forced in general to accept burdens such as subordination to the Florentine guilds; having to pay the latter a part of their income from matriculation fees, taxes, dues, and pecuniary fines; having to recognize the right of the Florentine guild consuls to hear appeals from local decisions; having their own rules of matriculation biased in favor of Florentines and foreigners residing in Pisa; and having to submit their corporate statutes to the Florentine guilds for approval.[90]

From this perpective, the design pursued in the late fourteenth and early fifteenth centuries by the Albizzi regime for the major manufacturing sectors emerged even more starkly. Silk manufacturing was concentrated in the capital city and was experiencing rapid growth: in 1419, a law was passed giving Florence dominion-wide monopoly of this activity, under threat of severe penalties.[91] For wool manufacturing, widespread throughout the territories but struggling in Florence itself, the strategies adopted were more complex. The most interesting aspect is that—perhaps not by chance, given the strong involvement of the Albizzi family in cloth production—the government chose here to allow the wool

87 Mallett 1968, 413.
88 On all this, Doren 1940, 1:167–170, remains fundamental.
89 Epstein 1996, 884.
90 For the details, see Franceschi 1996, 1355–1356.
91 The provision is reported in the statutes of the Florentine silk guild: Dorini 1934, Riforma del 1416, rub. 1, 443: "Nullus iurisdictioni Comunis Florentie quomodolibet subditus possit extra dictam civitatem laborare, tessere, ordire drappos de auro et sirico" (No one subject in any way to the jurisdiction of the Florentine commune may work, weave, or warp cloth of gold and silk outside the said city).

guild full freedom of action. With a series of measures later incorporated into the new statutes of 1428, the guild set out a fully fledged system of prohibitions, authorizations, and dispensations, with two main objectives: to prevent producers in the subject territories from competing with those in Florence, and to make them effectively subordinate to the system of guild controls. The new legislation imposed a division of labor on a territory-wide scale, structured on three levels. Florence naturally remained at the top: it held a monopoly on the production of luxury fabrics using English wool, and was also the site where Mediterranean wool was transformed into cloth. Then there were a few "castles, villages, and walled sites" (*castelli, terre, luoghi murati*) such as Prato (and, although not mentioned explicitly, Arezzo as well) to which the Florentine republic, by virtue of specific accords, granted the right to have a wool guild, whose members were permitted to use wool from North Africa, Majorca, and Minorca, and any other kind of raw material except English wool. Lastly, there were rural workshops authorized to produce only cheap cloth using solely local wool—a status to which the Pisan wool industry was effectively reduced.[92]

When Cosimo acceded to power, there was no interruption in direct and indirect support for Florence's two major manufacturing sectors, both prominent in the Medici bank's activities until its liquidation.[93] In the case of silk manufacturing, and the related activity of goldbeating—which in the second half of the quattrocento experienced further growth, attracting the interest of merchant-entrepreneurs such as the Gondi, the Portinari, the Corsi, the Da Verrazzano, the Ridolfi, and the Serristori[94]—the main thrust was a new and more concerted effort to develop production of raw silk within Florentine territory. Two pertinent pieces of legislation date from 1441. The stated aim of the first was to lure workers skilled in "reeling silk or raising the worms from which silk is reeled" (*trarre seta o fare filugelli di che si trae la seta*) with the promise of a twenty-year fiscal exemption.[95] The second ordered landowners in Florentine dominions to plant five mulberry trees and five almond trees every year until they had at least fifty of each kind, and entrusted the task of supervising the measure's application to the consuls of the silk guild, along with a recommendation that rectors in the *contado* and *distretto* should ensure its enforcement.[96] Among those complying with the injunction was Giovanni Rucellai, who had three to four thousand mulberries planted on his property at Poggio a Caiano.[97]

92 ASF, AL 7, lib. 3, rubb. 6–8, fols. 65r–66r; Franceschi 2011, 883–885.
93 See De Roover 1963, ch. 8.
94 Dini 1995c, 82.
95 "And whoever wishes to take advantage of this benefit," the deliberation goes on to state, "must register with the office of the Cinque del Contado," while the guild consuls were also instructed to check on these workers: Dorini 1934, Riforma del 1441, rub. 1, 552.
96 Dorini 1934, Riforma del 1441, rub. 2, 553.
97 Kent et al. 1981, 76.

But the principal goal of the legislation was to provide incentives for the return to Florence of workers who had emigrated, generally because of debt, by offering sizable fiscal advantages. Measures were accordingly adopted in 1439, 1443, 1468, and 1481, with each law confirming previous enactments.[98] As well as fearing the dispersal of specialist knowledge to competing manufacturing centers,[99] the Florentine government probably thought that spinners, weavers, dyers, goldbeaters, designmakers, and other artisans with previous experience in the city's workshops constituted human capital of even greater value than fresh immigrants.

In the wool sector, the climate was different: at the start of the Medici period, the cloth industry was in difficulty, as has been seen (143 ff.), and consequently demanded direct intervention in order to merely preserve its productive apparatus and existing markets. The measures adopted in 1439, 1451, and 1458 progressively barred the import into Florentine territory of foreign fabrics, which not only competed directly with local products but potentially damaged their image abroad, given that "it will not be believed elsewhere that the textiles of Florence are satisfactory if we ourselves use foreign imports."[100] The Balìa of 1393 had established a precedent by erecting high customs tariffs on certain textiles; the Balìa of 1458 carried this policy to an extreme with an absolute prohibition on the import of all articles not produced in Florence's territory. Such protectionism proved enduring, confirmed as it was in the sixteenth century.[101] There were only two dispensations: the free trade in *perpignan*, a light and cheap woolen cloth, originating in southern France and Catalan-Aragonese Spain;[102] and a separate customs regime for commercial goods in transit through Florentine ports. In the latter case, a new feature was a more accurate system of control, directly involving wool guild personnel.[103]

98 For 1439, see ASF, PR 129, fol. 277r–v; Dorini 1934, Riforma del 1439, rub. 1, 541–543. For 1443, see ASF, PR 134, fol. 154r–v; Dorini 1934, Riforma del 1443, rub. 1, 560–562. For 1468, see ASF, PR 159, fol. 112v; Dorini 1934, Riforma del 1468, rub. 1, 627–631. For 1481, see ASF, PR 172, fols. 124r–126v; Dorini 1934, Riforma del 1481, 659–662.

99 These competitors are explicitly identified: in 1443, for example, not only Venice and Lucca but Milan, Genoa, and Siena as well (ASF, PR 134, fol. 154r); in 1468, Siena, Perugia, Bologna, Naples, and Spain (ASF, PR 159, fol. 112v); in 1481, the Marches (ASF, PR 172, fol. 125r).

100 "non si può credere altrove che i panni di Firenze siano buoni usando noi panni forestieri": ASF, Balìe 29, fol. 18v.

101 See Malanima 1982, 182–183.

102 Hoshino 1980, 235–236.

103 ASF, Balìe 29, fol. 19r: "E acciò che intorno a questo s'observi l'effecto della presente legge si dice per consoli dell'arte della lana della città di Firenze si debba diputare uno o più che stia a Livorno e a Pisa e a Pistoia alle spese di detta arte e con salario condecente, il quale tengha diligente conto de' panni che si metteranno et trarranno per andare fuori de' terreni del comune di Firenze, e abbia cura che non rimanghino e non si taglino né usino né in Pisa né in alchuno luogho dove il comune di Firenze à preheminentia o iurisdictione né in Firenze." (And in order that the present law can effectively be observed, it is resolved that one or more persons should be chosen to reside at Livorno and Pisa and Pistoia, and paid appropriate salaries by the consuls of the wool guild of the city of Florence. There such a person should keep careful track of what shipments of cloth enter the customhouses and which ones exit the customhouses for export to destinations outside Florentine dominions. He should ensure that the cloth allowed out does not remain there, that

There was a significant change of direction in productive sectors such as cotton cloth, arms, and other metal objects, which the Albizzi regime had tried to encourage in 1426 with protectionist measures "to ensure the production of such items within communal territory in order to provide a living for the populace through manufacturing."[104] Exceptions, partial and temporary, began to be made in 1431,[105] and were frequently extended in the following decades, mainly on the grounds that the city and its territory could not be left bereft of the goods in question.[106] Sometimes exceptions were for the products from a particular city, as in 1446, when fustians from Cremona imported into Florentine territory were exempted from all taxation, but only so long as the city remained under the authority of Francesco Sforza,[107] Florence's and Cosimo de' Medici's ally. None of these exceptions was permanent, and in a deliberation of 1474, it was regretted that certain textiles made of cotton and cotton and linen blends (*guarnelli, spessini, bordi vergati, pignolati*) could not be brought into Florentine territory "without paying a heavy duty over and above the ordinary excise levied since 1426."[108]

What was the Medici regime's attitude toward industrial production outside Florence? Measures to protect the domestic market, so long as they did not discriminate between Florence's historic *contado* and the rest of the dominion, favored producers in the subject towns too, which thus were spared competition from abroad. But in the second half of the quattrocento, it is possible to catch a glimpse of the Florentine government looking to needs and interests beyond the center. In general, however, such measures concerned activities carried out in localities situated at the borders of the dominion, or not in a position to compete with similar activities in Florence. In this sense, and only to a limited degree, did legislation further the "natural" process of economic integration in Florentine Tuscany.[109]

An example (mentioned above) is the customs relief granted in 1458 to facilitate cloth production in Sansepolcro, a community that enjoyed a privileged fiscal regime from the very moment of its submission to Florence in 1441.[110] Another is the favor offered to Pisa's manufacturing sector: limits on importing Lombard

---

it is not cut or used either in Pisa, or anywhere else where the Florentine commune has preeminence and jurisdiction, or in Florence itself.)

104 "acciò che tali cose si lavorassino nel terreno del comune per havervi più manifacture per sostentatione del popolo": ASF, PR 165, fol. 71r.

105 See Molho 1971, 57.

106 ASF, PR 132, fol. 135v (1432); ASF, Balìe 25, fol. 71r–v (1434); ASF, Balìe 26, fol. 51r–v (1444); ASF, DF, Dogana antica e campioni 371, fols. 178r–179r (1440), 181r (1436), 184r (1441), 327v–328r (1472).

107 ASF, Balìe 26, fol. 145r.

108 "se non col pagamento d'una grave gabella oltra l'ordinaria, la quale fu posta nell'anno del XXVI": ASF, PR 165, fol. 71r.

109 For the bibliography on this question, which has preoccupied researchers since the 1970s, see Franceschi and Molà 2012.

110 Scharf 2003, 99.

fabrics to promote the local wool industry, and encouragement to the linen industry, both decreed in 1473,[111] but above all the detailed plan endorsed by Lorenzo the Magnicent and the seventeen reformers to repopulate Pisan territory and revitalize its economy.[112] In this case, the incentives mainly took the form of customs reductions or exemptions on trade in local articles, as well as tariff increases on corresponding products imported from abroad. They were for the tanning industry, always a mainstay of the Pisan economy, hat manufacture, and soap production[113] (nourished by the demand created by the galley voyages and already supported by laws in 1441 and 1442).[114] The same applies to Volterra's wool and tanning industries, which from 1491 were limited exclusively to the city and its immediate surroundings: after only ten years, citizenship was promised to immigrant tanners and wool workers coming into Volterra from its former *contado*.[115]

These measures concerned two cities hard hit economically by subjugation to Florence: Pisa, by having its textile industry downgraded to the status of rural manufacturing, and Volterra, by the confiscation of its mineral wealth after the sack of 1472.[116] If they cannot be interpreted as a form of retrospective compensation, at least they appear to show central government's desire to normalize relations. This is confirmed by another important initiative of the seventeen reformers. They noted the persistent conflict between Florentine and Pisan guilds over "jurisdiction, taxes, and matriculation fees" (*di iurisdictione et di taxe et di matricole*), questions not resolved even by measures taken in 1459 and 1475 to relax the restrictions on the Pisan guilds; as a result, they ended the subordinate status of Pisa's guildsmen, whom they brought under the supervision of the sea consuls.[117] Shortly afterward, even those engaged in economic activity in the former *contado*, with the exception of judges and notaries, were also released from the requirement to be matriculated in Florence.[118] The Florentine guilds were clearly the losers in this political-economic realignment, marginalized by a direct agreement between the producing classes in the subject communities and central government. A similar situation occurred in

111 ASF, PR 164, fols. 111r–v, 275v.
112 "Et perché si desidera che a Pisa vadino nuovi habitatori et conoscesi che chi non v'avessi exercitio non vi potrebbe vivere senza grande sinistro, et però essere necessario ridurvi qualche nuovo exercitio o veramente augumentare di quelli che fare vi si solevano" (And because it is desirable for new inhabitants to go to Pisa, and obviously without work there they could not live without great hardship, [it is] therefore necessary to bring some new industries to the town, or else bring about growth in the traditional ones): ASF, Balìe 39, fol. 66r.
113 Ibid., fol. 66r–v.
114 Mallett 1968, 425.
115 ASF, Balìe 39, fol. 85v.
116 See note 136 below.
117 ASF, Balìe 39, fol. 64v: "Pisarum artium quod non sint supposite artibus florentinis"; Lupo Gentile 1940; Mallett 1968, 421; Franceschi 1996, 1359.
118 ASF, Balìe 39, fols. 73v–74r. The Florentine guilds retained judicial authority over those practicing their trades in the former *contado* of Pisa; retention of this prerogative was regarded as necessary in order to ensure continuity of normal economic life and resolution of controversies arising from production and commercial activities. On all this, see Franceschi 1996, 1357–1360.

Arezzo during the 1470s, although here the Aretine guilds sought direct dialogue with Florence's chief authorities in order to win freedom from restraints imposed by their own commune.[119]

Promoting Innovation

Easier acquisition of citizenship, partial or total tax exemption, dispensation from guild enrollment, immunity from debt, the offer of material assets and tools of work, even the privilege of bearing weapons—such were the incentives held out to specialized laborers or experts with potential for innovating in established economic sectors, or of introducing new activities with positive market prospects. The textile sector both inside and outside Florence always enjoyed preeminence: it could employ a large segment of the population, stimulate the whole economy, and thereby help to guarantee social order. But initiatives were undertaken in other sectors as well. The city guilds themselves sought government intervention here: only public authorities could effectively confer privileges attractive to specialists. The attempt to establish silk-reeling at Florence in 1441 has already been noted, and similar action would recur in following decades.

In 1436, for example, in an attempt to promote the production of perpignan fabrics in Florence, the legislative councils granted *magister Petrus Jacobi Serrati*, who actually came from Perpignan, exemption from all taxation.[120] By 1470, the manufacture of these textiles had evidently not caught on as had been hoped, and so the government freed eventual producers from having to pay any guild matriculation fees,[121] besides prohibiting the import of foreign perpignan cloth into Florentine territory.[122] The wool guild, for its part, required its members, as in the past, to achieve an annual minimum production quota: 800 pieces in 1473; 1,500 in 1474; and 2,000 from 1475 onward.[123] The impact of these measures was immediate, as shown by, among other sources, a dyer's surviving account books: from May 1474 to May 1476, Piero di Giovanni Busini used more than 1,200 pounds of woad to color his cloth, of which 23 percent went to coloring or recoloring white *perpignans* (*cupi, isbiadati, bigi, trafilati, ispiumati*).[124]

In 1458, dispensation from enrollment in any guild, along with exclusive rights over his technology, were the inducements that won for Florence the services of the Bolognese Dante di Giovanni Dalla Lana. He assured the Florentines he could install and operate a new kind of machine "that spins, throws, gathers, and winds both wool and linen in one process," and was therefore judged "highly

---

119 See Franceschi 2012, 250.
120 ASF, PR 127, fols. 244r–245r.
121 Doren 1901, 567.
122 ASF, PR 164, fol. 159r (1472).
123 Hoshino 1980, 236.
124 Prato Biblioteca Roncioniana, Caccini-Vernaccia 765 (*Libro di Vagelli segnato B*).

useful because its throughput significantly exceeds that of a distaff."[125] Moreover, in 1463, the Venetian Luigi Bianco, already active in Florence for some time as a manufacturer of iron components for looms regarded as "better and more perfect than those of any rival master," won from the government, at the insistence of silk producers and their guild, ten years of protection against creditors or other claimants.[126]

But as well as overseeing initiatives launched by the guilds, the Florentine government intervened directly in the economy, as shown as early as 1422 when the sea consuls were required to report on the state of manufacturing throughout Florentine territory. The same policy priority is evident in 1447, when the *monte* officials—a magistracy created to administer the public debt, but which had gradually taken control over the most important sectors of public finance,[127] including customs and fiscal privileges[128]—were commissioned to "identify skills and trades currently unrepresented in Florence as well as their most proficient practitioners, trying to ensure that such skills and occupations gained a foothold in Florence."[129] Such directives suggest that, although the guilds might have had some influence on the introduction of innovative technology and might indeed have been asked for "consent"[130] in each case, they were now subordinated to central authority. So far no document with the findings of this commission has emerged, but it is clear that there was practical implementation of the policy: over the following decades, the *monte* officials functioned as the lead agency in attracting "experts" and promoting the exploitation of new resources, whether in bringing product innovation to the cloth industry or encouraging mineral exploration in Florentine territory.

As for textile manufacturing, a revealing example is the case of Cosimo Dini, a Florentine and longtime resident at Bologna, who in 1476 was persuaded to return to Florence to introduce the production of silk veils (*veletti di seta*), a light

125 "Per parte di Dante di Giovanni Dalla Lana da Bologna si dice lui avere notitia et scientia di sapere fare uno certo edificio et ingegnio il quale fila, torcie, raccoglie et inaspa lana et lino a uno tracto; la quale opera pe' consoli dell'arte della lana si riputa potere essere molto utile a questa città perché lavora assai più che non si fa a roccha": ASF, PR 150, fols. 2v–3r, at fol. 2v.

126 "di maggior bontà et di più perfectione che quelli d'alcuno altro maestro": Dorini 1934, Riforma del 1463, rub. 1, 621–623, at 622.

127 Conti 1984, 309; Goldthwaite 2009, 501–502.

128 See, for example, ASF, Monte comune 1122–1123 (1448–1450).

129 "investigare d'ogni arte et mestiero de' quali al presente nella città di Firenze non si ha notitia o artefice, e chi fosse experto in tale exercitio [. . .] condurre a fare et exercitare qualunche d'esse arti et exercitii nella città di Firenze": the relevant deliberation appears in ASF, PR 138, fol. 53r, but the text for the quoted passage comes from the *Liber legum palatii*, a register preserved in the archive of the wool guild: ASF, AL 13, fol. 136r.

130 "richiegendone non di meno e avutone consentimento da' consoli di qualunche delle XXI arti di Firenze a cui quel mestiero o artificio o suo membro appartenesse o potesse appartenere" (requiring nonetheless and obtaining the consent of the consuls of whichever of the twenty-one guilds of Florence that occupation or trade or its practitioner may or might belong to): ASF, AL 13, fol. 136r.

and low-cost fabric that was a traditional Bolognese speciality.[131] Cosimo's decision to return was the result of solicitations from highly placed individuals, whom he gratified by refusing the flattering and attractive offers of "various princes who had sought to recruit him."[132] In Florence, he undertook to teach the techniques of weaving, pleating, and bleaching *veletti*, and to keep at least thirty looms running. To this end, the *monte* officials put at his disposal the Mulinuzzo, an edifice on the Arno equipped with "throwing and spinning machines, and other instruments"[133] required by the process. Two hundred florins from the public purse were assigned annually for ten years to cover wages for the weavers and workers under his supervision. Finally, Cosimo Dini received authorization to bear arms and to hire up to four bodyguards. In this, as in numerous similar cases, it is hard to assess the results of the project, but it is telling that over the following decades, various kinds of records (legislative, fiscal, business) reveal that this sector survived, indicating foreign masters and workshops of *veletti* operating in the city.[134]

As for mineral prospecting, the first report of steps taken to favor *inventores metalli* dates from 1441, when the Florentine Astorre di Niccolò di Gherardino Gianni requested and was granted a license to search for and to exploit mineral resources throughout the dominion. Such licenses for extraction were conceded with increasing frequency over the following years, in response to requests from entrepreneurs and technical experts both domestic and foreign.[135] But the search for seams of buried metal received a sudden boost as a result of the controversy over alum deposits found at Sasso near Volterra, leading Lorenzo the Magnificent to take notoriously harsh measures against that city.[136] In 1472, with the effective incorporation into the Florentine dominion of Volterra's territory (rich in silver, copper, iron, sulphur, alum, and vitriol), Florence arrogated to itself all regalian rights previously vested in the commune of Volterra, and decreed that all contracts conceding mining rights stipulated by the latter would be renewed. The concessions currently extant included permission to exploit a copper mine at Caporciano, near Montecatini in Val di Cecina, awarded in 1469 to a company formed by the Florentines Gino Capponi, Tommaso di Lorenzo Soderini, Luigi di Piero Guicciardini, Paolo di Domenico dal Pozzo Toscanelli, Michele di ser Piero Migliorelli, and Tommaso di ser Bonifazio Marinai.[137] Between 1479 and 1484, this enterprise generated profits of almost twenty-two thousand florins.[138] The alum mine at Volterra, on the other

131 ASF, PR 167, fols. 112–113v. The provision also appears in Dorini 1934, Riforma del 1474, rub. 4, 653–657.
132 Ibid., 653.
133 Ibid., 654.
134 See Franceschi 2000, 421.
135 Pampaloni 1975, 6–7.
136 On the whole affair, see Fiumi 1948, 167–171, and the revisionist interpretation of Fubini 1996, 123–139, as well as Franceschi 2005, 148–153.
137 See Pampaloni 1975, 71–73.
138 Ibid., 110.

hand, proved a disappointment (by 1473, there were already complaints about low output)[139] and Florence shifted its attention to another mine at Campiglia, in the extreme south of the dominion, operated from 1484 by a Florentine company that included Lorenzo the Magnificent as a member.[140] Meanwhile, applications poured in from experts lured to Florentine territory by the concessions on offer: according to a law of 1484, so numerous were those granted "some privilege with respect to mineral extraction," and so many were "the places with exclusive rights to mineral extraction extending for miles round, that it might almost be said they had taken over the Florentine commune's entire jurisdiction."[141]

A Few Comparisons

In light of this sketch of Florentine government's economic policies during the fifteenth century, is it possible to detect any change of direction with the accession to power of Cosimo de' Medici and his successors? No simple answer is forthcoming: aspects of the problem remain unexplored, and sources such as the Medici correspondence have yet to be systematically combed for economic data. Before the Medici took power, the governing class had developed a clear economic policy: a tendency to centralize decision-making and to standardize legislation; a greater attention to the domestic market; support for and stimulus of textile manufacturing, regarded as the foundation of the Florentine economy; and protectionism on a massive scale to regulate in- and outflows.

The Medici regime carried on with much of this inheritance, and yet its economic policy appears less clear-cut, even self-contradictory at times. Contrasting with attempts at rationalization and streamlining, such as the *Dogana dei traffichi* in 1448, the *Legge dei passeggeri* of 1461, or the revised excise system at Livorno and Pisa in 1475, are repeatedly reversed decisions, as in the case of the *viai*, or the failure consistently to apply measures relating to cotton fabrics and arms trades. Some of these vacillations give the impression of heightened cautiousness and an attempt to mediate among needs and interests that were difficult to reconcile: between Florence and the rest of the dominion, between subject towns and their former *contadi*, between economic development and fiscal demands, between manufacture in Florence and the flow of consumer goods into the city. It has been observed that the Medici followed "a policy for preserving the dominion, rather than for structuring an administrative state able to (or intended to) counterbalance putative centrifugal tendencies in the pluralism of local territorial experiences."[142] Evidently

139 Boisseuil 2005, 112.

140 Ciasca 1927, 590.

141 "truovano in diversi tempi passati molti havere impetrato da' consigli qualche privilegio circa questa materia del cavare minere et havere disegnato tanti luoghi com prohibitioni di non si potere cavare vicino a quelli a tanto spatio di miglia, che si può dire che habbino preso tutta la iurisdictione del comune di Firenze": ASF, PR 175, fol. 104v.

142 Zorzi 2000, 21.

their concern to build consensus, and their realistic assessment of the difficulty of governing a territory in which conflict and resistance had not been eliminated, translated into economic policies more strongly marked by pragmatism, flexibility, and for that matter opportunism, than under the Albizzi regime. From this perspective, the granting of special prerogatives to individual communities within the dominion is comprehensible. For the most part, it was the result of negotiations in which members of the Medici family assumed an increasingly important role, marginalizing the role of territorial governors. The concession of the right to a fair or market, the award of greater guild autonomy, the concession of partial or full relief from the burdens of road maintenance, gabelles, and direct taxation—all these amounted to a "politics of privilege," seen to be an effective instrument of rule.

Such conclusions cannot be applied to all six decades of Medici rule: the governance of the economy felt the impact of the regime's internal evolution as well as of the overall political climate. With the strengthening of Medici power in 1458 came a policy shift: more incisive measures to improve the road and toll system, to protect the Florentine textile industry from outside competition, and to promote trade and public shipping; and more effort to achieve constructive dialogue with the economic forces of subject towns, above all with Pisa and its former *contado*, together with a slackening of the most punitive aspects of previous economic policy. This shift became more pronounced after the regime survived another crisis in 1466, which marked the "beginning of Medicean pre-eminence and hegemony, based on their successful exploitation of patronage networks,"[143] and found expression in the policy priorities of the Laurentian era, culminating in the activities of the seventeen reformers.

On these grounds, it is arguable that this change of direction gradually widened the gap between the policies of the Medici regime and the centralizing projects of the Albizzi regime, and aligned Medici economic policy more closely with that of other Italian states, especially the duchy of Milan. In Lombardy, both the Visconti and the Sforza displayed a notable capacity to intervene region-wide, for example, in connection with roads, waterways, tolls, and customs. But at the same time, aware that they were operating in an environment with a number of historic centers, these rulers also ensured that rural communities and minor centers received a flow of fiscal, commercial, and jurisdictional privileges aimed at stimulating the growth of local economies, reducing institutional barriers to trade, and above all, promoting a more balanced relationship between the capital city and the rest of the dominion.[144]

143 Salvadori 2000b, 219–220.
144 For a more detailed comparison extending to the other principal states of Renaissance Italy as well, see Franceschi and Molà 2012.

TEN

Lorenzo de' Medici and Foreigners
Recommendations and Reprisals

LORENZ BÖNINGER

IN THE FIRST BOOK OF the *Disputationes camaldulenses*, a philosophical dialogue written by Cristoforo Landino in the early 1470s, the young Lorenzo de' Medici delivers a lengthy oration in praise of the active life: a striking image is used, that of a *sapientissimus vir* (wisest man) who regulates access to the ideal state by sitting at the town gates (*ipse ad portas sedens*), deciding who should, or should not, be allowed in. According to these ideas, the perfect state always needs men who excel either in prudence or in craftsmanship (*prudentia artificiove*), for example, lawyers, orators, judges, medical doctors, military leaders, architects, sculptors, painters, and metal- and woodworkers. The exercise of these professions and occupations requires intelligence and diligence (*ingenio atque industria*). Bankers, merchants, cloth manufacturers, and workers with no specific skill (*laborem potius quam industriam*) are also welcome, such as the cloth-weavers, girdle-makers, tailors, or shoemakers; finally, there are the numerous occupations dedicated to feeding the populace. All of these activities contribute to the well-being of the perfect state; far more dubious, however, is the case of an idle and good-for-nothing philosopher.[1]

The idea that a single man presided over all foreigners passing through town came up again a few years later in a highly polemical context—that is to say, in the famous bull that Pope Sixtus IV issued on 1 June 1478, more than a month after

∞ I should like to thank Robert Black, Philippa Jackson, and the anonymous peer reviewers for their critical readings of this text and their many suggestions.
1   Landino 1980, 28–29. This entire image is taken from Maximus of Tyre: see Waith 1960.

the Pazzi conspiracy.[2] In his lengthy excommunication of the Florentine "tyrant" Lorenzo de' Medici, the *signoria*, and the *otto di pratica* (the foreign affairs magistracy), the pope enumerated among the many misdeeds of Lorenzo also the disrespect—*more Pharaonis* ("in the manner of a Pharaoh")—shown to certain pilgrims traveling for "devotional reasons" to Rome. Traditionally, such a charge had strong theological and canonical implications.[3] The bull refers especially to the recent case of three Germans who had been captured, jailed, and despoiled of their property by the Florentine authorities.[4] A couple of weeks later, Gentile Becchi in his equally famous reply, the *Florentina synodus*, stated more generally that Lorenzo had always—as every Christian prince should—defended the poor, pilgrims, and prisoners, but that what had been done in this specific case had been authorized by the apostolic see. In a cryptic manner, Becchi explained that, prior to this case, a Florentine merchant had been robbed in the native country of these "Rome-seekers" (the very term *romipetae* implied their protection by canon law) and that this merchant had as a result summoned them during their Florentine sojourn. In the end, they had been released paying nothing; Lorenzo de' Medici himself was hardly involved (*ad quem parum ea res pertinuit*).[5]

Becchi's response thus transferred the pope's general accusations from a political and personal level to that of a minor economic conflict; for him, it was a question of reciprocal commercial and financial relations with the Germanic countries in the 1460s and 1470s. In order to elucidate these issues, some cases of commercial and financial conflict between Florence and other states will be briefly examined, with a closer look at the widespread phenomenon of legal confiscations or reprisals (*rappresaglie*). The case of the three Germans' detention will then be analyzed in more detail. To return to Cristoforo Landino's image of a prince-citizen presiding over the influx of immigrants to Florence, it will finally be asked to what extent this image corresponded to reality as far as Lorenzo the Magnificent was concerned and whether and how he followed the ideals of the Christian prince in the protection of the poor, pilgrims, and prisoners.

First, it must be recognized that Renaissance Florence was not only a cosmopolitan city, but also a center "of tolerance based on humanism's core values"; the often repeated "appeal to humanity" became fundamental in dealing, for example, with Jewish moneylenders or merchants.[6] Furthermore, leading members of the Medici family never had the authority solely to decide immigration policy or the

---

2   Medici 1977–, 3:46–49.

3   Birch 1998. "Very grave censures," i.e., excommunications, were pronounced each year by the pope in a solemn ceremony on Maundy Thursday against anyone who impeded pilgrims or members of the curia from reaching Rome, as the college of cardinals reminded the Florentine *signoria* on 30 September 1482 (copy in ASF MAP 147, 9: "praeter gravissimas censuras quae adversus impedientes peregrinos et curiales Romam petentes quot annis in die cene Domini publicantur").

4   Daniels 2013a, 108.

5   Poliziano and Becchi 2012, 140–143; Daniels 2013a, 69, 141.

6   Brown 2012, 40.

treatment of foreigners passing through Florentine territory. These were traditionally matters for the whole Florentine ruling class and were thus subject to discussions in both institutional and informal meetings. A fundamental role in defining
workers' legal position in communal society was also played by the guilds (*arti*).

For most of the later Middle Ages, there was no institution that could effectively
oversee the influx of foreigners into Florence.[7] Nevertheless, the hierarchy of professions and the different grades of social prestige ascribed to them by Landino was
a fact of life in Florence as elsewhere. Lawyers, doctors, military leaders, and artists
showed a high level of mobility; they found favorable conditions there when they
decided to take up residence and establish a family.[8] While qualified workers in
unusual professions were eagerly sought, foreigners without skills were often seen
as a threat to public security. The norm was protection of the first group but conflict
with the second. This was already true at the time of the Ciompi revolt in 1378,[9] and
recurred repeatedly throughout the fifteenth century. In the midst of the political
crisis in 1466, the authorities published a decree requiring all nonresident foreigners to leave town and resident German and Flemish workers to stay at home.[10]

The process of professional and social integration of these immigrants was often
difficult. Many lived "at the margins" of the community and found few opportunities to socialize outside their national confraternities.[11] Sometimes these associations
sought eminent Florentine citizens as honorary members who could presumably, in
case of need, assume the role of advocates with the Florentine authorities on behalf of
their members. The confraternity of St. Barbara of the Flemish, Dutch, and Northern
Germans, for instance, accepted some members of the Neroni family, and, likewise,
the confraternity of the south German shoemakers welcomed two other patricians
close to the Medici, Agnolo and Sigismondo Della Stufa.[12]

Frequently, names of foreign immigrants can be found in the criminal records
of the Florentine state. Ordinary crimes were judged by the relevant communal
magistracies, usually the *podestà*; if, however, public order was in any way menaced,
the pertinent magistracy was the *otto di guardia e balìa*, established in 1378 to protect
the government then in power against declared "rebels." In the fifteenth century,
the *otto* gradually became the supreme criminal magistracy; all matters concerning foreigners and especially Jews fell under their authority.[13] Their sentences were
subject neither to communal statutes nor ordinary laws, but fell under the category

7   In Europe, close controls apparently became more common only in the sixteenth century: see
    Munck and Winter 2012.
8   For the "outsiders" among the lawyers, see Martines 1968, 498–505.
9   Böninger 2006a, 76–77.
10 "che qualunche forestiere per tempo dimora habbi sgombro la terra, et che e' tedeschi et fiaminghi
    stieno nelle case loro": Pampaloni 1962, 578.
11 Milner 2005a.
12 Böninger 2006a, 195, 217.
13 Antonelli 1953; Bellinazzi and Cotta 1992.

of "arbitrary justice." After 1478, the year of the Pazzi conspiracy, the *otto* became a particularly important instrument of Medicean "emergency rule."[14]

What was the official attitude on foreign immigrants to Florence? The letters of the first chancery at the end of Piero di Cosimo de' Medici's regime (d. 1469) and at the beginning of his son Lorenzo's partly answer the question.[15] In particular, the "private" presentation letters, for which subjects were usually charged a small sum, reflect not only literary commonplaces as derived from classical and medieval rhetoric, but also some fundamental concepts that regulated relations with foreigners living in the city. Modesty, personal integrity, and professional excellence were the three qualities mostly eulogized by the first chancellor Bartolomeo Scala and his associates. In May 1466, a Frenchman jailed in Siena (*Arrigus Iohannis filius homo est gallus*) was praised, for example, for his many friends in Florence and for his professional skills and intelligence (*carens multis civibus nostris ob industriam artis et ingenii liberalitatem*).[16] Another presentation letter was composed several months later for a Thuringian named *Georgius Fulclanth de Apolde*, who had worked in Florence for twenty-two years, married there, and had two children; from his initial "extreme poverty" he had become modestly prosperous. In supporting his wish to return home, the Florentine *signoria* praised him for both his industry and modesty.[17] Similarly in 1471 the *signoria* recommended *Simon Nicolai filius de Campis Brugensis* to his native city of Bruges for leading an upright and religious life in the convent of Santa Maria del Carmine.[18] Even philosophy was mentioned when, in 1470, the famous Flemish theologian of Santa Maria Novella, fra Domenico da Fiandra, was extolled not only for his virtues, doctrine, and modesty, but also for teaching philosophy to the Florentines.[19] Frequently, the foreigners were described as beloved by the Florentines "as if they were citizens."[20] Full citizenship, however, was rarely granted. When the *signoria* presented the Cypriot knight, humanist, and diplomat Filippo Podacataro to the duke of Milan in 1470, he was exceptionally identified as a Florentine "citizen by his own choice and by concession of a privilege from the people."[21]

14 Zorzi 1996, 1328; Isenmann 2011.
15 On the register mostly used here, BNCF Palatino 1103, see Brown 1979, 139–140.
16 BNCF, Palatino 1103, fol. 40r–v.
17 BNCF, Palatino 1103, fol. 60v.
18 "quantum publica fama fert, moribus vivit integris et relligiosis": BNCF, Palatino 1103, fol. 139v.
19 "cupimus remanere eum in civitate nostra ad hoc enim quod vitae exemplo perutilis est, eruditione certe homines nostros philosophie studiosos doctiores facit": BNCF, Palatino 1103, fol. 115v.
20 See, for example, in 1474, "maestro Ventura hebreo di Prato et huomo di stima per la sua doctrina et per la sua arte e a nnoi caro come fussi cittadino": BNCF, Palatino 1103, fol. 188v. Maestro Buonaventura had received a doctorate in medicine two years earlier: see Luzzati 1992.
21 "Philippus Potechaterus vir et militia et doctrina insignis ac plebiscito populi noster civis etsi natione cipriano [*sic*]": ASF, Signori, Minutari 9, fol. 153v. (The text "ac plebiscito populi noster civis etsi natione ciprianus" was added in the left margin. The final Italian version in BNCF, Palatino 1103, fol. 109v, reads: "nostro cittadino per sua electione et privilegio concedutoli dal nostro popolo.") Citizenship had been granted to him and the rest of his family in October 1461 by the council of the

If these letters present a conventional set of expectations for immigrants, other public letters show the daily conflicts that Florentine merchants had to face during their travels in these immigrants' native countries. Traditionally, merchants were considered the "blood and nerves" of the Florentine state, and therefore everything regarding them was considered a public affair.[22] On 6 July 1468, for example, the *signoria* wrote to the duke of Bavaria because, in 1467, the merchant Stefano di Berto Corsellini—who was probably on his way between Frankfurt and Nuremberg— had been imprisoned by the Franconian knight George of Rosenberg at his castle of Boxberg and was released only after paying a ransom of two hundred ducats, "as if he had fallen into the hands of enemies or pirates or robbers" (*tanquam si in hostium manus aut certe pirratarum et latronum incidisset*). The Florentines' surprise at the arbitrary behavior of the robber baron might have been more rhetorical than real, but the appeal to the Bavarian duke to restore obedience in his territory (*imperium*) was certainly sincere.[23]

Particularly insidious were legal confiscations of or reprisals against Florentine merchandise abroad, touching as they did not only political relations with the state where this confiscation had occurred, but also the very legal prerogatives of Florence, which claimed that, for any commercial conflict involving a Florentine citizen abroad, the appropriate court was in Florence, namely the *mercanzia* (commercial tribunal). Therefore, the *signoria* usually reacted vehemently when notice arrived of reprisals abroad. In most cases, either the Florentine consuls in that country or the *signoria* itself were able to resolve these problems, often with diplomatic missions.[24] In 1459, the first chancery directed no fewer than five letters to their ambassadors in Rome, to Pope Pius II, to his treasurer, to the papal governor of Rome, and to the Florentine archbishop, when Florentine goods had been sequestrated there.[25] Highly sensitive and complicated conflicts, resulting in economic reprisals against Florentine citizens in Ancona and in the duchy of Savoy, kept the chancery busy repeatedly in the 1460s.[26]

Studying the registers of Lorenzo the Magnificent's correspondence, the so-called *protocolli*, one notes several letters requesting the release of confiscated goods abroad that mirrored those sent by the first chancery sometimes on the

---

people (ASF, PR 152, fols. 185v–186v). For a discussion of a Cypriot doctor who in these years also received Florentine citizenship and had a successful professional career, see Contessa 2009.

22 See ASF, CP 60, fol. 146r; ASF, Signori, Dieci di Balìa, Otto di Pratica, Missive originali 4, fol. 79r.

23 ASF, Signori, Minutari 9, fol. 17v; BNCF, Palatino 1103, fol. 84r–v; on Corsellini, see ASF, Catasto 905, fol. 148v (1469). Boxberg was not actually Bavarian territory. War was declared against George of Rosenberg in 1470 by the archbishops of Mainz and Würzburg, and he was banned by the emperor in 1486; his line died out in 1542.

24 Martines 1968, 359–373.

25 Del Piazzo 1969, 35.

26 On the conflict with the duke of Savoy, see Lupi 1863, 284–285. Because of the Savoyard threat of reprisals, in 1467, Florentine merchants took a longer road to Lyon, that through Bern in Switzerland: see ASF, CP 58, fol. 229v.

same day.[27] In December 1473, when Florentine wares were retained (*sostenute*) at Turin in Savoy, however, Lorenzo the Magnificent alone wrote five letters to Milan to secure their release.[28] These must have been done the job: a few weeks later, he thanked the duke of Milan for their recovery.[29] Curiously, even Yolanda, duchess of Savoy, communicated how glad she was to have helped the Medici and other Florentines in this case, but there is no hint that Lorenzo had intervened directly with her.[30] The rapid resolution here must have increased his authority in similar cases. His role as ultimate mediator was put to use yet again during a dispute with Ancona in 1475: the Florentine merchant Carlo di Zanobi Buccelli decided to sue his ex-partner from Ancona in the *mercanzia*, and the *anziani* of Ancona turned to the Medici to block the action.[31]

Lorenzo's double role as political head and leading merchant banker was also highlighted by Bartolomeo Scala's first chancery. In September 1470, it attributed to him the epithet "magnificent" in order to persuade the viceroy of Sicily, Lupo Ximenes da Urrea, to free Medici goods there, especially in view of his rank (*qualità*).[32] In this choice of terminology, there presumably lay a deliberate reference to the aristocratic ethos prevailing among the Spanish elite; nearly two decades later, in dealings with Cardinal Rodrigo Borgia (later Pope Alexander VI), Lorenzo de' Medici still professed himself to be a "legal gentleman" (*legale gentile huomo*), meaning maybe a "loyal nobleman" (*leale gentile huomo*).[33] During 1472, in a similar social context, Lorenzo's Neapolitan banking partner, Agostino Biliotti, expressed with great "humanity"—that is to say, frankness—to the Venetian ambassador in Naples why it was advantageous (*convegniva*) for the Florentines to be governed by only one citizen.[34] The Venetians—especially in Naples—were sensitive to economic arguments and immediately comprehended the underlying needs. As a rule, international commercial disputes touched not only "public honor" but also required discreet resolution, as Lorenzo wrote many years later to a Florentine official in Pisa, Francesco Cambini, who had unknowingly confiscated goods that

---

27 Del Piazzo 1966, 497 (7 October 1473), 498 (13 October 1473), 499 (10 November 1473), 502 (1 December 1473), 503 (4 December 1473). See BNCF, Palatino 1103, fols. 172r–v (6 October, recommendation of Giovanni Canacci instead of Cesare Petrucci), 174r (for Giovanni Machiavelli "habita a Bologna"), 175r–v (9 November). The parallelism in the actions of the first chancery and those of Lorenzo de' Medici can also be observed in other cases.

28 Del Piazzo 1966, 504 (14 December 1473).

29 Ibid., 507 (3 January 1474).

30 Lupi 1863, 286–287.

31 ASF, MAP 26, 154 (11 January 1475).

32 "Sappiamo che di vostra natura date favore alla iustitia et a' nostri mercatanti, ma in questo di Lorenzo vi preghiamo lo facciate molto più perché molto più merita per la sua qualità, et noi ve ne resteremo obligatissimi": BNCF, Palatino 1103, fol. 103v. Ximenes had been an ambassador in Florence during May 1465: Trexler 1978c, 105; ASF, Signori, Risposte verbali di oratori forestieri 2, fols. 1r–3r.

33 Medici 1977–, 16:217 and n. 4 (with other references).

34 "perché ad ogni modo convegniva esser governata da qualche uno, et bisognava ne fusse uno maçor deli altri": Barbaro 1994, 256.

really belonged to the king of Portugal.[35] Protecting "public honor" in this sense meant not only safeguarding Florentine trade, but also avoiding open conflict and remaining on friendly terms with those sovereigns with whom relations were seen to be of vital strategic importance.

In the later Middle Ages, economic reprisals were seen as a justified means to achieve numerous aims, sometimes even political.[36] Almost all states or princes employed reprisals; in Florence, however, reprisals against foreign subjects were institutionally complicated, expensive, and not always successful. Jurisdiction here was in the hands of the *mercanzia* (four relevant registers from the early fourteenth century up to 1421 survive) and the sea consuls (before 1460).[37] In April 1421, for instance, the Florentine banker Gherardo di Jacopo Canigiani obtained a sentence of reprisal from the *mercanzia* and the five major guilds (*insieme co' consoli delle cinque magiori arti*) against the citizens of Camerino, with legal costs exceeding 102 gold florins added to the sum claimed.[38] Canigiani's confiscation of a Camerino merchant's villa and farmhouses outside Florence was, however, invalidated a year later, as decided in a long meeting of the *mercanzia* councilors together with thirteen "leading advocates," on the grounds that this latter merchant possessed full Florentine citizenship.[39] Another reprisal in favor of a citizen of San Gimignano against the commune of Gubbio was revoked on 19 January 1422, after the intervention of the *signoria* with the *mercanzia*.[40] As Alberto Del Vecchio and Eugenio Casanova demonstrated in their classic work more than a century ago, the right was still formally in the hands of the *mercanzia*, even after 1460, before becoming in the sixteenth century a prerogative of the "princes"—that is, the grand dukes of Tuscany.[41]

Throughout Europe, the tendency to delegate such a sensitive matter to the highest political authority or princely jurisdiction could be observed as early as the late fourteenth century.[42] It therefore comes as no surprise that Lorenzo the Magnificent became involved in the resolution of similar questions from the early 1470s. For example, at the beginning of 1473, the Spanish ambassador in Rome

35 Medici 1977–, 15:340–341.

36 Tanzini 2009; Tanzini and Tognetti 2012 (both with extensive bibliography).

37 On the *mercanzia*, see Astorri 1992; Zorzi 1996, 1327–1328; Goldthwaite 2009, 109–114. Although Bartolomeo Scala claimed in 1483 that this court "enjoyed great fame abroad, difficult cases being brought to it from all over the world, as people once used to consult the oracles at Dodona, Delphi, and Delos" (Brown 1979, 291), for many years it had been accused of serving only the rich and powerful: see Branca 1996, 120. Certainly its strict rules and procedural delays were the reason for the Savoyard reprisals after 1466 (see note 26 above).

38 ASF, Mercanzia 4353, fols. 20r–21v.

39 ASF, Mercanzia 4353, fols. 258v–161r. Venanzio di Pierozzo da Camerino in 1415 had been granted citizenship and from 1419 was related to the Pitti family; his villa of Rusciano later belonged to Luca Pitti. On the importance of the question of citizenship, see Tanzini 2009, 239 n. 95.

40 ASF, Mercanzia 4352, fol. 343v. These two cases seem to be the last reprisals mentioned in the Mercanzia series of "Cause straordinarie."

41 Vecchio and Casanova 1894, 80–85.

42 Ibid., 87 (on King Charles VIII of France); Tanzini 2009, 243 (on Venice).

complained to him and his brother Giuliano that the Florentines had used reprisals against some Spanish merchants in Pisa in reaction to the capture of a Florentine ship by unnamed "pirates" in the harbor of Cadiz; he therefore asked the two Medici brothers to intervene with the Florentine authorities to have these measures cancelled (*che dicte represaglie se levino in tucto*).[43] Likewise, Del Vecchio and Casanova published a letter from two citizens of Pietrasanta whom the *mercanzia* had arrested in 1476, as a consequence of reprisals conceded to a Florentine citizen against the Genoese: Lorenzo was now asked to use his influence with the *mercanzia* to resolve the case and to avoid jailing the two in the communal prison, the *stinche*.[44]

Two other examples of commercial conflict in which Lorenzo the Magnificent was directly involved will now be analyzed in more detail. The first regards an episode in which the commune of Bologna sequestered cargo belonging to Francesco Martelli's and Antonio Corsini's Florentine merchant company. In early 1478, Lorenzo directed several letters to the Bolognese ruler, Giovanni II Bentivoglio, as well as to another leading citizen of the town, Virgilio Malvezzi.[45] Other letters followed in April.[46] Malvezzi replied on 15 February, 19 February, 13 April, 19 April, and 21 April 1478.[47]

What was at stake? The exact date of Malvezzi's crucial first response is unfortunately unclear, but this letter obviously preceded the other five.[48] In his detailed account of the case, Malvezzi revealed a surprising scenario: the cargo of saffron that had been confiscated in Bologna did not really belong to the Florentines, but to an unnamed German merchant, for whom the two Florentines had only advanced payment; this not being, however, a question in which Lorenzo's own *utile et honore* was involved, Malvezzi did not refrain from explaining his own position. The story had begun with the move of a bankrupt German merchant from Venice to Bologna, where by law (*per legge commune*) he could not be charged or made liable by his numerous creditors.[49] One of these creditors was another German merchant who, without attempting to pursue his rights directly in Bologna, had then ordered the arrest of all Bolognese citizens passing through his home territory in Germany; the first of these had unfortunately been Annibale, the son of Virgilio Malvezzi himself. The confiscation of the saffron was therefore nothing but a consequence of this arrest and a means of exerting pressure in southern Germany.

---

43 ASF, MAP 139, 222 (22 February 1473). On foreign merchants in Pisa, see B. Casini 1996; on the episode of the Florentine galley in Cadiz in late 1472, see Mallett 1967, 101, 173.
44 Vecchio and Casanova 1894, 195–198.
45 Del Piazzo 1966, 38.
46 Ibid., 45, 47 ("per questi Martelli e Corsini, in causa de' zafferani sostenuti de' tedeschi").
47 ASF, MAP 34, 54; ASF, MAP 36, 195, 446, 468, 475.
48 ASF, MAP 73, 294.
49 This fact was obviously well known in Florence and might have been the reason why bankrupt Florentines such as Iacopo di Michele Sizzi and Lorenzo d'Ilarione de' Bardi fled to Bologna in those years: BNCF, Palatino 1103, fols. 110v–111r, 177v.

The episode is typical of the often difficult commercial relations with Germany. Luckily, in this case, there is detailed documentation of the capture of young Annibale Malvezzi in late 1477 near Kempten on Lake Constance, where he remained in prison for nearly two years.[50] Great resentment arose in Bologna, where German citizens had hitherto always been welcome; on 3 February 1478, the city government publicly decreed that German merchants and their goods ought to be safe in its territory,[51] although in the saffron episode this was apparently not the case.

Some weeks later, the government officially replied to the Florentines, the doge of Venice, the emperor, and the town of Augsburg to the effect that this confiscation and the imprisonment of a traveling merchant from Augsburg were fully justified.[52] It should be noted here that both Kempten and Augsburg were autonomous free imperial cities, and so not immediately subject to any ruler; their only direct link was common membership in the same communal federation. In 1479, Augsburg even turned to the Habsburg emperor Frederick III for help.[53] Presumably for this very reason and owing to the Bolognese case's legal weakness no formal sentence of any law court could ever be cited in all Malvezzi's letters, only the decision of the government, the *reggimento*.

The question was of obvious and vital political importance, a case touching both private and public repute, and so the confiscation and the arrest of the Augsburg merchant had been ordered by Bologna's highest magistracy, the sixteen reformers. By the end of 1479, the problem had been resolved, but it is unclear whether and in what way Lorenzo the Magnificent and the Florentine merchants ever accepted the compromise. In her study on the Bentivoglio family, Cecilia Ady not only mentioned the episode but also quoted from a contemporary Bolognese chronicler, who "comments with sympathy on the misfortunes of his fellow citizen, saying that he knew from experience the difficulties encountered by merchants in foreign lands, and the large sums which must be expended upon safe-conducts."[54]

To return to the presumed "pharaoh-like" persecution of the three religious pilgrims in Florence in 1477, this incident involved a similar case of economic reprisal. The registers of the *otto di guardia* reveal more details. On this powerful magistracy's orders, the first two pilgrims, *Bernardus Scultetus* (Schulz) and *Thimo Ulm* (Timme Holm) were transferred on 28 March 1477 to a separate part of the communal prison, the *mallevato*.[55] The crucial detail that they were not obliged to

---

50 Gorrini 1900, 53–54.
51 Ibid., 92–93.
52 Ibid., 101–108.
53 See Geffcken 2002, 135–136.
54 Ady 1937, 187.
55 ASF, Otto 44, fol. 42r. Until the early 1440s, the names of the prisoners in the *mallevato* were recorded in the so-called Libri del Giglio; by 1477, this was no longer the case. See ASF, Camera del comune, Provveditori poi Massai, Libri del giglio 66.

sustain the costs of their imprisonment—which had to be paid by their creditors—was a recurring theme in all cases of reprisal.[56] Curiously—and incorrectly—the *otto* identified both as citizens of Lübeck on the Baltic Sea (*Lubich*). Only on 12 July were the two men released.[57]

Such scarce information is typical of the way the *otto* handled sensitive issues. The whole story comes out only by way of several letters preserved in the Archivio Mediceo avanti il Principato, mostly written between 9 and 12 April 1477. Schulz originated in fact from Lauenburg in Pomerania and according to Cardinal Francesco Gonzaga was a member of the curia (a *cortigiano*) returning from Germany on the order of his patron, the papal nuncio and indulgence collector, Günther von Bünau.[58] In two other letters written on the same day, the apostolic protonotary Domenico Della Rovere urged Lorenzo the Magnificent to release the Germans, who were being detained in retaliation for the capture of the Burgundian-Florentine galley off Gravelines by the Hanse pirate Paul Benecke four years earlier.[59] Their detention was totally unjustified, so it was asserted, because Schulz and his companion came from entirely different parts of Germany;[60] furthermore, Della Rovere confirmed that the head of the mission was indeed an envoy of Sixtus IV who had been sent to the North to collect money for the crusade and was now on his way back.[61]

The most forceful intervention, however, came from Lorenzo the Magnificent's uncle, Giovanni Tornabuoni, a banker in Rome who, on 9 April, composed a letter of introduction for two special envoys, messer Theoderigo Clinrode and messer Hermanno Duker. They were both described as gentlemen and friends of the Medici who had recently been informed of their compatriots' detention in Florence, where it was believed that they were *istarlini*—that is to say, Hanseatic merchants.[62] Tornabuoni himself had gathered further information and not only confirmed that the two were indeed Germans, but added that several cardinals had asked him to

56 See Vecchio and Casanova 1894, 195. This rule corresponded to a law of 1474 according to which the creditors had to pay two soldi a day for their imprisoned debtors if the *soprastanti delle stinche* declared them to be indigent: ASF, PR 164, fol. 269r–v.

57 ASF, Soprastanti alle stinche 106, fol. 42v.

58 "rimandato in corte dal patrono suo domino Guntero cubiculario de la Sanctitate de Nostro Signore e collectore apostolico in Germania": Francesco Gonzaga to Lorenzo de' Medici, 12 April 1477, ASF, MAP 46, 448. On Schulz and Timme Holm, see Daniels 2013a, 113–114 nn. 23–25; on both Schulz and Günther von Bünau, see Volkmar 2008, 288–290, 306–307. I would like to thank Dr. Ulrich Schwarz (Wolfenbüttel) for valuable information on many of the Germans involved in this case.

59 ASF, MAP 35, 395, 400. On the capture of the Florentine galley in April 1473, see Mallett 1967, 98–102; De Roover 1963, 347–348.

60 "ob depredatum Florentinorum navigium a quibusdam pirattis in partibus Germaniae, unde ipse Bernardus non est": ASF, MAP 35, 400.

61 "pro sanctitatis sue pecuniis cruciate recuperandis in Germaniam destinatum et ea de causa ad sanctitatem suam redire": ASF, MAP 35, 395.

62 The word *sterlini/starlini* derives from the word employed for the Hanseatic merchants at Bruges and elsewhere (*Osterlinge* or *Esterlinge*), and not from the English monetary term.

write on their behalf; according to the date this letter was received, the two envoys must have arrived in Florence on 24 April 1477.[63]

On 29 April, after five days, the *signoria* responded to the arrival of both the papal brief and these distinguished German clerics and canon lawyers with a counter-mission to Rome.[64] The official statement of the Florentine position was entrusted to the prior of Santissima Annunziata, maestro Domenico da Viterbo OSM.[65] This Servite preacher was both well known in the curia and to the Medici family: Lorenzo the Magnificent's mother, Lucrezia Tornabuoni, had informed Domenico of his election to the priorate in 1476.[66]

In their official reply to Pope Sixtus IV and in further letters to the Florentine archbishop Rinaldo Orsini, to Domenico da Viterbo, and to Giovanni Tornabuoni, the *signoria* refuted all the opposing arguments, insisting that the Florentine merchants had a good case against the Hanseatic merchants (*per la giusta causa che hanno e mercatanti nostri contro agli sterlini*) and that the captured Germans were indeed *sterlini* and thus fully answerable for all these "barbarous and inhuman" crimes (*gentem illam barbaram atque immanem, ita ab omni humanitate alienam*).[67]

Why were the Florentines so sure about the real identity of the two merchants? It is likely that some of the exchange letters and other financial documentation carried by them had originated in Lübeck, a banking center where incoming papal taxes were traditionally collected and administered.[68] The Florentines themselves had

63 ASF, MAP 35, 378: "todeschi uhomini di bene et antichi amici della chasa, i quali ànno inteso che chostì sono stati presi Timo Holomo et Bernardo de Lombor a chagione della ghaleazza di Borghognia, stimando che fussino istarlini; il perché, avanti ve n'abbi voluto ischrivere, me ne sono voluto informare e truovo che i detti prigioni sono todeschi e che non n'ànno a ffare niente con detti starlini." On Klinckrode and Duncker, see Sohn 1997, 180–187, 364; on Klinckrode's links with Lübeck, see Schuchard 2009, 104–105. Bernhard Schulz died in 1510 in Rome; his portrait sculpture can still be seen there on his funeral monument in the church of Santa Maria dell'Anima. (My thanks to Dr. Eberhard Nikitsch [Rome], who is preparing a monograph on these monuments.)

64 The exact cause of an earlier mission of the Florentine *capitano del popolo*, Giovanni Calzavacca of Parma, to Rome in late April and May 1477 "pro negotiis comunis" is unfortunately unclear (ASF, Signori e collegi, Deliberazioni di ordinaria autorita, Duplicati, 19, fols. 280r, 300r).

65 This "praedicator insignis" had first been invited by the *signoria* in June 1471 to preach at Lent the following year (ASF, Signori, Minutari 9, fol. 268r), and had become prior of Santissima Annunziata following the provincial chapter convoked there in May 1476 (ASF, NA 611, fols. 127r–130v, 184r–187v). On 30 April 1477, the convent paid for fifty bunches of fennel to be presented by him at Rome to the order's cardinal protector, Giovanni Michiel (ASF, Corporazioni religiose soppresse dal governo francese 119, 696, fol. 40r) and on 10 June, wrote to him that he should return for the Florentine celebrations of St. John the Baptist, which he duly did (ibid., fols. 43v–44r). Vangelisti's (1959, 80) incorrect notice that from May 1477 maestro Domenico was ill in bed seems to have derived from a dating error in ASF, Corporazioni religiose soppresse dal governo francese 119, 196, fol. 277v (where 1478 instead of 1477 should be read). None of his letters from Rome have survived.

66 See maestro Domenico's response to Lucrezia Tornabuoni from Viterbo on 29 May 1476 in ASF, MAP 34, 329.

67 ASF, Missive 49, fol. 28r–v; ASF, Missive 47, fol. 57r.

68 Voigt 1968; in 1479, the papal collector Marino da Fregeno described the town as rich, beautiful, and governed by women ("hic mulieres regunt viros"), whereas the populace was garrulous, often drunk, and naturally hostile to the Roman Catholic Church (ibid., 194).

sent several bankers to Lübeck in the fifteenth century (but presumably there were none at this moment).[69] It is furthermore possible that some of the papers carried by Schulz and his companions were in one way or another related to the Hanseatic League.[70] The main purpose of their journey, however, must have been the delivery of the papal revenues, which were now almost certainly confiscated by the deposit bank of the *otto di guardia*, namely Lorenzo the Magnificent's Medici bank.[71]

After another two weeks, Sixtus IV put the final resolution of the conflict into the hands of Cardinal Giuliano Della Rovere (later Pope Julius II), who, however, never achieved a compromise between the two parties.[72] On 24 August 1477, Sixtus IV excommunicated Benecke and all residents of Danzig who would not help the Florentines recuperate their losses; in the papal bull, the Florentine reprisals were not mentioned.[73] Even Florentine sources remain surprisingly silent. If any discussion had taken place in the *pratiche*—as might be expected from the earlier intervention of the *signoria*—it was not recorded.[74] From a legal point of view, it may be noted that, apart from the generic reference to a "just cause," the Florentine procedure resembled that observed by the Bolognese government a few months later. A further parallel is that in both cases external arbitration was necessary. If economic reprisals were thus fully accepted in late fifteenth-century Italy, the particular role of Lorenzo the Magnificent in the 1477 dispute derived more from his direct involvement with the capture of the Florentine galley in the North Sea four years earlier than from his role as Florence's first citizen.

After the Pazzi war (1478–80), the dual role of Lorenzo as civic leader and merchant banker in his own right influenced Florentine politics even more. Official diplomacy served both his individual (*particolare*) and the public interest. In the decade following 1480, the Medici dedicated considerable time to the development and extension of commercial relations with both northern European and Mediterranean communities and merchants. In commenting on these issues, it is not always possible to draw a clear line between the public and private (for example, in Lorenzo de' Medici's protection of the Spanish merchants arriving after 1486

---

69 When on 30 January 1476 the chaplain of the Danish king Johannes Lang took a loan of ten ducats from the banker Guasparre di Nicodemo Spinelli in Florence, he promised to repay it in twenty-two and a half "marchae" of Lübeck, but directly to Marino da Fregeno (ASF, NA 1748, fol. 235v); see also Weissen 2011, 715–717.

70 See Schuchard 2009, 107, for the Hanseatic point of view in the case of the galley. The Florentines accused some of the Hanseatic towns such as Hamburg and Lübeck of double-dealing.

71 On the Medici bank here, see ASF, Otto 44, fol. 22v.

72 Giovanni Tornabuoni to Lorenzo de' Medici, 17 May 1477, ASF, MAP 34, 146: "Nostro Signore à chomesso al prefato San Piero in Vinchula il fatto della ghalea et fu presa de li sterlini et spaci[ato] in buona forma et da sperare ne seghua qualche buon fructo."

73 ASF, Diplomatico, Lunghe, 24 August 1477 (Mediceo; see Camerani Marri 1951, 14, 134–135). In addition, in September 1477, the Florentine *signoria* sent Cristofano Spini to the North with several letters of introduction; Pope Sixtus IV wrote a brief to Danzig in support of the Florentines' demands (Reumont 1861).

74 There is a gap between March and August 1477 in ASF, CP 60: see fol. 156v.

from the kingdom of Naples, among whom were some of real or presumed *marrano* origin). What is clear, however, is that these issues were usually negotiated in great secrecy and that even the Florentine inner circle might not always have been aware of all possible political implications. A more traditional initiative was launched in late 1489, resulting a year later in a treaty with the English crown that was meant to have secured "for Pisa a complete monopoly of the English wool trade to Italy."[75] Lorenzo played an active role in the preparation of this treaty and presumably had more than one meeting with the many English merchants passing through or living in Pisa and Florence at the time.[76]

Lorenzo's letters attest to the fact that what had previously been a prerogative of the first chancery now became his own—that is to say, the writing of letters of re-commendation or introduction for widows, for the poor, or for prisoners. Examples include his letter for *Valentino tedesco* to the Sienese *balìa* in 1486,[77] or the letter in favor of Despina Arianiti (Arniti) Comneno, the elderly princess of Macedonia, three years later.[78] These letters gave Lorenzo the chance openly to declare his "compassion" for the unjustly oppressed, assuming the image of a Christian prince, just as Gentile Becchi had written in 1477. Numerous other sources (mostly notar-ial) document cases in which Lorenzo de' Medici acted on behalf of poor widows or workers, among them also foreigners. In this, however, Lorenzo did not actually do more than what was expected of any leading Florentine citizen.

After 1478, the immigration of foreign workers to Florence suffered a serious decline owing to epidemics and warfare, and also because of the extremely strict control exercised by the *otto di guardia*, who stopped the influx.[79] Many foreign-ers whom Cristoforo Landino had identified as "laborers," such as the northern (wool-)weavers and shoemakers, had to leave Florence because of the economic crisis. As a consequence, the confraternity of south German shoemakers was forced to discontinue activity soon after 1478. Workers with more specific skills, on the other hand, were still eagerly sought after, such as the Spanish perfumers, for whom Lorenzo de' Medici wrote one of his carnival songs about 1490.[80]

Although political relations with the Hanseatic League never recovered in the fifteenth century, no more dramatic cases of detentions of foreigners passing through Florence, explicitly or implicitly identifiable as reprisals, can be found after 1477. The sources examined so far do not confirm Pope Sixtus IV's condemnation of Lorenzo the Magnificent as a tyrant or "pharaoh"; with regard to the control of

---

75 Mallett 1962, 261.

76 See Medici 1977–, 16:213–214.

77 Ibid., 9:354–355. On this interesting case, see also ASF, Otto 73, fols. 101v, 112v; ASF, NA 6088, fols. 71r–72r.

78 Medici 1977–, 15:369–370.

79 ASF, Otto 48, fols. 17r, 28r, 54r. See Böninger 2006a, 247.

80 "Siam galanti di Valenza / qui per passo capitati, / d'amor già presi e legati / delle donne di Fiorenza": Medici 1991, 62. Although Valence in France has been proposed in this case, at least one *Diegus de Scalona yspanus magister profumorum* is known in 1493: ASF, NA 5244, fol. 53r–v.

immigration and of reprisals, his authority does not seem to have gone beyond that of informal persuasion (which could often end in coercion) within a traditional institutional framework, formally conserving the prerogatives of the *signoria*, the *mercanzia*, and the *otto di guardia*. Lorenzo was kept informed of all their actions and so able to exert his influence up to a point. His quoting a popular saying against those who tried to have the city gates opened after dark by throwing stones was ungenerous because he held a particular privilege in this regard.[81] But if anyone was controlling immigration to Florence through these gates, it was the magistracy of the *otto di guardia e balìa*.

81 See Medici 1977–, 15:238, 258. In 1475, the only three exceptions that justified the brief opening of the city gates at night were the arrival of couriers on communal business ("pro factis comunis") or to the *otto di guardia* or to Lorenzo and Giuliano de' Medici (ASF, Signori e Collegi, Deliberazioni di ordinaria autorità, Duplicati 19, fol. 2r).

PART III
Religion and the Church

ELEVEN

The Albizzi, the Early Medici, and the Florentine Church, 1375–1460

DAVID S. PETERSON

THE RISE OF THE MEDICI can seem inevitable. Looking back across the fifteenth century from the pontificates of the Medici popes Leo X (1513–21) and Clement VII (1523–34) to Giovanni di Bicci de' Medici's (1360–1429) initial collaboration as papal banker with Baldassarre Cossa (Pope John XXIII, 1410–15), it is tempting to assume that the combination of papal and princely power achieved by the Medici in the early sixteenth century was a goal they had pursued deliberately from the outset. Certainly they were ambitious and opportunistic, and influence acquired in either the temporal or the religious sphere might indeed be used to enhance it in the other as well. But the rise of the Medici, and their relations with the church, were neither so linear nor so simple as hindsight might suggest.

The histories of Florence and the church over a long fifteenth century really fall into three parallel periods. That of papal weakness during the schism (1378–1417) corresponds roughly to the period in which Florence, led by the Albizzi oligarchy, expanded its territorial state and institutions. A second period from the 1420s to the death of Cosimo "il vecchio" (1389–1464) saw not only the Medici rise to dominance within the Florentine republic, but efforts by a reunited papacy to achieve significant church reform as a means of justifying the restoration of papal monarchy. Finally, the late fifteenth century witnessed the Renaissance papacy's retreat

∞ I wish to thank Robert Black, John Law, and the members of the Academic Committee for their gracious invitation to participate in this conference. Washington and Lee University provided a generous Lenfest Research Grant that facilitated the preparation of this chapter.

from reform into the princely self-absorption that helped precipitate the Protestant Reformation, while in Florence the magnificence of Lorenzo (1449–1492) in the end served as a foil to both Girolamo Savonarola's and Piero Soderini's efforts to restore the New Jerusalem and revive the Florentine republic.

Nor were political power and religious authority simply interchangeable. Certainly, state and church (*regnum et sacerdotium*) were juridical constructs meant even in theory to collaborate rather than to conflict with one other, and in social and political reality they often became intricately entwined. But within the institutional church it is possible, even in Guelf Florence, to distinguish between the papacy and a regional Florentine church, which, though certainly influenced by popes, by the Florentine republic, and by its leading families, nevertheless had interests and a history of its own and could act upon these parties in turn. Equally complex was the relationship between the church as a temporal power and its spiritual authority. Its wealth, courts, and benefices provoked efforts by Florentine governments to curb its power, but its sacral character made it a legitimizing institution as well, inspiring efforts by the city's rulers and leading families to embrace, control, and manipulate it. Too explicit a move to do so, however, risked voiding it of the spiritual credibility that gave it political value as a legitimating agency.[1]

The contrasting strategies of the Albizzi and early Medici regimes toward the church are evident in the two periods spanning, first, the papal schism and, then, the efforts at ecclesiastical reform and papal restoration that followed. Obviously, these regimes confronted the church—papal and Florentine—under significantly differing conditions of decline and (partial) regeneration. Like other Italian powers, Florence under the Albizzi expanded its territory over the course of the schism, bringing many more ecclesiastical institutions into its purview and devising means to place them under governmental supervision. The Florentine case was distinctive, however, because the schism was immediately preceded by Florence's failed war of the Eight Saints (1375–78) against Pope Gregory XI (1370–78) and the Ciompi revolt that promptly ensued. The war was an ideological rupture in Florence's Guelf tradition that stimulated the "civic" humanists' revaluation of the city's republican ideals. And it was accompanied by massive expropriations of ecclesiastical property that had an impact on local clerical finances and politics down to the mid-fifteenth century and cast a long shadow over Florentines' relations with their local church. Viewed as a profanation of the city's religious patrimony, the war called forth a variety of political efforts to resanctify the city as a whole.

The most notable point of continuity between the Albizzi and Medici regimes is therefore the effort both made to balance centralizing attention to delimit the operations of ecclesiastical institutions within Florentine territory with strategies to embrace the church as a source of political legitimation. The Medici and their partisans retained many institutions and practices devised by the Albizzi oligarchy

---

1   Trexler 1973b, 131; Peterson 1994.

to curb the church's judicial prerogatives and especially to monitor the movement of ecclesiastical wealth and benefices. To a greater extent than the Albizzi, however, the Medici aimed not simply to sanctify the city and legitimize their *reggimento*; more particularly, they aspired to justify their family's dominant position within both. Cosimo's vast wealth and extensive patronage network enabled him to identify his family with a variety of religious currents and institutions within the Florentine church. This may reflect signorial aspirations, but they were carefully adapted to a republican setting. The most explicit challenge to the Medici regime's legitimacy came at the moment of its consolidation in 1458 from Florence's archbishop Antonino Pierozzi (1389–1459), an Observant Dominican friar drawn from Cosimo's own favored convent of San Marco.

Gene Brucker aptly underscored the "ubiquity and propinquity" of the church's presence in fifteenth-century Florence.[2] There were 83 defining parishes within the city's baptismal parish (*pieve*) of San Giovanni Battista defining its urban space, while 60 large rural *pievi* articulated the landscape of the Florentine diocese, encompassing another 25 collegiate churches, 28 oratories, and 614 parish churches. These, like the 118 monasteries, hermitages, and friaries spread throughout the diocese, were important *loci* of family and parochial pride. Florentines' charitable impulses were manifest in 114 hospitals of various sorts, and penitential companies of *disciplinati* were increasingly prominent alongside traditional *laudesi* companies among 104 urban and rural confraternities. Including the six other dioceses of Fiesole, Pistoia, Arezzo, Volterra, Pisa, Cortona, and portions of Lucca, Florence's territory in the early fifteenth century encompassed over 270 *pievi*, 90 collegiate churches, 660 chapels and oratories, 290 monasteries, 275 hospitals, and 196 religious *compagnie*. The church's landed endowments constituted a quarter of some parts of the countryside, and clergy composed nearly 5 percent of the population.[3] The 1427 catasto of the Florentine clergy listed 40 institutions with capitalizations above 5,000 florins. These were impressive but not preponderant agglomerations of wealth in a community where 192 citizens were worth as much as, and 4 more than, 50,000 florins.[4]

Massive but not monolithic, the ecclesiastical establishment accommodated a remarkable variety of humanist, mendicant, charitable, and penitential strains of devotion, expressed publicly and privately, but it was marked by numerous rivalries and inequities of its own. When he toured the diocese in 1422, Amerigo Corsini (bishop 1411–19, archbishop 1419–35) found the cathedral chapter riven by the high-handed leadership of its provost, Amerigo de' Medici.[5] The dozen collegiate

2   Brucker 1983, 172. Figures following are from ASF, Catasto 195; on confraternities and hospitals, see Henderson 1994, 38–46, 297–306.
3   Conti 1965; Herlihy and Klapisch-Zuber 1978, 158–159.
4   Martines 1963, 365–378; I owe this comparative observation to Richard Goldthwaite.
5   Archivio Arcivescovile di Firenze, Visite pastorali 002.0 (1422), fols. 5r–12r.

churches that ringed the city center had become, like the cathedral chapter, hubs in a network of multiple benefice-holding. Tiny parishes here and in the countryside lay on the verge of extinction. While urban nunneries would expand their numbers over the fifteenth century, and "flagship" male institutions such as Camaldoli, Certosa, and Vallombrosa still flourished in the countryside, numerous other monasteries were reduced to a few poor members and efforts to reform the mendicants had split them. There was weakness at the center. The local church's fiscal and judicial prerogatives had been curbed by popular communal regimes in the thirteenth century, and episcopal authority had been undercut in the fourteenth by the expansion of papal provision to benefices, commendation of abbeys, and the creation of a network of tax collectorates that further fragmented local institutions.[6] While Florentines in the early quattrocento undertook the great ecclesiastical building projects that would shape Italy's artistic Renaissance, many sectors of the Florentine church were in decline and disarray.

Much of this decline resulted from plague, warfare, and schism that affected other regions of Italy as well. What set the Florentine case apart was the war of the Eight Saints (see above, 172). The generally collaborative relationship between Florentine bankers and the papacy that had prevailed since the Guelf entente of 1265–67 was upended when a regime dominated by new men (*gente nuova*) determined to block Gregory XI's return of the curia from Avignon to Rome and to defend Tuscan *libertas* by fomenting uprisings throughout the papal state.[7] Simultaneously, the Florentine councils passed a round of legislation further curbing the clergy's judicial immunities, extending communal supervision over ecclesiastical property, and prohibiting citizens from accepting appointment to the bishoprics of Florence or Fiesole.[8] The following year, 1376, Salvestro de' Medici, who would distinguish himself also during the Ciompi uprising, persuaded the councils to adopt a more radical measure: financing the war against the papacy by expropriating the estates of local clergy for sale to citizens.[9] There ensued the broadest liquidation of ecclesiastical landholdings conducted anywhere in Europe before the Reformation. Secular clergy were hit heavily and only nunneries went largely unscathed. Vieri di Cambio de' Medici alone purchased 288 florins' worth of the estates belonging formerly to his parish church of San Lorenzo.[10]

---

6   According to Francesco di Lorenzo Machiavelli, "al veschovado niente si fa": ASF, Catasto 17, fol. 603v. Thanks to Robert Black for this reference.

7   Becker 1962; Brucker 1962, 265–335; Trexler 1974. For what follows, see Peterson 2002.

8   ASF, PR 60, fol. 148r–v (8 January 1372/73); 62, fols. 76r–77v (22 June 1374); 63, fols. 69r–72v, 73r–75v (7 and 12 July 1375).

9   ASF, CP 14, fol. 86r (24 September 1376). The enabling legislation was ASF, PR 64, fols. 137r–140r, 153r–157r, 191r–192r (25 September, 13 October, and 5 November 1376).

10 ASF, Monte comune 1558, fols. 21v–22r. Anthony Molho called my attention to this valuable source. To gauge the depth of expropriations, I have contrasted the figures here with those in ASF, Catasto 195.

But extending the conflict against the papacy into an assault on the local church proved a massive political blunder. Public sentiment turned sharply against the war, sales of church property had to be forced, and in spring 1378 the republic sued for peace. Florence promised to pay Gregory's successor Urban VI (1378–89) an indemnity of 250,000 florins (though it paid little), to annul its anti-ecclesiastical legislation (which did not occur), and to reinstate the clergy's property.[11] The government devised a system of drawings by lot whereby clergy would gradually be returned their properties and citizens their purchase payments. Meanwhile, clergy were compensated with 5 percent interest-bearing shares in Florence's funded public debt, the *monte*. But the process, which did not get well under way until the restoration of the Guelf regime of 1382, was nearing completion only by the 1420s and not fully complete until 1451. Meanwhile, clerical finances were tied to those of the state while many laymen retained clerical property against their consciences.

War was followed by the papal schism and the Ciompi uprising of 1378. The chancellor Coluccio Salutati noted the conjunction, treating them as divine chastisements of Rome for its attack on Florentine *libertas* and of Florence for its assault on its church.[12] The shaken Guelf rulers who returned to power in 1382, led by the Albizzi, associated the Eight Saints with social revolution. To restore order, they encouraged the inquisition to combat a resurgence of *fraticelli* heretics.[13] Thereafter, the legislative councils passed occasional measures against possible conspiracies in confraternal *societates* in 1391 and 1419.[14]

More persistently, the Albizzi regime articulated a series of strategies aimed at resanctifying a profaned city and legitimizing their own oligarchic rule by embracing and orchestrating key strains of Florentine religious life. The completion of the cathedral and Orsanmichele were but the most visible of numerous Florentine civic projects to restore or redecorate leading churches and monasteries. Many others were granted *gabelle* exemptions or assistance in collecting testamentary bequests from the *mercanzia* or *monte* officials. Florence's legislative councils expanded the republic's calendar of religious holidays and from 1394 onward approved a series of oblations by the *sei di mercanzia* (the magistracy in charge of the *mercanzia*) and Florence's priors to the city's leading churches, convents, and friaries.[15] The government surpassed the episcopal curia in issuing new sumptuary legislation regulating such life-cycle sacraments as baptisms, marriages, and funerals; supervising women's dress and restricting gaming; and creating the *ufficiali dell'onestà* (officials for

11   ASF, Diplomatico, Lunghe, 28 July 1378 (Atti pubblici).
12   Salutati to Ubaldino Buonamici, 3 October 1383, Salutati 1891–1911, 2:122.
13   ASF, PR 71, fols. 175r–176r (13 December 1382).
14   ASF, PR 80, fols. 69r–70r (7 August 1391); ASF, PR 109, fols. 160v–162v (19 October 1419); Henderson 1985.
15   Beginning with Ognissanti, ASF, PR 83, fols. 141v–142v (5 October 1394); a list up to 1415 is in *Statuta* 1779–83, 3:287–370.

public decency) to police male sexuality and protect nunneries.[16] Though Florence had cardinals (and bankers) at both papal curias (Pietro Corsini at Avignon [1378–1405] and Angelo Acciaiuoli at Rome [1385–1408]), hosting the council of Pisa in 1409 was embraced as an opportunity to legitimize Florence's most recent territorial acquisition (Pisa was conquered in 1406) and to link the sanctification of the republic and its rulers to the broader conciliar effort to reunite a universal church whose own sanctity was in doubt.[17]

Meanwhile, Florence expanded its territory under Albizzi leadership, between 1384 and 1421 annexing Arezzo, Volterra, Pistoia, Pisa, Cortona, Montepulciano, Castrocaro, Livorno, and a myriad of minor centers.[18] Letters and embassies flowed from the republic's chancery to the Roman curia to support loyal Florentine candidates for bishoprics and abbacies and to defend regional institutions from foreign and papal exploitation. Salutati explained to Pope Boniface IX (1389–1404) the bishopric of Arezzo's importance as "a singular fortress and citadel of our state."[19] But as it developed its own system of vicariates, the government became concerned less with using bishoprics as agencies of direct territorial control than with circumscribing their administrative prerogatives.[20] Having imposed Florentine power so aggressively in Ghibelline Pisa, the *signoria* had second thoughts about similar rigor regarding the church, urging Bishop Giuliano Ricci (1418–61) to curb the severity of his curial initiatives.[21] The law prohibiting Florentines' appointment to their bishopric was invoked only once in 1385:[22] five of Florence's seven bishops over the course of the schism were native sons.[23] Boniface IX's removal of Onofrio dello Steccuto from the see in 1400 provoked indignation in the legislative councils, but Antonio Alessandri pointed out that "it is an ecclesiastical issue" and matters were left to stand.[24] For their part, popes resisted appointing scions of Florence's leading political families to the highest dignity of their church: Ubertino degli Albizzi (1426–36) and Donato de' Medici (1436–74) both ended their careers parked in the suffragan diocese of Pistoia.

The Albizzi regime was also concerned to defend the prerogatives of regional monastic institutions. Old legislation against lay spoliation and usurpation (*de*

---

16 E.g., *Statuta* 1779–83, 2:366–390; Rocke 1996.

17 Landi 1985; Lewin 2003, 136–167.

18 Zorzi 2000, 13.

19 ASF, Missive 26, fol. 21v (17 November 1403): "arx est, singulareque presidium nostri status."

20 Peterson 2000, 135.

21 ASF, Missive 32, fol. 180v (10 February 1429/30).

22 ASF, Missive 20, fol. 66r–v (22 October 1385).

23 Angelo Ricasoli (1370–82), Angelo Acciaiuoli (1383–85), Onofrio dello Steccuto (Visdomini, 1389–1400), Alamanno Adimari (1400–1), and Amerigo Corsini (1411–35).

24 ASF, CP 34, fol. 170r (23 March 1401/2): "quia res est ecclesiasticalis episcopatus, non videtur eis ad se pertinere."

accedendo) continued to be enforced.[25] But during the schism, the greatest menace was the impoverishment of the Roman popes themselves, who exploited their powers of provision and commendation to collect common service taxes by encouraging rapid turnover of benefices and increased absenteeism. In 1394, Florence's legislative councils created a commission to ensure that revenues of Florentine benefices held by foreigners went to the institutions themselves. A decade later, responding to Bishop Jacopo Palladini's (1401–10) lengthy absence in Rome, the councils directed the *monte* officials to sequester the incomes of episcopal properties. Two years later, the same *monte* officials were charged to impound the revenues of appointees who failed to take residence within five years, and the priors were authorized to tax the patrimonies of unbeneficed clergy.[26] Gregory XII's (1406–15) flagrant manipulation of benefices sparked proposals in the *pratiche* (advisory meetings) to assume direct supervision of appointments in Florentine territory. But the issue was dropped, partly to facilitate negotiations for the council of Pisa, but also for fear lest such control might stimulate partisan competition.[27]

With Alexander V's (1409–10) election at Pisa, the Florentine *reggimento* (regime) promptly began pressing for a scheme to redraw diocesan boundaries to align them with Florentine territory.[28] But it dropped the plan in exchange for a papal license to levy a 100,000-florin tax directly on the clergy. Though many clerics still awaited restitution of their expropriated property, Florence had quietly begun taxing clergy in the 1390s to meet rising military expenses. Gregory XII split a 30,000-florin levy with the Florentines in 1407. John XXIII, in turn, allowed the city to impose a forced loan (*prestanza*) of 10 percent on ecclesiastical revenues and 15 percent on clerics' patrimonial incomes, and himself imposed an 80,000-florin levy to be paid to Florence's *dieci di balìa* (ten of war) in 1413.[29] Meanwhile, to block fraudulent transfers of taxable property from laymen to tax-exempt (*non supportantes*) ecclesiastics, the councils enacted mortmain legislation, imposing a contract gabelle in 1407 on all lay benefactions to ecclesiastics and making the property transferred taxable.[30]

These laws were incorporated into a major codification of the Florentine statutes issued between 1415 and 1418. Integrating recent legislation regulating benefices and clerical wealth in the territory with older communal measures curbing ecclesiastical courts, the *Statuta* now included all within a single corpus of territorial law. Pope Martin V (1417–31), determined to assert the reunited church's prerogatives

25   ASF, PR 74, fols. 244r–245r (22 January 1385/86); ASF, PR 101, fols. 5r–6v (26 March 1412).

26   ASF, PR 83, fols. 212v–214r (10 December 1394); ASF, PR 93, fols. 71v–72v (18 July 1404); ASF, PR 95, fols. 57v–58r, 63r (8 and 15 June 1406).

27   ASF, CP 39, fols. 49v–58v (May–June 1408).

28   Chittolini 1980.

29   For taxation under Gregory XII, see ASV, RV 336, fols. 82v–83v (8 August 1407); under Alexander V, see ASF, PR 98, fols. 92r–93r (16 November 1409); under John XXIII, see ASF, PR 101, fol. 407r (23 March 1412/13) and ASV, RV 345, fols. 247r–248r (25 July 1413).

30   ASF, PR 96, fols. 68r–69r (17 July 1407).

in the aftermath of the schism, protested against this challenge to ecclesiastical liberty (*libertas ecclesiae*). In 1427, to facilitate negotiations for a further clerical tax, Florence's legislative councils agreed to strike down five old statutes restricting clerical judicial immunities. But they listed three other laws, concerning election to the bishopric, access to benefices, and supervision of lay bequests to ecclesiastics, that they absolutely refused to repeal.[31] Furthermore, two days later they established the *catasto*, a complete tax inventory of wealth in the territory including that of clergy.[32] The government thus created an additional bureaucratic instrument not only to monitor the movement of property from laymen to ecclesiastics, but to impose levies directly on the clergy themselves. Florence now had in place a coherent body of law regulating the activities of ecclesiastics throughout the territory and the bureaucratic apparatus to enforce it. Future dealings with the local church, and with Rome, could be conducted on the basis of Florentine institutional strength.

But by now tensions were approaching breaking points both within the Florentine church and the Albizzi regime. At the end of the schism, combined papal and Florentine fiscal exploitation of the local clergy brought to a head a crisis in diocesan government that had been deepening since the war of the Eight Saints. Deeply in debt and frustrated by decades of weak episcopal and papal leadership, determined to recover control of their finances, and inspired by the conciliar model of church government that had ended the schism at the council of Constance (1414–18), Florence's secular clergy in the 1420s undertook a unique experiment in diocesan self-government by forming a corporation (*universitas*) of their own to challenge the hierarchical authority of Archbishop Corsini. Featuring a representative assembly modeled on the recent council's and a collective executive resembling Florence's priorate, the clerical government fused conciliar principles with Florentine republican ideals. But ensuing struggles with Archbishop Corsini over liability for the clergy's debts soon split the urban and rural clergy, with the result that all parties appealed to Rome. Martin V dispatched the commissioners Giovanni Vitelleschi and Niccolò Mercatello, who imposed a settlement favorable to Corsini and the principle of church hierarchy.[33]

Five years later, Martin's successor Eugenius IV (1431–47) fled Rome, finding refuge in Florence in 1434, the same year in which Cosimo de' Medici returned from exile and expelled his Albizzi enemies. Eugenius was instrumental in persuading Rinaldo degli Albizzi to lay down arms. Cosimo returned the favor by arranging the papal consecration of Florence's new cathedral in 1436, in the process identifying himself with the completion of one of the city's greatest religious projects.

31 ASF, PR 117, fols. 35r–36r (19 May 1427) canceled *Statuta* 1779–83, vol. 1, liber 2, rub. 18 "De declinante," rubs. 21 and 22 on interdicts, and rub. 24 "De compromesso," 123–128. But it retained *Statuta* vol. 1, liber 3, rubs. 46 and 47, 262–264, and *Statuta*, vol. 2, "De extimis," rub. 40, 356.

32 ASF, PR 117, fols. 38v–43v (21 May 1427).

33 Peterson 2008.

What is more, he helped finance the transfer of the pope's ecumenical council from Ferrara to Florence in 1439.[34] This summit enabled Cosimo to showcase his diplomatic connections and Eugenius to assert his authority over his antipapal enemies at the rival council of Basel (1431–49) by securing a (short-lived) dogmatic reconciliation with the Greek Orthodox Church.

But Eugenius paid dearly for such Medicean support, as had his papal predecessors. Florentine banking ties to the papacy ran back to the Guelf entente of 1265–67. But the office of papal *depositarius* that John XXIII (Cossa) awarded Cosimo de' Medici's father, Giovanni di Bicci, at the beginning of the century gave the Medici bank a unique monopoly that it enjoyed without interruption (except for the years 1443–47) through Pius II's pontificate (1458–64).[35] This had not deterred the Florentine government from exacting massive levies on the clergy under John XXIII himself. Although Cosimo renewed the profitable relationship with Martin V, he also, as Florence's ambassador, reconciled the pope to Florence's revision of its ecclesiastical statutes in 1427 and secured permission for an additional 25,000-florin levy on the clergy.[36] While the Florentine government hosted the refugee Eugenius IV at the Dominican convent of Santa Maria Novella (1434–43), it imposed, without papal permission, three further substantial levies on the clergy of 25,000, 80,000, and 60,000 florins in 1432, 1438, and 1444.[37] Although his curial ties provided Cosimo with the wealth and influence underpinning his power, the decades of his predominance witnessed not a grateful or a collusive mitigation of Florentine policies toward the local church but rather a renewal of papal-Florentine disputes over ecclesiastical wealth and prerogatives. Eugenius began his Florentine sojourn protesting the *mercanzia*'s interference in clerical finances, but left Florence having tied clerical and papal finances more tightly to the *monte*, and appealing for the loan of Florence's *catasto* registers in order to impose his own levy on the clergy.[38]

Cosimo is famous for the quip ascribed to him by Niccolò Machiavelli that "states are not held with paternosters in hand."[39] But it seems he thought they might help. His father had served largely on civic building commissions (*opere*) at the cathedral, the baptistery, and Orsanmichele, and with his fellow parishioners at the collegiate church of San Lorenzo, where he paid for Filippo Brunelleschi's old sacristy and the double chapel at the south end of the transept. Cosimo and

34 Gill 1964, 195; De Roover 1963, 215–217; Molho 1990, 837–841.
35 Holmes 1968.
36 ASF, LC 7, fols. 66v–69v (18 November 1426), 73v–75r (8 April 1427); ASF, PR 117, fols. 308r–309r (18 August 1427).
37 ASF, PR 123, fols. 94v–96r (27 May 1432); ASF, PR 128, fols. 265r–267r (27 February 1437/38); ASV, RV 367, fols. 164v–165r (26 January 1444).
38 ASV, RV 374, fols. 10v–12r (4 December 1435); ASV, RV 367, fol. 164v (28 January 1444); Kirshner 1969.
39 Brown 1992a, 96–97 n. 7: "che gli stati non si tenevono co' paternostri in mano." (Machiavelli, *Istorie fiorentine*, 7.6; Machiavelli 2010, 637.)

his brother Lorenzo were more ready to undertake projects upon which they could affix the Medici arms (*palle* [six balls]).[40] They took over rebuilding the Observant Franciscan convent of Bosco ai Frati in their ancestral place of origin, the Mugello Valley, in 1417–19.[41] When the Observant Dominicans in San Domenico di Fiesole sought entrance to the city, Cosimo persuaded Eugenius IV to override his own reform commission and give them the Silvestrine convent of San Marco in 1435–36,[42] and proceeded to finance its extensive rebuilding and decoration. After his brother Lorenzo's death in 1440, when the San Lorenzo project stalled, Cosimo took over its funding entirely, reserving in exchange exclusive rights of family burial and the display of Medici arms.[43] His largesse extended in Florence to the novitiate's chapel at Santa Croce and the Camaldolese convent of Santa Maria degli Angeli, as well as in Fiesole to the reformed Augustinian Badia and to churches as far afield as Volterra, Venice, and Rome.

Ecclesiastical patronage was a patrician tradition in Florence, and Cosimo would have been mindful of the venerable Bardi and Peruzzi chapels and others at the Franciscan basilica of Santa Croce and at the Dominicans' Santa Maria Novella; Niccolò Acciaiuoli's construction of the massive Carthusian complex at Certosa di Firenze; and his rival Palla Strozzi's numerous contributions to rebuilding the Vallombrosan monastic church of Santa Trinita. But the breadth of Cosimo's patronage, though encompassing only a fraction of Florence's immense ecclesiastical establishment, was nonetheless unprecedented and touched a variety of ecclesiastical and devotional bases, old and new. In favoring the new observant orders, he signaled sympathy for emerging movements of reform and discipline and might have appreciated the freedom they offered from competing patrons.[44] Such endowments conveyed powerful political as well as devotional messages and did not go unremarked. The panegyric written by a grateful Abbot Timoteo Maffei of the Badia Fiesolana in the mid-1450s, *Against Those Who Disparage Cosimo de' Medici's Magnificence* (*In magnificentiae Cosmi Medicei Florentini detractores libellus*) signals possible resentment and at the very least a lively debate among Florentines whether Cosimo's benefactions reflected pious generosity or ostentatious religious politicking.[45] Cosimo's move in the early 1430s to claim a leading role in renovating Florence's ancient Badia was apparently rebuffed by the reforming Abbot Gomezio and other contributing families.[46] A scheme by San Lorenzo's canons in 1432 to secure Pope Eugenius's permission to wear tippets like those donned by the cathedral canons drew an angry protest from the chancellor Leonardo Bruni and the

---

40 See surveys by Kent 2000, 131–214; Paoletti 1992, 1995.
41 Robinson 1992.
42 Ripoll and Brémond 1729–40, 3:57.
43 Ginori Conti 1940, 236–240.
44 Rubinstein 1990.
45 See Fraser Jenkins 1970, 165; Howard 2012, 123–150.
46 Leader 2012, 91–96. Anne Leader generously shared her typescript with me before its publication.

signoria against this challenge to the primacy of the republic's cathedral.[47] The ousting of the Silvestrines from San Marco provoked an equally sharp protest: only recently, the legislative councils had put the convent under Florentine protection and entrusted it to the silk guild.[48] On the other hand, Cosimo may have exercised self-restraint, demurring from Brunelleschi's plan to orient the new Medici palace to face the basilica of San Lorenzo as "too grand" precisely because such a palace-basilica complex would have evoked the manner in which, in many Italian cities, the principal seat of civic or, especially, signorial government faced the cathedral.[49]

By 1445, when the archbishopric fell vacant, Cosimo was ready to attempt installing one of his own in Florence's highest ecclesiastical dignity. Had he been aiming at signorial power, this would have been the jewel in the crown of his already extensive ecclesiastical patronage network,[50] providing direct influence at the episcopal curia (with jurisdiction over usury cases), broad powers to supervise appointments to benefices throughout the archdiocese, confirmation of his family's status as head of a new *reggimento*, and proximity to the mantle of holiness itself. In early August, immediately following the death of the archbishop Bartolomeo Zabarella (1440–45), the first chancellor Carlo Marsuppini sent out letters supporting five Florentine candidates, and throughout the autumn dispatched a total of thirty-one to the pope and cardinals in what amounted to a veritable campaign.[51] It merits following in detail.[52] Notably, it was conducted through the republic's chancery rather than back channels in Rome; and despite expressions of deference to papal authority, it was framed as a defense of local ecclesiastical and civic prerogatives.

The first candidate put forward was Cosimo's second cousin, Donato de' Medici, bishop of Pistoia. Marsuppini urged the pope to appoint someone "from our citizenry, pleasing to the city and devoted to the present regime [*status*]." Donato fit the twin requirements of local birth and piety. He was, moreover, "descended from the celebrated [*clarissima*] family of the Medici . . . and by virtue of his parentage most pleasing and loyal to this regime [*fidissimus huic statui*]."[53] There are no positive grounds for doubting the first point. Donato had enjoyed a distinguished career, serving as parish priest (*pievano*) of Santa Maria a Dicomano, replacing his cousin Amerigo de' Medici as provost of Florence's cathedral chapter in 1432, and Ubertino degli Albizzi as bishop of Pistoia in 1436—a succession that cannot have gone

---

47 De Angelis 2006.

48 ASF, Missive 35, fol. 61r–v (17 July 1436); ASF, PR 107, fols. 52v–53r (24 April 1417); ASF, PR 117, fol. 254r–v (5 August 1427).

49 Hyman 1977, 109–121.

50 Kent 1978, 69–71; Molho 1979, 21–32; Bizzocchi 1987, 55–100.

51 Morçay 1914, 432–442.

52 Peterson 1989.

53 ASF, Missive 36, fol. 123v (8 August 1445): "aliquem e nostris civibus [. . .] civitati gratus et presentis status studiosus [. . .] ex clarissima medicorum familia ortus est [. . .] et familie genere gratiosissimus ac fidissimus huic statui sit."

unremarked. Family letters suggest that he was less active in ecclesiastical power brokering than either Cosimo or Cosimo's younger son Giovanni, who managed many appeals for patronage sent to the Medici by hopeful clergy. Donato indeed refused to grant numerous favors to Giovanni's clients.[54] Nor was Marsuppini necessarily disingenuous in citing Donato's piety. Chancery correspondence often reveals, alongside the desire to monitor benefices and to promote favorite sons, a belief that public stability and that of any regime (*reggimento*) were better served by reputable clergy than those who might provoke *scandalo*.

Marsuppini's second and third points concerning Donato's citizenship and family, however, were more delicate. Since the thirteenth century, Florence had prohibited citizens access to the bishopric precisely to avoid politicizing the office, and this principle had been reaffirmed in 1375 and 1427. Archbishop Corsini (1411–35), appointed under the Albizzi, was the last Florentine to have occupied the see: he had been succeeded by Giovanni Vitelleschi (1435–37) from Corneto and by Lodovico Scarampo (1438–39) and Bartolomeo Zabarella, both Paduans. The office had represented a mere step in their curial careers. The Florentine clergy had expressed frustration with failed episcopal leadership in the 1420s, and the Florentine laity might likewise have appreciated a committed prelate. Having resided in Florence for nearly a decade himself and attempted unsuccessfully to reform the city's monasteries by means of external apostolic commissioners, the pope might have been sympathetic to an internal appointment.

But Eugenius was being asked to appoint not just a Florentine, but one "loyal to this regime" (*fidissimus huic statui*). Already the councils had suspended the law prohibiting Florentines access to the bishopric in 1435 and 1439, "desiring that the cathedrals of Florence and Fiesole might be provided with citizens from the territory of Florence."[55] Cosimo had enjoyed close relations with the condottiere Vitelleschi and the diplomat Scarampo.[56] But Zabarella had been less accommodating, occasionally telling Cosimo to mind his own business.[57] One of the first measures of the *balìa* of 1444 was to repeal definitively the statute prohibiting Florentines from assuming the archbishopric.[58]

But there were no further letters on behalf of Donato. Vespasiano da Bisticci relates that Cosimo himself wrote to the pope urging him to choose a candidate appropriate to Florence, not mentioning Donato by name, and Eugenius coolly assured him that "he would elect such a pastor as would please them."[59]

---

54 E.g., ASF, MAP, 9:354 (11 February 1459); MAP 6–8 contain numerous petitions to Giovanni.

55 ASF, PR 126, fol. 163r–v (18 August 1435); ASF, PR 130, fol. 271r–v (18 December 1439): "Cupientes quod ecclesie cathedrali Florentine et Fesulane etiam de civibus comitatinis et districtualibus provideri possint."

56 On Vitelleschi, see Law 1998; on Scarampo, see Paschini 1939.

57 E.g., ASF, MAP 12, 215 (9 July 1444).

58 ASF, Balìe 26, fol. 62r (21 August 1444).

59 Da Bisticci 1970–76, 1:225–226: "elegerebe loro tale pastore che sarebono contenti."

Medici-papal relations had become strained. Florence's secret reconciliation with Francesco Sforza in 1441 had sacrificed papal interests in the Romagna, and in 1443 Eugenius relieved Roberto Martelli, head of the Medici bank's Rome branch, of his position as papal depositary general.[60] Meanwhile, the Florentine government, firmly under Medici control, had been tightening its grip on the local church. In January 1443, the legislative councils created a new commission to monitor the movement of property from laymen to ecclesiastics.[61] In February 1444, they curtailed the rights of office holders to meet in confraternal groups of *laudantes*.[62] That August, they prohibited foreigners from accepting benefices in Florentine territory without the *signoria*'s approval.[63] And in 1445, a 60,000-florin clerical levy that Eugenius had conceded the previous year collapsed in mutual recriminations, suspended by the pope until Florence paid overdue interest on his *monte* shares, which the Florentines protested they could not do without the revenues from the levy.[64]

Marsuppini nevertheless found grounds for promoting another Florentine candidate, Giovanni di Nerone di Nigi Dietisalvi. A Florentine cathedral canon trained in law, Giovanni also served as provost of the Fiesolan chapter and apostolic judge delegate for Tuscany. He was, moreover, the brother of Dietisalvi di Nerone di Nigi Dietisalvi, one of Cosimo's most devoted lieutenants.[65] On 16 August, Marsuppini sent another flurry of letters announcing that Giovanni had just been elected by Florence's cathedral chapter.[66] In fact, he had only narrowly defeated Francesco Legnamino, an apostolic treasurer.[67] The republic's support of a canonically elected candidate raised a delicate point. Florence's cathedral chapter, like most, had enjoyed little influence on episcopal appointments since the early fourteenth century.[68] In advancing Giovanni's candidacy, the canons may have hoped to exploit Eugenius's difficulties with the militantly conciliarist council of Basel in order to revive their former electoral prerogatives. Alternatively their motives may have lain closer to home. For decades, they had been objects of resentment from other clerics, who envied their privileges and felt they bore an insufficient share of ecclesiastical tax burdens. Eugenius himself had recently investigated their finances. They were annoyed by the pretensions of San Lorenzo's canons, but also objected to the

60 Partner 1968, 396–400; De Roover 1963, 198.
61 ASF, PR 132, fols. 328r–330r (16 January 1442/43).
62 ASF, PR 134, fols. 208v–209r (18 February 1443/44).
63 ASF, Balìe 26, fols. 61v–62r (21 August 1444).
64 ASF, LC 11, fols. 39v–40v (9 January 1444/45), 63r–64r (17 June 1445).
65 Kent 1978, 131–132.
66 ASF, Missive 36, fol. 126r (16 August 1445). Three other candidates appear to have been foils: Benozzo Federighi, bishop of Fiesole (1421–50); Roberto Cavalcanti, bishop of Volterra (1440–50); and Andrea di Domenico d'Andrea Fiochi, another cathedral canon (1427–52).
67 ASF, NA 11041 (ser Jacopo di Antonio di Jacopo da Romena, 1443–45), fols. 401r–406r (14–16 August 1445).
68 Rotelli 1974, 209.

republic's decision to enhance the cathedral's dignity by increasing their numbers. They were locked in a struggle too with the Dominican friars of Santa Maria Novella for precedence in the procession of Corpus Domini. But by the early 1440s, many of their families were allied to the Medici.[69] The republic's support of a Medici partisan, nominated by a faction of the cathedral chapter, thus presented Eugenius with a double challenge: a reassertion of Medici interests garbed in the prerogatives of the local church; and, conversely, the canons' effort to assert their bygone electoral rights and standing in the local church by aligning themselves with the Medici.

After five months' delay, Eugenius issued a bull on 10 January 1446 designating Antonino Pierozzi (1389–1459), an Observant Dominican who had just stepped down after six years as prior of San Marco, to succeed Zabarella as Florentine archbishop. In appointing Antonino, Eugenius satisfied the Florentines' avowed desire for a loyal native son and friend of the Medici. At the same time, he skirted round politics by reaching below the patriciate to tap an exponent of popular reforming and disciplinary impulses that had been increasingly evident since the turn of the century, indeed harnessing them to the papacy through the episcopate. The son of a prosperous Florentine notary, Antonino had been among the first Observant followers of the famous Dominican preacher and humanist-baiting conservative Giovanni Dominici, and had risen to serve in the Roman Rota before assuming the priorate of San Marco in 1438.[70] Although he and his Observant brothers owed much to Cosimo, he was not a Medici creation. His Lenten sermons and the circulation of his early *Confessionale* and *Consilia*, which became his *Summa moralis* and *Cronicon*, made him well known beyond Florence. In 1429, five years before Cosimo's return to the city, Bruni had acknowledged Antonino's popular appeal by urging the Dominicans to transfer him back to Fiesole.[71] Though he was not Cosimo's choice, as patron of San Marco he could scarcely object.

More than his patrician and curial predecessors in the archbishopric, Antonino epitomized the impulse of his humbler social peers to use religious institutions to impose discipline on the social orders above as well as below them. The *fraticello* heretic Giovanni Cani of Montecatini's death at the stake in front of the cathedral in 1450 was a terrifying display of Antonino's determination to assert ecclesiastical control over the city's religious life.[72] His rise as a political force derived from his success in reforming the clergy, which in turn depended on intervening between Florence and Rome to defend the prerogatives of a Florentine territorial church. In 1447, Florence's councils yielded to him, repealing the law sequestering the

69 Peterson 2001.
70 Orlandi 1959–60, 1:1–40, 2:1–187.
71 ASF, Missive 32, fols. 74v–75r (11 May 1429).
72 Baldovino Baldovini, "Vita di S. Antonino," Florence, BRF, MS 1333, fols. 62r–64v; Morçay 1914, 429–431.

incomes of foreign benefice holders.[73] In 1452, he was able to force modification of the legislation on confraternities as well.[74] When, in 1451, the councils imposed a 25 percent tax on all bequests by laymen to tax-exempt clerical institutions, Antonino intervened to force the measure's repeal.[75]

Responding to the financial needs that had spurred the clergy to experiment with corporate self-government in the 1420s, Antonino was able in turn to assert his authority over them. He was the first Florentine bishop since the war of the Eight Saints to issue a full set of constitutions for clergy and laymen, and whose court was sufficiently active to give them effect.[76] Touring the diocese, he stripped delinquent clerics of their benefices, and united impoverished rural parishes to form viable livings for priests.[77] His visitations and synods extended to neighboring dioceses, including Donato de' Medici's in Pistoia,[78] and he reformed monasteries throughout Florentine territory. Antonino's reform of the clergy prepared the laity to accept increased episcopal discipline of their religious lives as well. He curbed the growth of public religious festivals, wrote a widely circulated confessional manual for the laity, and reviewed the statutes of confraternities that were a vital link connecting ecclesiastical institutions, civic politics, and the penitential and charitable exercises of the laity.

Antonino maintained a delicate balance of interests, resisting Florentine legislation that limited ecclesiastical prerogatives while writing devotional manuals for Medici wives and widows. He was invited three times to represent the city before Emperor Frederick III (1452–93) and Popes Calixtus III (1455–58) and Pius II (1458–64).[79] This did not inhibit him from chastising Giovanni di Cosimo de' Medici when he sought episcopal favors for his clients: "In judicial affairs, no exception is made for persons. . . . Therefore I intend to take care of this matter properly, and not in a hurry."[80]

In July 1458, Antonino challenged the consolidation of Medici power publicly. Partisans led by Luca Pitti, frustrated by resistance in the legislative councils, determined to "retake the state (*ripigliare lo stato*)" by pressing for open rather than secret balloting in the councils.[81] Antonino intervened by posting a notice on the cathedral doors threatening excommunication of any councillors who acquiesced

73 ASF, CP 52, fol. 19v (14 July 1447); ASF, PR 138, fols. 112v–113r (8 August 1447).

74 ASF, PR 143, fols. 32v–33v (3 April 1452).

75 ASF, PR 142, fols. 216r–217r (9 September 1451). Antonino's protests and the law's repeal are recorded in ASF, Deliberazioni in forza di ordinaria autorità 74, fol. 23v (5 September 1452). The new commission's formation is recorded in ASF, Balìe 27, fols. 93r–95r (27 February 1452/53).

76 Trexler 1979; Brucker 1986.

77 Orlandi 1959–60, 1:136–178.

78 Documents in Morçay 1914, 414–420.

79 Guasti 1857.

80 ASF, MAP 6, 208 (8 December 1456): "In iudiciis personarum acceptio non est habenda [. . .] Maturamente adunque intendo di governare questa causa, e non in fretta."

81 Rubinstein 1997, 99–153, with quotation on 104.

in what he insisted was a violation of their sacred oaths of office.[82] Pitti and his allies were obliged to drop the measure and, in effect, their strategy of quiet intimidation. Instead they resorted to an open coup, convoking a public assembly (*parlamento*) at which, under the watchful eyes of troops, they set forth to Florence's citizenry the terms of their future control of the government by means of a new council, the 100 (*cento*). Antonino's intervention failed to block the Medicean reassertion of control. But by forcing the Medici to come out into the open to restore their grip on power, he exposed its illegitimacy; by spotlighting the sanctity of the oaths that had been violated, he underscored the regime's profanity.

Like the Albizzi oligarchy that preceded it, the Medici regime (*reggimento*) under Cosimo "il vecchio" deployed a balance of statist measures designed to curb the church's prerogatives while patronizing it in pursuit of political legitimacy. The Medici retained and reinforced many of the legislative and bureaucratic innovations developed by their Albizzi predecessors to monitor and circumscribe the operation of ecclesiastical institutions in Florentine territory. Circumstances differed, of course: the Albizzi faced a weak church divided by schism; the Medici confronted figures such as Eugenius IV and Antonino—ecclesiastical leaders determined to reform the church and to assert its independence of temporal power. Albizzi strategies for legitimizing their regime were tightly entwined with the broader civic project of resacralizing a city that had despoiled the clergy and profaned itself during the war of the Eight Saints. Medici patronage of the church aimed more narrowly at legitimizing their regime and, particularly, their position as its leaders. The unique financial ties between the Medici and the papacy not only enabled Cosimo to offer lavish patronage, but placed him in a position to mediate between Florence and Rome. On the other hand, the pursuit of religious legitimation opened the door to reformers such as Antonino to mediate not only among the papacy, Florence, and the local church, but also between the Florentine republic's Medicean elite and its increasingly subject citizenry.

Antonino's protest against open balloting in the councils in 1458 was a challenge from the highest and most credible level of the local church to the legitimacy of the methods being deployed by Cosimo's friends to consolidate their grip on the republic. It did not prevent the convocation of a *parlamento* later that year. Nor did it keep Giovanni di Nerone di Nigi Dietisalvi from being raised to the archbishopric in 1462. But having a client in the see did not necessarily guarantee the Medici religious legitimation. Giovanni was in fact forced to flee the city in 1466 after conspiring against Piero de' Medici.[83] Matters went little better for Lorenzo the Magnificent during the Pazzi conspiracy, incited and backed by clerical enemies at home and in Rome. The cardinalate he procured for his son Giovanni in

---

82 Morçay 1914, 429–430.
83 Calzolai 1970, 25.

1489 might have salved Medici relations with the papacy for the time being—but it did nothing to prevent the rise of anti-Medicean sentiment under Savonarola, who regularly invoked Antonino as a model reformer and defender of liberty.[84] When the Medici pope Leo X (1513–21) sought to appropriate Antonino's pious memory (while countering Savonarola's) by sponsoring Antonino's canonization, he succeeded only in provoking a resurgence of Savonarolan devotees (*piagnoni*).[85] By this time, the church's own religious credibility had become increasingly tenuous, both in Florence and throughout Europe. Having arrived at the papacy, it was the unenviable task of the Medici popes, Leo X and his cousin Clement VII (1523–34), to preside over the division of Christendom during the Protestant Reformation of the early sixteenth century.

84 Weinstein 1970, 247.
85 Polizzotto 1992.

TWELVE

Religion and Literature in Oligarchic, Medicean, and Savonarolan Florence

PAOLO ORVIETO

IN EVERY EPOCH, ESPECIALLY THAT of the Medici, power and culture are closely bound together, constituting what Michel Foucault called "discourses of power" that configure an organic cultural whole. The various fields of knowledge (literary, religious, philosophical, etc.) are programmatically linked to and refracted by one another, and are hence no more than facets of the epistemic system imposed, more or less consciously, by the dominant class or family.

I shall delineate the close relationship that arose in Florence over the course of the fifteenth century, and in particular under Medici domination, between religious choice, religious literature, and political power. In the fifteenth century, Florence was nominally a republic, but while there may have been upsurges of republican or pseudo-republican sentiment, the political culture was oligarchic, with power shared among a group of mostly noble or wealthy families. Out of this configuration, the Medici elevated themselves to the status of rulers. And yet even within the era of Medici power, two epistemic phases can be distinguished: one that prevailed from roughly 1473 to 1487, and another for the period after 1487. (This chronology is obviously approximate.) In each of these three periods, the "long" phase of oligarchic rule and the two shorter intervals of Laurentian domination, religious culture can be seen as growing from the underlying political soil. No piece of fifteenth-century Florentine literature is autonomous; each collaborates more or less openly with a political project, diffused and maintained by a cultural system that always has a literary and a religious aspect. Indeed, texts of importance were composed by the ruler himself, Lorenzo de' Medici.

The first religious phase represents traditional orthodox Catholicism, but accompanied by the equally medieval parodic infractions that Mikhail Bakhtin in his influential study *Rabelais and His World* called "carnivalization."[1] The century begins with the defense of classical poetry by the chancellor Coluccio Salutati, first against Giovanni da San Miniato and then against Giovanni Dominici (1356–1419), a Dominican and the author of *Lucula noctis* as well as of the *Regola del governo e della cura familiare*, in which he instructs a well-intentioned mother on education and the texts she should have her children read. Salutati (who was also author of *De seculo et religione*, in which he extols the monastic life's dedication to prayer) in the end yields some ground to his religious opponent, and recommends that faithful Christians should read "gentile" (i.e., pagan) writers with caution. In this phase, the early fifteenth century, there is a vast production of traditional religious literature. Among the authors, Feo Belcari stands out, composing *laude* (religious poems), lives of saints and blessed men and women (e.g., *Vita del beato Giovanni Colombini da Siena*), and mystery plays (*Annunciazione, San Giovanni nel deserto, San Pannunzio*, etc.). Of the latter, the best known is *Abraam e Isac*, staged in 1449 and dedicated to Giovanni di Cosimo de' Medici. Giovanni di Cosimo, who died in 1463, was a friend of Francesco d'Altobianco degli Alberti, of Belcari and of Burchiello (Domenico di Giovanni, known as "il Burchiello"), and so had links to representatives of an oligarchic and increasingly anti-Medicean culture. Perhaps the most typical authors of this first phase are the Pulci: Bernardo, author of an amorous *canzoniere* and mystery plays such as *Barlaam e Josafat*; Luca, poet and failed banker; Antonia, wife of Bernardo, also author of mystery plays (*Santa Guglielmina, Santa Domitilla, Figliol prodigo, San Francesco*); and, the most celebrated member of the family, Luigi, who came under the protection of Lucrezia Tornabuoni, Lorenzo the Magnificent's devout mother, and herself the author of biblical tales with mostly female protagonists (*La ystoria di Iudith vedova hebrea; La storia di Hester regina; La ystoria della devota Susanna; La vita di Tubia; La vita di sancto Giovanni Baptista*).[2] Hence, the Pulci were producing Catholic literature of a traditional kind (*laude*, mystery plays, religious tales and songs) permeated with medieval "carnivalization," a feature welcome to Lucrezia Tornabuoni, the "first lady" of Florence after the death of Cosimo in 1464, whom Luigi Pulci in *Morgante* (38, 131–136) celebrates as his own saintly protector. Characteristic is the "credo" of Margutte in *Morgante* (18, 115, 7–116, 5), at once a parody of the *Credo*, of the *Confiteor*, of God, of the Madonna and child, and of the Trinity:

> ma sopra tutto nel buon vino ho fede / e credo che sia salvo chi gli crede; /
> e credo nella torta e nel tortello: / l'uno è la madre e l'altro è il suo figliuolo; /
> e 'l vero paternostro è il fegatello, / e posson essere tre, due ed un solo, /
> e deriva dal fegato almen quello

1 Bakhtin 1979.
2 Tornabuoni 1978, 1992.

but above all in good wine I have faith / and I believe that he who believes in it is saved / and I believe in the *torta* and the *tortello*: / one is the mother and the other is her son; / and the true paternoster is fried liver, / which may be triple or double or single, / and that at any rate does derive from the liver.

His parodies sometimes provoked outrage, but by and large they were accepted by the ecclesiastical authorities as a salutary outlet for popular sentiment. The Pulci-Tornabuoni pairing perfectly represents the type of religion practiced in oligarchic, popularly orientated Florence, where the Medici were only *primi inter pares*.

Luigi Pulci, however, also wrote sonnets full of religious parody (*Costor che fan sì gran disputazione; In principio era il buio e buio fia; Poich'io partii da voi Bartolomeo*). These celebrations of the "mortality" of the soul are no longer mere carnivalization but genuine parody, not so much of traditional religion as of the new Neoplatonic religion endorsed by Marsilio Ficino.[3] At a certain point, "Pulcian religiosity"—traditional, popularly appealing, and yet oligarchic, a religious attitude shared by Piero di Cosimo de' Medici and his son the young Lorenzo the Magnificent[4]—comes into conflict not so much with the Catholic creed as with the new theology of Ficino, who was then writing his most important theological-philosophical work, *Theologia platonica de immortalitate animorum*, entirely centered on the soul, the immortal and unique medium between man and God. Pulci, by contrast, is capable of referring to the soul as if it were no more than a piece of salami in half a sliced sandwich.[5]

The first, "oligarchic" phase of Medici supremacy in Florence (from the last years of Cosimo "il vecchio," through his son Piero's brief predominance, and into the period of Lorenzo the Magnificent) is a rich mixture of traditional observance and heightened carnivalesque parody, which Lorenzo certainly supported. This period lasted until at least 1473–74. In 1466–67, Lorenzo was the author of the *Simposio*, a short poem in which he describes a long line of drinkers who arrive to guzzle from a keg of freshly tapped wine, a parody of Dante's *Commedia* (he similarly has two guides or *duci*) and of the voyage to paradise, which here ends in a disreputable establishment frequented by Florence's sots. There is even a parody of John's Gospel:

mai non si sazia sete naturale / come la mia, anzi più si raccende / quanto più béo, com'io beessi sale

natural thirst like mine is never quenched; indeed it reignites the more I drink, as though I were drinking salt

---

3 For Pulcian poetry as a genre, see Orvieto 1978; for Luigi Pulci's sonnets of religious parody, see Pulci 1986, 191–201.

4 On the typology of the religion and poetry of Luigi Pulci, see Orvieto 1978.

5 On the dispute between Pulci and Ficino, see Orvieto 1978, 213–321; Decaria 2009, 209–236.

e ha 'mparato che 'l maggior supplizio / ch'avessi in terra el nostro Salvatore, / è quando in sulla croce e' disse *sitio*

and he learned that the greatest torment that our Savior had on this earth was when, on the cross, he said "I am thirsty."[6]

One can also peruse Lorenzo's equally youthful novella *Giacoppo*, in which Giacoppo's confessor, fra Antonio della Marca, tries to persuade him to let another man, Francesco, have sex with his beautiful wife Cassandra. The friar interprets 2 Samuel 12:11 in sexual terms: *Non ha' tu sentito dire che il peccato della infamia e delle cose che l'uomo tiene contro a ragione non si può perdonare senza restituirle?* ("Have you not heard that the sin of infamy and the things a man holds contrary to reason cannot be pardoned without restitution?")[7] Hence Giacoppo, who believes himself guilty of having had sex with Francesco's wife Bartolomea (in reality a prostitute hired by Francesco to impersonate her), must, by Christian commandment, permit Francesco to take Cassandra to bed. The young Lorenzo also wrote extremely obscene dancing songs (it is widely asserted that he was the inventor of the genre of *canti carnascialeschi*, with their repeated sexual allusions) such as *Tra Empoli e Pontolmo*, in which the speaker halts at the inn of a lusty hostess, who offers him the female orifice of his choice; he happily chooses the one at the rear. This is religiosity of a popular and medieval kind, alternating effortlessly between traditional observance and carnivalesque parody, which, with Pulci and the young Lorenzo, belongs to the oligarchic period of Florentine history, when the Medici were becoming powerful, but were not yet comporting themselves as rulers of the city.[8]

There was a break in relations between Lorenzo and Pulci about 1473–74, when Pulci engaged in a fierce dispute with Marsilio Ficino. A new religion (or theology) was imposed from above, although received coolly by the people, who resented this move from a traditional, medieval religion, shared by the oligarchy, to a religion that established the absolute supremacy of theology over every other cognitive activity. This new religion was Ficinian Neoplatonic syncretism. But it was in substantial (albeit camouflaged) opposition to the orthodox and popularly accepted Catholic religion of the Roman Church, in that it removed any kind of mediation between man and God. Ficinian theology entailed the absolute impotence of priests, bishops, cardinals, and popes, and it portrayed Christianity (and the revelation of Christ) as merely the last link in an ancient sequence of divine revelations intended for initiates. Religious discourse was now shaped, via Medici power, into a virtual doctrinal manifesto that formed the basis for philosophy and literature, managed, so to speak, by Lorenzo. It was Luigi Pulci, famous for his

---

6   Medici 1992, 2:614, 627. The first passage parodies John 4:13–15, the second, John 19:28.
7   Medici 1992, 2:826.
8   See Orvieto 1978.

blasphemies, who paradoxically condemned the new religious creed, in a dispute that broke out in 1475–76. Pulci defamed its high priest, Marsilio Ficino (for Pulci the false prophet of a new creed), in four ferocious sonnets in which, it should be stressed, the target attacked is not so much Ficino as his philosophy (which is, in fact, a Platonic theology):

> Marsilio, questa tua filosofia / non se ne sente in bocca mai a persona, / che tu la metti donde il dopo nona / e riesce poi in chiasso o in pazzeria

> Marsilio, this philosophy of yours is never heard in any person's mouth, for you extol it to the skies,[9] and then it turns out to be babble or madness

> Che di' tu, che traduci Platone?—Sia col malan che Dio ti dia, / o tu bestemmi la filosofia

> What, do you say, that you are translating Plato? Let God visit you with misfortune, o you [who] blaspheme philosophy.

> Racconcia el lume un poco ch'è già spento; / cognoscot'io: tu se' filosofia. / Chi t'ha condutta qua, figliuola mia, / in tanto vituperio miseria e stento? / Condotta meschin m'ha, povera brulla, / cattivo scilinguato fatto prete, / promesso sposar, me' stavo fanciulla

> Adjust the light a little, for it has died out; I know you, you are philosophy. Who has brought you here, my daughter, in such shame, poverty and hardship? I, poor and penniless, have been brought to misery by a wicked stutterer made a priest, with a promise of marriage; I was better off as a maid.

As I wrote many years ago, Pulcian parody extends to *Morgante*, where in the final cantos the Saracen king Marsilio is none other than Ficino:

> Era Marsilio un uom che in suo segreto / credea manco nel Ciel che negli abissi: / bestemmiator, ma bestemmiava cheto; / [. . .] / ché e' sapea anche simulare e fignere / castità, santimonia e devozione, / e la sua vita per modo dipignere / che il popolo n'ebbe un tempo espettazione

> Marsilio was a man who in his heart believed less in heaven than in the underworld: he was a blasphemer, but blasphemed silently . . . for he knew

---

9   Note by the translator, William McCuaig: "In a private communication, the author has discussed the challenge to interpretation posed by the expression 'che tu la metti donde il dopo nona.' The translation supplied renders in the translator's English the author's best estimate of its general purport, as suggested by the context."

also how to simulate and feign chastity, sanctimony, and devotion, and present his own life in such a way that at one time much was expected of him by the people.[10]

There are various letters by Ficino, one in particular to his brother Bernardo, in which he in turn defames Luigi Pulci as a barking, heretical dog who has offended the sacred name not of Christ, but of Plato, while for Luigi Pulci the heretic is Ficino, who, albeit a priest, has shamefully betrayed his Catholic faith with a series of pagan demons and allegedly sacred texts, selling himself as an innovative theologian with hare-brained allegories and tangled, incomprehensible pseudo-philosophies. This was a head-on confrontation between two cultures that also represented two distinct religious beliefs. The victory was awarded by Lorenzo the Magnificent to Ficino, partly for political reasons.

The setting was a growing economic and political fissure between Florence and Rome in the period 1471–74. Pope Paul II had been succeeded on 25 August 1471 by Sixtus IV (Francesco Della Rovere). Lorenzo the Magnificent had high hopes of the new papacy, including confirmation of the alum monopoly as well as of the Medici's status as papal bankers, not to mention the cardinal's hat he already had in mind for his brother Giuliano. But on 16 December 1471, the pope nominated two of his own nephews as cardinals: Pietro Riario and Giuliano Della Rovere, the future Pope Julius II, closing the door on Giuliano de' Medici. Fearing Florence, Sixtus IV drew closer to Naples: when an illegitimate daughter of the Neapolitan king Ferrante passed through Rome on her way to Ferrara in order to marry Ercole d'Este, she was fêted for days on end, with a Lucullan banquet at the house of Pietro Riario, patriarch of Constantinople and archbishop of Florence, a man ever more powerful and ever less acceptable to Florence. Then, for his other nephew, Girolamo Riario, the pope acquired the *signoria* of Imola, and with it Caterina Sforza, the natural daughter of Galeazzo Maria, duke of Milan, as Girolamo's bride. Hence, the Riario were at the heart of a potentially anti-Florentine axis formed by the papacy, the Sforza, and the Aragonese in Naples. Lorenzo the Magnificent was extremely disturbed by the increasingly powerful Riario, and also by the forfeiture of Imola, which he had coveted for himself. On top of all that, the pope had acquired Imola with financial backing from the Pazzi, the Florentine banking rivals of the Medici. The Riario-Della Rovere alliance was on the point of winning hegemony at the heart of the peninsula, with the support of the king of Naples, Ferrante, who was rumored to have obtained a promise from Sixtus IV that he would be created king of Italy. In 1474, Giuliano Della Rovere led a military campaign in Umbria, a region under Florentine influence from time immemorial, crushing revolts in Todi, Forlì, and Spoleto and laying siege to Città di Castello and its despot Niccolò Vitelli.

10 The passage cited is from *Morgante*, 26, 118–119, 4. For the allegorical interpretation, especially the anti-Ficino slant, see Orvieto 1978, 244–283; Decaria 2012.

Città di Castello lay close to the Florentine town of Sansepolcro, and in response Lorenzo dispatched an army of six thousand men, forcing papal troops to withdraw. But the rupture between Florence and Rome was now irreparable. On 2 November 1474, Florence signed a defensive league with Venice and Milan, while shortly afterward Sixtus IV formed a league with Ferrante of Naples. Two opposing blocs were emerging: on one hand Florence, and on the other Rome, where the Pazzi replaced the Medici as papal bankers, causing the bankruptcy of the Medici bank's Roman branch. Sixtus IV also granted the Pazzi a license to export and sell alum, and at the end of 1474 he appointed Rinaldo Orsini as archbishop of Florence, against the wishes of Lorenzo the Magnificent, who had proposed other names, including once again his brother Giuliano's. Lastly, Sixtus IV named as archbishop of Pisa Francesco Salviati, a protégé of the Pazzi, an individual uncongenial to the Medici (and later a participant in the Pazzi conspiracy in 1478). In the same year, Sixtus IV declared that he would create no more Florentine cardinals.

Therefore, on one hand, the change in religious creed had the primary aim of signaling a cultural (and thereby political) break between the former oligarchic, ultrapopular tradition and the Medicean establishment of a religion for a remote elite. On the other, the inauguration of an alternative religious creed with its own "holy scriptures" signaled (how deliberately it is hard to say) an open ideological-political apostasy away from the church of Rome. Ficino made no overt display of abandoning Christianity, if only not to alienate popular feeling. In 1473, he was named parish priest of the church of S. Bartolomeo a Pomino at Fiesole, and, in the same year, he became a deacon and took holy orders. But long before, as Ficino was beginning his studies in the 1450s, Antonio degli Agli, future bishop of Fiesole and Volterra and a figure endowed with considerable foresight, had in his *De mystica statera* warned the young Ficino that his immersion in Platonic and Neoplatonic writings would distance him inexorably from the Christian religion.

With Ficino, and later with Giovanni Pico della Mirandola, a new religion was brought into being in Florence, de facto autochthonous and self-referential—one that excluded the mediation of the Roman Church and attributed to the city's ruler the charisma of a high priest, indeed a pontifex of sorts, an apostle of a new cult. There is an intricate set of links between the increasingly absolutist tendencies of the Medici, the theological and philosophical creed of Ficino, and Florentine literary production.

Although the earliest sponsor of this new theological philosophy was doubtless Lorenzo the Magnificent's grandfather Cosimo, it was Lorenzo who promoted it as a state religion (but only after 1473–74, when the reins of power were firmly in his grip), and it was Lorenzo who authorized the philosopher-priest Marsilio Ficino, a figure positioned close to the seat of power, to compose the new bible of a revolutionary, entirely Medicean, religion. Ficino, like Cristoforo Landino and Poliziano, all of them, tellingly, of humble birth, assumed the mission of creating an ostensibly apolitical form of culture that was actually ideologically supportive of Medici power. While still under the protection of Cosimo, Ficino transferred primacy among philosophers from the scholastic Aristotle to the new Medici rising star, Plato. The philosophers prized by the oligarchy were Aristotle and Cicero (and Ficino too had started off as an Aristotelian). Therefore giving the limelight to Plato and the Neoplatonists in their place is a philosophical initiative that can be interpreted politically: it signaled a challenge to the oligarchy. The Medici, operating through Ficino, chose to promote Plato. But to promote Plato was to put a cultural, hence moral, premium on the reclusive life of contemplation, and correspondingly to devalue practical activity. All absolutist regimes are Platonic in their way, seeking to impose on the phenomenal world a higher level of reality drawn from beyond, from the hyperuranian and metaphysical world of the ideas: every form of practical engagement with the world that exceeds the bare minimum needed in order to function is dismissed as useless, if not condemned as ethically blameworthy. Throughout this phase of Florentine history, the case that the contemplative is superior to the active life was pressed insistently.

The earliest extant testimony to a direct relationship between Ficino and Cosimo "il vecchio" is found in two letters from the closing years of Cosimo's life, 1462–64. At that time, Cosimo made Ficino a gift of manuscripts of Plato and Plotinus, and provided a house for Ficino's mother and another for Ficino himself not far from the Medici villa at Careggi. Here, the celebrated Accademia Platonica was founded as a center for the diffusion of the new creed. (Ficino himself, in dedicating his translation of the Plotinian *Enneads* to Lorenzo the Magnificent, backdated the initial contact between himself and Cosimo to 1452.) In the first letter, Ficino, who had been reading Hermetic texts since 1456, sent Cosimo a selection from his portfolio of translations, among them the complete Orphic hymn "to the Cosmos." From the second, it is learned that his portfolio already included nine of Plato's dialogues. The translation of the Platonic dialogues was a long and arduous process, begun in 1463–64 and pursued until 1468, with the addition of various *argumenta* (summaries) and the dedication of the whole corpus to Piero and then to Lorenzo de' Medici. They were revised between 1475–83 and printed in 1484, along with commentaries on the *Symposium* and *Timaeus*.

More significant even, from this perspective, than the famous Plato translations was Ficino's effort, with Cosimo's support, to promote the *Corpus Hermeticum*. These were ancient esoteric texts attributed to a mythical Egyptian priest, Hermes Trismegistus; another work closely associated with that corpus was the esoteric treatise *Asclepius*, attributed to Apuleius of Madaurus (second century CE). In 1463, Ficino was able to dedicate to Cosimo "il vecchio," on the latter's request, his Latin translation of *Pimander*, containing fourteen Hermetic texts (only the first of which actually bears the title *Pimander*; it was soon translated into the vernacular by Tommaso Benci). Ficino's source was a Greek codex brought from Macedonia by fra Leonardo da Pistoia. The *Corpus Hermeticum* was venerated in the Renaissance as a text originating in remotest antiquity; only in 1614 would Isaac Casaubon date it to the period to which it actually belonged—the second and third centuries CE.

But as Ficino continued to translate the Hermetic Corpus a hundred and fifty years earlier, he grew convinced that he was regaining contact with an ancient theology, an original revelation, the matrix of all faiths and doctrines. From this perspective, Christ was only the ultimate, albeit most prestigious, link in a long and unbroken theological chain that had begun centuries before. To the *Pimander*, Ficino added other translations from *prisci theologi* (ancient theologians), translations no longer extant but listed in a late letter to Martinus Uranius Preninger of Constance: *Orphic hymns*, hymns by Proclus, *Hymns* attributed to Homer, hymns from Hesiod's *Theogony* and from the *Argonautica* attributed to Orpheus, hymns from the *Aura verba* of Pythagoras, and the pseudo-Pythagorean *Symbola*. With these can be grouped the commentary on the *Oracula Chaldaica* attributed to Zoroaster, and the *Magica idest philosophica dicta magorum ex Zoroastri*, a work that Gemistus Pletho had already made known and that, according to the Cretan humanist George of Trebizond (d. 1472/73), promoted a "unique and entirely pagan religion." Out of this array of texts was woven an esoteric *prisca theologia* for (Florentine) initiates. Its pedigree ran as follows: "the first theologian is said to have been Zoroaster, chief of the Magi; the second Hermes Trismegistus, chief of the Egyptian priesthood; after Hermes came Orpheus; into the mysteries of Orpheus Aglaophemus was initiated; theology descended from Aglaophemus to Pythagoras, from Pythagoras to Plato, who in his writings confirmed, developed, and illustrated all their learning."[11]

Ficino's ancient theology conferred a new dignity on man, from whom the crushing burden of original sin was lifted, and who could lay claim to a birthright of potential divinity, of lordship and mastery over the world. As the *Asclepius* puts it, "a great miracle is man, worthy of veneration and honor, who takes on the nature of a god, as though he were himself a god."[12] This human dignity comes about through a species of self-regeneration or self-directed palingenesis: with his recognition of himself as the image of God, man, illuminated by the rays of the unique Sun, will be capable of reappropriating his original divinity, bypassing the sacramental channels regulated by the church. As early as his *Dialogus inter Deum et animam theologicus* (*Theological Dialogue between God and the Soul*), composed about 1462, Ficino had written suggestively of contact bordering on fusion between the soul of man and God. More than once he had adduced the Ovidian myth of Clytie (as would Lorenzo the Magnificent himself in his *Comento*): Clytie, who was transformed from a human being into a flower and lived on, her amorous gaze fixed on her beloved, the Sun (God); Clytie, who was thus, as it were, resurrected and united with the object of her desire.

11   Ficino 1970, 3:8:1, 148.
12   Ficino 1983, 1859.

The ancient theology also conferred a halo of new Platonic dignity on Lorenzo as ruler, magus, and philosopher, which legitimized, on the higher level of culture (higher, that is, than social rank), his primacy over other optimates. One particular passage from Plato was recited again and again by Ficino, by the humanist chancellor of Florence Bartolomeo Scala, and by the Florentine humanist Cristoforo Landino: "those republics will always be blessed, in which philosophizing men will rule, or those who rule will truly begin to philosophize."[13] Lorenzo the Magnificent became the prince of philosophers, and, given the coincidence of philosophy and theology, the promoter and virtual messiah of this new religious creed. Ficino began his celebrated commentary on Plato's *Symposium* of 1468–69 (immediately translated into the vernacular under the title *Il libro dell'amore*, a further demonstration of a program to spread Platonism among wider, more popular circles) with a symposium, at which Lorenzo presides, meant to honor Plato on the date of his birth, and so providing a telling indication of Lorenzo's and therefore Florence's exclusive conversion to Platonism. This apparently came about in 1473–74: as Sebastiano Gentile has shown, Lorenzo was not mentioned in the first draft, being introduced as Platonism's patron and as philosopher-ruler only in subsequent redactions.[14]

Again, it is not by chance that the Medici were increasingly depicted in the guise of Magi: for example in the 1459 fresco *Cavalcata dei Magi* by Benozzo Gozzoli in the Medici palace, and in the *Adorazione dei Magi* by Botticelli, now in the Uffizi Gallery, both with an almost complete cast of Medici family members. The Medici-Magi are both the guardians of an ancient theology preceding Christ's gospel, and mediators between the old and new revelations. Ficino asserted repeatedly that the Magi had been both kings and priests of an ancient Persian caste. Nor was it by chance that the Medici were all enrolled in the confraternity (or *compagnia*) of the Magi, which organized a procession in honor of the adoration of the Magi. In 1482, with the Medici-Magi identification fully established, Ficino composed the treatise *De stella magorum*.

The close affiliation of political power and religious charisma can be found in numerous passages by Ficino, for example, the *Argumentum* prefacing the eighth book of Plato's *Republic*. Just as a wise architect is needed to coordinate the labor of the workers in constructing a building (a reworking of the metaphor of the "great architect" of the edifice of the world, i.e., God), so a single "shepherd" (*pastor*, the ecclesiastical-evangelical term usually applied to Christ, or the pope) is indispensable for the management of the state, under whose guidance the golden age of felicity, the age of Saturn, can return. Power must be vested in one man alone (*unus ante omnes*), a wise and just helmsman of the ship of state, appointed by God without

---

13   "che sempre saranno beate le repubbliche nelle quali saranno al governo gl'uomini filosofanti, o veramente quegli che governano cominceranno a filosofare." Landino 1974, "Proemio al commento dantesco," 1:129.

14   Gentile 1981.

collaboration of others, including the pope—a king in fact, even if he lives as a private citizen. The Platonic monarch (Lorenzo) is such not by dynastic right, but because he is the depositary of superior "wisdom," charged with a religious magisterium (teaching function), as with the Egyptians. In 1482, Ficino dedicated to Lorenzo his most demanding and original work, the *Theologia platonica de immortalitate animorum*, composed between 1469 and 1474, but published only in 1482. In the proem, he pointed to Lorenzo as representing the Platonic unity of philosopher and king: Plato, he says, would salute the latter, "since what he had once hoped for especially from great men of the past, you have realized—the union of philosophy with the highest political authority."[15]

And yet this philosophy is, above all, a theocracy, with Lorenzo as its high priest. Through the syncretism of myriad religions, it proposes a new divine conversion without the mediation of church, priests, dogmas, and sacraments. Simply put, it inverts the process of creation: it reascends, step-by-step, the ontological hierarchichy of Plotinus, from the body to quality, to soul, to angelic mind, and finally to that which is "first" (the Good and the One that is God). This graduated ascent is described carefully by Ficino in *De raptu Pauli ad tertium caelum et animi immortalitate* (*On the Rapture of Paul to the Third Heaven and the Immortality of the Soul*), which dates from 1476 and was also soon translated into the vernacular by Ficino himself. All begins with God and terminates inexorably in God, an *itinerarium mentis sive cordis* ("itinerary of the mind or heart") of self-guided ascent and descent. This itinerary culminating in the sight of God (theophany) or religious creed treads close to outright heresy: in his catalogue of prophets or messiahs, Ficino mingled together on an equal footing Christians, pre-Christians, and Neoplatonists: "I have found, indeed, that the most important mysteries of Numenius, Philo, Plotinus, Iamblichus, and Proclus were transmitted by John, Paul, Hierotheus, and Dionysius the Areopagite."[16] This is a "concordance" of numerous revelations anticipating Giovanni Pico della Mirandola's thought; the syncretism becomes even more audacious when Ficino likens the creation in Genesis to the demiurgic creation in Plato's *Timaeus*, even hinting, in the *Compendium in Timeum* of 1483–84, at the equivalence between the three Plotinian hypostases and the Christian Trinity.[17]

---

15 Ficino 1970, 1:37.

16 "Io, di certo, ho trovato che i più importanti misteri di Numenio, Filone, Plotino, Giamblico, Proclo furono trasmessi da Giovanni, Paolo, Ieroteo, Dionisio Areopagita." Ficino 2005, 101–102.

17 Here, again from *La religione cristiana* (Ficino 2005, 79), is what Ficino had to say about the "prole angelica" (angelic offspring) chosen to mediate between God and the world: "Questa, Orfeo chiamò Pallade, nata soltanto dalla testa di Giove; a questo, nell'epistola a Ermia, Platone diede il nome di figlio del Dio padre. Nell'*Epinomide* lo chiamò *logos*, cioè ragione e verbo, dicendo: 'il logos, il più vicino di tutte le realtà, ha ornato questo mondo visibile.' Mercurio Trismegisto spesso menziona il verbo, ed il figliuolo di Dio, e anche lo spirito. Zoroastro, del pari, attribuisce una prole intellettuale a Dio." (Orpheus called her Pallas, born from the head of Jove alone; to him, in the epistle to Hermias, Plato gave the name of son of God the father. In the *Epinomis* he called it *logos*, meaning reason and word, saying "the logos, the thing closest to all realities, has

Ficino's philosophical-theological "discourse" became the official religion of the Medici, and so of Florence, only in the early 1470s, when Lorenzo put Ficinian Neoplatonism into verse. His *Comento* on his sonnets, entirely Ficinian in tone, has been mentioned, but even earlier, with *De summo bono* of 1473–74, Lorenzo as good as versified Ficino's epistle *De felicitate*: the relationship between the ruler and his intellectual mentor comes close to symbiosis. Beginning in the second *capitolo* of Lorenzo's little poem, Ficino himself is brought on stage and, to clarify the nature of the highest good, indicates the various steps in the ascent: from corporeal and fortuitous matter to contemplative virtue, to the contemplation of God, which, at the highest degree of fusion, comes about not through the intellect but through love. The poem ends with a religious hymn to the new Neoplatonic god, drawn from Ficino's *Oratio ad Deum theologica*:

> O venerando, immenso, eterno Lume, / el quale in te medesimo te vedi, / e luce ciò che luce nel tuo nume! [...] / tu accendi il disio, e da te viene / che la voglia è d'ogni bene ardentissima, / perché ogni ben se' tu, o sola spene / O vera luce micante e purissima, / te per te priego che la vista oscura / di caligine purghi, e sia chiarissima, / acciò che io vegga la tua luce pura; / perché tu nel mio cor la sete accendi, / tu fai che 'l ghiaccio suo s'infiammi et ura, ecc.

> O venerable immense eternal Light, which you see yourself in yourself, and which illuminates that which shines in your divinity! . . . you inflame desire, and from you it comes about that the will burns ardently for every good thing, for you are every good thing, o single hope, o true glittering and purest light; through you yourself I beseech you to purge my clouded sight of mist, so that it grows acute, so that I may see your pure light; because in my heart you kindle thirst, you cause its ice to catch fire and burn.

In short, this is an intimate relationship between man and God. Thirst kindles desire (the parodic slant given to thirst in the youthful *Simposio* will be noted), which inflames the heart with love, so that, blind before, it may contemplate the God-Sun in all its splendor (a recurrent comparison in Ficino). Of the sacraments, baptism, communion, confession, and the rest, nothing remains. Even Christ, the Bible, and Christ's representatives on earth have vanished from the religious panorama.

Finally, in the third cultural and religious phase, there is a return, evidently arising out of the altered historical and political situation in Laurentian Florence, to the Catholic faith. In 1488, Lorenzo the Magnificent married his fifteen-year-old daughter Maddalena to Francesco Cibo, the son (in the guise of nephew) of the new

---

adorned this visible world." Hermes Trismegistus often mentions the word, and the son of God, and also the spirit. Zoroaster likewise assigns an intellectual offspring to God.)

pope, Innocent VIII (enthroned on 29 August 1484). In 1488, too, his son Piero was married to Alfonsina Orsini. On 9 March 1489, the pope made Giovanni, Lorenzo's thirteen-year-old son, a cardinal, so bringing to fruition a campaign conducted by Lorenzo since 1487. Mario Martelli has shown that this third religious phase was conceived by Lorenzo in complete accord with Girolamo Savonarola. Savonarola was given the privilege of attending Lorenzo on his deathbed, as is recounted in the celebrated letter by Poliziano to Jacopo Antiquari (18 May 1492), in the company of Pico and Poliziano alone. Poliziano called him "a man distinguished for his learning and sanctity, an excellent preacher of celestial doctrines," and related that at the point of death Lorenzo sought pardon for his sins and holy blessing from Savonarola. It is noteworthy that Ficino was absent.[18] Despite (or because of) the support he had received from Cosimo and Lorenzo (with whom, incidentally, he enjoyed a conflicted relationship of subjection and betrayal), Ficino had taken his arcane Neoplatonic mysteries to extremes. Now he had to struggle to recover his good name as a Christian. In 1489, he addressed a belated *Apologia* to Piero Del Nero, Piero Guicciardini, and Piero Soderini, and in 1494, he welcomed Charles VIII as the Christian liberator of Italy and praised Savonarola as the savior of Florence and the single "divine voice" whom all should obey:

> Per virum santimonia sapientiaque praestantem Hyeronymum ex ordine praedicatorum, divinitus ad hoc electum [. . .] A Domino factum est illud, et est mirabile in oculis nostris. Reliquum est, optime mi Ioannes, ut deinceps salutaribus tanti viri consiliis obsequentes, non solum ego atque tu, sed omnes etiam Florentini [. . .][19]

> Through a man outstanding for sanctimony and wisdom, Girolamo of the order of preachers, divinely chosen to this end. . . the Lord brought this about, and it is a miracle before our eyes. It remains, my good Giovanni, that henceforth, in obedience to the salutary counsels of such a man, not just I and you but all Florentines as well. . . .

In the 1490s, Ficino even began a commentary on the Epistles of Saint Paul, accommodating himself to the shifts in prevailing philosophical-theological currents and to the changed literary and religious climate.

In 1491, Ugolino Verino, an intellectual unswervingly loyal to the Medici, who, like nearly all Medici intellectuals, had become a fervent follower of Savonarola, sent the latter (certainly with Lorenzo the Magnificent's full authorization) a poem consisting of 212 hexameters, *De christianae religionis et vitae monasticae felicitate* (*On the Felicity of the Christian Religion and the Monastic Life*), inquiring in the dedication

18   See Martelli 2009.
19   Ficino 1983, 963.

whether poetry had harmed or helped mankind. The perfectly Savonarolan conclusion arrived at is that the only beneficial poetry is that which celebrates the true (Catholic) religion and moral purity, to the exclusion of pagan and secularized humanist poetry—a conclusion converging with the teachings of Giovanni da San Miniato and Giovanni Dominici almost a century before. Savonarola replied with his *Apologeticus seu de ratione poeticae artis*: he is not absolutely averse to philosophy or poetry, but only to those who "prefer to utter the name of Jove rather than of Christ." This was a virtually direct allusion to Ficino's philosophy-theology, which had resuscitated the pagan gods and writers before Christ's revelation.

All the humanists, previously in every respect secularized, underwent conversions: unexpectedly, they composed sacred texts, although not, as in the earlier phase, for the people, but now for the elite. Pico and Poliziano, two intellectuals closely associated with the seats of power throughout their careers, are symptomatic. Pico, author of the nine hundred condemned *Conclusiones philosophicae, cabalisticae et theologicae*, did a volte-face with his *Apologia*, going on to become a faithful follower of Savonarola's, donning the Dominican habit, and planning a vast commentary on the Psalms. He also took a stand against Ficino, whom he branded an ecclesiastical heretic for his fascination with magic and astrological divination. Poliziano, previously indifferent to philosophy, now reversed the Platonic tendencies (of Ficinian theology) by delivering lectures at the University of Florence in the academic years 1490–92 on Aristotelian texts (*Nicomachean Ethics, Categories, De interpretatione, First and Second Analytics*). The same Poliziano, previously an unrepentent and secular-minded scholar of Greek and Latin classics, directed two hymns to the Virgin to Antonio Alabanti, the Servite general, in the summer of 1491; in the first half of 1492, he translated into Latin the portion of Saint Athanasius's commentary on the Psalms known as the *Epistola a Marcellino*.

Even Lorenzo the Magnificent embraced the new culture and religion, staging his *Rappresentazione di san Giovanni e Paolo* in 1491, besides composing for that year's holy week a few entirely traditional *laude* (spiritual poems), for example:

> Io son quel misero ingrato / peccator, che ho tanto errato. / Io son quel prodigo figlio / che ritorno al padre mio; / stato son in gran periglio / esulando da te, Dio; / ma tu se' sì dolce e pio, / che non guardi al mio peccato. / Io son quella pecorella, / che 'l pastor suo ha smarrito: / tu, Pastor, lasci per quella tutto il gregge, e m'hai seguito[20]

> I am that miserable ungrateful sinner who has erred so greatly. I am that prodigal son who returns to my father; in great peril have I been straying, God, from you; but you are so sweet and pious that you do not notice my sin.

20 Medici 1992, 2:1056.

I am that sheep that the shepherd has lost: Shepherd, you leave the whole flock for me, and have come after me.

An allusion to the two parables about the prodigal son and the lost sheep from Luke 15 is evident; in what follows there are references to the Psalms, the Pauline letters, the Song of Songs, and verses of Feo Belcari (virtually exhumed after decades of neglect). In other *laude*, entire passages from the sermons of Savonarola are quoted. Not least of the reasons for this religious reconversion was the progressive loss of favor with the people, who could hardly make sense of Ficino's *Theologia platonica*. For years these esoteric doctrines had brought glory and prestige to the Medici, but they were incomprehensible to a population powerfully tied to the traditional Catholicism (in religious observance as in literary production) of Lucrezia Tornabuoni and Feo Belcari.

THIRTEEN

A Cardinal in Rome

Florentine and Medici Ambitions

DAVID S. CHAMBERS

W HY WAS THERE NO CARDINAL of Florence for most of the fifteenth century, greatly to the loss, it was believed, of the city's honor and benefit? Why did it take so long, despite the fact that Florence even replaced Rome as the seat of the papacy in 1419–20 and from 1434 to 1444, that the papal bureaucracy and curial households were packed with canny Florentines, that Florentine banks for long periods controlled papal finances, and that Cosimo de' Medici was a personal friend of popes and cardinals?

For, although there had been several Florentine cardinals before and during the Great Schism,[1] after it ended in 1417, and after the death in 1422 of the last of them, only one Florentine was appointed before the underage Giovanni de' Medici in 1489,[2] the little known Alberto degli Alberti,[3] cardinal from 1439 to 1445. This long gap is all the more surprising since it was a period when Italian powers, not least signorial rulers, were eager and competitive about gaining red hats for their clerical protégés and relatives. This had less to do with ideas about national representation in the commanding heights of the church than with the urge to gain political influence there—at a time when the popes were consolidating their role as Italian princes—and the belief that a cardinal conferred prestige upon a regime.

---

1   Pietro Corsini (cardinal 1370–1405), Angelo Acciaiuoli (1385–1408), Alamanno Adimari (1411–22), and the Paduan canonist Francesco Zabarella, bishop and so-called cardinal of Florence (1411–17). See Chiffoleau 1983; D'Addario 1960a; Pàsztor 1960; also Ullmann 1948, 190–231.
2   Picotti 1928 remains essential.
3   D'Addario 1960b; see notes 14 and 38 below.

In the post-conciliar epoch, moreover, a new class of cardinal arose, Italian "princely cardinals," the first being Pius II's appointment in 1461 of the seventeen-year-old Francesco Gonzaga (second son of Ludovico III Gonzaga, marquis of Mantua and of Barbara of Brandenburg) in response to pressure not only from his parents (to whom the pope was obliged for hospitality at Mantua during the congress there in 1459), but also—after prompting—from Francesco's maternal relative, the emperor Frederick III.[4] A few years later, Marquis Guglielmo Paleologo of Monferrato was "very desirous that his brother, the protonotary Teodoro, should be promoted to the dignity of cardinal"; Teodoro was eventually appointed by Paul II in 1468.[5] Soon, King Ferrante of Naples was agitating to get his son Giovanni into the sacred college; this was expected in 1472, and Ferrante was so discouraged by failure that he thought of arranging a marriage for him instead,[6] but Giovanni finally achieved the red hat in December 1477, at the age of twenty-one. Meanwhile, already in 1471, Galeazzo Maria Sforza, duke of Milan, had been encouraged concerning his brother Ascanio, then only sixteen.[7] The youthfulness of all these princely candidates was not necessarily a drawback; youth implied relative innocence, whereas Ascanio had to wait until he was nearly thirty, and by then his character and career were tarnished enough to provoke objections from other cardinals. As Marco Pellegrini has shown, crucial to his prospects and eventual success was the support of Sixtus IV's nephew, Girolamo Riario, who had married Caterina Sforza, Galeazzo Maria's daughter.[8] Thus, a new if precarious route toward a prince cardinal's red hat was established—marriage alliance with the papal family—precarious because of the short term of most pontificates. Ascanio had just made it in 1484, a few months before Sixtus IV's death. But Milan already had two non-princely cardinals, Stefano Nardini and Giovanni Arcimboldi, while the republic of Venice had no fewer than seven in the period up to 1489, two of whom became popes.

So what was the matter? Was part of it that Florence was already so well connected in the papal court—Roberto Bizzocchi has drawn attention to the network of relatives and agents of the canons of Florence cathedral[9]—that the governing class

4   Pellegrini 1989, 215–218; Signorini 1974 and 1985, 34–41; Chambers 1992a, 11–18 and 1992b.

5   Sacramoro da Rimini to Duke Francesco Sforza, Rome, 11 October 1464, ASMi, Sforzesco 57, 219: "esso è molto desyderoso ch'el Reveren(do) d(omino) Theodoro suo fratello prothonotario apostolico sia promosso a la dignitate del cardinalato."

6   Sacromoro to Duke Galeazzo Maria Sforza, Rome, 3 June 1472, Medici 1977–, 1:427. Giampietro Arrivabene to Barbara of Brandenburg, marchesa of Mantua, Bologna, 28 February 1473, ASMn, AG 1141, 393: "dal papa e cardinali era expressamente data la negativa al re de fare el protonotario suo figliolo cardinale, et perché el re era intrato in pratica de darli mogliere."

7   Pellegrini 1989, 236. Galeazzo Maria mistrusted his brother, however, and became more urgent on behalf of Giovanni Arcimboldi, though in April 1476 he insisted on Ascanio if Giovanni of Aragon was to become a cardinal: Somaini 2003, 1:500–501.

8   Pellegrini 1989, 242; 2002, 1:67–107 passim.

9   Bizzocchi, 1984, 270, reckons that 94 of the 172 canons from 1417 to 1500 had offices or close ties in the curia.

thought they hardly needed the services of a native cardinal or feared one might become too powerful locally? Moreover, some prominent *porporati* (cardinals) in the 1430s and 1440s were extremely pro-Florentine: Giovanni Vitelleschi, archbishop from 1435 to 1437, was even referred to as the cardinal of Florence, though the *signoria* might ultimately have connived his downfall in 1440.[10] Vitelleschi's successor as archbishop and cardinal, the Paduan Lodovico Trevisan, later apostolic chamberlain, worked closely with the Medici bank and took a leading part in Florence's military victory at Anghiari (1440) against the condottiere Niccolò Piccinino and the Florentine exiles, for which services he received huge sums and a Florentine palace.[11] Later, the rich and powerful French cardinal Guillaume d'Estouteville (created by Eugenius IV in 1439) acted virtually as cardinal protector of Florence.[12]

Nevertheless, the appointment of a native Florentine cardinal was constantly solicited. Back in November 1422, and immediately after the death of Cardinal Alamanno Adimari, the *signoria* sent a long letter to the Florentine ambassador Bartolomeo de' Bardi and a follow-up letter to Pope Martin V, appealing for a new Florentine cardinal. The ambassador's instructions emphasized that since the deaths of the cardinals Zabarella and Adimari the city had been deprived of the dignity and honor for which it was deemed worthy.[13] Six names of possible candidates for the red hat were suggested: the archbishops of Florence and Pisa, Amerigo Corsini and Giuliano de' Ricci; the bishop of Fiesole, Benozzo Federighi; the general of the Dominicans, Leonardo Dati; a cathedral canon, Dino de' Pecori; and the theologian Ubertino degli Albizzi. It was all in vain. Only after seventeen more years had passed was there at last a Florentine cardinal, the aforementioned Alberti, whose appointment might have been an expression of papal gratitude for Florence's hosting, beginning in 1434, first the curia and then the general church council. Alberti cannot have been of much use to Florence since he was sent away on legations and died in 1445. But at least his name was invoked, over thirty years later, in a letter pointing out there had been no Florentine cardinal since his death.[14] No initiative to replace him seems to have been made in 1445, perhaps because attention was focused on a replacement for the deceased archbishop, and because relations with Eugenius IV had deteriorated.[15]

---

10   Rolfi 1994, 139–141. Vitelleschi was called "lo cardinale fiorentino" by Francesco Sforza, writing to Cosimo de' Medici, 20 July 1439: Fabroni 1788, 2:161–163; translated in Ross 1910, 44–46.

11   Paschini 1939, 48–52, 56–57.

12   On d'Estouteville, see Esposito 1993, 456–460.

13   "Come è suto piacere del Sommo Creatore a se à chiamato l'anima delle felici memorie in non troppo tempo de' reverendissimi signori cardinali di Pisa [Adimari] e di Ragugia [Zabarella] et di Fiesole [Bindo Guidotti, who was about to be promoted (Ughelli 1712–22, 3:260)] [...] et così la nostra città e communità rimane al presente privata di tanta dignità e honore che assai li reputiamo": ASF, Missive 31, fol. 12r, letter dated 22 November 1422; noted by Peterson 1989, 301 n. 2. The letter to the pope, 23 November 1422, does not repeat these names: ASF, Missive 31, fols. 52v–53v. I am grateful to David Peterson for transcripts.

14   See note 38 below.

15   Peterson 1989, 308–314.

There was a presumption that whoever was archbishop of Florence, or another bishop in Florentine territory, deserved to be made a cardinal. According to his tomb inscription, Archbishop Bartolomeo Zabarella was intended for the red hat in 1445, but died at Sutri on his way to Rome,[16] and Vespasiano da Bisticci wrote that Roberto Cavalcanti, bishop of Volterra, was so respected in the papal Curia that, had he not died in 1450, Nicholas V would have made him a cardinal.[17] Certainly the Dominican Antonino Pierozzi, archbishop since 1446 and in 1455 one of the ambassadors of the *signoria* sent to congratulate Calixtus III on his election, was proposed for the red hat. This must have been with the backing of Cosimo "il vecchio" de' Medici, since his son Giovanni was, they wrote, one of the "four [ambassadors] commissioned to speak to his holiness about promoting our monsignor archbishop to the dignity without his knowledge." Kneeling before the pope, they commended Antonino's learning, virtue, and reputation, stressing "our city has been provided with cardinals at other times … and this would bring the greatest joy to the Florentine people."[18] Their solicitations cut no ice, however, and probably would have appalled Antonino if he had ever heard of the proposal. On the contrary, his successor as archbishop, Orlando Bonarli, canon lawyer and auditor of the Rota, was said to be so keen to become a cardinal that, when this did not happen, the disappointment caused his death, in 1461.[19]

Candidates favored by the *signoria* for the cardinalate, as for other appointments, were not always preferred by the Medici, and vice versa. Cosimo "il vecchio" and his successors played their hand in this, as in other areas, more as a ruling family than as dominant citizens, and sought the red hat preferably for one of their kindred. A difficulty here was that there was no close relative, in Cosimo's time, who was suitable. His brother Lorenzo was a married layman, and died in 1440, though he did have his uses in the papal connection (for instance, he organized the removal of the council from Ferrara to Florence in December 1438 with Medici funds).[20] Cosimo's bastard son Carlo, thought to have been born of a Circassian slave, had been dispensed to hold minor orders and set up as provost of the collegiate church of Santo Stefano in Prato,[21] but Cosimo and his descendants evidently shrank from

16 Ughelli 1717–22, 3:260; Bizzocchi 1987, 209.

17 Da Bisticci 1970–76, 1:293.

18 Letter to the *signoria*, 7 June 1455: "Per mandare ad executione quanto fu commesso dalle vostre Signorie a noi quattro, in particularità di parlare al sancto Patre sopra a promuovere a dignità el nostro monsignor l'Arciveschovo, senza sua saputa fumo questa mattina a pie della Beatitudine del sancto Padre […] commendando et la scientia et virtù del prefato nostro Arciveschovo, et la reputatione che ha, et che la nostra città è stata provveduta ad altri tempi di cardinali […] et el sommo piacere che ne farebbe a tutto questo populo etc." Guasti 1857, doc. XI, 29, paraphrased by Morçay 1914, 235, who notes earlier Florentine cardinals (omitting Adimari and Alberti) and quotes Francesco da Castiglione's *Vita beati Antonini* (Castiglione 1680) that Antonino would have refused.

19 Piccolomini 1984, 1:398–401. On Bonarli, see Martines 1969; Bizzocchi 1987, 209–210.

20 Ross 1910, 42–44; Holmes 1992, 25.

21 Kent 2010, 197.

nominating him. Cosimo's two legitimate sons, Giovanni and Piero, were married and needed for secular services and to guarantee the regime's continuity, though Giovanni was sometimes sent to Rome on ecclesiastical business.[22] So Cosimo had to sponsor a more distant relative for the red hat. Among descendants of Vieri de' Medici were two rising prelates, Donato (born in 1402, bishop of Pistoia from 1436) and Donato's nephew Filippo (born in 1426), who became the favored candidate.[23]

Filippo de' Medici's rise was relatively rapid. He became an apostolic protonotary and was resident in the curia during the 1450s, and in 1456 he was appointed bishop of Arezzo. Many letters from Filippo survive from this period, mostly undated, but some suggest he was already ambitious for a cardinal's hat. In March 1458, he told Giovanni de' Medici that Pope Calixtus III was expected to make new appointments at Pentecost,[24] and assured Cosimo that his claim was strongly backed by the Milanese ambassador; the pope had declared that he wished to exalt the Medici, even though the *signoria* had been pressing for a different candidate.[25] Calixtus did not create new cardinals, however, and within a few months was dead. The five Florentine ambassadors sent to congratulate Pius II on his election were instructed on 28 September to praise Filippo as "worthy of the grandest dignity to bring honor to the city and to his deeply respected and beloved family."[26] They wrote on 12 October that Pius, almost laughing, simply expressed surprise that, among many recommendations, they had not mentioned Antonino.[27] Early in 1459, when the papal curia stopped at Siena on the journey to the congress of Mantua, Filippo's hopes rose again; he told Giovanni on 10 February that he was strongly supported by Cardinal d'Estouteville, and that warm letters from the *signoria* should be decisive.[28]

22 E.g., see note 18 above.

23 Luzzati 1964–66, especially 362–378. Some letters Luzzati cites from ASF, MAP have been renumbered.

24 Filippo de' Medici to Giovanni de' Medici, Rome, 12 March [1458?], ASF, MAP 11, 188: "credessi che al più tardi alla pentecoste farà quello a affare. Noi staremo attenti e con buoni modi cerceremo di fare e fatti nostri." In another, dated 29 March [1458?], ASF, MAP 7, 339: "sanza mancho si crede che a questa pentecoste farà qualche cosa."

25 Filippo to Cosimo, Rome, 21 March [1458?], ASF, MAP 12, 402: "Avendo avuto a questi dì una lettera da Giovanni nostro e con essa uno del duca al suo imbasciadore in mio favore e cercando molti per diverse vie d'essere promosso alla degnità del cappello, non ò voluto per negligentia essere lasciato adrieto. Onde avendo ieri exposto alla s(ignoria) n(ostra) tutto il bisognio et in buon modo ebbe gratissima risposta in questo effecto che la sanctità sua desiderava assai di fare cossa grata al duca et a voi." Filippo, bishop of Arezzo since January 1457, signed himself "aretinus."

26 "merita a ogni grandissima dignità essere assumpto [...] honore et gloria a questa città ne risulterebbe: pero che lui di quella famiglia è nato, la qual in questa città et apresso di tutti è in somma benivolentia et amore": Guasti 1857, 52; Morçay 1914, 273.

27 "si maravigliava che noi lasciassimo indrieto el nostro arcivescovo: et disse quasi ridendo": Guasti 1857, 56.

28 "che la Signoria scriva 3 lettere caldissime in diverse date, a ciò paia vogli ogni modo per me, non per altri [...] Otteremo ogni cosa coll'aiuto di mons. di Roano [d'Estouteville], il quale ha deliberato mettere la corazza per ottener questa posta": ASF, MAP 6, 347; Picotti 1912, 371; Luzzati 1964–66, 367.

Pius II made Filippo a referendary and in 1462 archbishop of Pisa, but was unimpressed by his claims for a red hat. In any case, the pope was irritated by perceived Florentine coolness over his crusade plans and tax proposals. From Siena, on 7 March 1460, he sent a polite brief to Cosimo citing the opposition of the cardinals to new promotions and—rather more of a put-down—the pressures upon him from the greatest princes of Christendom.[29] Later, in his *Commentaries*, he simply recorded that at Florence, on the journey back from Mantua early in 1460, he had been asked by Cosimo, quite modestly, to make his relative (*nepotem*) a cardinal, should he prove himself worthy.[30] Francesco Gonzaga's appointment a year later (and not Filippo's) was probably a blow, though Cosimo did not show it when the young Mantuan visited Florence on his way to Rome in March 1462. Racked with gout, Cosimo received him graciously, though he rather pointedly mentioned the king of Portugal's son as an exemplary young cardinal of royal blood. He also introduced Francesco Gonzaga to Filippo.[31] But the early 1460s were on the whole not a good time to solicit for a Florentine cardinal, even after Cosimo became more helpful about Pius II's crusade.[32] True, in 1463 Pius conferred the red hat on Niccolò Forteguerri from Pistoia, but Forteguerri, an old friend of the Piccolomini pope since their student days in Siena, seems to have been under few obligations to Florence or the Medici; only one letter to them, asking a favor of Giovanni, is known.[33]

For years, Filippo de' Medici continued to be the favored candidate of Cosimo, of his successor Piero, and of the *signoria*. Ottone del Carretto, Milanese ambassador in Rome, wrote to Francesco Sforza in December 1463 that Cardinal Ammannati had told Pius II that it was perhaps time to show some favor to Florence, and, if Filippo were appointed, "Cosimo could receive no greater pleasure and consolation in his old age, particularly for the grief suffered over the death of his son."[34] Filippo was present at Giovanni's death on 1 November 1463 and also that of Cosimo on 1 August the following year, but family bonds did nothing to help his cause. After the death of Pius II, also in 1464, the campaign nevertheless continued. Filippo headed the embassy of congratulation to the new pope, Paul II,[35] and could count on active support from the Medicean chancellor of Florence, Bartolomeo Scala, who wrote on his behalf in December 1466 (and again in 1471).[36] There were expectations that

---

29 "erant quippe pro multis preces porrecte et a maioribus christianitatis principibus": Pastor 1904, 120.

30 "petiitque, ma non sine modestia, ut nepotem inter cardinales assumi, si dignus videretur": Pius II 1984, 1:660.

31 Chambers 1988, 249–251.

32 Black 1973, 24–25; Black 1985, 279 ff.; Cardini 1979; Holmes 1992, 26.

33 Morici 1900.

34 "niuno magiore piacere potrebe ricevere cha de vedere questa consolatione el prefato Cosimo in questa sua vechieza, *maxime* per qualche ristoro de la mellanconia ricevuta per la morte de Giovanni suo figliolo": ASMi, Sforzesco 55.

35 Luzzati 1964–66, 370–373.

36 Brown 1979, 80 n. 55.

the pope would soon be appointing new cardinals the next spring, and Cardinal Gonzaga's secretary, Giampietro Arrivabene, wrote on 20 May 1467 that the pope had told the consistory he was under pressure from every nation, from signori and secular powers; there would need to be fifteen or at least twelve appointed. Arrivabene named six or seven likely candidates, but no Florentine.[37] On 14 June, another recommendation for Filippo de' Medici was sent by the *signoria*; this was the letter reminding the pope that there had been no Florentine cardinal since "our citizen cardinal Alberti of beloved memory whom your uncle Eugenius IV appointed."[38]

Was it just bad luck for Filippo that Popes Pius II and Paul II were unsympathetic to Florence,[39] aggravated not only by the matter of crusading funds, but by the city's pro-Angevin policy in the south, and perhaps by the protective role of the powerful French cardinal Guillaume d'Estouteville? Or were there some qualities lacking in Filippo de' Medici? Michele Luzzati dropped a hint of this—that he had merely some courtly or diplomatic skills,[40] and Riccardo Fubini drew attention to some negative opinions among contemporaries: a Franciscan friar, Francesco da Massa, wrote in July 1469 to Otto Niccolini, then ambassador in Rome,[41] that a powerful reason for there not being a Florentine cardinal was that no one worthy enough had ever been proposed. He suggested Paul II's Florentine secretary, Leonardo Dati, bishop of Massa. Dati might have been proposed once or twice by the *signoria*, but had little chance; according to Sacramoro da Rimini, the Milanese ambassador in Rome, writing in November 1470, he was a mortal enemy (*capitale inimico*) of the Medici.[42]

Or was perhaps part of the trouble in the failure of the Medici to get a cardinal that they did not count as princely signori? They were not officially a ruling dynasty nor in the first rank of Italian nobility—not in the same league to impress the court of Rome as the Gonzaga of Mantua, the Paleologi of Monferrato, the Aragonese royalty of Naples, or even the warrior Sforza or Visconti-Sforza of Milan.

Prospects improved, but only slowly, in Lorenzo the Magnificent's time. Lorenzo had early experience of the papal court. Sent there by his father Piero in

---

37 Arrivabene to Barbara of Brandenburg, Rome, 20 May 1467, ASMn, AG 843, 414–415: "nostro signore propose de volere fare cardinali [. . .] allegando la instantia grande che era fatta per ugni natione de cardinali novi e qui particularmente fece un discorso di dominii e potentie che ne dimandavano: concludendo che restringendo bene la cosa se ne bisognasse fare quindeci o almancho dodeci."

38 ASF, Missive 45, fols. 162v–163r: "ut per te [. . .] restituas tu tandem florentinae civitati eam dignitatem sine qua fuimus post decessum Alberti civis nostri cardinalis colendissime memorie quem divinus Eugenius quartus s(ummus) p(ontifex) patruus tuus cardinalem fecit." Another letter was sent on the same day to the college of cardinals (ASF, Missive 45, fol. 163v).

39 Picotti 1928, 161.

40 Luzzati 1964–66, 380.

41 Medici 1977–, 1:227. For Becchi's negative opinion of Filippo, see note 48 below.

42 Ibid. On Dati, see Ristori 1987. The *signoria* in 1455 and 1465 recommended him for high office, perhaps implying the cardinalate: Medici 1977–, 1:122.

1466 as ambassador along with his tutor Gentile Becchi, he made direct contact with Florence's friends, including Cardinals d'Estouteville and Ammannati,[43] and in 1467, negotiations began for his marriage (two years later) to Clarice Orsini.[44] This linked the Medici to one of the most powerful Roman families, providers of several popes and many cardinals in the past—and in the present, to Latino Orsini, who was soon to become apostolic chamberlain. Apparently Latino was encouraging Filippo de' Medici, who was back in Rome in 1468; Filippo wrote about this to Piero di Cosimo on 19 November, asking for supporting letters "in good ink."[45] He believed that eight new cardinals would be created at Christmas, noting likely names, and that, since many were Venetian, one Florentine might be allowed. Instead, two days later, Paul II appointed just a couple of nephews.

A month later, Filippo was commissioned by the *signoria* to take part, together with Otto Niccolini and Antonio Ridolfi, in welcoming the emperor Frederick III to Rome. They were to beg Frederick to beg Paul that "for a long time Florence had been without a cardinal and that the pope should act to make Florence equal to other Italian cities." The instructions went on to recommend Filippo, who in view of the family's nobility and his own virtues seems to us [the *signoria*] worthy of every honor.[46] Maybe someone remembered that the imperial gambit had worked for Francesco Gonzaga, but, if Frederick put in a word for Florence, it met with no success.

The campaign for Filippo nevertheless went on. In December 1470, Lorenzo the Magnificent was advised by Gentile Becchi that the honorable thing was to continue supporting him out of respect for the memory of his grandfather and father, Cosimo and Piero,[47] though it is difficult to see how the honor of Florence, which Becchi suggested was the overriding issue, was served by a candidate who continually failed to attract enough support in the curia and in any case had little rapport with the young Lorenzo. Some years later, as Fubini has shown, Becchi changed his tune, admitting his resentment at having to support Filippo, who had run up large debts in campaigning for himself and meanwhile had spoken badly of Lorenzo's regime.[48] As an alternative, Becchi had suggested Paul II's former tutor Antonio Agli, recently transferred as bishop from Fiesole to Volterra, though allegedly Agli

43 Rochon 1963, 77–79. On Becchi, see ibid., 31–35; Grayson 1970. On the connection with d'Estouteville, see Medici 1977–, 2:417.

44 Rochon 1963, 98–99.

45 ASF, MAP 16, 354. Luzzati 1964–66, 373, indicates the year was 1468.

46 ASF, Signori, Legazioni e Commisssarie, Missive 16, fol. 192r–v (Luzzati 1964–66, 374 n. 23), dated 17 December 1468, instructs the ambassadors, "pregherete la sua maestà che vogli pregare il santo patre che degni qualche volta in questa parte farci pari all'altre città di Italia alle quali noi né per observantia né religione ci reputiamo inferiori." Filippo's letter of 4 January 1468(9) is reticent: ASF, MAP 16, 384.

47 Luzzati 1964–66, 375, quoting Gentile Becchi to Lorenzo de' Medici, 3 December 1470, ASF, MAP 66, 35; Medici 1977–, 1:228 n. 2.

48 Fubini 1996, 341 n. 35.

had spoiled his chances of becoming a cardinal back in 1465, when he turned down the pope's offer of the bishopric of Ragusa (today Dubrovnik).[49]

The continuation of the story in Lorenzo the Magnificent's time has been discussed in the past by Angelo Fabroni, Giovanni Battista Picotti, Roberto Palmaroccchi, André Rochon, and others, and more recently by Fubini and succeeding editors of Lorenzo's letters. To summarize, soliciting for a Florentine cardinal became an urgent matter of prestige for the regime, and the *signoria* and chancellor Bartolomeo Scala put all their weight behind Medicean candidates. Filippo de' Medici at last left the scene, although late in 1473 he was still trying to pull strings for himself, injudiciously even approaching King Ferrante of Naples, no friend of Florence.[50]

The first novelty was the candidature of Lorenzo's younger brother, Giuliano. His age in 1472, eighteen, was perfectly acceptable for a princely cardinal, though he was not of course a prince. Lorenzo wrote directly to Sixtus IV in November 1472, stating frankly the family's (not explicitly the city's) long desire to have a cardinal.[51] Giovanni Tornabuoni, manager of the Medici bank in Rome, was in charge of negotiations and assured Lorenzo the following May that a Florentine cardinal would be appointed "from the heart of the regime,"[52] adding his opinion that Giuliano's appointment would restore confidence in the Medici bank. The advice of Cardinal Ammannati, however, was that the proposal would not go down well unless Giuliano was better prepared. He should be a protonotary for at least a month, have half the retinue of a cardinal, and on no account take any holy orders, for there was a risk to Medici preeminence in Florence should anything happen to Lorenzo and his brother was not available.[53] But after 1473, the worsening of relations with Sixtus IV over the sale of Imola to Girolamo Riario and other matters wrecked Lorenzo's hopes and might even have stoked fears of an anti-Medicean red hat being conferred on Francesco Salviati, Filippo's successor at Pisa.[54] In January 1476, Sixtus IV formally announced that at present he could not embellish the Florentine republic with a cardinal, though in April the *signoria* ordered Alamanno Rinuccini to go on trying.[55]

When the campaign resumed, the main Florentine candidate was Gentile Becchi. Although not a Medici or Florentine citizen, he did at least spring from expatriate Florentine stock in Urbino,[56] was totally loyal to Lorenzo, and familiar

49 Da Bisticci 1970–76, 1:295. On Agli, see also Fubini 1996, 248, 252–254.
50 Giovanni Tornabuoni to Lorenzo, 10 November 1473, quoted in Medici 1977–, 1:398–399.
51 "el lungo desiderio di casa nostra di avere un cardinal": Medici 1977–, 1:400–401; Fabroni 1784, 2:61; Ammannati Piccolomini 1997, 3:1699.
52 "del quorre di tutti e cittadini dello stato": ASP, MAP 137, 342; Medici 1977–, 1:398.
53 Fabroni 1784, 1:59–61; Ammannati Piccolomini 1997, 3:1706–1709; Medici 1977–, 1:425–427 n. 2.
54 Medici 1977–, 1:284–288; 2:269–270 n. 5; Fubini 1994, 276–277.
55 Rochon 1963, 29, 204–206; Rinuccini, Rinuccini, and Rinuccini 1840, ccxli.
56 Fubini 1996, 336–337.

with the papal curia; he was even on good terms with the pope's nephew, Girolamo Riario.[57] In February 1477, when a new creation seemed imminent, letters on Becchi's behalf were drafted in Lorenzo's name and addressed to the cardinals assumed to be Florence's most reliable friends and advocates. The one intended for Cardinal Latino Orsini restated the general problem: "the city asks for what has been promised long ago and granted to many lesser powers no less devoted to the apostolic see than we ourselves." It went on to beg, in Lorenzo's name, that Becchi be promoted because "the said bishop of Arezzo has been a second father to me."[58] Cardinal d'Estouteville was told he could have "no better occasion to confer honor on this city and especially on our house"[59] and Cardinal Ammannati, a close friend of Becchi's, was reminded that there were three interests involved: the public interest of the city, the family interest of the Medici, and the interest of Becchi himself.[60] But for some reason these and the other letters were never sent with Donato Acciaiuoli, the ambassador dispatched to plead for Becchi. The gossip in the curia, recorded by Cardinal Gonzaga's secretary, was that it would be hard for Becchi to succeed because of a scurrilous epigram he had written about the Della Rovere pope, Sixtus IV, and his family.[61] Perhaps Lorenzo hesitated because he still cherished some hopes for Giuliano.

The Pazzi conspiracy and the murder of Giuliano in April 1478, the suspected complicity of Sixtus IV and the aftermath of war, put the campaign for a Florentine or Medicean cardinal back by six years, until after the death of Sixtus IV in 1484. In the meantime, Gentile Becchi had further damaged his chances by leading the anti-papal defiance of the Florentine clergy.[62] Prospects did not improve until long after the election of Innocent VIII, until the Neapolitan Barons' War (over which the papacy and Florence took opposing sides) had ended, and until the deaths of several cardinals had occurred, thus reducing the total membership of the sacred college and modifying the ban on new appointments sanctioned during the conclave of 1484. By the middle of 1487, relations between Florence and the papacy, and on a personal level between Lorenzo the Magnificent and Innocent VIII, had greatly improved, and this trend was to continue thanks to the skill and constant application of the new Florentine ambassador, Giovanni Lanfredini, who arrived in June. In correspondence with Lanfredini, Lorenzo recommended both Gentile Becchi (now rehabilitated) and Clarice's brother Rinaldo Orsini (archbishop of Florence

57 Medici 1977–, 2:305 n. 5.
58 Ibid., 2:307 (ASF, MAP 42, 59).
59 Ibid., 2:311–314 (ASF, MAP 42, 61).
60 Ibid., 2:309–310 (ASF, MAP 42, 60).
61 Arrivabene to Ludovico Gonzaga, Rome, 13 February 1477, ASMn, AG 846, 14: "aspectasi Donato Acciaiolo ambasciatore firentino, la cui potissima casone comprendo sia per la impresa vol fare lo magnifico Lorenzo del cardinalato per lo vescovo de Arezzo, chi è d. Gientil da Urbino. Fu maestro suo ed è quello che dà li versi 'Dispersit gemmas etc.' arduum opus ad iudicio mio." For Becchi's epigram, see Medici 1977–, 2:71 n. 7; Fubini 1996, 343–345; Poliziano and Becchi 2012, 42.
62 Fubini 1996, 345. On Becchi and his "pericolosa tendenza polemica," see also Poliziano and Becchi 2012, 39–50, 90–169.

since 1474); he professed that, apart from his second son Giovanni, there was no one he wanted to see made a cardinal more than Rinaldo.[63] It is clear that Lorenzo was beginning to hope that Giovanni, now aged twelve, could be a serious candidate; writing on 10 July he insisted that no Florentine should be considered except those he had previously named to Lanfredini.[64]

Meanwhile, the Medici-Orsini connection was also being strengthened. Whether Lorenzo's wife Clarice was more committed to see her brother or her son become a cardinal is not clear, but early in 1487 she helped Lorenzo to arrange the marriage of Piero, their firstborn, to Alfonsina Orsini, which finally took place in May 1488.[65] Lorenzo's support for Rinaldo Orsini might have been purely tactical, and it cooled off after Clarice's death in July 1488. In any case, the pope was discouraging about him, saying that the cardinals would not favor a second cardinal from the Orsini family. Innocent suggested the name of Francesco Soderini, but Lanfredini was not keen.[66]

Another marriage negotiated in 1487 and finally celebrated in January 1488 was even more propitious than Piero's—that of Lorenzo's and Clarice's daughter Maddalena to Innocent VIII's ne'er-do-well son Francesco Cibo.[67] This bond with the papal family, involving financial support for Francesco from the funds of the Medici bank,[68] might seem greatly to have strengthened Giovanni di Lorenzo's prospects, but it was still not all plain sailing. Even if the pope himself was well disposed, he was not strong and decisive; some of his Genoese relatives were implacably anti-Florentine and there remained the need for a consensus among the cardinals. Lanfredini struggled on; from early in 1488, support was sought from Cardinal Giuliano Della Rovere, who was on his way back to Rome after a period of estrangement.[69]

But in 1488 progress was slow and there were some curious developments. Giovanni's age still remained a problem and Lorenzo again expressed worry on this point in January. It seems that Lorenzo might even have had the wild thought of substituting Piero for Giovanni, in spite of Piero's imminent wedding.[70] In March,

---

63 Picotti 1928, 167 n. 30. On 26 June 1487, Lorenzo wrote "facciate quanto faresti per messer Giovanni [...] facciate intendere ad l'arcivescovo [...] non ho homo al mondo in che desideri più questa dignità che nella persona sua": Medici 1977–, 10:361–363.

64 "vorrei che ad ogni modo ne accetase Sua Sanctità che non facesse fiorentino alcuni f[uori] quelli ricordati per mezo Vostro": Medici 1977–, 10:417.

65 Picotti 1928, 166, notes the union of the two families (*parentado*) was negotiated in February 1487. The nuptials were not until May 1488: Medici 1977–, 12:289.

66 Picotti 1928, 166–167, 170 n. 44, 177 n. 71; Medici 1977–, 10:399, 418. As late as February 1488, Lorenzo wrote, "La Clarice mi sollecita che io scriva per lo Arcivescovo": Medici 1977–, 12:22.

67 Picotti 1928, 165; Bullard 1994, 81–82, 136–138.

68 Medici 1977–, 12:ix.

69 Picotti 1928, 179–180; Medici 1977–, 12:x, 135–136, 473.

70 Medici 1977–, 11:640–643. Lorenzo wrote despairingly on 29 January 1488, "io non vorei passassi uno pontificato nel quale io ho tanta parte che non havessimo uno cardinale a nostro modo." (Ibid., 11:642)

however, Lorenzo was again inclined to back Becchi, proposing that his appointment would not spoil the chances of Giovanni, even if it meant waiting another few years; Giovanni would already have a foot in the door.[71] In June, Lanfredini made much the same point.[72] Soon after this, however, the death of Clarice occurred, and it appears from two letters from Lorenzo to Lanfredini, dated 16 August and 3 September (briefly mentioned by Palmarocchi), that Innocent VIII had even suggested making Lorenzo himself a cardinal. It is unlikely that the sacred college was consulted or would have approved, but as a widower Lorenzo was legally eligible, and he did not dismiss the idea outright. He told Lanfredini to consult Cardinal Marco Barbo, who emphatically opposed it.[73]

Lanfredini went on trying. In late July 1488, he went to Ostia to try and convince Cardinal Giuliano Della Rovere, who had seen Giovanni in Florence and admitted that he looked more than his age but remained dubious, suggesting it would be safer just to ask for Becchi, if Lorenzo still wanted him. In August, Lanfredini went to Palestrina to try to convince one of the most recalcitrant senior cardinals, Marco Barbo; he was unsuccessful but seemed determined not to give up.[74] The decisive stage came at last in the winter of 1488–89. Nofri Tornabuoni, who had for some time been collaborating with Lanfredini and been offering generous credit arrangements on behalf of the Medici bank, negotiated an enormous new loan—*il partito grande*—for the *camera apostolica*,[75] while Giovanni Lanfredini secured the support of Cardinal Ascanio Sforza. Ascanio brought with him the support of the other Lombard cardinals and the vice-chancellor Rodrigo Borgia, and obtained the consent of others, including a long-standing opponent of Giovanni's nomination, Cardinal Oliviero Carafa.[76] Even then an obstacle arose, since Ascanio's brother, Ludovico il Moro, the regent and effective ruler of Milan and the Sforza dominions, blackmailed him (at the peril of losing his status and benefices) into pressing for the simultaneous appointment of Federico Sanseverino. This son of the condottiere Roberto Sanseverino was a wholly inappropriate candidate for high office in the church, and anathema to the pope, but Ludovico dispatched a special ambassador to check that Ascanio was doing what he had been told. Eventually a compromise was reached, by which both Giovanni and Sanseverino would be

71 Ibid., 12:95 ("essendo lui in Collegio mi parrebbe havervi uno piè di messer Giovanni").
72 Ibid., 12:473 ("Havendo messer Giovanni perdete poi l'altro, et havendo l'altro, non perdete messer Giovanni benché indugiate due o tre anni").
73 Marco Pellegrini kindly directed me to the originals (ASF, MAP 59, 209, 219); Palmarocchi gave no archival reference (1952, 69). The still awaited volumes of Lorenzo's *Lettere* from July 1488 to February 1489 (Medici 1977–, vols. 13–14) will no doubt bring to light more about the final stages of Giovanni's progress toward the red hat. Many letters from Lanfredini survive in ASF, MAP 40: e.g., see note 74 below. Picotti cites some in his notes (1928, 212–227).
74 ASF, MAP 40, 361 (29 July 1488), 375 (24 August 1488), 379 (30 August 1488: "di non abandonare la impresa di messer Giovanni"). Picotti's account is extremely cursory (1928, 182).
75 Bullard 2008, 391–399.
76 Picotti 1928, 187–192, 660–661 (Ascanio's letter of 26 January 1489); Pellegrini 2002, 1:317–329; Medici 1977–, 12:135–136.

included secretly in the creation of new cardinals (officially announced on 9 March 1489), their names not to be made public for three years or until after the death of Innocent VIII, if sooner. So Giovanni finally made it, albeit on qualified terms, soon after his thirteenth birthday, though Lorenzo, dying in 1492, did not live to see his son recognized publicly as a cardinal, and Giovanni's career (though eventually triumphant with his election as pope) was to be hindered by a crisis in Florentine and papal politics as well as by foreign invasion of Italy.

Why had it taken so long for a Florentine to get the supreme ecclesiastical post of *honore et utile*—to use a catchphrase from Italian business and urban sources going back to the thirteenth and fourteenth centuries and particularly resonant in Medicean circles during the later 1480s and early 1490s.[77] I hope I have shown that the answer is not simple. Securing a cardinal's hat, especially for a member of a governing dynasty, was seldom a straightforward business. Apart from the need for a candidate acceptable to all parties, compatible foreign policies and good personal relations with individual popes and cardinals were important, as well as ambassadors possessing persuasive skills, keen intuitions, and effective contacts. Some of these conditions might at crucial times have been lacking for Florence. Ultimately—in addition to Lanfredini's successful lobbying of the cardinals and the *partito grande*, or Nofri Tornabuoni's massive credit arrangement to cover papal debts—*parentado* or marriage into the papal family was probably decisive for Giovanni's promotion, just as it had been for Ascanio Sforza's. Lorenz Böninger has pointed out that the Mantuan ambassador Giovanni Lucido Cattaneo consoled Marchese Francesco Gonzaga when his brother Sigismondo failed to be appointed in 1489, that all the candidates of secular rulers, including the emperor, had been refused, and that Giovanni de' Medici succeeded only because he was a relative of the pope.[78] In conclusion, the persistent angling to obtain a red hat for a Medici, rather than for any other Florentine, and the methods adopted, do seem to reflect the signorial or princely, if not necessarily despotic, pretensions of the family.

77 Bullard 1994, 133–151; Bullard 2008, 393–395; and particularly Frosini 2009, 5, 9, 17 and nn. 45 and 46.
78 Letters dated at Rome, 18–20 February 1489, ASMn, AG 846, 16–18; Medici 1977–, 15:3. See also Picotti 1928, 170; Bullard 1996, 264.

PART IV

The Medici and Their Image

FOURTEEN

Patriarchal Ideals, Patronage Practices, and the Authority of Cosimo "il vecchio"

DALE V. KENT

THERE ARE REMARKABLY FEW COMMENTS by authoritative Florentine contemporaries on the nature of Cosimo de' Medici's role in the republic, a fact of some significance in itself, as Alison Brown observed.[1] There are two writers who did record their views on this subject. One was Vespasiano da Bisticci, Cosimo's only biographer in his lifetime, who furnished books to many public figures of Italy, among them popes, princes, and Florentine citizens whom he knew well and described in his *Lives* of famous men. The other was Marco Parenti, who offered an extensive analysis of the Medici role in Florentine and Italian political life in his *Ricordi* (*Memoirs*), written in 1466 to explain the anti-Medicean reaction of many Florentine citizens after Cosimo's death in 1464.[2]

Both men focused on Cosimo's unique *autorità* (authority) over his fellow citizens. Parenti attributed Cosimo's status as "*sommo cittadino* [supreme citizen] of the city of Florence" to his wealth, prudence, authority, and power.[3] Vespasiano described him as "of great authority in his republic" and recounted episodes illustrating the nature of this *autorità*, which was such that Cosimo spoke his mind freely to others, from the factors of his business to leading citizens of the republic, but "no one dared talk back to him on account of his *autorità*." Although after his death "some considered impugning the reputation of his son Piero . . . while Cosimo

---

1   Brown 1961, 186.
2   Da Bisticci 1970–76, 2:167–211; Parenti 2001.
3   Parenti 2001, 57.

lived ... they did not dare to attempt anything against him, knowing how great was his *autorità*."[4] Piero inherited some of Cosimo's authority, and his son Lorenzo the Magnificent worked to place it on a firmer constitutional footing. Nevertheless, Lorenzo's claim in 1481, "I am not signore of Florence, but a citizen with a certain *autorità*,"[5] cannot be dismissed entirely as an example of the wordplay for which his grandfather Cosimo was notorious, in view of the weight of *autorità* in the language of Florentine political practice and its component cultural traditions—Christian, classical, and civic.[6]

I follow my teacher Nicolai Rubinstein, "maestro di coloro che sanno"[7] regarding the minutiae of Florentine government, in emphasizing the crucial importance of distinguishing between constitutional position and other forms of influence and power.[8] Cosimo's *autorità* drew strength from the Florentine reverence for *autorità* per se, particularly those forms of it that shaped his image and presentation of himself.[9] Chief of these were the patriarchal ideals that, as Francis William (Bill) Kent showed, dominated Florentine imaginations and made the family Florence's fundamental social institution, and the model for most other institutions and relationships.[10] Also important was the Aristotelian view, central to communal political thought, immortalized by Dante, and popularized also by Matteo Palmieri in his *Vita civile*, of the natural evolution from the governance and custodianship of family to that of neighborhood and city.[11] In this view, it was natural that Cosimo, paterfamilias of the Medici lineage, numbering twenty-seven households in 1427, should extend his patriarchal protection and promotion of his kinsmen to include *amici* (friends or allies) and *vicini* (neighbors), honorary kin to whom he was a patron or, in the parlance of the modern mafia, godfather: "dear as a father," as they wrote to him.[12] Eventually the Medici circle came to include a high proportion of the city's ruling group, and naturally Cosimo exercised over them an *autorità*, defined by Dante in his *Convivio* as that quality "worthy of faith and obedience," such as sons owed to their fathers.[13]

These associations are spelled out in the edict that recognized Cosimo after his death as *pater patriae* (father of his homeland),

4 Da Bisticci 1970–76, 2:167–168, 176, 195–196, 209.
5 Medici 1977–, 6:100.
6 Neri Capponi is said to have complained to Cosimo, "I wish you would say things clearly so that I could understand you." Cosimo replied, "Learn my language." Poliziano 1985, 57.
7 Dante, *Inferno* 4.131, speaking of Aristotle.
8 Rubinstein 1997.
9 On *auctoritas*, see Ascoli 2008, chap. 2; Dale Kent 2004, 166–167.
10 F. W. Kent 1977.
11 Dante, *Convivio* 4.4.4; Palmieri 1982, chap. 4, especially 161–163.
12 For example, ASF, MAP 2, 167, 246. On Cosimo's personal and political patronage, see Dale Kent 1978; 2000, especially 7–8.
13 Dante, *Convivio* 4.6.5.

because he conferred upon the Florentine republic innumerable benefits in times of both war and peace, and always with absolute piety preserved his *patria* (fatherland), aiding and augmenting it with his concern for its greatest profit and glory; up to the very last day of his life he conducted himself in all things as befitted the most excellent man and citizen (*civem optimum*), governing it with every care and concern and diligence as a paterfamilias does his own household, with the greatest virtue and benevolence and *pietas* (piety).[14]

Pietas, in the usage of the Roman republic that the Florentine ruling class so admired, signified a sacred duty of devotion to father and country (*pater, patria*). Florentines understood *auctoritas*, in the sense established by Cicero in his *Topica*, as the quality by which the ideal citizen or senator exerted his influence, in contrast to written law. *Auctoritas* derived from an individual's nature or character and depended largely on virtue, but "there are many things which lend authority, such as talent, wealth, age, good luck, skill, experience, necessity, and even at times a concurrence of fortuitous events." It was the duty of the virtuous *optimus civis* who possessed these qualities to exercise his *auctoritas* in the service and guardianship of the republic.[15] As Alamanno Rinuccini, by no means an unqualified admirer of the Medici, observed in 1465, Cosimo, "both as a private citizen and as a member of magistracies," was most useful to the republic "through his counsel and authority" (*consilio et auctoritate*).[16]

My espousal of Rubinstein's view of the nature of Cosimo's role in Florentine government as crucially different to that of the signori (rulers) of other Italian states, by contrast with that of Philip Jones, who was also my mentor, is not due to personal loyalty—"faith and obedience"—such as was expected of the partisans of Cosimo de' Medici. Rubinstein meticulously documented, through electoral records, laws, and government debates, how Cosimo's attempts, and those of more radical members of the Medici regime, to provide a constitutional foundation for his influence and the extension of their power through electoral controls and *balìe* (commissions with plenary powers) were constantly challenged, not only by the ancient republican councils of the people and the commune, but even by leading Mediceans, including the *accoppiatori*, who filled the electoral purses and were thus the chief instrument of electoral controls and the core of the Medici *reggimento* (regime). The terms of Cosimo's increasing authority had to be continually negotiated, and such extensions as were passed into law, often with the smallest majorities, were generally rescinded when the dangers by which they were justified abated—as in 1440, after the victory of the regime over its enemies, internal and external, at the battle of Anghiari, and in 1454, after the peace of Lodi brought an end to decades of

14 ASF, PR 155, fols. 261v–263v; on the decree and Cosimo's patriarchal image, see Kent 2000, 375–377.
15 Cicero, *Topica* 19.73–20.78; Rubinstein 1992, 7.
16 Rinuccini 1953, 126.

threatening and expensive peninsular wars in which the republic had relied heavily on Cosimo's financial and diplomatic strengths. Rubinstein stressed the definitive importance of the constitutional reforms of 1458, but also that they were achieved after a quarter century of effort following Cosimo's triumphant return from exile in 1434, and only six years before his death.[17]

Historians habitually refer to the Medici "domination" of Florence, as if their installation as dukes in the sixteenth century after the foreign conquest of Italy were somehow the foregone conclusion of Cosimo's rise to power and influence more than a century earlier, as if Cosimo's position in the republic were the same as Lorenzo's, and as if Cosimo's aims at the height of his power in the early 1450s and after the *parlamento* of 1458 were identical with those of the Medici *reggimento*—an assumption clearly contradicted by the challenge to Medici authority from their leading partisans in 1466. The provisions of 1458 were the essential basis for further accretions of power by Cosimo, Piero, Lorenzo, and the Medici regime, but, as other essays in this volume note, Lorenzo continued to be obliged, like his grandfather Cosimo, to negotiate the power he exercised with the Florentine people, who rejected the authority of his sons in 1494 in favor of a restored republic.[18]

How did Cosimo's patriarchal authority play out in practice? Historians often represent patriarchal authority as a vaguely benign, if condescending paternalism, but to quattrocento Florentines, a father was "a second God," who must be obeyed.[19] Visual exempla were at least as important to them as verbal injunctions, and the image of the father-son relationship most constantly before Florentine eyes was that of Abraham and Isaac, whose story represented the quintessential scriptural meditation on fathers, sons, and their relation to the Heavenly Father.[20] This was the subject of the 1401 competition for the contract to make a new set of bronze doors for the Florence baptistery, a landmark commission of the early Renaissance. The chief competitors were Filippo Brunelleschi and Lorenzo Ghiberti. Contemporary accounts differ as to the judges' decision, but Ghiberti received the commission. The bronze plaques they submitted both represented the climactic scene of the story, after Abraham had climbed the mountain, laid the wood in order, bound Isaac his son, and laid him on the altar upon the wood.

And Abraham stretched forth his hand, and took the knife to slay his son. And the angel of the Lord called unto him out of heaven ... and he said, "Lay not thine hand upon the lad, neither do thou anything unto him; for now I

17 Rubinstein 1997, especially 26–33, 117, 123, 137, 144–153.
18 See particularly the chapters by Alison Brown and Melissa Meriam Bullard in this volume. Also Jane Black observes that Francesco Sforza had similarly to negotiate with Lombard cities in his efforts to establish his rule: see her chapter in this volume.
19 Ficino 1937, 1:115.
20 For a fuller account of Florentine images of fathers and representations of Abraham and Isaac, see Kent forthcoming.

know that thou fearest God, seeing thou hast not withheld thy son, thine only son from me."[21]

Among other differences between them, the artists illuminated two different contemporary images of the father-son relationship, one emphasizing their mutual love, the other representing the son as appropriately in awe of his father's majesty, akin to that of God.[22] Ghiberti's Abraham, as Richard Krautheimer observed, "has raised the knife, but hesitates to strike; his left arm is placed lovingly around Isaac's shoulder (Fig. 1). The boy looks at his father, full of confidence; the angel floats down leisurely, sure to arrive in good time."[23] By contrast, Brunelleschi's panel is brutally direct (Fig. 2). Krautheimer notes "the dramatic force with which the angel rushes down from a massive cloud on the left, and his left arm shoots forth to grab Abraham's wrist, forcing it back from Isaac's throat—one feels the resistance of the surprised patriarch."[24]

Both panels were preserved, Ghiberti's in the audience hall of the Calimala guild, which had sponsored the 1401 competition and envisaged its use in a subsequent set of doors representing the Old Testament, eventually indeed executed by Ghiberti and known as the Gates of Paradise.[25] But it was the bold and ruthless realism of Brunelleschi's interpretation of Abraham's sacrifice of Isaac that persisted in the city's cultural consciousness. The panel was preserved, allegedly presented to Cosimo de' Medici by the artist, and certainly after 1421 installed on the altar of the old sacristy, commissioned by Cosimo's father Giovanni di Bicci de' Medici as his burial chapel, in the Medici parish church of San Lorenzo.[26] The dramatic force of Brunelleschi's image was translated into verse by another close friend and associate of the Medici, Feo Belcari. His was the most renowned of the many *sacre rappresentazioni* (sacred plays) on the theme of the sacrifice of Isaac, and it was dedicated to Cosimo de' Medici's younger son, Giovanni.[27] Belcari particularly emphasized the cruelty of the divine edict. Equally cruel is the boy's meek submission to his "revered father." Nevertheless, Belcari's essential message was clear: filial piety demands unquestioning obedience to fathers and to the Lord, and faith in the wisdom of their edicts. Abraham, "on his knees and stupefied," is made to say,

---

21 Gen. 22, especially 9–12.
22 On these various aspects of the father-son relationship, see particularly Trexler 1980b, chap. 5; Kuehn 1991, chap. 4.
23 Krautheimer 1970, 48.
24 Ibid., 44.
25 On the fate of the plaques and the controversy over which artist was the winner, see Hyman 1974, 50–51.
26 Kent 2000, 191–192.
27 On Belcari and this play, see Newbigin 1981.

1.

Lorenzo Ghiberti,
The Sacrifice of Isaac,
1401, bronze relief,
partly gilded,
46.5 × 40 cm
(including frame).
Museo Nazionale
del Bargello,
Florence. (Photo:
Art Resource,
New York.)

> Never should the servant of his good Lord / query the reason of his com-
> mandment; [Isaac replies to his] sweet father...I should never have been
> born / If I should ever wish to contradict the Lord / Or if I was not always
> ready / to want to obey you, my good father.[28]

When the Gates of Paradise were at last installed in 1452, the altercation between
Abraham and the angel in the Abraham and Isaac panel was much more in the spirit
of Brunelleschi and Belcari than of Ghiberti's plaque of 1401 (Fig. 3).

Like God, the patriarchal patron was both loved and feared. One of Cosimo's
partisans declared, "I have never desired anything else in life than to submit to your
authority" (*essere sotto le braccia vostre*),[29] evoking at once Isaac cowering beneath
Abraham's arm outstretched with knife in hand, and the very popular image of the
sheltering *Madonna della Misericordia* (Fig. 4), which emphasizes the protective and

28 Belcari 1872, 46, 51–52.
29 ASF, MAP 12, 27.

2.

Filippo Brunelleschi, *The Sacrifice of Isaac*, 1401, bronze relief, partly gilded, 46.5 × 40 cm (including frame). Museo Nazionale del Bargello, Florence. (Photo: Art Resource, New York.)

nourishing function of patriarchal patrons in heaven and on earth.[30] There was general agreement that a son's attitude to his father should include an element of awe, in its original sense the appropriate attitude of man in the presence of God. Otto Niccolini, perhaps the preeminent lawyer in mid-century Florence, and certainly a leading elder statesman of the Medici regime, was nevertheless in awe of Cosimo. In 1463, shortly before Cosimo's younger son Giovanni, to his great grief, predeceased him, Niccolini wrote from Rome, where he was serving as Florentine ambassador to the pope, to Antonio Pucci, one of the chief lieutenants of the Medici party,

> I haven't the courage to face Cosimo after this illness of Giovanni's, and indeed I never was able to cope in Cosimo's presence, or even when writing to him to be able to speak without *timore* (awe or fear). I know all too well that when I was nineteen and revered my father, to my great loss I defied him, as one does fathers, but now thirty years later, for more than three years I have believed that I have found a father, first for the city, and then for

30 Kent 2000, 135–136; see also McLean 2007, 55.

3.
Lorenzo Ghiberti,
*Story of Abraham, Gates
of Paradise*, 1425–52,
80 × 80 cm.
Baptistery of San
Giovanni, Florence.
(Photo: Art
Resource,
New York.)

myself, to whom I have never turned without faith and reverence, as you and many other wise men have done.[31]

The features of the earliest known portrait of Cosimo (Fig. 5), his expression cool and commanding in a three-quarter face sculpture now attributed to Antonio Rossellino, may help to account for Niccolini's awe and timidity.[32]

Both Vespasiano and Parenti stressed that Florentines feared Cosimo's *autorità*. It could be enforced through the ability of the powerful patron not only to aid, but also to discriminate against them in matters on which their prosperity and power depended, particularly the distribution of offices and taxes. Florentines expected constant intercession and intervention from fathers, both actual and honorary. Leon Battista Alberti described in his *Della famiglia* the duties of fathers, who "must stand ever prepared and ready to foresee and to know everything"; the paterfamilias, like a spider in the middle of his web, should "dwell ... alert and careful, so that with the slightest touch on the furthest filament, he feels it immediately,

31 ASF, CS, 1, 137, fols. 223r–224r.
32 Christiansen and Weppelmann 2011, 164–166.

4.
Piero della
Francesca, *Madonna
della Misericordia*,
1445–62, oil
and tempera on
panel, Pinacoteca
Comunale,
Sansepolcro.
(Photo: Art
Resource,
New York.)

apprehends it immediately, and immediately takes the necessary measures."[33] Such
a paterfamilias was considered an ideal model for the governance of social institutions: for example, Leonardo Bruni in his *Panegyric of the Florentine People* praised
the Guelf party for acting as a protective paterfamilias.[34]

33 Alberti 1969, 215–216.
34 Griffiths, Hankins, and Thompson 1987, 120.

5.
Workshop of Antonio
Rossellino, *Cosimo de'
Medici*, ca. 1460, marble, 36
× 32 cm (without frame).
Skulpturensammlung und
Museum für Byzantini-
sche Kunst, Staatliche
Museen, Berlin. (Photo:
Skulpturensammlung und
Museum für Byzantini-
sche Kunst, Staatliche
Museen, Berlin.)

Cosimo patently desired to pass on his *autorità* over both Florentine and foreign friends to his son Piero. The "succession" of two more generations of Medici
to Cosimo's authority over the republic has been seen as confirmation of Medici
"princely ambitions," and of Pope Pius II's opinion that, after 1458, Cosimo was
not so much a citizen as lord (*dominus*) of his *patria*.[35] It is clear from Cosimo's
personal letters and contributions to the *pratiche*, the councils advising the governing magistracy, the *signoria*, that he wanted increased control over the way the
republic was run, and was confident that he could run it better than anyone else.
However, he acknowledged the claims and pretensions of others, which set limits
to his own. Neri di Gino Capponi, a distinguished statesman and military commander, supported Cosimo in 1433–34 and the Medicean regime in the decades

35 Rubinstein 1992, 11; Rubinstein 1997, 145.

that followed. But he maintained a measure of independence from the Medici party, as did Agnolo Acciaiuoli, a senior Medici partisan from a distinguished family with long-standing ties to other Italian powers, particularly the kingdom of Naples.[36] Both these men were leaders, accustomed, like the senators envisaged by Cicero, to influence the course of the republic through their counsel and authority. Acciaiuoli's ambition to take over from Cosimo when he died is evident in his letters of the 1460s to his son Iacopo and to Francesco Sforza.[37] Like Cosimo, Capponi was well qualified for leadership by his expertise in war and diplomacy, and indeed in an inventory of a Florentine doctor's household there were portraits of both Cosimo and Neri Capponi—most unusual in a private citizen's house— along with portraits of Dante and St. Jerome, more conventional choices.[38]

According to Parenti, everyone "greatly respected [Capponi's] prudence and awaited his advice, and in serious decisions agreed with his opinions."[39] Cosimo himself was among Capponi's admirers. In 1454, he was asked by Iacopo Guicciardini, then a prior, to return from Careggi to deal with the crisis facing the Medicean regime. He responded that gout had him by the throat and he was too ill to move; he suggested Iacopo seek the advice of others whom he recommended: "Age and illness are attacking my intellect and sapping my spirit, and on this account I turn to the judgment of men whom I consider good and wise and lovers of their country." First among these he named Neri Capponi.[40] When Neri died in 1457, Cosimo instructed his son Piero to visit Neri's house to offer their condolences and to do all possible honor to one who so richly deserved it for his service to the republic.[41]

What distinguished Cosimo from his closest rivals was his unique combination of the characteristics of the ideal *optimus civis*, according to Cicero—skill, experience, and wealth, in which he was unmatched—with the enforceable *autorità* of the patriarchal patron.[42] In view of their achievements and popular reputation, Neri Capponi and Agnolo Acciaiuoli had the personal qualities and potential to rival Cosimo in *autorità*. But only Cosimo commanded a network of patronage effective enough to translate authority into power. When a group of Florence's principal citizens, the closest of Cosimo's former friends, challenged his son Piero's authority in 1466, it was Luca Pitti, not Agnolo Acciaiuoli, who was seen as the most feasible alternative, because he was a great patron. Cosimo had told Iacopo Guicciardini that Pitti was among those whom he could trust like a father: "He is a great friend of

36 For Capponi's complex relations with Cosimo, see Kent 2000, passim; on Acciaiuoli, see Rubinstein 1997, ad indicem; Ganz 2002, 2007.
37 For Acciaiuoli's letters to Iacopo, see particularly ASF, CS 1, 136; ASF, CS 3, 131. For his letters to Sforza, see ASMi Pot. est.; BA, MS Z 247 sup.
38 ASF, Otto 20, fol. 110r. This reference was kindly given to me by Alison Brown.
39 Parenti 2001, 112–113.
40 ASF, CS 1, 136, fol. 126r.
41 ASF, MAP 6, 300.
42 On this, see also Rubinstein 1992, 6–7, 14–17.

yours and understands the affairs of the city very well, though you should obtain his opinion separately."[43] Giovanni Rucellai described Luca Pitti as "a very great and powerful citizen (*grandissimo*) . . . with a great following, and, among other things, he was the most ardent and solicitous (*chaldo, amorevole*) man there was on behalf of his relatives and friends."[44]

Although it is now recognized that many of the constitutional innovations consolidating the power of the *reggimento* formerly credited to Cosimo were in fact initiatives of the once underrated Albizzi regime, none of its leading citizens had been able to match the patronage through which the Medici infiltrated the republic's offices in the 1430s. Similarly, in the 1460s, Cosimo's son Piero prevailed through his entrenched and extensive patronage network and the crucial support of his father's most powerful foreign friend, Francesco Sforza. The banker-statesman and the condottiere-prince, as Vincent Ilardi characterized Cosimo and Sforza at an I Tatti conference in the 1980s,[45] cooperated closely to increase their personal power and that of the states they came to dominate from the late 1420s, when Sforza was a talented mercenary captain who often fought in the pay of Florence. Florence and Cosimo himself financed Sforza's bid to become duke of Milan, which he did in 1450, and Sforza offered military support to the Medici regime, each, as Marco Parenti wrote, "lending the other his power and money, by which they made themselves feared by everyone else."[46]

While their alliance was obviously founded on mutual self-interest, they also had a close personal relationship, which they framed as that of father and son. Sforza's letters customarily addressed Cosimo as *magnifice tanquam pater carissime* ("magnificent like the dearest father"), and this patriarchal bond was extended to embrace not only their sons, Piero and Galeazzo Maria, but also the Milanese ambassador, Nicodemo Tranchedini, who was literally a member of the Medici household for long periods. The triangular relationship between Cosimo, Sforza, and the Florentine republic is documented in their letters and those of Tranchedini, preserved in the Milanese diplomatic archives. These show that, at least until the last decade of Cosimo's life, his was the authoritative and advisory patriarchal role, while Sforza was the respectful and often obedient son.[47] Sons commanded the love and loyalty of their fathers' friends, and inherited obligations to them: naturally when Medici leadership of the regime was challenged in 1466, Sforza protected Piero.[48]

43 ASF, CS 1, 136, fol. 126r.
44 Rucellai 2013, 20.
45 Ilardi 1989.
46 Parenti 2001, 106.
47 See ASMi, Pot est. 1464; BA, MS Z 247 sup., PBNF, MS Italien 1590; also ASF, MAP passim, especially *filza* 11. On the Medici-Sforza relationship, see Ilardi 1989; Kent 2000, 2005, and my forthcoming *Fathers and Friends: Patrons and Patriarchy in Early Medicean Florence*.
48 Cosimo's *amici* (allies), in professing allegiance or requesting protection, invoked the "buona memoria di vostro padre Giovanni di Bicci" (for example, ASF, MAP 2, 167), and Piero was inundated with similar protestations after Cosimo's death.

Letters written by Cosimo and his leading partisans in the 1460s reveal that they all saw the prospect of a second generation of Medici leadership in terms of a continuing patriarchal custodianship of the republic, but they disagreed about their respective roles in it. Nerone di Dietisalvi Neroni, another of the leaders of the anti-Medicean conspiracy of 1466, had written to Francesco Sforza a week after Cosimo's death, "While Cosimo was alive, decisions were left to him; now those who remain at the head of the regime are Piero and a number of citizens supporting him, who were brothers to Cosimo and who will now need to be fathers to Piero."[49] Cosimo used similar language in a letter he wrote to Agnolo Acciaiuoli shortly before his death. He assured Acciaiuoli that, despite Agnolo's recent long absences from Florence in Milan,

> I bear you the same love and affection as I always did in the past and would wish to do for that brief period of time which God may allow me to remain here, and so I believe most certainly Piero and Giovanni will always wish to do.... [He urged Agnolo to return to Florence] so that my sons may have once again another father in all their needs ... and for your own good and that of your sons, and for the good of our city and the satisfaction of your friends, which would give me the greatest pleasure I could have in this life, because it seems to me that if you decide to take care of the interests of the republic, our city will be preserved in that good and peaceful state in which it stands at present.[50]

After the failure of the conspiracy and Acciaiuoli's exile in 1466, he protested to Piero, "God has put it in your power to cancel all the accounts I have with you, and you do not know how to do so. For your father's sake my homeland (*patria*) and my status were taken from me; you are in a position to restore them." Piero responded in kind, "your friendship with my father and with us ... ought to have made you regard me as a son, and as such I considered myself ... I have pardoned every offense; the republic cannot and should not do so."[51]

The power of Cosimo's personal authority in the public sphere is apparent in the discussions of the *pratiche*, where leading citizens vied with one another to put their *autorità* at the service of the republic and its governors, the *signoria*. The pressing issues of Cosimo's era, 1434–64, were waging wars, financing them, and consolidating authority over these crucial matters in the hands of the Medicean regime.[52] Cosimo was uniquely fitted to advise on financial affairs; apart from his outstanding business acumen, reflected in the success of his bank, he and his closest friends

49 BA, MS Z 247 sup., 8 August 1464. Original text published by Rubinstein 1997, 156 n. 3, with a slightly different translation.

50 ASF, CS 1, 136, fol. 122r.

51 Fabroni 1784, 2:36–37.

52 See ASF, CP 50–58; Rubinstein 1997.

were the chief contributors to the republic's coffers, and the Medici bank was a major conduit of his and the city's pan-Italian influence.[53] The conduct of military affairs had always been a particular interest of Cosimo's, and his personal relationships with the condottieri who were signori of other states, among them Francesco Sforza, were central to Florentine diplomacy.[54]

These facts were clearly acknowledged in Cosimo's frequent appearances in the *pratiche* of the decade after 1434, when he held many major offices, particularly that of gonfalonier of justice (head of the *signoria*), and served on numerous war commissions. As spokesman for these offices, he openly asserted his leadership, firmly guiding debate and recommendations for action. His contributions were pithy and direct. In a debate of January 1436, he declared, "There are three things that should determine our actions," and went on to enumerate these.[55] Such pronouncements from Cosimo were as much orders as advice, and normally accepted with alacrity. Marco Parenti observed that, in the *pratiche*, everyone tried to guess Cosimo's opinion, which was followed with little or no further debate, so as not to displease him.[56] By the mid-1440s, Cosimo was less prominent in the *pratiche*, but participants were increasingly restricted to a small group of the closest supporters of the Medici regime, including a number of lawyers such as Otto Niccolini and Domenico Martelli, who added the authority of legal expertise to that of membership in the Medicean inner circle.[57] Among the most authoritative speakers were Orlando and Bernardo de' Medici; the latter, as joint military commander with Neri di Gino Capponi at the battle of Anghiari, had the status of a popular hero.[58] Thus Cosimo's policies were supported by his actual as well as his honorary family, and most became law. He did have trouble in persuading others to grant huge subsidies to Sforza, but eventually succeeded by invoking the Holy Grail of Florentine freedom from foreign domination, arguing that "if this is a bitter drink it has to be swallowed in the defense of liberty." As Francesco Bausi observes, Cosimo was seen as a prime defender of *Florentina libertas*.[59]

The crises within the *reggimento*'s inner circle over electoral controls began in the late 1440s and were exacerbated by a strong challenge to the regime in the mid-1450s. By this time, an aging Cosimo had ceased to exercise public office and no longer appeared in the *pratiche*. His views were expressed there by his closest partisans, or by his younger son, Giovanni. In September 1456, after Tommaso Soderini

53   See De Roover 1963; Molho 1971.

54   See Kent 2000, especially 268–277.

55   ASF, CP 51, fols. 15v–16r. For Cosimo's authoritative interventions, see also, for example, ASF, CP 53, fols. 27r–28v: "It is easy to give advice. It is difficult to make effective provisions."

56   Parenti 2001, 108.

57   See, for example, ASF, CP 53, fols. 142v–145v; on the role of lawyers in government, see Martines 1968.

58   See Kent 2000, 272.

59   ASF, CP 52, fol. 35r; Rubinstein 1992, 14–15; Bausi, this volume.

and Giannozzo Pitti, both from the innermost circle of the regime, had prepared the way, Giovanni intervened. He declared that "we must guard our *stato* (regime) and our *libertà*. A *balìa* is the way forward, and we must assume *auctoritas* in whatever way is acceptable to the people."[60] In January 1460, during a debate on how to respond to Pope Pius II, Giovanni relayed explicitly "the advice of Cosimo on these proposals," which was that "he should interpose his *autorità*," ingeniously arguing that, if Cosimo could not persuade the pope of the Florentine point of view, "he would take all the blame."[61]

From these debates it appears that, while Cosimo enjoyed immense authority over the leading citizens, he was far from exercising absolute control. In the last decade of his life, Cosimo disagreed with the "hawks" of the Medicean regime, most notably Agnolo Acciaiuoli. As he wrote to Iacopo Guicciardini in 1454,

> It does not seem to me that the affairs of the city are in such straits nor in such danger that we would want to use extreme remedies, and it does not seem to me in our interests to do so. And be aware that if it should come to this, it would be to the danger and the damage of the city's reputation and of the men who govern it. . . . And I believe that without too much difficulty we can maintain our hold on the affairs of the republic (*tenere le mani su' facti della republica*) and matters will resolve themselves on good terms if we do not seek to conduct them, as has been the case up until now, moved more by private passions than by the public good.[62]

As Giorgio Chittolini has observed, private and public elements were in constant interplay in the operation of the Renaissance state.[63] Private patronage networks augmented the power of patriarchal patrons in the public sphere. As Rubinstein pointed out in one of what he called his "little articles," which offered such rare and penetrating insights into the Florentine *mentalité*, citizens thought of *stato*, as they did of *autorità*, as an attribute, not so much of institutions, as of the persons who administered them. And insofar as a share of the *stato*, the opportunity to govern and counsel the republic, was seen as part of the patrimony of members of the ruling class, it was extremely difficult to distinguish in practice between public and private actions and authority, however much citizens such as Piero de' Medici, writing to Agnolo Acciaiuoli in 1466 (see above, 233), sought to do so when it suited them. While in Renaissance Italy *stati* were mainly principates, identical with the person of the prince, Florentines continued to identify the state with the *commune, città*, or *res publica*, envisaging a republican structure of political power and participation

60 ASF, CP 54, fols. 25v–29r; see Bernardo Giugni's remarks on 16 October 1465: ASF, CP 57, fol. 48r.
61 ASF, CP 56, fols. 39v–42v. For these debates and Cosimo's decisive behind-the-scenes influence, see Black 1973, 16 n. 63, 24 and n. 106; Black 1985, 280 n. 24.
62 ASF, CS 1, 136, fol. 126r.
63 Chittolini 1995.

in it by various members of the ruling class. Thus the close identification between private patrician and public interests persisted.[64]

However personal a bid for greater power by leading Florentine citizens, it was usually based on an appeal to the preservation of republican liberties, and this theme was so strong in political discussion that it cannot be dismissed as window dressing. To return to Parenti's analysis, those he really hated were the opportunistic Mediceans who acted only for their private advantage, "forgetting the city and the civil life, public honor, and the dignity of a free republic." He did not include Cosimo in this group. He recounted how, after the constitutional modifications of 1458, everyone waited with trepidation "to see how he would use his new power." In fact, Cosimo reformed the distribution of taxes and offices, and shored up the *monte delle doti* (dowry fund), which gave private citizens a financial stake in the state. He favored the merchants,

> and for a long time thenceforward the city enjoyed such prosperity that there was great rejoicing. . . . He maintained his household in a condition of great dignity, but one appropriate to a citizen, and maintained and fostered the peace and good order [*buono stato*] of Florence, and guided the government in an orderly and suitable fashion. And yet when he died everyone rejoiced, such is the love and desire for liberty, for it seemed to them that they had been in subjection and servitude under his governance.[65]

Rubinstein's preoccupation with the quotidian detail of political practice in fifteenth- and sixteenth-century Florence, where he saw continuity with communal and republican tradition constantly reasserted, was reaffirmed in the second, revised edition of *The Government of Florence*, which appeared in 1997. The same year saw the publication of Philip Jones's *The Italian City-State: From Commune to Signoria*. This masterly work surveyed the much larger canvas of the whole of Italy over the *longue durée* that saw the rise and fall of the communes, describing this in broad generalizations that submerged the particular concerns of individual societies and their members.[66] That Jones thought these ultimately unimportant was always clear. In the memorable conclusion to a 1965 article on "Communes and Despots," having observed with some justification that all Italian governments were "tyrannies"—of party, of class, of despots—he cited, as spokesman on the theme of political liberty, Dr. Samuel Johnson, who observed, "that is all visionary. I would not give half a guinea to live under one form of government rather than another."[67] Had Jones chosen instead to interrogate almost any fifteenth-century Florentine

---

64 Rubinstein 1980–81.
65 Parenti 2001, 117.
66 Jones 1997.
67 Jones 1965, 96.

statesman—arguably a better strategy for illuminating the attitudes and experience of the citizens of the Italian states—the answer would have been very different. Cosimo de' Medici, Neri Capponi, and Agnolo Acciaiuoli all dedicated their lives and fortunes with passionate conviction to the preservation and advancement of the Florentine republic, not just their own preeminence within it.

FIFTEEN

The Medici

Defenders of Liberty in Fifteenth-Century Florence

FRANCESCO BAUSI

IT IS COMMON IN FLORENTINE literature, political writing, and even official records of the fifteenth and early sixteenth centuries for the Medici to appear as defenders of Florence's free institutions and republican traditions, and as the city's saviors from the tyrannical and "subversive" machinations of their enemies. To give just a few examples, Giovanni Cavalcanti (in his *Istorie fiorentine*)[1] and Antonio Pacini (in his Latin translation of Plutarch's *Life of Timoleon*) both accused Rinaldo degli Albizzi of having forced Cosimo de' Medici into exile in order to make himself tyrant of Florence, the latter claiming that, if Cosimo had not returned in 1434, the city would never have regained its liberty.[2] Poliziano in his *Elegia al Fonzio* and the *Stanze*,[3] the anonymous author of a vernacular poem dating to the years 1466–68,[4] and indeed Donato Acciaiuoli in the dedication of his Latin version of Plutarch's *Life of Demetrius* to Piero de' Medici[5] depict Luca Pitti and his accomplices in 1466 as plotters preparing to subvert the republic and to deprive it of liberty, a coup foiled thanks only to the courage of Piero himself and of his young son Lorenzo. The *otto di guardia*, in a sentence passed on 4 August 1478, took a similar view of those who had organized and carried out the Pazzi conspiracy just three months before: they "conspired both to destabilize and overthrow the

1   Cavalcanti 1944, 264–265.
2   Brown 1961, 189.
3   Poliziano 1997, 1:31; 2003, 6–8.
4   Martelli 1988b.
5   Martelli 1988a, 86–87.

peaceful regime and liberty of the Florentine republic."[6] And in 1513, shortly after the Medici restoration, an anonymous and amateurish poet addressing Lorenzo di Piero, future duke of Urbino, described him as the man sent by God to free the city from an "evil tyrant"—an unequivocal reference to Piero Soderini, the life gonfalonier who had been overthrown a year before.[7]

But there are humanist texts in which this same celebratory topos is just one thematic strand in a more complex presentation of Medici power in the context of the Florentine republic. In such works, the exercise of Medici control is implicitly or explicitly compared to sovereign or autocratic power in a range of princely and monarchical regimes that flourished in other contemporary cities and states. Such *prises de position*, spanning all six decades of Medici predominance (1434–94), shed light on how both the perception of the Medici regime, and its image as portrayed and "propounded" by intellectuals (whether or not Florentine) with Medici connections, evolved over time. The authors in question may be considered particularly revealing witnesses, given that they were figures and literati who had, thanks to their varied experiences, acquired a more than superficial acquaintance both with "princely" government and with Medicean Florence. They were thus perhaps particularly well placed to throw into relief the Medici's unique position within the political-institutional panorama of Italy and Europe in the quattrocento.

First, the celebrated controversy between Poggio Bracciolini and Guarino Veronese concerning the relative merits of P. Cornelius Scipio Africanus (late third to early second century BCE) and Julius Caesar, which occurred between April and November 1435 in three stages. The first was a letter-treatise addressed by Poggio to Scipione Mainenti in April 1435, when Mainenti and Poggio were together in Florence as part of the entourage of Pope Eugenius IV, who had played a significant part in Cosimo de' Medici's seizure of power the year before. Its title was *De praestantia Caesaris et Scipionis* (On the Excellence of Caesar and Scipio) and it was passed on to Guarino by his patron, Duke Leonello d'Este of Ferrara. Guarino then replied directly to Poggio, who made a further ample riposte to Francesco Barbaro (cast in the role of arbiter) entitled *Defensiuncula* or *Defensio*.[8]

Poggio's letter to Mainenti leaves no doubt that he saw the comparison between Caesar and Scipio as particularly relevant to contemporary ideology and politics. There was a solid tradition, going back to the Middle Ages and persisting into the sixteenth century, of anti-Caesarism in Florence.[9] For Poggio, the two Roman leaders were not so much historical figures as symbols of two different forms of government—tyrannical and republican. Caesar, out of immoderate lust for power, destroyed the Roman republic's liberty and set absolute personal rule in its place;

6 "conspiraverunt insimul in perturbationem et eversionem pacifici status et libertatis rei publicae Florentine": Poliziano 1958, 77–78.

7 Bausi 2011, 124.

8 See Guarini 2001; Bracciolini 2001a, 2001b (and also Crevatin 1982, with excellent commentary).

9 Baron 1966, 47–54, 121–129, 146–159, and passim; Tanturli 1998; Russo 2008.

conversely, although Scipio had acquired immense authority thanks to the favor of his fellow citizens and to his own extraordinary virtues, he never ceased to show respect for the law, preferring to withdraw into voluntary exile rather than to cause harm to his country:

> What shall I say of the patriotic love that he demonstrated throughout his life and even at the moment of death, since the injuries he had received from his country he refrained from avenging except for the minimal gesture of calling Rome ungrateful? It was a sign of his magnanimity and his love toward his country that when his prominence appeared to overshadow Roman liberty, and his wealth had grown to the point that, as Seneca put it, "either Scipio must inevitably do injury to liberty, or liberty do injury to Scipio," he preferred to accept injury from his country rather than inflict such injury himself, and took voluntary exile in Liternum so as not to violate Rome's freedom by his presence.[10]

For Guarino, on the other hand, Caesar's unquestioned superiority had its counterpart in the supremacy of Ferrarese princely over Florentine republican government, and therefore in the superiority of the *optimus rex* (best king) Leonello over the *optimus civis* (best citizen) Cosimo. Indeed, in his reply to Poggio Guarino stated that the real tyrannies were those republics where overmighty citizens had seized power. The examples he gives are L. Cornelius Sulla and P. Clodius Pulcher (both first century BCE)—but behind them looms Cosimo—Guarino alluding to the repressive methods he had recently used to regain power, especially in exiling Palla Strozzi. Even Pompey, the paladin of anti-Caesarean opposition, is here accused by Guarino of "tyrannical violence" and labeled a "cunning adversary of liberty aspiring to one-man rule under the pretext of dictatorship."[11]

Guarino's response is notable too for accusing Poggio of ignoring and failing to exploit Greek historical sources. Guarino himself, in the effort to recast the figure of Caesar, drew largely upon Plutarch and Dio Cassius, whose testimony he regarded

---

10 "Quid loquar de caritate eius in patriam, quam cum per omnem vitam repraesentavit, tum etiam in morte, cum eius iniurias non nisi parvo titulo ultus fuerit, quo ingratam appellavit? Illud maximi animi et amoris erga patriam insigne indicium, quod, cum sua magnitudo libertatem obumbrare videretur eoque illius opes crevissent, ut refert Seneca, ut 'aut Scipionem libertati aut libertatem Scipioni iniuriam facere oporteret,' satius existimans patriae iniurias tolerare quam inferre, secessit Liternum in exilium voluntarium, ne libertatem publicam sua praesentia violaret": Bracciolini 2001b, 116. The Senecan quotation comes from the *Epistolae ad Lucilium* 86.3, which is the source of the entire passage given here (although the qualification of Rome as "ungrateful" derives from the epigraph Scipio composed for his tomb, as reported by Valerius Maximus in *Facta et dicta memorabilia* 5.3.2).

11 "tyrannica vis [. . .] astutum libertatis insidiatorem [. . .] monarchiae sub dictaturae specie studentem": Guarini 2001, 133. M. Porcius Cato the Younger (first century BCE) is also on the receiving end of harsh criticism from Guarino, who calls him an "instigator and nourisher of civil war" ("belli civilis [. . .] instigator et altor"): ibid.

as more objective and less partisan than the Latin sources. Thus he implicitly claimed not only personal cultural superiority over Poggio, but suggested Ferrara's superiority over Florence as well, refuting the assertion (going back to Leonardo Bruni and reprised by Poggio) that arts and letters blossom more readily on the fertile soil of republican liberty than on a monarchical terrain.[12] The battle between republics and principates and their supporters was always a battle of books too.

Poggio's letters to Cosimo de' Medici in November–December 1433 and on 28 October 1434 (the first to console him in exile, the second to congratulate him on returning to Florence)[13] drew a parallel between Scipio and Cosimo, presenting the latter as a wise and moderate *primus inter pares* (first among equals), attentive to and respectful of free civic institutions.[14] This fidelity to law, shared by Scipio and Cosimo, is seen in two circumstances: their great authority was not acquired (like Caesar's) through force and fraud but granted spontaneously by their fellow citizens; and both exercised restraint when forced into unjust exile, preferring to accept loss of personal liberty rather than unleash the havoc of civil war. The same two points were made in the controversy with Guarino, and served in Poggio's eyes to demonstrate the excellence of the "civic" Scipio in contrast to the "tyrannical" Caesar.

And yet Poggio's purpose in assimilating Scipio and Cosimo was not entirely encomiastic, but in some measure admonitory. The dichotomy between Caesar and Scipio was between two alternative paths down which Florence's new leader had the option of proceeding: the "tyrannical" route leading to the destruction of free institutions, and the "civic" path under the rule of law, winning infinitely greater glory (without sacrificing power and authority).

Poggio was attempting to provide an ideology for a leader who remained a private citizen in a formally republican state while acquiring and exercising de facto power equivalent to a prince's authority in a dynastic state, wielded not in person but through astute control of magistracies and electoral mechanisms. In *The Prince*, Niccolò Machiavelli labeled such a regime as a "civic principate" (*principato civile*).[15] Hence Poggio was able to present Cosimo (employing a common philo-Medicean tactic) as a new Scipio, the defender of liberty and the Florentine republic against the hidden maneuvers of an oligarchy intent upon tyranny. From such a perspective, some have descried in Poggio's portrait of Caesar a personification not just of Leonello d'Este but even of Rinaldo degli Albizzi, leader of the aristocratic opposition to Cosimo.[16]

12 Guarino's greater competence in Greek was indisputable and so Poggio in his *Defensio* was forced to parry with the stale topos (commonplace) of "lying Greeks," accusing Dio Cassius of adulation vis-à-vis the emperors (Bracciolini 2001a, 165).

13 Bracciolini 1984, respectively 181–188 (from Rome) and 192–197 (from Florence).

14 As Canfora 2001, 48, notes, "Scipio is no more than a veiled portrait" of Cosimo in Poggio's epistle, and the stance taken by Poggio amounts to a "vigorous defense of the Florentine model."

15 For the debate about the much-discussed Machiavellian notion of *principato civile* (*Principe* IX, "De principatu civili"), see Bausi 1985, 63–71; Larivaille 1989; Sasso 1988.

16 Oppel 1974, 237.

Poggio's letter to Mainenti had a noteworthy sequel: his son Jacopo (who would himself die on 26 April 1478 along with other Pazzi conspirators) incorporated the vernacular translation of his father's text into his own *Commento* on Petrarch's *Trionfo della fama* (Triumph of Fame), dedicated to Lorenzo de' Medici (a work written some years before its first edition in Rome of 1475 or 1476).[17] Jacopo's aim was to make the same political and ideological point his father had done in *De praestantia* in 1435, expressing esteem, loyalty, and praise in dedicating the commentary to Lorenzo, and characterizing Lorenzo as "the true and worthy heir" of Cosimo, who is explicitly compared to such Roman republican heroes as M. Furius Camillus (fifth to fourth century BCE), C. Fabricius Luscinus (third century BCE), and—of course—Scipio Africanus. In Florentine quattrocento literature, Camillus, Fabricius, and Scipio all represented the "eminent" citizen who nonetheless respected the law and preferred patriotic to private interests. It was to figures such as these, as well as to Aristides (fifth century BCE), Cicero, and M. Porcius Cato the Elder (third to second century BCE), never to Caesar, that literati and poets likened Cosimo[18] (although under Lorenzo there was no shortage of writers—such as Poliziano, Naldo Naldi, or Ugolino Verino—prepared to compare him explicitly to autocrats and emperors, ancient and modern, including Caesar).[19] In a Latin elegy (*Xandra* 3.15), for instance, Cristoforo Landino stressed the contrast between Cosimo and Caesar, preferring the former: "Great was Caesar, but Caesar was great in arms; / But you, O Cosimo, are greater in your city for your peaceful achievements [literally "for your toga"]. / He oppressed his country with arms and cruel tyranny, / liberty is the only care that concerns you" (vv. 43–46). These lines by Landino adopt Poggio's perspective both in limiting Caesar's greatness to military affairs (while denying him true virtue, thus presenting the dictator as a tyrant), and praising Cosimo as defender of liberty and true statesman with the strength of character not to abandon the sober demeanor of a private citizen. The point is stressed in a later couplet: "While holding the reins of the state / he maintained the bearing of a private citizen" (vv. 54–55).[20]

Second, in 1471, the humanist Platina (Bartolomeo Sacchi) wrote a political treatise entitled *De principe* (On the Prince), dedicated to Federico Gonzaga, son of

---

17 Bausi 2011, 105–193 (with a partial edition of the text, 168–193; the *editio princeps* appeared at Rome in 1475–76, the second printing at Florence in 1485).

18 Brown 1961; Coppini 2006–7.

19 Coppini 2006–7, 112–116. Ugolino Verino goes so far as to refer commonly in his letters to Lorenzo de' Medici as "Caesar."

20 "Magnus erat Caesar, sed magnus Caesar in armis; / at tu Cosme tua maior in urbe toga es. / Ille armis patriam saevaque tyrannide pressit, / te libertatis unica cura tenet"; "Nam qui magnarum rerum dum tractat habenas / privati potuit civis habere modum": Landino 1939, 118. The emphasis on the toga as the contrasting counterpart to arms was a way of associating Cosimo with Cicero, who in a famous verse from his lost short poem *De suo consulatu* (cited in *De officiis* 1.77 and *Philippicae* 2.20) had written "cedant arma togae" (let arms give way to the toga): Coppini 2006–7, 107–110.

(and seven years later the successor to) Marchese Ludovico III of Mantua. In 1474, Platina revised and rededicated the treatise to Lorenzo de' Medici, with the new title *De optimo cive* (On the Best Citizen). Among the alterations was the omission of the entire third book, devoted mainly to warfare and military discipline.[21] In addition, there was a change of genre from treatise to dialogue: in *De optimo cive*, the dialogic fiction (set sometime prior to Cosimo's death in 1464) is that the *optimus civis* Cosimo is instructing his grandson Lorenzo on the duties of an eminent statesman "in steering the city" (*in gubernanda civitate*). Proper civic conduct and proper civic models preoccupied numerous contemporary Florentine humanists (for example, Marsilio Ficino, Bartolomeo Fonzio, Ugolino Verino, and Benedetto Colucci). Cosimo had already been given the Ciceronian accolade *optimus civis* by Alamanno Rinuccini in a draft decree (dated 15 March 1465) honoring him with the title *pater patriae* ("father of his country").[22] In a speech delivered five days later, when the title was formally conferred, Donato Acciaiuoli had defined Cosimo, employing nautical imagery similar to Platina's, as the *gubernator* (steersman) of the Florentine vessel, emphasizing his "unceasing concern with preserving liberty."[23]

Besides switching dedicatees, Platina reworked his short treatise to dispel the misconception that Lorenzo's power was princely in nature, necessarily and inevitably leading to autocracy. In this respect, even the shift to the dialogue genre was probably not without ideological and political significance, given the powerful Florentine and republican tradition of political-moral dialogues (by the likes of Bruni, Poggio, Leon Battista Alberti, and Matteo Palmieri). Lorenzo is not a monarch, and neither can nor should he be: hence Platina has Cosimo instruct him on governing a republic as a "civic prince" and *primus inter pares*, respecting Florence's laws and political traditions. Lorenzo must defend such laws and traditions, above all the *libertas* and *aequalitas* always associated with the Florentine "popular republic" against malevolent citizens aspiring to tyranny, who need to be combatted and expelled from the city, following the Athenian example.

It is noteworthy that in the first chapter of *De principe*—later suppressed, of course, in *De optimo cive*—the Medici themselves appear among such malevolent citizens, not explicitly named but perfectly recognizable along with the Bentivoglio

---

21 Platina 1944. On this treatise (and the attendant problems of dating), see Rubinstein 1985, 1986; Vasoli 1983, 163–167.

22 Rinuccini 1953, 126.

23 Acciaiuoli 1789, 261: "perpetuum studium in libertate servanda" (see Rubinstein 1992, 8–9). In Platina's *De optimo cive*, Cosimo asserts that his grandson Lorenzo must follow the advice of the good and wise citizens of Florence "until he will first have learned to steer so large a ship" ("donec gubernare tantam navim prius ipse didicerit"): Platina 1944, 214. See too the poem by Gentile Becchi, *De laudibus Cosmi* 53–54: "his generous hand guided the ship of his country through unfriendly seas / and returned with the crew safe and sound" ("Larga manus patriam rexit per inhospita puppim / Et rediit salvo remige larga manus"): Becchi 2012, 217 as well as Ficino's *Epitome* of Plato's *Statesman*, which affirms that citizens are led to the common good by a pious and just king in the same way that sailors are led to port by the ability of a skillful steersman (Ficino 1576, 1295; the simile is already found in Plato, *Statesman*, 297d–299d).

of Bologna as examples of genuine tyrants, in contrast to the *optimus princeps*. Indeed, writing to Federico Gonzaga, Platina follows the example of Guarino's retort to Poggio, condemning the "civic principate" as tyrannical—with a leading family using money to corrupt the citizenry and foment division in order to achieve effective power:

> Nor does it matter in the least whether it is a single tyrant or several, such as in many cities in the past, especially Athens, or in the present, such as Bologna and Florence. Their concern—bereft as they are of virtue—is to deprive the citizens of arms and oppress or drive out all the best people and deplete the city of inhabitants, gaining security at the cost of desolation.[24]

The tables are turned in *De optimo cive*, where the eminent citizen now has the task of combatting "domestic tyrants" who mobilize the people against the nobility and "first gain a grip on princely status in their cities."[25] Here it is telling that Platina avoids modern examples, with the sole exception—neither Florentine nor strictly contemporary—of Ludovico Migliorati of Fermo, who had died in 1428. In the dialogue, Cosimo draws a contrast between such "domestic tyrants" and the virtuous citizens among whom Lorenzo will have to select his friends and collaborators, so as to make confident use of their learning and *peritia* (expertise) in public and private affairs. But the only names that emerge here from Cosimo's mouth are already familiar: Donato Acciaiuoli and Alamanno Rinuccini.

Nor was book three of Platina's *De principe* suppressed for trivial or arbitrary reasons: the role of military commander was regarded as unsuitable for a citizen of a free republic, because of the risk that a citizen in charge of soldiers might turn such military power against the state. Relevant here would be the fierce optimate resistance to Machiavelli's militia, which, so many would fear, might become an instrument of tyranny in the hands of the life gonfalonier Piero Soderini;[26] highly significant too would be the case of Lorenzo, future duke of Urbino, who in 1515 would become commander of the Florentine militia in the teeth of every precedent, a move that anti-Mediceans would see as confirmation of his unconcealed princely ambitions.[27]

And yet the "ambivalence" of Platina's treatise (enabling the author to address first a genuine prince and then an "eminent" citizen of the Florentine republic)

---

24 Platina 1979, 55–56: "Nec profecto refert unum pluresve tyrannos proponas, quales olim in multis civitatibus, maxime autem Athenis, nunc vero Bononiae ac Florentiae cernuntur. Horum enim cura haec est, cum virtute nequaquam muniti sint, et arma civibus suis adimere ac optimum quenque opprimere aut ex urbe pellere eandemque vacuam habitatoribus reddere, quo vastitate ipsa ac solitudine tutiores sint."

25 "in civitate sua primum principatum obtinent": Platina 1944, 192.

26 Ridolfi 1978, 131, 137, 465.

27 Albertini 1970, 31.

corresponds strikingly to the ambiguous character of the Florentine government under the Medici—a transitional regime ("stato di mezzo") as Machiavelli would later call it,[28] or more bluntly a *criptosignoria* that existed by inserting ever-growing authoritarian and autocratic elements into the increasingly hollow shell of the ancient communal institutions: a regime in which the same individual—as Poggio wrote of Cosimo in *De infelicitate principum* (1440)—simultaneously wore the masks of "preeminent prince" and "best and most valiant citizen."[29] Even in 1532, the title given to Alessandro de' Medici would be *duca della repubblica di Firenze* (duke of the Florentine republic).

Ambivalence of this kind can be detected when Benedetto Colucci (1438– ca. 1506), grammarian at the Florentine Studio (University) from 1473 to 1482, delivered his first academic prolusion, a *Declamatio* dating to early 1474, in which he depicted Lorenzo de' Medici as a prince "in a free city" (*in libera civitate*), comparing him to Epaminondas, Themistocles, and Scipio Africanus because he had assumed power peacefully, without subverting established institutions.[30] The prime example of a writer conveying such ambivalence is Marsilio Ficino. In dedicating his epitome of Plato's *Statesman* (also known at the time as *Politicus* or *De regno*) to Federico da Montefeltro about 1480, he gave him the features of the *optimus princeps* and philosopher-king who also, and unmistakably, bears many traits of the *optimus civis* Lorenzo (who is never explicitly mentioned).[31] The inclination shown by Florentine humanists to dedicate compositions to Federico da Montefeltro arguably betrays a veiled intent to celebrate the quasi-princely profile and power of Lorenzo the Magnificent.[32] Ficino states that whenever a man, even a private citizen, surpasses others in wisdom and justice, he has been invested by God with virtually regal power; that his power must be legitimated and controlled by a senate of leading citizens acting as a sort of "colleague to the king" (*collega regis*) and partner in the legislative process, so that the kingdom comes to resemble a republic of optimates; and that an authentic and legitimate king presents an aspect so mild and humane as to seem more a *concivis* (fellow citizen) than a *rex* (king)—a figure scarcely differing therefore from a *civilis vir* (an individual in a republic). From Ficino's epitome there seems to emerge the genuine figure of Lorenzo, particularly when he characterizes the empire of Octavian

28   In the *Discursus florentinarum rerum post mortem iunioris Laurentii Medices* of 1520–21 (Machiavelli 2001b, 631).

29   Bracciolini 1998, 8 (at 56, among those who "in their republic were princes of the city" ["in sua republica civitatis principes extiterunt"] Poggio cites Alcibiades, Themistocles, Pericles, Aristides, Hannibal, M. Furius Camillus, Q. Caecilius Metellus Numidicus, the Scipios, P. Rutilius Rufus, Julius Caesar, Pompey, Mark Anthony, M. Aemilius Lepidus, Sulla, and Marius). Bartolomeo Scala too defined Lorenzo as "citizen prince of the city" ("civem principem civitatis"): see Rubinstein 1992, 20.

30   Colucci 1939, 16.

31   Ficino 1576, 1294–1296.

32   Martelli 1996, 181–182.

Augustus—a time of peace and general prosperity—as *monarchiae umbra*, "a shadow of monarchy."[33]

The last text to be considered was begun in 1489. *Principatus* (or *regnum*, meaning "kingship" or "kingdom") and *res publica* might still be represented as a pair of scales, but the balance now tilted toward the princely side. Aurelio Lippo Brandolini (1454–1497) began his dialogue *Republics and Kingdoms Compared* (De comparatione reipublicae et regni) in 1489 in Buda. It was meant for King Matthias Corvinus of Hungary, who died, however, while Brandolini was still at work. Brandolini returned to Florence early in 1490, finishing the dialogue there, and dedicating it to Lorenzo de' Medici no later than autumn 1490.[34] No doubt if the *Comparison* had been completed in Buda and offered to King Matthias, the text might have been different. Nevertheless it is apparent that there were no fundamental alterations. The advocate of republican liberty is the elderly optimate, diplomat, and knight Domenico Giugni, in historical fact a confidant of Lorenzo's with firsthand knowledge of court life thanks to his frequent commercial and diplomatic visits to Hungary—qualities that made him well suited for Brandolini's purposes. His adversary and proponent of monarchy is King Matthias Corvinus himself, who delivers a devastating critique of Florence's republican constitution. Giugni is unable to counter the royalist arguments and in the end accepts unreservedly that kingship is the superior form of government.

The unaccustomed realism of the anti-Florentine arguments advanced by King Matthias is striking, especially in a humanist dialogue dedicated to Lorenzo the Magnicent. For anything similar before Machiavelli, it is necessary to turn to the writings of literati and historians outside the Medici ambit (such as Leon Battista Alberti in *De iciarchia* or Giovanni Cavalcanti in the so-called *Nuova opera*), or outright anti-Mediceans, such as Alamanno Rinuccini, whose *Dialogus de libertate* (1479) was carefully kept out of circulation.[35] Matthias, for example, forces Giugni to acknowledge that in Florence, *libertas*, *aequalitas*, and *iustitia* cannot coexist with the city's extreme socioeconomic inequality; that the much vaunted commercialism characteristic of republics is a font of moral, social, and cultural corruption; that Florentine government is inherently faction-ridden, inefficient, and chaotic—unable to guarantee impartiality or liberty; that the city is prey to intestine divisions, kept from exploding only through Lorenzo's authority and skillful management; that the artisans and merchants who sit as Florence's magistrates lack the requisite political experience and competence (in contrast to Venice, where, more successfully, only nobles can hold political office)—in short, that liberty, equality, and justice are better protected under a principate than in a republic. Brandolini's

---

33 Ficino 1576, 1295.

34 Brandolini 2009. On this (as yet little known) text, see Dionisotti 1980, 116–120; Viti 1992; Biagini 1995. James Hankins calls Brandolini "by far the most interesting humanistic writer on politics before Machiavelli" (2009, xxv).

35 Rinuccini 1957.

picture of Florentine republican corruption differs from Rinuccini's only in the
perspective adopted and the solution envisioned, which for the latter consists of
the elimination of the tyrant Lorenzo and the toppling of Medici power, whereas
Brandolini sees the *podestà quasi regia* (quasi-regal power, a Machiavellian expression used here deliberately)[36] of the dominant family as the only bulwark against
the degeneration of the city's republican order. For Brandolini (as for Machiavelli
more explicitly in the *Discursus florentinarum rerum post mortem iunioris Laurentii
Medices* [Discourse on Florentine Affairs after the Death of the Younger Lorenzo
de' Medici] thirty years later), conspicuously reinforced Medici authority is the
only means, albeit temporary and apparently paradoxical, of keeping alive whatever remains of *Florentina libertas*.

Brandolini (who in the 1470s, it may be noted, had dedicated to Ferrante of
Aragon a vernacular translation of Pliny the Younger's *Panegyric* to Emperor Trajan,
where he hailed Ferrante as supreme among princes) has King Matthias say what
Guarino had declared to Poggio when presenting Caesar not as a tyrant but as
the "restorer of Rome's lost liberty" against the "factious usurpers of indigenous
liberty."[37] Guarino had maintained that the real *optimus civis* was not Cosimo de'
Medici but Leonello d'Este, and that therefore the truly free state where justice and
equality actually prevailed was Ferrara, not Florence. Late in book one of *Republics
and Kingdoms Compared*, Matthias adopts the contradiction in terms *libertas regni*
(regal liberty) as opposed to *libertas reipublicae* (republican freedom); correspondingly, in his epitome of the *Statesman*, Ficino had declared that the subjects of a wise,
just, and pious king are the most perfectly free, subject neither to a tyrant's maltreatment nor to an elite's abuse of power nor indeed to arbitrary popular rule.[38]
In contrast, the portrait of Florence painted by King Matthias is of a city vexed by
vicious tyrants (its own plutocrats) and governed by a senate whose members, unac-
countable and with no prospect of reward for probity, are utterly selfish. Under a
monarchy, on the other hand, the sovereign acts as an objective judge and equitable
dispenser of rewards.

The superiority of principate over republic is shown as well, Matthias continues, by the fact that the most successful republics always ensure that a "monarchical" element is incorporated into their constitutions—in other words, that they are
"mixed governments," in the well-known expression of Polybius. Rome had annual
consuls, and could appoint a dictator in emergencies. Venice had a doge, "an image

36 In *Discorsi* 1.18.4 (Machiavelli 2001a, 117), where, without specifically mentioning the Medici,
Machiavelli alludes in general to the need to introduce a "strong" power of the princely type into
a "corrupt" republic in order to keep it functioning, thus shifting it "more toward a royal regime
than a popular regime" ("più verso lo stato regio, che verso lo stato popolare"). On the nature of
this *podestà quasi regia*, see Bausi 1985, 62–71.
37 "amissae libertatis reparator," "factiosos patriae libertatis occupatores": Guarini 2001, 137, 139.
38 Ficino 1576, 1295. Hankins (2009, xv) observes that Plato's *Statesman* and *Laws* are among
Brandolini's main sources.

and type of royal dignity" (*regie dignitatis speciem quandam et imaginem*). Florence had the gonfalonier of justice, similarly defined as a "distinguished figure and image of royal dignity" (*regie dignitatis non mediocrem effigiem atque imaginem*). Brandolini also sides with Guarino in denying the claim advanced by Poggio (and Leonardo Bruni before him) that culture flourishes under a republican regime; for him, the excellence of Florence here was due not to its form of government but to its numerous brilliant minds, due in turn to its mild climate and dulcet air.

The circle is squared in the dialogue's final part, doubtless written after Matthias Corvinus's death led to the Laurentian rededication, and so inevitably jarring with its earlier sections. Despite his hostility to republican government, Matthias is made to exempt the Florentine republic on account of Lorenzo's presence:

> *Mattias.* You yourself, who have often complained of the fact to me, know very well how your own republic was formerly disturbed by many tumults and many banishings too. If you did not have that excellent and outstanding citizen, Lorenzo de' Medici, who controls and rules the spirits of your citizens with his virtue and authority, you would now be experiencing, in my opinion, the greatest and most destructive acts of sedition among yourselves.
>
> *Domenico.* It is surely as you say, king. Whatever concord and felicity we enjoy, we have received from this one man; he is nevertheless so moderate and gentle that he arrogates to himself no more power or authority than is fair; indeed, he refuses much of what is rightly owed him, so that he seems to be not a single individual controlling everyone, but a single individual obeying and serving everyone.[39]

Lorenzo thus emerges as the preeminent citizen who with his virtue and authority guides and governs (*moderatur ac regit*) the Florentines. The two verbs speak volumes: Matthias might nod to tradition in declaring that Lorenzo upholds Florence's laws and institutions, never seeking official status and always conducting himself with complete moderation, but for Brandolini the equation *optimus civis = princeps* is now an undeniable fact, to the point that he calls Lorenzo

39 "*Matt.* Vestra vero respublica, quam multis etiam seditionibus olim agitata sit, quam multos cives eiecerit, ipse optime scis, qui mecum ea de re saepenumero conquestus es, quod nisi optimum illum et praestantissimum civem Laurentium Medicem haberetis, qui sua virtute atque auctoritate civium animos moderatur ac regit, maximas nunc quoque, ut opinor, inter vos et perniciosissimas seditiones excitaretis. / *Dom.* Ita profecto est ut dicis, rex. Quicquid enim concordiae felicitatisque habemus, illi uni acceptum ferimus; est tamen ipse ita moderatus ac mitis, ut nihilo plus sibi quam aequum sit vel potentiae vel auctoritatis arroget; immo, ex eo quod sibi iure debetur multum renuat, adeo ut non unus omnes moderari, sed unus omnibus parere ac subesse videatur": Brandolini 2009, 195–197 (English translation by James Hankins). The last words echo those used by Ficino in his epitome of the *Statesman*, where he declares that a king "lives not so much for himself as for all those who have been entrusted by God to his care" ("non tam sibimet, quam cunctis qui suae curae a Deo commissi sunt, vivet"): Ficino 1576, 1295.

"prince of the Florentine republic" (*Florentinae reipublicae princeps*) and "prince in the republic" (*in republica princeps*). Such expressions had, in fact, already been used earlier in reference to Cosimo (and would be adopted again by Machiavelli in the *Discourses on Livy*), with an unconcealed and deliberately equivocal play on the double meaning of the Latin word *princeps* ("leading citizen"/"head of state") not unfamiliar in quattrocento Florence.[40] The strategem of saying one thing and implying another was the semantic reflection of real political and institutional ambiguity.

Indeed, when Giugni converts wholeheartedly to monarchy at the end of *Republics and Kingdoms Compared*, Matthias urges him to honor and respect the native city in which he has had the good fortune to be born, striving to ensure that its laws and customs are upheld. The reason for this is that there are few truly excellent sovereigns at present, while Florence is a republic endowed with sound institutions and laws creating "a principate not inferior to the genuine royal kind" (*non deteriorem regio ... principatum*), "even [bearing] some resemblance to a genuine royal principate" (*aliquam etiam illius regii principatus imaginem*).[41] This wording is close to that which Matthias used to define the gonfalonier of justice. Now, at the close of the dialogue, it is cleverly recycled and reworded in a different context, with obvious allusion to Lorenzo's power, described as the image or shadow of a principate. It may appear, and indeed is, the usual portrait of the "civic prince," but in light of what has gone before in the dialogue, it is clear that Lorenzo's authority is being acknowledged as virtually that of a prince, and that his passage "from a republican to an absolute constitution" (*da lo ordine civile allo assoluto* in Machiavelli's formulation)[42] is not only desired, but regarded as imminent and inevitable, indeed already largely a matter of fact. In the end, it poses no real problem for a work arguing for the superiority of monarchies over republics—one originally conceived for a genuine king such as Matthias Corvinus—to be dedicated to Lorenzo de' Medici, a Florentine citizen.

Two points in conclusion. The first sheds light on Florence's evolution during the fifteenth century, both in and beyond the realm of culture. In 1490, immediately after dedicating his dialogue to Lorenzo, Aurelio Lippo Brandolini obtained a chair at the Florentine Studio—a sign that the work had pleased its dedicatee, and that the time was long gone when Cosimo de' Medici would shy at comparisons to dynastic princes or Roman emperors, claiming to be content with *civilis mediocritas* (civic moderation) and *repubblicana moderazione*;[43] or even when in November 1481 Lorenzo had articulated his position—not without egregious hypocrisy—to Pier Filippo Pandolfini: "I am not lord of Florence, but a citizen with

40 Rubinstein 1992, 10–11.
41 Brandolini 2009, 258.
42 Machiavelli, *Principe* 9.23 (Machiavelli 2013, 73).
43 Biagini 1995, 72.

some authority, which I must use with temperance and justification."[44] And for that matter, Brandolini asserts in his proem that the dialogue will supply Lorenzo with a faithful mirror of his own thinking and political actions (*suas cogitationes, suos labores, sua consilia*).[45]

Second, when he finished *Republics and Kingdoms Compared*, Brandolini had been away from Florence, as he himself states, for more than twenty years. As an expatriate, he had gained direct experience of a range of monarchical regimes, Italian and foreign (Rome, Naples, Hungary), evidently coming to believe that they functioned better than republics. He was also able to look upon Florence with detachment and with uncommon intellectual freedom (and perhaps also, as James Hankins notes,[46] with not a little resentment toward the city of his birth, which he had been forced to abandon in his youth on account of his father's bankruptcy). This may be the cause of his hostility to commercial activity cited above, an extreme position not without precedent (in Poggio's *De avaritia*, for example), but clearly inspired at least in part by Lippo's status as a Florentine outsider as well as by his religious convictions (shortly afterward, in 1491, he became an Augustinian friar). Such detachment facilitated the cogent critique of the city's institutions that Lorenzo, who had for some time been pursuing constitutional reforms meant to centralize ever greater power in his own hands and those of his inner circle, would have found welcome. For similar reasons, in 1505 or 1506, Aurelio's brother, the theologian Raffaelle Brandolini, was able to rededicate the dialogue to the exiled Florentine cardinal Giovanni de' Medici, Lorenzo's son, in the hope that the city's lost majesty and dignity would soon be restored with the return of the cardinal and his family to Florence.[47] From Matthias Corvinus to the future Leo X, by way of Lorenzo the Magnificent: the winding road of Brandolini's *Republics and Kingdoms Compared* ended with the hope that a Medici restoration was imminent, one that in twenty-five years would end in a permanent and official Florentine Medicean principate.

44 "Io non sono signore di Firenze, ma cittadino con qualche auctorità, la quale mi bisogna usare con temperanza et iustificazione": Medici 1977–, 6:100. On these words, see the commentary by the editor, Michael Mallett, ad loc., and the observations of Kent 1994a, 52.

45 Brandolini 2009, 8.

46 Hankins 2009, xxiv.

47 Raffaello's dedication to Giovanni de' Medici is in the appendix to Brandolini 2009, 260–265.

SIXTEEN

Medicean Theater

Image and Message

PAOLA VENTRONE

THE SPONSORSHIP OF SPECTACLES AND pageantry was a customary way for Renaissance princes to make an impression of magnificence (*magnificentia*). An exemplary and much-studied case is the activity promoted by Ercole d'Este, not just in celebration of his dynasty but every year also at carnival time. During these so-called Ferrarese festivals, the salons of the ducal palace provided the backdrop for vernacular performances of comedies by Plautus and Terence, or of dramatic texts newly composed for the occasion. At Ferrara, theatrical entertainment was one of the most visible and characteristic components of the humanist culture exhibited by the Este court as a badge of its distinction and nobility.[1]

In a princely state (*signoria*) such as Ferrara (or Milan, Mantua, or Bologna), the space granted to civic ceremonies was determined by the ruler, who tended to exert control over such displays of civic identity as festivals celebrating local patron saints and horse races through the city (*palio*).[2] In republican Florence, by contrast, especially after the oligarchic resurgence in 1382, civic identity—not to mention the preeminence of the families forming the ruling group—was celebrated[3]

---

1 Gundersheimer 1972, 1988; Zorzi 1977; Cruciani, Falletti, and Ruffini 1994.
2 For an initial comparison of how civic identity was fêted in three cities under different political regimes, see Ventrone 2003. For comparisons between Venice and Florence not specifically focused on festivals of civic identity, see Casini 1996; between Florence and Milan, see Garbero Zorzi 1989.
3 On civic pride in republican Florence and its persistence under the Medici regime, see F. W. Kent 2004b, 10–12.

above all during the festival honoring the city's patron saint John the Baptist: such occasions witnessed[4] a highly articulated system of spectacles, including exhibitions of chivalric prowess such as jousts and *armeggerie* (choreographed equestrian performances),[5] and flamboyant displays such as the procession of the Magi.[6] Here the protagonists were the citizenry as a whole, or the governing class, but never one family set apart from its supporters and relatives, much less a single individual.

The role that the fifteenth-century Medici played in sponsoring festivals and theatrical performances can shed light on whether they were in fact "princely rulers," or only first among equals. Such a perspective can elucidate, first, their ambiguous political position in the city; second, the limits placed by Florentine republican traditions (*vivere civile*) on their freedom of choice in matters of ceremony; third, the extent to which staged entertainment varied between the eras of Cosimo "il vecchio" and Lorenzo the Magnificent; and finally, the differences between theatrical patronage in a republican context as opposed to a genuine princely court.

When Cosimo de' Medici returned from exile in October 1434, the basic pattern of ceremonial and celebratory theater in Florence was already established and would remain virtually unaltered until the principate's inception in the 1530s. In the period before 1382, a variety of spectacles are documented: *corti d'amore* (open-air banquets, dancing, and cavalcades through the city) organized by groups of magnates (nobles prohibited from holding the highest political offices), especially in the May Day period; processions; chivalric games; and parades by the minor guilds.[7] But they never became a matter of routine, nor were they formalized: Florentines evidently did not wish to be reminded of the political conflicts out of which they grew. These displays constituted attempts—neither always effective nor welcome to the citizenry as a whole—to give the limelight to their organizers, often significant political and social actors. After 1382, such "experiments" in ceremonial performance tended to employ both chivalric and religious languages—two modes of discourse that often overlapped.[8]

The families making up the Albizzi regime regularized the city's festive calendar in the hope of giving Florence an image of ceremonial dignity and civic unity, in contrast to the factional strife and numerous regime changes that had occurred before 1382.[9] Beginning at the end of the fourteenth century, new feast days were

4   There are numerous studies of this Florentine festival: the classic is Trexler 1980b, 240–263; see Ventrone 2007a for previous bibliography.
5   Trexler 1980b, 215–235; Cardini 1997.
6   Hatfield 1970; Trexler 1978e.
7   See Trexler 1980b, 216–224.
8   I use the term "religious language" in relation to the institution in the 1390s of the oldest feasts and performances on religious themes of which we know, the *festa de' Magi* and that of the Ascension. These became regular features of the city's festive calendar in the fifteenth century, though not with identical regularity, affording important opportunities for display to both the confraternities in charge as well as to the individual families' members who played a part in their preparation and staging.
9   See Brucker 1962; De Vincentiis 2001, 2003.

instituted and the festival of St. John the Baptist, the major annual celebration of Florence's civic identity, was restructured.[10] Traditional chivalric displays continued, but were now organized so as to give starring roles to ruling family members: in jousts, or dances and mock combats (*armeggerie*) arranged by groups of youths (*brigate*), under instruction from the Guelf party to celebrate important events (such as the conquest of Pisa in 1406),[11] or visits by illustrious guests (such as Emperor Sigismund of Luxembourg's ambassadors in 1432).[12]

The first notice of a *festa dei magi* dates from 1390,[13] as does the earliest mention of a religious play in the church of Santa Maria del Carmine recounting the Ascension of Christ;[14] in later years there also were religious plays focused on the Pentecost and the Annunciation in the churches, respectively, of Santo Spirito and San Felice in Piazza.[15] At the *festa dei magi*, city dwellers could be dazzled by a cavalcade through the streets of eminent citizens in the regal dress of the magi, accompanied by a throng of squires and aristocratic youths, exotic animals, and carriages loaded with precious wares, while those attending the religious plays could be thrilled by avant-garde stage machinery of astounding complexity, later attributed by Giorgio Vasari to Filippo Brunelleschi.[16] Such plays enabled the faithful to visualize a new and impressive image of paradise, besides dramatizing the mystery of Christ's twofold nature, human and divine.[17]

The stance of the Medici regime vis-à-vis this rich panorama of spectacle was conservative. They continued oligarchic traditions without emphasizing (beyond what established custom would allow) their own family members' prominence, both in jousts and *armeggerie* and in religious and civic festivals. Cosimo "il vecchio" and his relatives and friends did, however, begin, not long after their return from exile, to affiliate themselves with the confraternities organizing such spectacles, either joining forces with, or taking the place of, the rich members and patrons who had helped to cover the costs under the previous regime.[18] A telling sign was Medici family membership in the company of the magi, whose annual procession through Florence had once conferred luster on the Albizzi regime's top families, and that now, immediately after the political revolution, became a conspicuous

---

10 Guasti 1908.

11 See Corazza 1991, 20–23.

12 For the frequency and solemnity of the chivalric ceremonies organized for important visits, see Petriboni and Rinaldi 2001. See also Trexler 1978c; and for the visit of the imperial ambassadors, Trexler 1980b, 236–238; Ventrone 2007b, 14–15.

13 Molho and Sznura 1986, 89; Hatfield 1970, 108–109; Trexler 1978e, 152–159.

14 Sacchetti 1970, 55, 188.

15 For these festivals, see Newbigin 1996a, vol. 2.

16 Vasari 1906, 2:375–378.

17 Ventrone 2015.

18 On this, see as well Kent 2000, 47, 65–66. The involvement of the Medici in the so-called *feste di Oltrarno* is confirmed by several sonnets of Feo Belcari, addressed to Cosimo and his sons and published most recently in Newbigin 1996a, 2:239 (*Annunciazione*), 2:253 (*Ascensione*).

opportunity for displaying Medici wealth and preeminence—indeed for regal transfiguration. Cosimo himself, luxuriously attired, not only took part in the celebration;[19] he also linked the magi's image indissolubly to his own lineage and of his leading political allies[20] with Benozzo Gozzoli's frescoes in Medici palace chapel on via Larga (today via Cavour), where the idealized portrait of the young Lorenzo as the magus Gaspare prefigured the leadership role that he was "dynastically" destined to fill.[21] The Florentine public was exposed to the sumptuous regality that still strikes viewers today in those paintings (deliberately entrusted to a leading practioner of the International Gothic style, the favored contemporary vehicle for representing the core notions of chivalric and princely nobility) mainly at "live" performances of the procession (though these were held infrequently):[22] access to the Medici chapel was a rare privilege reserved for select foreign visitors, or for the Medici's Florentine intimates. Thus the Medici projected an image of magnificence outside Florence, which they could keep deliberately subdued at home.

But at key political junctures Cosimo did not hesitate to promote displays illustrating his family's preeminence, without, however, ever overstepping the bounds of civic tradition. He simultaneously demonstrated keen awareness of theatrical communication's potency as an instrument of propaganda, showing acute sensitivity to the need to keep his own patronage sufficiently understated so as not to grate on other leading oligarchs' sensibilities. The two most significant moments at which Cosimo took the lead in staging spectacles were the ecumenical council of 1439 and the visit of Pope Pius II and Galeazzo Maria Sforza to Florence in 1459.

It is well known that the council summoned to reunite the Western and Eastern churches was transferred to Florence at the instance of Cosimo and his brother Lorenzo, providing support, and so deriving potent reinforcement of their family's prestige.[23] For the occasion, the coterie of humanists and theologians who were habitués of the Florentine church of Santa Maria degli Angeli put together, under the guidance of Ambrogio Traversari, an ambitious theatrical program in support of the unionist position of the Roman church, in the context of the traditional Annunciation and Ascension festivals. The stage sets of these religious plays were adapted so as to convey a visual endorsement of the *filioque* clause (at the

19   On Medici patronage of the *compagnia de' magi*, see Hatfield 1970, 135–141. In 1451, Cosimo received an expensive fur cape to wear during the festival: ibid., 136–137; Kent 2000, 65–66.

20   Including Galeazzo Maria Sforza and Sigismondo Pandolfo Malatesta, prominently portrayed in the foreground.

21   On Medici portraiture linked to the theme of the magi, see Chastel 1959, 240–248; Hatfield 1976. On the relationship between Lorenzo and his grandfather Cosimo, see F. W. Kent 2004b, 13–14, 17–18.

22   The feast of the magi was meant to take place every three and then every five years, but is attested only sporadically in the Medici period: 1439, 1447, 1451, and 1469, besides 1454 as a pageant during the San Giovanni festival: Hatfield 1970, 113–119. On the affiliation of leading writers and intellectuals (from Luigi Pulci to Poliziano and Marsilio Ficino) with the *compagnia dei magi* in the Laurentian years, see ibid., 115–117, 135–141; Trexler 1980b, 423–425.

23   On the council of Florence's historiography, see Viti 1994.

Annunciation play) and the principle of papal *plenitudo potestatis* (at the Ascension play).[24] The *Annunciazione* play in particular was designed to put the unionist message across, with an original stage setting never subsequently reemployed, and a changed location from the usual church of San Felice in Piazza to San Marco, then being remodeled by Michelozzi (with Cosimo's patronage) under a Dominican rector, Antonino Pierozzi, who was himself deeply involved in the conciliar debates. Given the synod's positive outcome (if only in the short term), these elaborate performances must have further buttressed the position of the Medici—but more on the plane of international relations than internal politics: the churches would have been packed not with the Florentine populace, but with local and foreign ecclesiastics and intellectuals attached to the council. None of the numerous Florentine sources and chronicles nor, so far as I know, any ambassadorial dispatches, mentions the plays, which in contrast are minutely described by Bishop Abraham of Suzdal, a member of the Russian delegation.[25]

During the two decades following the council, the Medici cannot be detected attempting to overshadow or upstage other elite family members at major festivals. But an important diplomatic event spurred the government to plan a program of civic festivities of unprecedented richness and variety. Pius II's visit, en route to the diet of Mantua to promote a crusade against the Ottomans, drew princes and diplomats to Florence from all over Europe—a mark of the central role the city now played on the wider political scene, especially after the peace of Lodi in 1454. As the herald, Francesco Filarete recorded in the *Liber cerimonialis*[26] that, in addition to a series of solemn receptions, visits, and banquets offered to the illustrious guests, the *signoria* (the chief Florentine magistracy) organized a joust in piazza Santa Croce,[27] a ball in the *mercato nuovo* (which was adorned with tapestries and silver to resemble a salon in a palazzo), and a wild animal hunt in piazza della Signoria.[28]

During these events, the Medici deliberately mingled with the other participating ruling families, maintaining a discreet presence so as to escape notice either in the official source (*Liber cerimonialis*) or in most private memoirs. Cosimo did however play the host in his own palace to Galeazzo Maria Sforza, the young heir

24 For this thesis, see Ventrone 2009, with previous bibliography and an assessment of the sources. On papal *plenitudo potestatis*, see Rizzi 2010.

25 His descriptions are published in Prokof'ev 1970, 205–208, 254–256, and, in a new Italian translation accompanied by the Cyrillic text, in Ventrone 2015.

26 Trexler 1978c, 74–78; Petriboni and Rinaldi 2001, 466–470.

27 Apropos of this joust, Cosimo wrote to his nephew Pierfrancesco di Lorenzo, who intended to participate on his own horse, "questa è festa della chomunità et fassi per honore della ciptà e non per altre leggieri chagioni come s'è chostumato più volte" (This is a community festival and is being held for the city's benefit and not for other frivolous reasons, as has often been the case): Kent 2000, 476 n. 310. On this joust, and in general on Florence's ceremonial apparatus on this occasion, see now Lurati 2012.

28 See Ventrone 1992, 147–165; Ricciardi 1992, 129–160.

of Duke Francesco Sforza, his main political ally,[29] sponsoring an *armeggeria* in his honor at which the ten-year-old Lorenzo, bearing the honorific title of *messere*, rode at the head of a *brigata* of youths—a way of presenting him as his grandfather's legitimate successor at the head of the Medici *consorteria* (lineage), and so of the city itself. Even here the Medici comported themselves ambiguously: on the one hand Lorenzo's first "public" appearance took place in an *armeggeria*, an activity that had given the elite's offspring the chance to swagger ever since the Albizzi period, but on the other the display's symbolic message was highlighted in a pageant, "conducted" by the noble youths and mounting a triumph of love (*amore*), the first such known in Florence.[30] The message was conveyed in a short poem—one of two dedicated by anonymous clients (*clientes*) to Lorenzo's father Piero and grandfather Cosimo: the people assembled were meant to understand "they all were subject to one lord [*signore*]."[31]

Encomiastic poetry of this type, linked to spectacles promoted by particular families, first appears in Florence, as far as I know, with the 1459 festivals, and more than official sources and private memoirs it highlights the fusion of civic and family interests that Dale Kent has identified as Cosimo's characteristic political style.[32] The two short poems describe the celebrations, organized by the *signoria*, and the equestrian display, mounted by the Medici, as exaltations of the city's and its rulers' wealth and political centrality. And yet despite their explicit eulogies, such compositions—preserved in single, usually dedication, manuscripts—were intended for a circumscribed audience, declaimed as they were exclusively for the dedicatees and their closest associates, and thus reflecting the dialogue between reality and appearance that had characterized the ruling family's double image since 1434: within the civic domain respectful of oligarchic tradition, and yet within the inner circle of their "relatives and friends" laying the basis of an identity on the wider

---

29 Visitors from abroad were customarily lodged with the Florentine elite; Galeazzo Maria stayed with the Medici obviously to emphasize, both in Florence and throughout Italy, the solidity of the Medici-Sforza alliance.

30 Petriboni and Rinaldi 2001, 469. The word used is *menare*, meaning "to lead" or "to conduct."

31 "Poi venne un giovanetto assai virile, / giovan di tempo e vecchio di sapere, / e tiene ancora di boce puerile. / Costui per più cagioni ha gran potere, / perciò che la sua casa molto puote, / e questo chiaro si puote vedere, / Figliuol di Piero e di Cosmo nipote; / però questi gentili il fan signore, / avendo inteso del tinor le note. / Ond'egli, come savio a tal tinore, / volle mostrare a tutta quella gente / ch'eran suggetti tutti a un signore" (Then there came a thoroughly manly youngster, a youth in years but a man in wisdom, still with a boy's voice. For many reasons he has great power because his house is potent, as is plain to see [for he is] the son of Piero and grandson of Cosimo; so these gentlemen make him signore, having understood the notes of the tenor. Whence he, understanding this tenor too, wishes to show to all the people assembled that they all were subject to one lord): *Ricordi di Firenze 1459*, BNCF, MS Magl. XXV.24, p. 31. The other short poem is *Terze rime* (BNCF, MS Magliabechiano 7.1121, published in Newbigin 2011): Biagini 1992, 152; Bessi 1992, 108–109. It has been repeatedly emphasized, ever since Chastel 1959, 241, that the golden tunic and turban worn by Lorenzo in this *armeggeria* resembled the young magus Gaspare's in the cavalcade depicted in Gozzoli's fresco—in other words, with the political message that the family's young scion was the city's future leader.

32 Kent 2009.

stage of interstate relations sufficiently elevated and noble to set them on a par with legitimate princely dynasties elsewhere.[33]

Encomiastic descriptions of spectacles staged on special occasions became the norm in the sixteenth century, when princely marriages or other significant moments in rulers' private lives assumed a public character in the civic celebratory calendar;[34] similar accounts are to be found in the previous century too, both in manuscript and in print, especially in courtly contexts.[35] While Medici sponsorship of displays and spectacles might have been quantitatively modest in comparison to similar events at Italian princely courts,[36] it is nevertheless significant that there are copious and precocious encomia for festivities featuring not just the Medici but their closest political allies too. Such compositions (especially when preserved in a single manuscript and obviously limited in circulation) helped to create a self-conscious awareness of the Medici regime's growing exclusiveness.[37]

The two short poems in terza rima on the 1459 festivities inaugurated a mode of marking the few spectacles publicly sponsored by the Medici: Filippo Lapaccini's tercets on the *armeggeria* of 1464, dedicated by Tommaso Benci to Marietta degli Strozzi;[38] Luigi Pulci's *Giostra* and a short poem, no longer extant, by Ugolino Verino for Lorenzo's jousting victory in 1469;[39] Poliziano's *Stanze* and the *Hexametrum*

33 An emblem of the Medici's double aspect, originating with Cosimo and maintained by his successors, is the monumental marble portal (on view today in the Museo d'Arte Antica at the Castello Sforzesco in Milan) that welcomed visitors to Medici bank's Milan seat—a building donated by Francesco Sforza. It features the sculpted Medici and Sforza emblems, emphasizing their parity in a way hard to imagine in Florence. The Medici's private and public status is confirmed by the embassy sent to Florence (26–27 February 1450) announcing Francesco Sforza's conquest of Milan, delivered both to "La comunità de Fiorenza" and "Cosmo de' Medici" in person: Colombo 1905, 95. With regard to the insignia conveying the "external" image of the Medici at the Bolognese marriage of Annibale Bentivoglio to Lucrezia d'Este in 1487, Lorenzo de' Medici's personal coat of arms figured among the Italian princes' heraldic crests adorning the reception room walls—demonstrating the signorial status, de facto if not de jure, accorded to him outside Florence: see Cazzola 1979, 24.

34 Molinari 1980; Mitchell 1990.

35 No specific and up-to-date study exists on the pamphlets published to celebrate marriages in the quattrocento. See in general Pinto 1971, which is now dated; for a selection of Sforza marriages, see Lopez 1976, 2008.

36 Even a cursory examination of the Mantuan ambassadors' letters while resident at the Milanese court between 1458 and 1482 will reveal that at carnival and Christmas time, during spring and summer, as well as for weddings, funerals, and the entrées of illustrious visitors, feasts, balls, hunts, banquets, and jousts were taking place almost daily. In Florence, such activities were rarer and almost always prompted (except for weddings and funerals) by important civic occasions. See Leverotti and Lazzarini 1999–; see too the chronology of Ferrarese spectacles in Cruciani, Falletti, and Ruffini 1994, 164–167.

37 Regardless of staged spectacles, the encomiastic poetry dedicated to the Medici (for example, Ugolino Verino's *Carlias*) could never be as explicit as, for example, Tito Vespasiano Strozzi's *Borsiade* or Francesco Filelfo's *Sphortias*, addressed respectively to the Estensi and the Sforza—another measure of the "distance that separated the Sforza and the Estensi—dukes and legitimate sovereigns—from Lorenzo, who exercised princely power in fact but not by right": Bausi 2006, 163.

38 Lapaccini 1973–75. On the political significance of this *armeggeria*, see Ventrone 2007b, 18–22, with bibliography.

39 Pulci 1986; on Verino's composition, see Bausi 1996, 358–359.

carmen de ludicro hastatorum equitum certamine ad Iulianum Medicem virum claris-
simum by Naldo Naldi for Giuliano's jousting triumph in 1475;[40] and the *Elegia in*
septem stellas errantes, sub humana specie per urbem florentinam curribus a Laurentio
Medice patrie patre duci iussas more triumphantium, also by Naldi, for the seven
planets' cavalcade sponsored by Lorenzo for the 1490 carnival[41]—to mention only
poems linked to spectacles. Such compositions reveal the political significance of
the events celebrated (although the message was for only a select circle able to deci-
pher the allusions' cryptic symbolism). Examples are the lines cited above from the
Terze rime alluding to the Medici's power,[42] or Pulci's verses explaining the meaning of Lorenzo's standard in the 1469 joust:

> E' mi parea sentir sonar Miseno,
> quando in sul campo Lorenzo giugnea
> sopra un caval che tremar fa il terreno;
> e nel suo bel vexillo si vedea
> di sopra un sole e poi l'arcobaleno,
> dove a lettere d'oro si leggea:
> "Le tems revient," che può interpretarsi
> tornare il tempo e 'l secol rinnovarsi.[43]

Lorenzo thus adhered to his grandfather's policy of dissimulation, at least until
the Pazzi conspiracy in 1478—itself a watershed, resulting in no public spectacles
for a decade.[44] The participation of the two Medici brothers in the jousts of 1469 and

---

40 Poliziano 1979; Naldi 1974, 117–133; Ventrone 1992, 189–205.

41 NALDI NALDII ELEGIA IN SEP/TEM STELLAS ERRANTES SVB/ HVMANA SPECIE PER VRBEM/ FLORENTINAM CVRRIBVS A/ LAVRENTIO MEDICE PATRIAE PATRE/ DVCI IVSSAS MORE TRI/VMPHANTIVM, BRF, Edizioni rare 572, the unique copy without indication of place or date of publication: see IGI, n. 6766. The *Elegia* is discussed and partly pub- lished in Ventrone 1990, 356–360.

42 See note 31 above.

43 Pulci 1986, lxiv, 86. "And it seemed to me I heard Misenus sound [his horn] when Lorenzo came onto the field riding a horse that made the ground shake. And on his fair standard could be seen a sun on high and then a rainbow, and these golden letters could be read: 'The time returns,' which may be taken to mean that time has returned and the world been renewed." For a "Caesarean" reading of these verses and of Lorenzo's standard, see Ricciardi 1992, 190–191.

44 This is clear from, among other sources, Piero da Bibbiena letter to Giovanni Lanfredini, in Fabroni 1784, 2:388: "Non voglio dimenticare di dire che più di dieci anni sono non si feciono edi- fici et trionfi, et in questi tali dì et per amore di sua Sig[noria Franceschetto Cibo] se ne sono fatti da sei che gli sono paruti meravigliosi e opera divina [. . .] È concorso questa volta in questa terra il maggior popolo che ci si ricordassi mai, in tal modo che da Palagio a S. Giovanni non poteron portare le cose pubbliche come ceri et similia. È stato continuo un numero infinito di persone, et quando questi famigli pubblici volevano rimuoverne alcuni, rispondevano gridando che erano venuti nella città per vedere il genero di Lorenzo, il figliuolo del papa, ché così parlavano." (Let me not forget to mention that it has been more than ten years since any [temporary] edifices or triumphs were mounted, and yet just recently, out of affection for his lordship Franceschetto Cibo, six have been put on, appearing to him marvelous and divine. . . . On this occasion the larg- est crowd within memory assembled in Florence, so that it was impossible to carry public items

1475 may have been notable for the splendor of their outfits and of the literary commemorations they received (which, however, remained entirely "in house," as we have seen),[45] but there was no rupture with the pattern of the oligarchy's traditional civic ceremonials. Lorenzo's understated style is evident as well on the particular occasion that, not only at princely courts but in Florence itself, shed most luster on ruling families: a wedding.[46]

Lorenzo's marriage to the Roman noble Clarice Orsini in June 1469, while celebrated magnificently in the *cortile* and in the garden of the Medici palace, and on a deck with lavish trappings erected in the street for dancing (as was customary among the Florentine oligarchy),[47] did not violate communal sumptuary regulations for such occasions: no solemn entrée with ephemeral architectural "sets" was organized at the city gates for the bride, and no theatrical spectacles or allegorical *entremets*, customary at princely courts,[48] were mounted. Luxury was judicious and sparing. As Marco Parenti recalled, "The food served was better suited to a *wedding* than to *splendid feasting,* and this I believe they did *on purpose,* to *set an example to*

such as *ceri* and the like from the Palazzo della Signoria to the Baptistry of San Giovanni. The immense crowd never thinned out, and when the communal employees tried to get some of them to move along, they responded with an outcry that they had come to town to see Lorenzo's son-in-law, the pope's son as they called him.) *Ceri* were not candles, but wood and papier-mâché constructions representing towns subject to Florence. They were called *ceri* because they were offered to the patron saint. They were large and carried by porters. For other reports, see Gori 1926, 193–195.

45 Scalini 1992; Ventrone 1992, 167–205.

46 Such a deliberate understatement also emerges during illustrious visits, for example by Galeazzo Maria Sforza and Bona of Savoy in 1471, and Eleonora of Aragon in 1473. In the first instance, as their host in his own palace, Lorenzo organized no special display or entertainment: it was the city that staged religious plays in the Oltrarno churches (Newbigin 1996a, 1:39–41). In the second, the greeting offered by the *signoria* and the citizenry to Ferrara's future duchess was combined with the San Giovanni Battista festival: she attended the processions, the various pageants (*edifizi*) in parade and the *palio* race, and was then welcomed at the Medici palace, where (as she herself recalled in a letter) there was a "domestic lunch at which Lorenzo and Giuliano served her [at table] as esquires"—a diplomatic way of marking their inferiority to her in rank (see Falletti 1988, 134). On both occasions, Lorenzo displayed no behavior in public that overstepped his status as "citizen" or overshadowed the *signoria*'s preeminence at official ceremonies.

47 Iconographic evidence, especially fifteenth-century marriage chests (*cassoni nuziali*), is more abundant than written. Since such furniture was intended for the newlyweds' bedrooms, it often depicted wedding feasts—a way to record the virtual "stage sets" (arches, decks, lavish decorations) erected in the street at Florentine weddings, as well as the table settings, and the finery worn, for their owners' future recollection. See Paolini and Parenti 2010, with bibliography.

48 *Entremets,* a word of Franco-Burgundian origin, was used in the fifteenth century to denote what would later be called interludes, pauses between the main courses of a banquet at court that might include both the service of some light dish and some brief staged entertainment, often allegorical. Examples of court banquets in Italy prior to Lorenzo's wedding are the Milanese wedding of Tristano Sforza and Beatrice d'Este in 1455 (Motta 1894, 57–66) and Ippolita Sforza's to Alfonso of Aragon, duke of Calabria, in 1465 (Rosmini 1820, 4:31–47). A subsequent example is the wedding of Eleonora of Aragon to Ercole d'Este in 1473 (Falletti 1988, 135–138). One custom the rich families of Florence did have was to assemble a mounted *brigata* of "the wedding youth" (*giovani delle nozze*) to accompany the bride from her father's house to her husband's. On Florentine wedding rituals, see Klapisch-Zuber 1979; Fabbri 1991, 175–193.

others to preserve the modesty and the middling approach appropriate to a wedding, since there was no more than one roast meat course."[49] Moreover, "no *credenziera* was installed for silverware,"[50] and even in the choice of table silver moderation prevailed in comparison not just to the princely weddings known to us, but to some festivities for other young Florentine patricians.[51]

Less caution about display was evident, for example, in June 1466 at Nannina di Piero de' Medici's and Bernardo Rucellai's wedding feast, which spilled over into the *piazzetta* facing Palazzo Rucellai and the loggia on which it bordered—a space joined together by an artificial "sky of deep blue fabric overhead, giving protection from the sun,"[52] and embellished with the two families' coats of arms. There was also a "rich *credenziera* laden with wrought silverware—the most beautiful and gracious ornament ever made for a wedding feast."[53] Although differing in political and cultural context, similarly sumptuous was Lorenzo Tornabuoni and Giovanna degli Albizzi's wedding in September 1486, celebrated with exceptionally rich

49 "Le vivande furono acomodate *a noze,* più tosto che a *conviti splendidissimi,* e questo credo che facessi *de industria,* per *dare exemplo agl'altri a servare quella modestia e mediocrità che·ssi richiede nelle noze,* peroché non die' mai più che uno arrosto." Parenti 1996, 247–250, at 248; italics mine.
50 "niuna credenziera v'era ordinata per arienti": ibid., 249.
51 This moderation probably betrays the intention to set an example of the sort of restraint formally stipulated by new sumptuary laws in 1473 intended to curb the display of luxury at weddings and other ceremonial occasions, as noted approvingly by Alamanno Rinuccini: "Questi signori feciono molte leggi a *ridurre la gente a buoni costumi e risecare la superfluità delle spese,* come fu la legge de' conviti, del giuoco, de' comparatichi, de' frodi delle gabelle, e molte *altre leggi utili pel ben vivere e risparmio del popolo,* come quella del limitare i conviti e i mortori e proibire il superfluo portare del bruno pe' morti, e altre molte" (These lords [meaning the *signoria,* not the Medici] made many laws *to turn people back to good customs restrict superfluous expenditure,* including the laws on banquets, on gaming, on godparenting, on excise fraud, and many *other laws that helped the people to live decently and spend less,* such as those limiting banquets and lavish funerals, and prohibiting the superfluous wearing of black mourning, and many others): Rinuccini, Rinuccini, and Rinuccini 1840, cxxii; italics mine. Rinuccini's assessment was more negative after Lorenzo's death in 1492, condemning him, whom he now considered as a "malign tyrant," and maintaining, "Tutte le cose che anticamente davano grazia e riputazione ai cittadini, come nozze, balli e feste e ornato di vestiri tutte dannava, e con exemplo e con parole levò via" (All the things that formerly imparted grace and reputation to citizens, such as weddings, balls, feasts, and highly adorned clothing, he condemned, and abolished by example and in words): ibid., cxlviii. On Rinuccini's political profile, see Martelli 1985. This sumptuary legislation illuminates the double, internal/external image of the Medici: by drastically limiting the opportunities for ostentation by oligarchic families, they seemingly put themselves on the same level as their peers, all the while nourishing their princely image abroad in other ways, such as Lorenzo's personal diplomatic and political relations with the leading European potentates (to which the multi-volumed edition of his letters bears witness), or his assembling refined collection of rare and precious objects that so greatly impressed his high-ranking visitors (Fusco and Corti 2006). The aura surrounding Lorenzo's collection of gems in the eyes of the princes to whom it was shown, or simply its reputation, is evident in their zeal to acquire the best pieces after the Medici's fall from power—for example Ludovico Sforza, Isabella d'Este Gonzaga, Ludovico Gonzaga, and Pierre de Rohan, the French king Charles VIII's ambassador. On the contracts to acquire such objects, see ibid., 325–333, documents 169–197.
52 "cielo di sopra per difesa del sole di panni turchini": Rucellai 2013, 107–108.
53 "una chredenziera fornita d'arienti lavorati, molto richa. La quale chosa fu tenuto il più bello e 'l più gientile parato che si sia mai facto a ffesta di nozze." Ibid., 108.

furnishings, banquets, dances, and jousts, and with a profusion of premium table-ware that tempted a light-fingered guest to make off with a valuable silver bowl.[54]

Abundant costly utensils at table, and especially a *credenziera*—a display cabinet with staggered shelves covered in finely embroidered cloth and containing expensive cutlery intended for admiration, not use—can reveal the self-image that patrons hoped to project—an object symbolically chosen to exhibit magnificence at princely weddings and regularly described and appraised as such by chroniclers and ambassadors.[55] It is perhaps no accident that the only surviving part of the sumptuous pictorial decor by Melozzo da Forlì and his assistants once adorning the banquet hall of Girolamo Riario's Roman palace (today Palazzo Altemps) is the imposing, life-size *piattaia* (a cabinet for displaying plates), which aptly conveys the visual effect once produced on illustrious guests.[56]

The matrimonial opulence practiced by families related or closely linked to the Medici, in contrast to the affected self-restraint of Lorenzo's own wedding,[57] can be viewed from two perspectives. On the one hand, it shows a reluctance, especially in the delicate circumstances of his probably imminent succession to his father Piero, to adopt forms of behavior too elitist toward his social peers,[58] especially given the choice of an aristocratic, non-Florentine bride. On the other, the lavish weddings of families with Medici ties suggests a concerted sharing of charisma within the narrow Medici circle, with the magnificence exhibited redounding to the ruling family's advantage too. It was a process that gathered pace, especially in the 1480s, in tandem with the authoritarian legislative measures following the Pazzi conspiracy,[59] through architectural and pictorial commissions not given directly by Lorenzo but entrusted to his closest supporters. Such commissions changed the aspect of the city and many of its religious buildings. Examples of architectural commissions include the Scala and Gondi palaces, erected in Albertian style by Giuliano da Sangallo, and Filippo Strozzi's palace by Benedetto da Maiano. Examples of pictorial commissions

54 The political importance of this matrimonial alliance, linking two lineages particularly close to the Medici, is emphasized in the *Nuptiale carmen* (*Wedding Poem*) commissioned by the families from the humanist (and Medici client) Naldo Naldi: see Sman 2010, 31–44.

55 On objects associated with court banquet ceremonial and symbolizing courtly magnificence, see Bertelli and Crifò 1985.

56 *Credenziere* are often depicted on wedding chests: see note 47 above; and see too the one prominently on view in the wall panel (*spalliera*) by Sandro Botticelli depicting the fourth episode of the *Storie di Nastagio degli Onesti* cycle, now in the Florentine Collezione Pucci.

57 It is significant that there are no reports of festivities in Florence for the weddings of Piero di Lorenzo with Alfonsina Orsini, nor of his sister Maddalena with Franceschetto Cibo, Innocent VIII's son—alliances politically essential for the Medici but viewed with suspicion by the wider Florentine elite. The aim was evidently to avoid spotlighting unions needed to consolidate Lorenzo's hegemony.

58 Parenti seems to suggest that no diplomats from other states were present, unlike courtly weddings. The only reference to an external political alliance, coded but significant for those in the know, was the palfrey given to Lorenzo by Ferrante of Naples for his joust, mounted by Clarice Orsini for the ride to her new husband's palace: Parenti 1996, 247.

59 Rubinstein 1997, 226 ff.

include the Sassetti chapel in Santa Trinita and the Tornabuoni chapel in Santa Maria Novella, both the work of Domenico Ghirlandaio, not to mention numerous suburban building projects.[60] In sum, during the last years of Lorenzo's hegemony, the Medici continued to be formally *primi inter pares*, but the number of *pares* (equals) continued to shrink and harden into a caste of loyalists who abandoned once and for all the Gothic and chivalric style once the badge of the traditional oligarchy, and embraced the languages (perhaps even more political than cultural and aesthetic) of classicism and Neoplatonic hermeticism.

And yet, despite the relative stability regained after the Pazzi crisis, Lorenzo never surrendered the cautiously understated attitude always characterizing his public and diplomatic conduct, evident in a particularly significant letter written to his son Piero when the latter, then just twelve years old, took part in the embassy to Rome following Innocent VIII's election to the papacy in 1484. Against this background, Lorenzo told Piero how to behave and what ceremonial protocol he should follow, emphasizing in particular the importance of heeding the counselors and adult associates accompanying him, and of maintaining an equable and modest demeanor consonant with his family's institutional role both locally and internationally: "At times and places where the other ambassadors' sons join you, bear yourself gravely and considerately toward your equals and make sure not to precede them if they are older than you, *for you may be my son, but you are still no more than a citizen of Florence, just as they are.*"[61]

At the end of the 1480s, especially after his son Giovanni's cardinalate, Lorenzo the Magnificent took an active interest in conceiving and organizing spectacles that aligned his own image with that of a "civic prince" dedicated to the common good, and, indeed, constrained by love of his homeland's liberty (*patria libertas*) to assume the burden of leadership.[62] Such was the message of the only public

60 Morolli and Acidini Luchinat 1992.

61 "Ne' tempi e luoghi dove concorrano gl'altri giovani degl'ambasciatori, pòrtati gravemente et con humanità verso gli altri pari tuoi, guardandoti di non preceder loro, se fussino di età più di te, *perché per essere mio figliolo non se' però altro che cittadino di Firenze, come sono ancor loro.*" Medici 1977–, 8:70; italics mine.

62 Notable are the remarks by Bartolomeo Cerretani, a Medici supporter, on Florence's flourishing state in 1490: "Il che tutto chausava lo 'ngegno, iuditio, animo et felice fortuna di Lorenzo de' Medici et di quella schuola di ciptadini savi che erano preposti al governare la ciptà, e quali non passavano il numero di 20, che chon deto Lorenzo asiduamente pratichavano l'onore utile et felicità della florentina republica. Et di già, havendo dato una sua figl[i]ola al signore Franchescheto figl[i]olo d'Inocentio ottavo [I correct Berti's erroneous reading *terzo*], et facto chardinale messere Giovanni suo sechondo figl[i]olo pareva che la ciptà per lui et lui per la ciptà, chon tutto il popolo felicitassi in asidue feste et popolari triomphi chon una optima contenteza universalmente et de' ciptadini et della plebe et finalmente di tutto lo 'mperio nostro." (The cause of all this was the intelligence, judgment, high spirits, and happy fortune of Lorenzo de' Medici and of that group of wise citizens who headed the city's government. They were no more than twenty, and together with Lorenzo they strove assiduously for the Florentine republic's honor, utility, and felicity. And having already given one of his daughters to signore Franceschetto, son of Innocent VIII, and with his second son messer Giovanni a cardinal, it was as if the city for him and he for the city took delight with all the people in ongoing festivals and popular triumphs, with the greatest

spectacles he is known to have directly designed and sponsored: the *Trionfo dei sette pianeti* (*Triumph of the Seven Planets*) for carnival in 1490, the *Trionfo di Paolo Emilio* for the Saint John the Baptist festival in 1491, and a *Rappresentazione di San Giovanni e Paulo* in the same year.[63] And yet notwithstanding the public exposure that such initiatives entailed for Lorenzo, he always had the common sense to retain his footing both in Florentine civic tradition (carnival, festivals for Saint John the Baptist, religious and sacred plays by confraternities) and in the groups and confraternities that traditionally organized performances (in these specific cases, the company *della Stella*, which organized carnival and the festival of Saint John the Baptist, and the company of the *fanciulli del Vangelista*, which organized the *Rappresentazione di San Giovanni e Paolo*), prudently exhibiting the comportment of a citizen (however particularly eminent) at odds with the signorial magnificence on view in the numerous wedding feasts that featured in the Italian princely courts during those years,[64] while treading the narrow path of equilibrium between reality and appearance: *primus inter pares* at home, yet prince abroad.

---

universal contentment of the citizens, and of the lower classes, and finally of our whole dominion.) Cerretani 1994, 183.

63   For an overview of these spectacles and their ideological and political significance, see Ventrone 1992. On the political testament evident in the *Rappresentazione di San Giovanni e Paulo* in particular, see Ventrone 2008, 346–348; 2015.

64   For example, the Milanese festivities for the three Sforza weddings between 1489 and 1491—Gian Galeazzo to Isabella d'Aragona, Ludovico il Moro to Beatrice d'Este, and Alfonso d'Este to Anna Sforza: Lopez 1976, Mazzocchi Doglio 1983.

SEVENTEEN

Sound Patrons

The Medici and Florentine Musical Life

BLAKE WILSON

THE SIXTY-YEAR PERIOD OF Medici de facto rule during the fifteenth century can be framed by two musical monuments that, appropriately, mark a beginning and an end. Guillaume Dufay's *Nuper rosarum flores* was commissioned and performed for the consecration of the Florentine cathedral in 1436, and, while this marked the end of a construction project that had begun in 1297, it was the beginning of Santa Maria del Fiore as a newly completed center of Florentine religious and civic life. At the far end of this period, when Lorenzo the Magnificent died in 1492, Heinrich Isaac and Poliziano collaborated in the creation of a sonic funeral monument, *Quis dabit capiti meo aquam*. The subsequent history of both works bears out their status as lasting memorials, for they remain among the best known and most frequently performed works of the Renaissance. It is perhaps significant that the first work bears no obvious traces of Medici references or emblems, while the second is entirely suffused with the image of Lorenzo, whom many had come to regard as a "Caesar" or "tyrannus."[1] This would appear to define an evolution of Medici rule from patron to signore, a thesis that appears in the pioneering work of Frank D'Accone on the fifteenth-century history of the Florentine polyphonic chapel, the Cantori di San Giovanni.[2] In fact, ruling families such as the

---

1 Kent 1994a, 53, 59–60. Though we do not know if Cosimo "il vecchio" commissioned Dufay to compose *Nuper rosarum*, he certainly played a significant (though largely covert) role in the dedication event in general, and probably met Dufay at this time to initiate what was to be a lasting relationship between the Medici and the composer.
2 D'Accone 1961.

Este, Sforza, and Aragonese house had pursued increasingly aggressive policies in the cultivation of polyphonic chapels, and, by the last quarter of the century, these had become de rigueur signs of courtly magnificence, cosmopolitanism, and dynastic ambition. Florence was alone among non-courtly centers in Italy to pursue this goal, and the Medici—Lorenzo above all—had much to do with this, but their image as princely patrons of music aspiring to the courtly model of their neighbors has not been seriously revaluated, nor has Medici patronage of polyphonic music and musicians been placed in the larger context of Florentine musical life and literary traditions, about which we now know a good deal more.

Cosimo and the Founding of the Cantori di San Giovanni

The history in Florence of a stable polyphonic chapel capable of performing Northern polyphony begins with the establishment of the Cantori di San Giovanni shortly after Cosimo's return from exile. Given Cosimo's broad network of friends and allies outside of Florence, particularly those cultivated during his exile in Venice, he can hardly have been ignorant of progressive musical currents in Italy,[3] but it is the activities of his sons Piero and Giovanni that provide the most direct evidence of the nature of early Medici musical patronage.[4] In 1438, they were certainly old enough (twenty-two and seventeen, respectively) to have been privy to the deliberations surrounding the recruitment of the first group of Northern singers, instigated by Cosimo, and conducted in person by their uncle Lorenzo in Ferrara.[5] Among the inaugural *cantori* were two French singers with solid credentials as polyphonic composers: the younger Benotto (Benoit [Benedictus] Sirede), who after leading the Florentine chapel for a decade would move on to serve at the Ferrara court and in the papal singers; and the more seasoned Beltrame Feragut, an Augustinian monk who had already served at the Malatesta and Este courts and as chapel master of Milan cathedral, and who by 1445 had left Florence to serve the court of King René d'Anjou. For them, as for the great majority of their successors in Florence, service to the public ceremonial life of a republic must have been novel interludes in careers that elsewhere were dedicated primarily to following princely protocols.

In the years surrounding the performance of Dufay's motet, the musical life of Florence can be described as rich in local traditions, but insular with regard to the more progressive and international developments circulating in Italy through

---

3   The Franco-Flemish composer Arnolfo Giliardi (Arnoul Greban) reportedly served Cosimo: see D'Accone 1970, 264–265, and more recently Smith 1994–2007, 7:1541–1545.

4   D'Accone 1994, 266–270. Despite Giovanni's evidently strong personal interests in music, it was Piero who would remain most closely involved with the affairs of the *cantori*, primarily, it appears, as the recipient of inquiries and requests: see especially Haar and Nádas 2011.

5   The commissioning letter to Lorenzo from the cathedral *operai* (supervisors)—which instructs Lorenzo to seek "as best he can to engage a *magister capelle* and three singers or more, as is deemed necessary for the chapel . . ."—is edited and translated in D'Accone 1961, 309–310. By the date of this letter, 6 December 1438, Piero and Giovanni had for several years been members of the wool guild, from whose members the cathedral *operai* were drawn: Kent 2000, 440–441.

the agency of northerners such as Guillaume Dufay. The founding of a polyphonic chapel in Florence certainly was undertaken in part to address this situation, for it was done in conjunction with events that thrust Florence onto a more international stage: not only the cathedral consecration, at which Pope Eugenius IV and his entourage (including Dufay) were in attendance, but also the transfer of the council for the reunion of the Greek and Latin churches from Ferrara to Florence in 1439, which temporarily infused Florentine society with a highly cosmopolitan population of clerics, scholars, statesmen, merchants, and travelers. The foundation of the chapel at this time marks the beginning of a continuous, if fluctuating, presence in the city of polyphonic singers and composers, most imported from outside Florence. But sustained by Medici money, subject to the shifting fortunes of Florentine political life, and liable to recruitment from more attractive centers, the chapel, the singers, and the art they represented can hardly be said to have thrived in Medicean Florence.[6] The adoption of Northern polyphonic practice appears to have been impeded by local conditions, including the absence of the court culture in which Northern polyphony arose, and the persistence of native Florentine musical and literary traditions that were not easily supplanted. Medici involvement with both, especially under Lorenzo's leadership, would lead to hybrid approaches involving both imported polyphony and a Tuscan vernacular that was rising in stature during the late fifteenth century.

Giovanni de' Medici's *Brigata*, ca. 1445–1447

Because Florence lacked the formal institution of a court and its attendant class of cosmopolitan aristocracy, international repertoire filtered into the city through the localized structures and networks of Florentine society, such as confraternities, mercantile courier services, the lending and copying of materials among friends and family, and the activities of *brigate*. The *brigata* was a loose consortium of young men from the ruling class whose interests and tastes might have been princely, but whose social network was built upon traditional Florentine ties of family and *amicizia* (friendship or alliance). A group of Medici letters from ca. 1445–47 reveal Giovanni de' Medici and his close companions Rosello Roselli and Ugo Della Stufa engaged in a project to have one of Giovanni's poems set to music. The new song was to be compared to a *ballata* by Rosello that he reports having been set to music "with great success." Rosello's poem, *Poy che crudel fortuna*, in fact survives in a musical setting attributed to the Franco-Flemish composer Gilles Joye, so that the interesting aim of this poetic *giostra* (joust) is in fact one of great historical significance, since it is what I believe stands at the heart of Medici interests in Northern music: the adaptation of Northern polyphony to Florentine poetic texts.[7]

---

6   On problems and gaps in the membership of the *cantori* during 1448–69, see Haar and Nádas 2011.

7   D'Accone 1994, 268. The incident and relevant documents are presented in Haar 2006, and more fully in Haar 2004. This agonistic spirit is typical of Florentine musical and poetic performance

But the enterprise was clearly in its infancy in the 1440s. The composer chosen to set Giovanni's text was none other than Antonio Squarcialupi, the cathedral organist and devoted Medici client. But Antonio struggled mightily, and produced such poor results that the *brigata* undertook several emergency measures: first, Della Stufa lent Squarcialupi a *libro di canti* that he had copied out himself, evidently a small collection of polyphonic *chansons* for Squarcialupi to use as models, and when this failed, the master of the Cantori di San Giovanni, Benotto (Sirede: see above, 268), was called in to fashion the final product, which was to be "given a character approaching something not differing from Binciois [Giles de Bins, dit Binchois (ca. 1400–1460)], one of the most famous polyphonic composers of the time]." Somewhere in the process, Piero de' Medici's wife Lucrezia Tornabuoni learned the *ballata* (it took her three days) and sang it, to assist the *brigata* members in their critiques, while Giovanni de' Medici (in Rome during this episode) had a copy of the piece tried out with some singer friends there.[8]

Several conclusions can be drawn from this episode: at least among this small circle of Florentines, the music of Binchois was known and considered the gold standard of Northern polyphonic style, and there were no Florentines who had yet mastered it. The whole episode also bears a remarkable resemblance to other *brigata* activity of the late 1480s (see below, 276), including a musical-poetic *giostra*, and the apparent freedom of the chapel musicians to moonlight beyond their contractual duties in churches. Benotto's role in Giovanni's *brigata* by itself might be judged simply to be an extension of privileges the Medici enjoyed as the behind-the-scenes patrons of the chapel, but in fact Benotto's first documented presence in Florence is in 1436–37, as "Benocto da Francia" in the payment records of the company of Orsanmichele, a *laudesi* confraternity where Benotto first would have encountered Squarcialupi (who was organist there).[9] At this time, Orsanmichele showed no signs of Medici intervention or control, and this level of freedom for Northern professionals to freelance in the city was without parallel in courtly settings (where

---

at this time, evident not only in a similar scene involving Heinrich Isaac described at the end of this chapter, but in the competitive exchange of epistolary sonnets, for example, that typified public arenas such as San Martino and at carnival time, when poetry and music were performed, exchanged, and compared. On the continuation of this practice in early sixteenth-century Florence, see Wilson 2012. For fourteenth-century precedents, see Robins 2006.

8 As will be apparent with the activities of the Da Filicaia *brigata* described below (276 ff.), this kind of aural *prova* (preview) with an ad hoc group of singers became a typical method for trying and judging a new polyphonic work: see also Wilson 2006, 110–128.

9 Wilson 1992, 84–85. Haar and Nádas 2008, 36, argue for Benotto's presence in Florence earlier as the Benedetto di Giovanni listed in a 1432 Orsanmichele payment record. Though Benotto later would be listed in Florentine documents as Benedetto di Giovanni, the 1432 document almost certainly does not refer to Benoit, whose first listings in the 1436–37 registers were attended by deference to his title (*magister/maestro*), and initial and inconsistent efforts to render his French name (Benoit) in Latin and Italian (Benoctus, Benotto). On the Medici's decidedly low-profile involvement with the *cantori*, see D'Accone 1961, especially 312–326; Wilson 2006, 116; Haar and Nádas 2008, 2011.

their services were more closely guarded), and was a distinct feature of the city's more diffused patronage environment.

Florentine Music Books

Mention of Della Stufa's *libro di canti* requires a brief digression on a development that went hand-in-hand with imported polyphony: the need and desire for music books. As keen book collectors, the Medici had to have been aware of just how sumptuous and prestigious a luxurious parchment music manuscript emblazoned with dynastic imagery might be, such as those produced for the French royal court by the workshop of Petrus Alamire.[10] A Florentine *chansonnier* now datable to the early 1470s was prepared for Margerita Castellani, either for or after her wedding to Bernardino Niccolini, for the decorated opening folio shows the two families' coats of arms impaled on a single shield.[11] But through Lorenzo's generation, the only fifteenth-century music manuscript for which Medici ownership can be securely established is a modest collection copied in the 1440s, owned by Piero by the time he gave it away in the 1460s.[12] Piero's book, in fact, has been proposed as the *libro di canti* lent by Squarcialupi to Della Stufa in the above episode, since twelve of its nineteen songs are attributed in the manuscript to "Bincoys" (Binchois), the composer whose style the *brigata* was trying to emulate.[13]

As Elisabetta Pasquini's research on music books in quattrocento Florence suggests, however, there was nothing special about any Medici music collection compared to other private collections catalogued during the second half of the century.[14] Certainly there were other Florentines interested in collecting French secular polyphony, an interest related to that in Flemish painting and tapestries which was stimulated by the personal experience of Florentine merchants and their agents in cities such as Bruges. It is mercantile, rather than aristocratic, collecting that accounts for the diffusion of this repertory in Florence during the second half of the century: there are more surviving polyphonic *chansonniers* from Florence than from any other Italian music center, some extremely modest in character, and a sizable repertory of this music was even absorbed into the city's oral tradition of devotional *lauda* singing.[15] In other words, if the Medici were at all concerned with collecting Northern polyphony as a sign of princely magnificence, they did little to distinguish themselves from their fellow citizens, despite their apparent interest in

10 Kellman 1999.
11 Berlin Staatsbibliothek, Kupferstichkabinett, MS 78.C.28; Gallagher 2007. For a list of Florentine *chansonniers*, see note 42 below.
12 It is probably the *libro di musicha piccholo* listed with two other larger music books in the 1456 and 1465 inventories of Piero's library: Pasquini 2000, 72.
13 Haar 2004, 2006, but first proposed by Ames-Lewis 1982; for a dissenting view, see D'Accone 1994, 267 n. 19.
14 Pasquini 2000, 80, 182–183, where a 1471 inventory reveals that Francesco Inghirami owned six books of *canto fighurato*.
15 Wilson 2009, 108–120.

Northern singers and repertories. By the last quarter of the century, the Florentine workshop of Gherardo and Monte di Giovanni was capable of producing such works, for example the Pixérécourt Chansonnier and Florence Banco Rari 229,[16] but no such manuscripts can be connected with the Medici, though they were certainly commissioning lavish copies of literary and philosophical texts.[17] It was not until after the Medici restoration in 1512, primarily through the patronage of the Medici pope Leo X, that Medici music books, liturgical or secular, were cultivated as emblems of princely magnificence.[18]

The Cantori to ca. 1469

A final observation regarding music patronage by the early Medici concerns the Cantori di San Giovanni and polyphonic music for the leading churches in Florence. James Haar and John Nádas have argued recently that a manuscript of liturgical polyphony now in a Modenese archive was assembled and copied by Benotto in Florence for use by the *cantori*. Whether or not this is the case, that collection probably left Florence with Benotto when he resigned from the chapel in 1448.[19] Thereafter, there is little evidence of the copying and preservation of liturgical polyphony in fifteenth-century Florence, nor did the *cantori's* performances appear to have much impact on Florentines, who are silent on the topic in their memoirs and chronicles.[20] And the Medici themselves appear not to have been particularly concerned with this aspect of Northern polyphonic practice in Florence. In a recent article, Haar and Nádas have concluded, "Piero di Medici and his young son Lorenzo are frequently addressed in correspondence regarding the [Cantori di San Giovanni]. They helped in the recruitment process by using branches of the Medici bank to fund the travel expenses of newly engaged singers; but they did not themselves hire them or pay their salaries, and there is little or nothing to suggest that they were concerned in a meaningful way with the level of performance of sacred polyphony in the churches served by the Cantori di San Giovanni."[21]

The Medici and the *Improvvisatori*

A complete picture of Medici involvement with and attitudes toward music is not possible, however, without accounting for the vital local culture of carnival song,

16 PBNF, MS français 15123; BNCF, MS Banco Rari 229 (ca. 1492).
17 Pirolo 1992.
18 Shephard 2010. On liturgical books for Santa Maria del Fiore bearing Medici emblems, see Tacconi 2003.
19 Haar and Nádas 2008, 77–84.
20 Planchart 1993, 105: "The liturgical music heard or known in Florence in the 1460s, 1470, and early 1480s appears to have disappeared without a trace." The few recorded reactions to liturgical polyphony in Florence are the negative responses of two Dominican reformers, Giovanni di Carlo in 1479, and Girolamo Savonarola in his sermons dating from 1494–96: see Macey 1998, 91–98.
21 Haar and Nádas 2011, 104.

devotional *laude*, and improvisatory solo singing. Florentines of all classes and quarters (and Lorenzo the Magnificent especially) were involved in all these activities, and their textual, melodic, and performance traditions were deeply embedded in the traditional civic culture of the late medieval commune from which they arose. Common to all these were the composition and performance (whether sung or recited) of vernacular poetry, and, in the spirit of the project of Giovanni's *brigata*, all three genres became sites for hybridizing efforts to adapt polyphony to Tuscan vernacular. Given the scope of this chapter, a few vignettes must serve to suggest something of the nature of Medici involvement with this public performing culture.

Concurrent with the events of the late 1430s described above, there rose to prominence a small piazza, San Martino al Vescovo (today piazza de' Cimatori), as the premier venue for public performances of vernacular poetry.[22] San Martino was widely known and attended by a broad range of Florentine society, in large part because it appears to have been located in the heart of the city's thriving wool district, in the thick of workshops, and separate from the larger piazzas that were subject to Marvin Trachtenberg's "dominion of the eye."[23] It was no place for charlatans and hacks, but a stage to which the city's best local poets and performers aspired. The closest thing to an impresario and manager of San Martino was the figure Michele del Giogante, accountant, copyist, and poet who was among the participants in the 1441 vernacular poetry competition, the Certame Coronario. In a letter of 1454, he described a teenaged Florentine "whom I had already put to singing improvisations on the bench at San Martino, of fine intellect and imagination, really gifted by nature with this skill..." The letter was addressed to Piero de' Medici, and Michele continued, "you have already heard him sing in Lionardo Bartolino's house, at a splendid dinner he gave for you, where I brought him, and he sang a few stanzas; you must remember it. I think you were also acquainted with his work when he brought with him an exceedingly pleasing little book that I made for him, and he had sung a good part of the material written in it at San Martino, including a little work maestro Niccolò [Cieco, from Arezzo] performed as a motet at San Martino, which made hundreds of people there weep in sympathy."[24] Michele was in fact appealing to Piero for support for the young *improvvisatore*, whose impoverished state had forced him to enlist in the Venetian army. As other documents confirm, Michele was on intimate terms with Piero, who himself was on familiar terms with San Martino's performers.

The nature of Michele's relationship to Piero emerges in another of Michele's *quadernucci* (little notebooks), this one a draft version of a small compilation

22 Wilson 2013.
23 Trachtenberg 1998. The quotation here reflects Trachtenburg's thesis that the piazza was part of the ruling regime's deliberately contructed "architectural apparatus for the spatio-visual production of power."
24 ASF, MAP 17, 108 (24 May 1454); Flamini 1891, 600–601, discussed on 241–242, and in Kent 2000, 47–48, where most of the letter is translated.

prepared by Michele for "Pier mio." It is a collection of letters, poems, and chronicles all related to the military exploits of Francesco Sforza, and presented in 1450 to Piero on the eve of his departure for Milan as part of a special embassy to honor Francesco's accession as duke. Included in the book are two stanzas in *ottava rima* (octaves) copied with a rubric explaining that these were performed at San Martino by a *fanciullo ch'aveva una gientil pronu[n]zia* ("boy with a refined diction"), presumably the same one mentioned above (273), but the broader relationship of the material in this book to San Martino is suggested in the book's dedicatory poem addressed to Piero. Here Michele explains that the contents were prepared *per tuo consiglio* ("for your advice"), by "having spent some time gathering them we know where / that source [i.e., San Martino] [is] from which these things always spring / and [which are] known to everyone."[25]

That such singers were privately engaged by the Medici is clear from documents relating to the career of the most famous San Martino performer, Antonio di Guido (d. 1486), whose memorable debut took place there in 1437. Writing to his father, Duke Francesco Sforza, a young Galeazzo Maria was dazzled by Antonio at a dinner hosted in 1459 by Cosimo at his villa in Careggi.[26] In attendance were not only Cosimo, his son Giovanni, and Galeazzo Maria, but members of the Malatesta and Este families, and the ambassador of the Neapolitan court. Antonio's moving and "learned" performance, which included an account of Sforza military accomplishments, was clearly calculated to highlight the Florence-Milan alliance. It is worth pointing out that this is precisely the elitist, convivial occasion for which professional musicians were engaged at this time, and, while Cosimo easily could have drawn on the services of several San Giovanni singers whose talents this particular gathering would have appreciated, he must have understood that they could in no way match Antonio's ability to deliver nuanced dynastic propaganda in such an agreeable manner.

Though Michele and Antonio were linked to the Medici, who could not have been unaware of the capacity of the *improvvisatori* to influence public opinion at San Martino, their activities appear to have been far from circumscribed or prescribed by the Medici. There is little trace, for example, of Medici partisanship in the surviving poetry of Antonio, and the same is true of another high-profile San Martino performer, Niccolò Cieco d'Arezzo. After a career in service to several popes, an emperor, and the governments of Venice, Perugia, and Siena, Niccolò settled in Florence about 1435, where he performed with great success (to crowds of foreign prelates in Florence for the council of Florence in 1439 as well) until his death sometime in the early 1440s. His poetry survives almost exclusively in

25 Kent 2000, 73.
26 The original letter is preserved in the PBNF, MS ital. 1588, fol. 226, edited in Orvieto 1978, 181, and translated in Baldassarri and Saiber 2000, 322–324 (though the "Antonio" here is misidentified as Antonio Squarcialupi).

Florentine sources, probably transcribed from live performances by the relatively literate crowds at San Martino, and apart from a handful of moralizing poems originating as local civic commissions, those copied repeatedly in Florentine *zibaldoni* and *canzonieri* were the large-scale works for foreign dignitaries composed prior to his Florentine residence.[27] In short, however much the Medici might have wished to control the message at San Martino, there is no sign they did so, and every indication that they respected the relative autonomy of the site and its singers, which in any case might have proved thoroughly resistant to any form of intervention.

Lorenzo the Magnificent

Lorenzo the Magnificent's relationship to music and musicians was more complex than that of his forebears, and there are several reasons for this. Polyphonic musical chapels grew larger and recruitment of Northern musicians escalated throughout Italy ca. 1470–92, the number of singers increased, and Lorenzo sometimes received unsolicited offers of service from them. Polyphonic procedures also changed significantly and became more broadly disseminated among Italians.

Lorenzo was also far more engaged than any of his kinsmen with the improvisatory singing of Italian verse, which was a natural adjunct to his literary interests. In August 1473, Lorenzo wrote from Vallombrosa to his secretary Niccolò Michelozzi in Florence, instructing him to find Antonio di Guido and to arrange for this *improvvisatore* to come to Lorenzo and bring his instrument and a sonnet that Lorenzo had sent him.[28] It is clear from the exchange, including Antonio's own response conveyed by Michelozzi, that Lorenzo relished this kind of singing (which he himself practiced), and that he prized Antonio's art and even his opinion and musical interpretations of Lorenzo's own poetry. This is borne out by subsequent evidence of Antonio's occasional place in Lorenzo's circles, and above all by the more elevated cultivation of this kind of accompanied solo singing of new poetry by members of Lorenzo's circle such as Marsilio Ficino, Poliziano, and Baccio Ugolini. Lorenzo's sons Piero and Giovanni inherited an enthusiasm for it as well, and it would be the latter's ample patronage of improvisatory singers in Rome as cardinal and pope that would embolden Raffaele Brandolini, another Florentine *improvvisatore*, to dedicate to him a treatise on poetry and improvisatory singing *ad lyram* (with lyre accompaniment) (*De musica et poetica*, 1513). Brandolini alludes to the especially strong Florentine roots of this practice, a premise also implicit in the dedication of such a treatise by one Florentine to another, and Leo X certainly understood it as a Florentine cultural practice with which his quattrocento predecessors closely identified. In fact, this humanist transformation of solo singing in Laurentian literary

27　See Lanza 1973–75 for the extant poems of Niccolò (2:167–213), as well as those of Antonio di Guido (1:169–240) and Michele del Giogante (1:667–681).

28　ASF, MAP 29, 575; in Medici 1977, 1:467–468. See also D'Accone 1994, 277–278; Volpi 1934, 122–123.

circles had brought that traditional Florentine practice of improvisatory singing even closer in line with Lorenzo's own deepening engagement with vernacular poetry.[29]

That these pursuits were strategically intertwined would be made explicit in the activities of the Florentine academies of the 1520s, where improvisatory singers, polyphonic composers, and local poets mingled, and the Italian madrigal emerged as the fruit of efforts to merge expressive solo singing, flexible polyphonic textures, and Italian poetry.[30] This project to adapt polyphony to Italian texts had its roots in the fifteenth century, and was driven by a strong Florentine engagement with the expressive power of sung vernacular poetry, with which the Medici closely identified. However tenuous those efforts were prior to Lorenzo's time, the activities of a Florentine *brigata* active during the late 1480s suggest that things had by then come a long way. The remarkable letters describing these activities were graciously brought to my attention by Bill Kent, who after publishing a short article on them in 2004 invited me to explore their musicological significance at greater length.[31] The *brigata* consisted of Ambrogio Angeni (the author of the above-mentioned letters), Antonio Da Filicaia (their recipient, living in Nantes, whom Ambrogio addresses on behalf of "la tua brigata"), a certain Zanobi (a composer), and Simone Orlandini (a copyist with some knowledge of music). The four shared a fascination with all kinds of new polyphonic music (French, Italian, sacred, and secular), but they were particularly concerned with polyphonic *canzoni*, that is, with settings of Italian secular texts. There was much posting of music in both directions: Antonio was eager for music from Florence, and much of what was sent were the latest *canzoni* by Heinrich Isaac (the great Flemish composer living in Florence); the *brigata* members in turn were the recipients of music from Nantes including, remarkably, a carnival song text written by the *brigata* that was sent to the North to be set by a local composer in Nantes and returned to the *brigata*.

With respect to the letters examined by Bill Kent, he observed that "Lorenzo is everywhere in and around" the events they describe.[32] But was he? The events surrounding the composition and performance of one of Isaac's most famous pieces, *Alla battaglia*, come to light in several of Angeni's letters, reporting that the work was being prepared for the 1488 carnival season, that it was a *gran fantasia* of great difficulty, and that its secrecy had been violated by a "good friend" who had obtained a copy.[33] Angeni promised to send Da Filicaia a copy, but withdrew his offer after he learned that the work had not been well received in performance. As I have argued elsewhere, the work's failure was clearly due to its inordinate length

29 Wilson, forthcoming, where I discuss the refashioning of the older civic tradition into Orphic singing to the lyre, a practice conceived in light of ancient models by Ficino and his colleagues.
30 Cummings 2004; Wilson 2012.
31 Kent 2004a; Wilson 2006.
32 Kent 2004a, 370.
33 Ibid., 368–369; Wilson 2006, 100–101, 148–149.

and polyphonic complexity, which violated the decorum of traditional Florentine carnival songs, but *Alla battaglia* is of great historical importance as an example of Isaac's more advanced experiments in the creation of Italian-texted polyphony (of which it is a stunning example).[34] In this regard, I am inclined to agree with Bill Kent that Lorenzo's guiding hand can be detected in the projects of Isaac, his favorite composer, particularly in the experimental style of this work, but this is less evident in the specific workings of this event. After describing the problems attending Isaac's *gran fantasia*, Angeni concluded, "I do not believe they will be able to perform it if Piero di Lorenzo does not return from Rome; I hope he will take on the enterprise, but otherwise it will not succeed because it is exceedingly expensive." This is a remarkable situation: the composer we assume to be Lorenzo's client is in fact engaged in creating an ambitious *fantasia* that is part of an expensive carnival project to celebrate the Florentine victory over the Genoese at Sarzana in 1487, and the whole "enterprise" was unfolding without direct Medici support (until perhaps the eleventh hour).[35]

The letters describe a number of events that reveal Isaac and other members of the Cantori di San Giovanni operating at a distance from Lorenzo. In September of 1488, Angeni informed Da Filicaia, "Niccolò di Lore... quit the chapel, and made an agreement with the king of Hungary, and Bartholomeus [de Castris] has done the same. Their departure without Lorenzo's knowledge has displeased him exceedingly."[36] These two musicians that Matthias Corvinus purloined from Lorenzo were capable Flemish singers who had been members of the Florentine chapel since 1482, and, while Lorenzo's authority over this institution seems beyond question here, his direct involvement and even control are another matter. Equally remarkable is the pretext for passing on this information: Angeni asked Da Filicaia if he knew of "some good bass, tenor, or contralto voice over there [in Nantes]," as if such an obscure figure was in a position to recruit for the city's polyphonic chapel.

Like Benotto some decades earlier, Isaac appears to have acted with remarkable independence in Florence, so much so that one can question to what extent he was Lorenzo's client in any manner at all resembling the quasi-feudal relationships that bound other Northern musicians to their employers at music-loving courts such as Milan, Ferrara, and Naples. Isaac and two of his chapel colleagues were often called upon by the *brigata* to read through newly acquired compositions, and after two of these occasions Isaac offered to make a three-voice composition *più dolce e buono* (sweeter and better) by adding a bass part. In a situation reminiscent of the aforementioned competition involving Roselli, Della Stufa, and Benotto, one of the resulting four-voice works was to be compared with another solicited from a certain

---

34 Wilson 2006, 108–110.

35 Lorenzo might have delegated the project to a friend or relative, but it clearly exceeded the financial resources of whoever was supporting it initially. It is also possible that the project originated with his son Piero, whose absence from the city might have precipitated the funding crisis.

36 Kent 2004a, 370; Wilson 2006, 116.

maestro in Nantes, and a copy sent to Angeni "in order to compare [and see] which one knows better...how to compose."[37] Although Lorenzo clearly prized Isaac's compositions, a selection of which he once proudly presented in 1491 to Girolamo Donato, the Venetian ambassador to Rome, the freeware status of Isaac's services and *canzoni* in Florence stands in contrast to the situation at Ferrara, for example, where Duke Ercole expressly forbade any music of the court to be sent out of the city.[38] No Northern composer aligned himself more permanently with an Italian city than Isaac did with Florence, but, as the recent research of Giovanni Zanovello has shown, his links went well beyond his documented connections to the Medici: his recorded salary payments as a singer came from Florentine churches (none from the Medici are documented), and later in life he clearly made provisions for his own welfare: he donated 104 gold florins to the hospital of Santa Maria Nuova in exchange for a lifetime provision of grain, salted meat, wine, and oil to him and his Florentine wife, and he enrolled in both the Flemish confraternity of Santa Barbara in Florence and the relatively autonomous musical chapel at Santissima Annunziata, whose friars were the executors of his will.[39]

If for the moment we can set aside the shaky premise that the absence of an obvious Medici (especially Laurentian) hand in musical affairs is the sign of a covert *modus operandi* on Lorenzo's part, the full range of evidence suggests a picture entirely different from the world of a signore, *tyrannus*, or Caesar. Though the patronage of music had prominently emerged elsewhere in late fifteenth-century Italy as a sign of princely magnificence and courtly refinement, this appears not to have been emulated by the Medici. The reasons are manifold. Though individual Florentines occasionally engaged in polyphonic chanson *collezionismo* as a status symbol, the evidence of interest in French-texted polyphony as such, even among the Medici, is at best inconclusive, nor did Florence's social or political topography provide congenial venues for its display.[40] Of the Latin liturgical polyphony that the Cantori di San Giovanni were recruited to sing in the city's churches there is little trace, and the concealment of the Medici role in its cultivation, however much this was dictated by their unofficial political status, suggests that it was intended by them more as an ornament to the city than to the family. Instead, the activities of both *brigate*, of Isaac's *canzona* composition, and even the dispersed operation of fitting devotional *lauda* texts to polyphonic frames (in which Lorenzo and his mother participated) point to a further motive for the patronage of Northern polyphonic practice in Florence: the cultivation and refinement of polyphonic settings of vernacular

---

37 Wilson 2006, 112.
38 Wegman 1996, 465. On Lorenzo's presentation to Donato of an Isaac collection, see Blackburn 1996.
39 Zanovello 2008, 2010.
40 The 1460 event at which Lorenzo's sister Bianca and a companion played and sang French *chansons* appears to have been exceptional: see Prizer 1991, 3–4.

texts. This same priority surfaces in the citywide practice of stripping the texts from French polyphonic songs, extracting some form of the music, and refitting it with Italian devotional texts.[41] This interest in the music apart from the French texts is also evident in the condition of many of the relatively numerous *chansonniers* copied in Florence, in which French texts are entered only as incipits (often mangled at that), or not at all.[42]

Lorenzo understood as well as his fellow citizens that vernacular poetry was a performative medium, and when Niccolò Valori later wrote of him that "he always honored all musicians, [being] himself an exceedingly skilled musician, to the point that he was deemed second to none," he was referring to Lorenzo's documented activity as a solo singer accompanying himself on the *lira da braccio*.[43] But in his music, as in his vernacular poetry, he sought to refine traditional Tuscan idioms through infusion with imported elements.[44] As early as 1467, Lorenzo's interest in polyphonic settings of his poetry can be inferred from his father Piero's efforts to commission a polyphonic setting of Lorenzo's *ballata*, *Amore ch'ai visto ciascun mio pensiero*. At Piero's behest, Antonio Squarcialupi initially approached Dufay with this request, explaining with regard to the young Lorenzo that, "because of the excellence of his divine talent, he enjoys [high] quality in all the arts, and thus he delights exceedingly in the greater refinement of your music, and for that reason he admires your art and respects you as a father."[45] In the event, the commission was fulfilled by another foreign polyphonist and Medici client, the English composer/theorist John Hothby, who had moved to Lucca in the 1460s to join the Carmelite community there and to become choirmaster of the cathedral.[46] When Lorenzo later pursued this direction through the primary agency of Isaac, especially in the public venue of carnival, he would not have forgotten that this was the natural extension

41 Wilson 2009. A more traditional interpretation of the Italian-wide phenomenon of polyphonic works copied without their texts is that these compositions were intended for instrumental performance, most likely the professional civic and court ensembles of *pifferi* (wind players) such as that retained by the Florentine *signoria*. In his study of the Florentine civic musicians, Timothy McGee admits that the evidence for a specific and identifiable repertory for the Florentine *pifferi* is "ambiguous," but he cites circumstantial evidence from other centers to argue that this repertory must have included "composed polyphonic vocal music" such as that found in the Florentine *chansonniers*: McGee 2009, 222–227 (where other relevant studies are also cited).

42 Three such Florentine *chansonniers* can be found in the Berlin Staatliche Museen der Stiftung Preussischer Kulturbesitz, Kupferstichkabinett, MS 78.C.28; BNCF, MS Magl. XIX.176; and BRF, MS 2356. The remaining *chansonniers* of Florentine provenance are BNCF, MS Banco rari 229; PBNF, MS franç.15123 (Pixérécourt Chansonnier); BAV, MS Cappella Giulia XIII.27; BNCF, MS Magl. XIX.178; and Bologna Civico Museo Bibliografico Musicale, MS Q17.

43 Valori 1991, 72: "Musicis omnibus semper plurimum detulit, musicus ipse peritissimus, adeo ut nulli secundus putaretur." D'Accone 1994, 271 n. 32, provides an Italian version less accurate than that made by Valori's brother Filippo, as published in Valori 1991, 127.

44 For a similar argument, drawn more broadly, see Dempsey 2012, where (as in his earlier works) he argues for the primary role of Florentine vernacular culture in the process of reimagining antiquity (a different sort of cultural import).

45 D'Accone 1994, 270–271.

46 Memelsdorff 2006, 20–23; Haar and Nádas 2007, 291–303; Brand 2010, 765–768.

of a personal and creative engagement with Tuscan poetry, which was strongly embedded in the Florentine communal past. Lorenzo's keen interest in poetry and the intensification of its power to communicate through music were bequeathed to the next generation of Medici, who were formative patrons of the early madrigal, and who set about aligning musical patronage with dynastic identity. Lorenzo's musical pursuits, however, were conditioned by factors that set him apart from both his predecessors and his successors. The ephemerality of musical performance and the persistent orality of native Florentine musical practices were not conducive to the creation of substantial monuments of the kind that would have enabled the fifteenth-century Medici to combine signorial splendor with civic pride (or to put it another way, the material culture of fifteenth-century Florentine music was relatively weak). On the other hand, Lorenzo's abiding interest in poetry and language steered his musical patronage, including the decision to favor a single, permanently installed Northern composer (Isaac), toward experiments in sung poetry more substantial than any imagined by his earlier relatives. This development was suspended by Lorenzo's death in 1492, but its continuation and consummation in the creation of the Florentine madrigal of the 1520s suggest that Lorenzo's musico-literary goals were both close to his heart, and inseparable from the city's enduring *res publica* of language and literature.

EIGHTEEN

The Medici Question

A Rhetorical "Special Case"?

STEPHEN J. MILNER

M Y AIM IN THIS CHAPTER is less to seek an answer to the question that has given rise to the current volume than to examine the framing of the debate and its genesis within the classical rhetorical tradition. My central contention is that the debate within postwar Anglophone historiography concerning the republican or signorial credentials of the Medici replicates a form of argumentation that would have been as familiar to pupils of the classical schoolroom as to the young Florentine patricians undertaking *pro/contra* rhetorical exercises in the school of Santa Maria in Campo under the tutelage of Cino Rinuccini in the 1380s or copying vernacular renditions of the *Declamations* (*Controversiae* and *Suasoriae*) of the elder Seneca and pseudo-Quintilian.[1] This is not to belittle the importance of the question by reducing it to "mere" rhetoric understood as style (*elocutio*). On the contrary, it is to stress the persuasive and probabilistic parts of invention (*inventio*) and arrangement (*dispositio*) that render rhetoric a medium for making sense in and of the world: rhetoric as a means of social cognition constituting and constructing what it purports to describe.[2] Such a focus provides a useful critical prism through which to begin interrogating some of the assumptions and beliefs that have conditioned the various readings of Medicean preeminence in fifteenth-century

---

1 Tanturli 1976; De Robertis and Resta 2005; Marchesi 1907. On the importance of vernacular renditions of classical rhetorical theory for use in communal contexts, see Milner 2009.

2 For some recent histories of rhetoric, see Olmsted 2006; Richards 2008; and, for Renaissance rhetoric in particular, Mack 2011.

Florence. Significantly, it also sheds light on the continuing debates concerning the status and the importance of rhetoric and representational practices in the past and how contemporary historians and cultural critics read them. Rather than attempting to disentangle the primary rhetorical figurations of the Medici from the secondary historical discourses of their historians, the intention is to demonstrate how these accounts fold back into each other. The aim, therefore, is not so much to answer the question as to chart its genealogy and to place it within the controversial framework of rhetorical argumentation: history understood as rhetorical invention in the finding of arguments and the making of meaning.

Taking Sides

In classical rhetorical theory, the topics of most speeches were known as *quaestiones civiles*, defined as speech topics that were generally comprehensible. The chosen topic would be formulated as a *quaestio* or *controversia* to be addressed by two parties who would take opposing points of view within a performance context that involved the three component elements of any speech act: speaker, topic, and listener. On the basis of the relationship of these three elements, a decision would then be made concerning which genre of speech topic to choose. If the topic was uncertain, *dubium*, the speaker addressed the listener as a decision-maker. If the topic belonged to the past, the listener was addressed as a judge. If it belonged to the future, the listener was addressed as a member of a political assembly. If, on the other hand, the topic was certain, *certum*, the speaker addressed the listener as a passive, entertained spectator.

On the basis of these classifications, a speaker could then decide which genre of rhetoric to deploy: forensic or judicial (*genus iudiciale*), deliberative (*genus deliberativum*), or demonstrative or epideictic (*genus demonstrativum*). Significantly, in the context of the current *controversia*, all three forms testify to the dialectical or controversial character of rhetorical disputation: guilty or not guilty; to do or not to do; to praise or to blame. As such, they all demand partiality on the part of those taking the relative sides of the question, what was known in the handbooks as the *utilitas causae* or "party interest."[3] In terms of developing a case, therefore, the rhetorical texts furnished plenty of guidance on where to find the relevant arguments, or so-called "places of invention," in order to present one's case as forcefully as possible in all three genres of rhetoric, whichever side was taken.

A further refinement that applies to the Medici case is made in Cicero's treatment of the subject in the *De inventione*, where he takes issue with the twofold division of invention proposed by Hermagoras between what he terms *questionae* and *causae*, understood as "general questions" and "special cases."[4] While both are controversial in seeking to answer a question, Cicero rejects general questions of the

3 See Lausberg 1998, 29–34.
4 Cicero 1976, 1.6.8.18–19; Corbeill 2002.

type "Can the senses be trusted?" as the domain of the philosopher rather than of the orator. "Special cases," *causae,* on the other hand, are considered the domain of the orator as they involve "controversy conducted by a speech with the introduction of definite individuals." Here the abstract *thesis* is differentiated from *hypothesis,* understood as the inquiry into a specific set of circumstances involving specific people. In terms of framing the debate, therefore, it would seem that, within the categories and terminology of classical rhetorical theory, the current debate is a classic example of an uncertain, *dubium,* special case: a controversy focusing upon the assessment of the actions of specific individuals. Having identified the nature of the case, the question remains of which genre to adopt in its treatment. As historians seeking to evaluate and interrogate a past, we are not in a deliberative context looking to decide policy for the future. But both the forensic and epideictic modes of argumentation can be applied: the Medici as signori—guilty or not guilty? The Medici as signori—to praise or to blame? Both sides of the debate can call on a well-established classical repertory of rhetorical tropes in their characterization of the Medici as either tyrants or exemplary citizens.

Rhetorical Controversies and Tyrannical Commonplaces

Before turning to examine this "special case" directly, it is worth considering how the controversial nature of rhetorical argumentation was evidenced prior to the Medici's ascendancy, for the articulation of Florentine republican values was itself developed through rhetorical disputation, or what vernacular rhetorical commentators from Brunetto Latini onward liked to refer to as *lite,* arguments.[5] One of the key catalysts in the evolution of a Florentine republican ideology was the city's rhetorical response to the perceived threat to Florentine liberty from outside, in the shape of successive dukes of Milan between 1385 and 1447 and especially during the rule of Gian Galeazzo Visconti (1351–1402). The respective cases for republican and signorial rule were worked out through the exchange of invectives, the most celebrated being those mainly between respective chancellors when Antonio Loschi's *Invectiva in Florentinos* of 1397 was rebutted first by Coluccio Salutati in the *Invectiva contra Antonium Luschum Vicentinum* of 1403 and again in Cino Rinuccini's *Risponsiva alla Invettiva di messer Antonio Lusco.*[6] In defending the Florentine republican constitution from rhetorical attack, such invectives constituted powerful statements of the values that constructed the Florentine communal belief system, its ideology, clarifying what Florence stood against. Simultaneously, in 1404, Leonardo Bruni, who would be Salutati's eventual successor as chancellor, wrote a panegyric, the *Laudatio florentinae urbis,* in praise of the city's laws, customs, and citizens, clarifying what Florence stood for.[7] Rhetorically, as the two faces of *epideixis,* such

5   See Latini 1968, 49, in his *La rettorica,* a partial commentary on the *De inventione.*
6   Witt 1970; 2000, 300–315.
7   Hankins 2000a; Lanza 1991.

position taking depended upon the marshaling of arguments through confirmation and refutation, also referred to as contradiction, literally "speaking against." Invective and panegyric were therefore the rhetorical means of articulating the values of civic republicanism and key in describing the attributes of the would-be tyrant bent on the suppression of Florentine liberties. As such, they reinforced a sense of shared purpose and identity in the face of external threat.

The same values also applied when turned inward to examine potential threats to Florentine liberty from within. Unsurprisingly, any signorial pretensions identified within republican Florence were perennially understood and represented by contemporaries in terms of tyranny as attempts to usurp political self-determination for personal profit, as Donato Acciaiuoli discovered in 1396.[8] To act like signori within a republican polity was to threaten the durability of the established political form of self-government. Almost the complete list of high-status Florentines exiled during the republican period is made up of individuals described as having manifested signorial or tyrannical pretensions in seeking to seize control of the state, the Medici included (and on more than one occasion).[9] The use of the commonplaces associated with the rhetorical tyrant, therefore, was central to the identification and description of overbearing citizens deemed a threat to the established order. When turned inward, invective was a means of exposing elite citizens to shame in the eyes of fellow citizens and, in judicial guise, was a means for confirming such suspicions in the minds of those who sat in judgment when considering a sentence of exile. As a result, the condemnation of leading Florentine citizens as would-be signori makes sense only when considered in the context of their Florentine citizenship. Virtuous monarchical or princely government had always constituted a perfectly legitimate form of political ordering within the classical typology of governmental forms. It was only when the question was considered within a republican form that the charge, and its associated lexis, assumed a pejorative sense.

The rhetorical construction of the would-be tyrant not only had its own illustrious history, but was also a well-established schoolroom exercise. Indeed, the figure of the rhetorical tyrant first emerged in the Roman adaptations of Greek tragedies before it entered the rhetorical canon in the works of Cicero, Sallust, Livy, and Tacitus—not without coincidence all chroniclers of the late republican period and the transition to imperial rule. In addition to the vices of *superbia*, *libido*, and *crudelitas* (pride, lust, and cruelty), other attributes also became commonplaces of invention in the kind of classroom *controversia* that described the tyrannical type: the wearing of purple clothing and a crown, the deployment of a bodyguard, difficulty of access, the denial of burial, and the use of banishment and murder in the removal of opponents.[10]

---

8 Milner 2005b.
9 Ricciardelli 2007.
10 Dunkle 1971; Koebner 1951.

While few contested the legitimacy and authority of the republican legal framework and its symbolic and rhetorical articulation, many questioned the motives and practices of those elected to administer and represent it. The translation of the identifiable attributes of the rhetorical tyrant from the classroom to the contested political realm of fifteenth-century Florence saw them deployed in a social world that has been consistently characterized by historical anthropologists as suspicious and lacking in trust.[11] Consequently, the exercise of the authority granted by the commune was under constant scrutiny as to its impartiality within a framework constructed to secure disinterested government on behalf of the common good, or *bene comune*. Once the inclusive corporatist experiments of the mid-fourteenth century gave way to the government of a more restricted patrician elite, rhetoric became increasingly important in securing consensus regarding their legitimacy as leaders. When political participation was institutionally restricted, the rhetoric of the *bene comune* evolved into the rhetoric of the *res pubblica*, which continued to characterize the commune as belonging to the people despite the proscription of the governing class: liberty was freedom from tyranny, equity in the granting of each his due, and justice the impartial administration of the law irrespective of station.

This dynamic has been described by John Najemy as a "dialogue of power," whereby opposition arose once sufficient participants in the political realm felt the elite could plausibly be charged with overriding the republic's constitution: "the measure of oligarchic power is the distance between the official ideology of how things were meant to work and the way they in fact did work."[12] The dialogue in Najemy's reading refers to the manner in which the institutions and the political ideology of the *popolo* conditioned what the elite were able both to do and imagine within a republican polity. But did the values of the *popolo* as they had been enshrined, for example, in Latini's writings really hold the Medici in check? What kind of a dialogue is it when the patriciate, and the Medici in particular, are in effect being charged with appropriating republican ideology as a mask to cover their quest for political domination? Rather than a dialogue, it would appear that what is at play here are two differing senses of ideology, the constitutive and the dissimulative. Najemy's reading in fact presents the tension less as a dialogue than as a controversy in which judgments and sentences fluctuated until the final victory of the Medici dynasty in 1532. There was no sense of reasoned dialogue leading to consensus through the accommodation of multiple voices.

When Florentines sought to describe corrupt government, therefore, they differentiated clearly between the corrupt agents and the reified laws and rhetoric, which in themselves were considered virtuous: just laws were unjustly administered and the rhetoric of virtue was spoken by the dissimulating tongues of

---

11 Trexler 1978a, 1980b; Weissman 1989.
12 Najemy 1991, 279; see Machiavelli, *Il principe*, ch. 5.

would-be tyrants.[13] To cite Latini again in his paraphrase of the late Roman rhetorician, Victorinus (fourth century AD):

> Et dice Vittorino che eloquenzia sola è appellata "la vista," perciò che ella fae parere che sapienza sia in coloro ne' quali ella non fae dimoro. Et queste sono quelle persone che per avere li onori e l'uttilitadi delle comunanze parlano sanza sentimento di bene; così turbano le cittadi et usano la gente a perversi costumi.[14]

> And Victorinus states that eloquence on its own is called "the visible," since it makes it appear that wisdom resides in those in whom it has no place. And these people are those who in order to secure the benefits of communal office speak without regard to what is good; in this way they stir up the populace and accustom people to wrong-headed practices.

Rhetoric deployed in this way was *superficies*, words devoid of substance, empty speech: "mere rhetoric." The good citizen's duty was to learn to differentiate the virtuous, assembling, communal orator from the dissembling, divisive orator as described in the opening of Cicero's *De inventione*.

Judging the Medici: Contemporary Witnesses

The language of internal political conflict therefore was wholly mediated through the places of invention of epideictic rhetoric and its controversial framework. Was Cosimo "il vecchio" the embodiment of Bartolomeo Platina's *De optimo cive*? Was Lorenzo the Magnificent the secular peacemaker presented in Marsilio Ficino's vernacular rendition of Dante's *Monarchia*?[15] Or were they the corrupt and tyrannical usurpers of republican liberty described in Francesco Filelfo's *Orationes in Cosmum Medicem ad exules optimates florentinos*, where the *pater patriae* and his followers become the *patriae parricidae*?[16] Was it mere coincidence that Filelfo's course at the Florentine Studio on Sallust's *Bellum Iugurthinum* and his bombastic public readings of Dante, another contested Florentine figure, were followed by a Medici attempt to murder him?[17] In this context, Sallust was a key source for those seeking to present their opponents as factious enemies of republican liberty, a fact not lost on Latini in his use of the Roman historian when seeking to stigmatize the dynastic magnate class in the same way that Cicero sought to drive out the

---

13 On the legal tyranny of the Medici, see Isenmann 2011.
14 Latini 1968, 28.
15 Platina 1944; Rubinstein 1992. On Ficino's translation of *De monarchia* and the Medici, see Shaw 1978; Fubini 1984, 11–12.
16 Filelfo, *Orationum in Cosmum Medicem ad exules optimates florentinos liber primus*, BA, MS V. 10 sup.
17 Filelfo, *Oratio in principio extraordinarie lectionis Salustii de bello Jugurthino*, Lucca Biblioteca Governativa, MS 1394.

decadent noble youths in Catiline's train.[18] The granting of the title *pater patriae*, conferred by the Roman senate on Cicero after the defeat of the Catiline conspirators, was readily applied to Cosimo and Lorenzo by their humanistic apologists. Implicit within such an assertion were the signorial pretensions of their opponents. In the Pistoiese grammarian Benedetto Colucci's *De discordiis Florentinorum*, for example, the description of the failed uprising by Luca Pitti and his associates in September 1466 was based on Sallust's *Bellum Catalinae*.[19] Poliziano, another pro-Medicean humanist, also modeled his *Coniurationis commentarium*, written in the immediate aftermath of the Pazzi conspiracy of 1478, on Sallust's text.[20] Alamanno Rinuccini, as an anti-Medicean, assumed the role of defense lawyer in viewing the same events from the opposite perspective, writing his account under the title *De libertate*.[21] In or out, the physical as well as political position of the reader as writer was of paramount importance in identifying his "party interest." Sacked as chancellor in 1456, Poggio Bracciolini wrote a public invective, the *Invectiva contra fidei violatores*, against the regime that had rejected him, presenting himself as the displaced guardian of communal values and a trustworthy citizen, and his opponents as the usurping communal tyrants themselves deserving exile.[22]

Nowhere is this spatial/ideological positioning more fully worked out than in the works of Giovanni Cavalcanti (1381–ca. 1451). His three works, which cover the period of the Medici and Albizzi struggle for ascendancy, chart his change of position as his anti-Medicean stance hardened over the years. While the *Istorie fiorentine* was penned in the mid-1440s, the *Nuova opera* and *Trattato politico-morale* were composed in the last years of the decade and the early 1450s.[23] The so-called eccentricity of Cavalcanti's work derives from the alteration in his judgment of the Medici between the majority of the *Istorie* and the remaining two works. Already within the final chapters of the *Istorie* his disillusionment with the consolidation of the Medici's preeminence is clear, but the transition from praising to blaming them is still marked and provides a unique instance of a single witness advocating both sides of an issue. However, this was clearly not an exercise in "mere rhetoric." The question of whether to praise the Medici or censure them was dependent upon their political comportment relative to the values implicit within the conceptualization of good and bad citizenship as understood by Cavalcanti. Cavalcanti despised the factional struggles of the late 1420s and 1430s and, in terms long familiar to Florentine chroniclers, he describes the inner circle of the *reggimento* as ruling in a manner "non politico ma tirannesco" (tyrannical rather than political), their

---

18 Milner 2005b, 172–175; Osmond 2000; Hands 1959.
19 Colucci 1747; and the comments in Phillips 1987, 247–250.
20 Poliziano 1958.
21 Rinuccini 1957.
22 Bracciolini, *Invectiva in fidei violatores*. BML, MS Plut. 90 sup. 7, fols. 94r–101r; Field 1988, 40–43. See Black 1985, 91–98.
23 Cavalcanti 1944, 1973, 1989.

decisions animated by their "sfrenata volontà" (unbridled caprice).[24] Rather than conducting public business in the public sphere, he notes, "il Comune era più governato alle cene e negli scrittoi che nel Palagio" ("the commune was governed more at dinners and in studies than in the palace of the *signoria*").[25] Self-regarding, willful, secret, and unrestrained: all the rhetorical commonplaces of would-be tyrants.

Such an alignment inevitably involved the judgment of the morality of speech. In the *Istorie*, Rinaldo degli Albizzi is described in terms redolent of Dino Compagni's portrait of Giano della Bella, "uomo senza paura ... il più valente cavaliere ... della città nostra, il quale portava l'onore della fiorentina eloquenza oltre al comune uso, giusto e costante" (a man who knew no fear ... the most valorous knight ... in our city, who championed Florentine eloquence beyond measure, and was both just and loyal). His fatal flaw, however, was the standard commonplace of all signorial types: his *superbia* (pride).[26] Similarly, Cavalcanti's revised judgment of the Medici is illustrated by his changed evaluation of Leonardo Bruni. Referred to as the "eccellente Lionardo d'Arezzo" in the *Istorie*, in the *Nuova opera* he becomes the apologist of factional interests, the eloquent man skilled in simulation who makes things appear other than what they are, "col suo ornato stile le cose vili e basse à fatte magnifiche e 'scelse colla sua eloquenzia" (with his ornate style he rendered what was iniquitous and shameful magnificent and lofty through his eloquence).[27] The corruption of the commune's institutions and customs by the Medici is reflected in the corruption of the mouthpiece of communal rhetoric, Bruni as chancellor. Cavalcanti's understanding of the characteristics of the virtuous citizen are laid out in his final work, *Trattato politico-morale*. True happiness, he argues, lies not in the pursuit of office nor the esteem of one's peers. Neither is it to be found in advantageous marriage alliances. Rather it lies in virtuous political behavior and the observance of justice and the laws.[28] It could be argued that his eccentricity lay in his constancy, his unswerving belief and application of republican civic values irrespective of the alterations within the *reggimento* (regime).

Recalling the Medici: Historiographical Praise

Praising and blaming political leaders, therefore, was far more than the act of "*littérateurs* rather than politicians whose praise ... was intimately connected with their work of recovering and translating classical texts"; it was a highly political activity.[29] The question is then posed as to how we, as historians, evaluate such evaluations. What are we to make of them? How do we interpret such interpretations? Guilty or not guilty? Or do we praise them and blame them by using the same rhetorical

24 On the figuration of tyrants in chronicles, see Green 1993.
25 Cavalcanti 1944, 20; Dale Kent 1979, 125.
26 Cavalcanti 1944, 172. On Rinaldo's rhetorical prowess, see Kent 1978, 215–217.
27 Cavalcanti 1989, 126.
28 For his discussion of justice, see Cavalcanti 1973.
29 Brown 1961, 188.

forms of argumentation and narrative invention? One way forward is to interrogate the rhetorical dimension of Medicean historiography, the history of its history, or what Hayden White has famously referred to as its "metahistory."[30] For here too we can see that the tropes and position taking of contemporary scholarship find their own genealogy within the commonplaces of classical rhetorical argumentation.

The Nicolai Rubinstein versus Philip Jones debate has an illustrious Victorian prehistory whose terms of reference were themselves predicated on the controversial foundations of ancient rhetorical practices. In Victorian Britain, the question of the Medici's credentials as republicans or signori was of little concern relative to their exemplary status as models of enlightened mercantile patronage. In writing a reception history of the Medici family through the ages, the chapters on the nineteenth and early twentieth centuries reveal an extensive literature documenting a continuing fascination with the Medici on the part of Victorian scholars and commentators. As northern England in particular began to grow and flex its industrial muscle in the nineteenth century, its industrialists saw the Medici as an appropriate historical example of the happy union of capital accumulation and enlightened patronage in the improvement and betterment of their respective cities.[31] With the advent of the industrial revolution and the startling growth of modern mercantile cities, the new merchant class looked back to the precocious examples of the German trading cities of the Hanseatic League and the merchant republics of northern Italy in seeking to associate themselves with key moments of accelerated urban growth and social progress.[32] As latter-day merchant princes, the Medici of Renaissance Florence furnished this new class with a cultural paradigm that enabled them to refute the charge of cultural philistinism in their pursuit of profit by deploying their newfound wealth in programs of public and private works, which involved the collecting of books and artefacts, the building of libraries and galleries, and the chairing of committees that oversaw the embellishment of the shock cities of modernity. As early as 1796, William Roscoe, a Liverpudlian lawyer, banker, politician, Unitarian, Italophile, and collector, had penned a biography of Lorenzo de' Medici, the "beneficent genius" who, he claimed, successfully "combined a state of high intellectual improvement with the tranquillity of well-ordered government."[33] Benjamin Disraeli, speaking at the Manchester Athenaeum in 1843, attacked the defamatory conjunction of mercantilism with philistinism, declaring that "the pages of history have shown that literature and the fine arts have ever discovered that their most munificent patrons are to be sought in the busy hum of industry," concluding that he was certain a future as great as the Florentine past was destined for those great cities of Lancashire.[34] The official magazine of the world's

30 White 1973.
31 Milner 2013.
32 Vaughan 1842; the articles in Kidd and Nicholls 1999.
33 Roscoe 1846, 333; Gaja 2005; Fletcher 2012.
34 Hunt and Whitfield 2007, 54.

first ever fine art exhibition held in Manchester in 1857, *The Art-Treasures Examiner*, opened its weekly coverage of the blockbuster show by proclaiming, Manchester now "steps forward in her aggregate character to emulate the glorious example of Florence of old, under her Prince-merchants the de' Medici, to display to the world the richest collection of fine arts the resources of the country allow."[35]

The mercantile adoption of the aristocratic grand tour, and the more widespread turn to Renaissance Italy during the nineteenth and early twentieth centuries, were a direct consequence of such identificatory impulses that resulted in the translation of part of the Medici's cultural patrimony to both Manchester and Harvard University. Enriqueta Rylands, the widow of Manchester's first cotton millionaire, John Rylands, not only purchased both the Spencer Collection of printed books from Althorp in 1892 and the manuscript portion of the Bibliotheca Lindesiana from the seat of the Earls of Crawford at Wigan in 1901, but also built a library in her husband's memory to house their collection, which contained numerous Italian medieval and Renaissance texts. It was this sense of shared genealogy that led the librarian of the John Rylands Library to attend an auction at Christie's in 1919 of the Medici archives, which had been placed on the market by marchese Cosimo and marchese Averardo de' Medici in 1918.[36] The original sale was postponed while the Italian government intervened to withdraw 174 lots for the nation, including numerous Laurentian autographs.

When the sale eventually took place, the ambition of the librarian to secure a large part of the archive was dashed by the enthusiastic intervention of another bidder. In settling for a mere 36 lots consisting of 198 pieces, the librarian noted in his annual report,

> We are glad to learn, however, that the remaining series of letters of Lorenzo de' Medici were sold in one lot, and that the collection of ledgers, account books, and memoranda of the Medici family as bankers and merchants are also to be kept together in this country, both lots having been acquired by Mr. Gordon Selfridge.[37]

Harry Gordon Selfridge's interest in the Medici was no doubt also born of the same sense of genealogy as that felt by the John Rylands Library. For the retail magnate and founder of the Selfridges chain of department stores was also the author in 1918 of *The Romance of Commerce*, a chapter of which describes the place of the Medici in a history of trade that stretched from the Phoenicians to the new shopping complexes of the twentieth century. "The House of the Medici," he wrote, "presents to

---

35 *The Art-Treasures Examiner* 1857, i.
36 See the two catalogues edited by Tyler 1918, 1919.
37 For news of the sale, see Guppy 1918–20. For the listing of the Manchester Medici holdings, see Fawtier 1924. The contents are listed on the National Archives database: http://www.national archives.gov.uk.

the world the noble spectacle of Commerce clothed in royal robes."[38] Their preeminence, which is described as "practically a kingship," was read as testament to their ability, influence, and commercial wealth, which enamored them to their fellow citizens. In 1927, Selfridge gifted the Medici papers to Harvard, where they are still kept in the Baker Library of Harvard Business School.[39] To these merchant historians, there were no differences of opinion, no anxieties concerning the legitimacy, or otherwise, of the Medici's preeminence in Renaissance Florence. Whether viewed as merchant-princes or kings in all but name, the overriding focus was on their cultural and civic leadership, their significance as models of beneficent paternalism, and as proud sponsors of their city's image both at home and abroad.

Recalling the Medici: Historiographical Controversy

Yet such a characterization of the Medici's heritage did not go uncontested, as the reception history of the Medici was also inextricably bound up with the simultaneous emergence of a political skepticism concerning the significance and intentions that lay behind the civic munificence of the new bourgeois merchant elite. Indeed, it was the abject poverty and social degradation of swaths of the urban poor whose manual labor was exploited by the new class of capitalists that led to the Marxist critique of political economy and its exposé of the strategic use made of cultural capital to add a veneer of respectability to capitalism's oppressive practices. Friedrich Engels, in his examination of the social condition of the working class in Manchester in 1844, described how the city was built "so that a person may live in it for years and go in and out daily without coming into contact with the working people's quarter or even with workers," the facades of the warehouse palaces built on Florentine models masking the social reality that lay behind them.[40] When such poverty did break through and manifest itself, it was promptly wrapped in what Engels described as "the cloak of charity." Such concerns with the relation of wealth to charity, as well as with the politics of palace building, are shared as much by historians of Renaissance Florence as they were by Renaissance Florentines themselves.[41]

From a Marxist perspective, therefore, the characterization of the new class of industrial capitalists as latter-day Medici can itself be read as a form of symbolic cloaking, a means of legitimating capitalist modes of production through identification with their bourgeois forebears who represented the apotheosis of urban cultural production. The town halls, libraries, cultural institutions, and educational programs of the self-appointed nineteenth-century philanthropists can all be read as a means of presenting an image of civic well-being, of commonwealth, which

---

38 Selfridge 1918, 63–78.
39 Selfridge purchased lots 77–310 and 491–568 from the 1919 catalogue. See Richards 1932.
40 Engels 1993, 57–59.
41 Kent 1987; Burroughs 2002; Sebregondi and Parks 2011. On the relation of charity to the urban elites of late medieval and Renaissance Italy, see Trexler 1973a.

masked the abjection of the alienated class of the disenfranchised urban poor. Viewed from this perspective, as appropriators and distorters, the nineteenth-century capitalists can be configured as the would-be tyrants of the new economic order, with the Medici as their model and the urban poor their subjects. It comes as no surprise that the subsequent tradition of cultural Marxism, from the advent of critical theory in the work of the Frankfurt School to the origins of cultural studies in the 1960s at the Birmingham School, led by Richard Hoggart and Stuart Hall, has sought systematically to interrogate and critique all forms of representation in order to reveal the political instrumentality of culture in the establishment and maintenance of power relations. [42]

The status of the Medici as either beneficent patrons or capitalist oppressors, therefore, stands at the heart of contemporary cultural criticism. The confluence of the nineteenth-century myth of the Medici with the origins of the Marxist exposé of cultural politics furnishes a case study in the ambivalence of symbolic reading that finds its own genealogy within the controversial rhetoric of the classical rhetorical tradition. Read positively, ideology can be understood as "the medium in which conscious social actors make sense of their world" and as a means of "identity thinking," which offers "a position for a subject." [43] In this guise, ideology is the medium through which individuals and groups can articulate the values that render their social being meaningful. Read negatively, ideology is presented as a means of generating false consciousness through the systematic manipulation and distortion of representation in the service of a dominant power—the Marxist position. These contrasting readings both find expression in the secondary literature on Renaissance Florence, for with the advent of Communism, National Socialism, and Fascism, a new generation of scholars turned to examine the aesthetics of power and the role of representation in the establishment of political domination, redefining in the process the terms of debate regarding the history of liberty and dictatorship in late medieval and Renaissance Italy.

Such impulses clearly lay behind Harvard professor Ephraim Emerton's 1925 volume *Humanism and Tyranny: Studies in the Trecento* and informed Hans Baron's *The Crisis of the Early Italian Renaissance* as evidenced in the subtitle: *Civic Humanism and Republican Liberty in an Age of Classicism and Tyranny*. Baron himself described the work as a study of the role of the Florentine Republic in "waging a protracted fight which succeeded in limiting the triumphant progress of Tyranny in Renaissance Italy." [44] What is of interest in the context of the current discussion, however, is the manner in which Baron's "thesis" itself became the subject of controversy. In the face of his positive reading of the ideology of "civic humanism" as produced by patriotic rhetoricians, he became involved in an exchange of articles,

42 Hall 1997; Rose 1987.
43 Eagleton 1991, 1–31.
44 Emerton 1925; Baron 1955, xxvi.

rather than letters, in *Past and Present* with Jerrold Seigel in 1966 and 1968, the charge being a familiar one: that humanists were simply hired pens producing "mere rhetoric," peddlers of false consciousness in the service of those in power.[45] Subsequent readings of Florentine social relations and political language have also stressed the role of the language of dissimulation in the dramaturgy of power, in keeping with the roots of such terminology in the symbolic interactionism of the Chicago School of sociology. For Ronald Weissman, for example, in the opening chapter of his study of Florentine ritual brotherhood, Judas was a Florentine perennially prepared to betray for financial gain, the theatricality of self-presentation necessitated by what he termed the "importance of being ambiguous" thereby raising the specter of the Medici as betrayers of the republic.[46] The widespread use of the terminology of masking and staging, with its assumption that a more concrete truth or reality lies behind such performance, and that the inner and outer self are somehow independent of each other, also owes a debt to classical rhetoric and Marxist skepticism concerning the integrity of the represented world.[47]

The genesis of the readings of Medicean preeminence forwarded by Jones and Rubinstein, therefore, lies squarely within a long-standing tradition of *controversiae*, albeit with a reduced political charge. Historians, for all their claims to impartiality, find a subject position for themselves and do some of their own "identity thinking," through their subjects of study. As latter-day apologists, Jones and Rubinstein took their respective sides just as Salutati and Loschi had done before them. For Jones, the outsider looking in, the mechanisms deployed by the Medici seemed no different from those used by the signori who had been the lifelong focus of his work. For Rubinstein the insider, however, the charge of being signori in all but name was to empty Florentine republicanism of all import and reduce it to a mask behind which the Medici hid their true intentions. The agency of rhetoric as a means of persuasion and catalyst for social action was never underestimated by Renaissance writers. It was precisely the political durability and significance of republican values as articulated rhetorically and symbolically, and the latent potential to recall those words, images, and institutions that conditioned Florentine political life during the republican period. Niccolò Machiavelli was not alone in his assessment in chapter five of *The Prince* that recourse to the name of liberty alone was sufficient to destabilize a regime.[48]

In many ways, the republican history of Florence can be read as a series of lurches from side to side between successive crises of identity rather than an unproblematic republican *longue durée* or enduring dialogue. From the defeat of the *primo popolo* (1260) until the establishment of the duchy of Florence, the perennial

45 Seigel 1966; Baron 1968.
46 Weissman 1982, 1985, 1989.
47 Brown 2000a.
48 Machiavelli 2013, 31–33.

fear of the usurpation of the communal realm by overbearing individuals acted as a catalyst in initiating upheaval and regime change. And nowhere is the partiality of those taking the relative sides of the question more clearly evidenced than in the successive alterations to the inscription under Cosimo de' Medici's tomb in the church of San Lorenzo. For it was here that the *pater patriae* inscription was altered to *tyrannus* in 1495, restored in 1512, erased again in 1528, and finally restored in 1532. On each occasion, the name alternated in harmony with the changes of regime, each overwriting the other's evaluation of past political actions in what can only be described as one monumental controversy.[49] While Rubinstein and Jones's controversy was one of intellectual leaning, for republican and signorial partisans in the fifteenth and sixteenth century it was a question of political life and its stability.

49 Rubinstein 1992, 19–20.

NINETEEN

Marking Time

Medici Imagery and Princely Iconography

ALISON WRIGHT

THE *Triumph of Time*, THE FIFTH OF PETRARCH'S *Triumphs*, opens with a vision of winged Sol issuing from his golden palace and driving the quadriga across the sky. Swifter than a falcon, he pursues the infinite cycle of day and night proclaiming,

> "Tal son qual era anzi che stabilita
> fusse la terra, dì e notte rotando
> per la strada ritonda ch'è infinita."
> Poi che questo ebbe detto, disdegnando
> riprese il corso più veloce assai
> che falcon d'alto a sua preda volando.[1]

The passage introduces a series of images that can be recognized in the Medici family's repertoire of devices alluding to time as they developed through the fifteenth century. The falcon was used as an impresa by Piero di Cosimo. Sol was identified with Lorenzo the Magnificent, who was praised as a reigning Apollo among the muses. Most consistently, the infinite round of time was implied by the Medici device of the diamond ring interwoven with the motto "SEMPER" (always).

---

[1] "'I am as erst I was, ere the earth itself / Was established, wheeling ever, day and night, / In my round course, that never comes to an end.' / Thus did he speak; and then disdainfully / He started on again, swifter by far / Than falcon plunging downward on his prey." Petrarca 1962, 96.

1.

Bertoldo di
Giovanni, attrib.,
pre-restoration
detail of the right
side of the portico
frieze, Poggio a
Caiano, early 1490s,
glazed terracotta.
(Photo: Warburg
Institute, London.)

The familiar objects, emblems, mottoes, and other devices adopted by the fifteenth-century Medici deliberately operated on an open register and are not simply to be associated with literary sources, and yet Petrarch's evocation of ancient, cyclical notions of time, his poetic persona, and his allusive language are, as I hope to show below, fundamental for the Medici family semiotics of time. They offered a culturally specific and yet widely recognized set of mythic claims on the ancient past and an indefinitely renewable future. Time, as controlled by the passage of the sun across the heavens, has an infinite circular structure: everything changes and yet returns.

It was in Lorenzo the Magnificent's last years that such temporal imagery was most explicitly put to work. On the terracotta frieze that fronts his villa at Poggio a Caiano, completed only after his death, the ancient narrative of the origin of a golden age closes, to the far right (Fig. 1), with an image of Apollo taking to the sky in his chariot: he is the apotheosis and the point of departure within an infinite round. The extended time metaphors of the frieze, adopted from Claudian's *De consulatu Stilichonis* (AD 400), allowed the flexible application of the universal myth to the specific moment of the early 1490s. Borrowing Claudian's device that linked Stilicho's (d. AD 408) military achievements in war to his predestined election by Phoebus/Apollo, the villa's owner was similarly associated with a new epoch of peace and cultural achievement. The precise status of the individual honored, as public servant or as autocratic ruler, is not articulated.

Whereas literary and visual encomiasts happily referred to him in princely, even heavenly, terms, Lorenzo himself had, up to this point, avoided any public alignment with regal iconography. His aim was to promote his family and faction's prosperity ("the safety of our friends and our possessions") and Florence's international reputation as a state.[2] Yet from the perspectives of both his person and the public good, his position was well served by myths and metaphors of dynastic protection that begged the question of whether the terms of that rule were despotic or not.[3] As Janet Cox-Rearick showed in her seminal study of themes of time and rule on the Poggio frieze, Augustan poetic imagery, as well as continued citation of the Roman foundation myths dear to Florence, were adapted under Lorenzo in the 1490s in a way both sophisticated and purposeful.[4] Their adaptation was neatly interwoven with already established personal devices such as the reflowering laurel branch and the motto *le tems revient* (time returns), a theme to which the present article will return at the end (308–309).[5]

At Poggio a Caiano, an unapologetically princely building, the tension implicit in Lorenzo's own position of unrivaled authority over the Florentine republic is brought to the fore by the employment of a rhetoric of peace associated with the emperor Augustus. Augustus, who rejected royal titles and styled himself as first citizen, had ostensibly restored the free republic under a Roman senate while in reality retaining autocratic power and military command. In the frieze, the tension is present at a thematic level: Mars, god of war, has been paradoxically presented as a god of the resurrection of the year in spring.[6] As Cox-Rearick argues, Mars Gradivus exits Janus's temple at the center not to unleash conflict but to represent the springtime month of March in the ancient Roman calendar, marking the beginning of the agricultural and, by extension, the Florentine year. Yet the bellicose implications of the opening of the temple door have not disappeared in this context. The central gathering of armed soldiers bearing *palle* (balls) and other Medici devices makes of Mars-the-bringer-of-peace a kind of doublespeak: the element of military force associated with the achievement of prosperity and security is present even in the context of a rural villa without obvious defensive purpose.

While control over troops is an overt sign of a ruler's authority, control over time is more elusive and striking since it appears as an intervention in what is perceived as natural or permanent. Lorenzo de' Medici, born on the first day of the year, had a limited impact on the Florentine calendar, though he did introduce innovations in,

---

2   See Lorenzo's *Ricordi* translated in Watkins 1978, 160; Hale 1977, 60–66. For examples of encomiastic literature favorably comparing Lorenzo to a king, see Fusco and Corti 2006, 151–154, 259–260 nn. 113–121; see also Bausi, this volume, 246 ff.

3   For charges of despotism against Lorenzo, see Brown 1994; Najemy 2006b, 342–344; for the same charge against Lorenzo's grandfather Cosimo, see Kent 2000, 117–118.

4   Cox-Rearick 1982, 195–202; 1984, 68–86.

5   See also for this theme Landi 1986 and (with some correctives) Draper 1992, 197–220; Cox-Rearick 1984, 15–23.

6   A tension between the cyclical and the narrative of apotheosis is arguably present at a structural level too. At the far left, the serpent devouring his own tail should encircle the entrance to the cave of eternity, but has been foreshortened to appear itself like the relief as a whole, as a frieze or lintel.

as well as restrictions on, festive culture.[7] In commemorating the defeat of the 1478 Pazzi conspiracy, which brought about a long suppression of public celebrations, Lorenzo showed a facility for crisis management, characteristically identifying a moment of family disaster—the assassination of his brother—with an attack on the republic as a whole. Giuliano's murder was presented on Bertoldo di Giovanni's commemorative medal as the reverse side of a fundamentally stable regime still presided over by Lorenzo (Fig. 2). The latter is associated with the sacred center of the Florentine cathedral and, as in Petrarch's *Triumph of Fame*, with the overcoming of death.[8] A moment that changes everything ultimately strengthens the *salus publica* (public welfare) brought to the city by continued Medici protection and is given a mythic gloss by Bertoldo's *all'antica* treatment of figures as seminude and rubbed down by time.[9]

Having begun with two Laurentian sculptural commissions, in the remainder of this chapter I shall draw attention to a range of objects, sites, and materials to substantiate the thesis that, while Medici adoption of imprese and strategies of display and representation sometimes looks like the common currency of Italian princely dynasties and must have been intended to do so, the Medici were exceptional among the families dominating northern states in at least two respects. The first is in the multistranded sophistication and relative coherence over decades of the semiotics that intimated their right to rule. The second is in the way in which their use of devices implied an identity of interests between their own fortunes and those of a stable republic.

To underscore this second point, we must turn to the diamond ring impresa. The significance of this device in Florence is complicated by the fact that it was

7   Trexler 1978d; 1980b, 450–452; Gaston 1987, 121–127; Ventrone 1992, 22–33; 1996, esp. 110–116; Newbigin 1996b, 128–130.

8   For the medal, see especially Draper 1992, 86–95; Rubin and Wright 1999, 128–129, cat. no. 2.

9   For the tightening grip of Lorenzo's regime after 1480, see Rubinstein 1997, 226 ff.; Najemy 2006b, 361–369.

3.
Window frame, with impresa of the diamond ring and feathers, Palazzo Medici, Florence. (Photo: Alison Wright.)

shared by the Medici and the Rucellai, with both families applying it publicly to architectural ornament and monumental tombs (Fig. 3). The Medici ring and feathers already appeared on the frieze of the Capella del Crocifisso at San Miniato al Monte, commissioned in 1448, and it seems telling for the Petrarchan resonance of early Medici imprese that, according to Francis Ames-Lewis, the ring device first appeared early in the 1440s in a Medici copy of Petrarch's *Triumphs*.[10] Giovanni Rucellai's ring is sometimes seen as a Medicean adoption after the families were allied through betrothal in 1461, but it is possible that the device was already granted to them as a literal sign of fidelity and friendship by the ruling Este family of Ferrara.[11] It appears already in the window spandrels and on the lowest frieze of the Rucellai palace as well as, later, on their loggia.[12] The Medici introduction of three feathers, frequently coded red/purple, green, and white, the colors of the theological virtues but also Este livery colors, might just add weight to the possibility that the Medici variant was taken from (rather than granted by) the Este. Cosimo and

10 PBNF, MS Ital. 1471, fol. 1v. Ames-Lewis 1979, 127 n. 22, 141. The interlocking diamond rings of Francesco Sforza also adorn a later Petrarch manuscript: Böninger 1993, 43, 52 n. 36; PBNF, MS Ital. 1023, fol. 1. Interestingly, the first visual interpretations of the theme of time (BML MSS Med. Pal. 72 and Strozzi 174; BRF, MS 1129; BAV, MS Urb. Lat. 683) all date to the 1440s: see Cohen 2000.

11 Ames-Lewis 1979, 130 n. 36; Perosa 1981, 150–151; Preyer 1981, 198–201; Kent 2000, 364, with a word of caution on the origin at 490 n. 120.

12 The ring with two feathers alternates with a hatband (*mazzocchio*) motif with three feathers on the palace frieze and on the facade of Santa Maria Novella.

4.

Designed by Leon Battista
Alberti, detail of facade
frieze and pilaster, with
impresa of the wind-
blown sail, 1470, Santa
Maria Novella, Florence.
(Photo: Alison Wright.)

his son Piero had had firsthand experience of their court practices in diplomatic
missions to Ferrara in the late 1430s.[13]

For the Rucellai, the personal device of the free-billowing sail (Fig. 4), representing the winds of Fortune, tempered the stable message of the ring. The Medici,
by contrast, anchored the message of permanence by interweaving the Latin motto
semper. Though it has been argued that the ring was a sign of legitimacy, suggesting the consensual relationship of Florence in submission to the Medici,[14] a ring,

13 On the Medici diamond ring and feathers as well as its existing use by other Italian families, see
    Ames-Lewis 1979, 129–130; Preyer 1981, 198–199; Cox-Rearick 1984, 16–17, 36–40; Borgia and
    Fumi Cambi Gado 1992, especially 224–229; Cardini 1992, 70–73. Böninger (1993, 42–44) argues
    that the ring impresa was granted to Piero de' Medici by Francesco Sforza in 1450, but the device
    already appears in a Medici manuscript of the early 1440s (see note 10 above).

14 Randolph 2002, 108–137, who notes Vasari's claim that the diamond was a reference to *dio amante*
    (loving God) and develops evidence that the pun on Piero's name, *petrus* (stone) was already made
    in relation to the diamond in the fifteenth century. For the stone pun vis-à-vis Piero di Lorenzo de'

and even interlocking rings, are inexplicit in this respect and can suggest a more generalized pledge of Medici fidelity. In this sense, the clustering of Medici rings at sacred sites such as the shrine at Santissima Annunziata or San Miniato al Monte is akin to Giovanni Rucellai's use of the ring at San Pancrazio (his local parish church in Florence) and Santa Maria Novella. What is clear is that, rather than representing the family's experience of changing fortune, as does apparently Rucellai's sail, the Medici ring was a purely ideological choice: it supported ideas of legitimacy but also antique stability, purity, and tenacity that had great social and political advantages for a family in their position.[15] The argument for Medici association with adamantine permanence and resistance to the blows of fortune is made most transparently in the surprisingly direct image of a shipwreck that appears as a frontispiece in Lorenzo de' Medici's illuminated *Triumphs* and *Sonnets* of Petrarch, now in Paris (Fig. 5).[16] The wind-filled sail of the ship has brought the young man to grief and it is only with the help of the firmly rooted Laurentian laurel and, in the *bas-de-page*, within the compass of the diamond ring, that he finds rescue and then shade.[17]

The physical and social contexts in which imprese were employed by the Medici within their city were necessarily different to those of princely dynasties such as the Este or their major allies, the Sforza rulers of Milan.[18] Like other established Florentine clans, the Medici youth joined *brigate* (parties of friends) and sponsored jousts where they could display military skills and employ pages with livery colors.[19] They did not quarter their arms with those of families allied by marriage, nor could they concede the use of family devices as signs of allegiance. Though Giovanni Rucellai pushed the boundaries in this respect, there is no equivalent in Florence for extended repeat patterns of imprese surrounding palace portals, still less their use as wall embossments, such as the eye-catching diamond facets of Sigismondo d'Este's Palazzo dei Diamanti in Ferrara. Many Florentine families distributed personal devices and coats of arms liberally over all manner of domestic, military, and liturgical objects, but they did not imitate the princely habit of dedicating

---

Medici and possibly also for Piero di Cosimo, see Butters 1996, 105–106. For the latter's use of the diamond ring impresa on civic shrines, see Liebenwein 1993, especially 261, 275–282.

15 See note 13 above.

16 PBNF, MS Ital. 548, fol. 1v. For this manuscript, see, for example, Garzelli 1985, 1:122–124; Marie Pierre Lafitte in Lenzuni 1992, 161–164; Rubin and Wright 1999, 131–132, cat. no. 3.

17 The laurel is also here the Petrarchan laurel of poetic inspiration and the author's beloved Laura. Even so, Garzelli's interpretation of the shipwrecked figure as either Petrarch or Lorenzo fits less well with the recognized imagery of Lorenzo de' Medici as provider of patronal shade.

18 Riccardo Fubini (1982) emphasized how the Sforza and the Medici required mutual support in the face of their questionable legitimacy. For Ferrarese government as divided between state and court appointments, but with the Este frequently appointing the key state officials, see Colantuono 2010, 198–202.

19 Carew-Reid 1995. The Medici palace inventory, fol. 59v (Spallanzani and Bertelà 1992, 122), refers to nine *giornee* (cloaks) embroidered with the device of Piero di Cosimo as well as three *ghonellini alla dovisa* (livery skirts) of purple and white velvet with the *bronconi* (laurel branches) and letters, and versions of the same outfits for boys (presumably pages). These apparently date from the 1469 joust of Lorenzo de' Medici.

5.
Francesco d'Antonio
del Chierico, scene of
shipwreck illustrating
Petrarch's *Triumphs*
and *Sonnets*, 1476, MS
Italien 548, fol. 1v,
Bibliothèque nationale
de France, Paris. (Photo:
Bibliothèque nationale
de France, Paris.)

entire rooms to single emblems, where repeated devices expanded like wallpaper. Examples recorded in the Palazzo del Corte of Ferrara under Leonello d'Este include the colorfully named *camere* of the *paraduri* (a type of flood-control device) of the *zenochiale* (knee armor) as well as the diamond.[20] The legibility of imprese on Medici clothing was also less apparent at home than on those occasions when the younger members attended the great events of signorial courts. Piero di Lorenzo de' Medici is recorded as having made a spectacular appearance in embroidered

20 Tuohy 1996, 62.

bronconi (laurel branches) at the marriage of Gian Galeazzo Sforza in 1489.[21] It is this chivalric habit that distinguishes the cavalcade of the kings depicted in the tiny Medici palace chapel, but it was rarely visible on the Florentine street.

As *primi inter pares*, the authority assumed by the Medici within Florence was less close to that of the Este than it was to the Bentivoglio, who, in the last third of the fifteenth century, claimed a permanent place on the ruling council of Bologna's tight civic oligarchy and made use of public displays to flaunt signorial powers within the republic.[22] Yet, even here, distinctions must be drawn since Bentivoglio self-assertion was also more brazen. Georgia Clarke has stressed the citywide, constant visibility of the Bentivoglio arms of the *sega* (saw) before their fall from power.[23] Equally, one need only to enter the Bentivoglio family chapel in San Giacomo Maggiore, whose decoration followed directly the crushing of a plot by the rival Malvezzi family, to find a courtly dynastic presence inscribed in the public space of the church.[24] The triumphant family gathering round the *Virgin and Child* (Fig. 6) is modeled on the hierarchy of the heavenly court, but also on that of neighboring states dominated by military families, such as the Gonzaga of Mantua or the Sforza to whom the Bentivoglio were allied in marriage.[25] Self-representation takes the overtly signorial form of mural group portraiture and it is significant that it was in this chapel that Giovanni Bentivoglio exercised his right to create knights.[26] The iconography of time is explicit in the two site-specific *Triumphs* derived from Petrarch in which members of the Bentivoglio family look on at the spectacle of fame and death. Though death takes all, the unusual representation of a type of wheel of fortune in the circle above fame suggests that Giovanni Bentivoglio and his advisers wished to present fortune as a positive force. The appropriateness of this celebration of the Bentivoglio as fortune's favorites proved, in fact, to be short-lived.[27]

For Florentines, including the Medici, the imagery of the *Triumphs* was a more domestic affair, though not without political significance.[28] In the far smaller and

---

21 Bullard 1994, 53–54.

22 For the major Bentivoglio jousts in a familial and civic context, see, for example, Bacci 1969, 65. See also Clarke 2004 for Bentivoglio political maneuvering in relation to other families of the oligarchy.

23 Clarke 1999 refers to the 1493 dedicatory letter of Filippo Beroaldo's commentary on Suetonius, in which the ubiquity of the Bentivoglio *sega* in the city is celebrated. Their removal was later ordered by the victorious Pope Julius II in 1506–7.

24 For relations between the Malvezzi and the Bentivoglio, see especially Belvederi 1967; for their earlier alliance and rivalry, see Clarke 2004, 165. For the chapel in the context of Bentivoglio power, see Nieuwenhuizen 1996; Drogin 2004, 85–89; 2010, especially 266–269.

25 Sante Bentivoglio (in 1454) first and then, ten years later, his successor Giovanni II Bentivoglio were married to Ginevra Sforza, Francesco Sforza's niece.

26 Wegener 1989, 185–186.

27 David Drogin (2010) recalls that the Bentivoglio-organized festivities for the civic feast of San Petronio (1490) included the triumph of fortune on a chariot, which was followed by the heir Annibale Bentivoglio. For the roundel, see Wegener 1989, 94–205; Ottani Cavina 1967.

28 For the Medicean triumph of love staged in 1459 for the visit of Pius II and Galeazzo Maria Sforza to Florence, see Eisenbichler 1990; also Ventrone 1992, 26, 50 n. 31, and Rossella Bessi in the same volume, 108–109.

6.

Lorenzo Costa, *Virgin and Child with Bentivoglio Family Members,* 1488, fresco, Cappella Bentivoglio, San Giacomo Maggiore, Bologna. (Photo: Archivi Alinari, Florence.)

less public chapel of the Medici palace painted in 1459, the position of the family portraits among the illustrious entourage reminds us that the conception of Benozzo Gozzoli's fresco is closely related to Petrarch's *Triumph of Fame,* which begins with Fame's rising, "like a star in the East." In the poem, fame's followers show their worthiness on their brows: Julius Caesar and Scipio Africanus head the ancient Romans, "followed by a grandson and a son / Who was unique and peerless in the world";[29] Petrarch leaves these successors unnamed, but the triumph of

29 "ed ecco i primi due, / l'un seguiva il nipote e l'altro, il figlio, / che sol, senza alcun pari, al mondo fue": Petrarca 1962, 74. The nephew is Scipio Africannus; the son, Octavian Augustus.

7.

Vesting table, late
1420s?, marble,
porphyry, and
bronze, Old
Sacristy, San
Lorenzo, Florence.
(Photo: © The
Courtauld Institute
of Art, London.)

fame follows a masculine dynastic structure of virtue (*virtù*) that is pursued down
the roster of Roman worthies, republican to imperial. In the Medici palace chapel,
the Medici generations follow the kings in time, in space, and in their aspirations as
donors and wise rulers. So much is clear. What is deliberately less explicit is whether
the glittering, youngest "king," set against a laurel, is a direct model for the future
ruler, since Lorenzo de' Medici's actual portrait appears elsewhere.[30]

One strategy that sets Medici use of temporal metaphors apart both from other
Florentines and from most contemporary signori is the distinctive argument from
materials that bring with them their own temporality and resistance. The diamond
device is a significant choice, but equally telling are the non-emblematic ways in
which actual hard stones were employed across generations. When, in the 1420s,
Giovanni di Bicci de' Medici built the Old Sacristy of the church of San Lorenzo
with his own burial place in mind, he carefully balanced the needs of the canons
with those of a family mausoleum. The massive slice of polished porphyry set into
the middle of the vesting table (Fig. 7), which, apparently from as early as 1430,
doubled as a canopy over his tomb, served both these constituencies.[31] With its
diameter mirroring the opening of the lantern in the dome directly above, it effectively inserted the site within the perspective of eternity and the cosmic sphere.
The *rota* (circle) was well known as a ceremonial marker in Roman basilicas and,

30 A cosmic and cyclical dimension is not as apparent in the Medici palace chapel as it is in Este fam-
    ily imagery, whether that of Leonello's *studiolo* at Belfiore (from ca. 1447) or later in the hall of the
    months painted for Borso d'Este at Schifanoia (ca. 1470). In the latter, Borso's court and his sub-
    jects completely dominate the lower walls, even as they act in harmony with the planetary heavens
    depicted above them: Lippincott 1990; Colantuono 2010, 214–219.

31 For date and function, see Caglioti 1996, 128 nn. 12, 15, 19, correcting the interpretation of Susan
    McKillop (1992a, 272, 289), and some earlier writers, of the table as an altar. See Olson 2000,
    47–55, for tondo symbolism in the Old Sacristy at San Lorenzo.

by its antiquity and position, it made an implicit claim for a return to pristine early Christian and imperial traditions.[32] It both looked back to the Holy Sepulcher and forward to the resurrection of the body (as do the "evergreen" bronze ivy fronds that creep up from columns below). The inscription on his father Giovanni's sarcophagus, commissioned by Cosimo, refers in Petrarchan terms to "Death conquering all," but the message of the roundel suggests rather the later triumphs of fame, time, and eternity.[33] Importantly, unlike later Bentivoglio chapel decoration, the message was non-iconographic and inextricable from its material embodiment. The language of colored marble, hard stones, and other durable materials such as bronze was markedly *all'antica* and sacralizing. It was also Florentine, recalling the materials of the supposedly Roman baptistery with its great doors and accretion of venerable monuments. The material choices at the heart of the old sacristy took on a dynastic character when they set the terms not only for Cosimo's tomb slab, but the exceptionally rich double-sided casket of his sons Piero and Giovanni under its triumphal arch.

Lorenzo de' Medici inherited a cumulative and invented tradition of permanence and Piero di Cosimo had his eyes set on greater things to come when he chose no less a theme than the triumph of fame for his eldest child's exceptional birth tray (Fig. 8). Raised upon a *palla* (ball) encircled by hailing knights, fame holds the center and the whole is framed by the Medici feathers (joined by three golden feathers) so that Lorenzo's potential for future greatness is proclaimed without any direct allusion to his birth. On the reverse, the device of the diamond ring and feathers with the motto *semper* dwarfs the Medici and Tornabuoni (Lorenzo's mother was Lucrezia Tornabuoni) family arms. The imagery and emblem taken together point to a dynastic formulation of ruling class prerogative that is, as in Petrarch's *Triumphs*, both Roman and chivalric. Moreover, beneath fame, the viewer's perspective opens to a wide panorama of land and sea that suggests an international scope. This trumpet blast on the theme of family ambition is effectively a gift to the infant Lorenzo rather than to his mother and shows the unrivaled adaptability of the tondo form and its claims on fame, time, and eternity in a Medici context.

After Lorenzo's death, the 1492 palace inventory refers to the birth tray as installed in the *camera* (chamber) decorated for his parents, alongside a pair of chests displaying Petrarch's *Triumphs* and a matching back board painted with gold falcons and coats of arms on a blue ground.[34] The falcon impresa is likely to be Piero's, though it was briefly borrowed by the young Lorenzo on the occasion of the 1459 *armeggeria* (mock combat) for Galeazzo Maria Sforza.[35] This adoption

32 Beyer 1993; McKillop 1992a, 289–291. For the temporality of hard stone pavements and the later tomb of Cosimo de' Medici, see Nagel and Wood 2010, 187–188.
33 For the inscription and its implications, see Kent 2000, 141, 190.
34 Spallanzani and Bertelà 1992, 26–27 (fol. 14 in the inventory).
35 See, for example, Ames-Lewis 1979, 135; Ricciardi 1992, 153.

8.

Giovanni di ser Giovanni Guidi
(called Lo Scheggia), childbirth
tray showing the *Triumph of Fame*,
ca. 1449, tempera, silver, and
gold on panel, 92.7 cm diameter.
The Metropolitan Museum
of Art, New York. (Photo:
Purchase in memory of Sir John
Pope-Hennessy: Rogers Fund,
The Annenberg Foundation,
Drue Heinz Foundation,
Annette de la Renta, Mr. and
Mrs. Frank E. Richardson, and
The Vincent Astor Foundation
Gifts, Wrightsman and Gwynne
Andrews Funds, special funds, and
Gift of the children of Mrs Harry
Payne Whitney, Gift of Mr. and
Mrs. Joshua Logan, and other gifts
and bequests, by exchange, 1995.)

was dynastically significant and has a later parallel in the way Annibale Bentivoglio was launched, so to speak, at the time of his marriage with the device of the falcon issuing from the nest and the none-too-subtle motto *nunc mihi* (now to me).[36] It seems telling for Lorenzo's external reputation that, by the time of this Bentivoglio-Este wedding in 1487, the emblematic sugar sculpture chosen as appropriate to him by his Bolognese hosts was a castle with a peacock on top, signifying, presumably, lordship in eternity.[37] Abroad, Lorenzo was an established signore.

The ring, falcon, and peacock belong to the imagery of nobility and chivalry and their precise origins in Medici family usage cannot be pinpointed.[38] Lorenzo's personal device of the reflowering laurel branch or *broncone* (see Fig. 5) seems, on the other hand, to have been introduced with a strong sense of its appropriateness to the moment at the 1469 joust preceding his own marriage, where it appeared on his standard.[39] Lorenzo's friend Luigi Pulci had already used the image for him

36 Bacci 1969, 81.
37 Ibid. Annibale Bentivoglio received a falcon, Federico da Montefeltro a fortress, and the marquis of Mantua a triumphal car. Given the problems of overlap and potential for diplomatic offense (the power of the emblem is relative and can be compromised by an unhappy juxtaposition), this must have been a delicate task.
38 See Ames-Lewis 1979, 132–134, for the peacock as symbol of incorruptibility but also magnificence. The latter sense apparently dominated in Medici manuscripts, associated with Giovanni di Cosimo, in which the peacock is accompanied by the motto *regarde moi* (behold me).
39 See, for example, Ricciardi 1992, 166–174.

in a pun-ridden prologue written after the death of Cosimo de' Medici, proclaiming Lorenzo *torni buona l'ombra ov'io mi fido ... Diamante sempre in mezzo a Palla e 'l Sole'* ("should make good again the shade in which I trust ... Diamond always between Pallas [*palle*] and the sun [or Apollo])." Not only was the diamond patron always reliable, but Lorenzo's laurel, a symbol of fame, would prove to be the *Florida fronda a far fiorir Fiorenzia* ("florid frond to make Florence flourish").[40] The tree lending its *ombra* (shade) used as a metaphor of patronage appears in Petrarch's Laura eclogues, which themselves imitate Virgil's. Thus, even as a Petrarchan device associated with love and fame, the rejuvenated, but in any case evergreen, laurel on Lorenzo's standard was as unequivocally political as the diamond ring. Equally, the golden age motto *le tems revient* accompanying it declared the heir apparent as a gilded youth whose fame, wisdom, and Apolline abilities would usher in a Medicean and Florentine spring that was endlessly renewable. Francesco Bausi has convincingly argued that Jacopo Bracciolini must have already dedicated his commentary on Petrarch's *Triumph of Fame* to Lorenzo in 1469–70 at the time of his succession, since it extols by turns both the ideology of republican equality of citizens and the value of a "civic prince" whose authority could ensure republican institutions.[41] Such a tension and a message are symptomatic of this precarious moment of transition in Florentine government.

Lorenzo's status at the time of his joust meant that the event invited coding in both universal and civic terms according to the example set by his "cosmic" grandfather and "Petrine" father. But in terms of poetic elegance, range of classical references, and personal appropriateness, the Laurentian laurel is easily the most eloquent of the Medici *imprese*. Offering the dynamism of a living form it did not, like other images of rejuvenation and purity such as the phoenix adopted by Francesco Sforza or the various fiery and watery devices preferred by the Este, have any association with preliminary destruction or the risk of inundation.[42] Continuity was an essential message and it was precisely the stability that the Medici regime seemed to offer the city that supposedly led Tommaso Soderini, republican kingmaker in 1469, to support Lorenzo's succession.[43] The evergreen but resprouting laurel is a dialectical image that preserves an interplay between the continuous and the new, just as the verdant laurel entered into a dialogue with the diamond, and the motto *le tems revient* both extended and modified the monolithic *semper*. It is only in the later acquisitions for Lorenzo's library that the princely habit

40 Pulci 1888, 170.

41 Bausi 1989, 73–103; for a defense of a later, mid-1470s dating, see Tateo 1999, 387 n. 38. For increasing critical attention to Petrarch's *Triumphs* in the second half of the fifteenth century, see Alessio 1990 (with earlier bibliography).

42 For Este imprese, see especially Toniolo 1997; Spaggiari and Trenti 1985, 45–52.

43 Machiavelli 2010, 674–675 (*Istorie fiorentine*, 7.24.3–8), states that Tommaso Soderini advised that the oligarchy should support the Medici in the interests of internal and external stability simply because the family had the advantage of established power and this left Lorenzo and Giuliano "come principi dello stato onorati." (Ibid., 675 [7.24.8])

of multiplying both the number and complexity of devices is embraced and three or four different emblems, with or without mottoes, might appear on the same manuscript page. New images that flirt with risk and fragility—butterflies round the flame, the parrot with *ne le set qui ne lessaie* ("he who has no experience cannot know" [Chrétien de Troyes, *Cligés*, v. 3048])—are more reminiscent of those of Lorenzo's princely allies.

All the Medici imagery that I have discussed, and the heraldic *palle* (balls) themselves, obey principles of symmetry and circularity and this is, I would argue, significant for the visual appearance of mottoes too. The shortened version of the French *le temps revient* dropping the *p* allows the letters to divide neatly between two sets of six to either side of the all-important *r* beginning *revient*. In light of this pattern, we might revisit Lorenzo's extraordinarily risky and self-assertive practice of inscribing the Latin form of his name LAV•R•MED on gems and hard stones that could have broken in the process of inscription.[44] This exercised a temporal transformation both upon Lorenzo's identity and on that of the work, permanently attaching the gem to him but also projecting that possessive identity into the past as well as the future of the object as "a future memorial for posterity of his royal splendor," as Bernardo Rucellai put it.[45] Ruth Rubinstein was right to see a love of symmetry in the isolation of the R between two stops, but the cutting into the name Laurentius surprises the attention and encourages the reader's search for meaning: it is precisely here, indeed, that the enunciation of a veiled princely ambition has been found by a number of scholars who have read the *R* as *Rex* for "King of the Medici" (king of his own family?) or, alternatively, "King of antiquity."[46]

There is no doubt that Lorenzo's avid acquisition of illuminated books and antiquities, and the collections themselves, were viewed by his contemporaries as regal.[47] An object such as the great sardonyx ewer, ringed by the massive letters LAV•R•MED and crowned with a diamond ring, itself containing a sphere covered with Medici *palle*, suggests that Lorenzo actively projected this princely aura through possession of works embodying exceptional taste, *virtù*, and magnificence, as well as durability. Another possibility opened up by the encircling letters on his hard stones and the isolated R is a reference, for cognoscenti, to the motto of golden age renewal or return. Arguably, LAV•R•MED anticipates the later motto,

---

44 Butters 1996, 142, suggests the possible responsibility of the gem carver Giovanni delle Corniole.

45 "futurum ad posteros regii splendoris monumentum": Fusco and Corti 2006, 1512, Doc. 247 (after 1495).

46 R. Rubinstein 1972. Fusco and Corti 2006, 150–155, summarize the various arguments and propose a reading that convincingly allows for both regal and republican possibilities. I am especially grateful to Caroline Elam, Alison Brown, and Angela Dillon Busi for references and suggestions with regard to this inscription. I have avoided proposing a specific Latin expansion for the R since I would argue it remains part of Lorenzo's name and, like Laurie Fusco and Gino Corti, consider that its further implication is deliberately elusive.

47 For the library as regal, see Lenzuni 1992, 16.

first appearing in a Laurentian copy of Lucan's *Pharsalia* (1485), of GLOVIS, which reads as SI VOLG[E] (one turns or it is turned) when revolved.[48] The broken R in the margin of this same manuscript is a cryptic device associated here, and elsewhere, with Lorenzo's eldest son Piero. When twinned with Piero's lute-with-the-broken-string device, the word/image suggests rupture or discord, a break that plays against the longer familial claim for continuity and return. What is distinctive in Lorenzo's own inscription is that it occurs only once in a surviving manuscript, but was otherwise exclusively carved into hard stones.[49] Here again, the medium is the message: the object's ancient substance is inscribed forever as Laurentian and, in the case of the vases, the sign of ownership appears to repeat endlessly when the work is revolved.

A number of recent art history textbooks have decided that Medici dominance in fifteenth-century Florence was that of a court in all but name.[50] Though the Medici may have benefited from, even encouraged, such an assumption about their status on the part of contemporary powers, their precise lack of a formal court and of legal title remain important distinctions. Few would deny that self-identification with the stability of the republic was a central pillar of Medici presentation and a legitimizing strategy that is distinctive in its application to devices and personal imagery. Motifs and mottoes of permanent rule and return have a paradoxical, indeed undermining, relation to the protection of actual republican values and it is also true that the family's commissions become increasingly princely from mid-century. But did Lorenzo himself ever aspire to be more than *civilis princeps*? It is arguable that he might have seen the disadvantages of doing so when existing communal institutions, robbed of any pretense to broader social participation by constitutional change and patronage, could be made to serve his family's own interests.[51] The language of mottoes and materials, being allusive rather than concrete, do not voice Lorenzo's precise ends and this was surely advantageous. There is an implication of the regal in LAV•R•MED, but to see *Rex* you need to be looking for it—as some of Lorenzo's supporters and his critics might well have done. To find in Lorenzo's carved name the laurel, reflowering from a Medici stem, is to see a play of allusions that underpinned more generally the cultural politics of the late fifteenth-century Medici. Inscribed here are Medici dynastic inheritance, Lorenzo's personal reputation, poetic myth, fame like that of the ancients', and the assertion of an authority not boundless, but endless.

---

48 BML, MS Plut. 35.2, fol. 1r; Cox-Rearick 1984, 29 and n. 55, in which she reads GLOVIS as "a cryptic version of Lorenzo's LE TEMPS REVIENT"; Lenzuni 1992, 138.

49 Truncated as LAV•R•ME (depicted as carved on a plinth for the Medici arms in BML, MS Plut. 16.1, fol. 1): see Lenzuni 1992, 137, illustrated at 136.

50 See e.g. Mateer 2000; and most recently Folin 2010.

51 In this volume, Melissa Bullard argues for the advantage Lorenzo could gain from denying, when it suited him, any special authority in Florence; Jane Black, on the other hand, highlights the strength afforded to the Medici in Florence, despite their lack of a legal title.

TWENTY

The Politics of Castellation

AMANDA LILLIE

THE TERM *casa da signore*, THE PHRASE MOST commonly used to refer
to a landowner's country house in the fifteenth-century Florentine *contado*,
encodes social distinction and hierarchy, separating the owner's abode from
those of the *lavoratori*, his farmworkers.[1] The phrase seems to imply that every
rural estate is a little fiefdom with a signore overseeing his microstate from the
power base of his own house. It is also possible to interpret the fifteenth-century
casa da signore in a less authoritarian light, to see it as the creation of a society in
which signori were allowed to proliferate and in which every landowner, whether
a successful artisan with a house attached to a small farm, or a magnate with a big,
inherited portfolio of estates, could inhabit the same category of house.[2] It might
seem as though, throughout the fourteenth and fifteenth centuries, the power
of the signore was shifting down the ranks and spreading through the countryside. This chapter, however, focuses on one end of the *casa da signore* spectrum—

1   I am extremely grateful to Anna Baj-Macario and Alberto Peroni for generously allowing me to
    see the Pazzi castle of Trebbio and for sharing their knowledge of the house and its history. Brenda
    Preyer, Daniela Lamberini, Mauro Mussolin, and Leonardo Dati offered valuable suggestions and
    resolved many thorny problems on-site. New plans and elevations have been supervised by Pietro
    Ruschi and were carried out by Eleonora Barsanti, Alberto Bartalucci, and Jacopo Simonetti.
    Thanks to their revelatory new survey, it is now possible to study the house in a more precise and
    rigorous way.
2   For a range of *case da signore* from modest to grand examples, including *case da lavoratori* con-
    verted into *case da signore* and vice versa, see Lillie 2005, 2–3, 24–29, 58–63, 80–87, 96–100, 105–132,
    151–154, 170–179, 220–239.

1.

Tower, Palazzo della
Signoria, Florence.
(Photo: Amanda Lillie.)

the end representing wealth, dynastic longevity, and political clout—and on the most widespread form of grand country house, the castellated *palagio*, which was indeed a proud, dominating, effectively defensible type of building that bore those unmistakable signs of signorial presence: towers, machicolated galleries, and crenellations.

Fifteenth-century Florence provides an intriguing case study of a republic's attitude toward a type of architecture deeply associated with the concepts of nobility nurtured by kingdoms, principalities, dukedoms, and courts. If a castle or fortified residence is an unmistakable sign of nobility, what happens when that society has attempted to dismantle its aristocracy, as Florence did when it created its popular governments and disempowered its magnates during the late thirteenth

2.

Tower, from the
entrance courtyard,
Acciaiuoli villa of
Montegufoni. (Photo:
Amanda Lillie.)

and fourteenth centuries?[3] A glance at the Palazzo della Signoria, the Florentine government's own iconic castellated *palagio*, may be a helpful first step in this inquiry. Although architectural historians have emphasized the ways in which Cosimo "il vecchio" de' Medici's new urban palace on the via Larga seemed to echo the Florentine seat of government—particularly its rustication[4]—far more obvious formal comparisons can be made between castellated *palagi* in the countryside and the Palagio della Signoria in town (Figs. 1 and 2). Indeed, castle owners most probably viewed the Florentine Palagio della Signoria, and Tuscan town halls and

3   Lansing 1991; Klapisch-Zuber 2009, 17–31.
4   Preyer 1990, 61–62; Bruschi 1998, 106.

seats of government (*palazzi communali* or *palazzi del podestà*) more generally, as prototypes and sought to imitate their towers, machicolated galleries, and crenellations on their country estates as signs of control or governance.[5] It could be further argued that private owners of fortified villas were mimicking communal buildings in order to align themselves politically with the popular government, or with the urban power base that held jurisdiction over the countryside.

Other motives underlay the continued favor accorded to castellated country houses. Since the construction of high towers was banned by statute in the city, it is likely that castle owners relished the freedom to build towers and crenellations in the country while they were forbidden to do so in town.[6] What was viewed as architectural *superbia* (pride), to be denigrated and suppressed within the city walls, became permissible as a defensive measure in the unwalled, vulnerable countryside. Above all, these features were part of a pan-European language of castellation that predated the palace of the Florentine commune, an idiom that was established not only in other government palaces and fortified town walls across Tuscany and Italy, but in private dwellings all over the Florentine *contado* by the late thirteenth and early fourteenth centuries.[7]

Trebbio, Cafaggiolo, and Careggi, the country houses inhabited for most of the fifteenth century by four generations of the main branch of the Medici, conform to this pattern and were all castellated (Figs. 3–5).[8] Even after Giovanni di Cosimo had built an unfortified house at Fiesole in the 1450s, this was a smaller, supplementary villa that was rarely, if ever, used for long stays by the Medici *brigata* (group of friends). When Lorenzo de' Medici bought the villa of Ambra at Poggio a Caiano in 1474, it was probably still a castellated house, and building the new villa (at least above ground level) seems to have started only in 1490—a house which Lorenzo never actually inhabited.[9] Why, then, did the Medici and other members of the Florentine ruling class, many of whom were building palaces in an *all'antica* mode in town, choose to retain, repair, and radically rebuild castellated villas in the countryside?

The fortified country palace stands at a nodal point in architectural historiography. It illuminates the flaws in the progressive model that constructs a

5 The tower imitating the Palazzo della Signoria in the Acciaiuoli's fortified enclosure at Montegufoni was probably built in 1386–89: Pestelli 2002, 34.
6 Caggese 1999, bk. 4, chap. 41, 305; *Statuta populi et communis Florentiae* 1779–83, 1:306–307, rub. 92–94. On the wide diffusion and continued favor accorded to fortified villas, see Burns 2012, 18–19, 29–33; on motives for retaining towers and castellation, see Lillie 1995, 199–200; 2000, 196–197.
7 Francovich 1976; Stopani 1977, 42–43; Pirillo 2007, 241–242, suggests that the influence could flow in the other direction and that communal palaces might have imitated private castles.
8 On the Medici villas, see Gori-Sassoli 1975; Ackerman 1990, 63–73; on Trebbio, see Carunchio 1998; Budini Gattai, Carrara Screti, and Agostini 2011; on Cafaggiolo, see Tiraboschi 1992; and on Careggi, see Zangheri 2006.
9 F. W. Kent 1979; 2004b, 135–145, 142–143; for archival evidence that Ambra at Poggio a Caiano was fortified, see ASF, Otto 10, fol. 53r, discussed below, 319 ff.

3.
Tower, Medici villa of
Trebbio, Mugello.
(Photo: Amanda Lillie.)

4.
Entrance facade, Medici
villa of Cafaggiolo, Mugello.
(Photo: Amanda Lillie.)

5.
East facade, Medici
villa of Careggi.
(Photo: Amanda Lillie.)

simple, linear chronology of architectural development. According to this model, the castle was a military, Gothic, and medieval form that was replaced by the civil architecture of the classical villa when the Renaissance arrived.[10] The castellated villa, however, fuses these artificially separated functions and perceptions. It is at the same time martial and defensive, but also civil and domestic. It is crucial to remember that these were dwellings, and that a strict functional divide between security and pleasure probably never existed. Furthermore, when it comes to their architectural form, apparently Gothic and classicizing features often coexisted within the same building and were even constructed simultaneously (Fig. 6). While their asymmetry, vertical emphasis, towers, machicolations, and crenellations may seem to align them with the Gothic, at the same time many fifteenth-century Florentine examples incorporated courtyards with loggias supported by columns and capitals, and grand interiors with lunette vaults and impost capitals like those to be found in contemporary urban palaces. Above all, the teleological model of stylistic development flies in the face of the archival and architectural evidence, which shows that castellated villas remained the most widespread grand type of country house, certainly until the 1460s and probably until the 1480s; and then they did not fall into disfavor, but were reinterpreted and remodeled, as important later examples such as the Medici villa of Petraia, the Villa Salviati at Ponte alla Badia, and the Ginori villa of Baroncoli all proclaim (Fig. 7).[11] The hybrid forms of fortified villas should not be interpreted as stylistic vacillation in a time of transition between the Middle Ages and the Renaissance, but as a confident and tangible declaration of a clear preference for what we might call a continuing process of modernizing castellation.

Although architectural historians have tended to perceive the survival and revival of castellated architecture as anticlassical, the fruit of an alternative, courtly, and chivalric tradition, more evidence is needed to show that it was perceived in this way in the fifteenth century.[12] The known existence of ancient Roman castles and ancient texts describing them means that castles per se need not have been perceived as anticlassical. On the contrary, as readers of Roman military treatises such as Vegetius's *Epitoma rei militaris* or Frontinus's *Strategemata*, castle builders and

10 Lamberini 1987, 1:132, charts a clear chronological and formal progression as fortified castles are replaced by unfortified villas in the fifteenth and sixteenth centuries; but see also her interpretation of the Baroncoli tower as a revival or "refined reinterpretation, in a sixteenth-century manner, of a glorious medieval tradition" of castellation: ibid., 1:261.

11 Pirillo 2007; on Petraia, see Chiostri 1972; the rebuilding of the Villa Salviati has been attributed to Giuliano da Sangallo: Ginori-Lisci 1950; and Baroncoli to Baccio d'Agnolo: Lamberini 1987, 1:259–265.

12 Ackerman 1990, 63–72, sees castles and villas as opposing architectural types in terms of both form and function: the fortified aspects of castles are "straightforward medieval elements" that served as "symbols of power and prestige." However, he describes the Medici's castellated houses of Trebbio, Cafaggiolo, and Careggi as villas and in order to explain their fortified character he tellingly suggests that "perhaps a little of the signori psychology affected the grand families of republican Florence when they left the dust of the city behind them": ibid., 65.

6.

Antonio Vannucci and Pietro Giovanni Fabbroni, Nerli villa of Soffiano, now known as Torre Galli, Scandicci, in a *cabreo* made for Angelo Galli Tassi, 1753, ASF Galli Tassi, 45, 3, Libro di piante no. 3. (Photo: Paolo Mariani "Fotomariani" for Archivio di Stato, Florence.)

7.

Villa Salviati, Ponte alla Badia. (Photo: Amanda Lillie.)

castle owners might have seen themselves as maintaining or reviving an ancient architectural type.

A key motive for the retention of fortification was undoubtedly the continued need (or perception of a need) for buildings in open countryside to be well defended. Ditches, towers, machicolated galleries, and crenellations were practical security measures, but the psychological effect created by the mere existence of a fortress was also emphasized in chronicles and treatises. Dino Compagni's *Cronica* (ca. 1310–13) articulates how the idea of a castle inspires fear: "when a fortress or castle is being built there are many who fear it for various reasons, and yet once it is built and finished their minds are reassured and they do not fear it at all."[13] Here, the act of building a castle is sufficient to arouse emotion in the local inhabitants. The castle in the mind is more powerful than the real thing.

Modern scholars have often cited Leon Battista Alberti's negative attitude toward castellation in private houses, appearing to encapsulate the modern or Renaissance approach. This is voiced in just two passages in *De re aedificatoria*. In book 8, Alberti notes, "Watchtowers provide an excellent ornament.... Yet I cannot recommend the mania prevalent two hundred years ago for building towers even in the smallest towns. It seemed that no head of a family could be without a tower; as a result forests of towers sprouted up everywhere."[14] More crucially, in book 9, Alberti writes, "I do not approve of turrets and crenellations on the houses of private citizens; such elements are foreign to peaceful citizens and the well-ordered state: they belong rather to the tyrant, in that they imply the presence of fear or of malicious intent."[15] This sentence presents castellation in domestic architecture as a belligerent, anti-civic way of building associated with despots, both deriving from and instilling fear. Turrets and crenellations exert a malign force.

It is clear, however, that, when the full text of Alberti's *De re aedificatoria* is considered, a holistic strategy is formulated with regard to defense and that his ideal of a peace-loving, benign civic architecture depends on an extensive network of cunningly designed, strongly built fortifications for the whole city and outlying towns. Although in book 5 Alberti makes important distinctions between the architectural choices of a king and a despot, in the end he brings them into close relation, stating that the king's palace must be linked to a fortress.[16] This is a crucial passage that demonstrates that the *arx* (fortress) remains a necessity, not only for tyrants, but for all rulers. The distinction is a question of residence: the civil, unfortified style is the one that the benign ruler should adopt for his own habitation, but he will still need to live next door to a fortress for protection.

In his treatment of defensive structures, Alberti's notion of the rhetorical power and active force exerted by buildings is at its most eloquent. Citadels not only "withstand assaults," but they "drive back attackers"; they should be "threatening, rugged, rocky, stubborn, and invincible."[17] The buildings are personified, taking on the character of an aggressor. Likewise in book 7, chapter 2, he recommends using "huge, irregular blocks of stone.... This is how I would build the city walls, that the enemy might be terrified by their appearance and retreat, his confidence

13   Compagni 2000, 108 (bk. 3, chap. 15): "Perché le cose si temono più da lunge che da presso, e pensa l'uomo molte cose sì come quando una forteza o uno castello si fa, molti sono che per diversi pensieri la temono."

14   Alberti 1966, vol. 2, bk. 8, chap. 5, 698–699; English translation in Alberti 1988, 257.

15   Alberti 1966, vol. 2, bk. 9, chap. 4, 808–809; English translation in Alberti 1988, 301.

16   Alberti 1966, vol. 1, bk. 5, chap. 1, 332–337; English translation in Alberti 1988, 117–118, 121–122.

17   Alberti 1966, vol. 1, bk. 5, chap. 3–4, 348–351; English translation in Alberti 1988, 122–123.

destroyed.... A projecting row of large stones ... without revetment ... preserving a rough, austere, and almost menacing appearance."[18] In what amounts to a theory of psychological warfare in which the weapon is architecture, Alberti emphasizes not so much the strength of this type of construction but the emotive impact of enormous, irregular blocks of stone. It is the appearance of the building, its "rugged air of antique severity," that will instill fear in the enemy. Thus, the fear-inducing effect, which was presented in a negative light in book 5 and deemed indecorous for the peace-loving king's residence, finds its rightful place in city walls.

Rather than interpreting Alberti's recommendations for domestic architecture as evidence that fortified houses were out of favor at the time, or even that they were being rejected by the cultural elite, it is more likely that the anxiety about security that seeps through *De re aedificatoria* was part of a widespread sense of vulnerability to attack in fifteenth-century society. The landowner with a castellated *palagio* in open countryside may be viewed as a small-scale ruler who needed his castle to protect his family and his estate, much as the commune or Alberti's king needed their *arx* and town walls.

An important document in the *otto di guardia e balìa* files in the Florentine Archivio di Stato, previously discussed by Paolo Pirillo, sheds light on fortified villas in 1409 and 1410—what we might describe as a pre-Medicean phase—and helps to establish how these buildings were regarded at this time of military threat during the war against King Ladislas of Naples (1409–14).[19] Volume 10 lists 117 owners or guardians of castellated *palagi* and fortresses in the countryside who were required to swear on oath that they would hold, guard, and save (*tenere, custodire et salvare*) their buildings for the defense of the commune.[20] Although the verbs *tenere, custodire*, and *salvare*, repeated in the formula for each fortified house, are military terms, they are surprisingly passive, since the commune could have demanded construction, repair, or reinforcement of buildings, or the addition of defensive structures such as earthworks or barbicans. The assumption was that, since castellated features already existed and the fortresses were in place, all that was required was to service them with no extra costs incurred.

The terms used to refer to these buildings are helpful in establishing the range of privately owned building types used to defend the approaches to Florence. By far the most common term is *fortilitia*, with 103 of 117 buildings being listed as such. Sixteen were also named as towers (*torre, torraccio, turris, turrini, turricella*), including one campanile. Nine of the 117 fortified houses are referred to as *palagio* or *palatium*, although these were almost certainly also castellated buildings; this confirms

18 Alberti 1966, vol. 2, bk. 7, chap. 2, 538–539; English translation in Alberti 1988, 192.
19 ASF, Otto 10 (1408–9); Pirillo 2001, 166–171. I am most grateful to Brenda Preyer, who first drew my attention to this document and to the research of Paolo Pirillo, whose fully annotated edition of these documents will soon be published. On the magistracy of the *otto di guardia*, see Antonelli 1953; Becker 1968, 221.
20 Pirillo 2007, 250–251.

that the word *palagio* was fully compatible, and probably closely associated with, the castle form, so that our modern notion of the palace as an unfortified architectural type did not pertain in the first decades of the fifteenth century.[21] Nor were the *palagi* in the *otto di guardia* document those we might expect to be described as grand residences. For example, the two Medici sites of Cafaggiolo and Trebbio, along with Ambra at Poggio a Caiano, are included in the list, but none of the three are referred to as *palagi*: they are all straightforwardly listed as *fortilitia*.[22]

The *otto di guardia* document conveys some sense of the sheer number of fortified houses spread through the Florentine countryside, for these 117 included only buildings on key routes and in border territories required for a particular military emergency in 1409 (namely, the war with King Ladislas).[23] Other castles, such as the Pazzi villa of Trebbio in a side valley above Pontassieve or the Nerli villa at Scandicci, were not regarded as strategically crucial in 1409 and were not included. We could extrapolate a much larger number—perhaps two, or even three times 117—to arrive at an extremely approximate total estimate of privately owned castles or fortified palaces surviving in the fifteenth-century Florentine *contado*.[24]

The evidence from *otto di guardia* volume 10 confirms that, in the first decade or so of the fifteenth century, these houses were regarded as key players in the defense strategy of the state and as working military structures. This was not play, or false, or purely decorative fortification. Nor is it likely that there would be a sudden switch from working castles, as we might describe them, to pretend castles, as if what was militarily effective in 1409 would suddenly become redundant in, say, 1450. As is evident from the texts of Dino Compagni and Alberti, architectural puissance was, in any case, a matter of potential, or what would now be described as the deterrent principle of visual impact and emotional effect, as much as martial operability.

To convey some sense of how fortified villas might have been regarded later in the fifteenth century, a glance at two contrasting examples shows how flexible

---

21   ASF, Otto 10: the nine fortresses also referred to as palaces are (fol. 48v) a Spinelli *palagio* at Fiesole; (fol. 62r) the Lippi's "il Palagio" near the Badia Fiesolana; (fol. 49r) the Bardi *palatium seu fortilitium* known as Monte di messer Cipriano; (fol. 51v) the Pulci *palatio* in the Mugello; (fol. 61v) the *palagio* of the Tedaldi at Sant'Andrea a Rovezzano; (fol. 63r) the Albergotti's two *palazzi* at Pieve a Quarto near Arezzo and Vitiano; (fol. 70v) a *palatio* at Panzano owned by Antonio di ser Luca da Panzano; and (fol. 82v) the Landini property of Monte Sano in Chianti also known as "il palagio di messer Niccolò Squarcialupi." Of these nine, it is significant that eight (all except the Bardi house known as Il Monte di messer Cipriano) were called "Il Palagio" (*dicitur il palagio*), so that *palagio* was part of the place-name, rather than a reference to size or grandeur. Of these nine *palagi*, seven were also described in the document as *fortilitia*, and so were certainly castellated structures, just as we probably can assume the remaining two were.
22   ASF, Otto 10, fols. 53r, 61v, 62v; Ambra belonged to Domenico di Piero de' Cancellieri of Pistoia at this time.
23   Pirillo 2001, 115, 166.
24   Francovich 1976, 9, lists 235 fortified villages or small towns (*castelli*) in the dioceses of Florence and Fiesole before 1300. But, although some of these became single dwellings or compact clusters of buildings that formed one large residence such as Montegufoni, no census of castellated private dwellings has been made.

8.

Strozzi villa
of Santuccio,
in a prewar
photograph
(Photo courtesy
of Giuliana
Salvadori.)

responses to castellation could be in the 1480s. From 1483 to 1484, Filippo Strozzi restored a tower with a machicolated gallery and crenellation at his villa of Santuccio, while at the same time subverting any defensive validity by adding an open loggia and upper *verone* (balcony) to abut the tower (Fig. 8).[25] As a patron, Filippo Strozzi was capable of being bold and innovative, as his commissions for the Palazzo Strozzi and his burial chapel at Santa Maria Novella demonstrate. But in the case of his main country residence, he chose to preserve a fortified tower once inhabited by his uncle. Maintaining the tangible presence of the clan in a form that declared their strength and longevity was probably the prime motive; but this villa was situated on the via Pistoiese guarding the approach to a bridge over the river Bisenzio, and so a genuine defensive reason might have bolstered Filippo Strozzi's decision.[26] A different response was voiced in the same year (1483) when Lorenzo de' Medici visited the castellated palace of Pitiana, announcing his plan to carry out a civil remodeling of the villa and its surrounding lands (Fig. 9).[27] The phrase *riducto con diversi disegni alla civile* shows that Lorenzo saw a distinction between the martial and civil styles, that his preference was for the civil, and that a transformation from martial to civil style would be easily accomplished with the help of *disegni* (drawings). If the Vallombrosan monks had complied, Pitiana could have become another Poggio a Caiano or Agnano.

25 Lillie 2005, 94–97, 105–132, figs. 43, 68, 74, 79, 87, 90, 100.
26 Ibid., 45–46, 48–49, fig. 20.
27 Elam and Gombrich 1988; Kent 2004b, 117–118.

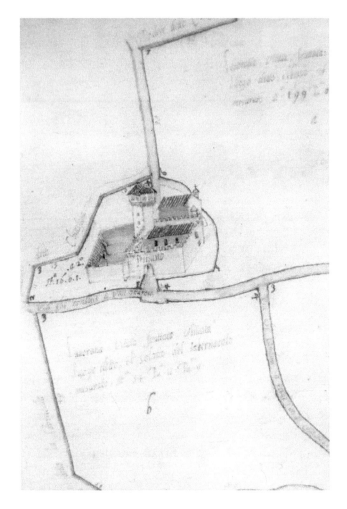

9.

Pitiana, detail
from ASF Comp.
Rel. Sop., 260, 136,
Piantario 1584–1586,
fols. 187v–188r.
(Photo: Amanda
Lillie.)

Does the *otto di guardia* list help us to understand whether castellation was perceived as signorial, as we would expect? Interestingly, there is a relatively weak correlation between magnate families and the castle owners in this list. Of those with surnames, sixty-six lineages are represented, of whom fourteen (21 percent) were magnates.[28] The Bardi, a powerful magnate family, do figure as the clan with the most fortified villas and they swore to defend ten in 1409. But mostly there is a mix of the old elite and powerful *popolani* families, with a cross section of the Florentine ruling class represented.[29] The Medici owned four of the *fortilitie* on the list (Montelezzanico, Ferriolo, Cafaggiolo, and Trebbio) and the Albergotti likewise had four, while the Castellani, Strozzi, Accaiuoli, and Bartoli—all of them *popolani* families—each had two castles (Fig. 10). One implication to be drawn

28   For lists of magnates, see Klapisch-Zuber 2009, 413–421; Lansing 1991, 239–242.
29   This tallies with Pirillo 2007, 242, 244, 247, citing Giovanni Villani on the integrated mix of *popolani* and *grandi* building country houses round Florence.

10.

Strozzi villa of
Loiano, Monte
Morello. (Photo:
Amanda Lillie.)

from this document is that the fortified *palagio* was indeed an elite building type, but one that could be said to link rather than separate magnates and *popolani*, or at least to render them architecturally indistinguishable.

Furthermore, since many of these castle owners were partly responsible for public defense, their fortified houses might have been associated with patriotic values and could even be perceived as architectural statements of loyalty to the commune. This is the opposite of how tower houses in the city had been perceived: as anti-civic, selfish, belligerent architectural forms designed to protect individual families or clans. In the case of their rural equivalent, the castellated form could celebrate and support the commune.

The Pazzi family's fortified *palagio* of Trebbio can serve as an illuminating comparison with the Medici villas, providing rich architectural evidence for castellation's long survival and especially how a key architectural patron such as Andrea di Guglielmino de' Pazzi (1372–1445)—best known for his commission of the Pazzi chapel at Santa Croce—approached the difficult task of reinventing an old castle (Fig. 11).[30] Unlike the Medici, who were *popolani*, the Pazzi were among the staunchest of Guelf magnates during the fourteenth century, identified as super-magnates by the rebel Ciompi government in 1378.[31] Yet in 1422 Andrea de' Pazzi petitioned the Florentine commune to relinquish his magnate status and become a *popolano*,

30   On the Pazzi, see Litta 1819–99, vol. 4, *Pazzi di Firenze*; Herzner 1976; Spallanzani 1987; Saalman 1993, 211–231, 441–449; Martines 2004, 62–82.
31   Brucker 1962, 34–35, 165, 185, 214–215, 235, 343, 370; Saalman 1993, 211–223.

11.

Pazzi villa of
Trebbio, Val di
Sieci, between
Pontassieve and
Santa Brigida.
(Photo: Amanda
Lillie.)

while managing to retain his family name and coat of arms.[32] Furthermore, for about fifty years, from the start of the 1420s until the 1470s, Medici-Pazzi relations were cordial and close. Andrea de' Pazzi was manager of Averardo de' Medici's Rome bank from 1421 to 1433; he was an *amico* and political supporter of the Medici, and was related to them by marriage.[33] When it came to choosing wives for his sons, Andrea ensured all three were married to Medici partisans. What light does the Pazzi's castellated villa shed on this interplay between the Medici and the Pazzi in the decades before the conspiracy of 1478?

The Pazzi villa of Trebbio is set on an outcrop of *alberese* (white Eocene marly limestone) overlooking the upper Val di Sieci, a fertile *altopiano* (plateau) into which streams flow from the ridge that separates the Arno valley from the Mugello, including the high hills of Monte Rotondo and the Giogo (Fig. 12).[34] Perhaps in the thirteenth century, when the first records for Trebbio appear, it was a strategic site,[35] but it was not among the 117 fortified palaces listed by the *otto* in 1409. A house existed on this site by 1311, when it was referred to as Lapo di Littifredo de' Pazzi's *palatium* (palace), inherited by his sons Bindo and Bartolomeo and shared with their mother monna Itta. It was clearly an important estate center at this date,

---

32 Saalman 1993, 220, 441–442, citing ASF, PR 112, fols. 37v–38v, 52.

33 De Roover 1963, 30, 38; Kent 1978, 60, 66 n. 14, 74 n. 14, 95 n. 57, 100 n. 75, 129, 285, 319; Andrea de' Pazzi married Caterina di Iacopo d'Alamanno Salviati, whose brother Alamanno Salviati married Caterina, daughter of Averardo de' Medici.

34 Carocci 1906, 1:30; Pucci 1939, 225–228; Righini 1956, 315–317; Amerighi 1977, 71; Acidini 2000, 158.

35 Lami 1758, 1:55–56, 67–69; Repetti 1833–46, 5:585, "Trebbio del Pontassieve"; Carocci 1880, 63–64; Pecchioni 1976, "Monte Rotondo e il Castello del Trebbio."

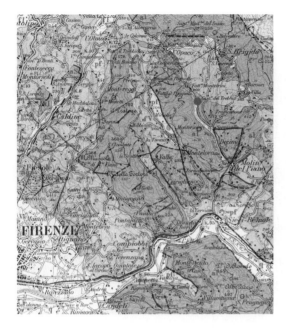

12.

Geological map of Florence (1:25,000), with Pazzi "Castello del Trebbio" northeast of the city, marked with a red dot. Areas of *alberese* limestone are shaded in khaki and labelled "al". (Photo reprinted from *Carta geologica d'Italia* [Florence: Servizio geologico d'Italia, 1962], fol. 106.)

encircled by about twenty farms.[36] Building on hard limestone had special advantages, both for structural reasons (to provide a strong, stable foundation) and, as Alberti emphasized, for defensive reasons, since enemies could not tunnel underneath or destabilize the fortress at its base.[37] The flattened bedrock was also exploited for agricultural purposes, creating a specially hard and durable threshing floor in the piazza between the signore's residence and the home farm of Croce di Via (Fig. 13). Above all, this outcrop of *alberese* provided superb building stone, which could also be ground and used for mortar.[38]

The need for building materials, their selection and manufacture are emphasized in the documents, helping to create some anchors in the fifteenth-century chronology of this complex building. In his 1427 tax return, Andrea de' Pazzi already declared his intention to build on the Trebbio site, claiming he needed a lime kiln at Trebbio "in order to carry out building works for himself."[39] That these building works referred specifically to the *casa da signore* was confirmed three years later when Andrea mentions the same kiln, described as adjacent to his residence at Trebbio, its purpose being to provide lime, bricks, and tiles to renovate his own

36 Nelli 1985, 31, 83, 85, 124.
37 Alberti 1966, vol. 1, bk. 5, chap. 1, 336–337; English translation in Alberti 1988, 123.
38 *Carta geologica d'Italia*, fol. 106, "Firenze," "Alberese," II^a edizione, 1962, 1:25,000; Rodolico 1995, 235–237, 244.
39 ASF, Catasto 80 (*campione*), parte 2, fol. 589r–v (1427): "perché la vuole per chuociere per murare per se." See also Andrea de Pazzi's *portata* of the same year: ASF, Catasto 57, fol. 684r. The *portate* were the personal returns filed by individuals, while the *campioni* were the summaries made by the *catasto* officials.

13.

Threshing floor or *aia* in front of the Croce di Via farmhouse, Pazzi villa of Trebbio. (Photo: Amanda Lillie.)

house (Fig. 14).[40] The use of the present tense (*adopero*) confirms that construction was underway in 1430. At the same time, in 1429 and 1430, Andrea was improving and extending his property holdings around Trebbio, building a new house for his *fattore* (farm manager), a further farmhouse and oil press, and buying nine farms and another *casa da signore*, as well as two mills on the river Sieci.

The 1442 tax return sheds further light on the Trebbio estate in the years between 1433 and 1442, showing how Andrea continued to invest in the area, acquiring six additional farms with their farmhouses and two further landowners' houses.[41] There are signs that major building was still continuing on the main house at Trebbio. The garden and meadow garden had been destroyed by building

---

40 ASF, Catasto 385 (Prima Parte, A–G), fol. 13r (1430): "Anchora presso alla detta chasa d'abitare ò fatto fare una fornacie da ffare chalcina e lavorio la quale a[d]opero per achonciare detta chasa per me." See also ASF, Catasto 478, fol. 86v (1433): "Una fornacie da fare chalcina posta in detto popolo e luogho chon suoi chonfini la quale dicie che è per adopera' per achoncimi della chasa sua di villa e non per altro."

41 ASF, Catasto 626, fols. 190r–191r (1442) (alternative foliation: 245r–246r).

14.

West facade,
Pazzi villa of
Trebbio. (Photo:
Amanda Lillie.)

work and needed to be recreated (*s'arragino fresche*), and, crucially, that year Andrea bought a large ruined residence (*abituro grande*) in a neighboring parish, which he declared was to be used as a supply of cut stone (*per llastra*), from which we can infer that building stone was still needed.[42] By 1446, the year after Andrea de' Pazzi's death, when a division was drawn up among his sons, Trebbio is referred to as *quod palatium pro maiori parte murari et seu edificari fecit dictus dominus Andreas* ("that palace, the greater part of which was ordered to be built or constructed by the said messer Andrea").[43]

The chronology for Trebbio's renovation—planned by 1427 and executed between ca. 1428 and ca. 1445—overlaps with the Pazzi chapel project at Santa Croce, which may have been planned as early as 1424, was allocated funds from 1427, and may have been partially built in the later 1420s, although its construction continued into the 1440s and its main cupola is inscribed with the date 1459.[44] Trebbio was assigned to Andrea's son Piero de' Pazzi in 1446 and, although its chapel entrance and interior were probably renovated by Piero (or by a later generation), no subsequent references have yet been found to major building works at the villa

42   ASF, Catasto 626, fols. 190v/245v (1442): "Uno abituro ghrande che si dicie a Chastello ch'è parte chaduto e rresto per chadere [...] chonperato questo anno [1442] da Matteo Ghuadagni per Fl. 350 di monte chomune che chostorono Fl. 56: in tutto e' rende pocho, ché si chonperò per llastra."

43   Saalman 1993, 443–445, provides a summary and partial transcription of the division between Antonio, Piero, and Jacopo de' Pazzi on 5 March 1446: ASF, NA 9273.

44   Laschi, Roselli, and Rossi 1962; Saalman 1993, 229, 232–233, 254; Bruschi 1998, 68 n. 55.

in the 1450s or 1460s, nor indeed during the rest of the fifteenth century.[45] After the Pazzi conspiracy of 1478, it either remained in the possession of the heirs of Piero's son Renato (hanged in 1478) or, most probably, was confiscated and reacquired, so that in 1498 Trebbio was still in Pazzi hands, while the town palaces had been burned or confiscated.[46]

Andrea de' Pazzi's investment in property over the whole district around Trebbio could be interpreted as a neo-feudal desire for control, which looks much like what the Medici were doing in the Mugello in the same period.[47] One reason for investment was agricultural profit. The yields of wheat in the Val di Sieci were huge, and there was the added advantage of combining arable crops not only with vineyards and olives, but also with herds of sheep, timber-producing woodland, and chestnuts on the mountain slopes. Yet Andrea's purchases do not seem to have been motivated purely by the desire for agricultural returns, as can be inferred from his acquisition of six grand old buildings round Trebbio, already partly ruined, including the *chasolare* at Torre a Decima,[48] the *abituro grande* bought for its building stone,[49] and a *casa da oste all'antica cattiva*, which Carlo de' Pazzi used to let for an annual rent of 11 florins (Fig. 15).[50] He or his son Piero also acquired the feudal rights (*feudatorio*) to the ruined tower on Monte Rotondo, together with the mountain itself, pasture, and woods, from the archbishop of Florence, to whom they paid a *feudo* of wheat every year (Fig. 16).[51] There is nothing like this series of castle acquisitions in the Medici's territorial expansion in the Mugello in the same period. For Andrea de' Pazzi, ruins appear to have been desirable assets, each of which he seems to have valued for a different reason. In the case of the *abituro grande . . . chonperò*

45 ASF, Catasto 682, fol. 913r (1446) (fol. 191r, pencil pagination at bottom right); ASF, Catasto 718, fol. 121r (1451) (no. 354, pencil pagination at bottom right); ASF, Catasto 829, parte 1, fols. 516r–517r (1457); ASF, Catasto 927, parte 2, fol. 504r (1469). Architectural features—including the chapel's exterior doorway and steps, its interior altar, its fresco attributed to Andrea del Castagno, the double-arched molding for the lavabo and staircase door in the east-facing *sala grande terrena* [large ground-floor saloon], and the doors with horizontal lintels and ovolo moldings opening onto the courtyard—were all probably part of a continuing process of modernization carried out by Piero de' Pazzi in the 1450s and 1460s.

46 ASF, Decima Repubblicana 31, fol. 600r (1498): "mona Francesca, donna fu di Renato de' Pazzi." On the confiscation of Pazzi property after the 1478 conspiracy, see Martines 2004, 199–213.

47 See Brucker 1962, 35, on the fourteenth-century Pazzi behaving like "feudal barons"; on Medici properties in the Mugello, see Franchetti Pardo and Casali 1978; Casali 1983; Diana 1983; Lillie 1993, 53–56.

48 ASF, Catasto 682, fols. 919r/197r (1446): "Uno chasolare tutto schoperto e lla magiore parte rovinato luogho detto la Torre a Decima [. . .] El quale chonprò messer Andrea, parte dalla famiglia de' Salteregli e parte d'Alamanno Salviati."

49 See note 42 above.

50 ASF, Catasto 626, fols. 190v/245v (1442), bought in December 1441.

51 ASF, Catasto 829, parte I, fol. 517r (1457): "Una torre schoperta che è a Monte Ritondo chon monte, pasture e boschi e uno boscho di chastagno, luogho detto Filichaie, posti a chonfini del Mugiello e di Val di Sieve, il quale è feudatorio dello arciveschovo di Firenze e da lui lo tengho in feudo." On ecclesiastical lordship in this area, see Davidsohn 1956–68, 5:351–353; Nelli 1985. The castle of Monte Rotondo had belonged to the Florentine bishops since 1227: see ibid., 7 n. 8, 22.

15.

Torre a Decima, near
Pontassieve. (Photo:
Eleanora Barsanti,
Alberto Bartalucci, and
Jacopo Simonetti.)

16.

Ruined tower, Monte
Rotondo. (Photo:
Amanda Lillie.)

per llastra, he further ruined the ruin and carried away its stone. The *casa da oste all'antica cattiva* was bought to retain an uninterrupted sweep of Pazzi property and perhaps for its *all'antica* qualities. The Torre a Decima *chasolare* and tower on Monte Rotondo, both linked to the history of the district, were venerable landmarks that were preserved by the Pazzi.

The authoritarian architecture of Trebbio and the retention of its exterior walls and castellated features seem consistent with Andrea's desire to take control of a whole mountain with its celebrated tower, to appropriate other historic castles in the district, and to step into the shoes of the Conti Guidi, the old feudal lords of the district.[52] This may seem surprising when we remember that Andrea de' Pazzi had petitioned to change his status from that of a magnate to a *popolano* in 1422, and it could be claimed that Trebbio visually contradicts Andrea's projection of himself as a newborn *popolano*.[53] But, as we have seen in the *otto di guardia* documents, private castellation and neo-feudal behavior could coexist with a *popolano* identity and support for government by the people. Indeed, Andrea de' Pazzi's Trebbio project, timed just as he was establishing his new political identity, provides crucial evidence for this interpretation. It also reveals a more complex behavior pattern, as Andrea was repudiating his magnate status in order to forge a more powerful social, political, and economic position in the city, at the same time as he revived his signorial identity in the countryside. This program of castle acquisition and rebuilding was arguably a compensatory act to ensure that his noble status and dynastic roots were strengthened in the Pazzi rural heartland at precisely the moment when they were under threat or diminished in Florence.

An examination of the building and comparison with the Medici villas of Cafaggiolo, Trebbio, and Careggi suggest that the Pazzi villa was a meticulously planned, wholesale renovation project that ingeniously managed to retain, extend, and regularize the existing external walls, which were then wrapped round a modernized interior. Today, the most obvious difference between the Pazzi villa of Trebbio and the Medici villas of Trebbio, Cafaggiolo, and Careggi is that the Pazzi house (unusually for a villa) is now unrendered, with its stone facades exposed to the weather, whereas the Medici villa facades have been plastered and replastered numerous times. Yet this may be a modern difference, since close inspection of the Pazzi *palagio* reveals the remains of intonaco on the north, east, and south facades, and a small section of plaster under the projecting eaves of the south front retains sgraffito decoration of fictive ashlar. It is not clear whether the entire outer walls of the villa were rendered, or whether the entrance (west and north) facades at ground-floor level were left unplastered to display their masonry, as was the case in many fifteenth-century Florentine palaces that had rustication at ground-floor

52 Fabbri 2005, 173–176.
53 Saalman 1993, 211–212, 220, 441–442, document 1. On complex responses to the loss of magnate status, see Klapisch-Zuber 2009, 251–254, 402.

17.

Alternating thin
and thick courses
of *alberese,* west
facade, Pazzi villa
of Trebbio. (Photo:
Amanda Lillie.)

level with intonaco above. Such a scheme would have revealed the regular alternating courses of thin and thick *alberese,* which is of higher quality on the lower levels of the main entrance facade (west) of the Pazzi Trebbio castle (Fig. 17). This type of facade design would not have been an option at the Medici castle of Trebbio, where the stone construction is a less refined combination of roughly hewn *pietra forte, alberese,* and rubble, visible in areas where the plaster has dropped off lower sections of the tower and the northwest facade.[54] The fine stonework at the Pazzi castle probably survives from the early fourteenth century since it closely resembles Carcherelli at Scandicci dated to the 1320s or 1330s,[55] although it was possibly part of Lapo de' Pazzi's *palatium* in 1311.[56] The same system of alternating bands of *alberese* continuing round the north facade is less regular and was possibly restored by Andrea de' Pazzi with stone from the nearby ruined castle, which he had bought as a sort of local *spolia, per lastra.* The prestigious qualities of the white stone are also emphasized by the highly distinctive alternating thin and thick bands, which closely resemble Vitruvius's description of *opus pseudisodomum,* with "rows of courses of different heights and lengths."[57]

54 Budini Gattai, Carrara Screti, and Agostini 2011, 8, 102.
55 Also known as Calcherelli and L'Acciaiolo. Lamberini 2002, 16: west curtain wall shown in figs. 23–24, 27, 53, 68. Dated before the death of the owner/builder Nardo di Bencivenni Rucellai in 1342.
56 Nelli 1985, 85.
57 Vitruvius 1511, bk. 2, 17, fig. b: "Pseudisodomum"; English translation in Vitruvius 2009, 51, 328 (fig. 4).

18.

Antiporta on west facade,
Pazzi villa of Trebbio.
(Photo: Amanda Lillie.)

The *antiporta* or projecting fortified gateway, providing a second layer of defense at the vulnerable entrance point, is one of the most significant security measures to survive and is a rare example of its type in rural domestic architecture, although Cafaggiolo sports a splendid towered example (Fig. 18).[58] The Pazzi bulwark is strikingly similar to the great *antiporte* added to the entrance facades of the Palazzo della Signoria in 1342 by Walter of Brienne, duke of Athens, during his short rule as signore of Florence.[59] In the fresco depicting his expulsion (Fig. 19), the *antiporte* feature as a demonstration of Walter's repression, just as the decision by the

58 *Antiporte* is Giovanni Villani's term for these fortified entrances: 1990–91, vol. 3, bk. 13, chap. 8, 309.
59 Rubinstein 1995, 15–16 n. 106; Ferrari 2013.

19.

Orcagna, attrib., detail of the Palazzo della Signoria with its *antiporte* in *The Expulsion of the Duke of Athens from Florence*, 1344–45, fresco, 257 × 290 cm. Palazzo Vecchio, Florence.

government of Florence to remove them after his departure was a significant political gesture, showing that the tyrant had left and that the Palazzo della Signoria and its government belonged once more to the people. That the Pazzi villa retained such a strong defensive measure—one clearly associated with despotism by the city of Florence—reveals much about this type of isolated country residence and particularly how the Pazzi viewed their position. A close examination of the juncture between the main facade and the *antiporta* shows that it was not built at the same time as the early fourteenth-century walls, but was perhaps added later in that century or the next, possibly at the same time as the north wing was constructed, with its great vaulted *sala*, chapel, and courtyard loggias, under the direction of Andrea de' Pazzi in the 1430s or early 1440s.

The Pazzi villa of Trebbio lacks a soaring tower of the type that dominated the Medici villas of Trebbio and Cafaggiolo villas, although the base of the northwest corner tower, which is clear in the plan with its thick walls, cross vault, and escarped buttress, suggests that it was an earlier structure, or at least part of the pre-fifteenth-century building (Fig. 20). Its outer walls, with their alternating courses of thin and thick *alberese* and semicylindrical string course, continue under the wall of the north wing, which they evidently predate (Fig. 21). In the machicolated gallery, the trilobe *pietra serena* brackets supporting pointed brick arches likely date from the second half of the fourteenth century, like their bilobed equivalents at the Medici Trebbio villa, dated between 1354–67 by Roberto Budini Gattai and Francesca Carrara Screti, although there remains the question of whether they are from the nineteenth century (Figs. 22 and 23).[60] There are, however, significant architectural differences in the details of the Pazzi machicolation, such as the projecting beveled blocks that rest on top of the brackets, forming an abacus to support the arches above, and the semicircular roll moldings of the string courses above and below that frame the sported out arcade, suggesting the presence of a more emphatic and carefully considered design. Like the Pazzi villa of Trebbio and the Palazzo della Signoria in Florence, the Medici villas of Trebbio and Cafaggiolo were provided with *cadutoie*, or murder holes, in their machicolated galleries, from which missiles could be hurled or boiling oil dropped on assailants.

Above all, the plan of the Pazzi castle is more regular and cohesive than those of the Medici villas of Trebbio, Cafaggiolo, or Careggi (Fig. 24). Its outer form is that of a great rectangular block, enclosing a courtyard that occupies about half the width of the main facade and is a regularly proportioned space. There are three key projecting features: the *antiporta*, the northwest corner tower, and the chapel in the northeast corner, but these are not so dominant in the plan as they are in elevation. In contrast, the Medici villa of Trebbio is a trapezoid structure enclosing a trapezoid courtyard (Fig. 25), while Cafaggiolo's outer walls are enlivened by larger projecting features enclosing three cramped courtyards (Fig. 26), and the regularity of Careggi's plan is compromised by the oblique slanting east front (Fig. 27).[61] The plan of the Pazzi villa revolves round the central courtyard, its U-shape enclosed on the west side by a double wall into which stairs were deftly inserted. The proportions of

60   Budini Gattai, Carrara Screti, and Agostini 2011, 54–56, 105, 107.

61   For an analysis of Careggi's plan, see Zangheri 2006, 10, 12, tav. 6; for Trebbio, see Budini Gattai, Carrara Screti, and Agostini 2011, 104–105; for Cafaggiolo, see Tiraboschi 1992, 101–108.

20.

North facade with northwest corner tower, Pazzi villa of Trebbio. (Photo: Amanda Lillie.)

21.

Base of northwest corner tower, Pazzi villa of Trebbio. (Photo: Amanda Lillie.)

the courtyard and the two great *sale* (dining halls) on the ground floor are striking and proclaim a radical, systematic planning campaign that must have been carried out for Andrea de' Pazzi between 1428 and 1445. To highlight briefly one or two salient features: the whole courtyard is divided into three almost equal parts, the dimensions of the two loggias and the open central space falling within a meter of the proportion of one to two, being about six meters wide and twelve meters long.[62]

62   For exact dimensions, see the plan by Eleonora Barsanti, Alberto Bartalucci, and Jacopo Simonetti, supervised by Pietro Ruschi, published here in Fig. 24. A full set of plans and elevations will be published in my forthcoming article for *Opus incertum*, edited by Gianluca Belli and Amedeo Belluzzi.

22.
Machicolation, Pazzi villa of
Trebbio. (Photo: Amanda
Lillie.)

23.
Machicolation, Medici villa of
Trebbio. (Photo: Budini Gattai
and Carrara Screti.)

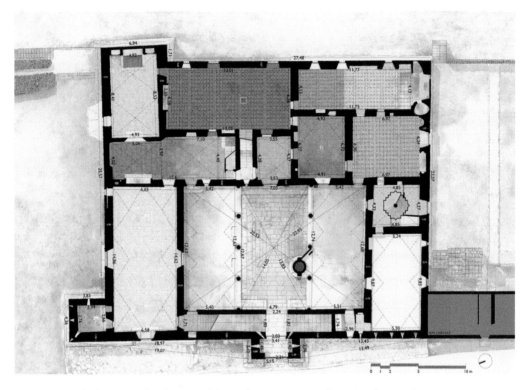

24. Ground plan, Pazzi villa of Trebbio. (Photo: Eleonora Barsanti, Alberto Bartalucci, and Jacopo Simonetti.)

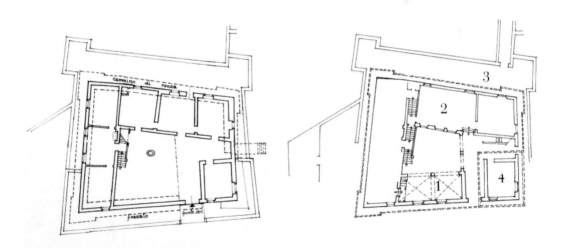

25. Ground plan, Medici villa of Trebbio. (Photo: Budini Gattai and Carrara Screti.)

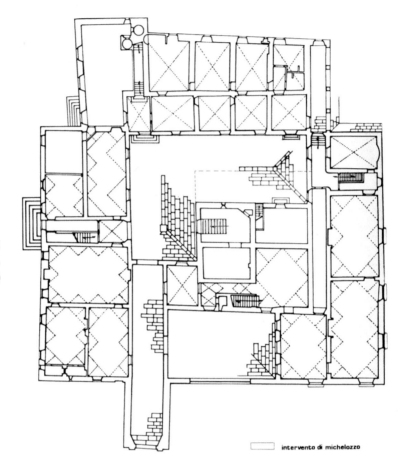

26.

Ground plan, Medici
villa of Cafaggiolo.
(Photo: Tiraboschi.)

intervento di michelozzo

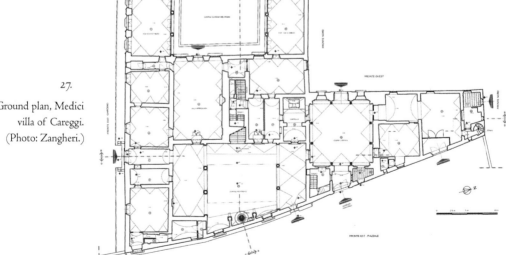

27.

Ground plan, Medici
villa of Careggi.
(Photo: Zangheri.)

28.

Courtyard, Pazzi
villa of Trebbio,
looking west
toward the main
entrance. (Photo:
Amanda Lillie.)

These dimensions and proportions are repeated in the main reception hall to the left of the entrance, and again in the second *sala terrena* on the east front, all of which are approximately six by twelve meters.[63] Were the rigorous mathematical proportions that govern the Pazzi chapel in Florence being applied here? Certainly a level of coherence and systematic consistency is apparent that would not normally be associated with villa architecture in the 1430s or early 1440s, nor with the rebuilding of old castellated structures. If the projecting tower, chapel, and *antiporta* are mentally sliced off, we might well be looking at the plan of an urban palace of the same date, or from a decade later, or even at the type of ideal palace plan related to the Roman house we find in later fifteenth-century architectural treatises such as Francesco di Giorgio's.[64]

The courtyard at first seems to encapsulate the defensive concerns of fortified villa owners at this date (Fig. 28). Its central axis, powerfully established by the severe *antiporta* with its dark entrance, arrow slits, and murder hole (Figs. 29 and 30), leads into a relatively narrow central court focused on the thirteenth-century *pietra serena* portal surmounted by the Pazzi *stemma* (Fig. 31).[65] This entrance axis is aligned for the arriving visitor, designed round the stern dynastic power of the Pazzi. But to either side, Andrea de' Pazzi's twin loggias with their *pietra serena*

63 The main *salone* to the left of the entrance is 14.7 meters long because it includes the staircase, which is nearly 2 meters wide.

64 E.g., Martini and Maltese 1967, 1:261, fol. 24, tav. 43. Turin, Biblioteca Reale, Codice Saluzziano 148, fol. 24r: "chasa sichondo el modo grecho."

65 This finely carved Pazzi coat of arms shows signs of having been attached to this wall at a later date and might have been brought here from another part of the villa or from another Pazzi property.

29.

Arrow slit in the wall of the *antiporta*, Pazzi villa of Trebbio. (Photo: Amanda Lillie.)

30.

Murderhole (*cadutoio*) in the roof of the *antiporta*, Pazzi villa of Trebbio. (Photo: Amanda Lillie.)

31.

Pazzi coat of arms in the
courtyard, Pazzi villa of
Trebbio. (Photo:
Amanda Lillie.)

columns transform this courtyard into a broader, more open, and more sociable
space in a more modern idiom, with a simplified version of composite capitals and
portals of the *all'antica* type (Fig. 32). Furthermore, in the plan, the narrow central
opening of the courtyard, especially when integrated into the proportional system
of the whole ground floor, invites interpretation as an atrium like those found in
reconstructions of Vitruvius's Roman house.[66]

An inventory survives from 1464 after Piero de' Pazzi had inherited Trebbio,
but it presents more difficulties than it resolves.[67] Either it is a full inventory of
Trebbio, in which case the house was richly furnished with intarsia *lettucci*, silverware, fine textiles, jewelry, a library of Latin texts, nine main *camere* and four *anti-
camere* as well as a tutor's room, a nursery (*camera delle fanciulle*), a room for the

66 Clarke 2003, 111–119. Many thanks to Howard Burns and Giovanni Santucci for their helpful comments on the plan.

67 ASF, NA 388, ser Andrea di ser Agnolo da Terranova, 1463–66, fols. 174r–186v. This document was
found by Howard Saalman and Anthony Molho; special thanks to Brenda Preyer for showing it to
me and for invaluable help with this and other Pazzi documents.

32.
North loggia of
the courtyard, Pazzi
villa of Trebbio.
(Photo: Amanda
Lillie.)

estate manager (*fattore*), and servants' rooms; or the first pages list the contents of
Piero de' Pazzi's town house, while the last pages refer to Trebbio, in which case the
grander items might all have been kept in town and only three *camere*, two *antica-
mere*, one *sala*, a *saletta*, kitchen, chapel, and the factor's and other servants' rooms
of this villa were included. The surviving building is considerably larger than the
latter more limited reading of the document's Trebbio pages would suggest. The
ground floor alone incorporates two great *sale*, at least four *camere* (Fig. 33), at least
one *anticamera*, and the chapel. The *sale* or dining halls are strikingly large, well
proportioned, and positioned for seasonal use—one clearly designed for summer,
cool with high vaults, its windows facing north, and its doors opening off the shady
courtyard loggia (Fig. 34); the second for colder weather, facing east, with a wooden
coffered ceiling and a vast fireplace (Fig. 35).

The interior planning and modernized courtyard of the Pazzi's fortified *palagio*,
with its provision for entertaining in spacious *sale* and deep loggias, its fine chapel incorporated into the fabric of the building, and its numerous *camere*, reveal an
aesthetic preference for systematically repeated regular proportions, with a concern as well for comfort. The chapel is interesting since it is more than merely a
room with ecclesiastical furnishings, in the manner of the Cafaggiolo or La Pietra
ground-floor chapels.[68] It is not only the semicircular pedimented portal on the
north facade that advertises the chapel's presence to passersby on the road and to
the wider rural community (Fig. 36), but its structure appears quasi-defensive, projecting from the east side of the building, with *alberese* quoins to mark its perimeter,

68 Lillie 1998a, 91–92, figs. 6, 9; 1998b, 20, 29–31, figs. 2.7, 2.8.

33.
South-facing *camera della loggia*,
Pazzi villa of Trebbio. (Photo:
Amanda Lillie.)

34.
North-facing *sala grande terrena*,
Pazzi villa of Trebbio. (Photo:
Amanda Lillie.)

35.
East-facing *sala terrena*, Pazzi villa of Trebbio. (Photo: Amanda Lillie.)

36.
North facade with chapel entrance, Pazzi villa of Trebbio. (Photo: Amanda Lillie.)

and with its own supportive bastion, like those of the tower and the *antiporta* and a small campanile above (Fig. 37). Furthermore, its orientation—its altar faces east, which is unusual in villa oratories or chapels—implies a devotional seriousness of purpose for this domestic chapel (Fig. 38).

If the Pazzi chapel at Santa Croce is an updated version of the Old Sacristy designed by Filippo Brunelleschi for the Medici at San Lorenzo, and elements of

37.

Exterior of chapel,
east wall, Pazzi villa
of Trebbio. (Photo:
Amanda Lillie.)

the Palazzo Pazzi [69] seem to mimic the Palazzo Medici (particularly its *bifore* windows and ground-floor rustication), what then do the fortified villas of the Pazzi and Medici add to this echoing narrative? Major renovation projects at the Medici villas of Trebbio (for Giovanni di Bicci de' Medici, ca. 1420–28) and Cafaggiolo (for Averardo de' Medici, ca. 1420–25) probably predate the reconstruction of the Pazzi Trebbio villa (ca. 1428–45) and might have offered inspiration. This was the period when Andrea de' Pazzi was employed in Averardo's bank and he would have known the Mugello villas well. It is therefore tempting to interpret his own villa as his first architectural tribute to the Medici. Yet all these fortified houses were already in existence, and it was perhaps intervilla dialogue or rivalry that spurred Andrea to modernize his castle interior in a more radical way. In any case, it is unlikely that

69 Built by Jacopo di Andrea de' Pazzi between ca. 1458 and ca. 1469, Palazzo Pazzi is on the south side of canto de' Pazzi, where the modern borgo degli Albizzi meets via del Proconsolo.

38.
Interior of chapel,
Pazzi villa of
Trebbio. (Photo:
Amanda Lillie.)

the Pazzi knights messer Andrea, his son Piero, and his other son Jacopo[70] would have displayed deference toward the Medici, even—or especially—in a visual or architectural form.

As we have seen, Pazzi property acquisitions across the Val di Sieci were broadly similar to the Medici activities in the Mugello. We should beware of interpreting evidence from the first half of the fifteenth century with hindsight, in the knowledge of the conspiracy to come; and it may, therefore, be misleading to view the Pazzi collection of castles as more belligerent and more anxious than the Medici's territorial expansion. The Pazzi may appear more concerned to "preserve the not-too distant

70 Salvemini 1896, 135, 145, 147: Andrea, knighted in 1442 by René of Anjou; Piero, knighted in 1462 by Louis XI but without the title of *dominus* or *messer*; Jacopo, knighted by the Florentine commune in 1469.

memory of feudal, magnate, authority,"[71] and to do so in a militarily effective fashion, as demonstrated by their refortified castle of Trebbio with its entrance bulwark (*antiporta*), arrow slits, machicolation, and murder holes (*cadutoie*), as well as their acquisition of an encircling group of other watch towers and *palagi*. But the Medici castle of Cafaggiolo sported a higher, more impressive bulwark at its entrance, and their castle of Trebbio also had murder holes round its tower and at the corners of its lower machicolation.[72] The 1498 inventory of the Medici castle of Trebbio included a room for soldiers to prepare cannonballs and a munitions room with a supply of arms.[73] The single addition of arrow slits at the Pazzi castle is scarcely sufficient architectural evidence to support the claim that their castle was more powerful or more noble, or more of a fortress and less of a villa.

These examples therefore serve to highlight the difficulties in distinguishing between the castellated villas and territorial identities of knightly ex-magnates, on the one hand, and politically powerful *popolani*, on the other. In the final analysis, their shared values seem greater than their differences. To take the argument a step further, if the architectural and territorial identities of the Pazzi and the Medici were indistinguishable in the arena where they would be most expected to differ— in the rural power bases associated with their dynastic origins—we may be justified in suggesting that they were intentionally interchangeable, as each group sought to appropriate the trappings of power associated with the other. This type of building is like a tangible exemplum of Philip Jones's view that we should not seek to distinguish land-based aristocratic society from urban republican merchants.[74] They all shared a predilection for the castle.

Perhaps the most arresting feature of the Val di Sieci Trebbio villa is that it shows how it was possible to radically modernize a fortified country house while simultaneously enhancing its historic aura and martial features. This is the sort of approach we associate with late nineteenth-century medievalizing—Gothic towers with bathrooms and electricity—rather than with the fifteenth century.

71 Kent 2004b, 125, 142.
72 Budini Gattai, Carrara Screti, and Agostini 2011, 102.
73 Ibid., 82–83.
74 Jones 1978.

TWENTY-ONE

Cosimo de' Medici and Francesco Sforza in Machiavelli's *Florentine Histories*

JOHN M. NAJEMY

NICCOLÒ MACHIAVELLI PONDERED THE NATURE of the fifteenth-century Medici domination of Florence, implicitly asking whether it constituted an exercise of power comparable to that of the signori of the avowedly princely regimes of northern Italy. In the *Discourses on Livy*, he suggests that the Medici were at least aiming at such power. In *Discourses* 1.33, Cosimo's rise to power is presented as the prime example of a citizen of a republic who gains "more power than is reasonable" (*più forze che non è ragionevole*) through a combination of his prudence and his fellow citizens' ignorance. Cosimo's political enemies recognized their "error" too late and imprudently exiled him when his faction—his *parte*—was already so strong in the city that soon thereafter it was able to force his return and make him *principe della republica*—*principe* of course in the sense of leading citizen, but obviously pointing to Medici ambitions for still greater power. In *Discourses* 1.52, Cosimo reappears in a discussion of the best way to "repress the insolence" of citizens who become too powerful. In corrupt republics, the most effective method of obstructing such a citizen is to "preempt the means he himself is seen to be using to arrive at the rank to which he aspires" (*preoccupandogli quelle vie per le quali si vede che esso cammina per arrivare al grado che disegna*). Cosimo realized his goal through "his tactic of favoring the people" (*lo stile suo, di favorire il popolo*), and his opponents should have done the same. In both these chapters, Cosimo is portrayed as nurturing and furthering immoderate ambitions dangerous to the Florentine republic.[1]

---

1 Machiavelli 2001a, 162–164, 244–245.

Throughout the *Discourses*, Machiavelli sees republics as inherently vulnerable to the ambitions of their own powerful citizens and liable to slide into home-grown tyranny. In 3.28, he warns that, although a republic needs "citizens of repute," they are also the "cause of tyranny."[2] Corrupt republics often degenerate into hybrid polities that share with *signorie* the dominating presence of a dangerously powerful *principe* who exercises power de facto in the one case and de jure (at least after the acquisition of vicariates and titles) in the other. This does not mean that Machiavelli did not distinguish republics from principalities. In *The Prince*'s opening sentence, he rigorously separates them, albeit without explanation.[3] In *Discourses* 1.55, he examines the contrasting social foundations of republics and principalities and on this basis gives a theoretical explanation of the political geography of Italy. In regions dominated by *gentiluomini*—nobles who live "idly" on the income from their landed possessions—and by *signori di castella*—lords who exercise jurisdiction over territories and have "subjects who obey them"—the hostility of these two classes of nobles to *ogni civiltà* ("civic way of life") makes republics impossible. This is why there "has never arisen any *republica* or *politico vivere*" in the kingdom of Naples, in the area around Rome, in the Romagna, and in Lombardy (which then meant the entire Po Valley). Tuscany, by contrast, has few *gentiluomini* and no *signori di castella*, but several republics and other cities that would like to regain their former liberty[4]—a strong suggestion of censure of Florence's policy of repressing the liberties of its subject cities.

From the standpoint of this conceptual distinction between republics and princely states, the Florentine republic and the Visconti-Sforza *signoria* in Milan belong to mutually exclusive categories. Yet, when viewing their development in the fifteenth century, Machiavelli emphasized less their differences than their converging similarities. His view of the evolution of the Florentine state is concisely presented in the 1520–21 *Discourse on Florentine Affairs after the Death of the Younger Lorenzo*, where he says that no Florentine government after 1393 had the *debite qualità* ("required characteristics") of either a republic or a principality. The Medici regime "leaned more toward a principality than a republic," but its weakness was in effect a residue of Florentine republicanism, namely, the need to consult with so many citizens, which several times almost caused Cosimo to lose control and forced him to resort to extra-constitutional assemblies (*parlamenti*) and the exile of opponents.[5] In this *Discourse*, Machiavelli sees the Medici regime more as a defective principality than as a corrupt republic. In the *Florentine Histories*, he reverses the perspective and views it as a failed republic, but here too Cosimo is portrayed (by his enemies) as aiming at a principality. In Niccolò da Uzzano's speech in *Histories* 4.27,

---

2   Ibid., 702.
3   Machiavelli 2013, 7: "Tutti gli stati, tutti e' dominii che hanno avuto e hanno imperio sopra gli uomini, sono stati e sono o republiche o principati."
4   Machiavelli 2001a, 265–267.
5   Machiavelli 2001b, 624–627.

Machiavelli has this respected leader of the opposing party explain that, although they would have preferred to exile Cosimo because of their "suspicion that he might make himself *principe* of this city," it was impossible to persuade the people of this, partly because they saw little difference between Cosimo's party and that of his oligarchic opponents, but also because "the actions of Cosimo that make him suspect to us are that he helps everyone with his money, not only private citizens but also the state [*non solamente i privati ma il publico*], not only Florentines but also the condottieri" employed by the government, that he "assists this and that citizen who need something from public officials" and promotes his friends into prestigious offices. "So it would be necessary to adduce as the reasons for banishing him that he is compassionate, considerate, generous, and universally loved.... And, although these are all methods that propel men flying toward the principate [*volando al principato*], nonetheless they are not believed to be such."[6] In the draft of this speech, Machiavelli first wrote "tyranny" (*volando a la tirannide*) before prudently replacing it with *principato.*[7] As he told Donato Giannotti, it is in the speeches of their opponents that we should look for opinions of the Medici that Machiavelli was unwilling to express in his own voice in a work whose commission was approved by Cardinal Giulio de' Medici.[8] Machiavelli's sustained critique of the political corruption that the Medici inflicted on Florence's already compromised republican institutions is well known.[9]

A significant measure of Machiavelli's judgment of the Medici, to which less attention has been paid, is the implicit parallel he develops in the *Florentine Histories* between Cosimo de' Medici and Francesco Sforza, whose rise to princely status in Milan was of particular interest to Machiavelli as the most notable example of the political ambitions of mercenaries and, moreover, as the one whose political career was most entwined with the Medici. Book four of the *Histories* recounts the ascendancy in Florence of Cosimo and his party, but Sforza is the central figure of books five and six. Although on the surface two more contrasting political figures could hardly be imagined—Cosimo, the citizen banker and behind-the-scenes manipulator of Florentine politics; Sforza, the noble mercenary captain who became duke of Milan—Machiavelli's narrative of Sforza's career underscores the parallel effects they had on the states they came to dominate.[10]

Sforza undergoes a remarkable transformation from *The Prince* to the *Florentine Histories.* In chapter seven of *The Prince*, he is Machiavelli's lone modern example of a new prince who acquires a state with his own arms and *virtù*, not through *fortuna* and the arms of others; he rose from a private station *con una grande sua virtù* to become duke of Milan, and what he gained "with infinite difficulties" he preserved "with little effort." Machiavelli contrasts Sforza with Cesare Borgia, who acquired

6   Machiavelli 2010, 430.
7   Ibid., 846.
8   Giannotti 1974, 35.
9   Najemy 1982b; Sasso 1993, 363–485; Marietti 2005, 137–162; Benner 2009, 19–24.
10   Marietti 2005, 156–157, calls it an "occulto parallelo"; see also Quint 2004.

his state with the *fortuna* of his father's influence and arms and lost it when that *fortuna* vanished.[11] It may be revealing of some ambivalence about Sforza, however, that Machiavelli says nothing more about him in this chapter and that elsewhere in *The Prince* he is remembered only for having allied with Venice to "oppress the Milanese"[12] and for mistakenly believing that the fortress he built in Milan (the Castello Sforzesco) would protect his family.[13]

In the *Histories*, Sforza's exemplary *virtù* disappears. Concluding the first book's survey of Italian history since the barbarian invasions, Machiavelli identifies the common weakness of the Italian states in the fifteenth century in the lack of their own arms and hence in dependence on hired mercenaries. Milan, Venice, the papacy, and the kingdom of Naples all followed this "custom of the Italians," and the Florentines "obeyed the same necessity," having destroyed their warrior "nobility" and put the republic in the hands of men "trained in commerce." Italian arms now belonged instead to "lesser princes" and *uomini senza stato* ("men without states"), who, immersed in military affairs from their youth, knew no other *arte* ("profession") and sought wealth and power in the exercise of arms—an echo of the scathing critique by Fabrizio Colonna in Machiavelli's *Art of War* of professional soldiers who make war their *arte*. Machiavelli names Carmagnola, Sforza, Niccolò Piccinino, Micheletto Attendolo (Sforza's cousin), Niccolò da Tolentino, and several others. Far from being the unique exemplar of *virtù* he is in *The Prince*, Sforza is here one of a group of soldier-nobles, who also include "the barons of Rome, the Orsini and Colonna," and other *signori e gentili uomini* of the kingdom of Naples and Lombardy, who entered into "a kind of association or conspiracy" (*come una lega e intelligenza insieme*) by which they agreed to delay and diminish military actions, with the result that in most wars the employers of both armies failed to gain their objectives. "So completely did they reduce war to such cowardice" (*viltà*), Machiavelli writes in a particularly angry sentence, "that any mediocre captain who possessed even a shadow of reborn ancient *virtù* would have humiliated them, to the astonishment of all Italy, which foolishly honored these men." He concludes the diatribe by telling his readers that "my history will be replete with such idle princes and cowardly arms."[14] As a judgment of Italian arms, this is perhaps exaggeratedly polemical, but the important point is that it is in this negative context and with this excoriation of the men who ruined Italy that Machiavelli introduces Francesco Sforza into the *Histories*.

Machiavelli's account of Sforza's rise to power emphasizes the myriad ways in which private ambitions determined his actions and decisions, including the rapidity with which he switched from one employer to another, the ease with which he

---

11 Machiavelli 2013, 42–43.
12 Ibid., 89 (chap. 12).
13 Ibid., 156 (chap. 20), an observation repeated in *Discourses* 2.24: Machiavelli 2001a, 466–467.
14 Machiavelli 2010, 185–188 (1.39).

broke promises and betrayed trust, and his determination to marry Duke Filippo Maria Visconti's daughter as the avenue to power in Milan. Machiavelli also highlights Sforza's dependence on fortune and on Cosimo de' Medici's money. Sforza first appears in the narrative in the employ of Filippo Maria, who sent him into Tuscany in 1430 to prevent Florence from subjugating Lucca. After he raided and burned several towns, the Florentines "had recourse to the solution that had many times saved them, knowing that, with mercenary soldiers, when force did not suffice, bribery would help" (*giovava la corruzione*). Florence offered Sforza fifty thousand ducats to hand over Lucca, but he simply took the money and left.[15] Machiavelli thus presents Sforza as a free agent who bargained for his own advantage, deceived the Florentines, and delivered little benefit to his Milanese employer. Still, in order to keep his cooperation, as early as the mid-1430s Filippo Maria dangled before Sforza the prospect of marriage to his daughter. Despite the *riputazione grandissima* the promised marriage gave him, Sforza left the duke's service and, motivated by *ambizione*, invaded the papal states, seized territories in the Marche, and forced Pope Eugenius IV to make him *gonfaloniere della Chiesa* ("military captain of the church") and to recognize him and his rival Niccolò Fortebraccio as *principi* in the areas they controlled.[16] Soon thereafter, Sforza signed on as captain of the Venetian-Florentine-papal league,[17] fighting against the Milanese army of Niccolò Piccinino and again devastating the countryside near Lucca, this time in support of Florence's attempt to capture that city.[18] Venice refused to open a second front in the north unless Florence let Sforza go there, but when he arrived in Lombardy he refused to cross the Po because "he did not wish to deprive himself of the hopes he had for the marriage alliance promised by the duke [of Milan]." Sforza quarreled with the Venetians and returned to Tuscany, where the Florentines hoped he would resume operations against Lucca, which he also declined to do. Duke Filippo Maria, believing that Sforza's refusal to cross the Po was motivated by *reverenzia* for him and by a desire to protect the promised marriage, now hoped for reconciliation with his former captain. The political benefits of marriage to the duke's daughter "had a strong hold" on Sforza (*moveva forte il conte*) "because, since the duke had no sons, [Sforza] hoped in this way to be able to make himself signore of Milan [*potersi insignorire di Milano*]. This was why he always obstructed Florentine war plans." Moreover, "wishing to possess securely his territories [*volendo vivere sicuro degli stati suoi*] . . . he needed to give thought to his own affairs and cleverly threatened to come to an agreement with the duke."[19]

Machiavelli introduces Cosimo into the narrative of Sforza's rise to power as the latter's crucial ally, even at a moment in which Sforza's "pretexts and deceptions"

15   Ibid., 422–423 (4.24).
16   Ibid., 452–454 (5.2).
17   Ibid., 454–456 (5.3).
18   Ibid., 471–477 (5.10–11).
19   Ibid., 478–481 (5.13).

greatly displeased the Florentines. He recounts that Cosimo personally went to Venice (in April 1438) to persuade the Venetians not to break Sforza's contract. His source for Cosimo's mission is Neri Capponi's *Commentarii*,[20] but the counterarguments attributed to the Venetians are reported in no source and presumably reflect Machiavelli's own view of Sforza. The Venetians tell Cosimo they are not in the habit of paying soldiers who serve others: so let the Florentines pay him if they wish, since he works for them. Venice seeks to enjoy its dominions in security and thinks it "more urgent to diminish [Sforza's] arrogance than to pay him; the ambition of men knows no bounds, and, if he were paid without providing service, he would soon demand something still more dishonorable and dangerous. They therefore think it necessary to curb his insolence [*insolenzia*] once and for all and not let it grow to the point of becoming incorrigible."[21] It is worth noting that *insolenzia* is ascribed both to Cosimo in the *Discourses*[22] and here to Sforza. Cosimo's mission, says Machiavelli, was a failure.

Sforza wavered over whether to abandon the Florentine-Venetian league, reluctant as he was to detach himself from Florence, no doubt because of Cosimo's financial and political support, but at the same time "desirous of finalizing the marriage alliance" with Visconti. Without breaking his ties to Florence, he entered into an agreement with Filippo Maria, promising not to aid Florence's war against Lucca.[23] Visconti assumed that this *nuova amicizia* with Sforza and the still promised marriage would keep him loyal (*fermo*)[24] and allow Milanese forces to occupy the Romagna. Fearing an expansion of Visconti power, Florence asked Sforza to return to Tuscany to bolster Florentine defenses. Once again, Sforza's "wish to see the marriage alliance . . . go forward kept him undecided [*sospeso*]." Visconti now toyed with Sforza: knowing his *desiderio*, the duke fed his hopes by several times making preparations for the wedding, only to cancel it with various pretexts, and then giving him the thirty thousand florins stipulated in the agreement in order to keep Sforza believing his promises.[25]

But both sides were capable of manipulating Sforza's fears. After Visconti's army under Piccinino inflicted losses on Venice, Florence tried to persuade Sforza that Venice's collapse would entail his own ruin, telling him that Filippo Maria had offered the marriage only because he needed and feared Sforza, which would no longer be the case if Venice were badly defeated. These arguments increased the "hatred" that Sforza, already feeling mocked (*sbeffato*) in the matter of the marriage, now conceived for Filippo Maria.[26] In early 1439, Sforza finally agreed to cross the Po and

20 As noted by the editors of ibid., 482 n. 10; see also Anselmi 1979, 129–132.
21 Machiavelli 2010, 482 (5.14).
22 Machiavelli 2001a, 244 (1.52).
23 Machiavelli 2010, 483 (5.14).
24 Ibid., 488 (5.17).
25 Ibid., 492 (5.18).
26 Ibid., 493–494 (5.19).

liberated Verona from Piccinino's siege.[27] Visconti blamed this setback on Florentine "money and support,"[28] presumably, at least in part, Cosimo's. Filippo Maria took the war into Tuscany, encouraged by Piccinino, whose real motive, says Machiavelli, was to attack Sforza's territories in the Marche, and also by the Florentine exiles, among them Rinaldo degli Albizzi, who assured Visconti that the people of Florence, "exhausted by taxes and by the *insolenzia* of the powerful," would rise against the regime.[29] Sforza refused Venice's demand that he also should liberate Brescia from besieging ducal forces.[30] Again worried about his territories in the Marche and determined to go south *a soccorrere la casa sua* ("to shore up his home base"), Sforza first went to Venice to explain to the doge (Francesco Foscari) that taking his forces south would benefit the Venetian-Florentine league, because Piccinino was going there and the war had to be fought where the enemy was. Following Capponi's account in the *Commentarii*,[31] Machiavelli has Sforza tell the doge that he "did not intend to abandon his subjects [*sudditi*] and friends," and that, "having entered Lombardy as a signore, he did not wish to leave as a condottiere." The doge replies that anyone who examines *saviamente* ("wisely") Visconti's decision to send Piccinino into Tuscany (implying that Sforza, blinded by his own interests, had not done so) can see that the objective is to remove Sforza and the war from Lombardy.[32] The speech Machiavelli has Sforza make before the doge reveals key aspects of his perception of Sforza: it is the possession of those territories in the Marche and in Umbria that makes Sforza a signore with *sudditi* and, therefore, one of those *signori di castella* described in the *Discourses* as mortal enemies of republics. Although on this occasion Sforza remained in Lombardy, Machiavelli regularly reminds the reader that protecting those territories was always foremost among his purposes and the foundation of further ambitions that governed his military maneuvers.

Sforza resumed operations in Lombardy, liberating Brescia from the Visconti siege,[33] while Piccinino raided the Mugello valley just north of Florence.[34] According to Machiavelli, although the Florentines "were not frightened" by the arrival of Piccinino's army, they took measures to "keep the regime stable" (*a tenere fermo il governo*),[35] which hints at potential problems of the sort predicted by the exiles. Machiavelli had written in an earlier chapter that the Medici regime had a *terrore grandissimo* of the exiles,[36] but now says it felt secure because of Cosimo's favor among the people and because major offices were restricted to a small group

27 Ibid., 499–508 (5.22–25).
28 Ibid., 509 (5.26).
29 Ibid.
30 Ibid., 514 (5.28).
31 Ibid., 515 n. 6.
32 Ibid., 515–516 (5.29).
33 Ibid., 523 (5.32).
34 Ibid., 518 (5.30).
35 Ibid., 519 (5.31).
36 Ibid., 495 (5.20).

of powerful men (*intra pochi potenti*), who "with severity" maintained tight control in the event that anyone sought political changes. Neri Capponi was returning to Tuscany with troops, and this "kept [the Florentines] alive with hope." Capponi found the city in *disordini e paure* ("disorder and fear")—an assessment rather at odds with the notion of tight control by a few. In any case, Capponi succeeded in stopping Piccinino's depredations and caused him to move to the Casentino,[37] where the Florentines defeated him at Anghiari. The importance of Capponi in the *Histories* has been amply recognized.[38] He is the exemplary citizen who served the republic with military valor, in contrast to Cosimo whose power rested on those "private" methods, favors, and friends through which he built his faction. The contrast between Capponi's *vie publiche* and Cosimo's *modi privati* is explicitly drawn at the beginning of book seven, but it is already implied in Capponi's successful resistance to Piccinino's incursion into Tuscany, events in which Cosimo plays no role. Although Machiavelli polemically belittles the battle of Anghiari in 1440 as barely a skirmish in which only one man was killed falling from his horse, he nonetheless says that control of Tuscany would have been lost to the Florentines if they had been defeated and praises the "commissioners," including Capponi, for their great *diligenzia* in disciplining the Florentine forces and bringing victory.[39]

After Anghiari, Visconti again sought reconciliation with Sforza, telling him it was not in his interest to weaken the Visconti state so much that Venice and Florence would no longer need him—the exact converse of the argument the Florentines had used in warning him not to allow the Venetian state to break apart and cause Filippo Maria to have no further need of him—and again dangling the marriage alliance before him. Sforza distrusted Visconti's overtures, especially concerning the marriage, "having many times been mocked over it," as Machiavelli again says.[40] Negotiations faltered and hostilities resumed between Visconti and Sforza.[41] As the latter was besieging Martinengo, south of Bergamo, Piccinino cut off his supply lines and put him "in greater danger" than that faced by the besieged town: *una manifesta vittoria* for Visconti, and *una espressa rovina* for both Sforza and Venice. Piccinino and Visconti were on the verge of a decisive victory over Sforza and the Venetians when, as Machiavelli's Milanese sources reported, Piccinino let himself be tempted by excessive *ambizione e insolenzia*, demanding that Visconti give him Piacenza as a reward for his years of service, boasting that it was in his power to make the duke *signore* of all Lombardy, and threatening to abandon him if his demands were not met.[42] Visconti reacted angrily and indignantly[43] and

---

37 Ibid., 519–520 (5.31).
38 Sasso 1993, 427–430; Anselmi 1979, 132.
39 Machiavelli 2010, 525–528 (5.33).
40 Ibid., 535–536 (6.2).
41 Ibid., 536–538 (6.3).
42 Ibid., 539–540 (6.4).
43 Ibid., 540 (6.4). Visconti's reaction is confirmed by Mallett 1974, 105.

immediately dispatched an envoy to Sforza to offer him a truce and marriage to his daughter without further delay. Sforza accepted, married Bianca Maria in October 1441, and signed the peace of Cavriana in November. Giovanni Simonetta, the chief source for this dramatic turn of events, says of Sforza's rescue from disaster by Piccinino's imprudent demands that "into so dangerous a situation, fortune unexpectedly brought a beneficial resolution" (*Sed attulit in re tam ancipiti salutare ex insperato fortuna consilium*).[44] Machiavelli rewrote this line, personifying fortune, as he liked to do, and attributing the reversal to "fortune, who never lacks for ways to favor friends and foil enemies" (*la fortuna, alla quale non manca modo di aiutare gli amici e disfavorire i nimici*).[45] Sforza, close to catastrophic failure, is rescued by "fortune"—not by his own arms or by any action or ability of his own.

Even after this seemingly definitive alliance between Visconti and Sforza, Machiavelli emphasizes their ongoing rituals of deception and betrayal. In 1444, Sforza, again close to defeat, "was in such peril" (*condotto … in estrema necessità*) that he "would have been vanquished" if Filippo Maria had not recalled Piccinino, who died shortly thereafter.[46] Visconti tried to sabotage Sforza by luring away one of his lieutenants, and as late as 1445–46 they were still fighting each other, despite the marriage alliance. Filippo Maria tried to recapture Pontremoli and Cremona, which had been part of Sforza's dowry, but Venetian forces under Micheletto Attendolo defeated the Visconti army (September 1446), crossed the Adda, occupied Cremona, and raided the countryside up to the city of Milan.[47] Visconti now appealed to Sforza for help, begging him not to "abandon his aged and blind father-in-law." Although offended by Visconti's aggression and deceit, Sforza also feared Venetian *grandezza*. Visconti offered him full command of the Milanese forces (*il principato di tutte le sue genti*), while the Venetians promised him Milan itself and permanent command of their army. After some hesitation, Sforza accepted Visconti's offer, reasoning that, if the Venetians controlled all of Lombardy, he would be *a loro discrezione* ("at their mercy"), a situation, as Machiavelli comments, to which "no prudent prince ever subjects himself except out of necessity." "Setting aside all doubts, he allied with the duke" (*posposti tutti i rispetti, si accostò al duca*).[48]

Closely following Simonetta's account,[49] Machiavelli describes Sforza as isolated and beset by *affanni* ("anguish") when Filippo Maria died in August 1447. With his forces ill-prepared, Sforza feared retribution from the Venetians for having betrayed them, feared Alfonso of Naples, *suo perpetuo nimico*, and trusted neither Florence nor the pope (Nicholas V). "Yet he resolved to show his face to fortune" (*mostrare il viso alla fortuna*) and "let himself be counseled" by whatever

44 Simonetta 1932–59, 107.
45 Machiavelli 2010, 539 (6.4).
46 Ibid., 549–550 (6.8).
47 Ibid., 555–556 (6.11).
48 Ibid., 556–558 (6.12).
49 As noted by the editors, ibid., 558 n. 5; see Simonetta 1932–59, 179.

unforeseen circumstances (*secondo gli accidenti*) fortune might bring. What fortune brought was revolution in Milan, which gave Sforza "great hope" and rescued him from his difficulties because he believed the Milanese could "turn to no other arms but his" in resisting Venetian attempts to seize as much of the Visconti state as possible. Machiavelli notes the political divisions within Milan: some preferred to "live under a prince," one faction supporting Sforza and another Alfonso, but those who wanted a republic were more united. The Ambrosian Republic failed, however, to gain the allegiance of the subject cities—Pavia and Parma desiring, as did Milan itself, *la loro libertà*; Lodi and Piacenza accepting Venetian rule—and Sforza successfully exploited this failure. With Venice occupying portions of the fragmenting territorial state, the republic engaged Sforza as its captain with the same terms under which he had served Visconti.[50] When Pavia realized it lacked the means to safeguard its newly declared independence, it offered itself to Sforza with the condition that he not subject the city to *lo imperio di Milano*. Sforza "desired to possess" Pavia as a solid beginning for the realization of his ultimate objective. He was held back "neither by fear nor by shame in breaking faith [with Milan]," because *gli uomini grandi* see shame "only in losing, not in acquiring by means of deceit." Yet he hesitated, fearing that, if he took Pavia, the indignant Milanese might ally with Venice, and that, if he did not, Pavia would submit to the duke of Savoy, depriving him in either case of the *imperio di Lombardia*.[51]

Sforza took Pavia, and the decision deeply distressed the Milanese because it revealed his true "ambition and the end to which he was aiming." Yet the Ambrosian Republic, having no one else to whom it could turn except the dreaded Venetians, stayed with Sforza, hoping somehow to "be free of him" once they no longer had to fear Venice.[52] Simonetta describes the anguish of the Milanese over the occupation of Pavia and their apprehensions about being at the mercy of military captains "who, as they suspected, were not sufficiently trustworthy."[53] Machiavelli adds to this their sudden awareness of Sforza's intention. The realization of the danger he represented, combined with powerlessness to repel it, is reminiscent of the moment in which Niccolò da Uzzano explains why his party, despite its full understanding that Cosimo was employing methods that would lead to princely rule (or "tyranny"), was incapable of taking action to prevent it. However different the circumstances, in both cases overweening ambition silenced and subjugated a republic, established a family dynasty, and turned all political opposition into conspiracy.

Despite Milanese distrust of Sforza, he continued the war against Venice, seizing and sacking Piacenza (November 1447), winning the battle of Caravaggio (September 1448), and laying siege to Brescia. Machiavelli recounts the background

---

50 Machiavelli 2010, 558–560 (6.13).
51 Ibid., 566 (6.17).
52 Ibid., 566–567 (6.17).
53 Simonetta 1932–59, 191: "in ducum praescriptu atque arbitratu, quos maxime non satis sibi fidos fore suspicarentur."

to Sforza's final betrayal of the Ambrosian Republic. The Venetians, knowing that the Milanese did not trust Sforza, reasoned that they could extricate themselves from the precarious military situation in which they found themselves after Caravaggio by coming to terms with either the republic or Sforza. They opted for a separate peace with Sforza, the treaty of Rivoltella (October 1448), which sealed the fate of Milan's republic: Venice would fund Sforza until he subdued Milan, and he agreed to restore captured Venetian territories.[54] In Simonetta's account, representatives of the betrayed republic go to Sforza to express the astonishment and sorrow of the Milanese people, whose former joy over the recovery of their liberty was now transformed into "the greatest mourning and tears" by Sforza's abandonment of "their friendship." They ask him to set aside his disdain and consider the good will of the many, not the transgressions of a few: "we beg and beseech you as fervently as we can" (*te oramus et quanto majore possumus studio obsecramus*) not to inflict harm on the Milanese and instead to fight with them against the common enemy. Milan, they say, will never deny him anything in its power to give.[55] This cringing and servile appeal reflects the purposes of Simonetta's history, a quasi-biography of Sforza written by a loyal chancery functionary, in legitimating the Sforza claim to rule.[56]

Machiavelli transforms Simonetta's version of what the Milanese ambassadors said to Sforza into an angry expression of aggrieved indignation and accusation. The republic sent these ambassadors, says Machiavelli, not because it believed "they could draw [Sforza] back from his ungrateful purpose with supplications or promises," but to see "with what face and words he accompanied this wickedness of his." Rebuking him for his *crudeltà*, *ambizione*, and *superbia*, the envoys remind him of the "benefits" he had received from the Milanese people and with "how much ingratitude" he repaid them. When Visconti died, so they tell him, Sforza had no allies, friends, or money, and no hope of maintaining his territories and reputation; only the naïveté (*semplicità*) of the Milanese saved him. "How unhappy," they exclaim, "are those cities that must defend their liberty against the ambition of those who desire to suppress it! Unhappier still [are] those that are forced to defend themselves with faithless mercenary arms like yours! May our example aid posterity, as the example of Thebes and Philip of Macedon did not aid us." (In chapter twelve of *The Prince*, Machiavelli had already compared Sforza's betrayal of Milan to Philip's subjugation of Thebes after he had defended the city.[57]) Machiavelli has the ambassadors blame the Milanese themselves for unwisely trusting Sforza: "your past life and your insatiable ambition" (*lo animo tuo vasto*)—echoing Sallust's characterization (*animus vastus*) of Catiline[58]—"never satisfied with any rank or title, should have warned us.... But our lack of prudence does not excuse your perfidy ... and will not

54   Machiavelli 2010, 568–573 (6.18–19).
55   Simonetta 1932–59, 251.
56   Ianziti 1988, 138–209; Black 2009, 81, 84–92.
57   Machiavelli 2013, 88–89.
58   Sallust, *Bellum Catilinae* 5.5; noticed in Machiavelli 2010, 576 n. 17.

prevent the righteous sting of your conscience from following you.... You yourself will judge yourself worthy of the punishment that parricides deserve." They warn him not to be confident of lasting victory: "be assured that the rule [*regno*] you have begun with deceit and infamy will end, whether for you or your heirs, in disgrace and disaster":[59] an allusion to the assassination of Galeazzo Maria Sforza in 1476, to the fateful miscalculations of Lodovico il Moro in 1494 that resulted in his expulsion by the French in 1500, and possibly also to the removal of Massimiliano, the puppet duke under Swiss control from 1512 until the French reoccupation of Milan in 1515.

A few pages later, Machiavelli reports the controversies in Florence over the support given to Sforza by Cosimo de' Medici, who is now revealed as Sforza's chief financial backer. In his moment of greatest danger when he lacked allies in 1447, says Machiavelli, Sforza "was compelled to seek help insistently from the Florentines, both from the government" (*publicamente allo stato*) and "privately from his friends, and especially from Cosimo de' Medici" (*privatamente agli amici, e massimamente a Cosimo de' Medici*). Privatization of political power and influence is Machiavelli's fundamental article of indictment against the Medici and the core of the corruption with which he believes they infected the Florentine republic. Dependence on Cosimo, "with whom [Sforza] had always maintained a steady friendship and by whom he had always been faithfully advised and generously subsidized in every undertaking," implicates Sforza in this corruption. "Nor did Cosimo abandon him in his time of great need, but as a private citizen provided him with ample funds" (*come privato copiosamente lo suvvenne*), encouraged him in his designs on Milan, and also pressured the Florentine government to assist him with public funds (*Desiderava ancora che la città publicamente lo aiutasse*). In Machiavelli's account, Neri Capponi objects and argues that a Sforza conquest of Milan would not be in Florence's interest: if Sforza was *insopportabile* as a count, the combination of *tante armi e tanto stato* ("so many arms and so much power") would make him *insopportabilissimo* as duke of Milan. It would be better for Italy if he remained a soldier and if Lombardy were divided into two republics (the Ambrosian and the Venetian). Machiavelli underscores the interdependence of Cosimo's and Sforza's ambitions when he writes that "Cosimo's friends" rejected Capponi's arguments and accused him of expressing such views, not because he believed his recommendations were in the best interests of the Florentine republic, but because it "seemed to him" that if Sforza, "Cosimo's friend," became duke of Milan, "Cosimo would become too powerful" in Florence.[60]

The historian Giovanni Cavalcanti briefly states in his *Trattato politico-morale* that Capponi supported Florence's traditional alliance with Venice, which implies that he might indeed have opposed the pact with Sforza to which Cosimo was inexorably pushing Florence.[61] But the detailed arguments that Machiavelli attributes

---

59 Machiavelli 2010, 573–577 (6.20).
60 Ibid., 582–583 (6.23).
61 Anselmi 1979, 139.

to Capponi and the rebuttal that he has Cosimo himself speak are apparently Machiavelli's own additions to the historical facts as he knew them. Assisting Sforza would indeed be beneficial to Florence and to Italy, says Cosimo, "for it is an unsound opinion to believe that the Milanese people can keep themselves free" (*era opinione poco savia credere che i Milanesi si potessero conservare liberi*). Cosimo concludes that Milan will fall either to Venice or to Sforza because "the conditions of its citizenry, their way of life, and their entrenched party divisions [*le sette anti-quate*] are inimical to any form of republican governance" (*ad ogni forma di civile governo contrarie*). These judgments echo Machiavelli's own in *Discourses* 1.17, where he adduces Naples and Milan, specifically citing the Ambrosian Republic, as examples of cities whose corruption is so advanced that republican liberty becomes unsustainable.[62] Corruption through factions and party divisions, of course, is also the condition to which Machiavelli says, in *Florentine Histories* 4.1, the Florentine republic had been reduced by the early fifteenth century: here too corruption pre-cludes liberty and causes Florence to alternate between tyrannical and anarchic (*licenzioso*) regimes, rendering it dependent on the *virtù e fortuna* of one man.[63] There is a cutting irony in having Cosimo, the chief corruptor of Florentine institu-tions, articulate Machiavelli's own analysis of Milanese corruption, a diagnosis as valid for Florence, in Machiavelli's view, as for Milan. Machiavelli also has Cosimo reject Capponi's warning that the Milanese might submit to Venice; they would not do so because Sforza, unlike the Venetians, had his *parte*—his faction—in Milan:[64] spoken by the master of party politics who knew the necessity of a strong faction with loyal clients in securing and maintaining power.

This revealing chapter of the *Histories* juxtaposes the corruption of the Floren-tine republic, dependent on Cosimo's wealth and private network of friends, and that of the Milanese state, dependent on its hired soldier—himself one of those *gentiluomini* who suffocate republics—and his *parte* of private supporters. From this angle, the constitutional differences between republican Florence and ducal Milan, although still real (otherwise, the revival of republicanism in Florence in 1494 would not have been possible), meant less and less as both became trapped in dependence on ambitious men, each also dependent on the other.[65] Machiavelli sees the weakness of both regimes in their fear, and occasional elimination, of potential opponents. In 1441, the Medici regime "diminished" the influence of Neri Capponi, "whose reputation Cosimo feared more than anyone else's," by murder-ing Capponi's ally, the soldier Baldaccio d'Anghiari.[66] In 1465, Francesco Sforza actively colluded in the murder of Jacopo Piccinino, Niccolò's son and successor,

62 Machiavelli 2001a, 109.
63 Machiavelli 2010, 374–375.
64 Ibid., 584 (6.23).
65 Quint 2004, 43–45.
66 Machiavelli 2010, 545–549 (6.6–7).

whose great popularity among the Milanese Sforza feared,[67] much as Cosimo had feared Capponi's prestige. Implying that such behavior was common among Italy's princes, and indirectly reminding readers of the strikingly similar earlier episode in Florence, Machiavelli comments on Piccinino's murder: "Thus did our Italian princes fear and extinguish in others the *virtù* they themselves lacked, so that, with no *virtù* remaining in anyone, they exposed [Italy] to the ruin that shortly thereafter afflicted and destroyed it" (*E così i nostri principi italiani quella virtù che non era in loro temevano in altri, e la spegnevano: tanto che, non la avendo alcuno, esposono questa provincia a quella rovina la quale, dopo non molto tempo, la guastò e afflisse*).[68] The vulnerability of both regimes to the hatred of many of their own leading citizens is likewise revealed in the juxtaposition, respectively, at the end of book seven and beginning of book eight, of the 1476 assassination of Galeazzo Maria Sforza[69] and the 1478 Pazzi conspiracy against the Medici.[70] Referring to the Milanese conspiracy, but clearly alluding to the Pazzi plot as well, and emphasizing in both the refusal of the people to follow elite conspirators, Machiavelli admonishes princes who create the conditions in which conspirators place hopes for their survival on the support of the multitude: "Let princes learn, therefore, to live in such a way, and to make themselves so revered and loved, that no one who kills a prince can hope to save himself."[71]

A few chapters before the account of Galeazzo Maria's assassination, Machiavelli describes and comments on the duke's 1471 state visit to Florence, whose purpose was to cement Medici-Sforza ties just two years after Lorenzo had assumed power. Although Lorenzo is not mentioned, his role and reputation hover over the chapter's denunciation of the deterioration, under his leadership, of the sober values of a republican society, with Florence now dominated, Machiavelli says, by idle and unbridled young men who spent large sums on fancy clothes, banquets, games, women, and *simili lascivie*. Like the princes that Machiavelli excoriates at the end of the *Art of War*, these young men thought of nothing except fancy attire and clever speech, and "the one who most skillfully maligned the others was considered the cleverest and most praiseworthy." These fashions were "reinforced" (*accresciuti*) by the courtiers of the duke of Milan, who "came with his wife and all the ducal court" and was welcomed with the ceremony due to "such a prince" and "friend" of the city. But the ducal entourage, says Machiavelli, offended Florentine custom by eating meat during Lent; and when the church of Santo Spirito went up in flames during a religious play in the duke's honor, many believed that God had "given this sign of his anger." Machiavelli concludes that, "if the duke found the city of Florence full of courtly frivolities and customs contrary to any well ordered polity, he left it

---

67 On the background to Jacopo Piccinino's murder, see Ferente 2005, 630–647.
68 Machiavelli 2010, 642–643 (7.8).
69 Ibid., 691–698 (7.33–34).
70 Ibid., 699–724 (8.1–10). On this juxtaposition, see Fasano Guarini 2010, 155–207.
71 Machiavelli 2010, 698 (7.34).

even more so" (*Se adunque quel duca trovò la città di Firenze piena di cortigiane deli-catezze e costumi a ogni bene ordinata civiltà contrari, la lasciò molto più*).[72] This judg-ment of the episode confirms Machiavelli's sense of the converging degeneration of Florence and Milan toward regimes whose corrupt foundations and tenuous legiti-macy led to perilous contraventions of custom, religion, and political morality that made them vulnerable to internal and external dangers. In both the republic and the duchy, power was seized by *principi nuovi*—Cosimo de' Medici and Francesco Sforza—who were initially perceived as pillars of Italian stability, but who actually created the conditions for subsequent disasters.

Because Machiavelli wrote his major works—from *The Prince* in 1513 to the *Histories*, presented in 1525 to Giulio de' Medici, now Pope Clement VII—at a time in which the major question in Florentine politics was whether the Medici might make themselves de jure signori of Florence, it was inevitable that the problem of how far Cosimo and the elder Lorenzo had prepared and furthered this possibility would surround everything he wrote about them. This is apparent in the audacious com-parison in *Discourses* 1.33 of the roles of Cosimo and Caesar in bringing about the "ruin" of the republics they helped transform into principalities. Machiavelli did not of course conclude that the fifteenth-century Medici were already signori in the same sense in which the Sforza ruled Milan. As noted earlier, he viewed the Medici hegemony of 1434–94 as an unstable hybrid, caught, like Rome in the age of Caesar, between a corrupt republic and overly ambitious first-citizen *principi*. In both cases, the political successors of these *principi*—in Rome, Caesar's adopted heir Octavian/Augustus; in Florence, the sixteenth-century Medici dukes Alessandro (most likely the natural son of Giulio/Clement) and Cosimo I (descended from both branches of the family)—ultimately transformed the republics into principal-ities, legitimating their new status by appealing to the memory of family founders and, ironically, to the fiction of the superseded republic as the source and founda-tion of their princely authority. Although Machiavelli did not live to see the formal transition of Florence from republic to principality, he was aware that the success of a Medici *signoria* would depend on how later members of the family adapted and built upon the foundations laid by the elder Cosimo and the elder Lorenzo.

Machiavelli strongly hints that both Cosimo and Sforza were tyrants—but for different reasons. Even if we did not have the draft of *Histories* 4.27, in which he has Niccolò da Uzzano say that Cosimo's methods were those of one "flying toward tyranny," the final text still delivers the devastating judgment that Florence's citi-zens were prepared, "partly through ignorance and partly through malice, to sell this republic" and that "fortune is so much their friend that they have found their

72 Ibid., 681–682 (7.28). Machiavelli's sources for the ducal visit are the chronicle of Giovanni di Carlo (see Hatfield 1972; Anselmi 1979, 147–148); and the Milanese historian Bernardino Corio 1978, 2:1379–1381.

buyer [*il comperatore*]."[73] Moreover, the full meaning of Machiavelli's comparison of Cosimo and Caesar in *Discourses* 1.33 emerges when juxtaposed with the inclusion of Caesar among the tyrants condemned in *Discourses* 1.10 (where he is also likened to Catiline) and with the characterization of Caesar as "the first tyrant in Rome" in *Discourses* 1.37.[74] Cosimo and Caesar bear comparison in Machiavelli's judgment because both led private factions that undermined the authority of republican government and usurped its powers. Like Caesar, Cosimo and the Medici represent the dominance of private power over law and public institutions.

Cosimo was not of course a general like Caesar, who led an army against a republic, but he did bankroll a mercenary general who did exactly that. In *Histories* 6.21, Machiavelli has representatives of the Milanese republic appeal to the Venetians for help against Sforza; Venice, they say, should follow the *costume delle republiche* ("custom of republics") and favor the cause of the liberty of the Milanese people and not that of a "tyrant [*tiranno*] whom they [the Venetians] will not be able to restrain if he succeeds in making himself lord" of Milan.[75] In the *Art of War*, when Fabrizio Colonna denounces mercenary captains who make war their permanent profession and who, being necessarily "rapacious, fraudulent, and violent," routinely commit acts of "robbery, violence, and murder . . . against friends as well as enemies," he recalls the freelance "companies" that "extorted money from cities and plundered the country," citing as his chief example Francesco Sforza, who, "in the age of our fathers, in order to live lavishly in times of peace, not only betrayed the Milanese people whose hired captain he was but also snatched away their liberty and became their *principe*." Such men, Fabrizio continues, "can by themselves reduce a state to corruption and are in every way the ministers of tyranny" (*solo essi sono la corruttela del suo re e in tutto ministri della tirannide*). Keeping such *gentili uomini* on the payroll even in peacetime is a "corrupt" system that can result in a "thousand problems" if they command sufficiently numerous forces, as was the case, Fabrizio notes again, with "Francesco and his father Sforza." Later he adds that a state that employs a mercenary captain will always fear him, "as what I said about Francesco Sforza a little while ago should remind you."[76] Albeit with different methods from those of the Medici, Sforza similarly represents for Machiavelli the subordination of law and public institutions to private interest and private power. The cancerous growth of private power is central to Machiavelli's notions of both corruption and tyranny, and he clearly saw the magnitude of the corruption that the Medici and the Sforza exacerbated not only in their own, but also in each other's, states.

73 Machiavelli 2010, 432.
74 Machiavelli 2001a, 71, 184.
75 Machiavelli 2010, 580.
76 Machiavelli 2001b, 41–42, 48, 50–52, 62.

TWENTY-TWO

Florence and Ferrara

Dynastic Marriage and Politics

CAROLYN JAMES

L ORENZO DE' MEDICI, UNOFFICIAL LEADER of the Florentine republic
from 1469 until his death in 1492, and Ercole d'Este, duke of Ferrara between
1471 and 1505, both married higher-born women, from a baronial and royal lineage respectively, for undisguised political reasons. The similarity of their marital choices is consistent with Philip Jones's view that behind the facade of Italian
republics and despotisms lurked "a common interdependent elite with shared ideals, social attitudes and political objectives."[1] However, it is also the case that ideological differences that still distinguished the Florentine republic from her signorial
neighbors shaped relationships within these similarly conceived political unions
in contrasting ways. Lorenzo de' Medici observed Florentine interpretations of
wedlock, while taking advantage of the economic and diplomatic benefits that his
Roman in-laws provided. Ercole d'Este, on the other hand, having spent a substantial part of his youth in Naples, embraced a political as well as personal union with
his Neapolitan wife, her Aragonese heritage providing a precedent for the couple's
wide-ranging collaboration.[2]

∞ I am grateful to the Australian Research Council and the Fondazione Cassamarca for financial
support of the research on which this chapter is based. I also thank my colleagues in the research
reading group at Monash University for helpful comments on an early draft of the article and
Alison Brown for more specialized advice. All translations are my own unless otherwise indicated.
1   Jones 1997, 648.
2   Chiappini 1956, 9–12. On the queens of the crown of Aragon assuming the position of lieutenant
general in their husbands' regimes, see Earenfight 2005.

The men's different approaches to the nuptial bond were no doubt partly related to the rapport established with their wives, but these were also responses to the particular challenges each faced in asserting and preserving his authority. While a noble and foreign wife could be a political asset in a princely state, in republican Florence such a choice invited censure from fellow citizens, sensitive to the implications of a dynastic marriage outside the city's elite and resistant to the idea that a woman could have a recognized political role alongside her husband. Contrasting attitudes to patrician women in the republics and courts of fifteenth-century Italy were even seen by some contemporaries as markers of the divide between republican and signorial regimes. Lorenzo de' Medici made a lordly marriage but he endeavored to convince nominal Florentine peers that his view of women was thoroughly republican.

I

The marriage policies of Italy's feudal clans, emerging princely dynasties, and mercantile elites might have had a similarly instrumental basis, but a complex blend of economic, political, and cultural considerations produced a variety of approaches to prospective alliances. While endogamous marriages were deployed in defense of the financial preeminence of a family, to bolster civic allegiances or to confirm cultural identity, exogamic unions promoted social mobility and new political partnerships. Patrizia Meli has analyzed how the Malaspina, rulers of Fosdinovo and lords of numerous small castles in the surrounding area, married within their own clan to concentrate economic resources, while extending their political reach as far as the republic of Florence through marital alliances beyond their territory. Larger neighboring states such as Milan and Genoa were consequently forced to take notice of the marquis of Fosdinovo, despite the comparatively modest area under his control.[3] The patterns outlined by Meli can be observed in relation to other Italian ruling houses: by the fifteenth century, exogamic became more common than endogamic marriages, as powerful political dynasties that had emerged through force of arms sought to ennoble themselves and to legitimize their regimes. Thus the rise of the Gonzaga of Mantua, who seized power from the Bonacolsi in 1328, was given a boost in the early fifteenth century by Lodovico Gonzaga's marriage to Barbara of Brandenburg. Her close links to the Holy Roman emperor facilitated Ludovico's acquisition of the title of marquis and provided useful allies north of the Alps. In the following generation, another German marriage, this time with Margherita Wittelsbach of Bavaria, further consolidated Gonzaga rule, just as Ercole d'Este strengthened his position in Ferrara by marrying Eleonora of Aragon, daughter of King Ferrante I of Naples.[4]

3 Meli 2008, 47–78.
4 On Ferrara, see Tuohy 1996. On Mantua, see Swain 1986; Antenhofer 2008.

In the republic of Florence, however, endogamic marriages remained predominant. As Anthony Molho has pointed out, most wealthy Florentines sought to preserve their honor and reputation, as well as the city's social and economic equilibrium, by marrying into local families whose status and circumstances were similar to their own.[5] Lorenzo de' Medici's betrothal to Clarice Orsini from a Roman baronial lineage with extensive lands in Lazio and excellent connections to the papacy was perceived as decidedly out of step with Florentine tradition.[6] Tommaso Soderini, a member of the ruling group closely related to the Medici through his marriage to Dianora Tornabuoni, Lorenzo's maternal aunt, responded competitively to the Orsini/Medici match by also looking beyond Florence and Tuscany for a suitable bride for his son Piero.[7] He chose the daughter of Gabriele Malaspina, marquis of Fosdinovo, whose wealth, like the Orsini's, came from feudal landholdings and military contracts. Argentina Malaspina brought her husband a dowry of four thousand ducats, not as much as Clarice Orsini's six thousand Roman florins, but still beyond contemporary Florentine patrician settlements.[8] Not surprisingly, both the Orsini/Medici betrothal formalized in Rome in early December 1468, a year before Lorenzo assumed leadership of the Florentine Republic, and that of the Malaspina/Soderini couple, announced in March 1469, generated controversy in Florence. On learning that negotiations with Clarice's father, Giacomo Orsini, had been finalized, the Milanese ambassador in Florence predicted in a letter to the duke of Milan that "it would give the people and some leading citizens plenty to talk about."[9] Several months later, he confirmed that the Soderini betrothal "is also the subject of some comment."[10]

The Florentine silk merchant Marco Parenti provides further evidence that the Medici alliance with the Orsini of Monterotondo was regarded with disapproval in Florence. In his *Ricordi storici*, the memoir he wrote to perpetuate the memory of a Florentine civic culture he felt was fast disappearing, Parenti criticizes the choice of an outsider on the grounds that it was a lost opportunity to create greater social cohesion. By acceding to Luca Pitti's desire to marry his daughter to Lorenzo, the Medici could have neutralized underlying enmities between themselves and a powerful rival. Pitti's suggestion was rejected by Piero de' Medici because, as Parenti put it, "he wished to reserve Lorenzo for a marriage with nobility, considering himself

---

5   Molho 1994, 233–297; Fabbri 1991, 81–110. On endogamous marriages within the Florentine mercantile community in Rome, see Fosi and Visceglia 1998, 205–206.

6   Lorenzo de' Medici was married by proxy to Clarice Orsini in December 1468, the wedding itself taking place in Florence in June 1469: Roscoe 1902, 106.

7   On Tommaso Soderini's relationship with the Medici, see Clarke 1992.

8   Meli 2008, 66; Roscoe 1902, 132. On Florentine dowry prices, see Molho 1994, 310–324. All these dowries were minuscule compared to Eleonora of Aragon's promised portion of eighty thousand ducats, eventually reduced to sixty thousand. See Chiappini 1956, 13–14.

9   "Secondo mi questa cosa darà da dire assay al populazzo et ad altri de quisti principali": Sacramoro da Rimini to Galeazzo Maria Sforza, 7 December 1468, Brown 1992d, 87 n. 57.

10 "anchor de questo se dice qualche cosa": Sacramoro to Sforza, 16 March 1469, Meli 2008, 65.

to be now more than a mere citizen, and he indeed went ahead, giving [his son] to a woman from the Orsini, great and ancient Italian lords and noble warriors."[11]

While news of the Malaspina/Soderini marriage does not seem to have elicited the same degree of criticism, three decades later the relationship became the focus of more intense Florentine scrutiny and speculation. During the troubled period of republican restoration following the fall of the Medici regime in 1494, Piero Soderini was appointed gonfalonier of Justice in 1502, not for the usual two months, but for life, the position resembling that of the Venetian doge, whose continual presence at the apex of government seemed to many Florentines the key to Venice's greater political resilience.[12] Since it was the custom for the gonfalonier and the other elected officials to remain in the Palazzo della Signoria for the whole period of their appointment, Soderini could hardly have been expected to forgo his wife's company permanently; in February 1503, therefore, Argentina Malaspina and her female attendants took up residence in the palazzo.[13] The reservations widely felt at the profound change in the Florentine constitution were heightened by the unprecedented sight of women at the windows and on the stairways of a building that had formerly been a completely male space.[14]

Marco Parenti's son Piero, who continued his father's practice of commenting on his city and times, reported in his chronicle that the presence of women in the Palazzo della Signoria was regarded as an "unworthy thing" (cosa indegna), while another contemporary observer, Bartolomeo Cerretani, expressed disgust in his memoir about the modifications made to the austere center of Florentine government to accommodate Soderini and his household.[15] The gonfalonier's new apartment and the roof garden created for the recreation of his wife and a coterie of female attendants heralded for many Florentines the infiltration of an alien courtly culture into the very heart of republican decision making. Nor were those who scrutinized Soderini for signs of exploiting the new post to accumulate signorial powers reassured by his relationship with his wife. The gonfalonier's obvious devotion to a beautiful and intelligent woman, to whom he delegated tasks of a political nature and allowed openly to dispense patronage, shocked Florentine observers. Argentina's expectations of marriage were perhaps shaped by the bond between her parents, Gabriele and Bianca Malaspina, whose fifty-two-year union

---

11 "Lorenzo si volse riserbare a imparentarsi con signori che già haveva l'animo sopra cittadino, come fece dipoi, che gli dette una degli Orsini, assai et antichi signori in Italia et nobili capitani." Parenti 2001, 141.

12 On the appointment of Soderini to gonfaloniere a vita, see Pesman Cooper 2002, 1–42.

13 Landucci 1883, 254.

14 In Venice, private areas within the seat of government were set aside for the doge and his family. Passageways were also constructed so that the dogaressa and other female members of the household could move from one part of the building to another, without passing through public space. See Hurlburt 2006, 89–93.

15 Piero di Marco Parenti, Storia fiorentina, BNCF, MS II.ii.133, fol. 88v (March 1503), in Rubinstein 1995, 44 n. 336; Cerretani 1994, 320.

was punctuated by periods of close political cooperation. The perception that Florence's most powerful citizen willingly acceded to his wife's interpretation of wedlock as a collaborative and seemingly egalitarian partnership was regarded by Cerretani as evidence that Soderini sought an excessive degree of authority and wished to adopt the ways "not of a gonfalonier but of a lord."[16]

The scandalized reactions of Cerretani and Parenti to Soderini's treatment of his spouse suggest not only that patrician Florentines preferred to marry each other, so acquiring relatives with shared civic values and traditions, but also that they formed at least a part of their republican identity through adherence to strict gender divisions. Women were told to confine themselves to the domestic sphere, female literacy was discouraged, and patriarchal authority was maximized through the practice of marrying young girls to mature, economically established men. It is little wonder, then, that the introduction into Florentine society of wives from baronial or princely dynasties, who might not adhere to the city's customs, and who all too clearly represented their husbands' efforts to forge political links without, rather than within, the republic, continued to be regarded with suspicion in Florence. Women meddling in public affairs and signorial regimes were becoming ever more firmly associated in Florentine minds as twin evils to be shunned: hence the fear about Argentina's removal to the Palazzo della Signoria. The evidence for such an unappealing association lay to the north and south of Florence in the princely and monarchical city-states of Italy.

II

The contrast in attitudes to highly born women between Florentine and courtly elites was particularly evident when the duke of Milan visited Florence in March 1471, bringing with him not only his treasury and five hundred lavishly attired courtiers, but also his wife, Bona of Savoy, who, to the astonishment of the Florentine population, rode by her husband's side. The Milanese were equally amazed that no women met their procession when they neared the city, waiting rather, as Florentine etiquette dictated, within the Medici palace, where there was an elaborate reception to greet the visitors.[17] Two years later, Eleonora of Aragon stopped in Florence on the journey from Naples to join her new husband in Ferrara. The city was again confronted by an unfamiliar model of femininity. Although the Florentine citizens lining the streets to catch a glimpse of Eleonora might not have been aware of the

---

16 "Gl'haveva la moglie im palazo e dimolte cose di partichulari rimetteva a llei e davagli reputatione assai, e più ciptadini quando andavano a parlargli se gli traevano di testa sempre chiamandola madonna, e lei bellisima ma atempata e savia si vendichava molti favori; e finalmente teneva, e lui e lei, vita e modi non più di g[onfalonie]re ma di signore." Cerretani 1993, 84. On Argentina's parents, see Meli 2008, 20–22. The Venetian Republic addressed the possibility that the doge's wife could wield political influence by requiring her to take a solemn oath that constrained her from exercising patronage. She was also discouraged from writing letters or acting as an intercessor in the manner of princely consorts. See Hurlburt 2006, 15–43, 115.

17 Fubini 1992, 171–172, 192–197.

full extent of her accomplishments, her brief address to the priors, delivered on horseback in front of the Palazzo della Signoria, must have been regarded as a discomfiting novelty in a city that did not permit women to speak formally in public.[18]

For both Eleonora and her sister Beatrice, future queen of Hungary, such speeches were routine features of the roles they were to assume as princely and royal consorts. Their mother Isabella di Chiaramonte had provided her daughters with a compelling example of how to interpret their future duties. According to the queen's late fifteenth-century biographer, Giovanni Sabadino degli Arienti, while King Ferrante defended his realm on the battlefield, Isabella ruled Naples for six years "with justice . . . tranquility and the love of citizens."[19] Perhaps with this maternal precedent in mind, Eleonora was educated, according to the Neapolitan courtier and bureaucrat Giovan Marco Cinico, "further than is customary for wellborn women to be instructed . . . so that she might be ignorant of nothing praiseworthy either practical or intellectual."[20]

Eleonora's tutor, Diomede Carafa, an experienced administrator and royal adviser, even dedicated to his pupil, about the time of her marriage, a treatise that assumed that a ducal consort would have a significant political role.[21] Although *I doveri del principe (The Duties of a Prince)* takes a conventional stance on the weaknesses of the female sex, warning Eleonora to control the womanly proclivity to gossip and to embrace the essential political virtue of taciturnity, the text is otherwise a standard guide to good government in the "mirror of princes" tradition, marginally adapted for its female dedicatee.[22] Shortly after her arrival in Ferrara, Eleonora had this treatise translated from Italian into Latin by the humanist scholar, Battista Guarini, thereby signaling to the educated elite of the city her intention to intervene actively in administrative and diplomatic affairs.[23]

Ercole's rule had been preceded by that of his half brothers Leonello and Borso, illegitimate sons of Niccolò III d'Este. Eleonora's rapid production of four boys, who survived childhood and thus secured the Este succession, contributed to the positive light in which the Ferrarese population was disposed to regard her.[24] Within the ducal castle and adjoining palace, the duchess could move easily between her own chambers and the chancery, allowing her to intervene in government business with little public awareness of the extent of her role behind the scenes. When the duke left Ferrara, he preferred to leave his affairs in the hands of his capable wife, obviating the risk that male relatives could exploit his absence to stage a coup and

---

18 Chiappini 1956, 15. On Eleonora of Aragon's life, see Messina 1993.
19 "Isabella per sei anni sola governò la città de Napoli, capo del regno, cum iustitia et tranquilità et amore de citadini." Sabadino degli Arienti 1887, 252.
20 Corradini 1998, 30.
21 On Carafa's career, see Petrucci 1976; Moores 1971.
22 Carafa 1988, 117.
23 Guerra 2005, 113.
24 Chiappini 1956, 19.

seize power for themselves. As time went by, the duchess's authority as her husband's deputy became more widely acknowledged both locally and abroad, thereby revealing a widening gap between courtly and republican attitudes regarding the participation of women in government.

As well as the convenient configuration of domestic and public space in the Ferrarese court, letter writing was central to Eleonora's ability to collaborate politically with her husband. Over a thousand letters exchanged by the duke and duchess survive in the Archivio di Stato of Modena. The collection documents the couple's evolving cooperation from June 1477, when Eleonora was in Naples for her father's remarriage, until her death in 1493.[25] By October 1478, Ercole was already delegating the oversight of many fiscal and organizational matters to his wife; from early 1479, he increasingly left details concerning the precise implementation of his orders to Eleonora's discretion.[26] Rather than merely a series of instructions from the duke and deferential reports of implementation by the duchess, the letters constitute a wide-ranging dialogue about every aspect of government. Family matters are mixed with political news, the epistolary evidence suggesting that Ercole respected his wife's opinion and often sought her counsel.

Eleonora took pride in demonstrating her executive ability to resolve administrative or judicial issues. The couple regularly shared diplomatic information, Eleonora briefing her husband in detail about incoming correspondence during his periods on the battlefield. The duchess also oversaw the provisioning of the court and made it her business to ensure that government officials carried out their work efficiently and loyally.[27] Besides traditional female tasks such as dispensing charity to the convents of the city and helping the poor and sick, Eleonora received petitioners, issued edicts, entertained dignitaries, and made diplomatic visits to neighboring states. She also organized more secure living quarters for herself and her children in the Estense fortress of Castelnuovo in the heart of the city.[28]

The memoir of the Ferrarese jurist Girolamo Ferrarini even documents the duchess's intervention in March 1479 to resolve a dispute at the University of Ferrara about whether an Italian or northerner from beyond the Alps should become rector.[29] All the while, Eleonora attended to her children's education and lobbied for their advancement as they grew into adults. Once her eldest daughter was betrothed to Francesco Gonzaga, heir to the marquisate of nearby Mantua, she assumed an occasional pedagogical role on behalf of her future son-in-law, offering

25 The letters between Ercole d'Este and Eleonora d'Aragona are preserved in ASMo, CS, boxes 67, 68, 131, 132.

26 On Ercole's willingness to allow Eleonora to make decisions about routine administrative matters on his behalf, see his letters of 8, 9 March and 4, 25, 31 May 1479, ASMo, CS, box 67, fols. 26, 27, 45, 50, 52. These examples are typical of many similar letters.

27 Chiappini 1956, 38–39, publishes a chancery document listing Eleonora's administrative weekly and monthly duties. See also Gundersheimer 1980a.

28 Folin 2008, 494.

29 Ferrarini 2006, 99–101.

political advice when the still young man assumed power on the death of his father in 1484 and writing regularly to him thereafter.[30]

During the war of Ferrara (1480–82), Eleonora displayed leadership and mental strength as the incursions of soldiers into the outlying areas of the city sparked unrest among the citizens. Her robust relationship with Ercole is apparent in a letter of May 1482 in which she berates him for failing to curb the violent behavior of troops under his command. Mercenaries were roaming the Ferrarese countryside, victimizing peasants, committing assaults, and even murdering whoever tried to resist their predations. The difficulties Eleonora faced in addressing such lawlessness tested her endurance, as she pointed out to her absent husband:

> I don't know where to turn to deal with so many failings and, apart from the inevitable anger of God, I foresee that the people would rise up against such misdeeds, and woe indeed if they occur again, for which reason I pray and beseech your excellency to deign to impose order on the chaos, even if you have to return here, to ensure those who commit such excesses are punished, . . . and promise that henceforth, if you have to go away from here, you will not leave me with so many troubles and worries, even should you have to depart without notice, because I could not endure them in addition to the other worries I face . . .[31]

The duke's replies suggest that he took the admonition to heart. Through efficient management of the court, attentive monitoring of ducal administration, and judicious interventions to help subjects *in extremis*, Eleonora contributed significantly to the stability of her husband's regime. Philip Jones argued that the key to Italy's signorial leaders' success in handing power to the next generation lay with their ability to provide stable and efficient government.[32] If a woman contributed to the same outcome, her unconventional role could have won similar approval from her husband's subjects.

Even when her political role was visible to the Ferrarese population, Eleonora seems to have been viewed benignly. In his entry for 1 September 1478, the Ferrarese chronicler Ugo Caleffini, reporting the departure of the duke from Ferrara to take up his command of the forces of the Italian League, related the duchess's initiatives as her husband's representative:

30 See, for example, Eleonora of Aragon to Francesco Gonzaga, 16 July 1484, Luzio 1908, 54–55.
31 "Io non scio dove voltarme per provedere a tanti manchamenti, li quali oltra la ira de Dio, che non el potria comportare, vedo questo populo doverse levare a tale remore, che guai se gli retrovarà, per la quale cossa prego et supplico Vostra Excellentia se digni de metterli tale ordine incontinente, se bene la dovesse venire fino qui, che siano puniti chi fano simili excessi, . . . certificando Vostra Signoria che da mo inanti partendossse Lei di qui, la non me lassarà in tanti guai et affanni, se bene me ne dovesse fuzire senza licentia alcuna, perché non gli poteria durare appresso li altri affanni in che me retrovo. . . .": Eleonora to Ercole d'Este, 29 May 1482, ASMo, CS, box 131, fol. 26.
32 Jones 1974, 321–322.

And the lieutenant of his Lordship was the Illustrious Madam Eleonora, his consort, who left the castle daily to give audience to the people, providing two separate hearings. And as soon as the duke left she had an edict issued forbidding anyone, including courtiers, from bearing arms.[33]

By 1484, Caleffini's chronicle indicates that Eleonora's occasional regency had become routine: "In this period the duke of Ferrara worried little about government; rather his illustrious madam duchess ruled over and governed everything, as she had done in the past."[34] In the winter of 1492, with food prices in the city rising because of extreme weather and crime increasing, Caleffini remained effusive about the duchess, whose response to the crisis was to dismiss the court jesters, to pray ardently, and to make herself available to hear the petitions of the hard-pressed population. She was, he concluded, "entirely saintly" (*tuta santa*).[35] On Eleonora's death in 1493, he summed up her contribution in glowing terms: "it is incredible how well she had governed the state of Duke Ercole, winning the love of everyone, with the result that the lord duke loved her most dearly because of her virtue and goodness...."[36]

To win such approval, the duchess had artfully manipulated her image as a sympathetic and devout mother to her people (which is not to deny her genuine piety). She was also associated with a number of philosophical texts, which aimed to justify an expanded cultural and political role for the female elite of courtly society. Although it is not known whether Eleonora directly commissioned these works, she did decorate her rooms with panel paintings of ancient heroines: Lucrezia, Portia, and the wife of Hasdrubal.[37] Such exemplars of wifely virtue, having been richly provided with courage, constancy, and fortitude, were often included in defense of women literature, and Eleonora doubtless intended the paintings' beholders to associate her with similar qualities. The duchess's political role in Ferrara might even have inspired writers such as Bartolomeo Goggio, a Ferrarese chancery notary, to break new ground in the contemporary philosophical debate about women's worth, arguing in his *De laudibus mulierum* (*On the Praise of Women*) that women were

---

33 "Et locotenente del signore rimase la illustrissima madama Eleonora, sua consorte, la quale ogno zorno usciva da castello et dava audientia al populo et facea due fiate il zorno examine. Et partito il duca, imediate fece fare crida che alcuno non portasse arme da li cortesani in fora." Caleffini 2006, 300. Some entries reporting similar departures by the duke include Sigismondo d'Este as co-regent. See, for example, ibid., 537, 697.

34 "In questo tempo el duca de Ferrara pocho niente se impazava del Stato suo, ma la illustrissima madama duchessa sua regieva et gubernava il tuto, come anche haveva facto per lo passato." Ibid., 640. See also similar reports of Eleonora's role as intermediary between the duke and his subjects in 1486 and 1487: ibid., 666, 683.

35 Ibid., 826.

36 "tanto bene havea gubernato il Stato del duca Hercule et cum amore de ogni persona che è incredibile. Sì che el signore duca multo la havea amata in vita per le sue virtute et bontade.": ibid., 892.

37 Franklin 2006, 131–148; Manca 2000; Cox 2009.

in many ways superior to men (nor was he the only author to write in this vein on Eleonora's behalf).[38]

By the time Eleonora died, the young Isabella d'Este, marchioness of nearby Mantua, had begun to follow in her mother's footsteps. Isabella was also associated with innovative treatises supporting the political role of well-educated princely consorts.[39] These, and similar texts issued from the ducal courts of Milan, Mantua, Ferrara, and, of course, Urbino, the setting of Baldassare Castiglione's famous work, *The Courtier*, wrestled with the challenge to convention posed by the increasingly evident participation of educated women in public affairs. The court, an environment sufficiently enclosed to resemble domestic space, allowed women to socialize respectably with their male peers. It was also open to the world, with diplomats, courtiers, and bureaucrats constantly coming and going. Such a combination was conducive not only to the emergence of new ideas about women's capacities, but also to a less rigid vision of relationships between the sexes.

III

In Florence, the model of female and marital virtue described by Vespasiano da Bisticci in his *Libro delle lodi delle donne* (*Book on the Praise of Women*) of the late 1470s remained largely unchanged. This work looked back to a golden age of republican sobriety where men and women observed traditional gendered and social hierarchies.[40] The very nostalgia for the past suggests that relations between Florentine husbands and wives were more complex than ideological versions of family life. Lorenzo the Magnificent's own parents, for example, shared the burden of maintaining the vast Medicean patronage networks fundamental to the regime's success.[41] In public affairs, the couple acted with discretion, and rightly so: on a rare occasion when Lucrezia Tornabuoni took an overtly diplomatic role, Medici enemies were quick to attack both her and her husband Piero, whose ill health was seen as an impediment to effective manly leadership. When Lucrezia went to Rome to explore the possibility of an Orsini marriage for her eldest son, Jacopo Acciaiuoli, a Florentine exile there, wrote to his brother Neri, criticizing Piero de' Medici for allowing his wife to act as his representative instead of the official ambassador, and mocking Lucrezia's choice of clothing for her audience with the pope: "She acts the lady and goes about dressed up as if she were fifteen years old," he wrote. "Some laugh at her but more at Piero."[42] Here again, signorial

---

38 On Goggio's *De laudibus mulierum* of 1487, see Gundersheimer 1980b; Fahy 1956, 33–36. On Cornazzano's *Del modo di regere e di regnare* (*On the Manner of Ruling and Reigning*), composed about 1478/79, see Musso 1999.

39 See Kolsky 2005, 148–169.

40 On this theme, see Lombardi's introduction in Da Bisticci 1999, lxvii–lxxvii.

41 Kent 1997, 11; Tornabuoni 1978, 13–14.

42 "Fàlla alla signorile e va lisciata come fussi di 15 anni. Ècci chi si ride di lei, ma più di Piero." Jacopo Acciaiuoli to Neri Acciaiuoli, Rome, 3 April 1467, in Tornabuoni 1993, 21 n. 77; Tomas 2003, 31; Kent 1997, 13.

pretensions are associated with an inappropriate degree of female autonomy, mobility, and sartorial display.

With his authority in Florence still precarious, Lorenzo was well aware of the dangers posed by being seen as a weak husband who could not control his wife's behavior or, worse still, harboring lordly ambitions suggested by his marriage to a baron's daughter. Twenty years old when he inherited his father's position as leader of the Medici regime, well short of the usual age of marriage and political eligibility for Florentine men, Lorenzo had to manipulate his image as a leader with care. Unlike Ercole d'Este and other Italian warrior princes, Lorenzo, lacking a military role, did not leave his wife in charge of coordinating public affairs in his absence. In the early phase of his ascendancy, he left Florence as little as possible: a still tentative authority required Lorenzo's physical presence in the city and constant personal interactions with fellow citizens. Later, as he managed to shift an increasing amount of government business away from republican committees to his personal control, he left oversight of the regime to a small group of bureaucrats and deputies, whose rise was indissolubly connected to his own political fortunes.[43]

Clarice's importance for Lorenzo lay in her ability to act as intermediary between him and the Orsini ecclesiastics and mercenary captains who figured so prominently in his political enterprises. In return, she expected her husband to accede to her requests on behalf of Orsini clients and relatives.[44] With few surviving letters between the couple, it is difficult to gain more than a superficial impression of their personal rapport. The correspondence that remains is formulaic and stilted, mediated by secretaries.[45] Unlike the duke and duchess of Ferrara, the Medici couple did not collaborate in day-to-day political administration; letters were therefore not a regular means of communication between them. There is epistolary evidence, however, of several marital battles, one well-known example involving Clarice's expulsion of Lorenzo's close friend Poliziano, tutor to the couple's children, from the Medici villa at Cafaggiolo.[46] This incident gives a sense that the relationship between Lorenzo and his wife may have been just as robust as Ercole and Eleonora's. By Florentine standards unusually close in age to her husband, Clarice seems never to have regarded the long-suffering and humble model of wifely virtue portrayed in Giovanni Boccaccio's tale of patient Griselda, which one scholar has suggested might have been staged as entertainment at her wedding as appropriate to her elevated status.[47]

Apart from the fact that Lorenzo would not have risked placing a woman from a baronial background in a position where her interventions in republican government could have inflamed public opinion, there was no need for his wife to

43 Brown 2011b, 23–32.
44 Kent 1997, 10; Tomas 2003, 59–62.
45 See Maguire 1927, 127–172; 1936, 69–100.
46 Maguire 1927, 154; 1936, 85–94.
47 Clubb 2005, 347.

provide relief from political burdens. As a number of scholars have shown, Lucrezia Tornabuoni was her son's adviser and an important broker of Medici patronage.[48] A Florentine from an ancient magnate family, Lucrezia was well versed in her city's political culture. As a widow she was the recipient of numerous supplications for administrative posts, ecclesiastical benefices, and legal interventions. It was normally a question of her intercession with Lorenzo, but government representatives in the Florentine territories sometimes looked to Lucrezia's interventions in administrative problems such as border disputes. Arguably, she had her own spheres of influence and a degree of autonomy, particularly in areas of Tuscany where she owned property and knew local conditions.[49] With her wide experience of Medicean rule over many decades, Lucrezia could offer advice and practical help to her son in the privacy of the family's palace and country villas. On her death in 1482, one Medici client summed up her role in a eulogy addressed to the grief-stricken Lorenzo:

> What part of the state did the wisdom of Lucrezia not see, take care of, or confirm! . . . Sometimes [your mother's] actions, from the political point of view, were more prudent than yours, for you attended to great things and forgot the lesser. . . . She advised the most important persons as well as the magistrates, and she also admitted the humblest to her presence and all she sent away happy and contented. She knew how to manage the most pressing affairs with wise counsel, and to succor the citizens in times of calamity.[50]

Apart from such an obviously exaggerated eulogy, Lorenzo himself corroborated his mother's political role in letters reporting her death to the duke and duchess of Ferrara. She was, he wrote to Eleonora, "an irreplaceable refuge from my many troubles" and a "source of relief from many burdens," while to Ercole he confided similarly that she was "the means by which I was relieved of many cares."[51]

Lucrezia also engaged in a literary campaign to promote and justify her political activities. While probably not so well educated as Eleonora of Aragon, Lucrezia was intelligent and culturally sophisticated. She enjoyed literary friendships with major figures such as Luigi Pulci and Poliziano, the former's *Morgante* having been written at her request. Instead of encouraging male clients to write philosophical treatises in defense of women's worth, as the duchess of Ferrara might have done,

---

48 Kent 1997; Tomas 2003; Tornabuoni 1993, 39–45.
49 Kent 1997, 17–18; Tornabuoni 1993, 23–27.
50 Tornabuoni 2001, 32. See also Tomas 2003, 65–66, 81 n. 223.
51 "io resto tanto sconsolato quanto la Excellentia Vostra po' pensare, havendo perduto non solamente la madre, ma uno unico refugio di molti mia fastidii et sublevamento de molte fatiche": Lorenzo de' Medici to Eleonora, 25 March 1482, Medici 1977–, 6:285–286. "io mi trovo tanto male contento quanto più se possa dire, perché oltra a l'havere perduta la madre, che solo a ricordarla me crepa il core, io anchora ho perduto uno instrumento che mi levava di molte fatiche": Lorenzo to Ercole, 25 March 1482, ibid., 6:287.

Lucrezia herself composed sacred narratives about the biblical heroines Judith, Susanna, and Esther.[52] These stories focus on the dilemmas faced by women treading a path between convention and autonomy, sufficient for them to act in the world. Her choice of Florence's patron saint, John the Baptist, for another of her narratives was calculated to remind her readers that she was a fiercely civic-minded Florentine. Like Eleonora, Lucrezia played a crucial role in convincing the local population that she was associated with a holy regime.[53] The cultivation by both women of a virtuous reputation, through attention to charity and to pacifying and reconciling litigants, deflected criticism of the political roles they assumed behind the scenes.

Through the collaboration with his Florentine mother and his Roman wife, Lorenzo de' Medici straddled two worlds, skillfully negotiating the ideological differences between republican and signorial regimes. He could rely on his mother to operate unobtrusively but efficaciously in Florence, where women were rarely seen and almost never heard in public, while allowing his wife to take a greater role in patronage within her own Roman and lordly milieu. Lorenzo managed public perceptions of his marriage shrewdly, largely neutralizing the danger that it would become the focus of Florentine suspicions about his princely ambitions. However, while tightening his grip on the Florentine Republic, Lorenzo began to arrange the marriages of others to his own political advantage, organizing for example, the union of his wife's sister, Aurante Orsini, to Leonardo Malaspina, nephew of Gabriele Malaspina, marquis of Fosdinovo, and of Gabriele's son to the daughter of Aurante. The following year, 1477, he engineered the betrothal of Gabriele's daughter Giovanna to Cosimo, son of his brother-in-law Bernardo Rucellai and Nannina de' Medici.[54] These and similar exogamic unions were part of an elaborate Medicean strategy to break down the city's insularity, so diluting the influence of its most prominent families.[55]

Lorenzo followed the well-trodden path of Italian lords in attempting to manipulate webs of kinship within the political class. However, tenacious republican ideology and Florentine traditions of marital homogamy meant that Lorenzo had to step slowly in following signorial precedents. Within his own family, Lorenzo organized a series of endogamic and exogamic unions for his children, hoping thereby to have the best of both worlds. However, in marrying his eldest son Piero into the Neapolitan branch of the Orsini, he created a situation where the heir to the Medicean regime was as much steeped in the baronial culture of his Orsini relatives as in the sensibilities of his fellow citizens. Lorenzo's premature death in 1492 left Piero with an uncertain political legacy and a hold on power that was to

---

52 Tornabuoni 1978, 41, 66; 2001, 50.
53 Kent 1997, 24–33.
54 Meli 2008, 67–72; Maguire 1936, 46.
55 According to Francesco Guicciardini, Lorenzo's control of the Florentine marriage market was formidable: "non si faceva parentado alcuno più che mediocre senza participazione e licenzia sua." Guicciardini 1931, 79. See Guidi Bruscoli 1997.

prove short lived. For Florentine traditionalists, the full consequences of Piero's marriage to Alfonsina Orsini became evident in mid-1515 when the couple's son Lorenzo di Piero, leader of the restored Medicean regime at home, led Florentine troops against the French, leaving his mother as de facto ruler of Florence. The prospect of an Orsini and a woman effectively in charge of the city vindicated long-held Florentine convictions that female interference in government, synonymous as it was with lordly regimes, was politically corrosive and augured ill for the future of the republic under Medicean domination.

Bibliography

ACCIAIUOLI, DONATO. "Oratio habita quando Cosmus Medices ex decreto publico factus fuit Pater Patriae." In *Magni Cosmi Medicei vita*, edited by ANGELO FABRONI, 2:260–262. Pisa, 1789.

ACIDINI, CRISTINA, ed. *Il Mugello, la Valdisieve e la Romagna fiorentina*. Milan, 2000.

ACKERMAN, JAMES S. *The Villa: Form and Ideology of Country Houses*. London, 1990.

ADY, CECILIA M. *The Bentivoglio of Bologna: A Study in Despotism*. London, 1937.

———. *Lorenzo dei Medici and Renaissance Italy*. London, 1955.

ALBERTI, LEON BATTISTA. *L'architettura (De re aedificatoria)*. Edited by GIOVANNI ORLANDI and PAOLO PORTOGHESI. 2 vols. Milan, 1966. Reprinted Milan, 1989.

———. *I libri della famiglia*. Edited by RUGGIERO ROMANO and ALBERTO TENENTI. Turin, 1969.

———. *On the Art of Building in Ten Books*. Translated by JOSEPH RYKWERT, NEIL LEACH, and ROBERT TAVERNOR. Cambridge MA, 1988.

ALBERTINI, RUDOLF VON. *Firenze dalla repubblica al principato. Storia e coscienza politica*. Translated by CESARE CRISTOFOLINI. Turin, 1970. First published Bern, 1955.

ALESSIO, GIAN CARLO. "The 'Lectura' of the *Triumphi* in the Fifteenth Century." In *Petrarch's Triumphs: Allegory and Spectacle*, edited by KONRAD EISENBICHLER and AMILCARE A. IANNUCCI, 269–290. Ottawa, 1990.

ALIGHIERI, DANTE. *La divina commedia*. Edited by NATALINO SAPEGNO. 3 vols. Florence, 1955.

AMERIGHI, CHIARA. *Mugello e Val di Sieve*. Florence, 1977.

AMES-LEWIS, FRANCIS. "Early Medicean Devices." *Journal of the Warburg and Courtauld Institutes* 42 (1979): 122–143.

———. "The Inventories of Piero di Cosimo de' Medici's Library." *La bibliofilia* 84 (1982): 102–142.

———, ed. *Cosimo "il Vecchio" de' Medici, 1389–1464: Essays in Commemoration of the 600th Anniversary of Cosimo de' Medici's Birth*. Oxford, 1992.

AMMANNATI PICCOLOMINI, JACOPO. *Lettere 1444–1479*. Edited by PAOLO CHERUBINI. 3 vols. Rome, 1997.

AMMIRATO, SCIPIONE. *Istorie fiorentine*. Florence, 1641–47.

ANDREOZZI, DANIELE. *Nascita di un disordine. Una famiglia signorile e una valle piacentina tra XV e XVI secolo*. Milan, 1993.

———. "La rivolta contadina del 1462 nell'episcopato di Piacenza." In *Proteste e rivolte contadine nell'Italia medievale*, edited by GIOVANNI CHERUBINI, 65–81. Rome, 1994.

———. "Il periodo sforzesco (1448–1499)." In *Storia di Piacenza*. Vol. 3, *Dalla signoria viscontea al principato farnesiano (1313–1545)*, edited by PIERO CASTIGNOLI, 133–166. Piacenza, 1997a.

———. *Piacenza, 1402–1545. Ipotesi di ricerca*. Piacenza, 1997b.

ANSELMI, GIAN MARIO. *Ricerche sul Machiavelli storico*. Pisa, 1979.

ANTENHOFER, CHRISTINA. "Il potere delle gentildonne. L'esempio di Barbara di Brandenburgo e Paula Gonzaga." In *Donne di potere nel Rinascimento*, edited by LETIZIA ARCANGELI and SUSANNA PEYRONEL RAMBALDI, 67–87. Rome, 2008.

Antiqua ducum Mediolani decreta. Milan, 1654.

ANTONELLI, GIOVANNI. "La magistratura degli otto di guardia a Firenze." *Archivio storico italiano* 112 (1953): 3–39.

ANTONIELLI, LIVIO, ed. *Le polizie informali. Seminario di studi, Messina, 28–29 novembre 2003*. Soveria Mannelli (Catanzaro), 2010.

ARCANGELI, LETIZIA, ed. *Milano e Luigi XII. Ricerche sul primo dominio francese in Lombardia, 1499–1512*. Milan, 2002.

———. *Gentiluomini di Lombardia. Ricerche sull'aristocrazia padana nel Rinascimento*. Milan, 2003.

———. "Appunti su guelfi e ghibellini in Lombardia nelle guerre d'Italia (1494–1530)." In *Guelfi e ghibellini nell'Italia del Rinascimento*, edited by MARCO GENTILE, 391–472. Rome, 2005.

———. "'Come bosco et spelunca di latroni.' Città e ordine pubblico a Parma e nello stato di Milano tra quattrocento e cinquecento." In *Le polizie informali. Seminario di studi, Messina, 28–29 novembre 2003*, edited by LIVIO ANTONIELLI, 65–89. Soveria Mannelli (Catanzaro), 2010.

ARIOSTO, LODOVICO. *Lettere*. Edited by ANGELO STELLA. Milan, 1965.

ARRIGHI, VANNA. "Gaddi, Francesco." *Dizionario biografico degli italiani* 51 (1998).

The Art-Treasures Examiner: A Pictorial, Critical, and Historical Record of the Art-Treasures Exhibition, at Manchester, in 1857. Manchester, 1857.

ASCHERI, MARIO, and DONATELLA CIAMPOLI. "Il distretto e il contado nella repubblica di Siena. L'esempio della Val d'Orcia nel Quattrocento." In *La Val d'Orcia nel medioevo e nei primi secoli dell'età moderna*, edited by ALFIO CORTONESI, 83–112. Rome, 1990.

ASCOLI, ALBERT RUSSELL. *Dante and the Making of a Modern Author*. Cambridge, 2008.

ASTORRI, ANTONELLA. "Note sulla mercanzia fiorentina sotto Lorenzo dei Medici. Aspetti istituzionali e politici." *Archivio storico italiano* 150 (1992): 965–993.

BACCI, MARSILIO, ed. *I Bentivoglio. Signori di Bologna*. Bologna, 1969.

BAKHTIN, MIHAIL MIHAJLOVIC. *L'opera di Rabelais e la cultura popolare. Riso, carnevale e festa nella tradizione medievale e rinascimentale*. Translated by MILI ROMANO. Turin, 1979.

BALDASSARRI, STEFANO, and ARIELLE SAIBER, eds. *Images of Quattrocento Florence*. New Haven, 2000.

BARBARO, ZACCARIA. *Corrispondenze diplomatiche veneziane da Napoli. Dispacci di Zaccaria Barbaro, 1 novembre 1471–7 settembre 1473*. Edited by GIGI CORAZZOL. Rome, 1994.

BARON, HANS. *The Crisis of the Early Italian Renaissance: Civic Humanism and Republican Liberty in an Age of Classicism and Tyranny*. Princeton, 1955. Revised edition, with epilogue, Princeton, 1966.

———. "Leonardo Bruni: 'Professional Rhetorician' or 'Civic Humanist'?" *Past and Present* 16 (1968): 21–37.

BAUSI, FRANCESCO. *I "Discorsi" di Niccolò Machiavelli. Genesi e strutture*. Florence, 1985.

———. "Politica e cultura nel commento al *Trionfo della Fama* di Jacopo Bracciolini." *Interpres* 9 (1989): 64–149.

———. "L'epica tra latino e volgare." In *La Toscana al tempo di Lorenzo il Magnifico. Politica, economia, cultura, arte*, 2:357–373. Pisa, 1996.

———. "La *Carlias* di Ugolino Verino." In *Paladini di carta. Il modello cavalleresco fiorentino*, edited by MARCO VILLORESI, 161–173. Rome, 2006.

———. *Umanesimo a Firenze nell'età di Lorenzo e Poliziano*. Rome, 2011.

BECCHI, GENTILE. "Carmina. Edizione critica, traduzione e commento." Edited by NICOLETTA MARCELLI. PhD thesis, Università degli studi di Firenze, 2012. (Accessible in BNCF and BNCR.)

BECKER, MARVIN. "Church and State in Florence on the Eve of the Renaissance (1343–1382)." *Speculum* 37 (1962): 509–527.

———. *Florence in Transition*. Vol. 2, *Studies in the Rise of the Territorial State*. Baltimore, 1968.

BELCARI, FEO. "Abram e Isaac." In *Sacre rappresentazioni dei secoli XIV, XV, e XVI*, edited by ALESSANDRO D'ANCONA, 1:41–59. Florence, 1872.

BELLINAZZI, ANNA, and IRENE COTTA. "Controllo sociale e repressione del dissenso. Gli otto di guardia e balia." In *Consorterie politiche e mutamenti istituzionali in età laurenziana*, exhibition catalog, Florence, Archivio di Stato, edited by MARIA AUGUSTA MORELLI TIMPANARO, ROSALIA MANNO TOLU, and PAOLO VITI, 151–167. Florence, 1992.

BELLONI, CRISTINA. "Prime indagine sulle relazioni tra Vigevano e il governo sforzesco durante il ducato di Francesco I (1450–66)." In *Vigevano e i territori circostanti alla fine del Medioevo*, edited by GIORGIO CHITTOLINI, 261–292. Milan, 1997.

BELLOSTA, ROBERTO. "Gli uffici ed il governo della città. Ricerche sull'amministrazione sforzesca a Piacenza al tempo di Francesco e Galeazzo Maria Sforza (1448–1476)." PhD thesis, Università degli studi di Milano, 2001. (Accessible in BNCF and BNCR.)

——. "Le 'squadre' in consiglio. Assemblee cittadine ed élite di governo urbana a Piacenza nella seconda metà del Quattrocento tra divisioni di parte ed ingerenze ducali." *Nuova rivista storica* 87 (2003): 1–54.

BELVEDERI, RAFFAELE. "I Bentivoglio e i Malvezzi a Bologna negli anni 1463–1506." *Annali della facoltà di magistero dell'Università di Bari* 6 (1967): 35–78.

BENIGNI, PAOLA, LAURETTA CARBONE, and CLAUDIO SAVIOTTI. *Fonti per la storia del sistema fiscale urbano, 1384–1533*. Rome, 1985.

BENNER, ERICA. *Machiavelli's Ethics*. Princeton, 2009.

BENTLEY, JERRY H. *Politics and Culture in Renaissance Naples*. Princeton, 1987.

BERETTA, RINALDO. *Appunti storici su alcuni monasteri e località della Brianza*. Monza, 1966.

BERTELLI, SERGIO. "Uno magistrato per a tempo lungho o uno dogie." In *Studi di storia medievale e moderna per Ernesto Sestan*, 2:451–494. Florence, 1980.

——. "Di due profili mancati e di un bilancino con pesi truccati." *Archivio storico italiano* 145 (1987): 579–610.

BERTELLI, SERGIO, and GIULIANO CRIFÒ, eds. *Rituale, cerimoniale, etichetta*. Milan, 1985.

BERTELLI, SERGIO, NICOLAI RUBINSTEIN, and CRAIG HUGH SMYTH, eds. *Florence and Venice: Comparisons and Relations; Acts of Two Conferences at Villa I Tatti in 1976–1977*. Florence, 1979–80.

——. *Florence and Milan: Comparisons and Relations; Acts of Two Conferences at Villa I Tatti in 1982–1984*. Florence, 1989.

BESSI, ROSSELLA. "Lo spettacolo e la scrittura." In *Le tems revient. 'L tempo si rinuova. Feste e spettacoli nella Firenze di Lorenzo il Magnifico*, exhibition catalog, Florence, Palazzo Medici Riccardi, edited by PAOLA VENTRONE, 103–117. Milan, 1992.

BEYER, ANDREAS. "Funktion und Repräsentation: Die Porphyry-Rotae der Medici." In *Piero de' Medici "il Gottoso" (1416–1469)*, edited by ANDREAS BEYER and BRUCE BOUCHER, 151–163. Berlin, 1993.

BIAGINI, LORENZA. "Terze rime in lode di Cosimo de' Medici." In *Le tems revient. 'L tempo si rinuova. Feste e spettacoli nella Firenze di Lorenzo il Magnifico*, exhibition catalog, Florence, Palazzo Medici Riccardi, edited by PAOLA VENTRONE, 152–153. Milan, 1992.

——. "Edizione critica del *De comparatione reipublicae et regni* di Aurelio Lippo Brandolini." PhD thesis, Università degli Studi di Firenze, 1995. (Accessible in BNCF and BNCR.)

BICCHIERAI, MARCO. *Ai confini della repubblica di Firenze. Poppi dalla signoria dei conti Guidi al vicariato del Casentino (1360–1480)*. Florence, 2005.

BIRCH, DEBRA J. *Pilgrimage to Rome in the Middle Ages*. Woodbridge, Suffolk, 1998.

BIZZOCCHI, ROBERTO. "Chiesa e aristocrazia nella Firenze del Quattrocento." *Archivio storico italiano* 142 (1984): 191–282.

——. *Chiesa e potere nella Toscana del Quattrocento*. Bologna, 1987.

BLACK, JANE. "Constitutional Ambitions, Legal Realities, and the Florentine State." In *Florentine Tuscany: Structures and Practices of Power*, edited by WILLIAM J. CONNELL and ANDREA ZORZI, 48–64. Cambridge, 2000.

——. *Absolutism in Renaissance Milan: Plenitude of Power under the Visconti and the Sforza, 1329–1535*. Oxford, 2009.

——. "Giangaleazzo Visconti and the Ducal Title." In *Communes and Despots in Medieval and Renaissance Italy*, edited by BERNADETTE PATON and JOHN E. LAW, 119–130. Farnham, Surrey, 2010.

———. "Double Duchy: The Sforza Dukes and the Other Lombard Title." In *Europa e Italia. Studi in onore di Giorgio Chittolini*, edited by PAOLA GUGLIELMOTTI, ISABELLA LAZZARINI, and GIAN MARIA VARANINI, 15–27. Florence, 2011.

BLACK, ROBERT. "La storia della prima crociata di Benedetto Accolti e la diplomazia fiorentina rispetto all'Oriente." *Archivio storico italiano* 131 (1973): 3–25.

———. *Benedetto Accolti and the Florentine Renaissance*. Cambridge, 1985.

———. "Piero de' Medici and Arezzo." In *Piero de' Medici "il Gottoso" (1416–1469)*, edited by ANDREAS BEYER and BRUCE BOUCHER, 21–38. Berlin, 1993.

———. "Lorenzo and Arezzo." In *Lorenzo the Magnificent: Culture and Politics*, edited by MICHAEL MALLETT and NICHOLAS MANN, 217–234. London, 1996.

———. "Arezzo, the Medici and the Florentine Regime." In *Florentine Tuscany: Structures and Practices of Power*, edited by WILLIAM J. CONNELL and ANDREA ZORZI, 293–311. Cambridge, 2000.

BLACKBURN, BONNIE. "Lorenzo de' Medici, a Lost Isaac Manuscript, and the Venetian Ambassador." In *Musica Franca: Essays in Honor of Frank A. D'Accone*, edited by IRENE ALM, ALYSON McLAMORE, and COLLEEN REARDON, 19–44. Stuyvesant NY, 1996.

BOISSEUIL, DIDIER. "L'alun en Toscane à la fin du Moyen Âge: Une première approche." In *L'alun de Méditerranée*, edited by PHILIPPE BORGARD, JEAN-PIERRE BRUN, and MAURICE PICON, 105–117. Naples, 2005.

BÖNINGER, LORENZ. "Diplomatie im Dienst der Kontinuität: Piero de' Medici zwischen Rom und Mailand (1447–1454)." In *Piero de' Medici "il Gottoso" (1416–1469)*, edited by ANDREAS BEYER and BRUCE BOUCHER, 39–54. Berlin, 1993.

———. *Die deutsche Einwanderung nach Florenz im Spätmittelalter*. Leiden, 2006a.

———. "La 'riforma laurenziana' di Santa Croce sull'Arno (11 giugno 1471)." *Archivio storico italiano* 164 (2006b): 319–324.

BORGIA, LUIGI, and FRANCESCA FUMI CAMBI GADO. "Insegne araldiche e imprese nella Firenze medicea del Quattrocento." In *Consorterie politiche e mutamenti istituzionali in età laurenziana*, exhibition catalog, Florence, Archivio di Stato, edited by MARIA AUGUSTA MORELLI TIMPANARO, ROSALIA MANNO TOLU, and PAOLO VITI, 213–238. Cinisello Balsamo, 1992.

BRACCIOLINI, POGGIO. *Epistolarum familiarium libri*. Edited by HELENE HARTH. Florence, 1984.

———. *De infelicitate principum*. Edited by DAVIDE CANFORA. Rome, 1998.

———. "Defensio de praestantia Caesaris et Scipionis ad Franciscum Barbarum virum clarissimum." In *La controversia di Poggio Bracciolini e Guarino Veronese su Cesare e Scipione*, edited by DAVIDE CANFORA, 141–167. Florence, 2001a.

———. "De praestantia Scipionis et Caesaris." In *La controversia di Poggio Bracciolini e Guarino Veronese su Cesare e Scipione*, edited by DAVIDE CANFORA, 111–118. Florence, 2001b.

BRANCA, VITTORE, ed. *Mercanti scrittori. Ricordi nella Firenze tra medioevo e rinascimento*. Milan, 1986.

———. *"Con amore volere." Narrar di mercatanti fra Boccaccio e Machiavelli*. Venice, 1996.

BRAND, BENJAMIN. "A Medieval *Scholasticus* and Renaissance Choirmaster: A Portrait of John Hothby at Lucca." *Renaissance Quarterly* 63 (2010): 754–806.

BRANDOLINI, AURELIO LIPPO. *Republics and Kingdoms Compared*. Edited and translated by JAMES HANKINS. Cambridge MA, 2009.

BROWN, ALISON. "The Humanist Portrait of Cosimo de' Medici, *Pater Patriae*." *Journal of the Warburg and Courtauld Institutes* 24 (1961): 186–221.

———. *Bartolomeo Scala, 1430–1497, Chancellor of Florence: The Humanist as Bureaucrat*. Princeton, 1979.

———. "Cosimo de' Medici's Wit and Wisdom." In *Cosimo "il Vecchio" de' Medici, 1389–1464: Essays in Commemoration of the 600th Anniversary of Cosimo de' Medici's Birth*, edited by FRANCIS AMES-LEWIS, 95–114. Oxford, 1992a.

———. "Lorenzo, the Monte, and the Seventeen Reformers: Public and Private Interest." In *The Medici in Florence: The Exercise and Language of Power*, 151–211. Florence and Perth, 1992b.

——. *The Medici in Florence: The Exercise and Language of Power.* Florence and Perth, 1992c.

——. "Pierfrancesco de' Medici, 1430–1476." In *The Medici in Florence: The Exercise and Language of Power*, 73–102. Florence and Perth, 1992d.

——. "Public and Private Interest: Lorenzo, the Monte, and the Seventeen Reformers." In *Lorenzo de' Medici: Studi*, edited by GIAN CARLO GARFAGNINI, 103–165. Florence, 1992e.

——. "Lorenzo and Public Opinion: The Problem of Opposition." In *Lorenzo il Magnifico e il suo mondo*, edited by GIAN CARLO GARFAGNINI, 61–85. Florence, 1994.

——. "De-Masking Renaissance Republicanism." In *Renaissance Civic Humanism: Reappraisals and Reflections*, edited by JAMES HANKINS, 179–199. Cambridge, 2000a.

——. "The Language of Empire." In *Florentine Tuscany: Structures and Practices of Power*, edited by WILLIAM J. CONNELL and ANDREA ZORZI, 32–47. Cambridge, 2000b.

——. "Women, Children, and Politics in the Letters of a Florentine Notary: Ser Pace di Bambello." In *Florence and Beyond: Culture, Society, and Politics in Renaissance Italy; Essays in Honour of John M. Najemy*, edited by DAVID S. PETERSON and DANIEL E. BORNSTEIN, 229–255. Toronto, 2008.

——. "Florentine Diplomacy on the Banks of the Po: Bernardo Ricci's Meeting with Lodovico il Moro in June 1493." In *Mantova e il Rinascimento italiano. Studi in onore di David S. Chambers*, edited by PHILIPPA JACKSON and GUIDO REBECCHINI, 301–314. Mantua, 2011a.

——. "Lorenzo de' Medici's New Men and Their Mores." In *Medicean and Savonarolan Florence: The Interplay of Politics, Humanism, and Religion*, 1–38. Turnhout, 2011b.

——. *Medicean and Savonarolan Florence: The Interplay of Politics, Humanism, and Religion.* Turnhout, 2011c.

——. "Dialogue or Dissent: Cultural Politics in Renaissance Florence." In *Umanesimo e università in Toscana (1300–1600)*, edited by STEFANO UGO BALDASSARRI, FABRIZIO RICCIARDELLI, and ENRICO SPAGNESI, 33–57. Florence, 2012.

BRUCKER, GENE A. *Florentine Politics and Society, 1343–1378.* Princeton, 1962.

——. *The Civic World of Early Renaissance Florence.* Princeton, 1977.

——. *Renaissance Florence.* New York, 1969. Reprinted Berkeley, 1983.

——. *Giovanni and Lusanna: Love and Marriage in Renaissance Florence.* Berkeley, 1986.

BRUSCHI, ARNALDO. "Brunelleschi e la nuova architettura fiorentina." In *Storia dell'architettura italiana. Il Quattrocento*, edited by FRANCESCO PAOLO FIORE, 38–113. Milan, 1998.

BUDINI GATTAI, ROBERTO, FRANCESCA CARRARA SCRETI, and ILARIA AGOSTINI. *Il Trebbio in Mugello. Terre, storia, architettura. Tre mila anni di un trivium.* Florence, 2011.

BULLARD, MELISSA MERIAM. *Lorenzo il Magnifico: Image and Anxiety, Politics and Finance.* Florence, 1994.

——. "Lorenzo and Patterns of Diplomatic Discourse in the Late Fifteenth Century." In *Lorenzo the Magnificent: Culture and Politics*, edited by MICHAEL E. MALLETT and NICHOLAS MANN, 263–274. London, 1996.

——. "Adumbrations of Power and the Politics of Appearances in Medicean Florence." *Renaissance Studies* 12 (1998): 341–356.

——. "'Hammering Away at the Pope': Nofri Tornabuoni, Lorenzo de' Medici's Agent and Collaborator in Rome." In *Florence and Beyond: Culture, Society, and Politics in Renaissance Italy; Essays in Honour of John M. Najemy*, edited by DAVID S. PETERSON and DANIEL E. BORNSTEIN, 383–398. Toronto, 2008.

BURKE, PETER. *The Historical Anthropology of Early Modern Italy: Essays on Perception and Communication.* Cambridge, 1987.

BURNS, HOWARD. *La villa italiana del rinascimento.* Costabissara, 2012.

BURROUGHS, CHARLES. *The Italian Renaissance Palace Facade: Structures of Authority, Surfaces of Sense.* Cambridge, 2002.

BUSER, BENJAMIN. *Die Beziehungen der Mediceer zu Frankreich während der Jahre 1434–1494 in ihrem Zusammenhang mit den allgemeinen Verhältnissen Italiens.* Leipzig, 1879.

BUTTERS, SUZANNE B. *The Triumph of Vulcan: Sculptors' Tools, Porphyry, and the Prince in Ducal Florence.* Florence, 1996.

CABRINI, ANNA MARIA. "La storia da non imitare. Il versante negativo dell'esemplarità nelle *Istorie fiorentine.*" In *Cultura e scrittura di Machiavelli. Atti del convegno di Firenze-Pisa 27–30 ottobre 1997*, 197–220. Rome, 1998.

———. *Un'idea di Firenze. Da Villani a Guicciardini.* Rome, 2001.

CADONI, GIORGIO, and FRANCO MARIA DI SCIULLO, eds. *Provvisioni concernenti l'ordinamento della repubblica fiorentina, 1494–1512.* 2 vols. Rome, 1994–2000.

CAGGESE, ROMOLO, ed. *Statuti della repubblica fiorentina.* Vol. 2, *Statuto del podestà dell'anno 1325*, edited by GIULIANO PINTO, FRANCESCO SALVESTRINI, and ANDREA ZORZI. Florence, 1999.

CAGLIOTI, FRANCESCO. "La tomba verrocchiesca dei 'cosmiadi' e la basilica di San Lorenzo. Antefatti e primi successi." In *Studi in onore del Kunsthistorisches Institut in Florenz per il suo centenario (1897–1997)*, 127–154. Pisa, 1996.

CALEFFINI, UGO. *Croniche, 1471–1494.* Edited by FRANCO CAZZOLA. Ferrara, 2006.

CALZOLAI, CARLO CELSO. "Vescovi e arcivescovi di Firenze." In *La chiesa fiorentina*, edited by CARLO CALZOLAI, 15–32. Florence, 1970.

CAMBI, GIOVANNI. *Istorie.* In *Delizie degli eruditi toscani*, edited by ILDEFONSO DI SAN LUIGI, vol. 21. Florence, 1785.

CAMERANI MARRI, GIULIA. *I documenti commerciali del fondo diplomatico mediceo nell'Archivio di Stato di Firenze (1230–1492).* Florence, 1951.

CAMMAROSANO, PAOLO. "Il comune di Siena dalla solidarietà imperiale al guelfismo. Celebrazione e propaganda." In *Le forme della propaganda politica nel Due e nel Trecento*, edited by PAOLO CAMMAROSANO, 455–467. Rome, 1994.

CANESTRINI, GIUSEPPE, and ABEL DESJARDINS. *Négociations diplomatiques de la France avec la Toscane.* 6 vols. Paris, 1859–86.

CANFORA, DAVIDE. *La controversia di Poggio Bracciolini e Guarino Veronese su Cesare e Scipione.* Florence, 2001.

CANZIAN, DARIO. "Condivisione del potere, modalità di successione e processo di dinastizzazione." In *Signorie cittadine e forme di governo personale nell'Italia comunale e post-comunale*, edited by JEAN-CLAUDE MAIRE VIGUEUR, 439–465. Rome, 2013.

CAPPONI, GINO. "Lettera scritta da Pietro di Lorenzo de' Medici a Dionigi Pucci... del dì 6 Maggio 1494." *Archivio storico italiano* 1 (1842): 343–347.

———. *Storia della repubblica di Firenze.* Florence, 1875.

CARAFA, DIOMEDE. *Memoriali.* Edited by FRANCA PETRUCCI NARDELLI. Rome, 1988.

CARDINI, FRANCO. "La repubblica di Firenze e la crociata di Pio II." *Rivista di storia della chiesa in Italia* 33 (1979): 455–482.

———. "Le insigne laurenziane." In *Le tems revient. 'L tempo si rinuova. Feste e spettacoli nella Firenze di Lorenzo il Magnifico*, exhibition catalog, Florence, Palazzo Medici Riccardi, edited by PAOLA VENTRONE, 55–74. Milan, 1992.

———. *L'acciar de' cavalieri. Studi sulla cavalleria nel mondo toscano e italico (secc. 13.–15.).* Florence, 1997.

CAREW-REID, NICOLE. *Les fêtes florentines au temps de Lorenzo il Magnifico.* Florence, 1995.

CAROCCI, GUIDO. *L'illustratore fiorentino.* Florence, 1880. Reprinted Florence, 1983.

———. *I dintorni di Firenze.* 2 vols. Florence, 1906. Reprinted Rome, 1968.

Carta geologica d'Italia, 2nd ed., 1962, 1:25,000.

CARUNCHIO, TANCREDI. "Michelozzo architetto 'restauratore' di fabbriche medicee. Il Trebbio." In *Michelozzo. Scultore e architetto (1396–1472)*, edited by GABRIELE MOROLLI, 73–80. Florence, 1998.

CASALI, GIOVANNA. "Le proprietà medicee nel Mugello." In *Il Mugello, un territorio, una presenza culturale. I beni culturali. Dalla conoscenza storica una prospettiva per il Mugello*, 159–168. Florence, 1983.

CASINI, BRUNO. "Brevi note sui mercanti forestieri operanti a Pisa nel settore delle importazioni e delle esportazioni nel semestre ottobre 1468–aprile 1469." *Le Apuane* 15, no. 29 (1996): 38–52; 15, no. 30 (1996): 78–95.

CASINI, MATTEO. *I gesti del principe. La festa politica a Firenze e Venezia in età rinascimentale.* Venice, 1996.

———. "Note sul linguaggio politico veneziano del Rinascimento." In *Politica e cultura nelle repubbliche italiane dal Medioevo all'età moderna*, edited by SIMONETTA ADORNI-BRACCESI and MARIO ASCHERI, 309–333. Rome, 2001.

———. "Fra città-stato e stato regionale. Riflessioni politiche sulla repubblica di Venezia in età moderna." *Studi veneziani* 44 (2002): 15–36.

CASTELNUOVO, GUIDO. "Offices and Officials." In *The Italian Renaissance State*, edited by ANDREA GAMBERINI and ISABELLA LAZZARINI, 368–384. Cambridge, 2012.

CASTIGLIONE, FRANCESCO. *Vita Beati Antonini.* Florence, 1680.

CASTIGNOLI, PIERO. "La dedizione di Piacenza a Francesco Sforza (27 ottobre 1448)." *Bollettino storico piacentino* 57 (1962): 126–154.

CASTRO, PAOLO DI. *Consiliorum sive responsorum.* 3 vols. Turin, 1580.

CAUCHIES, JEAN-MARIE, and GIORGIO CHITTOLINI, eds. *Milano e Borgogna. Due stati principeschi tra medioevo e rinascimento.* Rome, 1990.

CAVALCANTI, GIOVANNI. *Istorie fiorentine.* Edited by GUIDO DI PINO. Milan, 1944.

———. *The Trattato Politico-Morale of Giovanni Cavalcanti.* Edited by MARCELLA T. GRENDLER. Geneva, 1973.

———. *Nuova opera.* Edited by ANTOINE MONTI. Paris, 1989.

CAVALLAR, OSWALDO. "Il tiranno, i *dubia* del giudice, et i *consilia* dei giuristi." *Archivio storico italiano* 155 (1997): 265–345.

CAVALLI, CARLO. *Cenni statistico-storici della Valle Vigezzo.* 3 vols. Turin, 1845.

CAZZOLA, GABRIELE. "'Bentivoli machinatores'. Aspetti politici e momenti teatrali di una festa quattrocentesca bolognese." *Biblioteca teatrale* 23 (1979): 14–39.

CENGARLE, FEDERICA. *Immagine di potere e prassi di governo. La politica feudale di Filippo Maria Visconti.* Rome, 2006.

CERRETANI, BARTOLOMEO. *Ricordi.* Edited by GIULIANA BERTI. Florence, 1993.

———. *Storia fiorentina.* Edited by GIULIANA BERTI. Florence, 1994.

CHAMBERS, DAVID S. "Cardinal Francesco Gonzaga in Florence." In *Florence and Italy: Renaissance Studies in Honour of Nicolai Rubinstein*, edited by PETER DENLEY and CAROLINE ELAM, 241–261. London, 1988.

———. "Postscript on the Worldly Affairs of Cardinal Francesco Gonzaga and Other Princely Cardinals." In *Renaissance Cardinals and Their Worldly Problems*, by DAVID S. CHAMBERS, xi, 1–22. Aldershot, 1992a.

———. *A Renaissance Cardinal and His Worldly Goods: The Will and Inventory of Francesco Gonzaga (1444–1483).* Aldershot, 1992b.

CHASTEL, ANDRÉ. *Art et humanisme à Florence au temps de Laurent de Médicis: Études sur la renaissance et l'humanisme platonicien.* Paris, 1959.

CHIAPPINI, LUCIANO. *Eleonora d'Aragona, prima duchessa di Ferrrara.* Rovigo, 1956.

CHIESI, GIUSEPPE, ed. *Ticino ducale. Il carteggio e gli atti ufficiali.* Vol. 2, pt. 1, *Galeazzo Maria Sforza, 1466–1468.* Bellinzona, 1999.

CHIFFOLEAU, JACQUES. "Corsini, Pietro." *Dizionario biografico degli italiani* 29 (1983).

CHIOSTRI, FERDINANDO. *La Petraja. Villa e giardino. Settecento anni di storia.* Florence, 1972.

CHITTOLINI, GIORGIO. "I capitoli di dedizione delle comunità lombarde a Francesco Sforza. Motivi di contrasto fra città e contado." In *Felix olim Lombardia. Studi di storia padana dedicati dagli allievi a Giuseppe Martini*, 673–698. Milan, 1978.

———. "Ricerche sull'ordinamento territoriale del dominio fiorentino agli inizi del secolo XV." In *La formazione dello stato regionale e le istituzioni del contado. Secoli XIV e XV*, 225–265. Turin, 1979.

——. "Progetti di riordinamento ecclesiastico della Toscana agli inizi del Quattrocento." In *Forme e techniche del potere nella città. Secoli XIV–XVII*, edited by Sergio Bertelli, 275–296. Perugia, 1980.

——, ed. *Gli Sforza, la chiesa lombarda, la corte di Roma*. Naples, 1989a.

——. "L'onore dell'officiale." In *Florence and Milan: Comparisons and Relations; Acts of Two Conferences at Villa I Tatti in 1982–1984*, edited by Sergio Bertelli, Nicolai Rubinstein, and Craig Hugh Smyth, 1:101–133. Florence, 1989b.

——. "Cities, 'City-States,' and Regional States in North-Central Italy." In *Cities and States in Europe 1000–1800*, edited by Wim Blockmans, Giorgio Chittolini, and Charles Tilly, 689–706. Boulder, 1989c.

——. "Di alcuni aspetti della crisi dello stato sforzesco." In *Milano e Borgogna. Due stati principeschi tra medioevo e rinascimento*, edited by Jean-Marie Cauchies and Giorgio Chittolini, 21–34. Rome, 1990.

——. "Statuti e autonomie urbane. Introduzione." In *Statuti, città, territori in Italia e Germania tra medioevo ed età moderna*, edited by Giorgio Chittolini and Dietmar Willoweit, 7–45. Bologna, 1991.

——. "The 'Private,' the 'Public,' the State." In *The Origins of the State in Italy 1300–1600*, edited by Julius Kirshner, 34–61. Chicago, 1995.

——. *Città, comunità e feudi negli stati dell'Italia centro-settentrionale (secoli 14.–16.)*. Milan, 1996a.

——. "Civic Religion and the Countryside in Late Medieval Italy." In *City and Countryside in Late Medieval and Renaissance Italy: Essays Presented to Philip Jones*, edited by Trevor Dean and Chris Wickham, 69–80. London, 1996b.

——. "'Crisi' e 'lunga durata' delle istituzioni comunali in alcuni dibattiti recenti." In *Penale, giustizia, potere. Metodi, ricerche, storiografie*, edited by Luigi Lacché, 125–154. Macerata, 2007.

——. "Note sul comune di Firenze e i 'piccoli signori' dell'Appennino secondo la pace di Sarzana (1353)." In *From Florence to the Mediterranean and Beyond: Essays in Honour of Anthony Molho*, edited by Diogo Ramada Curto, Eric R. Dursteller, Julius Kirshner, and Francesca Trivellato, 193–210. Florence, 2009a.

——. "'Verae civitates'. Ancora a proposito del De iudiciis." In *Tra diritto e storia. Studi in onore di Luigi Berlinguer promossi dalle Università di Siena e di Sassari*, 449–461. Soveria Mannelli (Catanzaro), 2009b.

——. "Urban Population, Urban Territories, Small Towns: Some Problems of the History of Urbanisation in Northern and Central Italy." In *Power and Persuasion: Essays in the Art of State Building in Honour of W. P. Blockmans*, edited by Peter Hoppenbrouwers, Antheun Janse, and Robert Stein, 227–241. Turnhout, 2010.

——. "Le città e i loro territori. Alcune note comparative in relazione all'Italia centrosettentrionale tra medioevo ed età moderna." In *Le gouvernement des communautés politiques à la fin du moyen âge. Entre puissance et négociation. Villes, finances, état. Actes du colloque en l'honnneur d'Albert Rigaudière, Paris, 6–8 novembre 2008*, edited by Corinne Leveleux-Teixeira, 65–78. Paris, 2011.

——. "Milano 'città imperiale'? Note su due ambascerie di Enea Silvio Piccolomini (1447, 1449)." In *Il ritorno dei classici nell'umanesimo. Studi in onore di Gianvito Resta*, edited by Gabriella Albanese, Claudia Ciociola, Mariarosa Cortesi, and Claudia Villa. Florence, forthcoming.

Chittolini, Giorgio, Anthony Molho, and Pierangelo Schiera, eds. *Origini dello stato. Processi di formazione statale in Italia fra medioevo ed età moderna*. Bologna, 1994.

Christiansen, Keith, and Stefan Weppelmann, eds. *The Renaissance Portrait: From Donatello to Bellini*. New York and New Haven, 2011.

Ciasca, Raffaele. *L'arte dei medici e speziali nella storia e nel commercio fiorentino dal secolo XII al XV*. Florence, 1927.

CICCAGLIONI, GIOVANNI. "Il mare a Firenze. Interazioni tra mutamenti geografici, cambiamenti istituzionali e trasformazioni economiche nella Toscana fiorentina del '400." *Archivio storico italiano* 167 (2009): 91–125.

CICERO. *De senectute, De amicitia, De divinatione.* Translated by WILLIAM ARMISTEAD FALCONER. Cambridge MA, 1964.

———. *De inventione.* Translated by H. M. HUBBELL. Cambridge MA, 1976.

CIPOLLA, BARTOLOMEO. *Consilia criminalia.* Venice, 1555.

CLARKE, GEORGIA. "Magnificence and the City: Giovanni II Bentivoglio and the Architecture of Fifteenth-Century Bologna." *Renaissance Studies* 13 (1999): 397–411.

———. *Roman House—Renaissance Palaces: Inventing Antiquity in Fifteenth-Century Italy.* Cambridge, 2003.

———. "Giovanni II Bentivoglio and the Uses of Chivalry: Towards the Creation of a 'Republican Court' in Fifteenth-Century Bologna." In *Artistic Exchange and Cultural Translation in the Italian Renaissance City,* edited by STEPHEN J. CAMPBELL and STEPHEN J. MILNER, 163–186. Cambridge and New York, 2004.

CLARKE, PAULA C. *The Soderini and the Medici: Power and Patronage in Fifteenth-Century Florence.* Oxford, 1991.

———. "Lorenzo de' Medici and Tommaso Soderini." In *Lorenzo de' Medici. Studi,* edited by GIAN CARLO GARFAGNINI, 67–101. Florence, 1992.

CLUBB, LOUISE. "Staging Ferrara: State Theater from Borso to Alfonso II." In *Phaethon's Children: The Este Court and Its Culture in Early Modern Ferrara,* edited by DENNIS LOONEY and DEANNA SHEMEK, 345–362. Tempe AZ, 2005.

COGNASSO, FRANCESCO. "Istituzioni comunali e signorili di Milano sotto i Visconti." In *Storia di Milano.* Vol. 6. *Il ducato visconteo e la repubblica ambrosiana (1392–1450),* 449–544. Milan, 1955.

COHEN, RAYMOND. *Theatre of Power: The Art of Diplomatic Signalling.* London, 1987.

COHEN, SIMONA. "The Early Renaissance Personification of Time and Changing Concepts of Temporality." *Renaissance Studies* 14, no. 3 (2000): 301–328.

COLANTUONO, ANTHONY. "Estense Patronage and the Construction of the Ferrarese Renaissance, c. 1395–1598." In *The Court Cities of Northern Italy: Milan, Parma, Piacenza, Mantua, Ferrara, Bologna, Urbino, Pesaro, and Rimini,* edited by CHARLES M. ROSENBERG, 196–243. Cambridge, 2010.

COLÒ, GIUSEPPE. "Cronologia compendiata dei privilegi, decreti dominicali, ordini e rescritti del Contado di Bormio dal 1365 al 1777." *Periodico della società storica per la provincia e antica diocesi di Como* 9 (1892): 129–164.

COLOMBO, ALESSANDRO. "Vigevano e la repubblica ambrosiana nella lotta contro Francesco Sforza (agosto 1447–giugno 1449)." *Bollettino della società pavese di storia patria* 2 (1902): 315–337; 3 (1903): 2–38, 449–516.

———. "L'ingresso di Francesco Sforza in Milano e l'inizio di un nuovo principato." *Archivio storico lombardo* 32, no. 7 (1905): 33–101.

COLUCCI, BENEDETTO. *De discordiis florentinorum.* Edited by LORENZO MEHUS. Florence, 1747.

———. *Scritti inediti di Benedetto Colucci da Pistoia.* Edited by ARSENIO FRUGONI. Florence, 1939.

COMMYNES, PHILIPPE DE. *Lettres.* Edited by JOËL BLANCHARD. Geneva, 2001.

COMPAGNI, DINO. *Cronica.* Edited by DAVIDE CAPPI. Rome, 2000.

CONNELL, WILLIAM J. "Changing Patterns of Medicean Patronage: The Florentine Dominion during the Fifteenth Century." In *Lorenzo il Magnifico e il suo mondo,* edited by GIAN CARLO GARFAGNINI, 87–107. Florence, 1994a.

———. "'Il fautori delle parti': Citizen Interest and the Treatment of a Subject Town, c. 1500." In *Istituzioni e società in Toscana nell'età moderna,* edited by GIUSEPPE PANSINI, 118–147. Rome, 1994b.

———. "Appunti sui rapporti dei primi Medici con le comunità del dominio fiorentino." In *La Toscana al tempo di Lorenzo il Magnifico. Politica, economia, cultura, arte,* 3:907–916. Pisa, 1996.

———. *La città dei crucci. Fazioni e clientele in uno stato repubblicano del '400.* Florence, 2000a.

————. "The Humanist Citizen as Provincial Governor." In *Florentine Tuscany: Structures and Practices of Power*, edited by WILLIAM J. CONNELL and ANDREA ZORZI, 144–164. Cambridge, 2000b.

CONNELL, WILLIAM J., and ANDREA ZORZI, eds. *Florentine Tuscany: Structures and Practices of Power*. Cambridge, 2000.

CONTESSA, MARIA PIA. "La costruzione di un'identità familiare e sociale. Un immigrato cipriota nella Firenze del secondo Quattrocento." *Annali di Firenze* 6 (2009): 151–192.

CONTI, ELIO. *La formazione della struttura agraria moderna nel contado fiorentino*. Rome, 1965.

————. *L'imposta diretta a Firenze nel Quattrocento (1427–1494)*. Rome, 1984.

COPPINI, DONATELLA. "Cosimo *togatus*. Cosimo dei Medici nella poesia latina del Quattrocento." In *Incontri triestini di filologia classica* 6 (2006–7): 101–119.

CORAZZA, BARTOLOMEO DI MICHELE DEL. *Diario fiorentino (1405–1439)*. Edited by ROBERTA GENTILE. Anzio (Rome), 1991.

CORBEILL, ANTHONY. "Ciceronian Invective." In *Brill's Companion to Cicero: Oratory and Rhetoric*, edited by JAMES M. MAY, 197–217. Leiden, 2002.

CORIO, BERNARDINO. *Storia di Milano*. Edited by ANNA MORISI GUERRA. 2 vols. Turin, 1978.

CORRADINI, ELENA. "Medallic Portraits of the Este: *Effigies ad vivum expressae*." In *The Image of the Individual*, edited by NICHOLAS MANN and LUKE SYSON, 22–39. London, 1998.

CORTE, FRANCESCO. *Consilia*. Venice, 1580.

COSTA, PIETRO. *Civitas. Storia della cittadinanza in Europa*. Vol. 1. *Dalla civiltà comunale al Settecento*. Bari, 1999.

COVINI, MARIA NADIA. "'Alle spese di Zoan villano'. Gli alloggiamenti militari nel dominio visconteo-sforzesco." *Nuova rivista storica* 76 (1992): 1–56.

————. *L'esercito del duca. Organizzazione militare e istituzioni al tempo degli Sforza (1450–1480)*. Rome, 1998.

————. "*La balanza drita*". Pratiche di governo, leggi e ordinamenti nel ducato sforzesco. Milan, 2007.

————. "Bibliografia di Giorgio Chittolini 1965–2009." In *Europa e Italia. Studi in onore di Giorgio Chittolini*, xvii–xxxi. Florence, 2011.

————, ed. *Medioevo dei poteri. Studi di storia per Giorgio Chittolini*. Rome, 2012.

COX, VIRGINIA. "Gender and Eloquence in Ercole de' Roberti's 'Portia and Brutus.'" *Renaissance Quarterly* 62 (2009): 61–101.

COX-REARICK, JANET. "Themes of Time and Rule at Poggio a Caiano: The Portico Frieze of Lorenzo il Magnifico." *Mitteilungen des Kunsthistorischen Institutes in Florenz* 26 (1982): 167–210.

————. *Dynasty and Destiny in Medici Art: Pontormo, Leo X, and the Two Cosimos*. Princeton, 1984.

COZZI, GAETANO. "Domenico Morosini e il 'De bene instituta re publica.'" *Studi veneziani* 12 (1970): 405–458.

————. *Repubblica di Venezia e stati italiani. Politica e giustizia dal secolo XVI al secolo XVIII*. Turin, 1982.

————. "Domenico Morosini, Niccolò Machiavelli e la società veneziana." In *Ambiente veneziano, ambiente veneto. Saggi su politica, società, cultura nella repubblica di Venezia in età moderna*, 190–254. Venice, 1997.

CREVATIN, GIULIANA. "La politica e la retorica. Poggio e la controversia su Cesare e Scipione, con una nuova edizione della lettera a Scipione Mainenti." In *Poggio Bracciolini 1380–1980. Nel VI centenario della nascita*, 281–342. Florence, 1982.

CRUCIANI, FABRIZIO, CLELIA FALLETTI, and FRANCO RUFFINI. "La sperimentazione a Ferrara negli anni di Ercole I e di Ludovico Ariosto." *Teatro e storia* 16 (1994): 131–217.

CRUM, ROGER, and JOHN T. PAOLETTI. *Renaissance Florence: A Social History*. Cambridge, 2006.

CUMMINGS, ANTHONY M. *The Maecenas and the Madrigalist: Patrons, Patronage, and the Origins of the Italian Madrigal*. Philadelphia, 2004.

DA BISTICCI, VESPASIANO. *Le vite*. Edited by AULO GRECO. 2 vols. Florence, 1970–76.

————. *Il libro della lodi delle donne*. Edited by GIUSEPPE LOMBARDI. Rome, 1999.

D'ACCONE, FRANK. "The Singers of San Giovanni in Florence during the Fifteenth Century." *Journal of the American Musicological Society* 14 (1961): 307–358.

———. "Some Neglected Composers in the Florentine Chapels, ca. 1475–1525." *Viator* 1 (1970): 263–288.

———. "Lorenzo and Music." In *Lorenzo il Magnifico e il suo mondo*, edited by GIAN CARLO GARFAGNINI, 259–290. Florence, 1994.

D'ADDARIO, ARNALDO. "Acciaiuoli, Angelo." *Dizionario biografico degli italiani* 1 (1960a).

———. "Alberti, Alberto." *Dizionario biografico degli italiani* 1 (1960b).

DANIELS, TOBIAS. *La congiura dei Pazzi. I documenti del conflitto fra Lorenzo de' Medici e Sisto IV. Le bolle di scomunica, la "Florentina synodus," e la "Dissentio" insorta tra la santità del Papa e i Fiorentini.* Florence, 2013a.

———. "Poesia politica degli umanisti. Letteratura e propaganda dopo la congiura dei Pazzi." *Atti e memorie dell'accademia toscana di scienze e lettere, la Colombaria* (2013b): 89–108.

DAVIDSOHN, ROBERT. *Storia di Firenze.* Translated by E. DUPRÉ-THESEIDER. 8 vols. Florence, 1956–68.

DEAN, TREVOR. "The Rise of the *Signori*." In *Italy in the Central Middle Ages, 1000–1300*, edited by DAVID ABULAFIA, 104–124. Oxford, 2004.

———. "Philip James Jones, 1921–2006." *Proceedings of the British Academy* 161 (2009): 207–231.

DE ANGELIS, LAURA. "La fine della libertà pistoiese." In *Studi in onore di Arnaldo d'Addario*, edited by LUIGI BORGIA, FRANCESCO DE LUCA, PAOLO VITI, and RAFFAELLA MARIA ZACCARIA, 1:1157–1165. Lecce, 1995.

———. "Territorial Offices and Officeholders." In *Florentine Tuscany: Structures and Practices of Power*, edited by WILLIAM J. CONNELL and ANDREA ZORZI, 165–182. Cambridge, 2000.

———. "I canonici di San Lorenzo e loro disputa con i canonici della cattedrale." In *Il capitolo di San Lorenzo nel Quattrocento*, edited by PAOLO VITI, 21–34. Florence, 2006.

DE BENEDICTIS, ANGELA. "Lo 'stato popolare di libertà'. Pratica di governo e cultura di governo (1376–1506)." In *Bologna nel medioevo*, edited by OVIDIO CAPITANI, 899–950. Bologna, 2007.

DECARIA, ALESSIO. *Luigi Pulci e Francesco di Matteo Castellani.* Florence, 2009.

———. "Tra Marsilio e Pallante. Una nuova ipotesi sugli ultimi cantari del *Morgante*." In *L'entusiasmo delle opere. Studi in memoria di Domenico De Robertis*, edited by ISABELLA BECHERUCCI, SIMONE GIUSTI, and NATASCIA TONELLI, 299–338. Lecce, 2012.

DE LA RONCIÈRE, CHARLES M. *Florence, centre économique régional au XIV siècle.* 5 vols. Aix-en-Provence, 1976.

———. "De la ville à l'état régional. La constitution du territoire (XIVᵉ–XVᵉ siècle)." In *Florence et la Toscane, XIVᵉ–XIXᵉ siècles. Les dynamiques d'un état italien*, edited by JEAN BOUTIER, SANDRO LANDI, and OLIVIER ROUCHON, 15–38. Rennes, 2004.

———. *Firenze e le sue campagne nel Trecento. Mercanti, produzione, traffici.* Florence, 2005.

DELLA MISERICORDIA, MASSIMO. "Per non privarci di nostre raxone, li siamo stati desobedienti. Patto, giustizia e resistenza nella cultura politica delle comunità alpine nello stato di Milano (XV secolo)." In *Forme della comunicazione politica in Europa nei secoli XV–XVII*, edited by CECILIA NUBOLA and ANDREAS WÜRGLER, 147–215. Bologna, 2004.

———. "Como se tuta questa universitade parlasse. La rappresentanza politica delle comunità nello stato di Milano (XV secolo)." In *Avant le contrat social. Le contrat politique dans l'occident médiéval (XIIIᵉ–XVᵉ siècle)*, edited by FRANÇOIS FORONDA, 117–170. Paris, 2011.

———. "Uno officiale per gubernare questo paese. Considerazioni a proposito della giustizia dello stato e della comunità a partire dalle valli lombarde nel tardo medioevo." In *Medioevo dei poteri. Studi di storia per Giorgio Chittolini*, edited by NADIA COVINI, 245–274. Rome, 2012.

DEL MAINO, GIASONE. *Consiliorum sive responsorum.* 4 vols. Venice, 1581.

DEL PIAZZO, MARCELLO, ed. *Protocolli del carteggio di Lorenzo il Magnifico per gli anni 1473–74, 1477–92.* Florence, 1966.

———. *Il protocollo del carteggio della signoria di Firenze, 1459–1468.* Rome, 1969.

DELTREDICI, FEDERICO. "Lombardy under the Visconti and the Sforza." In *The Italian Renaissance State*, edited by ANDREA GAMBERINI and ISABELLA LAZZARINI, 157–176. Cambridge, 2012.

DELUMEAU, JEAN. *L'alun de Rome, XVe–XIXe siècle*. Paris, 1962.

DE MANDROT, BERNARD. *Dépêches des ambassadeurs milanais en France sous Louis XI et François Sforza*. 4 vols. Paris, 1916–23.

DEMPSEY, CHARLES. *The Early Renaissance and Vernacular Culture*. Cambridge MA, 2012.

DENLEY, PETER, and CAROLINE ELAM, eds. *Florence and Italy: Renaissance Studies in Honour of Nicolai Rubinstein*. London, 1988.

DE ROBERTIS, TERESA, and GIANVITO RESTA. *Seneca. Una vicenda testuale*. Florence, 2005.

DE ROOVER, RAYMOND. *The Rise and Decline of the Medici Bank, 1397–1494*. Cambridge MA, 1963. Reprinted New York, 1966 and 1968, and Washington DC, 1999.

DE ROSA, DANIELA. *Coluccio Salutati. Il cancelliere e il pensatore politico*. Florence, 1980.

DE VERGOTTINI, GIOVANNI. "Contributo alla storia della comitatinanza nello stato della chiesa." *Rivista di storia del diritto italiano* 26–27 (1953–54): 117–126.

———. "Vicariato imperiale e signoria." In *Scritti di storia del diritto italiano*, edited by GUIDO ROSSI, 2:535–584. Milan, 1977. First published 1941.

DE VINCENTIIS, AMEDEO. "Le signorie angioine a Firenze. Storiografia e prospettive." *Reti medievali rivista* 2, no. 2 (2001), http://www.rmojs.unina.it/index.php/rm/article/view/237/230.

———. "Politica, memoria e oblio a Firenze nel XIV secolo. La tradizione documentaria della signoria del duca d'Atene." *Archivio storico italiano* 161 (2003): 209–248.

———. "Storia e stile, 1343/1861. L'immagine del tiranno di Firenze." In *Condannare all'oblio. Pratiche della damnatio memoriae nel medioevo*, edited by ISA LORI SANFILIPPO and ANTONIO RIGON, 159–178. Rome, 2010.

DIANA, ESTHER. "Interventi medicei in Mugello." In *Il Mugello, un territorio, una presenza culturale. I beni culturali. Dalla conoscenza storica una prospettiva per il Mugello*, 169–193. Florence, 1983.

DILCHER, GERHARD, and DIEGO QUAGLIONI, eds. *Gli inizi del diritto pubblico*. Vol. 1. *L'età di Federico Barbarossa. Legislazione e scienza del diritto*. Berlin and Bologna, 2007.

DINI, BRUNO. *Arezzo intorno al 1400. Produzioni e mercato*. Arezzo, 1984.

———. "Le vie di comunicazione del territorio fiorentino alla metà del Quattrocento." In *Mercati e consumi. Organizzazione e qualificazione del commercio in Italia dal XII al XX secolo*, by BRUNO DINI, 285–296. Bologna, 1986.

———. "Aspetti del commercio di esportazione dei panni di lana e dei drappi di seta fiorentini in Costantinopoli negli anni 1522–1531." In *Saggi su una economia-mondo. Firenze e l'Italia fra Mediterraneo ed Europa (secc. XIII–XVI)*, by BRUNO DINI, 215–270. Pisa, 1995a.

———. "L'economia fiorentina dal 1450 al 1530." In *Saggi su una economia-mondo. Firenze e l'Italia fra Mediterraneo ed Europa (secc. XIII–XVI)*, by BRUNO DINI, 187–214. Pisa, 1995b.

———. "L'industria serica in Italia. Secc. XIII–XV." In *Saggi su una economia-mondo. Firenze e l'Italia fra Mediterraneo ed Europa (secc. XIII–XVI)*, by BRUNO DINI, 51–85. Pisa, 1995c.

———. "Mercati e piazze bancarie nel mediterraneo e in Europa nei secoli XIV–XVI. Presenze e strategie degli operatori economici fiorentini." In *Manifattura, commercio e banca nella Firenze medievale*, by BRUNO DINI, 102–124. Florence, 2001.

DIONISOTTI, CARLO. *Machiavellerie. Storia e fortuna di Machiavelli*. Turin, 1980.

DOREN, ALFRED. *Studien aus der florentiner Wirtschaftsgeschichte*. Vol. 1, *Die florentiner Wollentuchindustrie vom 14. bis zum 16. Jahrhundert: Ein Beitrag zur Geschichte des modernen Kapitalismus*. Stuttgart, 1901.

———. *Le arti fiorentine*. Translated by GIOVANNI BATTISTA KLEIN. 2 vols. Florence, 1940.

DORINI, UMBERTO, ed. *Statuti dell'arte di Por Santa Maria del tempo della repubblica*. Florence, 1934.

DRAPER, JAMES. *Bertoldo di Giovanni, Sculptor of the Medici Household*. Columbia MO, 1992.

DROGIN, DAVID J. "Bologna's Bentivoglio Family and Its Artists: Overview of a Quattrocento Court in the Making." In *Artists at Court: Image-Making and Identity, 1300–1550*, edited by STEPHEN J. CAMPBELL, 72–90. Boston, 2004.

———. "Art, Patronage, and Civic Identities in Renaissance Bologna." In *The Court Cities of Northern Italy: Milan, Parma, Piacenza, Mantua, Ferrara, Bologna, Urbino, Pesaro, and Rimini*, edited by CHARLES M. ROSENBERG, 244–324. Cambridge, 2010.

DUNKLE, J. ROGER. "The Rhetorical Tyrant in Roman Historiography: Sallust, Livy, and Tacitus." *The Classical World* 65 (1971): 12–20.

EAGLETON, TERRY. *Ideology: An Introduction.* London, 1991.

EARENFIGHT, THERESA. "Absent Kings: Queens as Political Partners in the Medieval Crown of Aragon." In *Queenship and Political Power in Medieval and Early Modern Spain*, edited by THERESA EARENFIGHT, 33–54. Aldershot, 2005.

EISENBICHLER, KONRAD. "Political Posturing in Some 'Triumphs of Love' in Quattrocento Florence." In *Petrarch's 'Triumphs': Allegory and Spectacle*, edited by KONRAD EISENBICHLER and AMILCARE A. IANNUCCI, 369–381. Ottawa, 1990.

ELAM, CAROLINE. "Lorenzo's Architectural and Urban Policies." In *Lorenzo il Magnifico e il suo mondo*, edited by GIANCARLO GARFAGNINI, 357–384. Florence, 1994.

ELAM, CAROLINE, and ERNST GOMBRICH. "Lorenzo de' Medici and a Frustrated Villa Project at Vallombrosa." In *Florence and Italy: Renaissance Studies in Honour of Nicolai Rubinstein*, edited by PETER DENLEY and CAROLINE ELAM, 482–492. London, 1988.

EMERTON, EPHRAIM. *Humanism and Tyranny: Studies in the Italian Trecento.* Cambridge MA, 1925.

ENGELS, FRIEDRICH. *The Condition of the Working Class in England.* Translated by WILLIAM HENRY CHALONER and WILLIAM OTTO HENDERSON. Oxford, 1993. First published Stanford CA, 1958.

EPSTEIN, STEPHAN R. "Stato territoriale ed economia regionale nella Toscana del Quattrocento." In *La Toscana al tempo di Lorenzo il Magnifico. Politica, economia, cultura, arte*, 3:869–890. Pisa, 1996.

———. *Freedom and Growth: The Rise of States and Markets in Europe, 1300–1750.* London, 2000a.

———. "Market Structures." In *Florentine Tuscany: Structures and Practices of Power*, edited by WILLIAM J. CONNELL and ANDREA ZORZI, 90–121. Cambridge, 2000b.

ERCOLE, FRANCESCO. *Dal comune al principato. Saggio sulla storia del diritto pubblico del rinascimento italiano.* Florence, 1929.

ESPOSITO, ANNA. "D'Estouteville, Guillaume." *Dizionario biografico degli italiani* 43 (1993).

EUBEL, CONRAD. *Hierarchia catholica medii aevi.* Vol. 2. Regensberg, 1901.

FABBRI, LORENZO. *Alleanza matrimoniale e patriziato nella Firenze del '400.* Florence, 1991.

———. "Patronage and Its Role in Government: The Florentine Patriciate and Volterra." In *Florentine Tuscany: Structures and Practices of Power*, edited by WILLIAM J. CONNELL and ANDREA ZORZI, 225–241. Cambridge, 2000.

———. "I Fiorentini tra Arno e Sieve. L'avanzata della proprietà cittadina in un territorio di frontiera." In *Antica possessione con belli costumi. Due giornate di studio su Lapo di Castiglionchio il vecchio*, edited by FRANEK SZNURA, 173–185. Florence, 2005.

FABRONI, ANGELO. *Laurentii Medicis Magnifici vita.* 2 vols. Pisa, 1784.

———. *Magni Cosmi Medicei vita.* 2 vols. Pisa, 1788.

FAHY, CONOR. "Three Early Renaissance Treatises on Women." *Italian Studies* 11 (1956): 30–55.

FALLETTI, CLELIA. "Le feste per Eleonora d'Aragona da Napoli a Ferrara (1473)." In *Spettacoli conviviali dall'antichità classica alle corti del '400*, 269–289. Viterbo, 1983. Reprinted in *Teatro e culture della rappresentazione. Lo spettacolo in Italia nel Quattrocento*, edited by RAIMONDO GUARINO, 121–140. Bologna, 1988.

———. "Centro e periferia, accentramento e particolarismi. Dicotomia o sostanza degli stati in età moderna?" In *Origini dello stato. Processi di formazione statale in Italia tra medioevo ed età moderna*, edited by GIORGIO CHITTOLINI and ANTHONY MOLHO, 147–176. Bologna, 1994.

FASANO GUARINI, ELENA. *Lo stato mediceo di Cosimo I.* Florence, 1973.

———. "Città soggette e contadi nel dominio fiorentino tra Quattro e Cinquecento. Il caso pisano." In *Ricerche di storia moderna*, edited by MARIO MIRRI, 1:1–94. Pisa, 1976.

———. "Centro e periferia, accentramento e particolarismi. Dicotomia o sostanza degli stati in età moderna?" In *Origini dello stato. Processi di formazione statale in Italia fra medioevo ed età moderna*, edited by GIORGIO CHITTOLINI, ANTHONY MOLHO, and PIERANGELO SCHIERA, 147–176. Bologna, 1994.

———. *Repubbliche e principi. Istituzioni e pratiche di potere nella Toscana granducale del '500–'600*. Bologna, 2010.

FAVREAU-LILIE, MARIE-LUISE. "Reichsherr-Schaft im spätmittelalterlichen Italien: Zur Handhabung des Reichsvikariats im 14./15. Jahrhundert." *Quellen und Forschungen aus italienischen Archiven und Bibliotheken* 80 (2000): 53–116.

FAWTIER, ROBERT D. "Hand-Lists of Charters and Deeds in the Possession of the John Rylands Library: III. The Medici Records." *Bulletin of the John Rylands Library* 8 (1924): 282–297.

FERENTE, SERENA. "'Soldato di ventura' e 'partesano'. Bracceschi e guelfi alla metà del Quattrocento." In *Guelfi e ghibellini nell'Italia del Rinascimento*, edited by MARCO GENTILE, 625–647. Rome, 2005.

———. *Gli ultimi guelfi. Linguaggi e identità politiche in Italia nella seconda metà del Quattrocento*. Rome, 2013.

FERRARI, MATTEO. Catalog entry no. 48 (Andrea di Cione detto Orcagna, *Sant'Anna e la cacciata del Duca d'Atene*). In *Dal Giglio al Davide. Arte civica a Firenze fra medioevo e rinascimento*, exhibition catalog, Galleria dell' Accademia, edited by MARIA MONICA DONATO and DANIELA PARENTI, 212–213. Florence, 2013.

FERRARINI, GIROLAMO. *Memoriale estense, 1476–1489*. Edited by PRIMO GRIGUOLO. Rovigo, 2006.

FICINO, MARSILIO. *Opera omnia*. Basel, 1576. Reprinted Turin, 1962 and 1983.

———. "Epistola ad fratres vulgaris." In *Supplementum ficinianum*. Edited by PAUL OSKAR KRISTELLER, 1:109–128. Florence, 1937.

———. *Théologie platonicienne de l'immortalité des âmes*. Edited by RAYMOND MARCEL. 3 vols. Paris, 1970.

———. *La religione cristiana*. Edited by ROBERTO ZANZARRI. Rome, 2005.

FIELD, ARTHUR. *The Origins of the Platonic Academy of Florence*. Princeton, 1988.

FINLAY, ROBERT. *Politics in Renaissance Venice*. New Brunswick NJ, 1980.

FIUMI, ENRICO. *L'impresa di Lorenzo de' Medici contro Volterra (1472)*. Florence, 1948.

FLAMINI, FRANCESCO. *La lirica toscana del rinascimento anteriore ai tempi del Magnifico*. Florence, 1891. Reprinted Florence, 1977.

FLETCHER, STELLA, ed. *Roscoe and Italy: The Reception of Italian Renaissance History and Culture in the Eighteenth and Nineteenth Centuries*. Farnham, Surrey, 2012.

FOLIN, MARCO. "Note sugli officiali negli stati estensi, secoli XV–XVI." *Annali della Scuola Normale Superiore di Pisa. Quaderni della classe di lettere e filosofia*, ser. IV, 1 (1997): 99–154.

———. *Rinascimento estense. Politica, cultura, istituzioni di un antico stato italiano*. Rome, 2001.

———. "La corte della duchessa. Eleonora d'Aragona a Ferrara." In *Donne di potere nel rinascimento*, edited by LETIZIA ARCANGELI and SUSANNA PEYRONEL RAMBALDI, 481–512. Rome, 2008.

———. *Courts and Courtly Arts in Renaissance Italy: Arts, Culture, and Politics, 1395–1530*. Woodbridge, Suffolk, 2010.

FOSI, IRENE, and MARIA ANTONIETTA VISCEGLIA. "Marriage and Politics at the Papal Court in the Sixteenth and Seventeenth Centuries." In *Marriage in Italy, 1300–1650*, edited by TREVOR DEAN and K. J. P. LOWE, 197–224. Cambridge, 1998.

FOSSATI, FELICE. "Rapporti tra una 'terra' e i suoi signori (Vigevano e i duchi di Milano nel secolo XV)." *Archivio storico lombardo* 41 (1914): 109–186.

FRANCESCHI, FRANCO. "Intervento del potere centrale e ruolo delle arti nel governo dell'economia fiorentina del Trecento e del primo Quattrocento. Linee generali." *Archivio storico italiano* 151 (1993a): 863–909.

———. *Oltre il "Tumulto". I lavoratori fiorentini dell'arte della lana fra Tre e Quattrocento*. Florence, 1993b.

———. "Istituzioni e attività economica a Firenze. Considerazioni sul governo del settore industriale (1350–1450)." In *Istituzioni e società in Toscana nell'età moderna,* edited by GIUSEPPE PANSINI, 76–117. Rome, 1994.

———. "Note sulle corporazioni fiorentine in età laurenziana." In *La Toscana al tempo di Lorenzo il Magnifico. Politica, economia, cultura, arte,* 3:1343–1362. Pisa, 1996.

———. "I forestieri e l'industria della seta fiorentina." In *La seta in Italia dal medioevo al Seicento. Dal baco al drappo,* edited by LUCA MOLÀ, REINHOLD C. MUELLER, and CLAUDIO ZANIER, 401–422. Venice, 2000.

———. "Vicende della regione boracifera volterrana nel basso medioevo." In *Il calore della terra. Contributo alla storia della geotermia in Italia,* edited by MARCO CIARDI and RAFFAELE CATALDI, 143–153. Pisa, 2005.

———. "Lane permesse e lane proibite nella Toscana fiorentina dei secoli XIV–XV. Logiche economiche e scelte 'politiche.'" In *La pastorizia mediterranea. Storia e diritto (secoli XI–XX),* edited by ANTONELLO MATTONE and PINUCCIA F. SIMBULA, 878–889. Rome, 2011.

———. "Aspetti dell'economia urbana." In *Arezzo nel medioevo,* edited by GIOVANNI CHERUBINI, FRANCO FRANCESCHI, ANDREA BARLUCCHI, and GIULIO FIRPO, 241–252. Rome, 2012.

FRANCESCHI, FRANCO, and LUCA MOLÀ. "Regional States and Economic Development." In *The Italian Renaissance State,* edited by ANDREA GAMBERINI and ISABELLA LAZZARINI, 444–466. Cambridge, 2012.

FRANCHETTI PARDO, VITTORIO, AND GIOVANNA CASALI. *I Medici nel contado fiorentino. Ville e possedimenti agricoli tra Quattrocento e Cinquecento.* Florence, 1978.

FRANCOVICH, RICCARDO. *I castelli del contado fiorentino nei secoli XII e XIII.* Florence, 1976.

FRANKLIN, MARGARET. *Boccaccio's Heroines: Power and Virtue in Renaissance Society.* Aldershot, 2006.

FRASER JENKINS, A. DAVID. "Cosimo de' Medici's Patronage of Architecture and the Theory of Magnificence." *Journal of the Warburg and Courtauld Institutes* 33 (1970): 162–170.

FRISI, ANTONIO FRANCESCO. *Memorie storiche di Monza e sua corte.* 3 vols. Milan, 1794.

FROSINI, GIOVANNA. "'Honore et utile.' Vicende storiche e testimonianza private nelle lettere romane di Matteo Franco (1488–1492)." *Reti medievali rivista* 10 (2009): 201–238.

FUBINI, RICCARDO. "Osservazioni e documenti sulla crisi del ducato di Milano nel 1477 e sulla riforma del consiglio segreto ducale di Bona Sforza." In *Essays Presented to Myron P. Gilmore,* edited by SERGIO BERTELLI and GLORIA RAMAKUS, 1:47–103. Florence, 1978.

———. "Appunti sui rapporti diplomatici fra il dominio sforzesco e Firenze medicea." In *Gli Sforza a Milano e in Lombardia e i loro rapporti con gli stati italiani ed europei,* 291–334. Milan, 1982.

———. "Ficino e i Medici all'avvento di Lorenzo il Magnifico." *Rinascimento* 24 (1984): 3–52.

———. "La rivendicazione di Firenze della sovranità statale e il contributo delle *Historiae* di Leonardo Bruni." In *Leonardo Bruni, cancelliere della repubblica di Firenze,* edited by PAOLO VITI, 29–62. Florence, 1990.

———. "In margine all'edizione delle lettere di Lorenzo de' Medici." In *Lorenzo de' Medici. Studi,* edited by GIAN CARLO GARFAGNINI, 167–227. Florence, 1992.

———. *Italia quattrocentesca. Politica e diplomazia nell'età di Lorenzo il Magnifico.* Milan, 1994.

———. "Politique et représentation dans le théâtre citadin. L'essor de Florence comme pouvoir souverain au début du XVe siècle." In *Représentation, pouvoir et royauté à la fin du moyen age,* edited by JOËL BLANCHARD, 109–118. Paris, 1995.

———. *Quattrocento fiorentino. Politica, diplomazia, cultura.* Pisa, 1996.

———. "'Potenze grosse' e piccolo stato nell'Italia del rinascimento. Consapevolezza della distinzione e dinamica dei poteri." In *Il piccolo stato. Politica storia diplomazia,* edited by LAURA BARLETTA, FRANCO CARDINI, and GIUSEPPE GALASSO, 91–126. San Marino, 2003.

———. *Storiografia dell'umanesimo in Italia da Leonardo Bruni ad Annio da Viterbo.* Rome, 2007.

———. *Politica e pensiero politico nell'Italia del Rinascimento. Dallo stato territoriale al Machiavelli.* Florence, 2009.

FUSCO, LAURIE S., and GINO CORTI. *Lorenzo de' Medici, Collector and Antiquarian*. Cambridge, 2006.

GAETA, FRANCO. "Storiografia, coscienza nazionale e politica culturale nella Venezia del Rinascimento." In *Storia della cultura veneta*. Vol. 3. *Dal primo quattrocento al concilio di Trento*, edited by GIROLAMO ARNALDI and GIANFRANCO FOLENA, 1–91. Vicenza, 1980.

GAJA, KATERINE. "Illustrating Lorenzo the Magnificent: From William Roscoe's *The Life of Lorenzo de' Medici Called the Magnificent* (1795) to George Frederic Watt's Fresco at Careggi (1845)." In *Victorian and Edwardian Responses to the Italian Renaissance*, edited by JOHN E. LAW and LENE ØSTERMARK-JOHANSEN, 121–144. Aldershot, 2005.

GALANTINO, FRANCESCO. *Storia di Soncino con documenti*. 3 vols. Milan, 1869–70.

GALLAGHER, SEAN. "The Berlin Chansonnier and French Song in Florence, 1450–1490: A New Dating and Its Implications." *Journal of Musicology* 24 (2007): 339–364.

GAMBERINI, ANDREA. "Cremona nel Quattrocento. La vicenda politica e istituzionale." In *Storia di Cremona. Il Quattrocento. Cremona e il ducato di Milano (1395–1535)*, edited by GIORGIO CHITTOLINI, 2–39. Azzano San Paolo, 2008.

GAMBERINI, ANDREA, JEAN-PHILIPPE GENET, and ANDREA ZORZI, eds. *The Languages of Political Society: Western Europe, Fourteenth–Seventeenth Centuries*. Rome, 2011.

GAMBERINI, ANDREA, and ISABELLA LAZZARINI, eds. *The Italian Renaissance State*. Cambridge, 2012.

GAMBERINI, ANDREA, and GIUSEPPE PETRALIA, eds. *Linguaggi politici nell'Italia del rinascimento*. Rome, 2007.

GANZ, MARGERY A. "Perceived Insults and Their Consequences: Acciaiuoli, Neroni, and Medici Relationships in the 1460s." In *Society and Individual in Renaissance Florence*, edited by WILLIAM J. CONNELL, 155–172. Berkeley, 2002.

———. "'Buon amici ma non per sempre'. Agnolo Acciaiuoli, Dietisalvi Neroni, Luca Pitti, Niccolò Soderini and the Medici, 1430s to 1460." In *Italian Art, Society, and Politics: A Festschrift in Honor of Rab Hatfield Presented by His Students on the Occasion of His Seventieth Birthday*, edited by BARBARA DEIMLING, JONATHAN K. NELSON, and GARY M. RADKE, 72–82. Florence, 2007.

GARBERO ZORZI, ELVIRA. "Le forme dello spettacolo in due città-stato del rinascimento. Firenze e Milano." In *Florence and Milan: Comparisons and Relations; Acts of Two Conferences at Villa I Tatti in 1982–1984*, edited by SERGIO BERTELLI, NICOLAI RUBINSTEIN, and CRAIG HUGH SMYTH, 2:271–285. Florence, 1989.

GARZELLI, ANNAROSA. *Miniatura fiorentina del rinascimento 1440–1525. Un primo censimento*. 2 vols. Florence, 1985.

GASTON, ROBERT. "Liturgy and Patronage in San Lorenzo, Florence, 1350–1650." In *Patronage, Art, and Society in Renaissance Italy*, edited by FRANCIS WILLIAM KENT and PATRICIA SIMONS, 111–133. Oxford, 1987.

GEFFCKEN, PETER. "Die Welser und ihr Handel 1246–1496." In *Die Welser: Neue Forschungen zur Geschichte und Kultur des oberdeutschen Handelshauses*, edited by MARK HÄBERLEIN and JOHANNES BURKHART, 27–167. Berlin, 2002.

GENTILE, MARCO, ed. *Guelfi e ghibellini nell'Italia del Rinascimento*. Rome, 2005.

———. "Discorsi sulle fazioni, discorsi delle fazioni. 'Parole e demonstratione partiale' nella Lombardia del secondo Quattrocento." In *Linguaggi politici nell'Italia del rinascimento*, edited by ANDREA GAMBERINI and GIUSEPPE PETRALIA, 381–401. Rome, 2007a.

———. "La formazione del dominio dei Rossi tra XIV e XV secolo." In *Le signorie dei Rossi di Parma tra XIV e XVI secolo*, edited by LETIZIA ARCANGELI and MARCO GENTILE, 23–55. Florence, 2007b.

———. "Aristocrazia signorile e costituzione del ducato visconteo sforzesco. Appunti e problemi di ricerca." In *Noblesse et états princiers en Italie et en France au XVe siècle*, edited by MARCO GENTILE and PIERRE SAVY, 125–155. Rome, 2009a.

———. "Casato e fazione nella Lombardia del Quattrocento. Il caso di Parma." In *Famiglie e poteri in Italia tra Medioevo ed età moderna*, edited by ANNA BELLAVITIS and ISABELLE CHABOT, 151–187. Rome, 2009b.

———. *Fazioni al governo. Politica e società a Parma nel Quattrocento.* Rome, 2009c.

———. "La volontà d'impotenza. Rapporti di forza e gestione del 'disordine' nel ducato sforzesco." In *Le polizie informali. Seminario di studi, Messina, 28–29 novembre 2003*, edited by LIVIO ANTONIELLI, 45–63. Soveria Mannelli (Catanzaro), 2010.

GENTILE, MARCO, and PIERRE SAVY, eds. *Noblesse et états princiers en Italie et en France au XVᵉ siècle.* Rome, 2009.

GENTILE, SEBASTIANO. "Per la storia del testo *Commentarium in* Convivium di Marsilio Ficino." *Rinascimento* 21 (1981): 3–27.

GHERI, GORO. "Lettere di monsignore Goro Gheri pistoiese governatore di Piacenza nel 1515 a Giuliano, Giulio e Lorenzo de' Medici e ad altri, scelte ed estratte dal codice Capponi CCLXXXIV ed annotate dal conte Bernardo Pallastrelli, con postille di Luciano Scarabelli." *Archivio storico italiano* 6 (1848), appendix: 9–135.

GHINZONI, PIETRO. "Informazioni politiche sul ducato di Milano." *Archivio storico lombardo* 9 (1892): 863–881.

GHISETTI GIAVARINA, ADRIANO. "Fancelli, Luca." *Dizionario biografico degli italiani* 44 (1994).

GIANNOTTI, DONATO. *Lettere italiane.* Edited by FURIO DIAZ. Milan, 1974.

GIBBONS, MARY. "Cosimo's *Cavallo*: A Study in Imperial Imagery." In *The Cultural Politics of Duke Cosimo I de' Medici*, edited by KONRAD EISENBICHLER, 77–102. Aldershot, 2001.

GILBERT, FELIX. "The Venetian Constitution in Florentine Political Thought." In *Florentine Studies: Politics and Society in Renaissance Florence*, edited by NICOLAI RUBINSTEIN, 463–500. London, 1968.

GILL, JOSEPH. "The Cost of the Council of Florence." In *Personalities of the Council of Florence*, 186–203. New York, 1964.

GINATEMPO, MARIA. "Uno stato semplice. L'organizzazione del territorio nella Toscana senese del secondo Quattrocento." In *La Toscana al tempo di Lorenzo il Magnifico. Politica, economia, cultura, arte*, 3:1073–1101. Pisa, 1996.

GINORI CONTI, PIERO. *La basilica di S. Lorenzo di Firenze e la famiglia Ginori.* Florence, 1940.

GINORI-LISCI, LEONARDO. *Baroncoli. La dimora rurale di Carlo il vecchio de' Ginori.* Florence, 1950.

GIONTELLA, MASSIMO, and RICCARDO FUBINI. "Inspiration and Execution of the Frieze in Poggio a Caiano Villa: The Role of Giovanni Pico della Mirandola and Antonio del Pollaiolo." *Humanistica*, forthcoming.

GIORGETTI, A. "Lorenzo de' Medici, capitano generale della repubblica fiorentina." *Archivio storico italiano*, 4th ser., 11 (1883): 194–215.

GIULINI, GIORGIO. *Memorie spettanti alla storia, al governo ed alla descrizione della città e campagna di Milano.* 7 vols. Milan, 1854–57.

GOLDTHWAITE, RICHARD A. *The Economy of Renaissance Florence.* Baltimore, 2009.

GORI, PIETRO. *Le feste fiorentine attraverso i secoli. Le feste per San Giovanni.* Florence, 1926.

GORI-SASSOLI, MARIO. "Michelozzo e l'architettura di villa nel primo rinascimento." *Storia dell'arte* 23 (1975): 5–51.

GORRINI, GIACOMO. *La cattura e prigionia di Annibale Malvezzi in Germania. Episodi delle lotte di rappresaglia in Bologna (1432–1494). Memoria storica con documenti inediti.* Bologna, 1900.

GRAYSON, CECIL. "Becchi, Gentile." *Dizionario biografico degli italiani* 7 (1970).

GREEN, LOUIS. *Chronicle into History: An Essay on the Interpretation of History in Florentine Fourteenth-Century Chronicles.* Cambridge, 1972.

———. "Galvano Fiamma, Azzone Visconti, and the Revival of the Classical Theory of Magnificence." *Journal of the Warburg and Courtauld Institutes* 53 (1990): 98–143.

———. "The Image of Tyranny in Early Fourteenth-Century Italian Historical Writing." *Renaissance Studies* 7 (1993): 335–351.

GREENWOOD, RYAN MARTIN. "Law and War in Late Medieval Italy: The *Jus Commune* on War and Its Application in Florence, c. 1150–1450." PhD thesis, University of Toronto, 2011.

GRIFFITHS, GORDON, JAMES HANKINS, and DAVID THOMPSON, eds. *The Humanism of Leonardo Bruni*. Binghamton NY, 1987.

GRIGNANI, MARIA ANTONIETTA, ed. *Mantova 1430. Pareri a Gian Francesco Gonzaga per il governo.* Mantua, 1990.

GRIMANI, GIULIO. "Bernardo Dovizi alla corte d'Alfonso II d'Aragona." *Archivio storico per le province napoletane* 25 (1900): 218–237.

GUALAZZINI, UGO. *Gli organi assembleari e collegiali del comune di Cremona nell'età visconteo-sforzesca.* Milan, 1978.

GUALTIERI, PIERO. *Il comune di Firenze tra Due e Trecento. Partecipazione politica e assetto istituzionale.* Florence, 2009.

GUARINI, GUARINO (GUARINO VERONESE). "De praestantia Scipionis et Caesaris." In *La controversia di Poggio Bracciolini e Guarino Veronese su Cesare e Scipione,* edited by DAVIDE CANFORA, 119–140. Florence, 2001.

GUASTI, CESARE, ed. *Due legazioni al sommo pontefice per il comune di Firenze presiedute da Sant' Antonino, arcivescovo.* Florence, 1857.

———, ed. *I capitoli del comune di Firenze. Inventario e regesto.* 2 vols. Florence, 1866–93.

———. *Le feste di San Giovanni Batista in Firenze descritte in prosa e in versi dai contemporanei.* Florence, 1908.

GUERRA, ENRICA. "Eleonora d'Aragona e *I doveri del principe* di Diomede Carafa." In *Donne di palazzo nelle corti europee. Tracce e forme di potere dall'età moderna,* edited by ANGELA GIALLONGO, 113–119. Milan, 2005.

GUICCIARDINI, FRANCESCO. "Elogio di Lorenzo de' Medici." In *Scritti politici e ricordi,* by FRANCESCO GUICCIARDINI. Edited by ROBERTO PALMAROCCHI, 223–228. Bari, 1933.

———. *Storie fiorentine dal 1378 al 1509.* Edited by ROBERTO PALMAROCCHI. Bari, 1931. Reprinted Bari, 1968.

———. *Dialogo e discorsi del reggimento di Firenze.* Edited by ROBERTO PALMAROCCHI. Bari, 1932.

———. *Maxims and Reflections of a Renaissance Statesman.* Translated by MARIO DOMANDI. New York, 1965.

———. *Storia d'Italia.* Edited by FRANCO CATALANO. 3 vols. Milan, 1975.

———. *Dialogo del reggimento di Firenze.* Edited by GIAN MARIO ANSELMI and CARLO VAROTTI. Turin, 1994a.

———. *Dialogue on the Government of Florence.* Translated by ALISON BROWN. Cambridge, 1994b.

———. *Ricordi.* Edited by CARLO VAROTTI. Rome, 2013.

GUIDI, GUIDUBALDO. *Il governo della città-repubblica di Firenze del primo Quattrocento.* 3 vols. Florence, 1981.

GUIDI BRUSCOLI, FRANCESCO. "Politica matrimoniale e matrimoni politici nella Firenze di Lorenzo de Medici. Uno studio del ms. 'Notarile Antecosimiano 14099.'" *Archivio storico italiano* 155 (1997): 347–398.

GUNDERSHEIMER, WERNER, ed. *Art and Life at the Court of Ercole I d'Este: The 'De triumphis religionis' of Giovanni Sabadino degli Arienti.* Geneva, 1972.

———. "Bartolommeo Goggio: 'A Feminist in Renaissance Ferrara.'" *Renaissance Quarterly* 33 (1980a): 175–200.

———. "Women, Learning, and Power: Eleonora of Aragon and the Court of Ferrara." In *Beyond Their Sex: Learned Women of the European Past,* edited by PATRICIA LABALME, 43–65. New York, 1980b.

———. *Ferrara estense. Lo stile del potere.* Modena, 1988.

GUPPY, HENRY. "Library Notes and News, April–November, 1919." *Bulletin of the John Rylands Library* 5 (1918–1920): 189–190.

HAAR, JAMES. "Rome, BAV, Ms Urb. lat. 1411: An Undervalued Source?" In *Manoscritti di polifonia nel quattrocento europeo*, edited by MARCO GOZZI, 65–92. Trent, 2004.

———. *Città del Vaticano Ms Urbinas latinus 1411*. Lucca, 2006.

HAAR, JAMES, and JOHN NÁDAS. "Johannes de Anglia (John Hothby): Notes on His Career in Italy." *Acta musicologica* 79 (2007): 291–358.

———. "The Medici, the Signoria, the Pope: Sacred Polyphony in Florence, 1432–1448." *Recercare* 20 (2008): 25–93.

———. "I cantori di San Giovanni a Firenze negli anni 1448–1469." *Rivista italiana di musicologia* 46 (2011): 79–104.

HALE, JOHN. "The End of Florentine Liberty: The Fortezza da Basso." In *Florentine Studies: Politics and Society in Renaissance Florence*, edited by NICOLAI RUBINSTEIN, 501–532. London, 1968.

———. *Florence and the Medici: The Pattern of Control*. London, 1977.

HALL, STUART. *Representation: Cultural Representations and Signifying Practices*. London, 1997.

HANDS, A. R. "Sallust and *Dissimulatio*." *Journal of Roman Studies* 44 (1959): 56–60.

HANKINS, JAMES, ed. *Renaissance Civic Humanism: Reappraisals and Reflections*. Cambridge, 2000a.

———. "Rhetoric, History, and Ideology: The Civic Panegyrics of Leonardo Bruni." In *Renaissance Civic Humanism: Reappraisals and Reflections*, edited by JAMES HANKINS, 143–178. Cambridge, 2000b.

———. Introduction to *Republics and Kingdoms Compared*, by AURELIO LIPPO BRANDOLINI, ix–xxvi. Cambridge MA, 2009.

HARPER, DOUGLAS. "Scrim." In *Online Etymology Dictionary*, http://dictionary.reference.com/browse/Scrim, accessed 24 July 2011.

HATFIELD, RAB. "The Compagnia de' Magi." *Journal of the Warburg and Courtauld Institutes* 33 (1970): 107–144.

———. "A Source for Machiavelli's Account of the Regime of Piero de' Medici." In *Studies on Machiavelli*, edited by MYRON P. GILMORE, 317–333. Florence, 1972.

———. *Botticelli's Uffizi "Adoration": A Study in Pictorial Content*. Princeton, 1976.

———. "Cosimo de' Medici and the Chapel of His Palace." In *Cosimo "il Vecchio" de' Medici, 1389–1464: Essays in Commemoration of the 600th Anniversary of Cosimo de' Medici's Birth*, edited by FRANCIS AMES-LEWIS, 221–244. Oxford, 1992.

HENDERSON, JOHN. "Le confraternite religiose nella Firenze del tardo medioevo. Patroni spirituali e anche politici?" *Ricerche storiche* 15 (1985): 77–94.

———. *Piety and Charity in Late Medieval Florence*. Oxford, 1994.

HERLIHY, DAVID, and CHRISTIANE KLAPISCH-ZUBER. *Les toscans et leurs familles: Une étude du "catasto" florentin de 1427*. Paris, 1978.

HERZNER, VOLKER. "Die Segel-Imprese der Familie Pazzi." *Mitteilungen des Kunsthistorischen Institutes in Florenz* 20 (1976): 13–32.

HOLMES, GEORGE. "How the Medici Became the Pope's Bankers." In *Florentine Studies: Politics and Society in Renaissance Florence*, edited by NICOLAI RUBINSTEIN, 357–381. London, 1968.

———. "Cosimo and the Popes." In *Cosimo "il Vecchio" de' Medici, 1389–1464: Essays in Commemoration of the 600th Anniversary of Cosimo de' Medici's Birth*, edited by FRANCIS AMES-LEWIS, 21–31. Oxford, 1992.

HÖRNQVIST, MIKAEL. "The Two Myths of Civic Humanism." In *Renaissance Civic Humanism: Reappraisals and Reflections*, edited by JAMES HANKINS, 105–142. Cambridge, 2000.

HOSHINO, HIDETOSHI. *L'arte della lana in Firenze nel basso medioevo. Il commercio della lana e il mercato dei panni fiorentini nei secoli XIII–XV*. Florence, 1980.

———. "Il commercio fiorentino nell'Impero ottomano. Costi e profitti negli anni 1484–1488." In *Industria tessile e commercio internazionale nella Firenze del tardo medioevo*, edited by HIDETOSHI HOSHINO, FRANCO FRANCESCHI, and SERGIO TOGNETTI, 113–123. Florence, 2001.

HOWARD, PETER. *Creating Magnificence in Renaissance Florence*. Toronto, 2012.

HUNT, TRISTAM, and VICTORIA WHITFIELD. *Art Treasures in Manchester: 150 Years On.* Manchester, 2007.

HURLBURT, HOLLY S. *The Dogaressa of Venice, 1200–1500.* New York, 2006.

HYMAN, ISABELLE. *Brunelleschi in Perspective.* Englewood Cliffs NJ, 1974.

———. *Fifteenth-Century Florentine Studies: The Palazzo Medici and a Ledger for the Church of San Lorenzo.* New York, 1977.

IANZITI, GARY. *Humanistic Historiography under the Sforzas: Politics and Propaganda in Fifteenth-Century Milan.* Oxford, 1988.

ILARDI, VINCENT. "The Banker Statesman and the Condottiere-Prince: Cosimo de' Medici and Francesco Sforza (1450–1464)." In *Florence and Milan: Comparisons and Relations; Acts of Two Conferences at Villa I Tatti in 1982–1984,* edited by SERGIO BERTELLI, NICOLAI RUBINSTEIN, and CRAIG HUGH SMYTH, 1:217–239. Florence, 1989.

ISENMANN, MORITZ. "From Rule of Law to Emergency Rule in Renaissance Florence." In *The Politics of Law in Late Medieval and Renaissance Italy,* edited by LAWRIN ARMSTRONG and JULIUS KIRSHNER, 55–76. Toronto, 2011.

JONES, PHILIP. "Communes and Despots: The City-State in Late-Medieval Italy." *Transactions of the Royal Historical Society,* 5th ser., 15 (1965): 71–96. Republished in *Communes and Despots in Medieval and Renaissance Italy,* edited by JOHN E. LAW and BERNADETTE PATON, 3–24. Farnham, Surrey, 2010.

———. *The Malatesta of Rimini and the Papal State.* Cambridge, 1974.

———. "Economia e società nell'Italia medievale. La leggenda della borghesia." In *Storia d'Italia.* Vol. 1, *Dal feudalesimo al capitalismo,* edited by RUGGIERO ROMANO and CORRADO VIVANTI, 187–372. Turin, 1978.

———. "Comuni e signorie. La città-stato nell'Italia tardomedievale." In *Economia e società nell'Italia medievale,* 503–526. Turin, 1980.

———. *The Italian City-State: From Commune to Signoria.* Oxford, 1997.

KELLMAN, HERBERT, ed. *The Treasury of Petrus Alamire: Music and Art in Flemish Court Manuscripts 1500–1535.* Ghent, 1999.

KENT, DALE V. "The Florentine 'Reggimento' in the Fifteenth Century." *Renaissance Quarterly* 28 (1975): 575–638.

———. *The Rise of the Medici: Faction in Florence, 1426–1434.* Oxford, 1978.

———. "The Importance of Being Eccentric: Giovanni Cavalcanti's View of Cosimo de' Medici's Florence." *Journal of Medieval and Renaissance Studies* 9 (1979): 101–132.

———. *Cosimo de' Medici and the Florentine Renaissance: The Patron's Oeuvre.* New Haven, 2000.

———. "Elites, Patronage, and the State." In *Italy in the Age of the Renaissance,* edited by JOHN M. NAJEMY, 165–183. Oxford, 2004.

———. "Personal Literary Anthologies in Renaissance Florence: Re-presenting Current Events to Conform to Christian, Classical, and Civic Ideals." In *Rituals, Images, and Words: Varieties of Cultural Expression in Late Medieval and Early Modern Europe,* edited by FRANCIS WILLIAM KENT and CHARLES ZIKA, 277–295. Turnhout, 2005.

———. "Medici, Cosimo de'." *Dizionario biografico degli italiani* 73 (2009).

———. "'La cara e buona imagine paterna di voi': Ideal Images of Patriarchs and Patrons as Models for the Right Ordering of Renaissance Florence." In *Florence 1350–1550: Essays in Honour of F. W. Kent,* edited by PETER HOWARD and CECELIA HEWLETT. Turnhout, forthcoming.

KENT, FRANCIS WILLIAM. *Household and Lineage in Renaissance Florence: The Family Life of the Capponi, Ginori, and Rucellai.* Princeton, 1977.

———. "Lorenzo de' Medici's Acquisition of Poggio a Caiano in 1474 and an Early Reference to his Architectural Expertise." *Journal of the Warburg and Courtauld Institutes* 42 (1979): 250–257.

———. "Palaces, Politics, and Society in Fifteenth-Century Florence." *I Tatti Studies* 2 (1987): 41–70.

——. "Patron-Client Networks in Renaissance Florence and the Emergence of Lorenzo as 'Maestro della Bottega.'" In *Lorenzo de' Medici: New Perspectives*, edited by BERNARD TOSCANI, 279–313. New York, 1993.

——. "*Lorenzo . . . amico degli uomini da bene.* Lorenzo de' Medici and Oligarchy." In *Lorenzo il Magnifico e il suo mondo*, edited by GIAN CARLO GARFAGNINI, 43–60. Florence, 1994a.

——. "'Un paradiso habitato da diavoli'. Ties of Loyalty and Patronage in the Society of Medicean Florence." In *Le radici cristiane di Firenze*, edited by ANNA BENVENUIT PAPI and FRANCO CARDINI, 183–210. Florence, 1994b.

——. "Sainted Mother, Magnificent Son: Lucrezia Tornabuoni and Lorenzo de' Medici." *Italian History and Culture* 3 (1997): 3–34.

——. "Lorenzo de' Medici at the Duomo." In *La cattedrale e la città. Saggi sul duomo di Firenze*, edited by TIMOTHY VERDON and ANNALISA INNOCENTI, 1:341–368. Florence, 2001.

——. "Heinrich Isaac's Music in Laurentian Florence: New Documents." In *Die Lektüre der Welt: zur Theorie, Geschichte und Soziologie kultureller Praxis; Festschrift für Walter Veit*, edited by HELMUT HEINZE and CHRISTIANE WELLER, 367–371. New York, 2004a.

——. *Lorenzo de' Medici and the Art of Magnificence.* Baltimore, 2004b.

——. "Lorenzo de' Medici and the Love of Women." *Spunti e ricerche* 22 (2007): 28–49.

——. "Prato and Lorenzo de' Medici." In *Communes and Despots in Medieval and Renaissance Italy*, edited by JOHN E. LAW and BERNADETTE PATON, 193–208. Farnham, Surrey, 2010.

——. *Princely Citizen: Lorenzo de' Medici and Renaissance Florence.* Edited by CAROLYN JAMES. Turnhout, 2013.

KENT, FRANCIS WILLIAM, ALESSANDRO PEROSA, BRENDA PREYER, ROBERTO SALVINI, and PIERO SANPAOLESI, *Giovanni Rucellai ed il suo zibaldone*. Vol. 2. *A Florentine Patrician and His Palace.* London, 1981.

KIDD, ALAN, and DAVID NICHOLLS. *Gender, Civic Culture, and Consumerism: Middle-Class Identity in Britain, 1800–1940.* Manchester, 1999.

KIRSHNER, JULIUS. "Papa Eugenio IV e il monte comune. Documenti su investimento e speculazione nel debito pubblico di Firenze." *Archivio storico italiano* 127 (1969): 339–382.

——. "Paolo di Castro on *cives ex privilegio*: A Controversy over Legal Qualification for Public Office in Early Fifteenth-Century Florence." In *Renaissance Studies in Honour of Hans Baron*, edited by ANTHONY MOLHO and JOHN A. TEDESCHI, 227–264. Florence, 1971.

KLAPISCH-ZUBER, CHRISTIANE. "Zacharie, ou le père évincé. Les rites nuptiaux toscans entre Giotto et le concile de Trente." *Annales. Économies, sociétés, civilisations* 34 (1979): 403–438.

——. *Ritorno alla politica. I magnati fiorentini, 1340–1440.* Rome, 2009.

KLEIN, FRANCESCA, and VANNA ARRIGHI. "Da mercante avventuriero a confidente dello stato. Profilo di Bongianni Gianfigliazzi attraverso le sue Ricordanze." In *Scritture e governo dello stato a Firenze nel Rinascimento. Cancellieri, ufficiali, archive*, edited by FRANCESCA KLEIN, 173–191. Florence, 2013.

KNAPTON, MICHAEL. "Il consiglio dei dieci nel governo della terraferma. Un'ipotesi interpretativa per il secondo '400." In *Atti del convegno Venezia e la terraferma attraverso le relazioni dei rettori*, edited by AMELIO TAGLIAFERRI, 237–260. Milan, 1981.

——. "'Nobiltà e popolo' e un trentennio di storiografia veneta." *Nuova rivista storica* 82, no. 1 (1998): 167–192.

KOEBNER, ROBERT. "Despot and Despotism: Vicissitudes of a Political Term." *Journal of the Warburg and Courtauld Institutes* 14 (1951): 275–302.

KOHL, BENJAMIN G. *Padua under the Carrara, 1318–1405.* Baltimore, 1998.

——. "The Myth of the Renaissance Despot." In *Communes and Despots in Medieval and Renaissance Italy*, edited by JOHN E. LAW and BERNADETTE PATON, 63–74. Farnham, Surrey, 2010.

KOLSKY, STEPHEN. *The Ghost of Boccaccio: Writings on Famous Women in Renaissance Italy.* Turnhout, 2005.

KRAUTHEIMER, RICHARD, with TRUDE KRAUTHEIMER-HESS. *Lorenzo Ghiberti.* 2nd ed. Princeton, 1970.

KUEHN, THOMAS J. *Law, Family, and Women: Toward a Legal Anthropology of Renaissance Italy.* Chicago, 1991.

LAMBERINI, DANIELA. *Calenzano e la Val di Marina. Storia di un territorio fiorentino.* 2 vols. Prato, 1987.

———, ed. *Il castello dell'Acciaiolo a Scandicci. Storia e rilievi per il restauro.* Florence, 2002.

LAMI, GIOVANNI. *Sanctae ecclesiae florentinae monumenta.* 4 vols. Florence, 1758.

LANDI, ALDO. *Il papa deposto. Pisa, 1409. L'idea conciliare nel Grande Schisma.* Turin, 1985.

LANDI, FABRIZIA. *Le temps revient. Il fregio di Poggio a Caiano.* San Giovanni Valdarno, 1986.

LANDINO, CRISTOFORO. *Carmina omnia.* Edited by ALESSANDRO PEROSA. Florence, 1939.

———. *Scritti critici e teorici.* Edited by ROBERTO CARDINI. 2 vols. Rome, 1974.

———. *Disputationes camaldulenses.* Edited by PETER LOHE. Florence, 1980.

LANDUCCI, LUCA. *Diario fiorentino dal 1450–1516.* Edited by IODOCO DEL BADIA. Florence, 1883.

LANFREDINI, GIOVANNI. *Corrispondenza di Giovanni Lanfredini, 1485–1486.* Edited by ELISABETTA SCARTON. Salerno, 2002.

———. *Corrispondenza dell'ambasciatore Giovanni Lanfredini I (13 aprile 1484–9 maggio 1485).* Edited by ELISABETTA SCARTON. Salerno, 2005.

LANGEDIJK, KARLA. *The Portraits of the Medici, Fifteenth to Eighteenth Centuries.* 3 vols. Florence, 1981.

LANSING, CAROL. *The Florentine Magnates: Lineage and Faction in a Medieval Commune.* Princeton, 1991.

LANZA, ANTONIO, ed. *Lirici toscani del Quattrocento.* 2 vols. Rome, 1973–1975.

———. *Firenze contro Milano. Gli intellettuali fiorentini nelle guerre con i Visconti (1390–1440).* Anzio (Rome), 1991.

LAPACCINI, FILIPPO. "L'armeggeria di Tommaso Benci." In *Lirici toscani del Quattrocento,* edited by ANTONIO LANZA, 2:1–17. Rome, 1973–75.

LARIVAILLE, PAUL. "Nifo, Machiavelli, principato civile." *Interpres* 9 (1989): 150–195.

LASCHI, G., P. ROSELLI, and P. A. ROSSI. "Indagini sulla cappella dei Pazzi." *Commentari* 13 (1962): 24–41.

LATINI, BRUNETTO. *La rettorica.* Edited by CESARE SEGRE. Florence, 1968.

LAUSBERG, HEINRICH. *Handbook of Literary Rhetoric: A Foundation for Literary Study.* Leiden, 1998.

LAW, JOHN E. "Verona in the Venetian State in the Fifteenth Century." *Historical Research* 52, no. 125 (1979): 9–22.

———. "Venice and the Problem of Sovereignty in the *Patria del Friuli,* 1421." In *Florence and Italy: Renaissance Studies in Honour of Nicolai Rubinstein,* edited by PETER DENLEY and CAROLINE ELAM, 135–147. London, 1988.

———. "Giovanni Vitelleschi: 'Prelato guerriero.'" *Renaissance Studies* 12 (1998): 40–66.

———. "The Venetian Mainland State in the Fifteenth Century." In *Venice and the Veneto in the Early Renaissance,* 153–174. Aldershot, 2000a.

———. *Venice and the Veneto in the Early Renaissance.* Aldershot, 2000b.

———. "Verona and Venetian State in the Fifteenth Century." In *Venice and the Veneto in the Early Renaissance,* 9–22. Aldershot, 2000c.

———. "John Addington Symonds and the Despots." In *Victorian and Edwardian Responses to the Italian Renaissance,* edited by JOHN E. LAW and LENE ØSTERMARK-JOHANSEN, 145–163. Aldershot, 2005.

———. "Communes and Despots: The Nature of 'Diarchy.'" In *Communes and Despots in Medieval and Renaissance Italy,* edited by JOHN E. LAW and BERNADETTE PATON, 161–177. Farnham, Surrey, 2010.

LAW, JOHN E., and BERNADETTE PATON, eds. *Communes and Despots in Medieval and Renaissance Italy.* Farnham, Surrey, 2010.

LAZZARINI, ISABELLA. *Fra un principe e altri stati. Relazioni di potere e forme di servizio a Mantova nell'età di Ludovico Gonzaga.* Rome, 1996.

LEADER, ANNE. *Reforming the Florentine Badia: Art and Observance in a Renaissance Monastery.* Bloomington, 2012.

LENZUNI, ANNA, ed. *All'ombra del lauro.* Exhibition catalog, Florence, Biblioteca Medicea Laurenziana. Milan, 1992.

LEVEROTTI, FRANCA. *Diplomazia e governo dello stato. I "famigli cavalcanti" di Francesco Sforza (1450–1466).* Pisa, 1992.

———. *"Governare a modo e stillo de'Signori…" Osservazioni in margine all'amministrazione della giustizia al tempo di Galeazzo Maria Sforza duca di Milano (1466–76).* Florence, 1994.

———. "Gli officiali nel ducato sforzesco." *Annali della scuola normale superiore di Pisa. Classe di lettere e filosofia,* ser. 4, no. 1 (1997): 17–77.

———. "Leggi del principe, leggi della città nel ducato visconteo-sforzesco." In *Signori, regimi signorili e statuti nel tardo medioevo,* edited by ROLANDO DONDARINI, MARIA VENTICELLI, and GIAN MARIA VARANINI, 143–188. Bologna, 2003.

LEVEROTTI, FRANCA, and ISABELLA LAZZARINI. *Carteggio degli oratori mantovani alla corte sforzesca (1450–1500).* 15 vols. Rome, 1999–.

LEWIN, ALISON WILLIAMS. *Negotiating Survival: Florence and the Great Schism, 1378–1417.* Madison NJ, 2003.

LIEBENWEIN, WOLFGANG. "Die 'Privatisierung' des Wunders: Piero de' Medici in SS. Annunziata und San Miniato." In *Piero de' Medici "il Gottoso" (1416–1469),* edited by ANDREAS BEYER and BRUCE BOUCHER, 250–290. Berlin, 1993.

LILLIE, AMANDA. "Lorenzo de' Medici's Rural Investments and Territorial Expansion." *Rinascimento,* 2nd ser., 33 (1993): 53–67.

———. "The Humanist Villa Revisited." In *Language and Images of Renaissance Italy,* edited by ALISON BROWN, 193–215. Oxford, 1995.

———. "Cappelle e chiese delle ville medicee ai tempi di Michelozzo." In *Michelozzo scultore e architetto (1396–1472),* edited by GABRIELE MOROLLI, 89–98. Florence, 1998a.

———. "The Patronage of Villa Chapels and Oratories near Florence: A Typology of Private Religion." In *With and Without the Medici: Studies in Tuscan Art and Patronage, 1434–1530,* edited by ECKART MARCHAND and ALISON WRIGHT, 19–46. Aldershot, 1998b.

———. "Memory of Place: *Luogo* and Lineage in the Fifteenth-Century Florentine Countryside." In *Art, Memory, and Family in Renaissance Florence,* edited by GIOVANNI CIAPPELLI and PATRICIA LEE RUBIN, 195–214. Cambridge, 2000.

———. *Florentine Villas in the Fifteenth Century: An Architectural and Social History.* Cambridge, 2005. Revised edition Cambridge, 2011.

LIPPINCOTT, KRISTEN. "The Iconography of the Salone dei Mesi and the Study of Latin Grammar in Fifteenth-Century Ferrara." In *La corte di Ferrara e il suo mecenatismo, 1441–1598,* edited by MARIANNE PADE and LENE WAAGE PETERSEN, 93–109. Modena, 1990.

LITTA, POMPEO. *Famiglie celebri italiane.* 18 vols. Milan, 1819–99.

LOPEZ, GUIDO. *Festa di nozze per Ludovico il Moro nelle testimonianze di Tristano Calco, Giacomo Trotti, Isabella d'Este, Gian Galeazzo Sforza, Beatrice de' Contrari, e altri.* Milan, 1976.

———. *Festa di nozze per Ludovico il Moro. Fasti nuziali e intrighi di potere alla corte degli Sforza, tra Milano, Vigevano e Ferrara.* Milan, 2008.

LUBKIN, GREGORY. *A Renaissance Court: Milan under Galeazzo Maria Sforza.* Berkeley, 1994.

LÜNIG, JOHANN CHRISTIAN, ed. *Codex Italiae diplomaticus.* 4 vols. Frankfurt and Leipzig, 1725–35.

LUPI, CLEMENTE. "Delle relazioni fra la repubblica di Firenze e i conti e duchi di Savoia. Memoria compilata sui documenti dell'archivio fiorentino." *Giornale storico degli archivi toscani* 7 (1863): 3–45, 81–129, 177–219, 257–322.

LUPO GENTILE, MICHELE. "Le corporazioni delle arti a Pisa nel secolo XV." *Annali della scuola normale superiore di Pisa. Classe di lettere e filosofia,* ser. II, 9, fasc. 3 (1940): 197–200.

LURATI, PATRICIA. "'In Firenze non si fe' mai simile festa'. A proposito del cassone di Apollonio di Giovanni con scena di giostra alla Yale University Art Gallery." *Annali di storia di Firenze* 7 (2012): 35–71.

LUZIO, ALESSANDRO. "Isabella d'Este e Francesco Gonzaga promessi sposi." *Archivio storico lombardo* 9 (1908): 34–69.

LUZZATI, MICHELE. "Filippo de' Medici arcivescovo di Pisa e la visita pastorale del 1462–1463." *Bollettino della societa pisana di storia patria* 33–35 (1964–66): 362–408.

———. *Una guerra di popolo. Lettere private al tempo dell'assedio di Pisa (1494–1509)*. Pisa, 1973.

———. *Firenze e la Toscana nel medioevo. Seicento anni per la costruzione di uno stato*. Turin, 1986.

———. "Dottorati in medicina conferiti a Firenze nel 1472 da Judah messer Leon da Montecchio a Buonaventura da Terracina e ad Abramo da Montalcino." *Atti e memorie della Deputazione di storia patria per le Marche* 97 (1994): 41–53.

MACEY, PATRICK. *Bonfire Songs: Savonarola's Musical Legacy*. Oxford, 1998.

MACHIAVELLI, NICCOLÒ. *Discorsi sopra la prima deca di Tito Livio*. Edited by FRANCESCO BAUSI. 2 vols. Roma, 2001a.

———. *L'arte della guerra. Scritti politici minori*. Edited by JEAN JACQUES MARCHAND, DENIS FACHARD, and GIORGIO MASI. Rome, 2001b.

———. *Opere storiche*. Edited by ALESSANDRO MONTEVECCHI AND CARLO VAROTTI. 2 vols. Rome, 2010.

———. *Il principe*. Edited by GIORGIO INGLESE. Turin, 2013.

MACK, PETER. *A History of Renaissance Rhetoric, 1380–1620*. Oxford, 2011.

MAGNI, CESARE. *Il tramonto del feudo lombardo*. Milan, 1937.

MAGUIRE, YVONNE. *The Women of the Medici*. London, 1927.

———. *The Private Life of Lorenzo the Magnificent*. London, 1936.

MAIRE VIGUEUR, JEAN-CLAUDE. "Il problema storiografico. Firenze come modello (e mito) di regime popolare." In *Magnati e popolani nell'Italia comunale. Quindicesimo convegno di studi, Pistoia, 15–18 maggio 1995*, 1–16. Pistoia, 1997.

———, ed. *Signorie cittadine nell'Italia comunale*. Rome, 2013.

MAJOCCHI, PIERO. *Pavia città regia. Storia e memoria di una capitale medievale*. Rome, 2008.

MALANIMA, PAOLO. *La decadenza di un'economia cittadina. L'industria di Firenze nei secoli XVI–XVII*. Bologna, 1982.

MALLETT, MICHAEL E. "The Sea Consuls of Florence in the Fifteenth Century." *Papers of the British School at Rome* 27 (1959): 156–169.

———. "Anglo-Florentine Commercial Relations, 1465–1491." *Economic History Review* 15, no. 2 (1962): 205–265.

———. *The Florentine Galleys in the Fifteenth Century*. Oxford, 1967.

———. "Pisa and Florence in the Fifteenth Century: Aspects of the Period of the First Florentine Domination." In *Florentine Studies: Politics and Society in Renaissance Florence*, edited by NICOLAI RUBINSTEIN, 403–441. London, 1968.

———. *Mercenaries and Their Masters: Warfare in Renaissance Italy*. London, 1974.

———. "Personalities and Pressures: Italian Involvement in the French Invasion of 1494." In *The French Descent into Renaissance Italy, 1494–1495: Antecedents and Effects*, edited by DAVID ABULAFIA, 151–163. Aldershot, 1995.

———. "Horse-Racing and Politics in Lorenzo's Florence." In *Lorenzo the Magnificent: Culture and Politics*, edited by MICHAEL E. MALLETT and NICHOLAS MANN, 253–262. London, 1996.

MALLETT, MICHAEL E., and NICHOLAS MANN, ed. *Lorenzo the Magnificent: Culture and Politics*. London, 1996.

MANCA, JOSEPH. "Constantia et Forteza: Eleonora d'Aragona's Famous Matrons." *Notes in the History of Art* 19, no. 2 (2000): 13–20.

MANNORI, LUCA. "Il 'piccolo stato' nel 'grande stato'. Archetipi classici e processi di territorializzazione nell'Italia tardo-medievale e proto-moderna." In *Polis e piccolo stato tra riflessione antica e pensiero moderno. Atti delle giornate di studio, 21–22 febbraio 1977, Firenze*, edited by EMILIO GABBA and ALDO SCHIAVONE, 48–66. Como, 1999.

MARCHESI, CONCETTO. "Il volgarizzamento italico delle *Declamationes* pseudo-Quintilianee." In *Miscellanea di studi critici pubblicati in onore di Guido Mazzoni dai suoi discepoli*, edited by ARNALDO DELLA TORRE and P. L. RAMBALDI, 279–303. Florence, 1907.

MARIETTI, MARINA. *Machiavelli. L'eccezione fiorentina*. Fiesole, 2005.

MARTELLI, MARIO. "Le due redazioni della *Laurentii Medicei vita* di Niccolò Valori." *La bibliofilia* 66 (1964): 235–253.

———. "Il *Libro delle Epistole* di Angelo Poliziano." *Interpres* 1 (1978): 184–255.

———. "Profilo ideologico di Alamanno Rinuccini." In *Culture et société en Italie, du Moyen-Age à la Renaissance: Hommage à André Rochon*, 131–143. Paris, 1985.

———. "Firenze." In *Letteratura italiana. Storia e geografia*. Vol. 2, *L'età moderna*, edited by ALBERTO ASOR ROSA, 25–201. Turin, 1988a.

———. "Una poesia di parte medicea per la guerra di Bartolomeo Colleoni." *Interpres* 8 (1988b): 270–275.

———. *Letteratura fiorentina del Quattrocento. Il filtro degli anni Sessanta*. Florence, 1996.

———. "La politica culturale dell'ultimo Lorenzo." In *Per Mario Martelli, l'uomo, il maestro e lo studioso*, edited by PAOLO ORVIETO, 93–158. Rome, 2009.

MARTIN, JOHN JEFFRIES, and DENNIS ROMANO, eds. *Venice Reconsidered: The History and Civilization of an Italian City-State, 1297–1797*. Baltimore, 2000.

MARTINES, LAURO. *The Social World of the Florentine Humanists, 1390–1460*. Princeton, 1963.

———. *Lawyers and Statecraft in Renaissance Florence*. Princeton, 1968.

———. "Bonarli, Orlando." *Dizionario biografico degli italiani* 11 (1969).

———. *Power and Imagination: City-States in Renaissance Italy*. New York, 1979.

———. *April Blood: Florence and the Plot against the Medici*. London, 2004.

———. *Scourge and Fire: Savonarola and Renaissance Florence*. London, 2006.

MARTINI, FRANCESCO DI GIORGIO, and CORRADO MALTESE, eds. *Trattati di architettura ingegneria e arte militare*. 2 vols. Milan, 1967.

MATEER, DAVID, ed. *Courts, Patrons, and Poets*. New Haven, 2000.

MATHEW, ARNOLD HARRIS. *The Life and Times of Rodrigo Borgia, Pope Alexander VI*. London, 1912.

MAZZACANE, ALDO. "Lo stato e il dominio nei giuristi veneti durante il 'secolo della Terraferma.'" In *Storia della cultura veneta*, edited by GIROLAMO ARNALDI and MANLIO PASTORE STOCCHI, 3, 1:577–650. Vicenza, 1981.

MAZZOCCHI DOGLIO, MARIANGELA. *Leonardo e gli spettacoli del suo tempo*. Milan, 1983.

MCGEE, TIMOTHY J. *The Ceremonial Musicians of Late Medieval Florence*. Bloomington, 2009.

MCKILLOP, SUSAN. "Dante and *Lumen Christi*: A Proposal for the Meaning of the Tomb of Cosimo de' Medici." In *Cosimo "il Vecchio" de' Medici, 1389–1464: Essays in Commemoration of the 600th Anniversary of Cosimo de' Medici's Birth*, edited by FRANCIS AMES-LEWIS, 245–301. Oxford, 1992a.

———. "L'ampliamento dello stemma medíceo e il suo contesto politico." *Archivio storico italiano* 150 (1992b): 641–711.

MCLEAN, PAUL D. *The Art of the Network: Strategic Interaction and Patronage in Renaissance Florence*. Durham NC, 2007.

MEDICI, LORENZO DE'. *Lettere*. Edited by LORENZ BÖNINGER, MELISSA BULLARD, HUMFREY BUTTERS, RICCARDO FUBINI, MICHAEL MALLETT, MARCO PELLEGRINI, and NICOLAI RUBINSTEIN. 14 vols. Florence, 1977–.

———. *Canti carnascialeschi*. Edited by PAOLO ORVIETO. Rome, 1991.

———. *Tutte le opere*. Edited by PAOLO ORVIETO. 2 vols. Rome, 1992.

MELI, PATRIZIA. *Gabriele Malaspina marchese di Fosdinovo. Condotte, politica e diplomazia nella Lunigiana del rinascimento*. Florence, 2008.

MELI, PATRIZIA, and SERGIO TOGNETTI. *Il principe e il mercante nella Toscana del Quattrocento. Il magnifico signore di Piombino Jacopo III Appiani e le aziende Maschiani di Pisa*. Florence, 2006.

MEMELSDORFF, PEDRO. "John Hothby, Lorenzo il Magnifico, e Robert Morton." *Acta musicologica* 78 (2006): 1–32.

MENZINGER, SARA. "Pareri eccezionali. Procedure decisionali ordinarie e straordinarie nella politica comunale del XIII secolo." *Quaderni storici* 131 (2009): 399–410.

MESSINA, PIETRO. "Eleonora d'Aragona, duchessa di Ferrara." *Dizionario biografico degli italiani* 42 (1993).

MILANI, GIULIANO. "Legge ed eccezione nei comuni di popolo del XIII secolo (Bologna, Perugia, Pisa)." *Quaderni storici* 131 (2009): 377–398.

MILNER, STEPHEN J. "Lorenzo and Pistoia: Peacemaker or Partisan?" In *Lorenzo the Magnificent: Culture and Politics*, edited by MICHAEL E. MALLETT and NICOLAS MANN, 235–252. London, 1996.

———. "Citing the *Ringhiera*: The Politics of Place and Public Address in Trecento Florence." *Italian Studies* 55 (2000a): 53–82.

———. "Rubrics and Requests: Statutory Division and Supra-Communal Clientage in Fifteenth-Century Pistoia." In *Florentine Tuscany: Structures and Practices of Power*, edited by WILLIAM J. CONNELL and ANDREA ZORZI, 312–332. Cambridge, 2000b.

———, ed. *At the Margins: Minority Groups in Premodern Italy*. Minneapolis, 2005a.

———. "Exile, Rhetoric, and the Limits of Civic Republican Discourse." In *At the Margins: Minority Groups in Premodern Italy*, edited by STEPHEN J. MILNER, 162–191. Minneapolis, 2005b.

———. "'*Le sottili cose non si possono bene aprire in volgare*': Vernacular Oratory and the Transmission of Classical Rhetorical Theory in the Late Medieval Italian Communes." *Italian Studies* 64 (2009): 221–244.

———. "Manufacturing the Renaissance: Modern Merchant Princes and the Origins of the Manchester Dante Society." In *Culture in Manchester: Institutions and Urban Change since 1850*, edited by JANET WOLFF and MICHAEL SAVAGE, 61–94. Manchester, 2013.

MITCHELL, BONNER. *1598: A Year of Pageantry in Late Renaissance Ferrara*. Binghamton NY, 1990.

MOLHO, ANTHONY. *Florentine Public Finances in the Early Renaissance, 1400–1433*. Cambridge MA, 1971.

———. "Cosimo de' Medici: Pater Patriae or Padrino?" *Stanford Italian Review* 1 (1979): 5–33.

———. "Patronage and the State in Early Modern Italy." In *Klientelsysteme im Europa der frühen Neuzeit*, edited by ANTONI MACZAK and ELISABETH MÜLLER-LUCKNER, 233–242. Munich, 1988.

———. "Fisco ed economia a Firenze alla vigilia del concilio." *Archivio storico italiano* 148 (1990): 807–842.

———. *Marriage Alliance in Renaissance in Late Medieval Florence*. Cambridge MA, 1994.

MOLHO, ANTHONY, and FRANEK SZNURA, eds. *Alle bocche della piazza. Diario di anonimo fiorentino (1382–1401)*. Florence, 1986.

MOLINARI, CESARE. "Delle nozze medicee e dei loro cronisti." In *Il teatro dei Medici*, edited by LUDOVICO ZORZI, 23–30. Florence, 1980.

MONTAIGNE, MICHEL DE. *Journal de voyage*. Edited by FAUSTA GARAVINI. Paris, 1983.

MONTORZI, MARIO. *Giustizia in contado. Studi sull'esercizio della giurisdizione nel territorio ponterese e pisano in età moderna*. Florence, 1997.

———. Preface to *Ad statutum florentinum. Esegesi statutaria e cultura giuridica nella Toscana medievale e moderna*, edited by DANIELE EDIGATI and LORENZO TANZINI, ix–xv. Pisa, 2009.

MOORES, JOHN. "New Light on Diomede Carafa and His Perfect Loyalty to Ferrante of Aragon." *Italian Studies* 26 (1971): 1–23.

MORBIO, CARLO. *Storia della città e diocesi di Novara*. Milan, 1841.

MORÇAY, RAOUL. *Saint Antonin, fondateur du couvent de Saint-Marc, archevêque de Florence, 1389–1459*. Paris, 1914.

MORELLI TIMPANARO, MARIA AUGUSTA, ROSALIA MANNO TOLU, and PAOLO VITI, eds. *Consorterie politiche e mutamenti istituzionali in età laurenziana.* Exhibition catalog, Florence, Archivio di Stato. Florence, 1992.

MORICI, MEDARDO. "Il cardinale Niccolò Forteguerri e Giovanni di Cosimo de' Medici." *Bullettino storico pistoiese* 2 (1900): 110–114.

MOROLLI, GABRIELE, and CRISTINA ACIDINI LUCHINAT, eds. *L'architettura di Lorenzo il Magnifico.* Exhibition catalog, Florence, Spedale degli Innocenti. Cinisello Balsamo, 1992.

MOROSINI, DOMENICO. *De bene instituta re publica.* Edited by CLAUDIO FINZI. Milan, 1969.

MOTTA, EMILIO. "I Sanseverino feudatari di Lugano e di Balerna, 1434–1484." *Periodico della società storica per la provincia e antica diocesi di Como* 2 (1880): 153–185, 193–310.

———. "Guelfi e ghibellini nel Luganese." *Periodico della società storica per la provincia e antica diocesi di Como* 4 (1884): 69–198.

———. *Nozze principesche nel Quattrocento.* Milan, 1894.

MOZZARELLI, CESARE. "Nota storica." In *Mantova 1430. Pareri a Gian Francesco Gonzaga per il governo,* edited by MARIA ANTONIETTA GRIGNANI, 13–37. Mantua, 1990.

MÜLLER, JOSEPH. *Documenti sulle relazioni delle città toscane coll'oriente cristiano e coi Turchi fino all'anno MDXXXI.* Florence, 1879.

MUNCK, BERT DE, and ANNE WINTER, eds. *Gated Communities? Regulating Migration in Early Modern Cities.* Farnham, Surrey, 2012.

MUSSO, ANNALISA. "*Del modo de regere e di regnare* di Antonio Cornazzano. Una institutio principis al femminile." *Schifanoia* 19 (1999): 67–79.

NAGEL, ALEXANDER, and CHRISTOPHER S. WOOD. *Anachronic Renaissance.* New York, 2010.

NAJEMY, JOHN M. *Corporatism and Consensus in Florentine Electoral Politics, 1280–1400.* Chapel Hill NC, 1982a.

———. "Machiavelli and the Medici: The Lessons of Florentine History." *Renaissance Quarterly* 35 (1982b): 551–576.

———. "The Dialogue of Power in Florentine Politics." In *City States in Classical Antiquity and Medieval Italy: Athens and Rome, Florence and Venice,* edited by ANTHONY MOLHO, KURT A. RAAFLAUB, and JULIA EMLEN, 269–288. Stuttgart, 1991.

———. "Civic Humanism and Florentine Politics." In *Renaissance Civic Humanism: Reappraisals and Reflections,* edited by JAMES HANKINS, 75–104. Cambridge, 2000.

———. "Florentine Politics and Urban Spaces." In *Renaissance Florence: A Social History,* edited by ROGER J. CRUM and JOHN T. PAOLETTI, 19–54. New York, 2006a.

———. *A History of Florence 1200–1575.* Oxford, 2006b.

NALDI, NALDO. *Naldi Naldii Elegia in septem stellas errantes sub humana specie per urbem florentinam curribus a Laurentio Medice patriae patre duci iussas more triumphantium,* Florence, Biblioteca Riccardiana, Edizioni rare 572 (the unique copy without indication of place or date of publication: see IGI, n. 6766).

———. *Bucolica, Volaterrais, Hastiludium, Carmina varia.* Edited by LEONARD W. GRANT. Florence, 1974.

NEGRI, PAOLO. "Studi sulla crisi italiana alla fine del secolo XV." *Archivio storico lombardo* 50 (1923): 1–135.

NELLI, RENZO. *Signoria ecclesiastica e proprietà cittadina. Monte di Croce tra XIII e XIV secolo.* Pontassieve, 1985.

NEWBIGIN, NERIDA. "Il testo e il contesto dell' *Abramo e Isac* di Feo Belcari." *Studi e problemi di critica testuale* 13 (1981): 13–37.

———. *Feste d'Oltrarno: Plays in Churches in Fifteenth-Century Florence.* 2 vols. Florence, 1996a.

———. "Politics in the *Sacre rappresentazioni* of Lorenzo's Florence." In *Lorenzo the Magnificent: Culture and Politics,* edited by MICHAEL E. MALLETT and NICHOLAS MANN, 117–130. London, 1996b.

———, ed. "Le onoranze fiorentine del 1459. Poema anonimo." *Letteratura italiana antica* 12 (2011): 17–135.

NIEUWENHUIZEN, PAUL. "Worldly Ritual and Dynastic Iconography in the Bentivoglio Chapel in Bologna, 1483–1499." *Mededelingen van het Nederlands Instituut te Rome* 55 (1996): 187–212.

NUBOLA, CECILIA, and ANDREAS WÜRGLER, eds. *Forme della comunicazione politica in Europa nei secoli XV–XVII. Suppliche, gravamina, lettere.* Berlin and Bologna, 2004.

OLMSTED, WENDY. *Rhetoric: An Historical Introduction.* Oxford, 2006.

OLSON, ROBERTA J. M. *The Florentine Tondo.* Oxford, 2000.

OPPEL, JOHN W. "Peace vs. Liberty in the Quattrocento: Poggio, Guarino, and the Scipio-Caesar Controversy." *Journal of Medieval and Renaissance Studies* 4 (1974): 221–265.

ORLANDI, STEFANO. *S. Antonino. Studi bibliografici.* 2 vols. Florence, 1959–60.

ORTALLI, GHERARDO. "Entrar nel dominio. Le dedizioni delle città alla repubblica serenissima." In *Società economia istituzioni,* 49–62. Caselle di Sommacampagna (Verona), 2002 (published by Cierre edizione and the Consiglio regionale del Veneto).

———. "Comunicare con le figure." In *Arti e storia nel medioevo,* vol. 3, *Del vedere. Pubblici, forme e funzioni,* edited by ENRICO CASTELNUOVO and GIUSEPPE SERGI, 477–518. Turin, 2004.

ORVIETO, PAOLO. *Pulci medievale. Studio sulla poesia volgare fiorentina del Quattrocento.* Rome, 1978.

OSMOND, PATRICIA J. "Catiline in Fiesole and Florence: The After-Life of a Roman Conspirator." *International Journal of the Classical Tradition* 7 (2000): 3–38.

OTTANI CAVINA, ANNA. "La cappella Bentivoglio." In *Il tempio di San Giacomo Maggiore in Bologna,* edited by CARLO VOLPE, 117–131. Bologna, 1967.

PALMAROCCHI, ROBERTO. "Lorenzo de' Medici e la nomina cardinalizia di Giovanni." *Archivio storico italiano* 110 (1952): 38–54.

PALMIERI, MATTEO. *Vita civile.* Edited by GINO BELLONI. Florence, 1982.

PAMPALONI, GUIDO. "Nuovi tentativi di riforme alla costituzione fiorentina visti attraverso le consulte." *Archivio storico italiano* 120 (1962): 521–581.

———. "La miniera di rame di Montecatini Val di Cecina. La legislazione mineraria di Firenze e i Marinai di Prato, secolo XV, seconda metà." *Archivio storico pratese* 51, no. 2 (1975): 3–169.

PAMUK, ORHAM. *My Name Is Red.* Translated by ERDA M. GÖKNAR. New York, 2002.

PANDIMIGLIO, LEONIDA. "Lorenzo Morelli (1446–1528) e le 'calamità d'Italia'. Presenza pubblica e memoria privata." In *I ceti dirigenti in Firenze dal gonfalonierato di giustizia a vita all'avvento del ducato,* edited by ELISABETTA INSABATO, 281–304. Lecce, 1999.

PANSINI, GIUSEPPE. "Le piante dei 'popoli e strade' e lo stato della viabilità nel granducato di Toscana alla fine del secolo XVI." In *Piante di popoli e strade. Capitani di parte guelfa, 1580–1595,* edited by GIUSEPPE PANSINI, 1:7–19. Florence, 1989.

PAOLETTI, JOHN. "Fraternal Piety and Family Power: The Artistic Patronage of Cosimo and Lorenzo de' Medici." In *Cosimo "il Vecchio" de' Medici, 1389–1464: Essays in Commemoration of the 600th Anniversary of Cosimo de' Medici's Birth,* edited by FRANCIS AMES-LEWIS, 195–219. Oxford, 1992.

———. "Strategies and Structures of Medici Artistic Patronage in the Fifteenth Century." In *The Early Medici and Their Artists,* edited by FRANCIS AMES-LEWIS, 19–36. London, 1995.

PAOLINI, CLAUDIO, and DANIELA PARENTI, eds. *Virtù d'amore. Pittura nuziale nel Quattrocento fiorentino.* Exhibition catalog, Florence, Gallerie dell'Accademia. Florence, 2010.

PARENTI, MARCO. *Lettere.* Edited by MARIA MARRESE. Florence, 1996.

———. *Ricordi storici, 1464–1467.* Edited by MANUELA DONI GARFAGNINI. Rome, 2001.

PARENTI, PIERO DI MARCO. *Storia fiorentina.* Edited by ANDREA MATUCCI. 2 vols. Florence, 1994–2005.

PARTNER, PETER. "Florence and the Papacy in the Earlier Fifteenth Century." In *Florentine Studies: Politics and Society in Renaissance Florence,* edited by NICOLAI RUBINSTEIN, 381–402. London, 1968.

PASCHINI, PIO. *Lodovico Cardinal Camerlengo.* Rome, 1939.

PASQUINI, ELISABETTA. *Libri di musica a Firenze nel Tre-Quattocento*. Florence, 2000.

PASTOR, LUDWIG. *Ungedruckte Akten zur Geschichte der Päpste vornehmlich im XV, XVI, und XVII. Jahrhundert*. Freiburg im Breisgau, 1904.

PÀSZTOR, EDITH. "Adimari, Alamanno." *Dizionario biografico degli italiani* 1 (1960).

PECCHIONI, ENIO. *Note sul piviere di Lobaco con l'oratorio della Madonna del Sasso*. Florence, 1976.

PECUGI FOP, MARIA. *Perugia in Toscana. I centri aretini e senesi sottomessi al comune di Perugia nel Trecento*. Perugia, 2008.

PELLEGRINI, MARCO. "Ascanio Maria Sforza, la creazione di un cardinale 'di famiglia.'" In *Gli Sforza, la chiesa lombarda, la corte di Roma*, edited by GIORGIO CHITTOLINI, 215–289. Naples, 1989.

———. *Congiure di Romagna. Lorenzo de' Medici e il duplice tirannicidio a Forlì e a Faenza nel 1488*. Florence, 1999.

———. *Ascanio Maria Sforza. La parabola politica di un cardinale principe del rinascimento*. 2 vols. Rome, 2002.

PEROSA, ALESSANDRO. "Lo zibaldone di Giovanni Rucellai." In *Giovanni Rucellai ed il suo zibaldone*, vol. 2, *A Florentine Patrician and His Palace*, edited by FRANCIS WILLIAM KENT, ALESSANDRO PEROSA, BRENDA PREYER, ROBERTO SALVINI, and PIERO SANPAOLESI, 99–152. London, 1981.

PESMAN COOPER, ROSLYN. *Pier Soderini and the Ruling Class in Renaissance Florence*. Goldbach, 2002.

PESTELLI, ANDREA. *The Castle of Montegufoni: From Its Origins up to the Present Day*. Florence, 2002.

PETERSON, DAVID S. "An Episcopal Election in Quattrocento Florence." In *Popes, Teachers, and Canon Law in the Middle Ages*, edited by JAMES ROSS SWEENEY and STANLEY CHODOROW, 300–325. Ithaca, 1989.

———. "Religion, Politics, and the Church in Fifteenth-Century Florence." In *Girolamo Savonarola: Piety, Prophecy, and Politics in Renaissance Florence*, edited by DONALD WEINSTEIN and VALERY HOTCHKISS, 75–83. Dallas, 1994.

———. "State-Building, Church Reform, and the Politics of Legitimacy in Florence, 1375–1460." In *Florentine Tuscany: Structures and Practices of Power*, edited by WILLIAM J. CONNELL and ANDREA ZORZI, 122–141. Cambridge, 2000.

———. "The Cathedral, the Florentine Church, and Ecclesiastical Government in the Early Quattrocento." In *La cattedrale e la città. Saggi sul duomo di Firenze*, edited by TIMOTHY VERDON and ANNALISA INNOCENTI, 1:55–78. Florence, 2001.

———. "The War of the Eight Saints in Florentine Memory and Oblivion." In *Society and Individual in Renaissance Florence*, edited by WILLIAM J. CONNELL, 173–214. Berkeley, 2002.

———. "Conciliarism at the Local Level: Florence's Clerical Corporation in the Early Fifteenth Century." In *The Church, the Councils, and Reform: The Legacy of the Fifteenth Century*, edited by GERALD CHRISTIANSON, THOMAS M. IZBICKI, and CHRISTOPHER M. BELLITO, 250–270. Washington DC, 2008.

PETERSON, DAVID S., and DANIEL E. BORNSTEIN, eds. *Florence and Beyond: Culture, Society, and Politics in Renaissance Italy; Essays in Honour of John M. Najemy*. Toronto, 2008.

PETRALIA, GIUSEPPE. "'Crisi' ed emigrazione dei ceti eminenti a Pisa durante il primo dominio fiorentino. L'orizzonte cittadino e la ricerca di spazi esterni (1406–1460)." In *I ceti dirigenti nella Toscana del Quattrocento. Atti del V e VI convegno, Firenze, 10–11 dicembre 1982, 2–3 dicembre 1983*, edited by DONATELLA RUGIADINI, 291–352. Monte Oriolo (Florence), 1987.

———. "Pisa laurenziana. Una città e un territorio per la conservazione dello stato." In *La Toscana al tempo di Lorenzo il Magnifico. Politica, economia, cultura, arte*, 3:955–980. Pisa, 1996.

PETRARCA, FRANCESCO. *The Triumphs of Petrarch*. Translated by ERNEST HATCH WILKINS. Chicago, 1962.

PETRIBONI, PAGOLO DI MATTEO, and MATTEO DI BORGO RINALDI. *Priorista, 1407–1459*. Edited by JACQUELINE A. GUTWIRTH. Rome, 2001.

PETRUCCI, FRANCA. "Carafa, Diomede." *Dizionario biografico degli italiani* 19 (1976).

PEZZANA, ANGELO. *Storia della città di Parma.* 5 vols. Parma, 1837–59.

PHILLIPS, MARK. *The Memoir of Marco Parenti: A Life in Medici Florence.* Princeton, 1987.

PICCOLOMINI, AENEAS SILVIUS [POPE PIUS II]. *Der Briefwechsel des Aeneas Silvius Piccolomini,* vol. 2, *Briefe als Priester und Bischof von Trient 1447–1450.* Edited by RUDOLF WOLKAN. Vienna, 1912.

———. *I Commentarii [di Pio II].* Edited by LUIGI TORTARO. 2 vols. Milan, 1984.

———. *Historia austrialis.* Edited by JULIA KNÖDLER and MARTIN WAGENDORFER. 2 vols. Hannover, 2009.

PICO DELLA MIRANDOLA, GIOVANNI. *De hominis dignitate.* Edited by EUGENIO GARIN. Florence, 1942.

PICOTTI, GIOVANNI BATTISTA. *La dieta di Mantova e la politica de' Veneziani.* Venice, 1912. Reprinted Trent, 1996.

———. *La giovinezza di Leone X.* Milan, 1928. Reprinted Rome, 1981.

———. "Alessandro VI." *Dizionario biografico degli italiani* 2 (1960).

PIERACCINI, GAETANO. *La stirpe de' Medici di Cafaggiolo.* 3 vols. Florence, 1924–25.

PIERGIOVANNI, VITO. "I rapporti giuridici fra Genova e il dominio di Genova." In *Genoa, Pisa e il Mediterraneo tra Due e Trecento,* 45–58. Genoa, 1984.

PINTO, OLGA. *Nuptialia. Saggio di bibliografia di scritti italiani pubblicati per nozze dal 1484 al 1799.* Florence, 1971.

PIRILLO, PAOLO. *Costruzione di un contado. I Fiorentini e il loro territorio nel basso medioevo.* Florence, 2001.

———. "Torri, fortilizi e 'palagi in fortezza' nelle campagne fiorentine (secoli XIV–XV)." In *Motte, torri e caseforti nelle campagne medievali (secoli XII–XV),* edited by RINALDO COMBA, FRANCESCO PANERO, and GIULIANO PINTO, 241–253. Cherasco, 2007.

PIROLO, PAOLA, ed. *Lorenzo dopo Lorenzo. La fortuna storica di Lorenzo il Magnifico.* Florence, 1992.

PIUS II: see PICCOLOMINI, AENEAS SYLVIUS.

PLANCHART, ALEJANDRO. "Northern Repertories in Florence in the Fifteenth Century." In *La musica a Firenze al tempo di Lorenzo il Magnifico,* edited by PIERO GARGIULO, 101–112. Florence, 1993.

PLATINA, BARTOLOMEO. *De optimo cive.* Edited by F. BATTAGLIA. Bologna, 1944.

———. *De principe.* Edited by GIACOMO FERRAÙ. Palermo, 1979.

POLIZIANO, ANGELO. *Stanze cominciate per la giostra di Giuliano de' Medici.* Turin, 1954.

———. *Della congiura dei Pazzi.* Edited by ALESSANDRO PEROSA. Padua, 1958.

———. *Stanze cominciate per la giostra di Giuliano de' Medici.* Edited by MARIO MARTELLI. Alpignano, 1979.

———. *Detti piacevoli.* Edited by MARIANO FRESTA. Siena, 1985.

———. *Poesie volgari.* Edited by FRANCESCO BAUSI. 2 vols. Rome, 1997.

———. *Due poemetti latini.* Edited by FRANCESCO BAUSI. Rome, 2003.

POLIZIANO, ANGELO, and GENTILE BECCHI. *La congiura della verità.* Edited by MARCELLO SIMONETTA; translated by GERARDO FORTUNATO. Naples, 2012.

POLIZZOTTO, LORENZO. "The Making of a Saint: The Canonization of St. Antonino, 1516–1523." *Journal of Medieval and Renaissance Studies* 22 (1992): 353–381.

PREYER, BRENDA. "The Rucellai Palace." In *Giovanni Rucellai ed il suo zibaldone,* vol. 2, *A Florentine Patrician and His Palace,* edited by FRANCIS WILLIAM KENT, ALESSANDRO PEROSA, BRENDA PREYER, ROBERTO SALVINI, and PIERO SANPAOLESI, 155–225. London, 1981.

———. "L'architettura del Palazzo Mediceo." In *Il Palazzo Medici Riccardi di Firenze,* edited by GIOVANNI CHERUBINI and GIOVANNI FANELLI, 58–75. Florence, 1990.

PRIULI, GIROLAMO. *I diarii (1494–1512),* edited by ARTURO SEGRE. In *Rerum italicarum scriptores.* vol. 24, pt. 3. Città di Castello, 1912–41.

PRIZER, WILLIAM F. "Games of Venus: Secular Vocal Music in the Late Quattrocento and Early Cinquecento." *Journal of Musicology* 9 (1991): 3–56.

PROKOF'EV, N. I. *Russkije khoždenija XII–XV veka.* Moscow, 1970.

PUCCI, ORAZIO. *12 itinerari dei dintorni di Firenze.* Florence, 1939.

PULCI, LUIGI. "Il driadeo d'amore." In *Poemetti mitologici de' secoli XIV, XV, e XVI,* edited by FRANCESCO TORRACA, 161–319. Livorno, 1888.

———. *Opere minori,* edited by PAOLO ORVIETO. Milan, 1986.

QUAGLIONI, DIEGO. *Politica e diritto nel Trecento italiano. Il "De Tyranno" di Bartolo da Sassoferrato (1314–1357).* Florence, 1983.

QUINT, DAVID. "Narrative Design and Historical Irony in Machiavelli's *Istorie fiorentine.*" *Rinascimento* 43 (2004): 31–48.

RANDOLPH, ADRIAN W. B. *Engaging Symbols: Gender, Politics, and Public Art in Fifteenth-Century Florence.* New Haven, 2002.

REDDITI, FILIPPO. *Exhortatio ad Petrum Medicem, con appendice di lettere.* Edited by PAOLO VITI. Florence, 1989.

REDON, ODILE. *L'espace d'une cité. Sienne et le pays siennois, XIIIᵉ–XIVᵉ siècles.* Rome, 1994.

REPETTI, EMANUELE. *Dizionario geografico, fisico, storico della Toscana.* 6 vols. Florence, 1833–46.

REUMONT, ALFREDO. "Di alcune relazioni dei Fiorentini colla città di Danzica." *Archivio storico italiano* 13, no. 1 (1861): 37–47.

RICCHIONI, VICENZO. *La costituzione politica di Firenze ai tempi di Lorenzo il Magnifico.* Siena, 1913.

RICCIARDELLI, FABRIZIO. *The Politics of Exclusion in Early Renaissance Florence.* Turnhout, 2007.

RICCIARDI, LUCIA. *Col senno, col tesoro e colla lancia. Riti e giochi cavallereschi nella Firenze del Magnifico Lorenzo.* Florence, 1992.

RICHARDS, GERTRUDE RANDOLPH BRAMLETTE. *Florentine Merchants in the Age of the Medici: Letters and Documents from the Selfridge Collection of Medici Manuscripts.* Cambridge MA, 1932.

RICHARDS, JENNIFER. *Rhetoric.* London and New York, 2008.

RIDOLFI, ROBERTO. *Vita di Niccolò Machiavelli.* 7th ed. Florence, 1978.

RIGHINI, GASPERO. *Mugello e Val di Sieve. Note e memorie storico, artistico, letterarie.* Florence, 1956.

RINUCCINI, ALAMANNO. *Lettere ed orazioni.* Edited by VITO R. GIUSTINIANI. Florence, 1953.

———. *Dialogus de libertate.* Edited by FRANCESCO ADORNO. *Atti e memorie dell'Accademia toscana di scienze e lettere "La columbaria"* 22 (1957): 267–303.

RINUCCINI, FILIPPO DI CINO, ALAMANNO RINUCCINI, and NERI RINUCCINI. *Ricordi storici di Filippo di Cino Rinuccini dal 1282 al 1460, con la continuazione di Alamanno e Neri, suoi figli, fino al 1506.* Florence, 1840.

DA RIPALTA, ALBERTO. *Annales placentini.* Edited by LUDOVICO ANTONIO MURATORI. In *Rerum italicarum scriptores,* vol. 20. Milan, 1731.

RIPOLL, THOMÁS, and ANTONIN BRÉMOND. *Bullarium ordinis fratrum praedicatorum.* 8 vols. Rome, 1729–40.

RISTORI, RENZO. "Dati, Leonardo." *Dizionario biografico degli italiani* 33 (1987).

RIZZI, MARCO. *"Plenitudo potestatis.* Dalla teologia politica alla teoria dello stato assoluto." *Annali di storia moderna e contemporanea* 16 (2010): 153–164.

ROBEY, DAVID, and JOHN E. LAW. "The Venetian Myth and the 'De Republica Veneta' of Pietro Paolo Vergerio." *Rinascimento,* 2nd ser., 15 (1975): 3–59.

ROBINS, WILLIAM. "Poetic Rivalry: Antonio Pucci, Jacopo Salimbeni, and Antonio da Ferrara." In *Firenze alla vigilia del rinascimento. Antonio Pucci e i suoi contemporanei,* edited by MARIA PREDELLI, 307–322. Florence, 2006.

ROBINSON, CRISPIN. "Cosimo de' Medici and the Franciscan Observants at Bosco ai Frati." In *Cosimo "il Vecchio" de' Medici, 1389–1464: Essays in Commemoration of the 600th Anniversary of Cosimo de' Medici's Birth,* edited by FRANCIS AMES-LEWIS, 181–195. Oxford, 1992.

ROBOLINI, GIUSEPPE. *Notizie appartenenti alla storia della sua patria.* 6 vols. Pavia, 1823–38.

ROCHON, ANDRÉ. *La jeunesse de Laurent de Médicis (1449–1478).* Paris, 1963.

ROCKE, MICHAEL. *Forbidden Friendships: Homosexuality and Male Culture in Renaissance Florence.* New York, 1996.

RODOLICO, FRANCESCO. *Le pietre delle città d'Italia.* Florence, 1995.

ROLFI, GIANFRANCESCO. "Giovanni Vitelleschi arcivescovo di Firenze. La sua azione miltare all'epoca dell concilio. "In *Firenze e il concilio del 1493*, edited by PAOLO VITI, 121–146. Florence, 1994.

ROMANIN, SAMUELE. *Storia documentata di Venezia.* Vol. 4. 3rd ed. Venice, 1973.

ROMBAI, LEONARDO. "Prefazione. Strade e politica in Toscana tra medioevo ed età moderna." In *Il libro vecchio di strade della repubblica fiorentina*, edited by GABRIELE CIAMPI, 5–36. Florence, 1987.

———. "Il sistema delle infrastrutture di comunicazione nella toscana fiorentina del XV secolo." In *La Toscana al tempo di Lorenzo il Magnifico. Politica, economia, cultura, arte*, 3:857–868. Pisa, 1996.

ROSCOE, WILLIAM. *The Life of Lorenzo de' Medici, Called the Magnificent.* London, 1846. Reprinted London, 1902.

ROSE, MARGARET. "Marx and the Study of Patronage in the Renaissance." In *Patronage, Art, and Society in Renaissance Italy*, edited by FRANCIS WILLIAM KENT and PATRICIA SIMONS, 313–319. Oxford, 1987.

ROSMINI, CARLO DE'. *Dell'istoria intorno alle militari imprese e alla vita di Gian-Jacopo Trivulzio.* 2 vols. Milan, 1815.

———. *Dell'istoria di Milano.* 4 vols. Milan, 1820.

ROSS, JANET. *Lives of the Early Medici, as Told in Their Correspondence.* London, 1910. Reprinted Boston, 1911.

ROSSI, G., ed. *Bartolomeo Cipolla. Un giurista veronese del Quattrocento tra cattedra, foro, e luoghi del potere.* Padua, 2009.

ROTELLI, ELENA. "I vescovi nella società fiorentina del trecento." In *Eretici e ribelli del xiii e xiv secolo*, edited by DOMENICO MASELLI, 189–213. Pistoia, 1974.

ROVEDA, ENRICO. "Istituzioni politiche e gruppi sociali nel Quattrocento." In *Metamorfosi di un borgo. Vigevano in età visconteo-sforzesca*, edited by GIORGIO CHITTOLINI, 55–116. Milan, 1992a.

———. "Le istituzioni e la società in età visconteo-sforzesca." In *Storia di Pavia*, edited by ANGELO CERRI, 3:55–115. Pavia, 1992b.

ROVELLI, GIUSEPPE. *Storia di Como.* 3 vols. Como, 1789–1802.

RUBIN, PATRICIA. *Images and Identity in Fifteenth-Century Florence.* New Haven, 2007.

RUBIN, PATRICIA, and ALISON WRIGHT. *Renaissance Florence: The Art of the 1470s.* Exhibition catalog, London, National Gallery. London, 1999.

RUBINSTEIN, NICOLAI. "The Beginnings of Humanism in Florence." In *The Age of the Renaissance*, edited by DENYS HAY, 11–42. London, 1967.

———, ed. *Florentine Studies. Politics and Society in Renaissance Florence.* London, 1968.

———. "Machiavelli and the World of Florentine Politics." In *Studies on Machiavelli*, edited by MYRON P. GILMORE, 3–28. Florence, 1972.

———. "Lorenzo de' Medici: The Formation of His Statecraft." *Proceedings of the British Academy* 63 (1977): 71–94.

———. "Le istituzioni del regime mediceo da Lorenzo il Magnifico agli inizi del Principato." In *Idee, istituzioni, scienza ed arti nella Firenze dei Medici*, edited by CESARE VASOLI, 29–46. Florence, 1980.

———. "*Stato* and Regime in Fifteenth-Century Florence." In *Per Federico Chabod (1901–1960)*. Vol. 1, *Lo stato e il potere nel rinascimento*, edited by SERGIO BERTELLI, 137–146. Perugia, 1980–81.

———. "The *De optimo cive* and the *De principe* by Bartolomeo Platina." In *Tradizione classica e letteratura umanistica per Alessandro Perosa*, edited by ROBERTO CARDINI, EUGENIO GARIN, LUCIA CESARINI MARTINELLI, and GIOVANNI PASCUCCI, 375–389. Rome, 1985.

———. "Il *De optimo cive* del Platina." In *Bartolomeo Sacchi il Platina (Piadena 1421–Roma 1481)*, edited by AUGUSTO CAMPANA and PAOLA MEDIOLI MASOTTI, 137–144. Padua, 1986.

———. "Lay Patronage and Observant Reform in Fifteenth-Century Florence." In *Christianity and the Renaissance: Image and Religious Imagination in the Quattrocento*, edited by TIMOTHY VERDON and JOHN HENDERSON, 63–83. Syracuse, 1990.

———. "Cosimo *optimus civis*." In *Cosimo "il Vecchio" de' Medici, 1389–1464: Essays in Commemoration of the 600th Anniversary of Cosimo de' Medici's Birth*, edited by FRANCIS AMES-LEWIS, 5–20. Oxford, 1992.

———. *The Palazzo Vecchio 1298–1532: Government, Architecture, and Imagery in the Civic Palace of the Florentine Republic*. Oxford, 1995.

———. *The Government of Florence under the Medici (1434 to 1494)*. 2nd ed. Oxford, 1997. First published Oxford, 1966.

RUBINSTEIN, RUTH. "The Treasure of Lorenzo de' Medici in Florence." *Burlington Magazine* 114 (1972): 804–808.

RUCELLAI, GIOVANNI. *Zibaldone*. Edited by GABRIELLA BATTISTA. Florence, 2013.

RUSSO, FRANCESCA. *Bruto a Firenze. Mito, immagine e personaggio tra umanesimo e rinascimento*. Naples, 2008.

RYAN, MAGNUS. "Bartolus of Sassoferrato and Free Cities." *Transactions of the Royal Historical Society* 10 (2000): 65–89.

SAALMAN, HOWARD. *Filippo Brunelleschi: The Buildings*. London, 1993.

SABADINO DEGLI ARIENTI, GIOVANNI. *Gynevera de le clare donne di Joanne Sabadino de li Arienti*. Edited by CORRADO RICCI. Bologna, 1887.

SACCHETTI, FRANCO. *Il Trecentonovelle*. Edited by EMILIO FACCIOLI. Turin, 1970.

SALUTATI, COLUCCIO. *Epistolario*. Edited by FRANCESCO NOVATI. 4 vols. Rome, 1891–1911.

SALVADORI, PATRIZIA. *Dominio e patronato. Lorenzo dei Medici e la Toscana nel Quattrocento*. Rome, 2000a.

———. "Florentines and the Communities of the Territorial State." In *Florentine Tuscany: Structures and Practices of Power*, edited by WILLIAM J. CONNELL and ANDREA ZORZI, 207–224. Cambridge, 2000b.

———. "Lettere dal dominio. I Medici e la Toscana nel Quattrocento." In *I Medici in rete. Ricerca e progettualità scientifica a proposito dell'archivio medicea avanti il principato*, edited by IRENE COTTA and FRANCESCA KLEIN, 249–260. Florence, 2003.

SALVEMINI, GAETANO. *La dignità cavalleresca nel comune di Firenze*. Florence, 1896.

SANDRI, GINO. "I vicariati imperiali perpetui di Enrico VII di Lussemburgo." In *Scritti di Gino Sandri*, edited by GIULIO SANCASSANI, 157–193. Verona, 1969. First published Venice, 1939.

SANTORO, CATERINA. *Gli uffici del dominio sforzesco*. Milan, 1947.

SASSO, GENNARO. "Principato civile e tirannide (1982–1983)." In *Machiavelli e gli antichi e altri saggi*, 2:351–490. Milan, 1988.

———. *Niccolò Machiavelli*. Vol. 2. *La storiografia*. Bologna, 1993.

SAVELLI, RODOLFO. *Scrivere lo statuto, amministrare la giustizia, organizzare il territorio*. Genoa, 2003.

SAVONAROLA, GIROLAMO. *Selected Writings of Girolamo Savonarola: Religion and Politics, 1490–1498*. Edited by ANNE BORELLI and MARIA C. PASTORE PASSARO. New Haven, 2006.

SCALINI, MARIO. "Il 'ludus equestre' nell'età laurenziana." In *Le tems revient. 'L tempo si rinuova. feste e spettacoli nella Firenze di Lorenzo il Magnifico*, exhibition catalog, Florence, Palazzo Medici Riccardi, edited by PAOLA VENTRONE, 75–102. Milan, 1992.

SCARTON, ELISABETTA. *Giovanni Lanfredini. Uomo d'affari e diplomatico nell'Italia del Quattrocento*. Florence, 2007.

SCHARF, GIAN PAOLO GIUSEPPE. *Borgo San Sepolcro a metà del Quattrocento. Istituzioni e società 1440–1460*. Florence, 2003.

SCHNETTGER, MATTHIAS. *"Principe sovrano" oder "Civitas imperialis": Die Republick Genua und das alte Reich in der frühen Neuzeit, 1556–1797*. Mainz, 2006.

SCHUCHARD, CHRISTIANE. "Lübecker und Hamburger Interessenvertreter an der päpstlichen Kurie im 14. und 15. Jahrhundert." In *Der Kaufmann und der liebe Gott: Zu Kommerz und Kirche in Mittelalter und früher Neuzeit,* edited by ANTJEKATHREIN GRASSMANN, 89–111. Trier, 2009.

SEBREGONDI, LUDOVICA, and TIM PARKS, eds. *Money and Beauty: Bankers, Botticelli, and the Bonfire of the Vanities.* Florence, 2011.

SEGOLONI, DANILO. *Bartolo da Sassoferrato e la "civitas Perusina."* Milan, 1962.

SEGRE, ARTURO. "I prodromi della ritrata di Carlo VIII, re di Francia. Saggio sulle relazioni tra Venezia, Milano e Roma durante la primavera del 1495." *Archivio storico italiano,* ser. 5, 34 (1904): 384–405.

SEIGEL, JERROLD E. "'Civic Humanism' or Ciceronian Rhetoric? The Culture of Petrarch and Bruni." *Past and Present* 34 (1966): 3–48.

SELFRIDGE, HARRY GORDON. *The Romance of Commerce.* London, 1918.

SESTAN, ERNESTO. "Le origini delle signorie cittadine. Un problema storico esaurito?" *Bullettino dell'istituto storico italiano e archivio muratoriano* 73 (1961): 41–69.

SFORZA, GALEAZZO MARIA. *Estratto dal poemeto di anonimo. Terze rime in lode di Cosimo de' Medici e de' figli e dell'honoranza fatta l'anno 1458 [sic] al figl.o del duca di Milano ed al papa nella loro venuta a Firenze.* Florence, 1907.

SHAW, PRUE. "La versione ficiniana della *Monarchia.*" *Studi danteschi* 51 (1978): 289–408.

SHEPHARD, TIM. "Constructing Identities in a Music Manuscript: The Medici Codex as a Gift." *Renaissance Quarterly* 63 (2010): 84–127.

SIGNORINI, RODOLFO. "L'elevazione di Francesco Gonzaga al cardinalato." *Mitteilungen der Kunsthistorischen Institutes in Florenz* 18 (1974): 247–249.

———. *Opus hoc tenue. La camera dipinta di Andrea Mantegna.* Mantua, 1985.

SILVA, PIETRO. "Pisa sotto Firenze dal 1406 al 1433." *Studi storici* 18 (1909): 133–183, 285–323, 529–579.

SIMONETTA, GIOVANNI. *Rerum gestarum Francisci Sfortiae Mediolanensium ducis commentarii.* Edited by GIOVANNI SORANZO. In *Rerum italicarum scriptores,* vol. 21, pt. 2. Bologna, 1932–59.

SMAN, GERT JAN VAN DER. *Lorenzo e Giovanni. Vita e arte nella Firenze del Quattrocento.* Florence, 2010.

SMITH, DARWIN. "Greban, Arnoul." In *Die Musik in Geschichte und Gegenwart,* vol. 7, *1541–1545,* edited by LUDWIG FINSCHER. Kassel, 1994–2008.

SOHN, ANDREAS. *Deutsche Prokuratoren an der römischen Kurie in der Frührenaissance (1431–1474).* Cologne, 1997.

SOMAINI, FRANCESCO. "Processi costitutivi, dinamiche politiche e strutture istituzionali dello stato visconteo-sforzesco." In *Comuni e signorie nell'Italia settentrionale. La Lombardia,* edited by GIANCARLO ANDENNA, 681–825. Turin, 1998.

———. *Un prelato lombardo del XV secolo. Il cardinal Giovanni Arcimboldi vescovo di Novara, arcivescovo di Milano.* 3 vols. Rome, 2003.

———. "Il binomio imperfetto. Alcune osservazioni su guelfi e ghibellini a Milano in età visconteo-sforzesca." In *Guelfi e ghibellini nell'Italia del Rinascimento,* edited by MARCO GENTILE, 131–215. Rome, 2005.

———. "Una storia spezzata. La carriera ecclesiastica di Bernardo Rossi tra il 'piccolo stato,' la corte sforzesca, la curia romana e il 'sistema degli stati italiani.'" In *Le signorie dei Rossi di Parma tra XIV e XVI secolo,* edited by LETIZIA ARCANGELI and MARCO GENTILE, 109–186. Florence, 2007.

———. "The Political Geography of Renaissance Italy." In *Courts and Courtly Arts in Renaissance Italy: Art, Culture, Politics, 1395–1530,* edited by MARCO FOLIN, 33–61. Woodbridge, Suffolk, 2011.

SORANZO, GIOVANNI, ed. *Cronaca di anonimo Veronese, 1446–1488.* Venice, 1915.

———. "Lorenzo il Magnifico alla morte del padre e il suo primo balzo verso la signoria." *Archivio storico italiano* 111 (1953): 42–77.

SPAGGIARI, ANGELO, and GIUSEPPE TRENTI. *Gli stemmi estensi ed austro-estensi. Profilo storico.* Modena, 1985.

SPALLANZANI, MARCO. "Le aziende Pazzi al tempo della congiura del 1478." In *Studi di storia economica toscana nel medioevo e nel rinascimento in memoria di Federigo Melis*, edited by AMLETO SPICCIANI, 306–320. Pisa, 1987.

SPALLANZANI, MARCO, and GIOVANNA GAETA BERTELÀ, eds. *Libro d'inventario dei beni di Lorenzo de' Medici*. Florence, 1992.

SPINELLI, MARINA. "Ricerche per una nuova storia della repubblica ambrosiana." *Nuova rivista storica* 70 (1986): 231–252; 71 (1987): 27–48.

———. "La repubblica ambrosiana (1447–1450). Aspetti e problemi." PhD thesis, Università degli Studi di Milano, 1988. (Accessible at BNCF and BNCR.)

Statuta civitatis Cremonae. Cremona, 1578.

Statuta populi et communis Florentiae. 3 vols. Freiburg, 1779–83.

STEFANUTTI, ANDREINA. "Jacopo di Porcia. Gli studi e le esperienze di un intellettuale." In *Saggi di storia friulana*, edited by ANDREINA STEFANUTTI, LAURA CASELLA, and MICHAEL KNAPTON, 43–67. Udine, 2006.

STOPANI, RENATO. *Medievali "case da signore" nella campagna fiorentina*. Florence, 1977.

SWAIN, ELISABETH WARD. "'My excellent and most singular Lord': Marriage in a Noble Family of Fifteenth-Century Italy." *Journal of Medieval and Renaissance Studies* 16, no. 2 (1986): 171–197.

SYSON, LUKE. "Bertoldo di Giovanni, Republican Court Artist." In *Artistic Exchange and Cultural Translation in the Italian Renaissance City*, edited by STEPHEN J. CAMPBELL and STEPHEN J. MILNER, 96–133. Cambridge, 2004.

TABACCO, GIOVANNI. "La storia politica e sociale. Dal tramonto dell'impero alle prima formazioni di stati regionali." In *Storia d'Italia*, vol. 2, *Dalla caduta dell'impero romano al secolo XVIII*, edited by RUGGIERO ROMANO and CORRADO VIVANTI, 3–427. Turin, 1974.

TACCONI, MARICA. "Appropriating the Instruments of Worship: The 1512 Medici Restoration and the Florentine Cathedral Books." *Renaissance Quarterly* 56 (2003): 333–376.

TAFURI, MANFREDO. *Ricerca del rinascimento. Principi, città, architetti*. Turin, 1992.

TANTURLI, GIULIANO. "Cino Rinuccini e la scuola di Santa Maria in Campo." *Studi medievali* 17 (1976): 625–674.

———. "Continuità dell'umanesimo civile da Brunetto Latino a Leonardo Bruni." In *Gli umanesimi medievali*, edited by CLAUDIO LEONARDI, 735–780. Florence, 1998.

TANZINI, LORENZO. *Statuti e legislazione a Firenze dal 1355 al 1415. Lo statuto cittadino del 1409*. Florence, 2004.

———. *Alle origini della Toscana moderna. Firenze e gli statuti delle comunità soggette tra XIV e XVI secolo*. Florence, 2007a.

———. *Il governo delle leggi. Norme e pratiche delle istituzioni a Firenze dalla fine del Duecento all'inizio del Quattrocento*. Florence, 2007b.

———. "Le rappresaglie nei comuni italiani del Trecento." *Archivio storico italiano* 167 (2009): 199–252.

———. "Emergenza, eccezione, deroga. Tecniche e retoriche del potere nei comuni toscani del XIV secolo." In *Tecniche di potere nel tardo medioevo. Regimi comunali e signorie in Italia*, edited by MASSIMO VALLERANI, 149–182. Rome, 2010a.

———. "Il magnifico e il turco. Elementi politici, economici e culturali nelle relazioni tra Firenze e impero ottomano al tempo di Lorenzo de' Medici." *RiMe–Rivista dell'istituto di storia dell'Europa mediterranea* 4 (2010b): 271–289.

———. "Potere centrale e comunità del territorio nello stato fiorentino alla fine del medioevo." In *Poteri centrali e autonomie nella toscana medivale e moderna*, edited by GIULIANO PINTO and LORENZO TANZINI, 83–107. Florence, 2012.

———. "Delibere e verbali. Per una storia documentaria dei consigli nell'Italia comunale." *Reti medievali rivista* 14 (2013a): 43–79.

———. "Forme di egemonia politica in una città repubblicana. Firenze tra Tre e Quattrocento." In *Le signorie cittadine in Toscana. Esperienze di potere e forme di governo personale (secoli XIII–XV)*, edited by ANDREA ZORZI, 323–348. Rome, 2013b.

TANZINI, LORENZO, and SERGIO TOGNETTI, eds. *"Mercatura è arte". Uomini d'affari toscani in Europa e nel Mediterraneo tardomedievale*. Rome, 2012.

TARTAGNI, ALESSANDRO. *Consiliorum seu responsorum*. 7 vols. Venice, 1610.

TATEO, FRANCESCO. "Sulla ricezione umanistica dei *Trionfi*." In *I Triumphi di Francesco Petrarca*, edited by CLAUDIA BERRA, 375–401. Bologna, 1999.

TENENTI, ALBERTO. "Il senso del mare." In *Storia di Venezia*, vol. 12, *Il mare*, edited by ALBERTO TENENTI and UGO TUCCI, 7–76. Rome, 1991.

TERNI DE GREGORI, GINEVRA. "La signoria cremonese di Bianca Maria Visconti." In *Atti e memorie del terzo congresso storico lombardo*, 79–88. Milan, 1939.

TIRABOSCHI, MATTIA. *Cafaggiolo. La villa de' Medici nel Mugello*. Florence, 1992.

TOGNETTI, SERGIO. *Il banco Cambini. Affari e mercati di una compagnia mercantile-bancaria nella Firenze del XV secolo*. Florence, 1997.

———. "Gli affari di messer Palla Strozzi e di suo padre Nofri. Imprenditoria e mecenatismo nella Firenze del primo rinascimento." *Annali di storia di Firenze* 4 (2009): 7–88.

———, ed. *Firenze e Pisa dopo il 1406. La creazione di un nuovo spazio regionale*. Florence, 2010a.

———. "Pisa, Firenze e il mare (metà XI–fine XV sec.)." In *Firenze e Pisa dopo il 1406. La creazione di un nuovo spazio regionale*, edited by SERGIO TOGNETTI, 151–175. Florence, 2010b.

TOMAS, NATALIE. *The Medici Women*. Aldershot, 2003.

TONIOLO, FEDERICA. "Stemmi, imprese, natura dipinta." In *La Bibbia di Borso d'Este. Commentario al codice*, edited by VINCENZO CAPPELLETTI, FEDERICA TONIOLO, et al., 2:483–497. Modena, 1997.

TORELLI, PIETRO. "Capitanato del popolo e vicariato imperiale come elementi costitutivi della signoria bonacolsiana." *Atti della reale accademia virgiliana di Mantova*, n.s., 14–16 (1924): 73–221.

TORNABUONI, LUCREZIA. *I poemetti sacri di Lucrezia Tornabuoni*. Edited by FULVIO PEZZAROSSA. Florence, 1978.

———. *La istoria della casta Susanna*. Edited by PAOLO ORVIETO and ORNELLA CASAZZA. Bergamo, 1992.

———. *Lettere*. Edited by PATRIZIA SALVADORI. Florence, 1993.

———. *Sacred Narratives*. Edited by JANE TYLUS. Chicago, 2001.

La Toscana al tempo di Lorenzo il Magnifico. Politica, economia, cultura, arte. 3 vols. Pisa, 1996.

TRACHTENBERG, MARVIN. *Dominion of the Eye: Urbanism, Art, and Power in Early Modern Florence*. Cambridge, 1998.

TREXLER, RICHARD C. "Charity and the Defence of Urban Elites in the Italian Communes." In *The Rich, the Well Born, and the Powerful: Elites and Upper Classes in History*, edited by FREDERIC COPLE JAHER, 64–109. Urbana, 1973a.

———. "Ritual in Renaissance Florence: The Setting." *Medievalia et humanistica*, n.s., 3 (1973b): 125–144.

———. *The Spiritual Power: Republican Florence under the Interdict*. Leiden, 1974.

———. "'Honor Among Thieves': The Trust Function of the Urban Clergy in the Florentine Republic." In *Essays Presented to Myron P. Gilmore*, edited by SERGIO BERTELLI and GLORIA RAMAKUS, 1:317–334. Florence, 1978a.

———. "Il Parlamento fiorentino del 1378." *Archivio storico italiano* 143 (1978b): 437–475.

———, ed. *The "Libro cerimoniale" of the Florentine Republic*, by FRANCESCO FILARETE and ANGELO MANFIDI. Geneva, 1978c.

———. "Lorenzo de' Medici and Savonarola, Martyrs for Florence." *Renaissance Quarterly* 31, no. 3 (1978d): 293–308.

———. "The Magi Enter Florence: The Ubriachi of Florence and Venice." *Studies in Medieval and Renaissance History* 1 (1978e): 127–218.

——. "The Episcopal Constitutions of Antoninus of Florence." *Quellen und Forschungen aus Italienischen Archiven und Bibliotheken* 59 (1979): 244–272.

——. "Florentine Theatre, 1280–1500: A Checklist of Performances and Institutions." *Forum Italicum* 14 (1980a): 454–475.

——. *Public Life in Renaissance Florence.* New York, 1980b.

TROMBETTI BUDRIESI, ANNA LAURA. "Bologna 1334–1376." In *Bologna nel medioevo*, edited by OVIDIO CAPITANI, 761–866. Bologna, 2007.

TUOHY, THOMAS. *Herculean Ferrara: Ercole d'Este, 1471–1505, and the Invention of a Ducal Capital.* Cambridge, 1996.

TYLER, ROYALL, ed. *Catalogue of the Medici Archives.* London, 1918.

——, ed. *Catalogue of the Medici Archives.* London, 1919.

UGHELLI, FERDINANDO. *Italia sacra.* 10 vols. Venice, 1717–22.

ULLMANN, WALTER. *Origins of the Great Schism.* London, 1948.

UZZANO, GIOVANNI DA. "La pratica della mercatura." In *Della decima e di varie altre gravezze imposte dal comune di Firenze della moneta e della mercatura de' fiorentini fino al secolo XVI*, edited by GIOVANNI FRANCESCO PAGNINI, vol. 4. Lisbon and Lucca, 1766.

VAGLIENTI, FRANCESCA M. "'Fidelissimi servitori de consilio suo secreto'. Struttura e organizzazione del consiglio segreto nei primi anni del ducato di Galeazzo Maria Sforza (1466–1469)." *Nuova rivista storica* 76 (1992): 645–708.

——. "'Per dicta pace realegrati'. Le trattative diplomatiche tra la Confederazione Elvetica e il duca Galeazzo M. Sforza per il rinnovo del Capitolato, l'investitura della Leventina e la cessione della Val Formazza (1466–1469)." *Archivio storico ticinese* 116 (1994): 125–166.

——. "*Sunt enim duo populi*". Esercizio del potere ed esperimenti di fiscalità straordinaria nella prima età sforzesca (1450–1476). Milan, 1997.

VALORI, NICCOLÒ. *Vita di Lorenzo de' Medici, scritta in lingua latina da Niccolò Valori, resa in volgare dal figlio Filippo Valori.* Edited by ENRICO NICCOLINI. Vicenza, 1991.

VANGELISTI, GUGLIELMO M., OSM. "Il beato Giovanni Angelo Porro a Firenze. Studio sui documenti." *Studi storici dell'ordine dei Servi di Maria* 9 (1959): 77–89.

VARANINI, GIAN MARIA. "Note sui consigli civici veronesi. In margine a una ricerca di J. E. Law (secoli XIV–XV)." *Archivio veneto* 112 (1979): 5–32.

——. *Comuni cittadini e stato regionale. Ricerche sulla terraferma veneta nel Quattrocento.* Verona, 1992.

——. "Aristocrazie e poteri nell'Italia centro-settentrionale." In *Le aristocrazie dai signori rurali al patriziato*, edited by RENATO BORDONE, GUIDO CASTELNUOVO, and GIAN MARIA VARANINI, 121–193. Rome, 2004.

——. "La terraferma di fronte alla sconfitta di Agnadello (1509)." In *L'Europa e la Serenissima. La svolta del 1509*, edited by GIUSEPPE GULLINO, 115–161. Venice, 2011.

——. "Public Written Records." In *The Italian Renaissance State*, edited by ANDREA GAMBERINI and ISABELLA LAZZARINI, 385–405. Cambridge, 2012.

VASARI, GIORGIO. "Vita di Filippo Brunelleschi." In *Le opere di Giorgio Vasari*, edited by GAETANO MILANESI, 2:327–394. Florence, 1906.

VASIC VATOVEC, CORINNA. "Lorenzo il Magnifico e i Gonzaga. Due 'viaggi' nell'architettura (con nuovi documenti su Luca Fancelli)." In *La Toscana al tempo di Lorenzo il Magnifico. Politica, economia, cultura, arte*, 1:73–101. Pisa, 1996.

VASOLI, CESARE. "Riflessioni sugli umanisti e il principe. Il modello platonico dell' 'ottimo governante.'" In *Immagini umanistiche*, edited by CESARE VASOLI, 151–187. Naples, 1983.

VAUGHAN, ROBERT. *The Age of Great Cities.* London, 1842.

VECCHIO, ALBERTO DEL, and EUGENIO CASANOVA. *Le rappresaglie nei comuni medievali e specialmente in Firenze.* Bologna, 1894. Reprinted Bologna, 1974.

VENTRONE, PAOLA. "Note sul carnevale fiorentino di età laurenziana." In *Il carnevale. Dalla tradizione arcaica alla traduzione colta del rinascimento*, edited by MIRYAM CHIABÒ and FEDERICO DOGLIO, 312–366. Viterbo, 1990.

——, ed. *Le tems revient. 'L tempo si rinuova. Feste e spettacoli nella Firenze di Lorenzo il Magnifico*. Exhibition catalog, Florence, Palazzo Medici Riccardi. Milan, 1992.

——. *Gli araldi della commedia. Teatro a Firenze nel Rinascimento*. Pisa, 1993.

——. "Lorenzo's *Politica festiva*." In *Lorenzo the Magnficent: Culture and Politics*, edited by MICHAEL E. MALLETT and NICHOLAS MANN, 105–116. London, 1996.

——. "Feste e rituali civici. Città italiane a confronto." In *Aspetti e componenti dell'identità urbana in Italia e in Germania (secoli XIV–XVI)*, edited by GIORGIO CHITTOLINI and PETER JOHANEK, 155–191. Bologna, 2003.

——. "L'immaginario cavalleresco nella cultura dello spettacolo fiorentino del Quattrocento." In *Paladini di carta. Il modello cavalleresco fiorentino*, edited by MARCO VILLORESI, 191–223. Rome, 2006.

——. "La festa di san Giovanni. Costruzione di un'identità civica fra rituale e spettacolo (secoli XIV–XVI)." *Annali di storia di Firenze* 2 (2007a): 49–76.

——. "Simonetta Vespucci e le metamorfosi dell'immagine della donna nella Firenze dei primi Medici." In *Simonetta Vespucci. La nascita della Venere fiorentina*, edited by GIOVANNA LAZZI and PAOLA VENTRONE, 5–59. Florence, 2007b.

——. "Politica e attualità nella sacra rappresentazione fiorentina del Quattrocento." *Annali di storia moderna e contemporanea* 14 (2008): 319–348.

——. "La propaganda unionista negli spettacoli fiorentini per il concilio del 1439." In *La stella e la porpora. Il corteo di Benozzo e l'enigma del Virgilio riccardiano*, edited by GIOVANNA LAZZI and GERHARD WOLF, 23–47. Florence, 2009.

——. *Teatro civile e sacra rappresentazione a Firenze nel rinascimento*. Florence, 2015.

VENTURA, ANGELO. *Nobiltà e popolo nella società veneta del Quattrocento e del Cinquecento*. Milan, 1993. First published Bari, 1964.

——. "Politica del diritto e amministrazione della giustizia nella repubblica veneta." *Rivista storica italiana* 94 (1982): 589–608.

VIGGIANO, ALFREDO. *Governanti e governati. Legittimità del potere ed esercizio dell'autorità sovrana nello stato veneto della prima età moderna*. Treviso, 1993.

——. "Il dominio da terra. Politica e istituzioni." In *Storia di Venezia. Dalle origini alla caduta della serenissima*, vol. 4, *Il rinascimento politica e cultura*, edited by ALBERTO TENENTI and UGO TUCCI, 529–578. Rome, 1996.

VILLANI, GIOVANNI. *Nuova cronica*. Edited by GIUSEPPE PORTA. 3 vols. Parma, 1990–91.

VILLARI, PASQUALE. *La storia di Girolamo Savonarola e de' suoi tempi*. Vol. 1. Florence, 1887.

VILLORESI, MARCO, ed. *Paladini di carta. Il modello cavalleresco fiorentino*. Rome, 2006.

VITI, PAOLO. "Aurelio Lippo Brandolini e Lorenzo de' Medici *florentinae reipublicae princeps*." In *Consorterie politiche e mutamenti istituzionali in età laurenziana*, exhibition catalog, Florence, Archivio di Stato, edited by MARIA AUGUSTA MORELLI TIMPANARO, ROSALIA MANNO TOLU, and PAOLO VITI, 124–126. Milan, 1992.

——, ed. *Firenze e il concilio del 1439*. 2 vols. Florence, 1994.

VITI, PAOLO, and RAFFAELLA MARIA ZACCARIA, eds. *Archivio delle tratte. Introduzione e inventario*. Rome, 1989.

VITRUVIUS. *De architectura*. Edited by GIOVANNI GIOCONDO. Venice, 1511.

——. *On Architecture*. Translated by RICHARD V. SCHOFIELD. London, 2009.

VIVOLO, CARLO. "Della Stufa, Angelo." *Dizionario biografico degli italiani* 37 (1989).

VOIGT, KLAUS. "Der Kollektor Marinus de Fregeno und seine 'Descriptio provinciarum Alamanorum.'" *Quellen und Forschungen aus italienischen Archiven und Bibliotheken* 48 (1968): 148–206.

VOLKMAR, CHRISTOPH. "Mittelsmänner zwischen Sachsen und Rom: Die Kurienprokuratoren Herzog Georgs von Sachsen am Vorabend der Reformation." *Quellen und Forschungen aus italienischen Archiven und Bibliotheken* 88 (2008): 244–309.

VOLPI, GUGLIELMO. *Ricordi di Firenze dell'anno 1459 di autore anonimo.* Città di Castello, 1907.

———. "Lorenzo il Magnifico e Vallombrosa." *Archivio storico italiano*, 7th ser., 22 (1934): 121–132.

WAITH, EUGENE M. "Landino and Maximus of Tyre." *Renaissance News* 13 (1960): 289–294.

WALEY, DANIEL. *Later Medieval Europe.* London, 1964. Reprinted, 3rd ed., with PETER DENLEY, London, 2001.

———. "The Use of Sortition in Appointments in the Italian Communes." In *Communes and Despots in Medieval and Renaissance Italy,* edited by JOHN E. LAW and BERNADETTE PATON, 27–33. Farnham, Surrey, 2010.

WATKINS, RENÉE NEU. *Humanism and Liberty: Writings on Freedom from Fifteenth-Century Florence.* Columbia SC, 1978.

WEGENER, WENDY J. "Mortuary Chapels of Renaissance *Condottieri*." PhD diss., Princeton University, 1989.

WEGMAN, ROB. "From Maker to Composer: Improvisation and Musical Authorship in the Low Countries, 1450–1500." *Journal of the American Musicological Society* 49 (1996): 409–479.

WEINSTEIN, DONALD. *Savonarola and Florence: Prophecy and Patriotism in the Renaissance.* Princeton, 1970.

WEISSEN, KURT. "La rete commerciale tedesca delle compagnie fiorentine *romanam curiam sequentes*, 1410–1470." *Archivio storico italiano* 169 (2011): 707–726.

WEISSMAN, RONALD F. E. *Ritual Brotherhood in Renaissance Florence.* New York, 1982.

———. "Reconstructing Renaissance Sociology: The 'Chicago School' and the Study of Renaissance Society." In *Persons in Groups: Social Behaviour as Identity Formation in Medieval and Renaissance Europe,* edited by RICHARD C. TREXLER, 39–46. New York, 1985.

———. "The Importance of Being Ambiguous: Social Relations, Individualism, and Identity in Renaissance Florence." In *Urban Life in the Renaissance,* edited by SUSAN ZIMMERMAN and RONALD WEISSMAN, 269–280. Newark NJ, 1989.

WELCH, EVELYN. *Art and Authority in Renaissance Milan.* London, 1995.

WHITE, HAYDEN. *Metahistory: The Historical Imagination in Nineteenth-Century Europe.* Baltimore, 1973.

WILSON, BLAKE. *Music and Merchants: The Laudesi Companies of Republican Florence.* Oxford, 1992.

———. "Heinrich Isaac among the Florentines." *Journal of Musicology* 23 (2006): 97–152.

———. *Singing Poetry in Renaissance Florence: The "Cantasi come" Tradition (1375–1550).* Florence, 2009.

———. "Poliziano and the Language of Lament from Isaac to Layolle." In *Sleuthing the Muse: Essays in Honor of William F. Prizer,* edited by KRISTINE K. FORNEY, 85–114. New York, 2012.

———. "Dominion of the Ear: Singing the Vernacular in Piazza San Martino." *I Tatti Studies: Essays in the Renaissance* 16 (2013): 273–287.

———. "*Canterino* and *Improvvisatore*: Oral Poetry and Performance." In *The Cambridge History of Fifteenth-Century Music,* edited by ANNA MARIA BUSSE BERGER and JESSE RODIN. Cambridge, forthcoming.

WITT, RONALD G. "Cino Rinuccini's 'Risponsiva alla Invettiva di Messer Antonio Lusco.'" *Renaissance Quarterly* 23 (1970): 133–149.

———. *Hercules at the Crossroads: The Life, Works, and Thought of Coluccio Salutati.* Durham NC, 1983.

———. *"In the Footsteps of the Ancients": The Origins of Humanism from Lovato to Bruni.* Leiden, 2000.

WRIGHT, ALISON. "A Portrait for the Visit of Galeazzo Maria Sforza to Florence in 1471." In *Lorenzo the Magnificent: Culture and Politics,* edited by MICHAEL E. MALLETT and NICHOLAS MANN, 65–92. London, 1996.

ZANGHERI, LUIGI, ed. *La villa medicea di Careggi e il suo giardino. Storia, rilievi e analisi per il restauro.* Florence, 2006.

ZANOVELLO, GIOVANNI. "'Master Arigo Ysach, Our Brother': New Light on Isaac in Florence, 1502–1517." *Journal of Musicology* 25 (2008): 287–313.

———. "Heinrich Isaac, die Medici, und andere Florentiner." *Musik-Konzepte*, n.s., 148, no. 9 (2010): 5–19.

ZENATTI, ALBINO. "Il poemetto di Pietro de' Natali sulla pace di Venezia tra Alessandro III e Federico Barbarossa." *Bullettino dell'istituto storico italiano per il medioevo e archivio muratoriano* 26 (1905): 105–198.

ZORZI, ANDREA. "Giusdicenti e operatori di giustizia nello stato territoriale fiorentino del XV secolo." *Ricerche storiche* 19 (1989): 517–552.

———. "L'organizzazione del territorio in area fiorentina tra XIII e XIV secolo." In *L'organizzazione del territorio in Italia e in Germania. Secoli XIII–XIV,* edited by GIORGIO CHITTOLINI and DIETER WILLOWEIT, 279–349. Bologna, 1994.

———. "Progetti, riforme e pratiche giudiziarie a Firenze alla fine del Quattrocento." In *La Toscana al tempo di Lorenzo il Magnifico. Politica, economia, cultura, arte,* 3:1323–1342. Pisa, 1996.

———. "Gli ufficiali territoriali dello Stato fiorentino (secc. xiv–xv)." In *Gli officiali negli stati italiani del Quattrocento,* edited by FRANCA LEVEROTTI. *Annali della scuola normale superiore di Pisa,* ser. 4, Quaderni, 1 (1997): 191–212.

———. "The Material 'Constitution' of the Florentine Dominion." In *Florentine Tuscany: Structures and Practices of Power,* edited by WILLIAM J. CONNELL and ANDREA ZORZI, 6–31. Cambridge, 2000.

———. *Le signorie cittadine in Italia (secoli XIII–XV).* Milan, 2010.

———. "Rileggendo la 'Cronica' di Dino Compagni. Comuni, signori, tiranni." In *Roma e il papato nel medioevo. Studi in onore di Massimo Miglio,* edited by AMEDEO DE VINCENTIIS, 33–44. Rome, 2012a.

———. "Un problema storico non esaurito. Le signorie cittadine. Rileggendo Ernesto Sestan." In *Uomini paesaggi storie. Studi di storia medievale per Giovanni Cherubini,* edited by DUCCIO BALESTRACCI, ANDREA BARLUCCHI, FRANCO FRANCESCHI, PAOLO NANNI, GABRIELLA PICCINNI, and ANDREA ZORZI, 2:1247–1264. Siena, 2012b.

———, ed. *Le signorie cittadine in Toscana. Esperienze di potere e forme di governo personale (secoli XIII–XV).* Rome, 2013a.

———, ed. *Tiranni e tirannide nel Trecento italiano.* Rome, 2013b.

ZORZI, LUDOVICO. "Ferrara. Il sipario ducale." In *Il teatro e la città. Saggi sulla scena italiana,* 3–59. Turin, 1977.

Contributors

Francesco Bausi, Professore Ordinario di Filologia Italiana, Dipartimento di Studi Umanistici, Università della Calabria

Jane Black, formerly Lecturer in History, York College

Robert Black, Emeritus Professor of Renaissance History, University of Leeds

Lorenz Böninger, formerly Editor, Lettere di Lorenzo de' Medici

Alison Brown, Emerita Professor of Italian Renaissance History, Royal Holloway, University of London

Melissa Meriam Bullard, Professor of History, University of North Carolina at Chapel Hill

David S. Chambers, Emeritus Reader in Renaissance History, Warburg Institute, University of London

Giorgio Chittolini, formerly Professore Ordinario di Storia Medievale, Università Statale di Milano

Franco Franceschi, Professore Associato di Storia Medievale, Dipartimento di Scienze della Formazione, Scienze Umane e della Comunicazione Interculturale, Università degli Studi di Siena

Riccardo Fubini, formerly Professore Ordinario di Storia Moderna, Università degli Studi di Firenze

Marco Gentile, Ricercatore, Dipartimento di Lettere, Arti, Storia e Società, Università degli Studi di Parma

Carolyn James, Casamarca Associate Professor, Monash University

Dale V. Kent, Honorary Professorial Fellow, School of Historical and Philosophical Studies, University of Melbourne

John E. Law, Reader, Department of History and Classics, Swansea University

AMANDA LILLIE, Reader, History of Art, University of York

STEPHEN J. MILNER, Serena Professor of Italian, University of Manchester

JOHN M. NAJEMY, Professor of History, Cornell University

PAOLO ORVIETO, formerly Professore Ordinario, Dipartimento di Italianistica, Università degli Studi di Firenze

DAVID S. PETERSON, Professor of History, Washington and Lee University

GIAN MARIA VARANINI, Professore Ordinario di Storia Medievale, Dipartimento di Tempo, Spazio, Immagini, Società, Università degli Studi di Verona

PAOLA VENTRONE, Ricercatore, Dipartimento di Storia Moderna e Contemporanea, Università Cattolica di Sacro Cuore di Milano

BLAKE WILSON, Professor of Music, Dickinson College

ALISON WRIGHT, Reader, History of Art, University College London

ANDREA ZORZI, Professore Ordinario di Storia Medievale, Università degli Studi di Firenze

Index